Crime and Globalization

International Library of Criminology, Criminal Justice and Penology - Second Series
Series Editors: Gerald Mars and David Nelken

Titles in the Series:

Gender and Prisons
Dana M. Britton

Quantitative Methods in Criminology
Shawn Bushway and David Weisburd

Computer Crime
Indira Carr

Insurgent Terrorism
Gerald Cromer

Criminal Courts
Jo Dixon, Aaron Kupchik and Joachim J. Savelsberg

Crime and Immigration
Joshua D. Freilich and Graeme R. Newman

Crime and Security
Benjamin Goold and Lucia Zedner

Crime and Regulation
Fiona Haines

Recent Developments in Criminological Theory
Stuart Henry and Scott A. Lukas

Gun Crime
Rob Hornsby and Dick Hobbs

The Criminology of War
Ruth Jamieson

Crime and Globalization
Suzanne Karstedt and David Nelken

The Impact of HIV/AIDS on Criminology and Criminal Justice
Mark M. Lanier

Burglary
R.I. Mawby

Domestic Violence
Mangai Natarajan

Women Police
Mangai Natarajan

Surveillance, Crime and Social Control
Clive Norris and Dean Wilson

Crime and Social Institutions
Richard Rosenfeld

The Death Penalty, Volumes I and II
Austin Sarat

Gangs
Jacqueline Schneider and Nick Tilley

Corporate Crime
Sally Simpson and Carole Gibbs

Green Criminology
Nigel South and Piers Beirne

Crime, Criminal Justice and Masculinities
Stephen Tomsen

Crime and Deviance in Cyberspace
David S. Wall

Crime and Globalization

Edited by

Susanne Karstedt

University of Leeds, UK

David Nelken

Macerata University, Italy, University of Cardiff and University of Oxford, UK

With assistance from Matthias Koch

University of Bielefeld, Germany

Routledge
Taylor & Francis Group
LONDON AND NEW YORK

First published 2013 by Ashgate Publishing

2 Park Square, Milton Park, Abingdon, Oxfordshire OX14 4RN
711 Third Avenue, New York, NY 10017

Routledge is an imprint of the Taylor & Francis Group, an informa business

First issued in paperback 2018

British Library Cataloguing in Publication Data
A catalogue record for this book is available from the British Library.

The Library of Congress has cataloged the printed edition as follows: 2012949907

ISBN 978-0-7546-2805-7 (hbk)
ISBN 978-1-138-38357-9 (pbk)

Contents

PART III LOCALIZING THE GLOBAL: CITIES, MARKETS AND CRIME

PART IV CROSSING BORDERS: GLOBAL MOVEMENTS, CRIME AND CONTROL

PART V GLOBAL TRADES: AT THE INTERSECTION OF LEGAL AND ILLEGAL BUSINESS TRANSACTIONS

PART VI GLOBALIZATION AND VIOLENCE: GLOBAL FORCES AND LOCAL VIOLENCE

Acknowledgements

Ashgate would like to thank our researchers and the contributing authors who provided copies, along with the following for their permission to reprint copyright material.

American Society of Criminology for the essay: Carole Gibbs, Edmund F. McGarrell and Mark Axelrod (2010), 'Transnational White-Collar Crime and Risk: Lessons from the Global Trade in Electronic Waste', *Criminology and Public Policy*, 9, pp. 543–60. Copyright © 2010 American Society of Criminology.

American Sociological Association for the essay: Ronen Shamir (2005), 'Without Borders? Notes on Globalization as a Mobility Regime', *Sociological Theory*, **23**, pp. 197–217. Copyright © 2005 American Sociological Association.

American Studies Journal for the essay: Saskia Sassen (2000), 'The Global City: Strategic Site/New Frontier', *American Studies*, **41**, pp. 79–95.

Cambridge University Press for the essay: Rosaleen Duffy (2007), 'Gemstone Mining in Madagascar: Transnational Networks, Criminalisation and Global Integration', *Journal of Modern African Studies*, **45**, pp. 185–206. Copyright © 2007 Cambridge University Press.

Ifeanyi Ezeonu (2008), 'Crimes of Globalization: Health Care, HIV and the Poverty of Neoliberalism in Sub-Saharan Africa', *International Journal of Social Inquiry*, **1**, pp. 113–34. Copyright © 2008 Ifeanyi Ezeonu.

John Wiley & Sons for the essays: Dick Hobbs (2002), 'Going Down the Glocal: The Local Context of Organised Crime', *Howard Journal of Criminal Justice*, **37**, pp. 407–22; Liza Weinstein (2008), 'Mumbai's Development Mafias: Globalization, Organized Crime and Land Development', *International Journal of Urban and Regional Research*, **32**, pp. 22–38. Copyright © 2008 Liza Weinstein; Arjun Appadurai (1998), 'Dead Certainty: Ethnic Violence in the Era of Globalization', *Development and Change*, **29**, pp. 905–25.

Oxford University Press for the essays: David Nelken (1997), 'The Globalization of Crime and Criminal Justice: Prospects and Problems', *Current Legal Problems*, **50**, pp. 251–77. Copyright © 1997 David Nelken; Staci Strobl (2009), 'Policing Housemaids: The Criminalization of Domestic Workers in Bahrain', *British Journal of Criminology*, **49**, pp. 165–83. Copyright © 2009 Staci Strobl.

Sage Publications for the essays: John W. Meyer (2000), 'Globalization: Sources and Effects on National States and Societies', *International Sociology*, **15**, pp. 233–48. Copyright © 2000 Sage Publications; Carolyn Nordstrom (2000), 'Shadows and Sovereigns', *Theory, Culture & Society*, **17**, pp. 35–54. Copyright © 2000 Sage Publications; James Holston (2009), 'Dangerous Spaces of Citizenship: Gang Talk, Rights Talk and Rule of Law in Brazil',

Planning Theory, **8**, pp. 12–31. Copyright © 2009 Sage Publications; Katja Franko Aas (2007), 'Analysing a World in Motion: Global Flows Meet "Criminology of the Other"', *Theoretical Criminology*, **11**, pp. 283–303. Copyright © 2007 Sage Publications; Jo Goodey (2008), 'Human Trafficking: Sketchy Data and Policy Responses', *Criminology and Criminal Justice*, **8**, pp. 421–42. Copyright © 2008 Sage Publications; Asafa Jalata (2005), 'State Terrorism and Globalization: The Cases of Ethiopia and Sudan', *International Journal of Comparative Sociology*, **46**, pp. 79–102. Copyright © 2005 Sage Publications; Pat O'Malley (2002), 'Globalizing Risk? Distinguishing Styles of "Neo-liberal" Criminal Justice in Australia and the USA', *Criminal Justice*, **2**, pp. 205–22. Copyright © 2002 Sage Publications.

Social Justice for the essays: David O. Friedrichs (2007), 'Transnational Crime and Global Criminology: Definitional, Typological, and Contextual Conundrums', *Social Justice*, **34**, pp. 4–18; Nikos Passas (2000), 'Global Anomie, Dysnomie, and Economic Crime: Hidden Consequences of Neoliberalism and Globalization in Russia and Around the World', *Social Justice*, **27**, pp. 16–44; Simon R.M. Mackenzie (2007), 'Transnational Crime, Local Denial', *Social Justice*, **34**, pp. 111–23; Dawn L. Rothe, Christopher W. Mullins and Kent Sandstrom (2008), 'The Rwandan Genocide: International Finance Policies and Human Rights', *Social Justice*, **35**, pp. 66–86.

Springer for the essays: Dawn L. Rothe (2010), 'Facilitating Corruption and Human Rights Violations: The Role of International Financial Institutions', *Crime, Law and Social Change*, **53**, pp. 457–76. Copyright © 2010 Springer Science & Business Media B.V.; Leslie Holmes (2009), 'Good Guys, Bad Guys: Transnational Corporations, Rational Choice Theory and Power Crime', *Crime, Law and Social Change*, **51**, pp. 383–97. Copyright © 2009 Springer Science & Business Media B.V.; Fernanda Mena and Dick Hobbs (2010), 'Narcophobia: Drugs Prohibition and the Generation of Human Rights Abuses', *Trends in Organised Crime*, **13**, pp. 60–74. Copyright © 2010 Springer Science & Business Media B.V.; Bill Dixon (2004), 'In Search of Interactive Globalisation: Critical Criminology in South Africa's Transition', *Crime, Law and Social Change*, **41**, pp. 359–84. Copyright © 2004 Kluwer Academic Publishers; Nicholas Dorn and Michael Levi (2008), 'East meets West in Anti-Money Laundering and Anti-Terrorist Finance: Policy Dialogue and Differentiation on Security, the Timber Trade and "Alternative" Banking', *Asian Criminology*, **3**, pp. 91–110. Copyright © 2008 Springer Science & Business Media B.V.

Taylor & Francis Group for the essay: John Hagan and Wenona Rymond-Richmond (2007), 'The Mean Streets of the Global Village: Crimes of Exclusion in the United States and Darfur', *Journal of Scandinavian Studies in Criminology and Crime Prevention*, **8**, pp. 54–80. Copyright © 2007 Taylor & Francis; Susanne Karstedt (2007), 'Creating Institutions: Linking the "Local" and the "Global" in the Travel of Crime Policies', *Police Practice and Research*, **8**, pp. 145–58; Copyright © 2007 Taylor & Francis.

University of Nebraska Press for the essay: Jessica Livingston (2004), 'Murder in Juárez: Gender, Sexual Violence, and the Global Assembly Line', *Frontiers: A Journal of Women Studies*, **25**, pp. 59–76. Copyright © 2004 Frontiers Editorial Collective, Inc.

Every effort has been made to trace all the copyright holders, but if any have been inadvertently overlooked the publishers will be pleased to make the necessary arrangement at the first opportunity.

Publisher's Note

The material in this volume has been reproduced using the facsimile method. This means we can retain the original pagination to facilitate easy and correct citation of the original essays. It also explains the variety of typefaces, page layouts and numbering.

Preface to the Second Series

The first series of the International Library of Criminology, Criminal Justice and Penology has established itself as a major research resource by bringing together the most significant journal essays in contemporary criminology, criminal justice and penology. The series made available to researchers, teachers and students an extensive range of essays which are indispensable for obtaining an overview of the latest theories and findings in this fast-changing subject. Indeed the rapid growth of interesting scholarly work in the field has created a demand for a second series which, like the first, consists of volumes dealing with criminological schools and theories as well as with approaches to particular areas of crime criminal justice and penology. Each volume is edited by a recognized authority who has selected twenty or so of the best journal essays in the field of their special competence and provided an informative introduction giving a summary of the field and the relevance of the essays chosen. The original pagination is retained for ease of reference.

The difficulties of keeping on top of the steadily growing literature in criminology are complicated by the many disciplines from which its theories and findings are drawn (sociology, law, sociology of law, psychology, psychiatry, philosophy and economics are the most obvious). The development of new specialisms with their own journals (policing, victimology, mediation) as well as the debates between rival schools of thought (feminist criminology, left realism, critical criminology, abolitionism etc.) make it necessary to provide overviews that offer syntheses of the state of the art.

GERALD MARS
Honorary Professor of Anthropology, University College, London, UK

DAVID NELKEN
Distinguished Professor of Sociology, University of Macerata, Italy

Introduction

Introducing an Emerging Field

Globalization has engaged the criminological imagination for more than two decades. In imagining and predicting a global future for crime and criminal justice, criminologists have closed ranks with and followed the trail of international policing experts, international organizations, politicians and journalists who all predicted a yet unseen surge in organized transnational crime across the globe. This vision included increasingly powerful criminal actors who were on the brink of ruling if not the world then at least the most vulnerable countries and failed states. From this perspective, crime represents the 'other' or 'dark' side of globalization (Abraham and van Schendel, 2005) and illegal transactions thus mirror the 'bright side' of globalization with its enormous opportunities for exchange, trade, communication and business. As illegal entrepreneurs take advantage of these opportunities, organized and transnational crime overtakes and takes over the legal global economy. A recent report issued by the United Nations Office on Drugs and Crime rates transnational organized crime as a most serious threat and 'one of the world's most sophisticated and profitable businesses' (UNODC 2010, p. ii). Global crime was and is seen as equally thriving on the 'inability of the criminal law to globalize' (Nelken, 2004, p. 381) and to generate global and transnational instruments of crime control and criminal justice. Notwithstanding two decades of proliferation of national and international instruments on combating transnational organized crime the recent UNODC report states that 'purely national responses are inadequate' (UNODC, 2010, p. ii).

Prevailing concepts and theories of globalization have shaped this perspective. The idea of globalization proceeds from a 'premise of universality' and of globalization and global forces leading to convergence and homogenization of both crime and criminal justice across the globe. Within such a framework there is little space for the nation-state and consequently global forces are supposed to have a direct and imminent impact on local crime and national justice policies, whether these are neo-liberal market policies, new communication technologies or configurations of 'post- or late-modernity' (Aas, 2007). Claims of governance 'through globalised crime' (Findlay, 2008) were made; the role attributed to neo-liberal economic policies in the proliferation of crime, and expectations as to the global spread of US mass incarceration and policies of 'zero tolerance' of deviant behaviour, were mainly based on the premise of the global as a universalizing force. Trends towards convergence as well as the growth of transnational crime were considerably overrated, as was globalization as their foremost cause. In sum, a veritable 'moral panic' took hold of criminologists, analysts and policy-makers.

As is often the case with moral panics, a realistic perspective prevails in the end. Already in 1997, Nelken (Chapter 2 in this volume) had warned against exaggerated fears and an underrating of the capacity of the international community as well as of nation-states to counter such threats with new instruments of criminal justice, which were, as Nelken pointed out, not without dangers in themselves. Over the past decade, forecasts of the growth of transnational terrorism and cyber crime, of infiltration of organized crime into the legal economy and polity, and estimates of the size of illegal drug markets have been reduced to lower and more realistic levels (for example van Duyne and Levi, 2005; UNODC, 2010). In addition, considerable efforts have addressed the deficiencies of international and transnational law enforcement, and have led to UN and regional conventions and instruments against corruption, transnational organized crime, terrorism and international crimes (Sheptycki, 2000; Andreas and Nadelmann, 2006; Goldsmith and Sheptycki, 2007; Karstedt, 2012a). Networks and international institutions of transnational policing have evolved, often regionally confined but with considerable reach across the globe (Bowling, 2010).

Simultaneously, more differentiated conceptualizations of globalization have emerged with a focus on global processes, and on actors and networks; the local and the nation-state are increasingly seen as spaces where the global is taking hold and emerges in distinctly localized ways (Fourcade and Savelsberg, 2006; Nelken, 2011a). According to Sassen (2007, p. 5), globalization combines 'two distinct sets of dynamics', which are salient in both crime and criminal justice. One involves the evolution of global interdependence and interconnectedness through flows of goods, people and communication, and the formation of global institutions and global norms, as, for example, in the International Criminal Court and international conventions and instruments responding to global crime problems. Transnational crime is part of this set of global dynamics. The other set of global processes involves those that take place inside territories and societies, and consequently in subnational settings like cities and regions. Crime problems at the local, city and nation-state level thus are representations of the global enshrined in the local, and particularly visible in global cities with their confluence of illegal and legal flows and transactions of goods, services and people (Aas, 2007; Muncie *et al.*, 2010). The exclusive authority of the nation-state over its territory, jurisdiction and its system of criminal justice is key to understanding the intricate relationship between local and global crime and criminal justice. Processes of global convergence coincide with 'domestic divergence' in time and space (Carruthers and Halliday, 2006). Far from being a unifying force, globalization sharply delineates spaces of deficits of security and justice along a deepening North–South divide (van Dijk, 2008).

Criminologists have redirected their attention to such simultaneity of global and local dynamics and the resulting divergence rather than convergence of crime and justice on a global scale. Thus, comparative and cross-national approaches to crime and justice have not been made obsolete by globalization, and they did not turn out as incapable of capturing the full complexity of crime and justice issues on a global scale, as some had argued (Larsen and Smandych, 2008: p. xi). Rather to the contrary, they are in high demand, as it is only through the comparative lens that the difference in scope and scale of the impact of globalization can be assessed, and globalization can be localized and contextualized. Rather than assuming unambiguously convergent trends in crime and criminal justice, the role of regional networks and actors, models and travel of policies is increasingly recognized (Johnson and Zimring, 2009; Karstedt, 2012b). Global pressures towards harmonization in crime prevention and criminal justice have made comparative perspectives an 'intrinsic part' of the search for 'best practice' (Nelken, 2010, p. 2). In sum, the global perspective needs a solid underpinning from the comparative enterprise in criminology.

Friedrichs (2007, 2011) suggests a typology of global crime that roughly follows the two sets of global dynamics as outlined by Sassen. It comprises four types: a) *local and national crime problems* that are defined and addressed within the border of the nation-state; b) *transnational or border crossing crimes* that are mainly linked to organized crime, and increasingly addressed at the international level; c) *international crimes* that are defined by international law and its institutions, for example genocide, war crimes and crimes against humanity; and, finally, Friedrichs (2011, p. 172) adds '*globalised crimes*', which refer to the 'policies and practices of international financial institutions ... that have demonstrably harmful consequences' and as such are not (yet) legally crimes or fall under a legally binding definition of crimes even if some of their activities violate national and international laws.

Transnational and border crossing crimes are the crimes most obviously linked to processes of globalization and the forces of interdependency that it feeds. The flows of illegal and legal goods, migrants and communication mostly follow similar routes from the global South to the global North. The world's biggest trading partners, the G8, are also the world's biggest markets for illicit goods and services, and most illicit flows go to and/or emanate from major economic powers. Global interconnectedness exposes people, criminal justice systems and governments to problems and pressures of crime in two distinct ways. First, the global illicit economy links illegal production with illegal markets and organized crime groups in the global North and South. The global dynamics of transnational crime translate into very different crime patterns and problems at the local, national and regional levels. Consumption of illegal goods and services is mainly located in the rich countries of the global North, while production and transport affects the countries of the global South, and both give rise to a different mix of crime problems. While criminalized consumers and small traders are typical of markets in the North, as are the concomitant violent and property crimes, the production and transportation of illegal goods are linked to serious and rampant violence, gang crimes and corruption in the producer and transit countries of the global South (van Dijk, 2008, ch. 6; UNDOC, 2010).

The second way in which globalization affects local and national crime patterns involves processes of simultaneous and parallel change that are initiated, accelerated and forced upon nation-states and societies through globalization. Changes in the economy and the welfare systems within nation-states are driven by global economic forces and competition as much as by policy models and powerful international actors. In addition, new technologies that deeply change the lives of people spread around the globe. Both have a profound impact on the social order of (national) societies, on their institutional arrangements and populations, values and social hierarchies. As these global forces reside in societies and nation-states, they should generate more uniformity of crime problems across nation-states or cities worldwide. This globalization model of convergence of crime comprises two partially interrelated trajectories, both of them expansions of earlier models of global forces: *neo-liberalism* and *late modernity* represent the latest configurations of global capitalism and modernity. However, neither the global spread of neo-liberalism nor late modern conditions necessarily imply convergence in terms of crime and related fears and insecurities, nor the persistent increase in violence and crime that has been projected. Empirical evidence therefore points towards significant differences rather than convergence in terms of institutional patterns, social disorganization and related crime rates (Messner *et al.*, 2013). Imposition of neo-liberal policies seems to account for massive violence in the global South, and their differential adoption for widely diverging approaches to criminal justice policies in even culturally similar countries like the US and Australia (see O'Malley, Chapter 28 in this volume).

Cities are the most important subnational space where the global resides. As global networks cross borders and can bypass national states, cities constitute the nodes in global networks of actors and activities; they link subnational spaces globally. Immigration is the key process in urban spaces 'whereby global elements are localized, international labour markets are constituted and cultures are … deterritorialized' (Sassen, 2007, p. 124). In this process, the major cities of the North and the South have emerged as social orders of sharp economic, social and ethnic segmentation and polarization. These are entrenched in the fragmentation of urban space, its centres and margins; the ghettos of the US, the banlieues of Europe and the favelas of Latin America are 'ethnospaces' (Appadurai, 1996) where the global is nested within the city. As segmentation produces huge imbalances and large pockets of neglect in the political economy of urban space, violence and crime are concentrated in deprived neighbourhoods. The continuous though uneven decline of crime rates in the global North since the 1990s demonstrates that any such potential impact of globalization seems to have been attenuated and mitigated by other factors. In contrast, crime rates, in particular violent crime, persist at high levels in the cities of the global South.

Responses to urban crime and insecurity seem to have travelled with the global flows of ideas, models and policies, and models that promised competitive advantages were rapidly adopted. It is in the realm of security where globalization has changed the face of cities in distinct and presumably lasting ways (Karstedt, Chapter 27 in this volume; Aas, 2007, ch. 3). Surveillance of public and semi-public spaces has increased across the globe though on different levels. 'Gated communities' shield their middle- and upper-class inhabitants from crime and insecurity, while marginalized ghettos are left to the control of gangs (Holston, Chapter 13 in this volume; Body-Gendrot, 2000; Caldeira, 2000; Hagedorn, 2006). As integrative mechanisms of global cities failed, vigilantism and private security industries thrived, with little regulation and control through the rule of law (Johnston and Shearing, 2003).

Crime and justice are inevitably seen as sensitive indicators of the state of nations, the moral condition of societies, civilizing efforts and the quality of governance and government. The contemporary global landscape of crime and justice presents itself with deep divisions and fault lines that run between the global North and South, between the centre and periphery, and along post-colonial trajectories of dependence and influence. The North–South divide of security and justice is equally visible in the global economy, where harmful consequences of mostly legal transactions affect countries, regions and citizens mostly in the global South. When large multinational companies or small cyber entrepreneurs take advantage of the differentials of political and economic power of citizens as producers and consumers, of differences in regulation and oversight, or of weak institutions on a large scale, this has dangerous consequences for product and consumer safety, health and financial security (Karstedt, 2007). Crime and justice are significant concerns for the global community that still need to be addressed at the level of national jurisdictions, and major efforts at the global level are simultaneously required to improve global and local justice.

The selection of essays in this volume aims to provide an overview of the conceptualization, theorization and research of the nexus between globalization and crime across roughly the last two decades. It addresses the themes, problems and perspectives as outlined above in order to give the most comprehensive view of contemporary thinking from a range of disciplines, inevitably based on a small number of leading and path-breaking publications. The focus of the collection is on publications that explicitly link globalization and its dynamics to crime in conceptually and theoretically innovative, meaningful and state-of-the-art ways, often building upon theories and concepts outside of criminology. The editors wanted to capture a range of perspectives on globalization and crime that can lead us into the next decade, and also chart the road that authors and researchers have taken since roughly the 1990s. The volume brings to the fore the different forces at work in globalization, and looks at convergence as well as difference, at comparative and global perspectives. It has a particular focus on incorporating the local where possible and appropriate, as crime is a profoundly local phenomenon; in order to achieve a truly global perspective, research and analyses from all continents have been included.

The volume addresses seven systematic themes that are emerging in the most avant-garde literature. As volumes on organized crime, cyber crime, terrorism and international crimes and justice have already been published in this series, crimes of these types were mostly not included in this collection, and only if the essay added a particular framework, conceptual tool or perspective on the global context. Each of the seven parts starts with a more general and introductory essay that frames the processes of globalization at work. Part I, 'Globalization and Crime: Charting New Territory', gives an overview of globalization and perspectives on crime in a globalizing world. Part II, 'Power, Harm and Crime: Global Actors and Crimes of Globalization', provides seminal work on what has been termed the crimes of globalization, on harm and powerful actors within the global sphere beyond the reach of the nation-state. Part III, 'Localizing the Global: Cities, Markets and Crime', focuses on the 'glocality of crime' in the cities and the decisive nodes that cities constitute in the global illegal economy. It comprises seminal essays on illegal markets, organized crime groups and crime and security challenges in global cities. Part IV, 'Crossing Borders: Global Movements, Crime and Control', brings together an interdisciplinary range of writing on the most decisive changes that globalization has entailed, namely migration and mobility across borders, and its impact on crime, criminalization and victimization. Part V, 'Global Trades: At the Intersection of Legal and Illegal Business Transactions', comprises analyses that link legal and illegal business and explore the grey zones where these meet in the global economy and its localized contexts. Part VI, 'Globalization and Violence: Global Forces and Local Violence', addresses one of the most pressing problems of globalization. The increase of intergroup and interpersonal violence and the proliferation of mass atrocities and mass violence has been a major challenge for the international community since the end of the Cold War and the early 1990s (Karstedt, 2013). The concluding Part VII, 'Global Networks of Knowledge and Practice: Globalizing Criminology and Criminal Justice', addresses the global in our discipline and policy-making, and charts future trends and opportunities.

The editors have made their selection with an eye on its use for teaching national and international students, mainly at a postgraduate level where courses on international criminology and globalization are increasingly being established and included in the syllabus.

The editors have used and tested all the material included in their teaching. In March 2012, Susanne Karstedt taught a course on 'International Criminology: Globalization, Crime and Justice' in the International Masters Programme of the International Institute of the Sociology of Law, in Oñati in the Basque country. This course, nearly fully based on this collection, was delivered to a group of 15 students from 13 countries and four continents, Latin and North America, Asia, Africa and Europe. The students critically engaged with the essays and their thoughtful and thought-provoking comments and heated debates showed that the selected essays appealed to their sense of internationalization as well as to their engagement with and in their home countries.

The work on selection has been collaborative from the start, and even if focused on Europe, the collaborative efforts span three countries: David Nelken at home in Italy and the United Kingdom; Susanne Karstedt in the UK, where she migrated from Germany; and Matthias Koch, whose invaluable search efforts made the volume possible, at home in Germany.

Globalization and Crime: Charting New Territory

Essays in Part I of the volume provide a range of frameworks in which we can situate and from where we can explore the nexus between crime and globalization. In Chapter 1 John Meyer introduces concepts of globalization that are seminal for the analysis of crime and justice. His 'world society perspective' focuses on the normative aspects of globalization, where globalization shapes universal norms and values with wide repercussions on the nation-state and national societies. David Nelken was one of the first criminologists to outline the contours of the global landscape of crime and justice. In Chapter 2, written in 1997, he perspicaciously charts the prospects and problems for crime and criminal justice in the dawning era of globalization. Carolyn Nordstrom (Chapter 3) takes Meyer's perspective further and moves closer to the phenomena of global crime; she analyses those networks and flows in the shadow that have become a powerful force in processes of globalization and in particular in the increase of global and transnational crime. In Chapter 4 David Friedrichs canvasses the field of global criminology and redirects our notions of crimes as they enter the global sphere. John Hagan and Wenona Rymond-Richmond, in Chapter 5, provide a cutting-edge comparative perspective for a global criminology that links crime in the global North and South in an innovative way.

In Chapter 1, 'Globalization: Sources and Effects on National States and Societies', John Meyer argues that although globalization presumes local identities this is limited to expressive matters. He makes a number of important observations about the effects of globalization on states and societies, arguing that it produces 'high correlations over time collectively and low correlations across units cross-sectionally' (p. 14). In the absence of a world state, common models of social order are imposed by constituting common cultural principles. These are based on the most admired social models and are able to produce the desired actions in subunits of the world society. The role of non-governmental organizations and of their (apparently) scientific assessments is central to this process. And 'the individual' emerges as a new standardized unit of measurement in the work of these agencies. But the spread of global standards – in places differently able to apply them – often involves hypocrisy as it entails uncontrolled and uncontrollable costs for the actors being monitored.

In Chapter 2, 'The Globalization of Crime and Criminal Justice: Prospects and Problems', David Nelken begins by asking 'Can criminal law and justice be globalized? Or is this already happening?' and 'How are transnational crime and the fear of such crime pushing developments in criminal justice?' (p. 20). The essay counterpoises fear of transnational crime (we could now add terrorism) with the opposite worry of what an overblown reaction to this threat does to rights and freedoms of citizens and prospective immigrants. It goes on to analyse what is meant by globalization, and the ways this can be related to crime and to criminal justice, especially in relation to the possible implications of greater integration and/or homogenization. This is an essay that foreshadows the moral panics ensuing around globalization and transnational crime, and simultaneously promotes a realistic perspective on the globalizing strategies of organized criminals. As it anticipates much of contemporary discussion on globalization and crime it provides the 'long view' of today's problems (see Nelken, 2004, 2011b).

In 'Shadows and Sovereigns' (Chapter 3) Carolyn Nordstrom points to the many social groups that exist outside the formal state system and play a vital role in world markets concerning offshore finance, arms trade, smuggling and so on. She characterizes the networks that organize such traffic as 'non-formal' and seeks to uncover the 'social principles' that govern them. Her main point is that both legal and illegal goods and activities are inextricably linked: they do not belong to different worlds or flow just between military thugs. In many poor African or Asian countries some of the most lucrative – and illegal – commodities pass at some point through the hands of poor people such as workers, petty smugglers or housewives (see also Duffy, Chapter 21 in this volume). Nordstrom argues that the massive size of legal and illegal non-formal commerce has significant implications for the world economy as well as for the local collaboration between the power groups and brokers that keep a sort of order. Using Angola as a case study, she shows how these groups steal local resources under the very eyes of development agencies.

Chapter 4, 'Transnational Crime and Global Criminology: Definitional, Typological, and Contextual Conundrums', by David Friedrichs, offers a division between four areas of study: comparative criminology, transnational criminology, international criminology and global criminology. He also shows that we may need to make analytical distinctions in examining topics even within these fields. In terms of global criminology what, if anything, is there in common between harms perpetuated by international financial and trade institutions such as the World Bank, the International Monetary Fund and the World Trade Organization and crimes committed by nation-states, terrorism and human trafficking? He suggests that we should distinguish between the role of states in the global sphere as criminals, as sources of repression and as corrupt or criminally negligent actors. He is critical of the current institutions of governance in a globalizing world where international bodies may be as much part of the problem as of the solution.

John Hagan and Wenona Rymond-Richmond, in Chapter 5, 'The Mean Streets of the Global Village: Crimes of Exclusion in the United States and Darfur', set out to show the similarities as well as the (more obvious) differences in state-based systems of selective exclusion found in the global North (United States) and in the South (Sudan). The policy of killing fighting-age males in parts of Africa parallels, in demographic terms, the pattern of incarcerating the young adult leaders of drug gangs in the US. Likewise large numbers of homeless adults and children are denied the basic human right to secure shelter in the nations of both the global North and the global South. The fear-driven exclusivity of the North pushes back against the successive waves of forced displacement and pleas for sanctuary/asylum from the South. Yet the fate of each is linked by the shrinking and interconnected dimensions of the joined worlds in which we live. The authors conclude by calling for the institution of better international criminal law to narrow the distance between these worlds.

Power, Harm and Crime: Global Actors and Crimes of Globalization

The essays in Part II explore the crimes of globalization – that is, those crimes that are committed by powerful global actors in pursuit of global interests and policies. Transnational corporate crime, states and international institutions figure large in these accounts of harm done and crimes committed with impunity. These range from collusion with corrupt regimes (Chapters 7 and 8), denying health and safety to vulnerable populations (Chapter 6) to the pursuit of cross-border drug prevention policies (Chapter 9). Actors involved are states, transnational corporations (Chapter 8) and international organizations like the World Bank (Chapter 7), who are in a powerful position to impose harmful policies on communities in the global South and exploit their position as powerful global (and local) players through a range of harmful and often illegal activities.

In Chapter 6, 'Crimes of Globalization: Health Care, HIV and the Poverty of Neoliberalism in Sub-Saharan Africa', Ifeanyi Ezeonu sets out to reveal the dynamics of market economics and its criminogenic effects, especially in economically challenged regions like sub-Saharan Africa. He argues for a definition of crime that incorporates issues of social harm and justice and goes beyond the proscriptions of the criminal law. Adopting the approach of critical criminology as advocated by Friedrichs, he cites the structural adjustment programme of the International Monetary Fund and the World Bank in sub-Saharan Africa as having led to the victimization of vulnerable populations, especially a rise in deaths and illness among the poor. In general, Ezeonu argues that the policies of international agencies influenced by the dictates of neo-liberalism must be framed in terms of what he calls the 'ecology of poverty' (p. 131).

Chapter 7, 'Facilitating Corruption and Human Rights Violations: The Role of International Financial Institutions', by Dawn Rothe, also focuses on the harms committed by financial institutions. Rothe points to the World Bank's 'pressure to lend' culture and the entailing reward structure at the internal organizational level, both fostering violations of the very principles of these organizations in observing human rights and ending corruption. She illustrates her argument by focusing, for example, on the Structural Adjustment Programmes by which the Senegalese government was forced to cut spending in many areas, including its ferry programmes, which were central to transportation in the country. This had a direct impact on the upkeep of the Le Joola ferry which capsized, resulting in the deaths of 1,863 passengers. Rothe also points to the knowing acceptance of Rwanda's and Uganda's illegal expropriation of the Democratic Republic of Congo's gold and diamonds, as well as the linkages between international financial institution policies and rampant corruption that can be seen in the liberalization and privatizations that have occurred in Pakistan.

In Chapter 8, 'Good Guys, Bad Guys: Transnational Corporations, Rational Choice Theory and Power Crime', Leslie Holmes argues that transnational corporations exert exaggerated power in the contemporary world which is often at the expense of the nation-state. They may force states to collude with companies in securing important foreign contracts or in protecting important defence industries. He shows that many corporations, including some from countries with otherwise high domestic standards on such matters, have engaged in such corrupt behaviour. But he also points out that other corporations, such as Motorola and IKEA, have resisted pressures to enter such agreements. Holmes claims that rational choice models or the effects of 'neo-liberalism' are insufficient to explain such apparently contradictory behaviours by corporations. He ends by insisting that such collusive behaviour represents a serious danger to democracy, the rule of law and public security.

In 'Narcophobia: Drugs Prohibition and the Generation of Human Rights Abuses' (Chapter 9), Fernanda Mena and Dick Hobbs explore the impact of the war on drugs in the global North on human rights abuses in the global South. They argue that prohibition driven by moralism creates a black market that is regulated by violent entrepreneurs. This in particular affects developing countries, where this trade often offers the only feasible employment option. Using as illustrations Bolivia, Colombia and Brazil they show how the militarization of prohibition enforcement has hindered the advancement of democracy and increases violence and human rights abuses. The northern war on drugs leads to the corruption of law enforcement officials and monopolizes the efforts of the criminal justice system so that it is starved of resources to fight the crimes of robbery, theft and assault that mostly affect poor citizens. The authors end by insisting that issues of drug production and trade need to be dealt with by better regulation from within a development perspective.

Localizing the Global: Cities, Markets and Crime

Global cities are spaces where the global and the local meet, and where the global is embedded and intricately intertwined with the local. Contemporary cities are, as Saskia Sassen puts it in Chapter 10, 'strategic sites' and a 'new frontier' in a globalizing world. Citizens increasingly experience crime as a threat to their well-being and security, as they live with historically unprecedented levels of diversity. Part III opens with Chapter 10, a seminal essay by Saskia Sassen on the global city, which provides a framework for the dissection of contemporary crime and security challenges in urban spaces. This framework helps to understand the ways in which organized crime and illegal markets are deeply embedded in local urban structures (Chapters 11 and 12) and give rise to hybrid cultures and unprecedented urban discourses on global norms (Chapter 13).

In 'The Global City: Strategic Site/New Frontier' (Chapter 10), Saskia Sassen focuses on the *practices* that constitute economic globalization and global control, by which she means 'the work of producing and reproducing the organization and management of a global production system and a global marketplace for finance' (p. 189). She argues that the spatial dispersal of economic activities at the metropolitan, national and global levels has contributed to a demand for new forms of territorial centralization of top-level management and control operations. Many of the resources necessary for global economic activities are not hyper-mobile but, rather, deeply embedded in places such as global cities and export processing zones. But while the downtowns of cities and business centres in metropolitan areas receive massive investments in real estate and telecommunications the low-income urban and metropolitan areas are starved of resources. Financial services produce super profits while industry and industrial services barely survive. Women and immigrants provide a cheap labour supply while trapped in their deprived economic positions and neighbourhoods. It is within this 'glocal' and highly segregated urban space that crime and violence thrive.

It is this 'glocal' context of organized crime that Dick Hobbs addresses in Chapter 11, 'Going Down the Glocal: The Local Context of Organised Crime'. Like Nelken in Chapter 2, he was one of the first to take a more sober view of transnational organized crime, at a time when exaggerated and gloomy accounts of its global power predominated. Organized crime is essentially parochial and local, and 'firmly entrenched in the locations, working practices, occupational cultures and oppositional strategies' (p. 211) of the social and ethnic groups that are involved. Hobbs gives a vivid ethnographic account of the scene and environment, actors, networks and activities of organized crime in English working-class communities. These communities are equally threatened by globalization as industries and jobs migrate to other regions and globalization offers new opportunities for criminal business, which rarely deserves the label 'transnational'. These communities react in different ways, and their protagonists navigate diverse routes in the rapidly changing environment of local organized crime activities.

Chapter 12, 'Mumbai's Development Mafias: Globalization, Organized Crime and Land Development', by Liza Weinstein, provides a case study from the global South of what is happening in the type of global cities being discussed by Sassen. Weinstein traces the rise and transformation of Mumbai's major organized crime groups since the 1950s and argues that their recent entrance into land and property development is a product of the liberalization and globalization of the Indian economy. Mumbai's criminal organization has transformed from paternalistic local crime bosses into well-financed, globally reaching organizations. Extended now from the Persian Gulf to Malaysia, and with linkages identified in London, Johannesburg and New York, the strength of the city's large organized crime cartels is based on their ties to political parties, embeddedness in antagonistic religious communities and their increasingly global reach. In the real estate business, they are presently closely linked to the state, which has become dependent on these organizations to carry out its own development objectives using these same mafias to clear the city of street vendors and maintain control in particular poor neighbourhoods.

In the final essay in Part III, 'Dangerous Spaces of Citizenship: Gang Talk, Rights Talk and Rule of Law in Brazil' (Chapter 13), James Holston observes an unexpected emergence of human rights discourses in the urban spaces of extreme poverty in Brazil. The criminal gangs who run some of the poorest neighbourhoods of the urban peripheries distribute summary execution along with diapers, milk, medication and employment, but use the language of human rights to justify prison rebellions as well as their own usurpation of power and to criticize repressive actions by representatives of state justice alike. Holston's explanation of these contradictions is that urbanization and neo-liberalization have destabilized entrenched social, spatial and economic regimes. Differential citizenship has created legal and extralegal inequalities, and in the 'disjunctive democracies' (p. 246) large institutional spaces are left without governance and oversight. In the urban spaces of abject poverty the economic forces of globalization intersect with the normative impact of the international human rights regime and its proliferation, creating improbable alliances and normative discourses against the backdrop of 'world society'.

Crossing Borders: Global Movements, Crime and Control

Globalization has been most commonly described as an unprecedented flow of goods, people, capital and communication across the globe. Illegal migration and trafficking of people and goods are deemed one of the most pressing challenges for transnational control and are subject to intense monitoring and criminalization across borders. Far from being less important, borders signify the processes of globalization more than ever, and have a decisive role in the control of migration. The first two essays in Part IV frame globalization as a drive towards new 'mobility regimes', where new technologies of control across and within borders are developed (Chapter 14), and new forms of exclusion arise within societies (Chapter 15). Human trafficking affects vulnerable groups, and migrants are exposed to exploitation, exclusion and harassment from criminal justice (Chapter 16). As women represent the largest groups of migrants (see Sassen, Chapter 10), they are also the most vulnerable, and are victimized by traffickers, employers and criminal justice agencies (Chapter 17).

In his theoretical contribution 'Without Borders? Notes on Globalization as a Mobility Regime' (Chapter 14), Ronen Shamir treats globalization as a highly contradictory set of cultural and normative pressures, involving tensions between capitalism and democracy, the North and the South, the haves and have-nots, empire and multitude, as well as between 'globalizers' and a variety of so-called anti-globalization movements. Globalization imposes growing restrictions on movement even as it leads to hyper-mobility for a small minority and produces its own 'principles of closure' that operate as a counterbalance to the normative principle of global human rights. A 'paradigm of suspicion' (p. 265) has arisen that brings together the perceived threats of terrorism, crime and immigration and relies on finely tuned screening mechanisms. It transforms mobility into a public performance. The individual is located within collective categories of suspicion and subject to public scrutiny, simultaneously as a universal rights-bearer and as a universal threat.

In Chapter 15, 'Analysing a World in Motion: Global Flows Meet "Criminology of the Other"', Katja Franko Aas expands on these themes from a decisively criminological perspective. Demands for control of global mobility flows create a complex dynamics between the nation-state and the emerging 'world risk society'. A society connected by its shared awareness and fear of 'de-bounded' global risks produces recurrent moral panics about terrorism, crime by immigrants and asylum seekers, global paedophile and trafficking networks, cyber crime and so forth. The border is now everywhere, and regulating the various forms of transnational mobility is increasingly merged with the regulation of deviance in contemporary governance. The so-far privileged position of the state and the national as the primary field of criminological reference is increasingly overshadowed by various transnational and subnational configurations.

The focus of Jo Goodey's essay, 'Human Trafficking: Sketchy Data and Policy Responses' (Chapter 16), is on a realistic assessment of global trafficking. She casts doubt on available data, in particular as these provide the foundation for policy responses, and her sceptical view has been corroborated by recent reports and estimates on the extent of global trafficking (UNODC, 2010). After providing a brief overview of the various instruments defining trafficking, she draws attention to the fact that policy formation and responses have been dominated by sex trafficking, at the expense of other types such as labour exploitation and child trafficking. Policy responses are shifting into the direction of addressing it as a 'victim-centred' crime, even as they are inextricably linked to the migration-crime-security nexus. Notwithstanding the importance of trafficking in international and national policy responses and global law-making, essential knowledge is missing concerning the role of demand, the mechanisms of transactions and the modus operandi of traffickers. Trafficking as a global crime needs to be addressed on all these levels, and with sufficient evidence base (see Nelken, 2011c).

Finally, Chapter 17 by Staci Strobl, 'Policing Housemaids: The Criminalization of Domestic Workers in Bahrain', focuses on women as victims and controllers of migrants and migration. Globalization has given rise to a particular dependency on female labour as individual women attempt to survive within the global context of economic transformation. Strobl explains the increase in numbers of policewomen in the Bahraini police force as less a sign of progress towards more gender quality than a consequence of their task in the heavy policing of domestic workers. Themselves employing such workers, they almost always side with employers in conflicts with their workers or in cases where they decide they wish to be rid of them. Based on her observations at local police stations, Strobl identifies five types of 'constructed' characterizations of housemaids in such conflicts: the amicably departing housemaid, the thieving housemaid, the runaway housemaid, the indiscrete housemaid and the violent housemaid. The study demonstrates the importance of case studies in the exploration of the global and local dynamics of migration and crime, as outlined by both Ronen Shamir and Katja Franko Aas.

Global Trades: At the Intersection of Legal and Illegal Business Transactions

As global trade in goods and capital increased at an unprecedented scale, the spread of neo-liberal ideology meant that this was not balanced by a strategy of regulation. The global economy thus presented unparalleled opportunities for illegal business practices and forged linkages between legal and illegal markets, as legal markets incorporated illegal enterprises and illegal markets captured legal flows of goods and capital. Part V comprises analyses that explore the impact of globalization on illegal practices embedded in and connected to legal business transactions. The scale of illegal opportunities took its toll on the normative underpinnings of the legal global economy. As Nikos Passas puts it in Chapter 18, 'global anomie and dysnomie' are pervading the global economy, and traders, for example in the antiquities market, navigate global and national norms with idiosyncratic (im)moralities

(Chapter 19). Newly emerging trades are susceptible to linking up with transnational organized crime and pose considerable challenges for regulation (Chapter 20). The essay by Rosaleen Duffy on illegal gemstone mining in Africa (Chapter 21) presents a different perspective: it demonstrates that as previously legal trades are illegalized in the course of globalization, this has a detrimental impact on the livelihood and traditions of indigenous populations in the global South.

In Chapter 18, 'Global Anomie, Dysnomie, and Economic Crime: Hidden Consequences of Neoliberalism and Globalization in Russia and Around the World', Nikos Passas tries to go beyond what he calls the 'drastic' crime fighting methods used to respond to transnational crime in investigating the causes, structure, extent and effects of serious cross-border criminal conduct. He builds upon classical anomie theory and sees globalizing neo-liberalism as a key element in the causation of such crime. The 'market is best' ideology – allied to the global promotion of the American way of life – has led to what he calls' global anomie'. Increasing communications and connections between richer and poor parts of the globe make poor countries less content with their cultures. Ever greater economic, political, legal and cultural asymmetries between and within countries give rise to 'means-ends discrepancies' (p. 354) that generate motives for criminal activity and weaken social controls. Passas applies his approach to Russia, where a small elite in collusion with criminal organizations and legal companies learned how to exploit the transition and emerging illegal opportunities, and engaged in widespread corrupt practices.

In Chapter 19, 'Transnational Crime, Local Denial', Simon Mackenzie explores the global 'field' of law and morality, and the ways in which the normative underpinnings of market transactions evolve for a global niche market – the trade in antiquities. Even if small on a global scale, this is a trade of highest importance for the wider field of international relations and power structures. The increasingly contested nature of the trade in antiquities, and the conflicts between countries of origin and countries, where owners and museums are located, mirrors the global South–North divide in legal and illegal markets. Actors in this field respond with carefully crafted strategies that link legal and illegal business and adapt to the shifting nature of regulations, political constraints and economic advantages and disadvantages. Strategies of local denial in markets are accompanied by carefully constructed ethics, and legal advice, indicating a high level of collusion between providers, sellers and buyers in this market that defies law and regulation.

Carole Gibbs, Edmund McGarrell and Mark Axelrod argue in Chapter 20 that legal and illegal global business have more in common than is generally assumed. The causes of the financial crisis of 2008 are similar to those of global illegal trading, in particular the huge opportunities created by a lack of regulation and oversight. Their essay 'Transnational White-Collar Crime and Risk' draws lessons from the global trade in electronic waste. This is an innovative perspective not only in terms of the links and parallels between the financial crisis and this emerging type of trade, but also in terms of the analysis of an alarming increase in the global trade in e-waste, the discarding and disposal of electronic equipment of all kind. Importers and exporters can take advantage of differential regulation and oversight of the disposal of such waste, little to none worker safety in the handling of highly dangerous materials and their disposal in ways that cause severe health hazards in developing countries. This provides huge incentives and opportunities for risky and fraudulent global transactions in e-waste in a grey zone of global non-regulation, which have a lot in common with the financial transactions that finally culminated in the global crisis of 2008. The authors argue that only 'smart regulation' in the domestic and international sphere can provide viable responses to both types of risky and fraudulent business.

Finally, in Chapter 21, 'Gemstone Mining in Madagascar: Transnational Networks, Criminalisation and Global Integration', Rosaleen Duffy demonstrates the highly variable impacts of globalization in sub-Saharan Africa. She argues that distinct categories such as global/local, legal/illegal and traditional/modern have lost much of their explanatory power in the context of highly interlinked networks of actors involved in a wide range of exchanges that exist outside the formally recorded economic system and constitute a non-formal economy (according to Nordstrom, see Chapter 3 in this volume). Far from being distinct categories, they are indivisible and constitute a single complex that produces enormous wealth, coupled with high degrees of poverty and marginalization in precisely the same locations. Describing the interrelated global and local networks involved in informal, or extra-legal, gem trading and extraction in Madagascar Duffy shows how the contemporary state in Africa is characterized by alliances between elites with global economic interests, including private business, NGOs, donors and illicit trading networks. Thus gemstone miners are interlinked with globalized networks of international dealers who ensure that the stones can be illegally exported, linking rural areas with the global economy. These networks have gained control over the local economy through the use of symbolic or actual violence. Duffy points to the negative effects of this global-local economy for the growth of prostitution, AIDS, pollution and the destruction of forests.

Globalization and Violence: Global Forces and Local Violence

During the first decades of globalization, violence soared across the globe. Mass atrocities and massacres took place mostly as part of a resurgence of ethnic violence, and affected citizens in Europe, Africa, Latin America and Asia; cities in the global North as well as in the global South suffered from soaring levels of violence in particular during the 1980s and 1990s, and transnational organized crime was accompanied by extraordinary levels of violence in its strongholds. Since the beginning of the twenty-first century violence has subsided, including both conflict-related mass violence and interpersonal violence (Karstedt, 2012c). The invocation of globalization as the dominant and overarching cause has given way to more differentiated analyses of the connection between globalization and violence, which take into account different types of violence and dissect global processes and local contexts. The Indian sociologist Arjun Appadurai was one of the first to look back at two decades of globalization and a concomitant increase in ethnic violence; in a seminal essay (Chapter 22) he related extreme as well as intimate violence to the structural, physical and moral pressures of globalization. Two essays in Part VI detail the role of the state (Chapter 23) and of international financial institutions and business in genocides in Sudan and Rwanda (Chapter 24). In Chapter 25, Jessica Livingston explores the ways in which global pressures give rise to intimate and gendered violence, typically at the 'border', and in the infamous border city of Juárez.

Chapter 22, Arjun Appadurai's 'Dead Certainty: Ethnic Violence in the Era of Globalization', written in 1998, is grounded in an anthropological perspective of both globalization and violence. It takes a longer view of the processes of globalization and identifies at its core the emergence of divergence as well as homogenization, of 'categorical mixture' (p. 442) and imposed closure of ethnic categorization. Expanding upon Mary Douglas's (1966) classic link between 'purity and danger', Appadurai describes globalization as a process that questions and threatens ethnic identities and spaces, their institutional formations and economic foundations. Violence is inscribed on the body, and the 'body ethnic' has come under pressure and been threatened by the transnational processes and transregional contacts that have combined into contemporary globalization since the 1970s. Globalization creates doubt, uncertainty and indeterminacy about, and of, identity, belonging, entitlements and the 'other'. Violence – from interpersonal encounters and gendered violence to large-scale genocidal events and massacres – is deeply rooted in such uncertainty, and restoring certainty creates chain reactions of escalating violence – a dead end of deadly certainty.

In Chapter 23, 'State Terrorism and Globalization', Asafa Jalata provides a congenial application of Appadurai's framework of globalization and violence, with a focus on the role of the state and state formation in the violent processes of globalization. Since according to most accounts globalization puts the nation-state under immense pressure, problems should exacerbate where states are composed of highly divergent ethnicities, religions and cultures, and are essentially overwhelmed by problems of ethnic identity and conflict. Jalata links early colonial and contemporary globalization in the exemplary cases of Ethiopia and Sudan, as both processes have accelerated racialization and ethnicization of these states. In the move towards internal domination and external self-determination after colonial rule, both states have engaged in racializing ethnic identities; they have marginalized the indigenous African population and been involved in ethnic cleansing. These processes have been set in motion and sustained by state terror and extreme levels of state violence, which the elites in both states engaged in for their legitimacy and survival, with external support from the international community.

In a similar vein, in Chapter 24, 'The Rwandan Genocide: International Financial Policies and Human Rights', Dawn Rothe, Christopher Mullins and Kent Sandstrom start their analysis of the Rwandan genocide with the pressures put on the sovereignty and stability of African states by international financial organizations and the imbalances of power created through globalization. They target the policies the World Bank and the International Monetary Fund have imposed on African states like Rwanda since the 1980s, in particular the rescheduling of debts and the forced adoption of neo-liberal and open market policies. They demonstrate the huge discrepancy between the actual powerlessness of Rwanda at the international level and in the decision-making of these institutions, and the far-reaching impact that these policies had on the agricultural basis of the Rwandan economy. The Rwandan genocide of 1994 was preceded by a deepening economic crisis that directly resulted from these policies and affected the subsistence farming and livelihood of both leading ethnic groups. The subsequent creation of a climate of economic and political insecurity in Rwanda and Burundi exacerbated the ethnic conflicts on both sides of the border and erupted in massacres and finally the genocide.

Gendered violence is a defining characteristic of contemporary mass atrocities and ethnic conflicts. However, as Arjun Appadurai argues, intimate and interpersonal violence are equally and inevitably gendered and linked to the global processes that profoundly change gender as well as ethnic identities. In Chapter 25, 'Murder in Juárez', Jessica Livingston looks into the violent crime scene of Ciudad Juárez, across the border from El Paso in Texas, which became infamous for a series of murders of women between 1993 and 2002, with about 300 victims and more missing. This lethal violence was accompanied by an extraordinarily high number of rapes and other forms of violence against women. Nearly all of the victims were migrant workers from rural parts of Mexico, who were attracted by the thriving export economy, based on cheap and exploitative labour, mainly provided by female migrants. Globalization thus generated a gendered economy, with exploitative gender relationships that were extended into all realms of life, and could rely on traditional gender structures. Simultaneously the feminized labour market threatened male dominance and men's jobs. In the upsurge of extreme gendered violence in Ciudad Juárez the global economy intersected with local conditions and traditions, and created a dynamic of lethal insecurities for women.

Global Networks of Knowledge and Practice: Globalizing Criminology and Criminal Justice

Globalization raised expectations that criminological knowledge, institutional practice and criminal justice policies would easily travel around the globe. As for modernity in the previous decades, it was assumed that globalization itself would act as a force towards convergence not only through the coincidence of economic and social pressures but also through the adoption of institutions and practices that had proven successful. The institutional hegemony and domination of European models and practices of justice meant that they were rolled out, often without much consideration of their detrimental impact (Cohen, 1982). Only very slowly has the transfer of criminological knowledge and institutional practice changed direction, with theories and practice beginning to emanate from the South rather than travel from the North. In addition the importance of local conditions and national contexts is becoming increasingly recognized. On the other hand, contemporary global criminal justice is faced with universalizing pressures from the norms of the human rights regime, and its impact on local justice. Further to this, the international community has geared up activities to combat transnational crimes, which force national and local jurisdictions to implement particular instruments and institutions within an environment that often is not prepared for such design (van Dijk, 2008). As these processes simultaneously evolve, criminological paradigms, criminal justice institutions and practices converge as well as diverge, thus testifying to the different cultures, societies, polities and economies where they are established. The essays in Part VII thus illuminate the different forces behind global diversity and convergence in criminal justice policies. In Chapter 26, Bill Dixon analyses the travel of criminological paradigms from the global North to the South in highly reflexive and interactive processes. Susanne Karstedt, in Chapter 27, follows the routes and locales of criminal justice institutions as they are adopted from different national jurisdictions and institutional regimes. The following two essays reveal how the impact of global political, economic and social pressures on national jurisdictions produce a diversity of reforms and institutions that owe as much to national, cultural and social patterns of criminal justice and policing as to globalizing and universalizing forces, as Pat O'Malley stresses in Chapter 28. In Chapter 29, Nicholas Dorn and Michael Levi demonstrate the role of regional and national interests (Europe and Asia) and the importance of processes of coercion, power-broking and competition in the adoption of anti-money laundering policies in developed and developing countries.

In Chapter 26, Bill Dixon searches for and indeed finds a story of 'interactive globalization' in his account of the adoption and adaptation of critical criminology in South Africa. He follows the 'selective and disjointed history' (p. 542) of South Africa's engagement with critical criminology, starting from distorted applications in the 1930s up to the development of new models of informal justice and policing of and by communities since the 1990s. This history is deeply embedded in and distinctly shaped by the history of apartheid, the struggle for liberation and the final transition to democracy. As Dixon finds, the momentum in particular of the Zwelethemba project, a model of informal community policing and justice, comes from the periphery as much as from the centre, and the flows of ideas, practices and institutions emanate from South Africa as much as from Northern Ireland, as they were implemented in both post-conflict environments. Dixon detects a continuing process of interactive globalization in particular since the end of apartheid, with models and theories mirrored back and offered to the global North.

In Chapter 27, her essay on the 'travel' of crime policies, Susanne Karstedt takes issue with the notion that particular crime policies inevitably emerge as globalization takes hold. Rather she starts from a (neo)-institutional perspective that focuses on the role of the travel, import and export of institutions and practices, as well as 'crime policy packages' like community policing. She argues that the success and failure of such global travel is much less shaped by the specific features of the institutions and practices that are 'on the road' than by the institutional environment and context at the final 'destinations'. Criminal justice is deeply parochial and embedded in belief and value systems that are instantiated in its institutions and practices. They are less guided by principles of efficiency than by other principles, among these the human rights regime. Institutional travel and transfer fail where safeguards are lacking or engrained cultures of corruption and illegal violence are paradoxically encouraged rather than constrained by institutional transfer. For example, the introduction of zero-tolerance policies from the US into Brazil led to an increase in police brutality in Brazil, with soaring numbers of killings of street children.

Pat O'Malley takes this argument further in Chapter 28, 'Globalizing Risk?', his comparison of 'neo-liberal' criminal justice in Australia and the US. Like Karstedt he critically examines the assumption of global adoption and subsequent convergence, and bases his argument on the emergence and spread of risk-based models and frameworks of justice. Both the US and Australia at least in rhetoric have adopted 'actuarial models' of justice with a shift towards risk management of offenders that replaces other rationales for punishment. However, rather than adopting the model and in particular its repressive and incapacitating practices, Australia takes a decisively different route towards risk management, which is embedded in local contexts and social conditions. O'Malley corroborates his argument by juxtaposing the US 'war on drugs' with the 'harm minimization' strategies adopted for drug offenders and drug addicts in Australian states. These strategies digress so far from the US model that this raises severe doubts concerning global generalizations about such policies and their 'simple transportability'.

In Chapter 29, 'East Meets West in Anti-Money Laundering and Anti-Terrorist Finance', Nicholas Dorn and Michael Levi (re-)introduce the more traditional concepts of international relations into this debate, and thus provide a distinctly global rather than locally focused perspective. They analyse the field of power relations and security preferences and concerns, and the impact of these on the adoption or rejection of policies against transnational crime. Interests in global trade and market shares shape the adoption and implementation of anti-money laundering and anti-terrorist financing strategies. The negotiations between two different economic and jurisdictional regions, Europe in the global North and Asia in the global South, are defined by different interests and industries, as responsibilities for implementation and prosecution are assigned to the regions, and blame is distributed between the actors. Policy preferences are subject to dominating financial and economic interest, and presently Asian policy preferences are hardly accommodated in the global policy dialogue. International cooperation against transnational crime, monitoring and control is confronted with 'structural impediments, grounded in economic interests and political sensibilities' (p. 599) that mirror underlying (traditional) power relations rather than global dynamics.

References

Aas, K.F. (2007), *Globalization and Crime*, Los Angeles and London: Sage.

Abraham, I. and Schendel, W. (eds) (2005), *Illicit Flows and Criminal Things: States, Borders and the Other Side of Globalization*, Bloomington: Indiana University Press.

Andreas, P. and Nadelmann, E. (2006), *Policing the Globe: Criminalisation and Crime Control in International Relations*, Oxford: Oxford University Press.

Appadurai, A. (1996), *Modernity at Large: Cultural Dimensions of Globalization*, Minneapolis and London: University of Minnesota Press.

Body-Gendrot, S. (2000), *The Social Control of Cities: A Comparative Perspective*, Oxford: Blackwell.

Bowling, B. (2010), *Policing the Caribbean: Transnational Security Cooperation in Practice*, Oxford: Oxford University Press.

Caldeira, T. (2000), *City of Walls: Crime, Segregation and Citizenship in Sao Paulo*, Berkeley: University of California Press.

Carruthers, B.G. and Halliday, T. (2006), 'Negotiating Globalization: Globalization and the Construction of Insolvency Regimes in East Asia', *Law & Social Inquiry*, **31**, 3, pp. 521–84.

Cohen, S. (1982), 'Western Crime Control Models in the Third World: Benign or Malignant?', *Research in Law, Deviance and Social Control*, **4**, pp. 85–119.

Douglas, M. (1966), *Purity and Danger. An Analysis of the concepts of Pollution and Taboo*, London and Boston: Routledge and Kegan Paul.

Findlay, M. (2008), *Governing Through Globalised Crime: Futures for International Criminal Justice*, Cullompton: Willan.

Fourcade, M. and Savelsberg, J. (2006), 'Introduction: Global Processes, National Institutions, Local Bricolage: Shaping Law in an Era of Globalisation', *Law & Social Inquiry*, **31**, 3, pp. 513–19.

Friedrichs, D.O. (2007), 'Transnational Crime and Global Criminology: Definitional, Typological and Contextual Conundrums', *Social Justice*, **34**, pp. 1–19.

Friedrichs, D.O. (2011), 'Comparative Criminology and Global Criminology as Complementary Projects', in D. Nelken (ed.), *Comparative Criminal Justice and Globalisation*, Farnham: Ashgate, pp. 163–82.

Goldsmith, A. and Sheptycki, J. (eds) (2007), *Crafting Transnational Policing: Police Capacity-Building and Global Policing Reform*, Oxford: Hart.

Hagedorn, J. (ed.) (2006), *Gangs in the Global City*, Chicago: University of Illinois Press.

Johnson, D.T. and Zimring, F.E. (2009), *The Next Frontier: National Development, Political Change, and the Death Penalty in Asia*, Oxford and New York: Oxford University Press.

Johnston, L. and Shearing, C. (2003), *Governing Security: Explorations in Policing and Justice*, New York: Routledge.

Karstedt, S. (2007), 'From Crimes of the Powerful to the Crimes of Power: An Uncomfortable Situation', *Monatsschrift für Kriminologie und Strafrechtsreform*, **90**, 2/3, pp. 78–90.

Karstedt, S. (2012a), 'Globalization and Crime', in G. Ritzer (ed.), *Blackwell Encyclopedia of Globalization*, vol. I, Oxford: Blackwell, pp. 343–52.

Karstedt, S. (2012b), 'Comparing Justice and Crime Across Cultures', in D. Gadd, S. Karstedt and S. Messner (eds), *The SAGE Handbook of Criminological Research Methods*, Los Angeles, London and New Delhi: Sage, pp. 373–89.

Karstedt, S. (2012c), 'Globalisation, Mass Atrocities and Genocide', in F. Pakes (ed.), *Globalisation and the Challenge to Criminology*, Abingdon: Routledge, pp. 146–64.

Larsen, N. and Smandych, R. (eds) (2008), *Global Criminology and Criminal Justice: Current Issues and Perspectives*, Peterborough, CA: Broadview Press.

Messner, S.F., Rosenfeld, R and Karstedt, S. (2013), 'Social Institutions and Crime', in F.T. Cullen and P. Wilcox (eds), *Oxford Handbook of Criminological Theory*, New York: Oxford University Press, pp. 405–23.

Muncie, J., Talbot, D. and Walters, R. (eds) (2010), *Crime: Local and Global*, Cullompton: Willan.

Nelken, D. (2004), 'Globalisation and Crime', in P. Kennett (ed.), *A Handbook of Comparative Social Policy*, Cheltenham: Edward Elgar, pp. 373–82.

Nelken, D. (2010), *Comparative Criminal Justice*, Los Angeles and London: Sage.

Nelken, D. (2011a), 'Afterword: Studying Criminal Justice in Globalising Times', in D. Nelken (ed.), *Comparative Criminal Justice and Globalisation*, Farnham: Ashgate, pp. 183–210.

Nelken, D. (ed.) (2011b), *Comparative Criminal Justice and Globalisation*, Farnham: Ashgate.

Nelken, D. (2011c), 'Human Trafficking and Legal Culture', *Israel Law Review*, **43**, pp. 479–513.

Sassen, S. (2007), *A Sociology of Globalization*, New York and London: W.W. Norton.

Sheptycki, J. (ed.) (2000), *Issues in Transnational Policing*, London and New York: Routledge.

UNODC (United Nations Office on Drugs and Crime) (2010), *The Globalization of Crime: A Transnational Organized Crime Threat Assessment*, Vienna: UNODC.

Van Dijk, J. (2008), *The World of Crime*, Los Angeles and London: Sage.

Van Duyne, P.C. and Levi, M. (2005), *Drugs and Money: Managing the Drug Trade and Crime-Money in Europe*, London and New York: Routledge.

Part I
Globalization and Crime: Charting New Territory

[1]

Globalization

Sources and Effects on National States and Societies

John W. Meyer
Stanford University

abstract: The world polity and cultural system are relatively stateless, but they legitimate strong nation-state identities as the dominant actors. This produces very strong tendencies for the adoption of common models of modernity, despite extraordinary differences in resources and local culture. Local distinctiveness is also legitimated, so long as it is not inconsistent with homogeneity on the main dimensions of stratification and identity.

keywords: actor identities ✦ decoupling ✦ global models ✦ glocalization ✦ legitimation

Globalization has a number of dimensions. First, it means the increased political and military interdependence of a set of sovereign nation-states and the expanded and strengthened set of organizations involved: here, states are the main actors conceptualized. Second, it means the increased economic interdependencies of a set of national or subnational economies and the relevant multilateral and international public and private organizations: here, states and firms are the main originating actors. Third, it means an expanded flow of individual persons among societies through socioeconomic migration, travel and political expulsion: states and individuals are the main actors discussed.

Fourth, globalization means the expanded interdependence of expressive culture through intensified global communication. Themes from music to ethnic revival spread like fads through the world society, and organizational structures arise to spread them. All types of actors from individuals to organizations to national states are involved.

Fifth, globalization means the expanded flow of instrumental culture around the world. Put simply, common models of social order become authoritative in many different social settings. This article focuses on this dimension of globalization: on why it arises, how it is organized and what consequences it has.

The Phenomenon

There is, by now, little dispute about the facts of the matter. In many areas of social life, common models organized in world discourse arise and penetrate social life worldwide. At the nation-state level, the theme is highly developed (see the review by Meyer et al., 1997a).

1. The world society creates, increasingly, common models of national state identity and purpose (McNeely, 1995). These scripted forms, as they change over time, show up in national constitutions (Boli, 1987), depiction of national purpose (Fiala and Gordon-Lanford, 1987; McNeely, 1995) and data systems (Ventresca, 1995). Essentially, all national states now define their fundamental purposes as having to do with socioeconomic development or welfare and individual justice, rights and equality.
2. Common models of socioeconomic development are also scripted, and national policies change with changes in world scripts. Thus science is seen as central to development, and associated policies and investments expand and spread rapidly (Finnemore, 1996; Schofer, 1999). The same holds for population control in a mid-century reversal from pro-natalist to anti-natalist doctrines (Barrett and Frank, 1999); actual demographic patterns follow similar paths (Bongaarts and Watkins, 1996). Economic policies change in worldwide waves (Hall, 1989), including recent waves that stress markets and privatization. A huge wave of policy and practice change is created by the recent world environment movement (Frank et al., 1999; Meyer et al., 1997b). Broad shifts, such as a great expansion in numbers of national parks, are worldwide; so are narrow ones in the spread of environmental impact assessment policies.
3. Common models of human rights are also scripted and produce waves of national policy and practice changes in areas such as the status of ethnoracial minorities or women (Bradley and Ramirez, 1996; Berkovitch, 1999; McNeely, 1995). Movements such as current efforts to extend rights to gays and lesbians are worldwide in character and produce waves of local social organization and national policy (Frank and McEneaney, 1999). More broadly, a general world wave emphasizing both human rights and democratization has had much impact.
4. Education, linking both ideologies of human rights and of social progress, has been highly scripted with enormous impact on educational expansion around the world (Riddle, 1993; Meyer et al., 1992a).

Educational curricula show the same scripted and standardized qualities, both at the mass and at the elite levels (Meyer et al., 1992b).

If we shift from the national to the organizational level, it is more difficult to find comparative and longitudinal research. Most work in this field is intranational. But, clearly, much cultural globalization is going on, as organizations in many different societies come under the influence of standard models of organizing, and consulting firms and professionals helping them to do this spread very rapidly. In areas like accounting, sweeping reforms take a worldwide character (Olson et al., 1998). This is also true of information systems, management styles, organizational training programs and modern models of proper formal organizational structure. Schools, hospitals, businesses and government agencies come to see themselves – and to be analyzed by others – as organizations and actors of a generally universalized sort and thus as subject to standardizing rationalization (Brunsson and Sahlin-Andersson, 1997).

At the individual level, many analyses also suggest rather sweeping forms of modernization – the reconstruction of the individual as a standardized unit with standard rights and capacities (Inkeles and Smith, 1974; see the review by Jepperson, 1992). This is aided by the very rapid expansion of systems of universal mass education (Meyer et al., 1992a), which is known to play a dominant role in constructing the standard 'modern' individual. At the global level, of course, highly elaborated standard models of the rights and standing of the human and citizen individuals are developed. These build into something like law – in both liberal models of the human as an authoritative participant in society (freedoms of speech, association, religion, culture and the like) and more corporatist versions of the human as a bundle of welfare rights.

The overall phenomenon is clear: global models of the instrumental structure and actorhood of nation-states, organizations and individuals have much impact in the contemporary system. The intellectual questions are now not about the phenomenon itself but about its explanation. These questions are addressed in this article. First, why do these global structures arise? Second, how are they organized at the global level? Third, through what mechanisms do they impact national societies?

Forces for the Globalization of Models of Actorhood

The globalization of instrumental models of actorhood follows from the structure of world society, as it has become more integrated over time. Two core properties of this society are central: the fact that the modern world is stateless; and the fact that it is made up of strong, culturally constituted actors.

First, as is commonly recognized, the world society is a stateless polity. It has no central, controlling political organizations in it – no state organization with legitimate sovereignty over or responsibility for the whole. There are some important organizations such as the UN system and the World Bank/IMF. But these are not sovereign – they derive such authority as they have from delegation by the sub-unit nation-state actors that make them up. There are also some rather dominating sub-unit actors, such as very powerful nation-states and some very strong economic actors, but these, too, have no direct or authoritative sovereignty over the system as a whole.

Two important consequences follow from the statelessness of the world polity. First, almost all the interests that push for sociopolitical regulation in the world work toward building a broad world polity of shared rules and models, rather than trying to assemble a stronger world state bureaucracy. These interests may reflect the goals of nation-states, of business firms, of concerned human individuals and of all sorts of specialized groups. For instance, as concerns arise about the world environment, they are channeled principally toward the construction of rather binding cultural (mainly scientific) rules and models, not toward the formal imposition of bureaucratic authority by (non-existent) world state organizations. As concerns arise about the stability and growth of the (increasingly recognized) world economy, these are channeled into the creation of appropriate common economic models for states. As concerns arise about human rights and welfare, they are channeled similarly. In all these areas, there is no point to imagining a controlling world state. It is more reasonable to try to construct common cultural principles that can produce the desired actions in sub-units of the world society.

Thus, from every side, candidate models for appropriate action by national states, organizations and even individuals are produced at a very rapid rate. The exponential growth in this cultural material is indicated by the extraordinary expansion in international governmental and non-governmental associations in the current period (Boli and Thomas, 1997). It is also indicated by the explosion in scientific activity, covering the widest variety of domains, in the current system (Schofer, 1999).

Second, there is no central controlling structure to regulate or stop the expansion in world political culture that is produced. Faced with a knowledge system and groups that give attention to a problem with the ozone layer, an older (e.g. Chinese) imperial system could resort to simple suppression of the intellectuals and groups involved thus eliminating the problem. The statelessness of the current system means that nobody is in a position to stop an environmental, human rights or expansive economic development model.

Thus a great deal of cultural material – much of it imposing extraordinary costs on the actors involved – is produced in the contemporary system, with few mechanisms for control. Indeed, the intellectuals and concerned associations that are involved gain much prestige, importance and so on by developing costs for actors. For instance, the social scientists who discover new forms of unjust inequality (among countries, genders, classes, ethnic groups, races or persons of varying disabilities) gain world attention and preferment – prizes go to such people. They do not bear the costs of correction: the sub-unit nation-state and organizational actors in the system do.

Second, world society is itself stateless and lacks much of a collective actor. But it contains much cultural and associational material that defines itself as made up principally of very strong and highly legitimated actors. These arise from a rationalized (scientific) analysis of nature as universal and lawful and thus suited to rational and purposive action.

They arise even more from a secularized analysis of a universal and lawful moral or spiritual authority: the high god no longer acts in history, but sacralized human actors do, carrying legitimated agency for their own actions under valid and universal collective principles (Meyer and Jepperson, forthcoming). There are the modern nation-states. There are human and citizen persons, who now carry the banner of legitimated individuality and actorhood. And there are many types of formalized organizational actors, ultimately constituted by individuals and/or by states.

Modern culture and the strongest modern social theories define social life as the product of these actors in all sectors of social life: the economy, the political system and other institutional domains. Each actor is empowered, and the empowerment is highly legitimated, so that, in principle, they are all to respect the actorhood of the others.

Tremendous premiums in the modern system go with actorhood, so that social life tends to be reorganized around its claims. Essentially every society now forms itself around the model of autonomous nation-state actorhood. Within and among societies, individuals mobilize around principles of actorhood (e.g. human rights). And all sorts of social structures reform themselves as formal organizations and thus as legitimated actors.

The claims of actorhood are rewarding, exorbitant and utterly unrealistic. Under elaborate, standardized and very general rules, actors are thought to have clear purposes, means–ends technologies and analyzed resources. They are to have unified decision sovereignty, effective control over their internal activities and clearly defined boundaries. They are to have complete and accurate analyses of their environments. They are, in short, to be little gods. And all of this occurs under universalized legitimating rules and in a rationalized and standardized environment. So proper actors have a great deal in common and are exposed to a common wider environment.

In this situation, real social actors, because of the exorbitant claims built

International Sociology Vol. 15 No. 2

into their identities, face very great uncertainty about every property of their actorhood, from sovereignty and purpose to needed technologies to effective control systems to analyses of their environments. Real social entities of a more traditional kind, unconstrained by the claims of actorhood, might face the same uncertainties but would have no obligation to deal with them. The pretenses of actorhood require and facilitate mobilization.

Faced with now-rationalized uncertainties and the legitimated requirements of actorhood to deal with these uncertainties, modern actors stabilize themselves by creating and using rules of various kinds. This is a driving force for globalization. The point is that the first 'interest' or problem of the modern actor is – not to accomplish prior goals of some sort – but to be an actor. This requires discovering goals, technologies, resources, sovereignty, control and boundaries. It is much easier to do this if wider stabilizing rules can be created and utilized.

So modern actors create and consult collective rules. Nation-states employ common definitions of nation-state goals: principally socioeconomic development and justice or equality. They consult and respect wider cultural analyses about how to accomplish these goals and use common analyses (e.g. accountings) of their resources. They mobilize standardized ways of organizing sovereignty and control. And while none of these things work very well, they are at least legitimate demonstrations of actorhood which is, after all, the core purpose. Actors, in short, establish their existence by adopting common forms and by supporting the creation of such common forms (even when these forms might be quite costly to them).

Organizations, as is well known, follow similar patterns, structuring themselves – with the aid of elaborate consulting machineries – around common and established models: they devote many resources to the construction of such models. Individuals, too, in the modern system consult a myriad of external rule systems (lawyers, therapists, accountants and the like) in propping up their individuality. One achieves strong status as a rational actor by becoming much like everyone else.

The drive to the creation of common globalized models of instrumental culture, in other words, is produced by a system that defines actorhood as a core principle. It feeds on itself: each step forward in globalization produces more and more definitions of the requirements and responsibilities of effective actorhood (e.g. modern environmental principles), which motivates actors even further to support the construction of more demanding theories of their responsibilities.

Global Conflict

The extreme dependence of modern actors on wider legitimating models that sustain their actorhood generates much global instrumental culture.

The cultural models in question vary, but they rest on common rationalistic (e.g. scientific) assumptions and there is more integration than is commonly supposed. But absent a unifying state, there is a good deal of conflict too. The issues take great importance, since sub-unit actors depend on the wider models for legitimation. So differences that might otherwise seem small can loom very large, and modern global conflict is often about variations among fairly similar models of modernity. The Second World War, for instance, can be seen to have been about variations between more corporatist and statist models of individual and society. The Cold War can be seen to have been about modest variations in models of the social control of the economy. At present, similar fractionating lines appear between older western models and emerging, more fundamentalist Islamic ones. It is important to note that these conflicts are only secondarily about the 'interests' of the rational actors of the system: they are principally about the properties of proper actorhood and thus have a constitutive or religious character.

Otherhood: The Nature of the Globalized Cultural System

We have discussed the modern system's drive for or demand for a globalized instrumental culture and turn now to analyze the supply of this material. A core factor arises from the nature of modern actorhood. This actorhood involves two components (Meyer and Jepperson, forthcoming). First, mainly derived from the modern scientific analysis of nature, there is the recognized existence of physical and social entities with natural interests and functions: actors are entities with rights. These are not only individuals, societies and functional groups within society (like 'labor'), but also many entities outside society – like whales or other species, or the ecosystem as a whole, or social entities not yet proper actors (fetuses, unformed indigenous social groups and so on).

Actorhood proper arises from an additional principle mainly derived from western and now worldwide moral law. Actors are entities with rights or interests *and* with the assigned right and capacity to represent these interests. Actors, thus, are assigned agency – derived mainly from the moral universe: it is in this sense that they are small gods. Agency is, in effect, moral action and occurs with a great deal of universalized standardization. There are proper ways to set goals, choose technologies, organize effective sovereignty and self-control and to relate rationally to the environment. And the good agent, since legitimated agency is derived from a common moral frame, has a great deal in common with other agents: the rational state, rational organization and rational individual have a great deal in common (and often consult the same therapeutic authorities).

International Sociology Vol. 15 No. 2

Modern actors thus have great capacities to transfer their agency to others; in short, they function as Others. Modern individuals do this to others, sometimes for pay and sometimes for free. They also do it to the organizations they serve and to national states. Modern individuals are renowned for their ability to opine to each other and the wider world (including surveying social scientists). Similarly, states and other organizations serve as advising Others for each other and for individuals. Collective action of this sort is endemic in the modern system, contrary to realist theories.

All this activity occurs under the moral law: consultants and agents are to reflect the wider truths of the law in acting as Others to actors. In extreme cases, as with the sciences and professions, elite participants serve as agents almost purely of the wider extrasocial truths: agents for the Mind of God as reflected in nature (the sciences) and/or the moral universe (as in the legal professions and their kin).

Agency of this sort is very highly valued in the modern system, and the most virtuous and admired participants are those who serve most purely as agents of general truths. Indeed, in the modern stratification system, occupations are valued in terms of their nearness to pure Otherhood and their distance from self-interested actorhood. Unadmired roles are those that involve real work and the exercise of real narrow power. Consultant Others are more admired. Most admired, worldwide, are the Others who act as agents of the high truths of science and law: these are the ones who get the high prizes (Meyer, 1994).

Thus modern world society is filled with eager participants in the formation of universalized global culture. These are the direct creators of the general principles of social progress and social equality, the analysts of technologies for actors to accomplish their ends, the therapists who create general principles of sovereignty and self-control and all the scientific analysts of the wider natural environment.

Organizational Forms of Globalized and Rationalized Otherhood

Nation-state, organizational and individual actors are seeking models of their actorhood. And these structures – equipped with and valuing universal agency – readily supply Othering on a global scale.

Most directly, the modern system is seen as an explosion of scientific and professional activity and the organization of this activity on a global scale. Scientific and professional organizations, of both governmental and non-governmental sorts, have expanded exponentially (Schofer, 1999). So have investments in these activities, and so have the numbers of personnel trained in them. The activities and ideologies involved make global, universalistic claims and are used in just these ways. They provide grounding for globalized environmental and technological Othering, globalized instruction on human rights and personhood and global instruction on the proper organization of society (e.g. the market economy, the democratic political system and proper intrafamilial social relationships).

Between the pure Otherhood that is involved in the scientific and professional contemplation of universal law and the practical world of actors, a thick layer of applied professionalism arises. This is the most significant area of scientific expansion at the global level (Schofer, 1999). And it generates huge, global consulting industries that instruct national states, organizations and individuals on procedures for properly agentic actorhood. This is one of the most rapidly expanding industries in the world, and its services are widely utilized by claimant actors. It is an industry that almost entirely rests on universalized scientific and professional assumptions, so its output can, in principle, be used everywhere and by all actors.

It should be noted that a certain role distance between the purer Otherhood of the elite sciences and professions and the more applied Otherhood of the agentic consultants is maintained. Pure theory is too unclear and inconsistent to be used effectively by those who maintain the faith in practically agentic actorhood. So application fashions and fads arise and provide simplifications, for instance, in the contemporary 'standards' and 'quality assurance' programs supplied to modern organizations or in the recipes for the production of economic development by national states or in the therapies promoted for individuals. But the claims of the particular advocates rest almost entirely on the assumptions of true, universalized laws.

Then, on a more concrete level, it can be seen that agentic Othering is produced by a welter of international governmental and non-governmental associations. These have expanded exponentially in the current period (see the reviews by Boli and Thomas, 1997, 1999). They are built by agentic state and non-state actors, who (often eagerly) participate in their formation. They contain codified recipes and models for proper actor structuring and activity in all the areas of recognized instrumental social life: very few of them are concerned with arational or expressive domains of social life. They share models of medicine, science, education, economic organization, human rights, environmental protection, technical development, rational political and social organization and so on. The models put forward rest on rationalized scientific and professional analyses, and this justifies their putative universality, though the purely theoretical scientists and professionals often have little direct involvement. The spirit is applied and practical and often highly professionalized, but behind it is the mobilization of the true faith in a wider rationality.

Participation in these globalized associational networks is known to be a strong predictor of proper mobilized actorhood: this is true not only of national states (Meyer et al., 1997a) but also of formal organizations and, undoubtedly, of individuals too. At the individual level, the promotion of globalized actorhood is most dramatic through national educational systems which expand isomorphically around the world and which tie individuals into globalized models of modernity: education tends to be the main predictor at the individual level (Inkeles and Smith, 1974, and many others).

Next, these associations shade over into wider social movements, varying in degree of formal organization. All sorts of agentic human actors support as universalizing Others: discursive models of human rights, social organization in all its areas and the wider natural environment. Elaborate languages, universalized and often resting on very general scientific or professional ideologies, support the rapid expansion of human rights into unforeseen areas (e.g. gay and lesbian rights – see Frank and McEneaney, 1999) or the generalization of environmental principles to quite elaborate levels.

Finally, the actors themselves, in their eagerness to demonstrate universality, put their own models – often heavily edited by transmitting scientists, professionals and consultants – forward for general emulation. And, eager for stabilization, other actors try to copy the most admired ones. National states searching for models of proper individual welfare have beaten pathways to Sweden, which has been most happy to be copied. Others, searching for the true route to economic development, have often tried to copy the USA (which clearly finds self-enhancement by advancing itself as a model; but the recent tendency to try to copy Japanese models has abated). At the organizational level, admired firms put themselves forward as models, and whole sets of consulting firms and business school academics make a business out of aiding in the diffusion.

All this increasingly rapid 'diffusion' of models of actorhood rests on underlying assumptions that rational human actorhood is and should be a universal matter (Strang and Meyer, 1993), and that successful models must represent some sort of scientific truth.

Rationalistic and realist theories treat the sorts of collective action discussed above as rare and difficult (Olson, 1965; Coleman, 1986). In fact, it is routine in global society and makes for globalization. The theoretical issue is simple: if rational actorhood is a prior and natural state, as realist theories assume, then collective mobilization is likely to be difficult (unless built into the genetics or prior socialization of the actors). If, as we assume, rational actorhood is an elaborate sociocultural construction and at great odds with actual human life and possibilities, then collective action is a very natural outcome.

Meyer *Effects of Globalization on States and Societies*

Mechanisms of Transmission

The core mechanism by which the wider global instrumental culture is transmitted to sub-units, as outlined above, is through the structuring of actor identities. Once national societies enter the world as nation-state actors, they acquire proper identity and purpose and rather eagerly seek out approved forms. Once social groups have been reorganized as formal organizations, they come to be open to wider models of rationalization. Once persons become modern individuals, they eagerly acquire the forms of modern individualism.

Thus standardized purposes, technologies, resource definitions, sovereignty and control forms and analyses of the wider environment are quickly adopted. Nation-states, organizations and individuals, at least in their formal identity claims, tend to be very nice. Of course, this is all enhanced by the active Otherhood provided by the global system and floods of (also very nice) consultants, international associations and scientific and professional bodies. This is, in realist analyses, seen as imposed and potentially oppressive: the surprise of the modern world, obvious in our analyses, is how eagerly the forms of modernity (e.g. universal education) are sought out, and how little they are resisted. The core mechanism here is the identity mechanism which opens up essentially the whole social structure of the world to rather rapid penetration.

Beyond this, the models of modern actorhood are simultaneously supplied to national states, organizations (e.g. interest groups) and individuals. These various actor-levels affect each other a great deal, so that states which neglect to incorporate an approved model from the global system come under much pressure from world-legitimated internal actors to do so. Similarly, modernizing states press their internal actors (e.g. firms) to conform to proper models of actorhood.

Some Consequences for Actors

A first and obvious consequence of the globalized system of instrumental culture for actor sub-units is unexpected isomorphism. Societies vary by factors of 100 to 1 in resources and enormously in their own traditions. But they adopt surprisingly similar forms of modernity (in the state, the educational system and the economy). Bradley and Ramirez (1996), for instance, consider the world expansion in female participation in higher education. If this took place in developed countries only, realist theories could make sense of it: if it were slowed in Islamic ones, standard cultural theories would fit. In practice, it has been worldwide, and types of countries vary little in the matter.

A second consequence is the high internal structuration of modern actors: their extreme tendency to organize, to plan, to make policy and to posture around the goods of modern actorhood. Even Third World national states and rather functionally simple organizations and quite marginal individuals adopt rationalized structures of plan. A modern university, for instance, will have a much more elaborate structure than a university of the same size and diversity in an earlier period. So will a modern state, firm or individual person (who can now spell out [e.g. to an interviewer, or occasionally in the mass media] all sorts of matters a more traditional person would have left implicit). Structuration follows from the great inconsistency between high models of complete, rational actorhood and the practical capabilities and resources of actual putative actors. Core national states, for instance, can often simply carry out forms of modernity without too much centralized structuration. Semi-peripheral strugglers have to mobilize structure and peripheral ones to plan. The countries in the furthest periphery, with little capacity to do anything, then write the new forms into their identities, and their national constitutions are often some of the most progressive documents in the world (Boli, 1987).

A third consequence of globalization is local decoupling. Actors adopt high forms but are unable to carry them out in practice (e.g. human rights). They adopt inconsistent structures from different global sources (e.g. educational and labor market policies). They adopt symbolic frames without substantive meaning and so on. The exalted character of global frames of actorhood virtue naturally mean that hypocrisy – the respect vice pays to virtue – is enlarged in the modern system.

Analysts of decoupling often take it to mean that nothing really changes with the adoption of modern forms of actorhood, but this is unrealistic. In a Durkheimian way, local relationships between modern institutions and between these institutions and practices (e.g. between attitudes and actions) are very weak, but over time both systems are penetrated by wider models. For instance, Bradley and Ramirez (1996) show that the spread of world standards that encourage female participation in universities affects both national policy adoptions and actual enrollments, but these two variables are themselves little related. The point is that wider global changes penetrate all levels relatively independently, so that there are high correlations over time collectively and low correlations across units cross-sectionally.

In practice, the extensive decoupling characteristic of the modern system provides fertile soil for the discovery of social problems and social inconsistencies and the construction of much reform. Reform is, in fact, endemic and stimulates both local and global expansive change in modernity. New problems are discovered in the environment, socioeconomic development and human conditions (e.g. inequalities and injustices);

these provide the fuel for further expansive reform. Global models expand faster than any possible correction, so the system is in a kind of permanent crisis that calls for more rapid expansion and reform.

The Construction of the Local: Glocalization

The mobilization of social entities, in the modern system, around legitimated global models of actorhood is built on the principle that the local actors in fact have their own distinctive identities on which their nominal choices are rooted. Standardized actorhood arises around the principle of actor unique identity. Thus, with globalization, actors systematically generate and expand their own self-conscious, unique bases. But they do this within global models of effective instrumental action. This Tocquevillian phenomenon is called by Robertson (1992) 'glocalization'. Nations celebrate their unique heritages while moving into standardized models. Organizations, as they become standard, rational structures, dramatize their supposedly unique organizational cultures. Individuals parade their individual subjectivities.

The cultures produced and celebrated face the problem that true agentic actorhood has a standardized-model character in instrumental ways. This means that uniqueness – the dramatization of the local – inevitably takes an expressive character. Nation-states do not usually direct their uniqueness toward the arational and unique character of their divisions of labor, their forms of state structure, their educational or medical systems and the like. Too much uniqueness on such matters violates the principles of rational actorhood.

Uniqueness and identity are thus most legitimately focused on matters of expressive culture: variations in language, dress, food, traditions, landscapes, familial styles and so on. These are precisely the things that in the modern system do not matter, which is to say they have no direct, rational relation to instrumental actorhood. Nation-states and organized ethnic groups within them do not claim to have their own styles of wife- or child-beating, of economic production and so on. Such claims would violate global principles and pressures, and actual traditions along these lines are suppressed in reconstructions or revitalizations of history and tradition.

Conclusion

The globalization of instrumental culture is a striking empirical feature of the modern system, as models of proper actorhood for national states, individuals and organizations spread around the world. The empirical phenomenon is difficult to contest – we have concentrated on its explanation.

Globalization of instrumental culture is a product of a stateless world that is filled with 'social actors' who are legitimated in rationalistic and universalistic terms. Actorhood is a high and constructed form, far beyond the capacities of real social units. These units thus work to create stabilizing rules at the collective level, providing legitimacy to their structures and activities. They do this even when costs are high. The rules involved, of course, are rationalistic and universalistic and apply everywhere.

The supply of globalized models also expands with socially constructed actorhood. The legitimated agency of social actors readily transforms itself into agency for others or for the natural and moral universe beyond society: modern world society is, in a sense, dominated by its clergy. Thus globalized models are produced by the sciences and professions (the highest status groups in the modern national and world stratification system) by rapidly expanding international associations that rest on scientized and universalized pretenses, by social movements on a global scale and by actors themselves who present their forms as universal models.

The adoption of actor identities by national states, organizations and individuals produces units that are eager and ready to adopt legitimating global models. This is, of course, facilitated by the available Otherhood in a world of helpful consultants. It is also facilitated by the multilayered character of actorhood in the modern system, as individuals and organizations press national states (and conversely) to assume their world-legitimated responsibilities.

Consequences include massive unexpected isomorphisms among social units, the high structuration of these units and a great deal of internal decoupling within them. They also include the empowered production of much subjectivity and uniqueness within each constructed actor: scripted expressive culture that is edited to be consistent with the more instrumental models of global culture.

Note

This article is based on a paper that was prepared for the conference on 'Globalizations: Dimensions, Trajectories, Prospects', Stockholm 1998. It derives from collaborative work done over the last decade. I am indebted for the help of a number of colleagues. For a summary see Meyer et al. (1997a).

References

Barrett, Deborah and Frank, David John (1999) 'Population Control for National Development: From World Discourse to National Policies', in J. Boli and G. Thomas (eds) *Constructing World Culture*, pp. 198–221. Stanford, CA: Stanford University Press.

Berkovitch, Nitza (1999) 'The Emergence and Transformation of the International Women's Movement', in J. Boli and G. Thomas (eds) *Constructing World Culture*, pp. 100–26. Stanford, CA: Stanford University Press.

Boli, John (1987) 'World Polity Sources of Expanding State Authority and Organization, 1870–1970', in G. Thomas et al. (eds) *Institutional Structure*, pp. 71–91. Beverly Hills, CA: Sage.

Boli, John and Thomas, George (1997) 'World Culture in the World Polity: A Century of International Non-Governmental Organization', *American Sociological Review* 62: 171–90.

Boli, John and Thomas, George, eds (1999) *Constructing World Culture: International Nongovernmental Organizations Since 1875*. Stanford, CA: Stanford University Press.

Bongaarts, John and Watkins, Susan (1996) 'Social Interactions and Contemporary Fertility Transitions', *Population and Development Review* 22(4): 639–82.

Bradley, Karen and Ramirez, Francisco (1996) 'World Polity Promotion of Gender Parity: Women's Share of Higher Education, 1965–85', *Research in Sociology of Education and Socialization* 11: 63–91.

Brunsson, Nils and Sahlin-Andersson, Kerstin (1997) *Constructing Organizations*, Working Paper. Stockholm: Stockholm Center for Organizational Research.

Coleman, James (1986) *Individual Interests and Collective Action*. New York: Cambridge University Press.

Fiala, Robert and Gordon-Lanford, Audri (1987) 'Educational Ideology and the World Educational Revolution, 1950–1970', *Comparative Education Review* 31(3): 315–32.

Finnemore, Martha (1996) *National Interests in International Society*. Ithaca, NY: Cornell University Press.

Frank, David John, and McEneaney, Elizabeth H. (1999) 'The Individualization of Society and the Liberalization of State Policies on Same-Sex Sexual Relations, 1984–1995', *Social Forces* 77(March): 911–44.

Frank, David John, Hironaka, Ann, Meyer, John W., Schofer, Evan and Tuma, Nancy Brandon (1999) 'The Rationalization and Organization of Nature in World Culture', in J. Boli and G. Thomas (eds) *Constructing World Culture*, pp. 81–99. Stanford, CA: Stanford University Press.

Hall, Peter, ed. (1989) *The Political Power of Economic Ideas*. Princeton, NJ: Princeton University Press.

Inkeles, Alex and Smith, David (1974) *Becoming Modern*. Cambridge, MA: Harvard University Press.

Jepperson, Ronald (1992) 'National Scripts: The Varying Construction of Individualism and Opinion across the Modern Nation-States', PhD dissertation, Yale University.

McNeely, Connie (1995) *Constructing the Nation-State: International Organization and Prescriptive Action*. Westport, CT: Greenwood.

Meyer, John W. (1994) 'The Evolution of Modern Stratification Systems', in D. Grusky (ed.) *Social Stratification*, pp. 28–54. Boulder, CO: Westview Press.

Meyer, John W. and Jepperson, Ronald (forthcoming) 'The "Actors" of Modern Society: The Cultural Construction of Social Agency', *Sociological Theory*.

Meyer, John W., Ramirez, Francisco and Soysal, Yasemin (1992a) 'World Expansion of Mass Education, 1870–1980', *Sociology of Education* 65(2): 128–49.
Meyer, John W., Kamens, David and Benavot, Aaron (1992b) *School Knowledge for the Masses: World Models and National Primary Curricular Categories.* London: Falmer Press.
Meyer, John W., Boli, John, Thomas, George and Ramirez, Francisco. (1997a) 'World Society and the Nation-State', *American Journal of Sociology* 103(1): 144–81.
Meyer, John W., Frank, David John, Hironaka, Ann, Schofer, Evan and Tuma, Nancy Brandon (1997b) 'The Structuring of a World Environmental Regime, 1870–1990', *International Organization* 51(4): 623–51.
Olson, Mancur (1965) *The Logic of Collective Action.* Cambridge, MA: Harvard University Press.
Olson, Olov, Guthrie, James and Humphrey, Christopher, eds (1998) *Global Warning: Debating International Developments in New Public Financial Management.* Oslo: Cappelen Akademisk Forlag.
Riddle, Phyllis (1993) 'Political Authority and University Formation in Europe', *Sociological Perspectives* 36(1): 45–62.
Robertson, Roland (1992) *Globalization: Social Theory and Global Culture.* London: Sage.
Schofer, Evan (1999) 'Science Associations in the International Sphere, 1875–1990', in J. Boli and G. Thomas (eds) *Constructing World Culture*, pp. 249–66. Stanford, CA: Stanford University Press.
Strang, David and Meyer, John (1993) 'Institutional Conditions for Diffusion', *Theory and Society* 22: 487–511.
Ventresca, Marc (1995) 'Counting People when People Count', PhD dissertation, Stanford University.

Biographical Note: John W. Meyer is Professor of Sociology at Stanford University. He studies the impact of cultural and organization aspects of world society on nation-states and other organizations. He has written extensively on organizational theory and comparative analyses from neoinstitutional perspectives.

Address: Department of Sociology, Stanford University, Stanford, CA 94305-2047, USA. [email: meyer@leland.stanford.edu]

[2]

THE GLOBALIZATION OF CRIME AND CRIMINAL JUSTICE

Prospects and Problems

David Nelken

Earlier this year the following letter from a Mr Ali al Feel, a postgraduate student in Iraq, arrived for me at University College:

Dear Mr Nelken
I am Ali from Mosul. I am studying for a Masters of Military Criminal Law. My thesis is about Nolle Prosequi and the discontinuance of military criminal proceedings by the Ministry of Defence under military criminal law. I wish for you to reprint and send me modern reports and research about it as soon as possible.

Unfortunately, Ali was asking the wrong person if he hoped to find an expert in military criminal law. But his letter reminds us how law is both the most local and the most universal or globalized of cultural phenomena. Ali's letter might be though naïve because it carries the assumption of law as somehow being so beyond local culture that it becomes feasible to turn to a very different society as the potential source of useful ideas about how military criminal law could be developed in Iraq. But we should not be so quick to limit law's reach. Just such a spreading of legal ideas has occurred in the past (I live in Bologna not far from the tombs of the glossators whose rediscovery of Roman law helped shape the destiny of Europe), and something similar is happening today in the emergence of a new *lex mercatoria* for international business transactions or in the attempt to extend human rights law. The issue is rather that some forms of law do seem to travel better than others. Criminal law for example is usually seen as very much a quintessential part of national sovereignty, and not for nothing the

European Union has moved with extreme caution about urging harmonization in this area of law.

Thus the topic for this article. Can criminal law and justice be globalized? Or is this already happening? And how are transnational crime and the fear of such crime pushing developments in criminal justice? These are rather large questions and I cannot offer anything more than an introduction to some of the issues which they raise, around which there is a rapidly growing, though as yet unsynthesized, literature. I shall begin by evoking the fears which focus either on the spread or the response to transnational crime as examples of the type of problems associated with the globalization of crime. I shall then say something about the meaning of globalization and the various ways this phenomenon relates to criminal justice more generally. Finally I shall consider more carefully the claim that organized crime is globalizing, drawing also on my empirical research into organized frauds against the subsidies programmes of the European Union started many years ago when I still worked in University College.[1] I should say that it is not my intention in this article to debunk concern over the spread of organized crime as no more than a new 'moral panic'. If only it were that simple! Descriptions of the growth of this type of crime can be exaggerated, as can descriptions of the threat posed by the organization of police efforts to deal with it.[2] But calling for caution is unlikely by itself to have much influence over rapidly evolving events. What needs to be carefully questioned is the single-mindedness of policy-making which claims to rely on an allegedly irrefutable logic: since crime now knows no frontiers, it follows that systems of criminal justice can no longer afford to be based on the nation state but must do their best to form a common front.

[1] See N. Passas and D. Nelken, 'The Legal Response to Agricultural Fraud in the European Community: A Comparative Study' (1991) 6 *Corruption and Reform* 237, and 'The Thin Line Between Legitimate and Criminal Enterprises: Subsidy Frauds in the European Community' (with N. Passas) in (1993) 20 *Crime, Law and Social Change* 223.

[2] See K. G. Robertson, 'Practical Police Cooperation in Europe: the Intelligence Dimension' in M. Anderson and M. den Boer (eds.), *Policing across National Boundaries* (London, 1 994), 106 at 117 ('the conspiracy theorists of European policing are wrong when they see a vast surveillance State, for the reality is that a true intelligence system is not an easy monster to produce but is one of the rarest of creatures').

Instead, I shall try to show why the relationship between globalization, crime, and criminal justice is a lot more complex than this thought captures.

Two Opposite Fears

It is possible to detect two types of anxiety in current writing about the globalization of crime. The first of these stems from the argument that globalization is a process out of control, or even beyond control, which is creating enormous opportunities for business and organized crime which locally based criminal justice systems are struggling to keep up with and perhaps are always destined to be behind. The old-new category of 'transnational crime' is taken to embrace a wide variety of threatening behaviours including terrorism, espionage including industrial espionage, drugs and arms trafficking, the international wholesaling of pornography and prostitution, smuggling and trade in people and body parts, counterfeiting, crimes related to computer technology, international fraud and other financial crimes, tax evasion, theft of art, antiques, and other precious items, crimes against the environment, trade in endangered species, and internationally co-ordinated racial violence. What is more, much of this transnational crime is assumed (rightly) to be organized by foreign criminal enterprises such as the Sicilian Mafia, the Colombian drug cartels, the Yakuza in Japan, the Chinese and Taiwanese Triads, or sophisticated fraudster networks in Nigeria. Increasingly, attention is also being paid to the challenge represented by the Mafias of Russia and other countries in Eastern Europe who are seen as amongst the main beneficiaries of the break-up of the former Soviet Union, the run down of the Red Army, the privatization programmes or foreign investments and aid payments, and so on.

As is confirmed by the recent redeployment in Britain of the secret services to carry out intelligence against them, organized criminals have slipped easily into the slot of public enemy number one which was previously reserved for the anti-democratic menace of communism. And this is even more true of the United States. As Louise Shelley, an influential American expert on organized crime, argues, the world is now facing a new non-state based form of authoritarianism which subjects people to coercion, corrupts law, privatizes weak states for its own goals, and threatens those journalists—and criminologists—who try to expose it.[3] Her conclusion (these arguments always arrive at the same one) is that 'the legal institutions of the world are still bound to the nation state but the forces of coercion are transnational; existing state based legal systems therefore cannot protect citizens from the new authoritarian threat provided by transnational organised crime'.[4] According to this view the globalization of crime thrives on the inability of the criminal law to globalize. And the European Union is the best illustration of this. As another American writer put it:

> crooks were the last item on the European Community's agenda in 1990. Engrossed in plans to make money, economic leaders had given scarcely a thought to the opportunity for criminals to do likewise—no common police academy or training existed, each country had its own laws on extradition, rights of asylum, hot pursuit, exchange of police and intelligence information, undercover agents, controlled drug deliveries, jail terms for drug traffickers, money laundering or phone taps.[5]

But there also mirror image fears. The claim here is that police forces are in fact using these fears about transnational crime to forge alliances which are not democratically accountable. America has long been in the lead here in exporting abroad its war against drugs and terrorism, but in Europe this is also well illustrated by the inter-state TREVI or EUROPOL policing agreements; the European Commission itself only has observer status, the European Parliament still less say. Criminal justice is thus globalizing along with everything else (and in the same way) and efforts at transnational police action represent a real danger to democratic structures which themselves presuppose the national state. As one author claims 'it is by looking at the enforcement practices of the transnational law enforcement enterprise that we can best come to understand the political form of the emergent transnational world system'[6] or, as

[3] L. Shelley, 'Transnational Organized Crime: The New Authoritarianism', paper presented at the Law and Society Conference, Glasgow, 13 July 1996.

[4] *Ibid.*, 3.

[5] C. Sterling, *Thieves' World: The Threat of the New Global Network of Organised Crime* (New York, 1994), 40.

[6] L. W. E. Sheptycki, 'Law Enforcement, Justice and Democracy in the Transnational Arena: Reflections on the War on Drugs' (1996) 24 *International Journal of Sociology of Law* 61, 64. See also L. W. E. Sheptycki, 'Transnational Policing and the Makings of a Postmodern State' (1993) 33 *British Journal of Criminology* 613; E. Nadelman, *Cops across Borders* (London, 1993); M. Anderson and M. den Boer

Rosa Luxembourg is alleged to have said, 'the police are the one true International'. What is more, powers and techniques which are demanded or taken in order to deal with the threat of menacing forms of organized crime often end up being used against more low level or local forms of criminality. Insofar as borders are defended the focus is often on keeping out those immigrants who in the present economic climate are once again assumed to be surplus to requirements;[7] thus illegal immigration is now included alongside drugs and terrorism as one of the three major threats against which what is increasingly being called *Fortress Europe* needs to be defended. For these commentators on transnational policing the solution is often worse than the problem—not only because it is symmetrically authoritarian—but also because there is ample evidence that unaccountable policing can itself involve illegality or engage in crime in its own account.

So far the differences between systems and the obstacles to international collaboration are as significant as the moves to common forms of policing and punishment. But even if progress to a unified order of international criminal law is so slow, or perhaps just because it is so slow, we should also note that measures taken to deal with transnational criminality by *individual* nation-states already have serious implications for civil liberties. If INTERPOL is said to have files on 130,000 people of whom 80,000 are drug offenders; researchers quote the police in Britain alone as claiming to have records on the 60 per cent of Colombians living in London who, they say, are involved in the drug trade (as many as 42,000 out of a total of 70,000).[8] An intelligence agent was recently quoted in the *Sunday Times* as saying, 'We are one of the very few countries in the world to have legislation that allows us to work very aggressively overseas . . . We take the view that stealing money from a crook is a good thing and if it's from an account in a foreign country who cares? We are hardly likely to be sued, and anyway

(eds.) n. 2 above; M. Anderson et al. *Policing the European Union* (Oxford, 1995); C. Fijnaut and G. Marx, *Undercover: Police Surveillance in Comparative Perspective* (The Hague, 1995).

[7] The current politics of exclusion of immigrants to the European Community is the subject of large literature which I cannot summarize here, but there is still much to be studied about the relationship between this pattern of exclusion and internal forms of exclusionary social control.

[8] Sheptycki, 'Law Enforcement . . . .' n. 6 above.

there are no fingerprints to lead back to us'[9] (according to the report these remarks allegedly met with the approval of a leading London legal academic). The 1992 decision of the American Supreme Court in the *Alvarez Machain* case seemed to authorize state kidnapping of a drug dealer from Mexico. In the same year in the decision in *R.* v. *Governor of Pentonville Prison, ex p. Chinoy*[10] the English courts refused to took at illegalities which had allegedly occurred in the gathering of evidence in France. In sum, whatever globalization may or may not be doing to crime, talk about globalization is increasingly serving as a means by which national criminal justice systems seek to augment their resources and (re)legitimate themselves.

How far can discussions about globalization help us to place these fears about organized crime and transnational enforcement in some wider context so as to give us a better grasp of what is happening? Certainly there have been other periods, such as the early years of this century, which witnessed widespread levels of concern about international drug traffic—though it is worth remembering that Britain, and even more Holland, were then counted amongst the countries accused of profiting from the trade. This and other campaigns against foreign threats were accompanied by a level of xenophobia and fear of immigration even more severe than that being witnessed today. What difference does globalization make? Certainly it would be important if we could show that organized criminals engaged in transnational crimes were simply responding to the pressures and opportunities which were reshaping legal and illegal enterprise alike. For if we were to treat globalization as the real villain of the piece, we could hardly assume that transnational policing could provide the answer. It could certainly do little to offset the many other effects of globalization on levels of crime in different countries and cities. Rather than setting the secret services on the trails of the Mr Bigs of organized crime, the challenge we would face would be better analysed as having to do with the political choice whether to regulate or deregulate globalization processes more generally (together with the problem of whether and how such regulation could be made effective).

[9] *Sunday Times*, 17 Nov. 1996.

[10] [1992] 1 All ER 317.

Understanding Globalization

But what exactly is meant by globalization? Is it just the latest jargon phrase wheeled out so as to describe a series of otherwise unrelated matters or is it the magical key to making the connections which otherwise are so hard to find when living through a period of rapid change? The term is now being used in a variety of academic disciplines. I have the space here to say only a little about some of the definitions, aspects, and theories of globalization which I have gleaned from the literatures of sociology and management science. Because it is rare to find much specific reference to crime and criminal justice in these discussions our task will be to tease out the implications of globalization for our subject (as well as to consider how developments in crime and criminal justice and criminology may themselves affect globalization).

In a recent social science text with this title, Malcolm Walters[11] defines globalization as 'a social process in which the constraints of geography on social and cultural arrangements recede and in which people become increasingly aware that they are receding'. Thus globalization has both objective and subjective elements. However, though Walters tends to see these as going together it will sometimes be useful for our purposes to distinguish them. Starting from a concern with criminal justice we might want to ask—does globalization really destroy the local basis for allocating blame? In particular could it be one of the functions of criminal justice, for better or worse, to reflect or attempt to recreate a sense of group solidarity which does not coincide at all with changing economic constraints?

Anthony Giddens similarly defines globalization as 'the intensification of social relations which link distant localities in such a way that local happenings are shaped by events occurring miles away and vice versa'.[12] What this means for our argument is that what happens in a local neighbourhood of a city, including of course its levels of crime, is increasingly likely to be influenced by factors such as world money and commodity markets which operate at an indefinite distance from the neighbourhood itself. For

[11] M. Walters, *Globalisation* (London, 1995), 3.

[12] A. Giddens, *Consequences of Modernity* (Oxford, 1990), 64, and cf. A. Giddens *Modernity and Self Identity* (Oxford, 1991).

Giddens globalization should be treated as part of the process of modernization (not postmodernization), a secular trend through which time and space come to be separated from a person's location or the cycles of the seasons. It represents a further stage in the lifting out of social relations from local contexts of interaction and their restructuring across time and space through symbolic tokens such as money, media and expert systems. Those who live in modern times trust their societies and lives to be guided by such impersonal flows of expertise so that to know what to do it is necessary to have resort to a constantly changing forms of knowledge. (In the jargon without which sociology would become too user-friendly this is known as 'time-space distanciation', 'disemebedding', and 'reflexivity'). Each of these changes in the relationship of the individual to her social world has potential implications for crime and its control. A recent attempt to draw conclusions for criminology[13] suggests that Giddens has described a world of relativized and individualistic choices which helps weaken social controls and makes it more difficult to define and reinforce outer boundaries of cultural and legal systems. What replaces these boundaries is our drawing on expert systems so as to create bubbles of security in defined areas of housing and shopping malls which have to be fortified against the risks posed by those members of the population who have been displaced from the economy by processes of global change.

Globalization has manifold economic, political, and cultural aspects and there is predictable disagreement about which of these is driving the others.[14] As compared to what are described as more culturalist approaches other authors lay more stress on economic factors. Wallerstein argues that the world capitalist system has always been integrated not by nation-states but by global commercial and manufacturing relationships which determine which countries belong to the core, semi-periphery, or periphery of this system.[15] In these terms, changes in the dependent nation-state

[13] A. Bottoms and P. Wiles, 'Crime and insecurity in the City' in C. Finjaut, J. Goetals, T. Peters, and L. Walgrave (eds.), *Changes in Society, Crime and Criminal Justice in Europe*, Vol. I (The Hague, 1996).

[14] See M. Featherstone (ed.), *Global Culture* (London, 1990).

[15] I. Wallerstein, *The Capitalist World-Economy* (Cambridge, 1979): for another attempt to situate globalization in historical perspective see also R. Robertson, *Globalisation, Social Theory and Global Culture* (London, 1992).

system, world military order, and the international division of labour and trading relationships can all be expected to have consequences for the type and levels of crime. Another leading writer stresses the importance of transnational global companies, the transnational capitalist class, and the cultural ideology of consumerism and focuses in particular on what he calls the 'key transnational practices' which characterize globalization.[16] These practices, which originate with non-state actors and cross state borders, involve among others major capitalist institutions, globalizing bureaucrats, executives of transnational companies, and professional and consumerist elites in the first and third worlds. From a criminological perspective it would certainly be relevant to examine how the spread of consumerist ideology increases expectations without necessarily providing the income to satisfy them.

A similar stress on political economy, though without the Marxist flavour, is found in the management science literature.[17] It argues that the increasing integration of the world economy is an objective trend which can be measured by descriptive indicators such as price and interest rates convergence. Economic actors are increasingly having to take greater account of the way their actions in one nation state influence their actions in another. The State loses influence because political action is increasingly dominated by world financial and real goods markets and governments encounter particular difficulties in pursuing policies of regulation which are out of line with other countries. New forms of interdependence also pose governments with other problems such as how to tax information flows (though no doubt they will find out how to do so one day). In part as a reaction to these difficulties there is an increasing number of regional groupings, not only the EU or NAFTA, but also the IMF, which has grown in membership from forty-four to 178 countries. This literature is specially useful when we come to consider the globalization of organized crime as an aspect of how and why legitimate businesses are integrating world wide.

Where is globalization leading? What would a fully globalized

[16] L. Sklair, *The Sociology of the Global System* (Hemel Hempstead, 1991).

[17] See the entries on globalization in M. Warner (ed.), *International Encyclopedia of Business and Management* (London, 1996).

society look like? Walters[18] tells us it would exhibit a high level of differentiation and multicentricity and there would be no tight set of cultural preferences and prescriptions. Insofar as culture is unified it will be extremely abstract, expressing tolerance for diversity and individual choice. Importantly for the future of criminal justice, we are told that territoriality will disappear as an organizing principle for social and cultural life. But looking that far ahead is not all that convincing. We would do better to concentrate on trying to clarify our ideas about what is happening now to crime and criminal justice as it is shaped by or tries to resist these trends.

Globalization and Crime

In trying to apply theories of globalization it is all too easy to go from the sublime to the meticulous. On the one hand we have sweeping futuristic visions; on the other all too concrete descriptions of what is happening on the ground in police co-operation or the emergence of new forms of transnational crime, with only an impoverished account of how this relates to wider social changes. We lack a middle-range theory which makes developments in crime and criminal justice central to its concerns. But is it even plausible to expect to find one theory which would successfully explain all types of crime linked to globalization—from genocide to insider trading to computer 'hacking'—and which could also succinctly explain the common denominator of globalizing moral panics from pædophilia to political corruption (though current developments in Belgium suggest that there can be surprising and disturbing links between such apparently unrelated crimes)? What we can do is at least try to provide a framework which could help us to sort out the various relationships between globalization and developments in crime and criminal justice.

Which should be the axis of such a framework? One important distinction to bear in mind is that between increasing homogenization and increasing interdependence (of other kinds). On the one hand there is the phenomenon of the 'global village' (which we can call *homogenization*), in which up to 800 million of the world's population can be found watching an American superbowl game on television whilst eating pizza and drinking coca cola—or the

[18] N. 11 above.

scene in Nani Moretti's film *Dear Diary* where an Italian devotee of soap opera desperately shouts at some American tourists visiting the Etna volcano to find out what has happened in the latest instalments of his favourite soap which had been broadcast in the USA, but not yet in Italy. The spread of American films, television series, and novels which feature (particular) images of crime and criminal justice illustrates this sort of globalization. On the other hand there is the *interdependence* vividly illustrated by the Chernobyl nuclear disaster or the way a military coup in Nigeria affects the price of oil in Rotterdam and brings about a collapse of prices on the Tokyo Stock exchange. In the sphere of crime we could consider the part played by organized crime pyramid frauds in the recent collapse of order in Albania, or the multiple consequences of reckless or fraudulent speculation by merchant banks or other players on the commodities markets.

Globalization may further either or both of these processes. What is important is to see that interdependence does not necessarily presume or produce homogeneity.[19] As sociologists of modernity from Durkheim to Luhmann have emphasized, it thrives on difference and differentiation. But there is also a further distinction which needs to be made which is obscured in many discussions of globalization which describe growing interdependence. It is often unclear whether such interdependence is something planned as a *strategy* of integration (for example under the impetus of multinationals such as McDonalds), or whether it is rather (by definition) a process which is beyond control, as in the way money flows to where it can obtain the best return. Of course both of these processes may sometimes be relevant for different purposes, but all this needs careful sorting out. To allow this we need a framework which helps us to see how globalizing processes may involve homogenization and integration in varying degrees.

One final note of caution. We must not assume that developments in crime and criminal justice are merely a *consequence* of globalization; they may also, as already noted, be one of the causes

[19] See S. Yearley, *Sociology, Environmentalism, and Globalization* (London, 1996), 23: 'A global world is not a uniform world. But it is one in which key processes—manufacture, food production, cultural transmission—are increasingly being organized at a transnational level.'

of whether or not people feel part of a global order. Notoriously, criminal law functions by creating boundaries between insiders and outsiders; by responding to real or constructed threats it helps define enemies or create scapegoats.[20] Whilst this will often, and perhaps typically, tighten the definition of who can count as an insider, attempts to extend the reach of the law, as for example through the creation of the International War Crimes tribunals, or in legislation aimed at dealing with 'sex tourists' who victimize children abroad, may also broaden this definition of who counts as an offender or a victim. In addition, discourse about crime, like that about victims, is itself one of most universalizing of current ideologies—after the alleged death of merely political ideologies. As its influence spreads, criminology, like other types of expertise, can also be seen as a bearer of globalization, though it puts one in mind of Beck's remark that expertise secures its survival as much through its failure as its success.[21]

Globalization may even *constitute* and not simply cause or facilitate crime. Typically this will be when it increases the levels of criminalization of certain types of behaviour which not long before had been considered as acceptable, or at least containable, within acceptable limits, especially as long as they were confined to local insiders. One interpretation of the move to legislate against a crime which is aptly named 'insider trading', which accompanied the so-called 'big bang' liberalization of the London stock exchange, is in terms of the need to ensure predictability and trust in the globalized City of London once it was opened up to outsiders. As Clarke puts it, 'it would have perplexed leading members of these institutions up to the end of the 1950s to be told they were doing anything reprehensible in acting on such information. It was precisely because of access to such information that one was part of the city, and one was part of the city in the clear expectation of making a considerable amount of money'.[22] Similarly, it is not easy to decide how much the campaigns against political corruption of the 1990s merely reflect an increase in such misbehaviour in the 1980s or also the effects of globalization in making such conduct ' more 'costly'

[20] Cf. J. O'Neill, 'Aids as a Globalizing Panic', in n. 13 above, 329–42.

[21] U. Beck, *The Risk Society: Towards a New Modernity* (London, 1992).

[22] M. Clarke, *Business Crime: Its Nature and Control* (Oxford, 1990), 162.

or increasing the centrality of penal law as a political resource.[23]

Table 1: Crime, Criminal Justice and Two Aspects of Globalizing Processes of Interdependence

1. High homogenization, Low integration

Global spread of criminal techniques e.g. car ramming and strategies of control e.g. technological methods of surveillance;

Developments and fashions in criminal justice e.g. the decline of rehabilitation, fixed sentencing, community policing, local crime prevention, 'victim's rights', mediation, (the 'reintegrative shaming' approach in criminology).

Global spread of images of crime ('Miami Vice') and criminal justice ('Perry Mason'). Influence of (American) criminology and the Anglo-American concept of 'criminal justice'.

2. High integration, High homogenization

Greater flows of illegal trade e.g. of pornography, drugs, etc., as well as more opportunities for financial crime, as part of increased legal trading;

New criminal laws to fight counterfeiting, to protect new information property rights, regulate financial markets, computer 'hacking', the use of the INTERNET etc.

Development of international criminal law, creation of war crimes tribunals, international and regional policing agreements e.g. *Schengen*

3. Low integration, Low homogenization

Local differences in types and levels of crime in countries, cities (and parts of cities) in the core, semi periphery, and periphery of the 'world system' which result from market- and technology-driven changes in the flows of trade, information, and people.

Other effects of the 'hollowing out' of the State and of 'localization' as a reaction to (or aspect of) globalization.

[23] See e.g. D. della Porta and Y. Meny (eds.) *Corruzione e Democrazia: Sette paesi a confronto* (Naples, 1995); D. Nelken and M. Levi, 'Introduction' in M. Levi and D. Nelken (eds.), *The Politics of Corruption and the Corruption of Politics* (Oxford, 1996); and A. Garapon and D. Salas (eds.), *La République Pénalisée* (Paris, 1996).

4. High integration, Low homogenization

Pax Mafioso—strategic agreements between organized crime groups exploiting national differences in law and sentencing. The export of hot money, arms, dangerous waste, unsafe products and working practices by state/organized/business criminals. Competition for 'hot money' and money laundering, growth of tax havens.

Pax Americana—American foreign crime policy in Latin America and elsewhere. Fortress Europe: *TREVI*, *EUROPOL*; IMF and world bank pressures on developing countries.

Table 1 sets out the four cells of the framework which I have been outlining, with some illustrative examples (many more could of course be added) showing how increasing global interdependence may influence or be influenced by crime and criminal justice. It allows us to draw a number of lessons for the currently popular claim that the crucial threat which globalization represents is the way it facilitates the integration of organized crime (to which the only answer is a similar response by the international forces of order).

In the first place, and most importantly, it suggests the complexity of teasing out the connections between crime and globalization. While some forms of crime result from processes of integration, others belong more to homogenizing processes and some aspects of globalization cannot be fitted into either of these categories. Criminal justice or other agencies need to be aware of this variety; even more, their responses are themselves part of the phenomenon that needs to be understood.

More specifically, the table shows us why an exclusive focus on the threat of transnational criminals fails to capture many of the other ways globalization may affect opportunities for crime. As cell 3 suggests, many of the problems caused by globalization have nothing to do with deliberate integration by organized criminals but result from the differential effects of globalization on different countries, cities, or parts of cities which governments cannot or will not attempt to control. From a criminological point of view the drive to economic integration can, and often will, lead to social and anomic disintegration. It will therefore be of small help to integrate at the level of criminal justice responses whilst leaving the underlying causes untouched. The disintegrative effects of economic integration may even be exacerbated by some of the homogenizing globalizing processes which affect criminal justice (as can be seen in cell 1). It is enough to think of the way the rehabilitative approach to punishment fell widely out of favour just at the same time as the welfare state faced fiscal pressures because of changes in global competitiveness and oil prices.

We also need to question the assumption that there is an inverse relationship between the problem posed by organized crime and success in achieving agreement on the harmonization of national systems of criminal law and enforcement. The table reminds us that some homogenization of criminal justice (the increasing adoption of the accusatorial model for example) is already taking place as a result of globalization, despite the alleged dependence of criminal law on the nation state and local culture. But a comparison of cells 2 and 4 should again remind us of the limits of law as a response, whether uniform or not. It is true that organized crime is able to organize strategically to exploit differences in the economic and legal order—just as these differences are exploited and reinforced also by *legitimate* business in its 'forum shopping' for favourable legal systems and the way it puts pressure on weak states to soften regulatory regimes. But organized and economic crime has also benefited from the opportunities opened up by increasing *homogenization* of the world economic and legal order (including the enormous increase in the issue of bonds consequent on the internationalization of the banking system). Greater harmonization of legal procedures and penalties (even apart from the conceptual difficulties this raises) will do little as such to change the balance of incentives which lead to the world wide distribution of crime even if it may help in the processing of the few who are apprehended. And, in practice, integration of enforcement efforts usually tends to involve subordination rather than homogenization, as in the way the United States attempts to enforce its priorities in South America.

The dialectic between crime and control will not be understood as long as we stick to the idea that the forces of order are waging a losing war against an insidious foreign enemy. Increasing certain sorts of control efforts may even act as an incentive to criminal action, as in the case of drugs and other illegal products and activities in which organized crime specializes. Insofar as crime and control can, for some purposes, be separated this will depend on our ability to distinguish the dynamics of criminal behaviour and of changes in criminal justice which are highlighted in each of the four cells. How far do crime and control evolve by following the same or different logics? What are the organizational and inter-organizational challenges which each face? How far is it true that organized crime strategies reflect a strictly economic logic whereas the growth of international policing responds to more political considerations at both national and international levels? And what are the implications of any such differences?

Trend, Tactic, or Trope?

Before concluding this brief, and necessarily oversimplified, overview of the relationship between globalization and criminal justice there is one further reflection which can be drawn from the social science literature. This warns us to be wary of taking globalization to be something inevitable. There is certainly some evidence to justify talking about globalization as a current trend, just as it made sense—a generation ago—to talk about the economic and cultural 'convergence' between nations that would inevitably eventually be produced through their common reliance on modern technology. But, as that counter-example shows, historical inevitability is not so easily discerned (the move towards market systems in the former communist states may be more attributable to their failure to keep up in the technological battle). Presupposing the inevitability of globalization is itself a loaded description of current developments. Insofar as globalization is to be defined not simply or always as a process out of control, but also as a strategy or tactic which is followed by determinate economic and political actors, there will almost always be some room for alternative strategies and resistance.

The progress of globalization is thus not determined simply by the extension of new technologies in communication and transportation but is also the result of social and political action, including decisions (and non-decisions) by governments about regulating and deregulating the national and international economy. Talking about globalization as if it were inevitable is itself often a tactic for gaining resources, for favouring one or other policy choice—or what is often the same thing, making an alliance with one or other national or international actor or set of actors. It is precisely *not* the case that 'Global economic interaction poses an identical legal and law enforcement dilemma for industrialized and newly industrializing nations—opening their borders, economy, and society to the free exchange of people, capital, and goods, without sacrificing domestic order and protection of the international interests of their citizens'.[24] Even allegedly global environmental problems do not have the same costs for all, just as some countries or groups pay a higher price for trying to deal with them.[25] In particular there are likely to be systematic differences in judgments of globalization from the perspective of members of countries in the semi-periphery or periphery of the capitalist world system—as they experience its effects as packaged by the IMF and the world bank in its curious mixture of economic liberalism and human rights.

This point is often lost sight of because of the way talk about globalization has become a trope or metaphor which carries arguments over all or any obstacle. Take, for our own topic, the following quotation from the same article published in an allegedly radical criminological journal. 'Economic and social change', we are told, 'is apparent across the face of a transformed globe, reshaped by technological winds blowing across the global landscape as forcefully and as steadily as the Trade winds carried explorers and colonists to reshape the New World. Virtually every institution within industrialized and newly industrializing economies is undergoing rapid evolution to keep pace with the speed of technologically induced social and political change save *one*, law and law enforcement'.[26] With this type of metaphoric reasoning it is no surprise to find that our author later assumes, rather than demonstrates, the happy arrival of global consensus when he asserts blandly that organized crime (his concern is the Chinese and Taiwanese variety) 'imperils the attainment of international objectives like political harmony and economic advancement through free trade'.[27]

Less scholarly (even less scholarly!), though more widely read

[24] W. H. Myers III, 'The Emerging Threat of Transnational Organised Crime from the East' (1996) 24 *Crime, Law and Social Change*, 181, at 182. Myers himself immediately acknowledges that 'the economic burdens and social effects of maintaining this tension fall unequally upon industrialized and newly industrializing nations' but (illogically) insists nonetheless that 'all nations have an equal share in the consequences of failing to act'.

[25] See Yearley, n. 19, above.

[26] W. H. Myers III, n. 24 above, 182.

[27] *Ibid.*, 213.

accounts of organized crime—which one suspects may influence or echo even more closely some levels of official thinking—make regular resort to questionable metaphors rather than sober evidence. Crime, we are told, 'skids out of control around the globe'.[28] In particular the European Union 'faces an uncontrollable invasion of migrants from every direction'[29] and, in 1992, 'every kind of criminal was riding in on this human tide' so that 'Western Europe lay like a vast open city under murderous criminal bombardment'.[30] Even what purports to be evidence in such accounts is far from meeting minimum requirements, as in the claim that 'crime is the fastest growing industry in Britain' or the fatuous assertion that Holland, 'an island of civility on a turbulent continent', 'has more crimes per capita than . . . the United States'.[31] Nobody had told our author (an American living in Europe)—assuming she was in good faith—that it is the high level of bicycle theft in that country which so biases its crime statistics.

The Strategy and Culture of Organized Criminals

The exaggerations of those trying to grab our attention with metaphors should not be taken as an excuse to conclude that there is nothing to be worried about regarding organized crime or that globalization is irrelevant to its strategies. But if we are to take seriously both the fears mentioned at the outset of this article what can be done about the real threat of organized crime other than entrust the police and the intelligence services with ever-increasing (and uncontrollable) powers?

The first step must be to understand more about the changing strategies of organized criminals.[32] The management science

[28] N. 5 above, 38. [29] *Ibid.*, 39. [30] *Ibid.*, 41.
[31] *Ibid.*, 38.
[32] There is no space here to expound on the many differences between organized crime groups. But it is at least worth noting that describing organized crime as a new authoritarian menace to the democratic state fails to bring out the contrast between organized crime groups, or strategies, which aspire to military control over a territory (offering or exacting protection) and those, on the other hand, which thrive on the collusion of complicit weak States which allow them to accumulate wealth (e.g. through international frauds or drug smuggling) without drawing attention to their criminal activities.

literature, for example, explains the advantages of global integration for business multinationals in terms which can apply equally well to organized crime. Thus we read of alliances, protection from competition, economies of scale, the securing of stable supplies and markets, assistance in diversification and bringing products to market, the possibilities of taking advantage of expertise and local knowledge, the reduction of risks, the financing of large-scale projects, and the acquisition of technology.[33] The opportunities which globalization has opened up for organized crime also reflect the extent to which such crime enterprises have integrated not only with other organized crime groups but also with legitimate and semi-legitimate international business. For example only 5 per cent of the more than 175 billion dollars a day of international transactions is connected to flows of world trade directly.[34] The remainder is made up of capital on the look out for short-term liquid or semi-liquid speculative investments. This total has grown enormously as a result of the internationalization of banks and holding companies since the 1960s, the elimination of restrictions and controls on foreign investments and currency swaps, and the impact of electronic technology on the individual national capital markets. As important as the globalization of markets or the technological marvels of electronic money transfer is the development of privileged territories where transactions of huge dimensions can take place without any form of regulation and control—the tax havens and Eurodollar markets at the intersections of main routes of legal and illegal trade. In order to recycle their illegal profits organized criminals have thus increasingly established relationships with the institutions and locations harbouring homeless capital and bought themselves into systems of offshore banks and holding companies.

But the dirty money derived from illegal activity is only a minor part of all the 'hot money' ready to move from one end of the globe to the other at the smallest change in interest rates, legal

[33] See M. Warner, n. 17 above.

[34] P. Arlacchi, 'Corruption, Organized Crime and Money Laundering World Wide' in M. Punch et al., *Coping with Corruption in a Borderless World* (The Hague, 1993), 89. The best discussion of these matters is still R. T. Naylor, *Hot Money and the Politics of Debt* (New York, 1987).

regulations, economic policies, or political regimes. There are two other main sources of hot money apart from that produced from illegal transactions. A second source is the profit produced in the underground or informal economy which runs at 10–15 per cent of gross product in developed countries. This money, made by those otherwise law-abiding, cannot be declared because it is the result of transactions organized to avoid paying tax. It needs to flow out of the country until it can reappear safely. A third source of hot money is so-called 'flight capital' leaving indebted countries in the third world. In the period 1973–81, for example, multinational bank managers came to depend on the volume, not the quality of, loans extended without deposits. Highly-placed members of foreign governments spent the loans on public works, armaments, and luxurious consumer goods but a large part returned to Western countries in the form of illegally exported capital often deposited with the very banks that gave the credits in the first place. The short-sighted complicity of the largest banks in the world revealed itself as short-sighted when countries began defaulting. But when the banks curbed the credit flow to the developing world from 1981 the problem grew worse as frightened members of the middle classes began expatriating their savings; something like 200 billion dollars was allegedly transferred between 1976 and 1985 to the USA and the tax havens of Europe, Asia, and the Caribbean, leaving their own countries without foreign exchange reserves.

In some parts of the world the destinies of legal and illegal commerce now (again?) seem to be fatally intertwined. One chapter of a recent biography of Pablo Escobar (the former Colombian drug baron) begins:

> Every morning, on the fifth floor of the north Bogota headquarters of one of Colombia's biggest financial and industrial conglomerates there arrives a fax from its main office in the United States. The fax gives the daily US dollar price of cocaine on the streets of New York. Immediately the information is keyed into a computer performance chart. Two parallel lines run across the middle of the graph. When the price spikes through the upper line, it indicates a supply blockage. The scarcity of cocaine in New York means a scarcity of US dollars in Colombia. The company's domestic sales are damaged. When the price bursts through the lower line it heralds the presence of a major new cocaine supplier and a spate of killings and informant related seizures until the supply drops back to normal levels. In the meantime with US dollars flooding to Colombia, it is a good moment to

buy them cheaply. According to a technician who worked for the conglomerate, the chart was installed in 1986.[35]

Earnings from the illegal drug trade in Colombia are said to be the same as that from legal exports and to have helped to save the economy from debt-related torment, hyper-inflation, and economic stagnation which affected so many other countries in South America in the 1980s.[36]

Even in the most developed Western countries there is a blurring of legal and illegal commerce, as in the arms trade,[37] and this is as often sustained as attacked by the police and intelligence services. A good example is provided by the collapse of the Bank of Credit and Commerce International.[38] The BCCI grew to be the World's seventh largest private bank with assets of $23 billion and operations in seventy-two countries. The criminal enterprises it helped fund included smuggling, drug trafficking, money laundering, illegal arms trade, transfer of nuclear technology, public corruption and capital flight, illegal ownership of US banks, financing of terrorism, frauds against depositors, and the methods adopted ranged from false accounting to the use of violence. The bank's main beneficiaries were 3,000 powerful customers who included the Colombian drug lords, ruthless dictators such as Duvalier, Somoza, Saddam Hussein, Marcos, and Noriega. But the uses made of the bank by the CIA and other Western secret services also played an important part in postponing its hour of reckoning. As Passas argues:

> in order to better understand and fight organized international crime groups, one has to explore their links with legitimate organizations and (Western and other) government policies that provide crime facilitative conditions and/or create demands such as those fulfilled by BCCI. BCCI reflects and is deeply rooted in the world's structural problems and conflicts.[39]

There are ever more reports of research findings which illustrate the increasing overlap between organized crime, corporate crime,

[35] S. Strong, *Whitewash*, (London, 1996).

[36] *Ibid.*

[37] R. T. Naylor, 'Loose Cannons: Covert Commerce and Underground Finance in the Modern Arms Market' (1995) 22 *Crime, Law and Social Change* 1.

[38] N. Passas, 'BCCI?' (1996) 23 *Crime, Law and Social Change* 293–300, at 308.

[39] *Ibid.*, 245.

and ordinary business.[40] But whilst it is essential to explore the full extent of symbiosis between legitimate business and organized crime I am uneasy about the temptation in some parts simply to *equate* business and organized crime or to treat organized crime as no more than a special form of capitalist enterprise.[41] It seems to me that, for all the similarities in strategy, there are also significant differences in culture, differences which could perhaps be exploited in seeking to contain the threat posed by this form of criminality. Interviews carried out under my guidance with members of organized crime groups in Italy who are involved in defrauding the European Union, for example, show that there is an uneasy relationship between the locally based organized criminals and the more cosmopolitan legal and accounting experts on whom they have increasingly to rely.[42] There also persisting, if subtle, differences in philosophy between organized criminals and businessmen (notwithstanding the now widely-accepted accounts of the affinity between the approach of the New Mafia and that of business entrepreneurs).[43] The following extract from a longer interview with two members of the Mafia responsible for organizing European Union fraud in Sicily reveals, amongst other things, a fatalistic zero-sum approach to life which is, in some ways, far from the capitalistic ethic.

The interview was carried out at the height of the judges' attack on corruption in Italy. Asked whether the judges' campaign was bad for business the senior of the two men replied:

> all the screaming and excitement can never go on for very long—still less can it cause any permanent damage except to those who allow themselves to be frightened. You stop your activities for a moment and wait while the crows scream and get all excited. Then everything returns as it was before.

[40] See e.g. N. Passas and D. Nelken, 'The Thin Line . . .', n. 1 above; P. Van Kuyne 'Implications of Cross-border Crime Risks in an Open Europe' (1993) 20 *Crime, Law and Social Change* 99; and P. Van Duyne and A. A. Block, 'Organized Cross-Atlantic Crime: Racketeering in Fuels' (1995) 22 *Crime, Law and Social Change* 127.

[41] D. Gambetta, *The Sicilian Mafia: The Business of Private Protection* (Oxford, 1993); V. Ruggiero, *Organised Crime and Corporate Crime in Europe* (Aldershot, 1996); cf. D. Nelken, 'White-Collar Crime', in M. Maguire, R. Morgan, and R. Reiner (eds.), *Oxford Handbook of Criminology* (2nd edn.) (Oxford, (forthcoming).

[42] The following extracts are taken from D. Nelken, 'Inflated Claims: Organised Crime and European Union Fraud' in A. Febbrajo, D. Nelken, and V. Olgiati (eds.), *European Yearbook of Sociology of Law* (forthcoming).

[43] P. Arlacchi, *Mafia Business* (Oxford, 1995).

No-one (Nothing) can fundamentally upset [the order of] the forest: trees may dry up and die but other ones just the same will take their place, animals die, but others are born. Things can change their position and form but always remain essentially the same.[44]

Q But the world, the larger society in which we live, isn't actually a forest, and man is not only an animal . . .

A1 Man can be any of the things you want but in the end he remains nothing other than an animal. He can wear any type of clothes imaginable, and non-imaginable, but under these clothes the only concrete, real and true thing is his body which needs to eat, drink, piss, fuck, kill, defend itself, work, steal, win, dominate, and command.

Q . . . And, above all, love.

A1 Why, do you think that he who kills is unable also to love? It all depends what values we associate or give to love and what rules or concepts we relate it to. Love comes in infinite forms and substance!

A2 These ways of talking don't do any one any good. Everyone has their own way of thinking about this subject. Everyone loves and behaves according to his own lights. In the end it is always the strongest who triumphs.

Q It depends what you mean by 'the strongest'. . . . In any case Don . . ., (as you conceded) when the crows shout and get excited you do need to stay a little quieter and therefore you will be suffering losses. How do you make up for or at least limit these losses?

A1 You always want to understand, to discover. Don't let your brain overwork or your stomach will complain of hunger.

Q There are those who are satisfied by meat and others who are only sated by thoughts and discoveries. You can give me to eat the food that is best suited to my digestion . . .

A1 You really are the son of . . . a really good woman! . . .[45] Well, we always get to know much in advance if the crows are about to start their screeching. We have men who are predisposed for this role, planted in the appropriate positions. We invest major capital expenditures so as to maintain these special observers who are above suspicion. We always know to stop in time, before the rumpus starts. And so we are able to freeze every activity in time, and destroy any path that might lead to us. In those cases where it is necessary we also set in motion manoeuvres or entire apparatuses aimed at throwing the investigators off the scent.

[44] This is the well known thesis of *Il Gattopardo*.
[45] A way of saying 'you son of a whore'.

A2 Sometimes one is also obliged to throw someone or something to the crows so as to quieten them down.

A1 But nothing is decided on the spur of the moment. The less hasty decisions are taken the more one can be certain that the world will carry on going as it always has.

Q Doesn't the very use of the word 'truffa' (fraud/ swindle) bother you?

A1 And why on earth should it? It is a 'truffa'. But watch out, my boy, not everything that you think of as wrong really is so. It all depends, as I said before, on which rules you follow. For you the EEC is a legal and good system, for me it is itself nothing other than a 'truffa'. A real fraud just because it is so accepted and well defended . . . but come and visit me one day and we will speak at greater length about this. Real honesty is so rare as to be almost Utopian. On this earth perhaps only one man has ever succeeded in being really honest—and we put him on the cross. Meanwhile we all go to Mass and listen to the words of men who swindle and mislead us . . . Have you ever asked yourself why we and the Church keep going trying always not to step on each others toes. This is because at bottom we are both systems which, with different rules and rites, seek similar or even identical goals. But let's not speak any more about this now, otherwise you would be capable of wearying me with questions until tomorrow morning. . . .

Q You pursue power and wealth, but it seems to me that you never get the chance to relax and enjoy its fruits because you are always obliged (to fight to) hold on to it and to defend yourselves from everyone and everything. You have to watch out both for institutionalised legality and your own many internal enemies. So doesn't it all seem without any sense?

A1 But this is just what life is! All systems are forced to fight to survive and to defend themselves continuously. Man's only choice is whether to be essentially the hunter or the prey. All this is natural. And perhaps we (Cosa Nostra) are the most quintessentially natural of all systems . . .

A2 It is not easy to change a system. And it would in any case be useless and unproductive to try because no system could ever be really and deeply different from what came before. Revolutions only change the form of things but the substance always remains the same. So it is better to continue with what there has always been. Why waste energy uselessly?

Interviews with members of the Camorra-based organized crime groups in the Campagna region of Italy also provide equivocal evidence of the effects of globalization on the culture of organized criminals. Here is a member of the New Camorra confirming the changes brought about over the past few years.

A1 . . . The old Camorra had difficulty in getting beyond regional boundaries, and rarely went beyond national frontiers. Its links were with local politicians, together with a very few national politicians and Euro parliamentarians. It preferred to concern itself with matters that happened in its own backyard, in the political locality: contraband, prostitution, (protection) rackets, extortion, the 'pizzo',[46] illegal gaming, illegal football pools, betting as well as other similar 'businesses' and enterprises of various kinds. The New Camorra, on the other hand, has preferred to modernise itself, to turn itself into a full scale industry, and to organise at national and (even) international level. As a result its 'connections' have grown considerably both in number and sophistication. Our mode of operating nowadays is surgical, almost scientific.

On the other hand, listen to these comments by an accountant compromised into working for the Camorra—the only hopeful signs in his generally bleak picture of the dominance of this crime group in his part of Italy.

A . . . The children of those entrepreneurs who rely on this fraudulent way of running their business are beginning to rebel against their parents. These young people all come from studying at the University where they have had the chance to acquire an approach to business which is ethically correct, and relies on management skills. They have been made aware of the [rules of the] market, of market equilibrium at both national and international level. Furthermore, all of them, even if some more than others, having had experience of industries in the North (of Italy), have had the chance to come across their way of doing things and so come to understand that the way things are done where they grew up is completely mistaken. They feel humiliated both personally and in their role as businessmen. That is the reason therefore why, when they take over the reins of their father's business, they rebel against the compromises with organized crime to which their fathers have sunk. But this rebellion is enclosed for the time being within the walls of the home. Word of it never comes out. It is within the family that the young are fighting to change things, even at the price of being killed. I myself have many times been a witness to bitter family arguments in the homes of my industrialist friends. And I have seen the force, the courage and the determination of these young people. They choose to fight these battles out in the privacy of the home so as not to undermine the image of a united family in the eyes of acquaintances and the larger community.

[46] The 'pizzo' is the widespread practice of demanding a rake-off or 'cut' from all business activities in areas under control and/or subject to the threats or blandishments of organized crime.

It is thus worth remembering that globalization may help undermine the opportunities for some crimes as well as increase them. European Union fraud, like many other of the activities of organized crime in fact thrives on protective legislation rather than on globalized market freedom—in this case the common agricultural policy which is explicitly designed to keep out competition from food producing nations outside the European Union.

Think Global, Act Local?

I have no pretensions in this article to offer any worked out solutions to the new challenges of transnational crime. My task has been the more modest one of trying to clarify what is at stake and warn against over-simple remedies. Relying on increased police enforcement is likely to be illusory,[47] though there is much more to be done in seeking to reconcile the values of accountability and effectiveness in reshaping the role of the police at national and international level. But if we are not just to leave the battle against organized crime to the police there may be a need for more, rather than less, local action. The slogan of 'thinking globally and acting locally' adopted by the green movement has had deserved success in raising ecological consciousness about the wider implications of local action for the fate of common resources. There may be a need for similar consciousness-raising in order to see the links between organized crime and the financial and other choices made by businesses, banks and ordinary consumers of illicit services.[48] What could also repay further investigation is the extent to which organized criminals are really orientated to *local* cultural values; we could even say that organized crime 'thinks locally even as it acts globally'.

And what about the attempt to think globally in the letter sent by Ali from Masul? In my reply, I supplied him with information

[47] See G. Farrell, K. Manshur, and M. Tullis, 'Cocaine and Heroin in Europe 1983–93: A Cross-national Comparison of Trafficking and Prices' (1996) 36 *British Journal of Criminology* 255 who argue, at 279, 'the implications of this analysis for increasing the effectiveness of European law enforcement are not encouraging. The balance of evidence suggests increasing enforcement will impact only marginally upon prices due to rapidly diminishing marginal returns'.

[48] See M. Levi, 'Pecunia Non Olet: Cleansing the Money-Launderers from the Temple' (1996) 16 *Crime, Law and Social Change* 217, who notes the difficult practical and policy issues involved.

about two more appropriate experts to help him with his research. The handbook of the Society of Public Teachers of Law provided me with the name of a scholar in Liverpool who specializes in military law. But I also sent Ali the name of a law professor at Tel Aviv active in defending soldiers in military trials who refuse to obey orders they regard as illegitimate. The chances that a law student in Iraq dare write to a law professor in Israel are admittedly low, but then that too tells us something about how far the trend to globalization still has to go.

[3]

Shadows and Sovereigns

Carolyn Nordstrom

ONE DAY the political scientist Ed Garcia showed me a letter he had received from a well-established group that had been fighting for autonomy against government repression for several decades. The authors explained that, as they did not constitute a state, they were cut off from many opportunities most take for granted. Without the status of state, they were not recognized by the other states of the world as a formal trade partner, as part of political and military associations, or as being a signatory in economic treaties. They were not represented in the international banking system, nor could they receive IMF state-based loans. They had no seat at the United Nations, no inviolable land to attract multinational businesses. Yet their people required food, clothing, household goods, jobs and cars like anyone else in the world. They required travel visas and the means to travel. They needed access to the resources to set up industries and exchange their products on the world's open market. Not an easy thing for a group at war with a state. The state-based nature of the world's politics and economy forced them to rely on non-formal markets. How, they wanted to know, would it be possible to function in the world's formal economy?

It will be obvious to note that as I read this letter, I saw the role of states in determining the kinds of political and economic access people and populations have in the world. But I was in fact struck by something more subtle: I saw the vast international machinery that kept this group clothed and fed and armed and in business for all these decades, a machinery that functions outside of the world's formal markets and politics – one invisible to government's formal policies but equally powerful in shaping the course of the world's progression, a machinery capable of sustaining entire populations and creating new nations.

This article will explore a series of shadow powers, international by definition, that – while capable of shaping world economies and policies – remain largely invisible to formal analysis. The heart of this study is ethnographic in nature. In the 15 years I have been conducting fieldwork in war zones,[1] I have charted the ways in which people gain the necessities to wage war and create peace – necessities that range from major weapons systems to basic medicines and goods. An equally important aspect of this equation concerns the ways in which people pay for these goods and services: gold, diamonds, drugs, precious metals, human labor, sex workers, timber and even seafood move out of war zones into world markets to purchase everything from AK-47s and M-16s to satellite-linked computer communications and weapons systems, from antibiotics to basic grains. A large part of this trade takes place outside formal state and legal channels. As war gives way to peace in the conflict zones in which I have worked, I have also charted the ways in which people begin to rebuild war-devastated economies. Here, too, people often rely on buying and selling the same goods they did during war, along the same non-state channels – both to gain life's necessities and to acquire the finances and supplies to rehabilitate livelihoods and industries. Those most successful at this non-state trade amass economic fortunes that can be translated into political power, fortunes that can reshape social, economic and political landscapes (Nordstrom, 1995, 1997; Nordstrom and Robben, 1995).

This study of the shadows is not merely a study of extra-state transactions. The finances and power wielded by these shadow networks challenge academics to rethink our theories on states, sovereignty and the loci of power. It is not the story of individual people operating in the shadows, but a study of the vast networks of people who move goods and services worldwide – networks that broker power comparable to, and in many cases greater than, a number of the world's states. I have come to this research through the study of war zones, where non-state actors and transactions are perhaps most visible. But, as this study will show, vast extra-state networks expand across war and peace, and across all the world's countries. I have chosen to use the word 'extra-state' in defining the shadows to underscore the fact that while these networks are not comprised by states themselves, neither are they entirely distinct from, or opposite to, states – they work both through and around formal state representatives and institutions. This point is critical to the theory developed here: states and shadow networks exist simultaneously, each phenomenologically different, each representing distinct forms of authority and politico-economic organization.

I use the term 'shadows' (rather than criminal or illegal) as the transactions defining these networks are not confined solely to criminal, illicit or illegal activities – but they do take place outside formal state institutions. The relationships of power and exchange I am concerned with here cross various divides between legal, quasi-legal, gray markets and downright illegal activities. I do not use the term 'informal', but instead use 'non-formal', as the former in many definitions, the International Labor Organization's included, refers expressly to small-scale, low-income, low-tech and subsistence level activities. Shadow should not be taken to mean insubstantial: these transnational networks, taken together, employ millions of people and generate more than a trillion dollars annually.

Shadow networks, licit or otherwise, are more than sprawling value-neutral international market networks (Appadurai, 1996). They fashion economic possibilities, they broker political power and, importantly, they constitute cultures, for these networks of power and exchange are governed by rules of exchange, codes of conduct, hierarchies of deference and power – in short, they are governed by social principles, not merely the jungle law of tooth and claw. Shadow networks, as I define them here, and as this article will develop:

- are more formalized, integrated, and bound by rules of conduct than studies of the gray and black markets that focus on high-risk items like armaments and drugs, or studies that focus on basic informal markets like foodstuffs, imply;
- are by definition international – they entail societal systems that cross-cut national, linguistic and ethnic collectivities;
- are not simply (shadow) markets or economies (Ayers, 1996) – but a compilation of political, economic and sociocultural forces;
- benefit from analyses like those of William Reno's (1995, 1998) that look at 'shadow states' – nation-based systems of power and patronage paralleling state power – but focus on a different, and more distinctly international, set of criteria that constitute a set of 'institutional frameworks' in their own right;
- are not marginal to the world's economies and politics, but central. While little in-depth work exists on estimates of the sums generated per year through extra-state activities, initial inquiries seem to place them in the trillions. To give some examples of how these figures add up, the following examples run from the tragically exploitative to the remarkably mundane. As much as 20 percent of the world's financial deposits are located in unregulated banks and offshore locations (Lopez and Cortwright, 1998). UN estimates of illicit drugs earnings run at US$500 billion a year (UNRISD, 1995). Illicit weapons sales area also placed at US$500 billion a year (Ayers, 1996; Castells, 1998). As a single country, India's black economy in the early 1980s was placed at more than US$60 billion, and has grown since then (Gupta, 1992). India is not unusual: in Peru, 48 percent of the economically active population works in the informal sector, and that figure rises to 58 percent in Kenya, and perhaps even higher in Russia (Greif, 1996). Prostitution brings in scores of billions of dollars annually, and people-smuggling brings in equally large amounts. In a study on money laundering, Pasuk Phongpachit of Chulalongkorn University in Bangkok estimated that people-smuggling earns US$3.2 billion a year in Thailand alone, and that solely from Thai women smuggled into Japan, Germany and Taiwan for prostitution. Profits to Chinese triads smuggling illegal immigrants into the USA alone is placed at US$2.5 billion a year (Strange, 1996). As to the more mundane, 1 million tonnes of oil was smuggled into China in the first six months of 1997: the standard savings to smugglers per single standard cargo of 30,000 tonnes

amounts to US$1.8 million (Singapore Newsroom, 1997). Freon smuggling is a classic example of the mundane and often overlooked that reaps huge profits – in Miami alone, illegal freon smuggling has exceeded drug-trafficking in volume and may soon rival it in revenues (Tyson, 1995).

We do not know how these vast sums affect global (stock) markets, economic (non-)health and political power configurations. What we can surmise is that these extensive transnational transactions comprise a significant section of the world's economy, and thus of the world's power grids. If all these industries were to collapse overnight, the world's economies would be in chaos.

Ethnographic work on these networks prompts a reassessment of basic theoretical ideas concerning the nexus of legality/illegality, state/non-state and formal/non-formal power relations. Susan Strange writes that social scientists cling to outmoded and inappropriate theories that are rooted in a belief in a more stable and orderly world than the one we live in. Arguing that academics need to rethink the nature and sources of power, Strange (1996: 4) states:

> The argument put forward is that the impersonal forces of world markets, integrated over the post-war period more by private enterprise in finance, industry and trade than by the cooperative decisions of governments, are now more powerful than the state to whom ultimate political authority over society and economy is supposed to belong.

Organized crime, for Strange, is an undeniable part of the world market. Sassen (1998), and Castells as well, find informal and criminal networks central to our understanding of global power. Castells (1998: 166) writes:

> Crime is as old as humankind. But global crime, the networking of powerful criminal organizations, and their associates, in shared activities throughout the planet, is a new phenomenon that profoundly affects international and national economies, politics, security, and, ultimately, societies at large.

Like Strange, Castells (1998: 167–8) notes that: 'There is a general acknowledgment of the importance and reality of this phenomenon, and a wealth of evidence. . . .Yet the phenomenon is largely ignored by academics.'

Ethnographic interviews yielded another possible explanation for the dearth of formal research on illicit economies. When I was in southern Africa in the second half of the 1990s, I interviewed several leading United Nations Development Fund (UNDF) economists about why formal economic indicators did not take account of non-formal economies when they so significantly affected the outcomes of any policy, from development to peace accords. For example, in both Mozambique and Angola in the mid-1990s, fully half of the nations' resources were taken out of the country through extra-legal channels.[2] I asked the UNDF economists why these figures were seldom represented, even in passing, in formal research and policy documents. 'We cannot study this', the senior economist from a European office replied, 'it is not in our mandate.' I clearly did not understand, replying that retooling mandate priorities would be a good idea. After a few moments, the senior economist asked me to consider where all those millions of dollars worth of seafood goes – to whose factories and whose tables? Where do all the billions of dollars worth of precious gems, gold and diamonds end up? They purchase hard currency, weapons and luxury items, from whom? 'The countries', he answered, 'who write our mandates.' Or, as he and his colleagues concluded, who write things out of the mandates.

Strange and Castells have explored the development of organized crime and the increasing numbers of alliances among major mafias, cartels and triads in the world; and Sassen looks at the increasing importance and complexity of informal markets in major cosmopolitan 'global cities' – and all chart the impact these activities have on global economic and political realities. My research both draws upon and supports these conclusions.

What is different in this study is the ethnographic component that demonstrates links across arenas of politico-economic activity that are traditionally divided in theory and analysis – links that show complex socio-cultural and political as well as economic organization in these networks of exchange and association.

Linkages – Theoretical and Ethnographic

Theory has generally disaggregated:

- illegal and dangerous goods (drugs, weapons, mercenaries);
- illegal and immoral practices (child labor, sexual slavery, exploitation of non-legal immigration);
- illicit and non-dangerous goods (gems, precious minerals, entertainment electronics);
- non-legal and informal goods and services (clothing, food, basic supplies).

Analyses tend to concentrate on single discrete categories: there are studies that focus on mafias (Italy, the new Russian criminals); on drugs (narco-trafficking, the opium trade); on illegal immigration, forced prostitution or women's markets in Africa. These studies tend to be restricted to their field of inquiry: those investigating weapons transfers do not tend to look at the linkages with prostitution or immigration; those writing on narcotraficking do not tend to explore the links to informal market economies or illicit trade in minerals and high-tech electronics.

Each category tends to be approached as a distinct set of networks, and is ascribed a distinct ethical and politico-theoretical domain. The outcome is that it appears each network represents a different, closed and bounded, category – drug cartels are international criminal organizations; gem runners are international profiteers; and non-licensed clothing vendors operate in informal sectors that are neither as dangerous nor as ethically compromised as those of drug runners, nor as cosmopolitan and illicit as those of gem runners.[3] Each is taken as a distinct domain.

In reality, in markets, and in people's lives, these arenas of non-legal and extra-state activities are not so clearly disaggregated. For example, it is not enough to discuss the illegal arms trade as a distinct sphere of activity, separate from the lives of those who transport a weapon from point A to point B. To say only that the illegal arms industry generates US$500 billion worth of profits a year, and to discuss ways of curtailing this trade, gives the impression that these caches of weapons circulate as an indistinct mass through shadowy brokers to militias and criminals – and avoids the observation that each weapon exchanges hands, individual to individual, for very specific reasons. A criminal buying an illegal weapon to commit a crime is not equivalent to a hungry African woman who trades an AK-47 for a chicken to feed her family. Neither, my fieldwork has demonstrated, is the exception to the rule of illicit weapons transfers. Each, theoreticians can argue, belong to a different moral universe. Both make up the arena of illegal sales of dangerous goods.

I am not arguing we collapse categories here, either morally or analytically – quite the opposite, I am arguing for a greater nuancing and understanding of complex international extra-state realities. The same complexities of analysis adhere to, by way of another example, the gem trade. While the illicit gem trade runs in the billions of dollars a year (Angola and Sierra Leone alone each generate US$500 million a year), it is not confined to a nebulous world of profiteer business people. Gem miners can be local families plying the only trade they can in a war-devastated economy; or, as Paul Richards (1996) discusses, men with university education who are unable to find any other work in conflict zones where unemployment can run at 50 percent. Gems don't flow in a vacuum – they flow along informal food and supply lines, along illegal drug and weapons routes, along undocumented immigration passageways, along legal diplomatic channels.

By uncritically disaggregating the various spheres of extra-state activities analyses not only miss the overlapping connections among the various networks, but also fail to add up the sum total of extra-state phenomena and their impact on global finances, security, politics and economic systems. Castells (1998) and Strange (1996) are both careful to point out that, while organized crime is not new to the world, the degree to which different organized crime networks in the world are creating alliances, partnerships and the non-legal equivalent of transnational corporate organizations is new, and is changing the face of international markets and state systems of authority. Networks overlap. The dangerously criminal, the illicit and the informally mundane cannot, in actual practice, be always or easily disaggregated. Castells (1998: 167) reminds us:

> In addition, is everything that receives added value precisely from its prohibition in a given institutional environment: smuggling of everything from everywhere to everywhere, including radioactive material, human organs, and

illegal immigrants; prostitution; gambling; loan-sharking; kidnapping; racketeering and extortion; counterfeiting of goods, bank notes, financial documents, credit cards, and identity cards; killers for hire, traffic of sensitive information, technology, or art objects; international sales of stolen goods; or even dumping garbage illegally from one country to another (for example, US garbage smuggled into China in 1996).

What I want to add to Castell's equation are shadow goods, services, and networks that form not only because they are prohibited, but because they are basic to survival. Angola provides a good example. Large-scale illicit networks operate to bring military supplies into a country that has been at war for several decades, and pay for these supplies with luxury resources like gems. But also, because of the disruptions of war, 90 percent of Angola's economy, by UN estimates, is non-formal. Average people, to survive, must trade outside formal state channels. This, as the letter to Ed Garcia points out in the introduction to this article, is true of rebel groups and war zones worldwide.

Following the Complexities of the Shadows in the Example of Angola – From Informal Economies to Global Power

Angola has been at war for decades, first for independence from the Portuguese, and then in a civil war between the rebel forces Unita and the MPLA government (Maier, 1996; Human Rights Watch, 1994, 1999; Minter, 1994). Many people and countries worldwide have vested interests in the outcome of the war: Unita was long supported by the United States and by the apartheid South African Defense Forces; the MPLA by the socialist bloc of the Cold War. In addition, powerful international profiteers and transnational companies, ranging from interests in diamonds and oil to timber and seafood, have wild-catted enormous profits made possible by the political dislocations of war. The civil war has gone through cycles of peace accords and the re-eruption of war throughout the 1990s. At the turn of the century, the war has escalated dramatically: in 1999 there were 1.7 million internally displaced people inside the country, and hundreds of thousands more fled to other countries. Over a million people have been killed since hostilities began. In terms of governance, there are really two Angolas: the MPLA holds the major cosmopolitan areas and the major infrastructure (roadways, airports, oil production); Unita holds the rural areas and the food-producing regions. Thus people in the government areas have goods but suffer a lack of food while those in Unita-held zones have food but lack basic goods.

To focus on the highly profitable gem trade sustaining Savimbi's forces is to understand only a fragment of the complexities of extra-state networks. To understand the interconnections between power, politics, economics and survival that define Angola and its relationships within larger global systems it is critical to follow the complex linkages of state/non-state, legality/illegality and formal/informal *beyond* mere discussions of (a) large-scale gems and weapons networks; and (b) small-scale informal economies (Nordstrom, 1998).

First: *profitable trade in illicit and dangerous goods is intricately tied to informal trade*. Savimbi's weapons systems do not emerge out of a vacuum into the hands of his soldiers, nor do the gems and goods to pay for these flow straight from the mines into the hands of international smugglers. Each shipment is carried along a complex network of people – many, like the women who trade automatic weapons for food or the university graduates who work in the mines, do so in order to meet daily necessities. Savimbi's weapons and gems *depend* on these people, these linkages with informal networks. In war zones civilians and soldiers alike need food, clothing, medicines, daily supplies, etc., and supplying these requirements generally flows, like weapons and illicit goods, along extra-state routes – and often along the same extra-state routes. Like the harsh realities of survival, the complexities of trading illicit goods for survival are an ethically challenging issue for many of the people involved.

Second: *clear distinctions between legal and illegal, state and non-state, or local and international are often impossible to make*. Extra-state activities and the power politics that support them can not be easily divided into opposing separate spheres of state/legal and non-state/illegal. Like gems and weapons, everyday goods can follow international channels of production and distribution that may intersect with states, but are not bounded by them. They can partake of official channels, non-formal production systems, quasi-legal gray markets and downright illegal enterprises. A state actor can function simultaneously as a formally recognized official, a non-state actor (say, in his or her role as family member or service organization volunteer), a state-recognized manufacturer and a black-marketeer. A state actor can simultaneously vote sanctions into law and then ignore them for profit or power.[4] Disenfranchised civilians and wildcatting entrepreneurs bring everything from grains to industrial equipment through non-formal routes that link the cosmopolitan centers of the world with its hinterlands – hinterlands that may well be seen as the 'breadbaskets' of the world's states for precious minerals and fuels, food and timbers, labor and raw materials. As Strange (1996: 117) writes:

> The fact is that while financial crime has grown enormously . . . it remains, legally and morally, an indeterminate gray area. The dividing line is seldom clear and is nowhere the same between transactions which are widely practiced but ethically questionable and those which are down right criminal. . . . The need to use such secret or covert financial channels is not only a prerogative of organized and economic criminal groups – but also of terrorist and revolutionary groups and indeed of many individuals and economic operators engaged in activities which are not necessarily illicit. Investigations into the biggest financial scandal of the last fifteen years, the bankruptcy of the Bank of Credit and Commerce international, showed that BCCI was engaged in 'reserved' or illicit financial services for a very varied groups of clients, including Colombian narco-traffickers, Middle East terrorists and Latin American revolutionary groups, as well as tax evaders, corrupt politicians and several multinational companies (United States Senate, 1983, 1992).

These intersections of power, legality/illegality, non-legitimacy, and formality/non-formality are characteristic of shadow networks.

Third: *illicit and extra-state trade is, ironically, linked to development.* I have traveled to towns in the interior of Angola on several occasions. Many were among the most war-damaged I have seen in two decades of studying political violence. Roadways were heavily mined and beset by predatory armed bands, formal trade was virtually non-existent, banks were closed and state infrastructure was decimated. Yet in these besieged towns I found sophisticated electronic and computer equipment, transport vehicles, industrial supplies and other cosmopolitan goods. This involved trade that linked these remote areas to the major industrial centers of the world. It involved payments, not in the local Angolan kwanza (which does not trade on the international market), but in convertible 'currencies' like gems, precious resources, luxury items like hardwoods and seafood, and possibly drugs and weapons. As dangerous and illegal as drug and illicit weapons trade may be, it is often the means by which citizens gain the currency to buy industrial necessities, agricultural supplies and development goods. Such illicit goods purchase hard currency, they broker power, they allow investments into land, legal industries and political partnerships. They spawn and support subsidiary industries, both legal and illicit. And, of course, daily necessities like clothing, textbooks and medicines follow these same trading trajectories. If development is to take place without relying on illicit trade in dangerous goods, viable ways of making goods, services and payments available in these difficult circumstances need to be created.

Fourth: *illicit transaction and development link with political power.* The people in Angola who are adept at manipulating the junctures of licit/illicit markets to gain wealth often invest in legal enterprises in their countries. Illicit money, as Castells (1998) reminds us, must be laundered into legality. As business people amass economic power and status, they gain the ability to stand for political office. As influential business people, they may have the stature to work with international nongovernmental organizations, hold a position with the United Nations, consult for the World Bank. Business people who profit from shadow transactions are unlikely to give up shadow sources of power, profit and supply as they develop legitimate enterprises, and in fact, their success may depend on keeping these networks current.

Fifth: *the junctures of licit/illicit economy shape formal global markets.* In countries like Angola during the war, it may be impossible to conduct business without exploiting extra-state transactions. But it is important to remember all the goods that enter countries outside formal state channels constitute profits for legitimate businesses in industrial centers of the world. All US$500 billion worth of illicit weapons sold annually constitute a profit for legal arms industries in the industrial centers of the world. Angola is not unique: 50 percent of Italy's, 60 percent of Russia's, and up to 30 percent of the United States' economies are non-formal (Ayers, 1996). This vast set of global shadow exchanges affects global pricing, stock markets, interest rates and exchange rates, though these effects are as yet little researched or understood.

When we look at the networks that make such diamond/armament transfers possible, we are talking about thousands of people and billions of dollars annually, from a single diamond locale such as Angola alone. If we expand this to the other gem-producing regions of the world, and the armaments they purchase, the figures rise to millions of people and multi-billions of dollars. The number of people involved can rival populations of states. The revenues generated can far surpass the GNP of smaller nations. The power the leaders in these extra-state empires wield can rival that of state leaders. These vast networks shape the course of international affairs to as great a degree as the formal state apparatuses of some countries. When we expand out from gems and armaments to add in all extra-state industries, we are discussing a series of power grids that shape the fundamental economic-political dynamics of the world today.

Observations from another Fieldsite[5]

War zones are defined by contradictions: the immense suffering and impoverishment of people fleeing ruined towns exist side by side with the immense profits of business people manipulating war economies. An example from my own field data can help introduce the latter. I often fly with emergency relief cargo planes when I am at the epicenters of conflict. These emergency airlifts are quintessentially international enterprises. They receive aid money, both from governments and large international non-governmental organizations (INGOs). They require international alliances: airlifts are very expensive and cross a host of political, legal and technical jurisdictions. On a few occasions when I was preparing to ride with these cargo planes, I found the flights abruptly canceled with no explanation; but the planes departed at dawn, destination unknown. This in itself is unusual in airlift culture. Flight plans may not exist, pilots may give researchers unauthorized rides, but among colleagues (and this can extend to itinerant researchers) information is a commodity freely exchanged: staying safe in war zones depends on this.

I began to research these flight cancellations, and the facts turned out to be a study in power. A group of business people had requisitioned the plane (that means canceling not one, but five or six airlifts per day) to fly goods across the country: business goods, telecommunications equipment, war-related supplies, (stolen) motor vehicles, VCRs, luxury items, precious resources – the 'hard currency' of war zones. These people not only had the money to 'requisition' an airlift plane for personal use, they had the power to make sure the entire machinery that supported the airlift – from governmental to intergovernmental aid organizations and personnel (in this case, USAID among others was providing monetary support in the millions of dollars, though I doubt they were aware of the non-aid uses the plane was being put to) – was kept uninformed or unconcerned. Under cover of dark, planes were sometimes 'requisitioned' to cross international borders surreptitiously, collect state-of-the-art computers and military supplies (with planes, we are talking not pounds, but tons of cargo) and fly them back into the country to top military bases.[6]

These aspects of 'business as usual' raise the larger analytical issue of currency markets. In war zones, currencies often collapse, and black market (or 'street') currency exchanges are the norm. Those who control the black market money exchanges also control the exchange rates. These are, in effect, more powerful than formal institutions: they set the 'true' currency prices for an entire nation. The rates change daily, the product of complex monetary calculations. This itself represents an interesting study in power: in the midst of a war zone where all telecommunications and electricity were knocked out with frequency, business people at various ends of the country would work in unison, along with many others in a world economy, to calculate and set daily currency prices countrywide. These are extra-state calculations, they do not run through the banks and the government institutions of the country. These currency markets are very international: business people are calculating money indices based not only on internal conditions, but on a host of global market factors that range from the accessibility of goods and their worth to international exchange rates for hard currencies.

These fundamental financial systems can be found in many guises worldwide. Take, for example, the extra-state 'banking systems' in Asia. People often think of offshore financial interests and their relationship to money laundering when thinking of extra-state banking systems. But a far more mundane, yet powerful, 'informal' banking system is in place throughout the world. A customer, for example, chooses an informal 'bank' in one country in Asia and can send any amount of money to a receiving 'bank' in another country in Asia to hold for anyone the sender designates. Cash, goods and credit flow along these banking lines. This system may be non-formal, and the 'banks' little more than storefronts, but the system is both vast and powerful, transmitting untold fortunes through family and ethnic linkages, business partnerships and triad associations.

The Defining Characteristics and Cultures of Shadow Networks

One of the more interesting questions regarding these vast economic-political networks is how such massive amounts of goods and money, which follow such a complex set of exchange routes and political associations, flow as smoothly as they do. In plain words: Savimbi's gems get to Antwerp, Belgium and then on to rings on our global fingers without a great deal more, and sometimes less, murder and mayhem than state-based transactions do. The billions that flow through the informal banks of Asia function quite a bit like state-supported banks in that their customers do not usually lose their money. In a nutshell, the system works. But *how* is another matter. Many people I have spoken to about this respond that the system works because if it does not, people are simply killed. That may or may not be true: the fact is, it is an assumption, people have not collected representative data. We simply do not know how these vast billion- to trillion-dollar systems function on a day-to-day basis.[7]

Part of the answer lies in the fact that extra-state networks are not haphazard collections of people in ad hoc groups circling like moths around the light of profit. There is an explicit assumption in many analyses of state and non-state actors that states are somehow supra-communities, born of unique institutions of leadership that are not replicated outside the formal institutions of the state. No matter how successful or large a non-state collectivity, it will never approximate the moral community of the state. However true the existential answer to this is, practicalities demand a more nuanced assessment.

From diamonds to drugs, dominions exist that follow hierarchies of authority, rules of conduct, ways of punishing transgression and codes of behavior. Within these dominions, communities form, ideologies evolve and worldwide alliances and antagonisms are developed. These cannot be confused with states, but such interrelated transnational associations do have governing structures, law-like apparatuses and security forces. The people populating international extra-state networks forge trade agreements, foreign policy and currency exchanges. Susan Strange (1996: 112) discusses the 'transnational diplomacy between national mafias' that operates worldwide today. The people forging these networks set up the transport routes, communication linkages and banking systems to sustain their interactions.

Profiteers, smugglers and black/gray market merchants are not isolated actors loosely linked into a web of profit. Farmers who plant drug-related crops or miners who harvest gems have families and children they must provide for, in a variety of ways, from paying mortgages to celebrating birthdays. Truckers who transport illicit goods need tires and tune-ups for their trucks, and dental work for themselves and their families the same as if they were ferrying post-toasties cereals. Pilots trained at accredited airschools fly smuggled goods, often wearing professional pilot's emblems and uniforms. The banker that launders the money and the college student who buys a smuggled diamond-studded Rolex watch or deals a few drugs to pay his or her tuition may not fit the image of the dangerous drug lord, but they are as essential to the whole enterprise as the growers and the transporters. All of these people are deeply immersed in society and civil life.

I am not arguing an ethical point here, nor am I arguing that there is a moral equivalency between people who operate in the shadows and those who operate in formal state systems.[8] I am, instead, exploring the theoretical implications of the defining realities of shadow non-state systems. My goal is to challenge simplistic notions of non-state networks as 'merely' markets – devoid of social, cultural, political and legal ramifications. It is also to challenge 'mere' outlaw notions that non-state systems operate on the sheer violent rule of tooth and claw. Neither of these approaches can explain how these vast networks operate across up to a third of global transactional exchanges.

One of the answers to the question of how these vast international extra-state networks operate as coherently as they do is that people in these systems generally trust (and trust implies interpersonal and cultural definition) that the transaction will occur as predicted, and that they will remain safe (Gambetta, 1988a). The fact that large-scale massacres, wars and trails of dead bodies are found with far less regularity within these shadow networks than in and among the wars of states attests to the fact that the systems do work. This is no mean feat when we consider we are talking of millions of people exchanging billions of dollars worth of goods and services.[9] Ernest Gellner (1988: 147) provides an interesting take:

> The Hobbesian problem arises from the assumption that anarchy, absence of enforcement, leads to distrust and social disintegration . . . but there is a certain amount of interesting empirical evidence which points the other way. The paradox is: it is precisely anarchy which engenders trust or, if you want to use another name, which engenders social cohesion.

In a powerful irony, even Hobbes recognized that networks of self-interest were grounded in cultural codes of trust (Gambetta, 1988b: 215). Right or wrong, Gellner asks us to understand how what is taken to be anarchy becomes imbued with pattern and value. Chingono (1996: 114), writing on the war in Mozambique, captures well the paradoxes that can describe the complex intersections of legality/illegality and the state:

> Although operating within these constraints, the grass-roots war economy was more predictable and rational in many respects than the official one. Illegal and unrecorded trade was not haphazard but institutionalized, operating according to a system of rules known to all participants. Examples included the standardized equivalences observed for barter transactions, the set rate for paying border guides, the arrangements set up for the terms of clientage, and the reciprocal obligations of other personal ties. The organization of a grass-roots war economy depended to a great extent on these reciprocal obligations of personal ties. The trust and confidence inspired by personal relations or common cultural background provided the reliability and predictability that were so conspicuously lacking in the official economy. To some extent, therefore, the grass-roots war economy generated alternative economic opportunities for people as well as an alternative society, with parallel religio-economic institutions alongside official ones.

How large, and how interrelated, are shadow networks; how many networks operate at any given time around the globe? Pat answers are, obviously, impossible. But several key observations are possible. Informal economies (small-scale subsistence), large-scale gray and black markets (from arms through luxury items to oil and freon), and state industries and personnel (from sanctions-breaking technology to corrupt customs officials) are more interrelated than neoclassical theories suggest. I have sought to show in the examples such as Angola and of the business people commandeering aid flights and setting international currency exchange rates how running gems, for example, links within larger international exchange networks ranging from armaments through high-tech computers and industrial equipment to basic foods and medicines. Strange (1996: 111) observes that 'what is new and of importance in the international political economy is the networks of links being forged between organized crime in different parts of the world.' The lines between state and extra-state power can easily blur here: 'At the heart of the system', writes Castells (1998: 167), 'there is money laundering by the hundreds of billions (maybe trillions) of dollars. Complex financial schemes and international trade networks link up the criminal economy to the formal economy.' As I have discussed, such wealth and influence – straddling licit/illicit lines – can translate into significant political authority.

At the same time these networks are not all-inclusive: the gem runners in Angola may have nothing to do with the drug runners in Colombia or the non-state banking ventures in Asia. Neoclassical theory tends to postulate non-state networks as quite discrete: there are smugglers, there is official corruption and there are informal subsistence economies and, essentially, never shall these three meet.

In fact, judging from my data, it would seem that integrating networks internationally is viewed as desirable in practice. A clear indication of this can be shown in exploring the question of why some drug smuggling networks based in Latin America and Southeast Asia send drugs to Europe via Africa. Any number of ports, from remote Namibia to urban Nigeria, broker drugs from these drug-producing regions on their way to western destinations. The logic of markets and rational analysis would assume the routes with the least number of stops and locations where illegal goods can be confiscated and the carriers arrested or executed would be the most desirable – in other words, a route straight from Latin America or Asia to Europe makes the best sense. No matter how easy it is to get illegal goods into an intermediate port, it is just as hard getting them into Europe from Asia, Latin America or Africa. Why, then, route through Africa? A part of the equation might be that the heavy flow of precious minerals and gems, ivory, weapons, mercenaries, food and medicines in and out of Africa provides more avenues for other types of goods to travel along, speaking to the interrelatedness of diverse networks. But this is only part of the answer, for such exchanges route worldwide. Another part of the answer is that in a different kind of market and political logic, associations of extra-state networks (and their state linkages) are more productive and powerful than smaller, isolated coalitions of people and profit. Routing drugs through Africa links Africa with the goods and power politics of Latin America and Asia, and provides the latter with the rich resources and human power of Africa. Each country and continent gains more by its association with others than it could hope to achieve alone – much like multinationals.[10]

Networks, like the markets and the politics that gird them, are constellations of economic, political, demographic, historical and cultural processes (Appadurai, 1996; Greif, 1996). As such, they are dynamic, not static, phenomena: as the patterns of the constellations of factors that define networks change over time and circumstance, so too do the defining characteristics of the networks. Perhaps the very extra-state flexibility and fluidity of these exchange systems are a factor in their success.

A Question of Sovereignty

There is a general tendency to postulate that the non-formal markets of eastern Europe, the former Soviet States, Africa and Asia are the result of a combination of changing political regimes, social transitions and economic opportunism. The belief is that as these countries settle down in the course of normal state development their economies will become increasingly defined by state-regulated formal economies. In this view, while illicit markets and mafias will always exist in the countries of the world, they comprise a marginal part of the world's real power structures and economy. My research suggests we need to rethink these assumptions. I can stand in the most remote war zones of the world and watch a veritable supermarket of goods move into and out of the country along extra-state lines. Tracing the supply routes of these goods takes one through both major and minor economic centers of the world. The sanctions-regulated laptop satellite-linked computers I see on the battlefields of Africa are made in major cosmopolitan centers of the world, and the precious resources and human labor that pay for these commodities move along the same channels back to those cosmopolitan centers. Tanks, watches, industrial components, VCRs, electronic equipment, books, covert information, pornography and uranium travel these same routes. At the bottom line, it would appear non-formal economies play a formidable role in countries like Japan, Germany and the USA as well as in areas of more rapid economic and political change and development.

Given the complex social, cultural, political and legal, as well as economic, characteristics defining the vast international networks I discussed in the last section, and the enduring global nature of these networks described in the paragraph above, the question of the very nature of the power adhering to shadow networks arises. Tilly (1985: 169) opens his article 'War Making and State Making as Organized Crime':

> If protection rackets represent organized crime at its smoothest, then war making and state making – quintessential protection rackets with the advantage of legitimacy – qualify as our largest examples of organized crime.

Tilly argues that war-making, extraction and capital accumulation interacted in shaping the development of the European state, and asserts that 'banditry, piracy, gangland rivalry, policing, and war making all belong on the same continuum' in this state-making process (1985: 170; see also Gallant, 1999; Heyman, 1999). Distinctions of legitimate/illegitimate force are of little importance in this process. States seek to monopolize the use of force over all others – and what, Tilly (1985: 173) asks, distinguishes the violence employed by states from the violence produced by anyone else?

> Eventually, the personnel of states purveyed violence on a larger scale, more effectively, more efficiently, with wider assent from their subject populations, and with readier collaboration from neighboring authorities than did the personnel of other organizations. But it took a long time for that series of distinctions to become established.

Tilly is discussing the period of state-making in Europe, a time now relegated to the historical past. Yet vast networks continue to link war zones, banditry and extraction. Perhaps the links between war-making, banditry and extraction are necessary to the continued success of the state. But Tilly is clear about the fact that the state gains legitimacy because it ultimately wields force more effectively than competing systems. If Strange (1996) and Castells (1998) are correct in their observations that criminal organizations are forming an unprecedented set of developmental alliances that are producing global networks, then it becomes logical to ask if the ability of the state to maintain its legitimacy and sovereign status will be challenged. Both authors see the ultimate authority of the state being undermined by these transnational associations.

Such questions prompt inquiries into the ultimate definition of sovereignty and its relationship to power. Is it possible to speak of non-state sovereignty in any aspect? Do coherent shadow networks – as transnational social, cultural, political and economic systems – operate as distinct power configurations which have full, or sovereign, authority – over which no larger power has control? Robert Latham's (1997) concept of social sovereignty is useful in this context. His work on social sovereignty revitalizes dynamic definitions of sovereignty as complex domains of power and exchange that move the concept out from under a purely state-based focus. Latham asks: 'But if the sovereign nation-state is a particular form of state, why cannot the state be a particular form of sovereignty?' and goes on to question the supposed monopoly of sovereignty by the state and according to territoriality. Latham's concern in this analysis is with globalizing financial market systems and the 'social sovereignty' that can explain internationally based collectivities. But the definition he applies to sovereignty fits well the 'shadow' power grids I have been discussing. Latham (1997: 23) asks:

> When does the web of global financial markets – or any given domain for that matter – constitute a sovereignty? . . . [T]here is one key marker of a sovereign domain or social sovereignty. The degree to which upon entering the domain an agent is assigned or feels compelled to occupy or resist a role or place within the webs of codes, practices, and significances that constitute the domain. Thus, constitutive capacities rest exactly on the capacity to mark and code phenomena – from bodies and materials, to communications and values – that enter a relevant domain.

Latham (1997: 29) concludes:

> Sovereignty, not just as an attribute of the state but as a basic dimension of modernity, serves as a compass for directing attention to questions about accountability towards, responsibility for, and authority over setting the terms of social existence.

As this study has pointed out, shadow networks forge economic policies, they operate within political realms, they fashion foreign policy. These networks have developed dispute resolution systems and systems of enforcement. They have codes of conduct and rules of behavior set in social and cultural systems. They are not states, but they share these attributes with states. And perhaps they share the status of sovereignty – a social sovereignty in this case – as well. Studies of states are abundant while studies of the shadows are underdeveloped: what theory lacks is an understanding of the ways in which shadow networks function in daily international life – *how*, for example, disputes are settled and judgments enforced; *who* wields authority in the junctures of state/non-state transactions; and *how* extra-state realities shape global markets and fashion political power.

States, Tilly reminds us, first forged power and the means to protect this power, and then fashioned legitimacy. Sovereignty was a product of this process, not a natural attribute of a natural political unit. The links of war-making, banditry, extraction and state-making continue. Who will be most effective at mobilizing economies and the force to protect them in the future is as yet an unanswered question. What is certain is that sovereignty, authority and power are shaped today by shadow systems. A better understanding of the shadows might provide us with the tools to understand the Asian market collapse, failed states and the dynamics of in/equality affecting the future potential of people globally.

Notes

1. I have conducted extended fieldwork in Sri Lanka (1979, 1981, 1982–3, 1985, 1986, 1988, 1991), Mozambique (1988, 1989, 1990–91, 1994, 1995, 1996, 1997, 1998, 1999), South Africa (1995, 1996, 1997, 1998, 1999) and Angola (1997, 1998, 1999); shorter visits to countries in Southern Africa and Southeast Asia in the years 1979–91; and shorter visits to Southern Africa and Central Europe in the 1990s.

2. Personal communication, senior economists and resident representatives of UNDP and World Bank offices in Mozambique and Angola; and senior economists of UN offices at the European headquarters.

3. The implications of this are extensive. For example, researchers are well aware that rebel goups do not have access to state taxes for the purchase of their military supplies and governing costs, and must raise money outside formal state channels. Given the tendency to disaggregate extra-state activities into distinct ethical categories, researchers often find it difficult to investigate these money-raising and weapons-purchasing actions if they support the group in any way. Thus, researchers who view a rebel movement in a favorable light often do not discuss extra-state illicit transactions for weapons, while those less supportive of the movements they study point out the links between weapons, drugs and illicit goods in the political economy of the rebel group.

4. Few people are surprised today by the degree to which state actors can be embroiled in illegal or extra-state activities. From the popular culture of Mel Gibson's movie *Air America* to the politically charged problems defining US–Mexico relations on drug and drug enforcement issues concerning the degree of state involvement, the pull of high profits and power is well recognized. Another example is less widely recognized, but equally influential in shaping ground-level politics. UN peace-keepers have been praised for providing solutions to intractable wars, and their work is often exemplary. But the story is more complex than that. Sarajevo provides an apt example, where during the worst of the war when UN peace-keeping troops were stationed there, a large percentage of Sarajevo's economy was diverted into black marketeering through UN troops (Fetherston and Nordstrom, 1995). 'The UN soldiers are making themselves and the Sarajevo mafia rich. The locals are the middlemen for a trade in cigarettes, alcohol, food, prostitution and heroin, worth millions of pounds' (O'Kane, 1993). Not only luxury items flowed along these channels. Tanks and weapons rumbled along these pathways, from states through peace-keepers to fighting forces, each nationality following the alliances of their states, or, more obscurely, the alliances of profiteering.

5. Given the sensitive nature of the information discussed in this section, I have intentionally left this location unnamed.

6. The story is sometimes much bigger: in one case a major emergency airlift run by an international organization and paid for by such donors as USAID (who, I am sure, was unaware of any untoward activities) was headed by a European man who was both an international smuggler and a profiteer. The planes actually did fly many tons of cargo to bombed-out townspeople for months on end, but a number of other less altruistic activities were taking place as well. This one airlift operation in this one war zone grossed considerable sums of money, though few know how high those figures actually are.

7. I have done interviews with United Nations officials and lawyers alike asking what actual data they have on what rules of conduct define these systems and how they are 'enforced'. Each one – from the UNDP officers (Dr Aboagye, Dr Clements, Dierckx de Casterle) to academic economists (Professors Dutt and Melber) – said that the question was fascinating, but the data non-existent. And, lawyers and UN staff alike assured me, lawyers and economists do not 'do' fieldwork; without primary data, theory can not emerge.

8. For a discussion of the negative impact of illicit networks, see Nordstrom (1999).

9. Gambetta (1988b: 230) stresses a key consideration here in writing: 'What is at issue is not the importance of exploring in greater depth the causality of those forms of cooperation which are independent of trust, but the fact that economizing on trust is not as generalizable a strategy as might at first appear, and that, if it is risky to bank on trust, it is just as risky to fail to understand how it works, what forces other than successful cooperation bring it about, and how it relates to the conditions of cooperation. Considering the extremely limited literature on this crucial subject it seems that economizing on trust and economizing on understanding it have been unjustifiably conflated.'

10. This is not a phenomenon solely of drug shipments. For example, Strange (1996: 111–12) notes: 'What is new and of importance in the international political economy is the network of links being forged between organized crime in different parts of the world. While the Sicilian and American Cosa Nostras were the growing point, as it were, of this network, they no longer operate alone. There are half a dozen

other major transnational criminal organizations.... The expansion of illegal markets has fostered a wider and more frequent interaction among the major organized gangs. Drugs, arms or illegal immigrants often pass through the hands of to ten or twelve different operators attached to various national gangs. Inter-group bartering of illegal commodities has also become very common since such deals help conceal the origin of the profits for the state authorities. *As various criminal groups (like the multinationals) have expanded their activities outside their home territories, the illegal markets within state boundaries have joined together horizontally to form a single world market*' (emphasis added).

References

Appadurai, Arjun (1996) *Modernity at Large: Cultural Dimensions of Globalization.* Minneapolis: University of Minnesota Press.

Ayers, Ed (1996) 'The Expanding Shadow Economy', *World Watch* 9(4): 11–23.

Bureau for International Narcotics and Law Enforcement Affairs (1997) *International Narcotics Control Strategy Report 1996.* Bureau for International Narcotics and Law Enforcements Affairs, Washington, DC: US Department of State, March.

Castells, Manuel (1998) *End of Millennium.* London: Blackwell.

Chingono, Mark (1996) *The State, Violence and Development.* Brookfield: Avebury.

Fetherston, Betts and Carolyn Nordstrom (1995) 'Overcoming Conceptual Habitus in Conflict Management: UN Peacekeeping and Warzone Ethnography', *Peace and Change* 20(1): 94–119.

Gallant, Thomas (1999) 'Brigandage, Piracy, Capitalism, and State-Formation: Transnational Crime from a Historical World-Systems Perspective', pp. 25–61 in Josiah Heyman (ed.) *States and Illegal Practices.* Oxford: Berg.

Gambetta, Diego (ed.) (1988a) *Trust: Making and Breaking Cooperative Relations.* Oxford: Basil Blackwell.

Gambetta, Diego (1988b) 'Can We Trust?', pp. 213–37 in D. Gambetta (ed.) *Trust: Making and Breaking Cooperative Relations.* Oxford: Basil Blackwell.

Gellner, Ernest (1988) 'Trust, Cohesion, and Social Order', pp. 142–57 in D. Gambetta (ed.) *Trust: Making and Breaking Cooperative Relations.* Oxford: Basil Blackwell.

Greif, Avner (1996) 'Contracting, Enforcement, and Efficiency: Economics Beyond the Law', pp. 239–65 in M. Bruno and B. Pleskovic (eds) *Annual World Bank Conference on Development Economics 1996.* Washington, DC: World Bank.

Gupta, Suraj B. (1992) *Black Income in India.* New Delhi: Sage.

Heyman, Josiah (ed.) (1999) *States and Illegal Practices.* Oxford: Berg.

Human Rights Watch Arms Project and Human Rights Watch/Africa (1994) *Angola: Arms Trade and Violations of the Laws of War Since the 1992 Elections.* New York: Human Rights Watch.

Human Rights Watch Arms Project and Human Rights Watch/Africa (1999) *Angola Unravels.* London: Human Rights Watch.

Latham, Robert (1997) 'States, Global Markets, and Social Sovereignty', paper presented at the Social Science Research Council conference Sovereignty and Security, Notre Dame, 18–20 April.

Lawson, Tony (1997) *Economics and Reality.* London: Routledge.

Lopez, G. and D. Cortwright (1998) 'Making Targets "Smart" from Sanctions', paper delivered at the International Studies Association meetings, Minneapolis, 18–22 March.

Maier, Karl (1996) *Angola: Promises and Lies*. Rivonia: William Waterman.

Minter, William (1994) *Apartheid's Contras: An Inquiry into the Roots of War in Angola and Mozambique*. London: Zed Books.

Nordstrom, Carolyn (1995) 'Contested Identities/ Essentially Contested Powers', in K. Rupesinghe (ed.) *Conflict Transformation*. London: Macmillan.

Nordstrom, Carolyn (1997) *A Different Kind of War Story*. Philadelphia: University of Pennsylvania Press.

Nordstrom, Carolyn (1998) 'Out of the Shadows: Post-War Transformations and Extra-State Realities', presentation at the European University Institute, Florence, Italy, 28–9 March.

Nordstrom, Carolyn (1999) 'Visible Wars and Invisible Girls: Shadow Industries and the Politics of Not-Knowing', *International Feminist Journal of Politics* 1(1): 14–33.

Nordstrom, Carolyn and Antonius Robben (eds) (1995) *Fieldwork Under Fire: Contemporary Studies of Violence and Survival*. Berkeley: University of California Press.

O'Kane, Maggie (1993) 'The Soldiers Are Out of Control: They Are Feasting on a Dying City', *The Guardian Weekly* 5 September.

Reno, William (1995) *Corruption and State Politics in Sierra Leone*. Cambridge: Cambridge University Press.

Reno, William (1998) *Warlord Politics and African States*. Boulder, CO: Lynne Rienner.

Richards, Paul (1996) *Fighting for the Rainforest: War, Youth and Resources in Sierra Leone*. Oxford: James Currey.

Sassen, Saskia (1998) *Globalization and its Discontents*. New York: The New Press.

Singapore Newsroom (1997) WWW posting +65 870 3571.

Strange, Susan (1996) *The Retreat of the State: The Diffusions of Power in the World Economy*. Cambridge: Cambridge University Press.

Tilly, Charles (1985) 'War Making and State Making as Organized Crime', in P.B. Evans, D. Rueschemeyer and T. Skocpol (eds) *Bring the State Back In*. Cambridge: Cambridge University Press.

Tyson, Rae (1995) 'Freon-Smuggling Latest Miami Vice', WWW reprint of 1995 *Detroit News* report.

United Nations Research Institute (1995) *States of Disarray: The Social Effects of Globalization*. London: UNRISD.

Carolyn Nordstrom is Associate Professor of Anthropology and a Fellow of the Kroc Institute for International Peace Studies, at the University of Notre Dame. Her books include *A Different Kind of War Story*, *Fieldwork Under Fire: Contemporary Studies of Violence and Survival*, *The Paths to Domination, Resistance and Terror*. She is also the author of several dozen articles on political violence, gender and cultural theory. She has done extensive fieldwork in Southern Africa and South Asia.

[4]

Transnational Crime and Global Criminology: Definitional, Typological, and Contextual Conundrums

David O. Friedrichs

Introduction

EARLY IN THE 21ST CENTURY, A SPECTER HAUNTS THE FIELD OF CRIMINOLOGY: THE specter of globalization. Throughout most of its history, criminology has been principally preoccupied with crime and its control as a local phenomenon. During the course of the 20th century, criminologists increasingly found it necessary to attend to crime in a national (or federal) context, and the control of such crime as a federal endeavor. In particular, organized crime and white-collar crime (especially in its corporate form) were recognized to transcend local and state borders (e.g., Cressey, 1969; Clinard and Yeager, 1980). In the most recent era, and with spiraling intensity at the outset of the new century, a small but growing number of criminologists have focused upon crime as a transnational or global phenomenon (e.g., Karstedt and Bussmann, 2000; Sheptycki and Wardak, 2003). In conjunction with the recognition of transnational and global dimensions to crime, criminologists increasingly recognize the limitations of traditional criminal justice institutions—local, state, and federal—in addressing such crime (e.g., Reichel, 2005; Sheptycki, 2002). Accordingly, we are now witnessing the emergence of a global criminology.

Who are the criminologists at the forefront of the shift to a global framework for the field of criminology? Disproportionately, they are criminologists whose ideological orientation falls on the progressive side of the spectrum. There are several reasons for this. Progressive (or leftist) criminologists are by definition especially focused upon the crimes of the powerful as opposed to the crimes of the powerless. Transnational crime is disproportionately the crime of relatively powerful organizations and entities, in part because some level of power or resources

---

DAVID O. FRIEDRICHS is Professor of Sociology/Criminal Justice and Distinguished University Fellow at the University of Scranton. He is author of *Trusted Criminals: White Collar Crime in Contemporary Society* (Thomson/Wadsworth, 1996; 2004; 2007) and *Law in Our Lives: An Introduction* (Roxbury, 2001; 2006) and editor of *State Crime, Volumes I and II* (Ashgate/Dartmouth, 1998). He has also published on such topics as the legitimation of legal order, radical/critical criminology, violence, narrative jurisprudence, postmodernism, crimes of states, and white-collar crime. In 2005, he received the Lifetime Achievement Award of the Division on Critical Criminology of the American Society of Criminology.

is necessary to commit crime effectively on a global scale. Second, progressive criminologists are collectively less likely to do the type of work that is dependent upon major grant support, and the principal funding entities are oriented toward funding projects focused upon conventional forms of crime and its control. Third, progressive criminologists are especially likely to be engaged with the large-scale issues of the global political economy that are inevitably entangled with issues of transnational crime and its control.

If specialization of focus is the norm within academe, my own interests are about as far removed from such a focus as possible. The contribution I propose to make here goes to fundamental definitional, conceptual, and typological issues, and the provisional "mapping" of an emerging scholarly terrain. At the outset, it is necessary to provide some perspective on the criminological enterprise itself.

Criminological Parochialism and States of Denial

Early in the 21st century, it remains the case that conventional forms of crime and their control, within a local context, persist as the dominant focus of criminological inquiry. The principal concern with this dominant focus of mainstream criminology is one of proportionality and the relative neglect of alternatives to conventional crime as sources of significant social harm. In a parallel vein, mainstream criminology has studied primarily the traditional criminal justice system in relation to crime, and not alternative institutions of social control. Altogether, an inverse relationship exists between demonstrable levels of harm caused by various activities of individuals and social institutions and the level of criminological attention to the form of harm. These different levels of attention are also reflected in the allocation of research grant funds. If a 21st-century criminology is to transcend such parochialism and attend much more fully to transnational forms of crime and their control, and the global context within which such crime and its control occurs, the specific sources of this parochialism must be identified. They surely include: patterns of personal and professional socialization, and a commitment to traditional disciplinary boundaries; the reward structure within the discipline; the higher probability of "successful" outcomes for conventional research projects, relative to those addressing more complex global issues; and a "state of denial" about the complicity of powerful entities and individuals in criminal conduct.

Criminology as a field may well be too wedded to the theories, methods, and substantive concerns that emerged principally in the mid-20th century period, a time very different from the present. Other, cognate areas of intellectual inquiry may well be adapting more fully to a rapidly evolving, globalized, postmodern environment than is the case with criminology. For some time now, various commentators have suggested that criminology is in crisis, in some sense (e.g., Braithwaite, 1989; Chan, 2005; Cohen, 1988; Nelken, 1994). It is here claimed that critical or progressive criminology has been more responsive to the rapidly evolving global social environment than is the case with mainstream criminology.

But some objections have either been voiced or can be anticipated in response to the call for greater criminological attention to transnational forms of crime and criminal justice, and a global context. First, by virtue of their training criminologists do not have the professional competence to address the relevant phenomena on a sophisticated level, and simply become "commentators" in relation to such matters. Then, if criminologists address phenomena outside their traditional areas of competence, the question arises whether this will diminish respect for criminology per se, and even inspire direct attacks from those who believe that criminologists are infringing on their turf. Furthermore, it could be objected that a shift by criminologists to global concerns would be a counterproductive allocation of finite criminological resources. As suggested earlier, the practical challenges of researching transnational forms of crime and justice are likely to be considerably greater than is the case with conventional, domestic forms of crime and justice. In the context of graduate programs in criminology, is it ethically problematic to encourage graduate students to explore transnational and global crime issues if such work is less likely to enhance their employment and tenure prospects?

The foregoing may all be legitimate concerns. Nevertheless, the guiding premise here is that if criminology as a field is to remain relevant as the 21st century progresses, it must increasingly adopt a global framework and increasingly concern itself with transnational forms of crime and criminal justice. If a global criminology is still at a rather early stage of development, it seems especially desirable to establish a potent and coherent conceptual framework for such a criminology. This article aspires to contribute to the constructive development of such a framework.

Global Criminology in Relation to Other Macro-Criminological Perspectives

Criminologists who address transnational forms of crime and the control of such crime have adopted different terms for the criminological enterprise with which they are engaged. This generates a certain level of confusion. I wish here to propose some possible resolutions of such confusion. First, we have *comparative criminology and criminal justice* (e.g., Beirne and Nelken, 1997; Dammer and Fairchild, 2006). Comparative criminology addresses the nature of the crime problem and the form and character of the criminal justice system in countries around the world. Comparative criminology has in fact been a recognized strain of criminological inquiry for many decades. Courses on comparative criminology and criminal justice are quite widely offered. Some foundational knowledge in comparative criminology would appear to be an essential prerequisite for the study of transnational forms of crime and justice, although in the narrow sense a comparative criminology need not focus on such forms of crime or justice.

Second, we have a *transnational criminology* (e.g., Andreas and Nadelmann, 2006; Sheptycki and Wardak, 2003). Such a criminology is focused principally upon transnational or cross-border forms of crime, and endeavors on various levels to control or respond effectively to such crime. Recognition of the growth and significance of such crime is certainly widely diffused, and at least some forms of such crime have inspired a fair amount of attention from criminologists and from government entities. Students of organized crime, in particular, have focused upon the increasingly transnational character of many forms of such crime, including drug trafficking, arms trafficking, human trafficking, and money laundering (e.g., Edwards and Gill, 2003; Galeottie, 2005). Entities such as Interpol play a significant role in addressing such crime (DeFlem, 2001).

Third, we have an *international criminology* (e.g., Morrison, 2005; Rothe and Mullins, 2006). The focus here is on international crime—or crime that is specifically recognized widely across nations as a crime against humanity—and international law, as well as on the institutions of international law. The Nuremberg trials following World War II were an important landmark in the emerging recognition of the international character of certain forms of crime. With various international tribunals addressing genocidal actions in Kosovo and Rwanda, among other places, and the recent establishment of the Permanent International Criminal Court, recognition of the specifically international character of some forms of crime and justice has intensified.

Finally, the term *global criminology* is best applied to the study of the evolving societal context within which crime and criminal justice now exist (e.g., Barak, 2000; Findlay, 1999). Here the focus is on globalization and its consequences in relation to crime and criminal justice, and the role of the global economy and its regulation in this regard. The harms perpetrated by international financial—and trade—institutions such as the World Bank, the International Monetary Fund, and the World Trade Organization have been little attended to by criminologists, but are part of the subject matter of a global criminology (Friedrichs and Friedrichs, 2002; MacKenzie, 2006).

Other terms have been used to encompass the criminological study of the forms of crime and their control that concern us here. *Macro-Criminology*, for example, is a term applied to the study of large-scale criminological phenomena. To date, however, this term has been applied principally to macro-dimensions of conventional forms of crime and criminal justice. Also, the term *Supranational Criminology* has been adopted by a group of European criminologists, with a base at the University of Maastricht, who have been interested in large-scale forms of harm such as genocide, and the control of such crime (see Friedrichs, 2007).

Admittedly, there is considerable overlap between the forms and foci of the different nontraditional "criminologies" just identified, and sometimes these terms have been applied quite interchangeably. Certain questions arise in this context: Can one move toward a resolution of this terminological confusion? Can one achieve some consensus on the optimal use of such terminology? What is the interrelationship of the key foci of these different forms of emergent criminologies? Can "canonical" works within each of the criminological approaches delineated here be identified, and does such an exercise bring commonalities and differences between them into sharper focus?

In many of the growing number of surveys of different forms of transnational crime there is often a lack of coherence in the ordering of the topics subsumed under that heading: e.g., terrorism, organized crime, sex trafficking, crimes of states, and so forth. Is there a logical ordering for this range of activities? Is the *transnational* element proportionally equivalent for all these forms of crime? Can this be reliably measured? Does it make a difference in terms of analysis?

What is the status of attention to the types of concerns identified here in graduate programs in criminology and criminal justice? Although courses in comparative criminology are relatively common, and have been for some time, courses specifically on transnational, international, and global issues seem to be less common. A number of readings on transnational crime have now been published, but to date there are no textbooks in the conventional sense on transnational, international, and global criminology. A new journal, *Global Crime,* is now published, although its focus is currently on transnational organized crime. Criminology and criminal justice as fields continue to remain wedded principally to a 20th-century local/state/federal framework and this is reflected in graduate curriculums. But just as the law schools have increasingly recognized in recent years their need to transform their programs to more fully reflect a globalized world, the same will surely be true of graduate programs in criminology and criminal justice.

A Provisional Genealogy for a Global Criminology

It may be a useful exercise to engage in a genealogy of criminological concerns. What is the "ancestry" of emerging criminological specialties or lines of inquiry? Historical approaches in the field of criminology most typically focus upon the development of theories, criminological personalities, or criminological institutions. Much less attention has been directed to the emergence of different substantive interests.

A global criminology that focuses on crimes of powerful entities (including states) in the context of a transnational framework surely has its seminal roots in Edwin H. Sutherland's (1940) 1939 American Sociological Society Presidential Address. His call for attention to white-collar crime challenged the almost exclusive criminological focus upon conventional forms of crime that was the norm up to this time, and remained the case for some time afterwards. Sutherland's book (1949), *White-Collar Crime*, addressed the crimes of major U.S. corporations, and in this regard also extended the scope of criminological inquiry from individuals and gangs to organizations, and from predominantly local entities to national entities.

It took several decades before scholarship on white-collar crime achieved some real momentum—sometime in the 1970s. Sutherland's original conception of white-collar crime was restricted, however, to private-sector activity, principally of corporations. Some of the surveys of white-collar crime that began to appear by the early 1980s had a more inclusive conception of crimes of the powerful, to embrace the crimes of public officials (e.g., Simon, 2006). In the late 1980s, most specifically with William Chambliss' (1989) 1988 American Society of Criminology Presidential Address, we get the more formal emergence of attention to what he labeled state-organized crime, or crimes of states. The 1990s witnessed further development of a criminology of such crime, into the new century (e.g., see Rothe and Friedrichs, 2006). The publication of Penny Green and Tony Ward's (2004) *State Crime* represents another formal stage in the establishment of a full-fledged criminology of crimes of the state. These developments surely encompass and provide a point of departure for the various emerging lines of inquiry now being pursued within the framework of a transnational, international, or global criminology.

Obviously, some other strains of criminological inquiry have contributed as well, especially comparative criminology and the criminology of organized crime. To a limited extent, global criminology may draw upon the criminological investigation of professional crime. Nonetheless, neither mainstream criminological exploration of conventional forms of crime and juvenile delinquency, nor traditional forms of criminal justice, contribute in a measurable way to this lineage.

Within the context of the sparse and concise genealogy outlined above, some basic questions arise. Which variables impede, and which promote, the growth of a particular field of inquiry? Why was the emergence of a substantial criminology of white-collar crime so limited until the 1970s? What kinds of factors would contribute to a more rapid development of a transnational or global criminology?

State-Corporate Crime, Crimes of Globalization, and Finance Crime as Transnational, Hybrid Forms of White-Collar Crime: A Typological Approach

I strongly favor a typological approach to the understanding of crime. All typologies are problematic, and incorporate some distorting and artificial dimensions. Yet they are necessary to reduce incoherence and confusion. A useful typology clarifies more than it obfuscates. Furthermore, a typology should adopt some scheme for ordering or grouping related types of crime, on criteria such as level of harm.

In my typological approach to white-collar crime (Friedrichs, 2007), I differentiate between core types of white-collar crime and cognate, hybrid, and marginal forms. Corporate crime and occupational crime are the core types. For a global criminology, however, cognate and hybrid types of white-collar crime are especially significant, and accordingly some of these types are identified and discussed here.

Governmental crime—or crime that occurs within the context of government—is the principal cognate form of white-collar crime. *State crime* (or crime of the state) is macro-level harm carried out on behalf of the state or its agencies; *political white-collar crime* is crime carried out by individuals or networks of individuals who occupy governmental positions and seek economic or political advantage for themselves or their party.

I have formulated a typology of crimes of the state, centered upon the "core" criminal activity of the particular state. Accordingly, I differentiate between a *criminal state*, with a central project of a crime against humanity such as genocide (exemplified by the Nazi state); a *repressive state*, with a core project of systematic denial of basic rights to citizens or some group of citizens (exemplified by the case of Apartheid South Africa); a *corrupt state*, with systematic looting of the state for the benefit of the leadership and relatives or associates of the leadership (exemplified by Suharto's Indonesia); and a *negligent state*, characterized by a basic failure to alleviate forms of suffering that the state could address (exemplified by a wealthy United States with homeless people and many people with AIDS).

Admittedly, this typology is contentious and open to challenge on the claim that any such classifications are either politically biased or fundamentally arbitrary, or both. Some states—for example, Saddam Hussein's Iraq—could be said to combine in almost equal measure elements of each of these core projects. My conviction remains, however, that a typology of this sort at least provides a solid point of departure for exploring more fully each of the principal forms of harm associated with the activities of state officials acting on behalf of the state.

The concept of *state-corporate crime* was introduced by Ronald Kramer and Raymond Michalowski in 1990, with core contributions to the literature on this topic now brought together in an edited collection (Michalowski and Kramer, 2006). Such crime, involving a cooperative venture between the state and private-sector actors, must increasingly be addressed in terms of transnational dimensions within a global context. It may be useful to break this concept down further to capture who initiates and takes the lead in the cooperative venture, and whether organizational or individual benefits are central.

The term *crimes of globalization* addresses the demonstrable harm that results from the policies and practices of the international financial and trade institutions, principally the World Bank, the International Monetary Fund, and the World Trade Organization (Friedrichs and Friedrichs, 2002; MacKenzie, 2006). Criminologists have almost wholly neglected such crime. The original inspiration to explore this form of crime came from the experience of the author's daughter living among and working with Thai fishing people whose way of life was being destroyed by a World Bank-financed dam.

The international financial and trade institutions are inherently transnational in their operations. They put themselves forth as engaged in productive activities and as combating political corruption, but they are themselves sources of destructive outcomes and foster some forms of political corruption while tolerating other forms. The international financial institutions are inherently criminogenic because they reward getting out loans for projects, not attention to long-term human and environmental consequences of the funded projects. Furthermore, the international financial institutions operate without formal oversight on their policies and practices.

The term *finance crime* refers to the large-scale illegal and unethical policies and practices occurring in the higher echelons of our financial system: e.g., consumer and investment banks, the mutual funds industry, and the insurance industry. The term reflects a perception that many of the activities that occur in this context are not best captured by either "corporate crime" or "occupational crime." Finance crimes often involve networks of elites acting cooperatively, increasingly across borders. Individuals and groups of individuals use their control over organizational policies and practices to benefit themselves principally, and their organization secondarily, if at all. Disentangling organizational from individual benefit can be a challenge in these cases. But the nature of large-scale financial institutions and enterprises in crimes in a globalized world calls for more criminological attention.

The Adoption of a Global, Postmodern Context

A basic premise here is that our world is infinitely complex, and becoming ever more complex. Furthermore, any efforts to characterize the present state of the world—and there appears to be an exponential increase in the number of books doing so—will be incomplete or distorted in some sense, due to the complexity and dynamic character of our world today. Some efforts to characterize the world today are essentially descriptive, some are analytical, and some are polemical. Some such efforts are more persuasive than others.

Another premise is that any endeavor that analyzes transnational or global crime must adopt some version of a characterization of our world to provide a context for such analysis. What are the criteria for our adoption of a particular characterization of our world, and is such adoption in any sense objective? Should the adoption of a characterization aspire to be objective? A characterization that is coherent, persuasive, and supported by incontrovertible facts is worthy of adoption.

Globalization is indisputably one key dimension of understanding the world today. Some broad themes pertinent to globalization can be stated. First, it is a "buzzword" of our era. Salient dimensions include the acknowledgment that there are new and enduring elements of globalization. It has political and cultural dimensions, as well as economic dimensions. Transnational corporations and international financial institutions play a central role in an increasingly globalized world, but are fundamentally undemocratic. The global market has expanded, and has complex and contradictory tendencies. Although there are both winners and losers in an expanded neoliberal global economy, benefits are very unequally realized, and inequalities are expanding. Intensified global interconnections and communication are central. In the view of some, globalization is a new form of colonialism. The claim of "free trade" in a globalized world is hypocritical and misleading, since the trade policies are rigged to favor the developed countries and the corporations based in those countries. Many aspects of a Western, corporate, and IFI-dominated globalization have inspired atavistic rage toward the West. The earlier optimistic assessments of globalization's potential have eroded.

An ever-expanding globalization is only one dimension—although an especially important one—of our present evolving context. A steady increase in *postmodern* elements is another important dimension. Concisely, this refers to a shift from the central role of such distinctive features of modern society as industrialization, urbanization, bureaucratization, mass communication, and mobilization to a post-modern society, where computers (as opposed to machines), virtual communities (as opposed to physical communities), adhocracies (as opposed to less flexible bureaucracies), interactive communication (as opposed to traditional forms of mass communication), and fluidity—or movement in and out (as opposed to conventional forms of geographical and social mobility)—become increasingly dominant. In *traditional* societies, crime and its control are largely local and individual; in *modern* societies crime and its control are increasingly national and organizational; in *postmodern* societies, crime and its control are increasingly global and a function of networks.

Although the notion of a postmodern society should not be directly confused with postmodern philosophy, two concepts of Baudrillard's (1994) that emerge from this literature may be especially helpful in making sense of some aspects of transnational financial crime. First, the concept of *hyperreality* holds that reality has collapsed and has been replaced by image, illusion, and simulation. Second, the concept of *intertextuality* refers to a complex and infinite set of interwoven relationships, with everything related to everything else. If one considers some of the major corporate crime cases of the recent era—such as Enron—one cannot help but be struck by the central role of simulations in some sense at the core of Enron's operations, as well as the complex networks of parties (including auditors, stock analysts, investment bankers, and corporate lawyers) complicit in some way in the fraudulent activity (see Friedrichs, 2004a). Surely, concepts of this nature can also be applied to an understanding of transnational crime and its control. Students of transnational crime in a rapidly evolving world must engage quite fully with the literature on globalization and the postmodern, as well as with other endeavors to characterize this world. In the recent era, for example, we have claims that we now live in a "risk society" or a "network society" (Beck, 1992; Castells, 1996). Such characterizations need not be accepted uncritically, but should be addressed in any effort to provide an appropriate framework for the understanding of transnational crime and its control.

The Declining World Order and Transnational Crime

Beyond the need to address the broader global and societal context within which transnational crime and its control occur today, it seems useful to me to also adopt a more specific characterization of this world. An escalating number of books have been published—and continue to be published—that attempt to do this. Needless to say, these characterizations are hardly uniform, and may clash on some key issues. Richard A. Falk's (2004) *The Declining World Order: America's Imperial Geopolitics* seems to me an especially persuasive, coherent, and factually sound characterization of our world today. First, Falk usefully identifies different forms of globalization: *corporate* (neoliberal), supporting maximum autonomy for market forces; *civic*, the various alternatives to the neoliberal model put forth by its critics; *imperial*, post-September 11 U.S.-dominated global governance; *apocalyptic*, the Islamic fundamentalist vision; and *regional*, signified by such regionalizing endeavors as the European Union. For Falk (2004: *x*),

> the framing of world order is a more tenuous and contested reality, particularly influenced by the behavior of various kinds of transnational networks, ranging from criminal to religious, by global corporations, banks, hedge funds, financial traders, by regional actors, by the leaders of the first "global state"...and by a constellation of civil society actors pursuing an assortment of global policy agendas.

Falk (p. 4) goes on to identify, I believe quite correctly, some of the most salient "post-Westphalian" developments: the rise and fall of Eurocentrism, colonialism and decolonialism, the advent of weapons of mass destruction, the establishment of international institutions, the rise of global market forces, the emergence of global civil society, and revolutionary new technologies. All of these developments should be integrated in some form into the analysis of transnational crime and its control. Falk (p. 3) also identifies some significant new trends in the world today, including the resurgence of global religion, the emergence of transnational social forces, the rise of transnational crime, the expansion of legal and illegal migration patterns, the diffusion of global, integrated television, and the militarization of the planet. Falk includes the "rise of international crime" on his list of such trends. His book then examines the key attributes of our contemporary global circumstances in some depth. He concludes with a provocative claim that the foreign policy pursued by the George W. Bush administration is increasingly taking on the form of "global fascism." The emergence of an U.S. global empire with a fascist character has immense implications, and is also part of the context within which transnational crime and its control must be understood.

Sovereignty, Nationalism, and Legitimacy

Some concepts that traditionally have not figured significantly in the vocabulary of criminology have greater prominence in relation to an emerging global criminology. *Sovereignty* is one such concept. Despite the term's various meanings, central in this context is the state's exclusive control over the territory bounded by its borders. The term "jurisdiction" is part of conventional criminal justice discourse and parallels that of sovereignty in certain respects. In a world of increasing globalization and transnational crimes, however, sovereign claims become increasingly problematic or irrelevant—e.g., in the case of the Chernobyl catastrophe, aerosol in relation to global warming, etc. (Sands, 2005: 1; 5–16). Sovereignty claims are now an illusion in terms of their traditional meaning. They are increasingly invoked to justify various forms of state-organized lawbreaking. Criminologists must attend to sovereignty issues as they intersect with transnational crime and its control.

Nationalism is another concept little addressed within criminology. In the sense of putting one's own nation's interest and cultural values first, nationalism has a long and problematic history. Nationalism in one view is a form of socio-pathology in the context of a world of weapons of mass destruction. Criminology as a field has studied individual and gang pathologies quite extensively. Which principles can be applied to the pathologies of nations? Significant points of intersection exist between issues of nationalism and transnational crime and criminal justice. Nationalistic tendencies promote or deter transnational crime. How is nationalism directly complicit in some forms of transnational crime? Do transnational crime and the promotion of international criminal justice contribute to a resurgence of nationalism?

Finally, the concept of *legitimacy* refers to an order of authority perceived to be valid and deserving of compliance. This concept has been important in macro-level analyses within sociology and political science, and an aspect of law-related scholarship, but not within criminology. Legitimacy becomes increasingly complicated in a globalized, postmodern world. Legitimacy claims become increasingly problematic and contested as one moves from the local to the global. On what specific grounds are the legitimacy claims of international tribunals based? What are the consequences for their effectiveness if legitimacy is largely withheld from such institutions? How do globalization and emerging postmodern tendencies foster legitimacy crises domestically? How do legitimacy crises create conditions conducive to promoting certain forms of transnational crime?

International Tribunals, International Law, and Global Governance

Although criminologists and criminal justicians have written quite extensively on local, state, and federal courts and trials, international tribunals have been largely neglected by such scholars. However, a small number of criminologists have begun to examine such tribunals. John Hagan's (2003) *Justice in the Balkans: Prosecuting War Crimes in the Hague Trial* adopts an essentially mainstream framework to examine the workings of this particular tribunal. Dawn Rothe and Christopher W. Mullins' (2006) *The International Criminal Court: Symbolic Gestures and the Generation of Global Social Control* applies a critical perspective to an understanding of the procedural, conceptual, and practical dimensions of the International Criminal Court. Both the potential and the limitations of such tribunals should engage the interest of a growing number of criminologists in an increasingly globalized world. Criminologists should be able to provide useful insights into the issues arising in relation to the international tribunals and trials by undertaking systematic comparisons with the operations of traditional (domestic) criminal courts and trials.

Historically, criminology and criminal justice have focused upon local, state, and federal law, not international law. In 2003 the new dean of the Yale Law School, Harold Hongju Koh, noted that just as law schools shifted attention from state to national law late in the 19th century, now law schools must shift more attention from national to international law (Santora, 2003). Criminology and criminal justice, in terms of their curriculum and their scholarly focus, must undertake a parallel shift.

The problem of crime, and the justice system response to it, has been addressed traditionally within the context of local, state, and federal governments. One of the big questions going forward is whether an ever more interconnected global world will also lead in the direction of global governance. The notion of a global government is, of course, immensely problematic, and generates serious concerns across the ideological spectrum. The performance of the United Nations as a rudimentary institution of global governance has all-too-often disappointed its adherents and outraged its detractors. According to Anne-Marie Slaughter (2004), a very real form of global governance is in place today through the international network of diplomats and other government officials who work together cooperatively on many matters of international concern. But criminologists will find it increasingly necessary to engage with the evolving debate on global governance, especially in relation to the implications of such governance for transnational and international forms of crime, and their control.

Conclusion: An Agenda for Global Criminology

First, an emerging global criminology should attempt to arrive at some consensus on defining itself coherently. It should identify the parameters of expanded criminological concerns within the context of globalization. It should address the definition of crime issue anew within this context. It should attend to defining the key terms associated with an emerging global criminology clearly and cogently. It should develop a coherent typology of global crime or transnational crime, and of the institutions of control of such crime.

A global criminology needs to address systematically the formidable methodological issues that arise in relation to studying global and transnational crime. It should adopt a credible "world order" framework within which transnational forms of crime and its control can be analyzed. It should identify optimal strategies for promoting a broader awareness within the discipline of the need to adopt a global framework. It should identify viable and useful empirical projects that can advance the understanding of transnational crime and its control. It must also identify optimal strategies for securing funding and support for such projects. It needs to identify the major policy issues that now arise in relation to transnational crime and its control, and the optimal resolution of these issues. Finally, it needs to delineate the relationship of an emerging criminology to a range of disciplines—including international law and comparative politics—that address some of the same concerns.

Acknowledgments: This article was originally drafted while I was serving as Visiting Professor of Law at Flinders University in Adelaide, Australia. I appreciate the support of the law school, as well as a faculty research grant from my home institution, the University of Scranton.

REFERENCES

Andreas, Peter and Ethan Nadelmann
2006 *Policing the Globe: Criminalization and Crime in International Relations*. New York: Oxford.

Barak, Gregg (ed.)
2000 *Crime and Crime Control: A Global View*. Westport, CT: Greenwood Press.

Baudrillard, Jean
1994 *Simulacra and Simulation*. Ann Arbor: University of Michigan.

Beck, Ulrich
1992 *Risk Society: Towards a New Modernity*. London: Sage.

Beirne, Piers and David Nelken (eds.)
1997 *Issues in Comparative Criminology*. Dartmouth: Ashgate.

Braithwaite, John
1989 "The State of Criminology: Theoretical Decay or Renaissance?" *Australian and New Zealand Journal of Criminology* 22,12: 9–137.

Castells, Manuel
1996 *The Rise of the Network Society*. Cambridge, MA: Blackwell.

Chambliss, William J.
1989 "State-organized Crime." *Criminology* 27: 183–204.

Chan, Janet
2005 "Globalization, Reflexivity and the Practice of Criminology." J. Sheptycki and A. Wardak (eds.), *Transnational and Comparative Criminology*. London: Glasshouse Press.

Clinard, Marshall B. and Peter C. Yeager
1980 *Corporate Crime*. New York: The Free Press.

Cohen, Stanley
1988 *Against Criminology*. New Brunswick, NJ: Transaction Books.

Cressey, Donald R.
1969 *Theft of the Nation: The Structure and Operation of Organized Crime in America*. New York: Harper and Row.

Dammer, Harry R. and Erika Fairchild
2006 *Comparative Criminal Justice Systems*. Third edition. Belmont, CA: Thomson/Wadsworth.

DeFlem, Mathieu
2002 *Policing World Society: Historical Foundations of International Police Cooperation*. New York: Oxford University Press.

Edwards, Adam and Peter Gill
2003 *Transnational Organized Crime: Perspectives on Global Security*. New York: Routledge.

Falk, Richard A.
2004 *The Declining World Order: America's Imperial Geopolitics*. New York: Routledge.

Findlay, Mark
1999 *The Globalization of Crime*. Cambridge, U.K.: Cambridge University Press.

Friedrichs, David O.
2007 "Towards a Criminology of International Crimes: Producing a Conceptual and Contextual Framework." R. Haveman and A. Smeulers (eds.), *Towards a Criminology of International Crimes*. Antwerp: Insentia. Forthcoming.
2004a "Enron et al.: Paradigmatic White-Collar Crime Cases for the New Century." *Critical Criminology* 12: 113–132.
2004b *Trusted Criminals: White Collar Crime in Contemporary Society*. Third edition. Belmont, CA: Thomson/Wadsworth.
Friedrichs, David O. and Jessica Friedrichs
2002 "The World Bank and Crimes of Globalization: A Case Study." *Social Justice* 29,1: 3–36.
Galeottie, Mark (ed.)
2005 *Global Crime Today: The Changing Face of Organized Crime*. Cambridge, U.K.: Cambridge University Press.
Green, Penny and Tony Ward
2004 *State Crime: Governments, Violence and Corruption*. London: Pluto.
Hagan, John
2003 *Justice in the Balkans: Prosecuting War Crimes in the Hague Tribunal*. Chicago: University of Chicago Press.
Karstedt, Susanne and Kai-D. Bussmann (eds.)
2000 *Social Dynamics of Crime and Control: New Theories for a World in Transition*. Portland, OR: Oxford.
Kramer, Ronald C. and Raymond J. Michalowski
1990 "State-Corporate Crime." A Paper Presented at the Annual Meeting of the American Society of Criminology, Baltimore (November): 7–12.
Mackenzie, Simon
2006 "Systematic Crimes of the Powerful: Criminal Aspects of the Global Economy." *Social Justice* 33:1: 162–182.
Michalowski, Raymond J. and Ronald C. Kramer (eds.)
2006 *State-Corporate Crime: Wrongdoing at the Intersection of Business and Government*. New Brunswick, NJ: Rutgers University Press.
Morrison, Wayne
2005 *Criminology, Civilization and the New World Order*. London: Cavendish Publishing.
Nelken, David (ed.)
1994 *The Futures of Criminology*. London: Sage Publishing.
Reichel, Philip (ed.)
2005 *Handbook of Transnational Crime and Justice*. Thousand Oaks, CA: Sage.
Rothe, Dawn and David O. Friedrichs
2006 "The State of the Criminology of Crimes of the State." *Social Justice* 33,1: 147–161.
Rothe, Dawn and Christopher Mullins
2006 *The International Criminal Court: Symbolic Gestures and the Generation of Global Social Control: The International Criminal Court*. Lanham, MD: Lexington Books.
Sands, Philip
2005 *Lawless World: Making and Breaking Global Rules*. London: Penguin.
Santora, Marc
2003 "Battling the Darkness with the Law as His Lamp." *New York Times* (November 11): B2.
Sheptycki, James
2002 *In Search of Transnational Policing: Towards a Sociology of Global Policing*. Dartmouth: Ashgate.
Sheptycki, James and Ali Wardak (eds.)
2003 *Transnational and Comparative Criminology*. London: Glasshouse.

Simon, David R.
2006 *Elite Deviance*. Eighth edition. Boston: Allyn and Bacon.
Slaughter, Anne-Marie
2004 *A New World Order*. Princeton: Princeton University Press.
Sutherland, Edwin H.
1949 *White-Collar Crime*. New York: Holt, Rinehart and Winston.
1940 "White-Collar Criminality." *American Sociological Review* 5: 1–12.

[5]

The Mean Streets of the Global Village: Crimes of Exclusion in the United States and Darfur

JOHN HAGAN[1] AND WENONA RYMOND-RICHMOND[2]

[1] Northwestern University, American Bar Foundation, Evanston, Illinois, USA

[2] University of Massachusetts, Amherst, Massachusetts, USA

Abstract

This paper considers similarities as well as differences in state-based systems of selective exclusion found in the United States and Sudan. Albeit in different ways and to different degrees, large numbers of homeless adults and children are denied the basic human right to secure shelter in the nations of both the Global North and the Global South. Homelessness and imprisonment are pervasive forms of social exclusion in the late modern Global North, while forced migration and mortality are persistent forms of social exclusion in the contemporary Global South. The domestic policies of exclusion in the North—with their legalized use of arrest, due process, conviction, incarceration and homelessness—are a world apart from the policies of criminal exclusion in the Global South—with their death squads, militias, disappearances and displacements. Yet both depend on repression rather than restoration. Mass incarceration and genocidal death and displacement display an awkward symmetry along the mean streets of the global village, and the fragile and disrupted families of the North parallel the destroyed and displaced families of the South. They are parallel faces of vulnerability. The mean streets of the United States and Sudan are not the same, but their risks and vulnerabilities involve parallel and failed policies of punishment, repression, and exclusion.

KEY WORDS: Displacement, Darfur, Exclusion, Genocide, Homelessness, Imprisonment, Killing, Mortality, Rape, Sudan

The Global North and South

Should it be entirely surprising that a country, the United States, with a history of importing African slaves and genocidally killing and displacing its indigenous people, would four centuries later respond in ambivalent ways to an African country, Sudan, that has enslaved, killed and displaced its own indigenous population? Perhaps these countries are not as entirely different as they might at first seem. There may be lessons of broader relevance in the seemingly disconnected but in some ways similar and overlapping experiences of the United States and Sudan. Criminology is an important venue for the development of such lessons.

Our starting point is two jarringly different images of the consequences of Sudan's recent genocidal history. The first image is the well told story in Megan Mylan and Jon Shenk's documentary, *The Lost Boys of Sudan*, and in Dave Eggers' novel *What Is What*. This is the true tale of the thousands of young boys who when confronted with terrifying choices in the early 1990s between being child soldiers, slaves, and death, chose to flee from southern Sudan to refugee camps in Ethiopia. When life proved desperate there too, many of these same youth fled back through the still raging killing fields of southern Sudan, winding up in refugee camps in Kenya. Finally, in 2000, the US govern-

Figure 1. *Lost Boys of Sudan (www.lostboysfilm.com).*

ment began bringing some of these youth to the United States where they received help, often from church groups, in negotiating a challenging inclusion and reintegration into more normal lives in the Global North (Cheadle and Prendergast 2007). This outcome was an enormously important accomplishment of restorative justice for the fortunate few who survived their early lives as child victims and soldiers in Sudan.

The second image is a less uplifting and more sobering reflection of the exclusionary stigma and punitiveness that more often has confronted refugees from Sudan's genocidal policies. This second image appeared in a colour photo 'above the fold' on the front page

Figure 2. *One Sudanese refugee, left, crying out as he was grabbed by riot policemen, as another, right, tried to hand over his child through a bus window after both were arrested by Egyptian security troops. (New York Times December 31, 2005) Courtesy of AP Images/Ben Curtis.*

of the New York Times, on New Year's eve, 2005. The picture was of a Sudanese man crying out as another man tried to deliver his infant child to safety through a bus window as they were forcibly removed by Egyptian police from a protest in Cairo. The police killed at least 23 adults and children that day, when hundreds of Sudanese refugees refused to leave a public park they had occupied to protest denials of their refugee claims by United Nations officials. The officials implausibly told thousands of Sudanese camped in the small park across from their offices that they were ineligible for relocation because it was safe to return to their 'homes' in Sudan.

> When the officers charged, women and children tried to huddle together, and to hide under blankets as some men grabbed for anything—tree limbs, metal bars—struggling to fight back, witnesses said. The police hesitated, then rushed in with full force, trampling over people and dragging the Sudanese off to waiting buses... (Allam and Slackman 2005:1)

Those who survived were bused away and later released on the streets of Cairo with no possessions and nowhere to go (Allam and Slackman 2005)—yet again the victims of social exclusion.

No reports followed as to what became of the latter group of refugee claimants and their children, but it is reasonable to imagine that their fates on the streets of Cairo were far less favourable than those of the lost boys of Sudan who were allowed sanctuary in the United States. Of course, the Global North has its own problems of social exclusion, notably including homelessness and imprisonment, and the field of criminology has copiously researched the life course outcomes of young as well as older persons who are treated with analogously punitive (e.g. arrest and imprisonment) as opposed to reintegrative policies (e.g. shelters, alternative school and work programs) in North America. We can learn much from this criminological research in the Global North, and we argue in this paper that the implications of this work are instructive for our understanding of the Global South as well as the Global North—not just because our fates are linked by the shrinking and interconnected dimensions of the joined worlds in which we live, but also because even more fundamental aspects of our geographically separate lives may be more intertwined than they ordinarily seem.

In particular, we argue that there are lessons from the experiences of homeless youth and families in the Global North that can make the Global South, including the life prospects of the displaced and dispossessed in Darfur, more understandable. This paper ultimately considers similarities as well as differences in the state-based systems of selective exclusion found in the United States and Sudan. Readers may wish to jump ahead to Table I below for a summary statement of where this discussion is heading. Our discussion begins with a more broadly based comparison of policies of social exclusion in the Global North and Global South.

The criminology of two hemispheres

Albeit in different ways and to different degrees, large numbers of homeless adults and children are denied the basic human right to secure shelter in the nations of both the Global North and the Global South. For some, this form of social exclusion is a cause of involvement in crime, while for others it is a form of criminal victimization in itself. For many, it is both. Homelessness and imprisonment are pervasive institutions of social exclusion in the late modern Global North, while forced migration and mortality are persistent institutions of social exclusion in the contemporary Global South. We have already seen that the shrinking dimensions of world history and worldwide population shifts interconnect these institutional trends, often yielding conflict, as when the fear-driven exclusivity of the North pushes back against the successive waves of forced displacement and pleas for sanctuary from the South. These hemispheric processes beg for comparative research and understanding, and criminological theory and research can speak to this need.

Major contributions of late modern criminology speak in useful ways to the themes of social exclusion and inclusion that we explore in this paper. Any accounting is highly selective, but brief mention of some of the most notable contributions of recent recipients of the Stockholm Prize in Criminology can help to make this basic point. For example, John Braithwaite (1987, 2002) explains how stigmatic social exclusion and more inclusive and reintegrative shaming policies can characterize opposing regimes of punishment and strongly influence the life paths of those who experience them. Alfred Blumstein (2006) explains how an exclusionary period of escalating imprisonment and confinement of young, black males linked to a perceived drug epidemic in the United States has prolonged the challenge of encouraging desistance from lifelong criminal careers. Losel and Schumucker (2005) explains how social cognitive treatment programs in community settings can reduce persistent criminality. Moffit (1993) explains how adolescent-limited involvements in antisocial behaviour followed by social reintegration and inclusion can be distinguished from life course persistence in antisocial behaviour and its exclusionary developmental consequences.

This contemporary criminology builds further on the shoulders of giants. For example, when we elaborate the developmental concept of antisocial behaviour with Robert Merton's classic sociological typology that highlights 'innovation' and 'rebellion' as forms of criminalized deviance, we have the foundations of a late modern criminology that has much to tell us about the causes and consequences of not only the street crimes of the Global North, but also about crimes against humanity and the responses they provoke in the Global South. What we have learned in the North can tell us much about the South, while the lessons of the South may also be consequential for the North, if only partly as a result of the forces of displacement and immigration already noted.

We begin in the more familiar terrain of North American criminology, before returning to the urgency of current lessons from the Darfur region of Sudan. We review research indicating that reintegrative and restorative justice policies providing shelter and assistance are successful in limiting life course persistence in delinquency and crime. Alternatively, comparative research reveals more punitive and stigmatic policies are more likely to produce enduring criminal careers. Yet leading late modern states in the Global North, such as the United States and Great Britain, have trended toward increasingly punitive and stigmatizing justice system policies (Garland 2001). These are policies of legalized social exclusion. We consider new evidence that the collateral intergenerational consequences of this kind of institutionalized legal exclusion of parents are to increase family disruption, homelessness, educational detainment, delinquency and crime (Foster and Hagan 2007). We argue that underwriting all of this are distinctive alternative collective framings of groups, such as the homeless and displaced, in exclusive as contrasted with inclusive terms. The difference is as distinctive as the alternative collective framings in the nations of the Global North of '*street youth* who can be helped' and '*street criminals* who must be punished'.

If trends in the Global South are especially dire, they are foreshadowed by the often downward trending experiences of the Global North. The challenge is to see the countertrends in what otherwise too often seems an accelerating downward descent. Out of this mixed story comes a rich research agenda for a changing criminology, including a better understanding of some of the most desperate criminality of the Global South.

Street youth and street criminals in three cities

Two cities in the Canadian Global North, Toronto and Vancouver, adopted contrasting inclusive and exclusive policies in relation to homeless youth in the 1980s and 90s. The result was a research opportunity for the first author of this book to consider how alternative policies of inclusion and exclusion impact on homeless youth and street crime in the late modern urban settings of the Global North (Hagan and McCarthy 1997). A further study undertaken at the turn of the millennium in Glasgow, Scotland (Fitzpatrick 2000), provides a subsequent opportunity to confirm and extend some of the findings of the Canadian research—many thousands of miles away in another part of the Global North. We begin with Toronto and Vancouver.

On the one hand, Toronto had many features of an inclusive and restorative social welfare model that framed youth living on the streets and away from home in the developmental vernacular of 'street youth' or 'street kids'. In Toronto, provincial legislation allowed youth who lived apart from their families and without parental consent to receive emergency and longer-term public shelter and financial assistance. Thus in the 1990s, there were four hostels in Toronto reserved exclusively for youth aged 16 through 21. Although these hostels had their problems, and some youth preferred to live on the streets, most youth clearly valued the shelter and other services provided by these youth-oriented settings.

The situation in Vancouver was far different. Vancouverites worried about the enticements of their city's mild climate and unique coastal location. They foresaw security threats in an unceasing onslaught of westward migration. In the 1990s, the province and city's welfare policies were restrictive and exclusionary. Family and welfare legislation required that youth living apart from their families in Vancouver could only receive publicly funded support in unusual circumstances. Care providers could only offer shelter to youth if they first had parental permission to be away from home—an unrealistic precondition for youth in violent conflict and often hundreds or even thousands of miles away from their parents. Beyond this, authorities in Vancouver refused to implement a framing of 'street youth' that was separate and apart from 'street criminals'. Thus in the 1990s, there was no developed system of hostels, shelters, or safe houses for the short-term housing of homeless youth in Vancouver. Very few settings provided support for these youth on the street. They were stigmatized as 'ordinary street criminals' and socially excluded.

The situation in Vancouver made the police the first responders to homeless youth. The police responded either by returning youth to their families, who were liable to criminal prosecution if they refused to accept and promise to support their children; or by placing the youth in government care and sending them to a foster or group home; or by preemptively arresting and jailing these youth. These options did not offer promising solutions to problems that caused these youth to leave their homes in the first place.

Our panel survey interviews with the youth in the two cities confirmed that the settings and alternative policy models made a difference. This was reflected most clearly by a strong effect of being in Vancouver as contrasted with Toronto on involvement in crimes of theft, drugs, and prostitution. The results further highlighted another key difference in outcomes between these cities, one that further diminished involvement in street crimes in Toronto. Toronto's inclusive social welfare model of providing access to overnight shelters and social services reduced exposures to the criminal opportunities of street crime networks and subcultures, whereas Vancouver's exclusionary crime control model and absence of assistance made these exposures more common. Heightened exposure to the street and its criminal opportunities intensified a movement toward the fulfillment of criminalized expectations, including embeddedness of these youth within criminal networks and without legally employed peers (Hagan 1993). Vancouver youth were also more likely to be charged by the police for their involvement in street crime, which is, of course, also consistent with an exclusionary crime control model, a framing as street criminals, and inconsistent with getting and keeping jobs.

More generally, the direct and indirect effects of taking to the streets in Toronto's more inclusively and Vancouver's more exclusively framed policy settings illustrate the significant roles that macrolevel policies play in determining life outcomes. Inclusive and exclusionary framings and their connected policies can determine life paths that lead further into or away from the criminally networked subcultures of the streets that pervade cities of the Global North.

Confidence in the preceding conclusion is increased by a fascinating year-long intensive study of the lives of homeless youth across the Atlantic on the streets of Glasgow, Scotland (Fitzpatrick 2000). By the year's end, this ethnographic field study confirmed that those youth who avoided the 'homeless subcultures' of city centres and stayed in youth-specific ('street kid') shelters were also able to take advantage of social services and achieve better employment outcomes. These latter youth who participated in the specialized programs designed to reintegrate them into work and school programs and to reframe them as conventional adolescents were better able to avoid the 'downward spiral' experienced by youth who remained outside this sphere in adult-dominated hostels. The latter youth spent much of their time hanging out on street corners with other homeless youth who saw themselves and were seen by others as street criminals.

From North to South

What can the street experiences of homeless youth in the Global North tell us about the Global South? In the Global South, late modern economic policies imported from the Global North often combine with the strengths and weaknesses of local nation states in ways that threaten family survival and intensify youth problems. Latin and South America are sites of prodigious homelessness yielding corresponding levels of family disruption and heightened risk behaviour among young people, who as in the Global North are most often seen as street criminals. Also as in the Global North, the latter problems peak in late adolescence and early adulthood.

Of course, some Latin and South American as well as African nations are also victims of direct forms of social exclusion, including state-led military and paramilitary regimes that organize massive 'disappearances' as well as full-fledged massacres, resulting in even more extensive family displacement and destruction. Sub-Saharan Africa is today the epicentre of such one-sided, state-led violence against civilians and families. The Middle East and North Africa are also sites of surges in multisided violence against civilians (Liu Institute for Global Issues 2006:Chapter 2). Rebellion against these circumstances is a predictable result, and again the demography of age and crime informs the shape and form of this rebellion. Darfur, of course, is our focus.

The challenge of the remainder of this paper is to use new evidence from selected sites in Darfur to illustrate the range of consequences that assaults on the lives of African youth and their families are creating for current and future generations. There are, of course, differences of kind as well as degree between the experience of genocidal victimization in Darfur and the problems of youth in the Global North that we have thus far emphasized. Yet related life course challenges exist for high-risk youth throughout the world (Osgood et al. 2005). Our argument is that these separate but related problems of youth present an urgent new research agenda that underlines the need for a reconstituted and more internationally focused science of crime.

To introduce as well as provoke this new research agenda, we present in Table I a comparative snapshot of similarities as well as differences in the state-based systems of selective exclusion we argue characterize the US and Sudan. We acknowledge that other countries should be included in this comparison. For example, China probably should occupy a place in this figure between the US and Sudan, while Canada and many European countries are likely to be to the left of the US. Elaborations of this figure await further research. We focus first on the US and Sudan.

Racial selectivity is a pervasive feature of both the US and Sudan state-based systems of exclusion. Polarized racial images are prominent in both countries, resulting in practices of differentiation if not oppression. For example, the New York Times columnist Bob Herbert (2007) recently observed that in the United States 'No one is paying much attention, but parts of New York City are like a police state for young men, women, and children who happen to be black or Hispanic. They are routinely stopped, searched, harassed, intimidated, humiliated, and, in many cases, arrested for no good reason'. Of course, Herbert qualified his observation by drawing 'likeness' and not 'equivalence' between the US and police states elsewhere.

Selective practices characteristically are implemented indirectly in the US and directly in Darfur, which can be a crucial difference. Thus in the United States, racial differentiation is customarily legalized through recourse to juridical procedures, which may or may not

Table 1. *State-based systems of selective exclusion (institutionalized forms of removal and relocation)*

Example states:	United States	Sudan
Exclusionary method:	Indirect	Direct
Selection mechanism:	Racial differentiation	Racial oppression
Institutional authority:	Legal/juridical procedure	Political/military and paramilitary chain of command
Operational mode:	Individualized	Collectivized
Putative rights and protections:	Domestic constitutional, civil, and criminal law	International humanitarian and criminal law
Forms of exclusion:	Police harassment, Arrest and conviction; Incarceration; Homelessness; Disenfranchisement; Death penalty	Mass killings and rapes; Displacement; Deportation; Property loss; Refugee status
Theoretical metaphors:	Crime as war ('war on drugs')	War as crime (genocide)
Predictable consequences:	Criminal innovation, recidivism, and mass incarceration (street crimes)	Organized attacks, armed rebellion, and counterinsurgency (war crimes)

prove to be discriminatory in themselves. The Sudanese state organizes racial oppression more visibly and directly in Darfur: through the unchecked command chains of the polity and military and paramilitary forces. This difference implies individualized punishment in the US and collective punishment in Darfur. However, both forms of punishment create collateral consequences (Hagan and Dinovitzer 1999).

Ideally, there should be checks on practices of racial differentiation. Of course, these due process checks and procedures depend on the enforcement of domestic constitutional, civil, and criminal law protections in the US, while in Darfur there is (thus far) an ineffective reliance on international humanitarian and criminal law. Organizations like the American Civil Liberties Union and Human Rights Watch have limited success in delivering protection in both places, but especially via the International Criminal Court in Darfur.

Weaknesses in legal and other protective measures in both the US and Darfur result in extensive racial disparities. These follow in the US from discriminatory practices of police harassment, arrest, conviction, incarceration, homelessness, and disenfranchisement. The resulting racial differentiation, including wrongful convictions, leads to misapplications of the death penalty and massive disproportionality in the incarceration of African Americans. Meanwhile, the racial oppression in Darfur is catastrophic. The racial consequences of the use of the political and military and paramilitary command structures of the Sudanese state to organize militia attacks on African groups in Darfur are genocidal in scale. The results are hundreds of thousands of killings and rapes, displacement, deportation, property loss, and the confinement of millions of homeless Africans in internal displacement and refugee camps.

These similarities as well as differences in the US and Darfur are reflected in the parallel policy metaphors describing them respectively in terms of 'war against crime' and 'war as crime'. In the US, the crime metaphor is intermittent but often explicit, and is expressed in such policies as the 'war on drugs', which had its modern beginning in the Goldwater US Presidential campaign of 1964 and was implemented in the Nixon Administration in the 1970s. Ironically, it is the Bush Administration which has extended the crime metaphor to Darfur with an ambivalent labelling of this armed conflict as genocide and an abstention from the UN's referral of the Darfur case to the International Criminal Court.

Our thesis is that these wars of exclusion in both the US and Darfur have enormously harmful and predictable consequences. In the US, Blumstein (2006) has explained how the massive reliance on incarceration in a 'war on drugs' against the crack epidemic in the 1980s resulted in the exclusionary imprisonment of older gang leaders and the creation of vacancy chains for new recruits to meet continuing demands for drugs. The vacancies were filled by not only new but younger and characteristically more violence-prone recruits who set off spiralling increases in gun deaths and subsequent surges in imprisonment in the US. This produced the worst of several possibilities: an age-based and network-fed subcultural process in which mass incarceration led to more violent forms of crime through the 1980s and into the early 1990s.

As we see next, an exclusionary process with some notable parallels is at work in Darfur—in this case involving state-led and -supported violent attacks on African groups that have intensified an armed rebellion that features the young male children of the targeted victims. In the same sense that mass incarceration aggravated a surge in violent youth crime in the US, in Darfur military and paramilitary attacks are intensifying an armed rebellion among newer and younger recruits. Again, this is an age-based and network-fed subcultural process in which exclusion is leading to more violence, in this case armed rebellion. If the past is predictive, this increasingly youth-driven rebellion will span war crimes in its own right. Criminology is experienced in enumerating and explaining such processes of racial differentiation and violence.

Desperation and defiance in Darfur

Should it be entirely surprising that in a country with a region like Darfur, where scorched earth tactics of ethnic cleansing against African groups are epidemic, would produce a violent and defiant rebel movement that is especially attractive to the youth whose families are

Figure 3. *Young rebel soldier in Darfur.*

viciously victimized? We argue that this violent subcultural response is exactly what should be predicted by a tradition of labelling and conflict theory in criminology, including, for example, Laurence Sherman's (1993) late modern version of defiance theory. The more uplifting alternative prospect, of course, is the fate of the *Lost Boys of Sudan*, with whom we started this paper.

Yet the true tale of the *Lost Boys of Sudan* is a restorative story of inclusive turning points that is even less likely for the boys of Darfur than are the parallel probabilities of ghetto youth on the urban playing fields of America becoming successful professional athletes. As we demonstrate below, age-related patterns of death and displacement are the far more likely outcomes in Darfur. The lesson of defiance theory is that rebellion is too often the more plausible alternative for disadvantaged youth confronted with sobering life choices in the killing fields of nations as different as the United States and Sudan.

The larger lesson of defiance theory is the unanticipated self-perpetuating rage and rebellion that is the product of repressive policies in many social settings, especially settings that provide too few peaceful pathways to success or even survival. It is in such circumstances that opportunities and strain theories classically predicted innovation and rebellion. The age-connected forms of this innovation and rebellion are foreshadowed in the criminological research already considered. Again, there may be lessons of broader relevance in the seemingly disconnected but in some ways similar and overlapping experiences of the United States and Sudan, and criminology is an important venue for the development of these lessons.

Our starting point is thus a third image, part myth and part reality, to consider in juxtaposition to the two we have already considered in this paper. This image is of the adolescent and young adult males in Darfur referred to in the Sudanese conflict with the demonizing imagery of 'Tora Bora'. The Sudanese government has simultaneously identified the Tora Bora with the history of the Western frontier of the United States and the American pursuit of Osama Bin Laden (i.e. into the same named mountain range on the Afghanistan border with Pakistan). The goal of the Sudanese government is to create the image of a scourge worth fighting by brutally repressive means.

The Sudanese government in press releases by its embassies and through other news media describes the Tora Bora as armed robbers and smugglers who prey on the Arab groups in Darfur, much as in the history of the settlers in the lawless American West:

> Historically, these groups have been existent in Darfur's extreme rural areas for many centuries conducting acts of highway robbery. The situation here is reminiscent of the 18th and 19th century American robber... in the Wild West. The highway robbery is an ancient practice in nomadic societies which are not unique to Darfur. It is to be found in communities or similar circumstances in different parts of Africa. Groups such as the Tora Bora... emerged as new fledglings conducting the old practice of highway robbery (El Talib 2004).

Threatening activities of the Tora Bora are thus said to be an important source of the self-defense-motivated actions of the Arab Janjaweed militias. The argument is that 'the major function and the raison d'être for this militia are to protect herds of nomadic tribes in western Sudan from attacks of looters, highway robbery and particularly, attacks of rival nomadic tribes at times of conflict on pastures and water' (El Talib 2004).

As noted, the Tora Bora also are linked to Islamic extremism in Sudanese government news releases. 'Any study of the conflict in Darfur', a government source reports, 'can no longer ignore the clear involvement of Islamic extremists in fermenting rebellion in western Sudan' (El Talib 2004). The evidence for this assertion, which is refuted below, again features the Tora Bora images, noting that 'amongst the rebels there is a self-styled "Tora Bora" militia—named after the Afghan mountain range in which Osama Bin Laden, al-Qaeda, and the Taliban fought one of their last battles, and from which Bin Laden escaped American capture' (Ali-Dinar 2004).

It is true that groups of young rebels sometimes also describe themselves as Tora Bora and are a small but growing part of the Darfur conflict. These youth are part of the large number of child, adolescent and young adult soldiers in Africa. Although young males may always have fought wars in the largest numbers, they are an increasingly important and vicious part of African armed conflicts. The reasons are likely little different than in the Global North, where youth as well are valued in gangs for their loyalty, fearlessness, willingness to take risks and readily renewable availability as new recruits (Gettleman 2007). Also like gang members in the Global North, these youth often are recognizable by their adopted symbols. In Darfur and elsewhere in Africa, these menacing images include dreadlocks, wraparound sunglasses, displays of weapons and sometimes small leather pouches worn with string around their necks and containing good luck pieces. They often ride into conflict in rocket-equipped pickup trucks and gun-laden land cruisers.

It is important to emphasize the polarized racial identification of the Tora Bora in Darfur. There is a clear linkage between the rising racial polarization of everyday life in Darfur, represented in the reports of racial epithets heard during Janjaweed militia attacks in Darfur. We make this and related points in the remainder of this paper by drawing on a survey conducted by the US State Department with Darfur refugees in Chad in July and August of 2004 (see Hagan et al. 2005).

Figure 4 presents a summary based on this survey of the rise in the explicit expression of racism in Darfur. The figure presents three-month moving averages of the reports from Darfur refugees of hearing racial epithets from spring–summer 2003 to the same period in 2004. This was a period of rise and fall in killings, which peaked at the beginning of 2004 in Darfur.

Figure 4 similarly shows a peak in reported racial epithets just before a widely observed peak in killing, at the end of 2003. However, this figure also shows that when attacks continued to occur in 2004, the level of reported racial epithets remained high, with about 40% of the respondents hearing these taunts, compared to about 20% at the beginning of the time series. We will see below that the Tora Bora references were nearly always accompanied by racial epithets when they were heard during the attacks. The racial and Tora Bora taunts are joined expressions of a racial demonology. In classical terms of labelling and subcultural crime theory, or Sherman's defiance theory, the youth who take on the Tora Bora role are acting as if to say, 'we are everything you say we are, and worse'. They have adopted what Edwin Lemert (1967) called the 'symbolic appurtenances' of the demonized cultural frame.

The question is thus less about the existence or size of these rebel groups than about the sources and sequences of their development in settings like Darfur. There is no doubt that rebel groups such as the Tora Bora exist and pre-date the current conflict in Darfur. The most prominent of the organized rebel groups, the Sudan Liberation Army (SLA) and the Justice and Equality Movement (JEM), announced their existence in February and March of 2003. The SLA and JEM rebels joined forces in a seven-hour attack on the al Fasher air base with 33 land cruisers in April of 2003, destroying a number of Sudan air force bombers and gunships. The rebels killed more than 75 Sudanese soldiers and lost only 9 of their own. This attack is usually cited as the

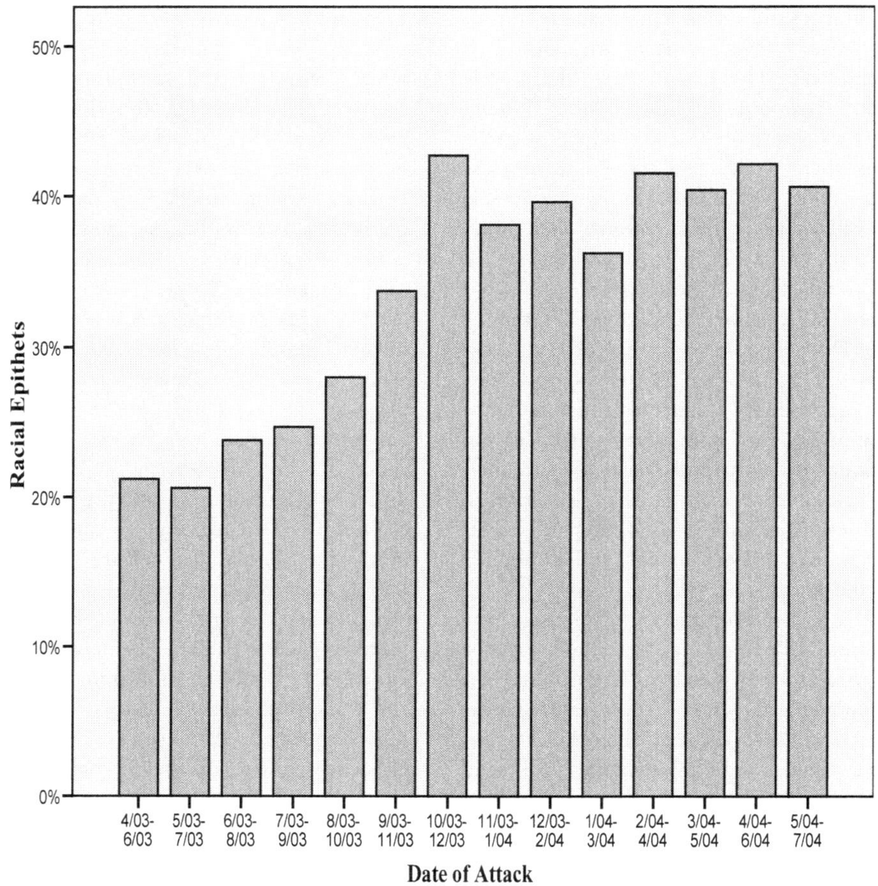

Figure 4. *Moving average percentage of refugees from Darfur who reported they heard racial epithets during attacks, by date of departure (Atrocities Documentation Survey, Summer 2004).*

beginning of the current conflict (Flint and de Waal 2005).

Yet the most exhaustive survey of reported attacks by both sides in Darfur reveals a very one-sided picture of this armed conflict, with few although increasing rebel attacks over time (Petersen and Tullin 2006). This survey is based on 178 witness statements/accounts and reports of attacks involving 372 sites in Darfur from January 2001 to September 2005. Although the accounting is certainly not exhaustive, it makes use of all known available sources. It begins by revealing at least eight significant attacks on African villages before the first major rebel attack on the al Fasher air base in the spring of 2003. In total, the survey reveals only 13 attacks by rebel forces

(3% of the total). All of the remaining attacks (97%) were conducted by Janjaweed militia groups, Sudanese government forces and/or aircraft, or a combination of these groups. Perhaps of even greater interest, however, is that while 3 of the 13 rebel attacks each are reported in 2003 and 2004, the remaining 7 attacks are reported in 2005. Six of these seven attacks are reported in South Darfur, with only one in North Darfur. It is very doubtful that this reporting of attacks is comprehensive, but it may well be representative of the relative distribution and sequence of the attacks, with the rebel attacks increasing over time.

This evidence is consistent with reports that the numbers of rebels seem to be growing along with the frequency of rebel actions, both against Arab targets and between rebel factions. This begs the question of who the rebels are and where they come from. Our answer is that they are usually the victims and sometimes also the perpetrators of war crimes, as well as more common crimes of subsistence. They come from all the targeted African groups—most notably the Zaghawa, Fur and Masaleit. They are mostly young, and some are under 18. All of the rebel groups—the SLA, JEM, and the newer National Movement for Reform and Development (NMRD) — are predominately made up of males in their later teens and twenties. As many as 80 Fur boys under 18 are known to have been in the ranks of the SLA and have been seen with weapons by Human Rights Watch observers (Human Rights Watch 2004a). Sudan is a ratified signatory to the Optional Protocol to the Convention on the Rights of the Child, which established 18 as the minimum age for forced recruitment and calls on states to assist with the rehabilitation of child soldiers.

Yet any thoughts of rehabilitation or restorative justice ignores the reality that the Sudan government's strategy of counterinsurgency in Darfur is a policy of collective stigmatization and exclusionary punishment concentrated on the families of the African farmers and villagers who are the targets of the joined government and Janjaweed militia attacks. An important Human Rights Watch (2005) report uses the term collective punishment to aptly describe the brutality we further describe below in the southwestern part of West Darfur state:

> These tactics—which were replicated throughout much of Darfur—were supplemented by other particularly brutal crimes in three Wadi Saleh, Mukjar, and Shattaya localities as a form of collective punishment—and total subjugation—of the civilian population for its perceived support of the rebel movement (Human Rights Watch 2005: 11).

Understanding the nature and dimensions of this collective punishment requires a further look at the pattern of victimization associated with the rebellion in Darfur. A key to understanding the consequences of collective punishment as a counterinsurgency strategy involves seeing its impact on families.

The collective punishment of families in West Darfur

An important way of understanding the impact of the counterinsurgency policy

Table II. *Darfur families before and after attacks (Atrocities Documentation Survey, Chad, 2004)*

Settlement	Average family size before attacks	Average number of family killed	Percent males killed	Percent reporting rapes	Average family size after attacks
Abu Gumra	25.66	19.94	56	20	5.71
Al Genina	9.29	2.43	87	45	6.86
Beida	22.62	16.31	55	14	6.31
Bendesi	6.75	2.19	92	38	4.56
Foro Burunga	6.68	1.44	78	41	5.24
Garsila	6.81	1.44	96	38	5.38
Habila	8.63	2.15	90	41	6.48
Kabkabiyah	8.63	2.18	95	33	6.45
Karnoi	17.88	11.68	64	31	6.21
Koulbous	8.39	1.23	94	0	7.15
Kutum	7.51	2.44	79	26	5.07
Masteri	9.59	2.33	76	47	7.22
Seleya	7.79	1.37	87	27	6.43
Sirba	7.23	1.13	89	29	6.10
Tine	7.13	1.13	97	22	6.00
Umm Bourou	8.66	2.69	77	27	5.96
Near Karnoi	8.56	2.44	87	23	6.13
Adar	10.06	3.88	76	35	6.18
Tandubayah	6.59	0.65	72	6	5.94
Near Tine	9.33	1.87	86	0	7.47
Girgira	8.44	1.06	53	0	7.38
Near Abu Gumra	7.76	2.12	91	12	5.64
Total	10.44	4.19	69	29	6.25

of the Sudanese government in Darfur is to reconstruct the numerical changes in family composition and how they have occurred as a result of attacks on farms and villages. We do this first by looking at all 22 settlements represented by the 932 refugees interviewed in the State Department Survey in Chad. Table II provides a before and after picture of the average families in these settlements, in terms of their mean size, loss of life and experiences of rape over the 18 months before the 2004 survey.

This table indicates that across the 22 settlements, the average family size before the attacks included more than ten persons (10.44). By the time these families reached the refugee camps in Chad, however, they consisted of just over six persons (6.25)—having lost on average more than four family members (4.19). Nearly 70% of these lost family members were males (69.2%), while nearly 30% of the respondents (29.1%) reported that rapes occurred during the attacks. These latter numbers reflect a pervasive pattern of killing men and raping women. The averages are influenced by especially high numbers of reported lost family members in several settlements, most notably Abu Gumra, Beida and Karnoi. For unknown reasons, these settlements which report the highest numbers of lost family members report somewhat lower rates of rape.

The best documentation of the patterns of death, disappearances and destruction in Darfur is in the southwestern areas of West Darfur known as Wadi Salih and Mukjar. These are among the most fertile land areas of Darfur, and the Mukjar area includes the strategically important Sindu Hills where rebel forces have often sought refuge. Four settlements in this region are included in Table II: Bendesi, Foro Burunga, Garsila and Habila. Although the numbers of lost family members are somewhat lower in this area than elsewhere in Darfur, we will see that the overall destruction of African group life, which has led to an increase in rebel recruitment and activity, is overwhelming. This area thus provides an important illustration of genocidal victimization and its consequences in Darfur.

The damage to family life in the about four settlement clusters included in Table II shows a consistent pattern. On average, the family sizes varied between six and more than eight members (6.68 to 8.63) before the attacks. Families on average lost from about one to two members (1.44 to 2.19), so that after the attacks the average family ranged in size from about four to six members (4.56 to 6.48). About 40% of the respondents from these families reported that rapes occurred during the attacks on their settlements (38%–41%). Three of the four settlements reported that more than 90% of the lost family members were male, while the fourth settlement reported that 78% of those lost were male. Thus the loss of family members was pervasive, and the direct or indirect experience of rape was extensive. However, the narrative accounts we consider next make it even more clear how devastatingly comprehensive the destruction of group life was in this southwestern area of West Darfur.

The destruction of Bendesi

The town of Bendesi is an instructive example of genocidal victimization in the southern part of West Darfur. Except where otherwise indicated, the quoted interviews come from the US State Department survey referenced and described above (see also Hagan et al. 2005).

Tensions grew between Arab herders and African farmers for at least two years before intense violence broke out in this Wadi Salih locality in August of 2003. For example, a refugee interviewed in Chad reported an early attack on the village of Kaber, south of Bendesi, in December of 2002 and several times thereafter. The attackers were Arab and dressed in khaki uniforms. An Umdha (i.e. tribal leader) and several others were killed, including several children who were thrown into a nearby river. The refugee reported that during the attack 'they tried to defend themselves, and when they did they were defeated'.

Four persons were killed and cattle were taken when Kaber was hit again in June and in the first days of August

2003. A plane dropped bombs on the village in the 3 August attack. As a woman fled this attack, she 'stopped at my father's shop and found him dead and the shop looted. I also saw the body of my ex-husband. My cousin was shot too, and died later of the injury'. Another village, Bamboi, was bombed and strafed in early July, with the attacking Janjaweed militia calling their victims 'Nuba [Arab for black slave] dogs'. Another respondent reports two killings on the road to Bendesi. These 'pre-attacks' were taken as warnings, and the populations of Bendesi and Mukjar began to swell as farmers and villagers in smaller centres began to move toward what they hoped would be the safety of larger settlements (Physicians for Human Rights 2006:24).

The population of Bendesi was seven to ten thousand before widespread violence broke out in the area. The vegetation around the town is lush, and the surrounding region is a fertile growing area. In the past, Arab nomads often passed through the area and stayed with their herds near the town of Bendesi. They frequently were seen in the markets of this and surrounding towns. The town of Mukjar is located 25 kilometers to the northeast.

Arab herders have long regarded land more generally in Darfur as belonging to Allah, with rights of use and settlement contingent on mutually advantageous exchange relationships (de Waal 2006). From the farming season of approximately July to February, the nomadic herders traditionally kept their livestock off the cultivated land and on established migration routes. Farmers in the Bendesi area complained that Arab herders were increasingly allowing their livestock to graze on their crops during the growing season. The effects of desertification and scarcity of grazing opportunities likely fueled the growing tensions. In 2002, a dispute followed an attempt to negotiate this disagreement and resulted in the shooting of four African men. For the next two years, Arab groups were accused of looting and shooting African farmers in this area (Physicians For Human Rights 2006: 23–4).

The African groups of this area—who are mainly Fur but also Masaleit and Zaghawa—began to arm and defend themselves. A resident of Bendesi remarked that negotiation with the Arab herders was futile: 'Anyone who tried to dispute them was shot... Also during this time, it became very unsafe for young women to go outside the village... Many young women were beaten and raped and were killed if they refused' (Physicians For Human Rights 2006:24). The local African tribes began to secretly arm and train themselves as a defense measure. An Umdha (i.e. a ranking leader in the Fur group) reported that arms became more readily available in the area following the civil war in Chad. Local Tora Bora rebels reportedly were smuggling them across the border. These rebels also attacked the local police and army barracks. In early August, the SLA attacked and stole weapons and a radio from the Bendesi police station, killing two Arab men. Similar raids occurred in Mukjar and surrounding villages (Human Rights Watch 2005:6).

Tension mounted in the early weeks of August, 2003, as the government began to actively recruit local Arabs into more formally organized militias. There was a public call for recruits, but only Arab volunteers were taken, and Africans were explicitly turned away. Ali Kushayb, an Arab militia leader charged with crimes against humanity by the International Criminal Court, led this recruitment effort, integrating the militia members into the structure of the Public Defense Forces of the region. The local African groups identified these militias as Janjaweed, characterizing them as highwaymen and robbers—the mirror image of the Sudanese government's depiction of the Tora Bora.

Ahmed Harun, a middle-level Sudanese ministerial official responsible for Darfur and also charged with crimes against humanity by the International Criminal Court, was seen on numerous occasions during this period in the Bendesi/Mukjar area. The Umdha interviewed in the Chad refugee camp recalled that 'I was at a meeting where he announced that those that disrespected the government should be cleansed away by the government'. He reported that 'the government has a propaganda program against blacks... which tries to show that all blacks are rebels and should be fought'. Harun is identified in the interviews as the government architect of the strategy of collective punishment which held all the African civilians in the Bendesi area responsible for the scattered local rebel attacks on police stations and government installations. Harun used the analogy that these farmers and villagers were the 'water' in which the rebel 'fish' swam and survived (International Criminal Court 2007).

As noted in the Chad State Department interviews cited above, smaller villages surrounding Bendesi were attacked in the first weeks of August, in a lead-up to the assault on Bendesi on 15 August, 2003. Reports of more planned attacks circulated in the markets and among mothers and children. For example, one woman reported that 'I heard about that in the market, and also from children who heard it from Arab children while herding. They were saying, "We're going to eliminate all the Nuba and just leave the trees—we'll even eliminate the ants" (Physicians for Human Rights 2006:25). The major government-organized attack in the Bendesi area began on 15 August, 2003.

Witnesses reported to Court investigators that the Arab militia leader, Ali Kushayb, was seen leaving Mukjar on 15 August in a vehicle with Janjaweed militia (International Criminal Court 2007:73). He was seen later the same day in Bendesi in military uniform and issuing orders to the Janjaweed. The Janjaweed arrived at the Umdha's house and indicated they would be back later to collect 'zakat'—an Islamic tax. A refugee in Chad from Bendesi recalled that 'at 7 a.m., six land cruisers with mounted guns of the Sudanese military force arrived and on a loudspeaker announced that everyone had to bring their goods and be assessed for taxes in a central area'. The government troops on the land cruisers with machine guns were accompanied by Janjaweed on horses, camels and on foot. The combined force included more than 500 men.

The government troops and Janjaweed simply waited an hour or two while the people of Bendesi gathered with their possessions for 'tax collection' and then attacked. The government soldiers had land vehicles with fixed machine guns and rockets, while the Janjaweed attacked on horseback and camels. As they rode and fired into the crowd, a refugee remembered they were shouting 'Tora Bora' and 'we don't want any blacks in this area'. This woman described seeing many people killed and injured and that as she was fleeing it felt like she was 'running on dead bodies'. This same woman saw a 12-year-old girl raped by five men in Bendesi. The girl was abducted and later returned to Mukjar where the woman saw her again, now covered in blood. She died soon after.

Another refugee in Chad from a village near Bendesi counted 32 persons killed and that girls were raped, abducted, and returned days later. Although some respondents offered exact counts of persons killed and raped, others emphasized that the attacks were too chaotic and terrifying to allow such counts. A woman observed that 'they rode into the village and were screaming "exterminate the Fur, kill the Fur!". It was total destruction. I saw people dead. I saw them raping women. But I didn't have time to count how many were killed or raped' (Physicians for Human Rights 2006:25).

A sheik said he and other sheiks were arrested and accused of being Tora Bora. He described being taken to a military base and tortured. 'The conditions were terrible—37 men in a small room about four by three metres. We were all lying down, tied up, some on top of each other.' He was detained for seven days and heard later that three of the men died as a result of the torture. During the attack on his village, a mile from Bendesi, he heard Janjaweed shouting 'kill the Nubas' and that 'the young Fur and Masaleit should be eradicated'. Many fled from the area of Bendesi to Mukjar, but to little avail. For example, a refugee in Chad said 'we stayed in Mukjar... but it was very dangerous for men. I didn't leave the house because the soldiers were arresting and killing many men suspected of being rebels'.

Respondents consistently recalled hearing a mixture of racial epithets along with the allegations of being Tora Bora. A refugee who tried to flee but was caught in Bendesi described the Janjaweed saying to him 'you were at Tora Bora', which meant to him that he was from the rebel group. His captors wanted information about the sheik and information about rebels. Another respondent from a nearby village said he was told he was 'protective of the Tora Bora'.

The attack on Bendesi that began on 15 August, continued for five days, and followed a pattern that was repeated in many parts of Darfur. After the initial assault, members of the armed forces and Janjaweed went through Bendesi in a door-by-door fashion, searching for remaining residents and killing those they found. Then, over the following days, witnesses described seeing 'the attackers divide into three groups: one burned the village; one collected animals and broke into houses; and the third chased the people who were running away... Witness DFR-023 stated that she heard the attackers say that they had been sent "to kill every black thing except the Laloba and Daylabe trees which are also black" (International Criminal Court 2007:74).

During this period, and over much of the next month, rapes and killings continued. A refugee in Chad was able to identify over 50 young men who were shot and killed between 15 August and 8 September in the Bendesi area. All together, he knew of 229 men who were killed. Young men were repeatedly arrested and taken into custody, where they were often tortured. Ali Kushayb was prominently involved in the operation of police stations and military bases for these purposes.

A refugee in Chad also reported more than 30 girls were abducted and raped by the Janjaweed in the Bendesi area. 'Of these, two had their throats slit, one was strangled, and one was shot when they resisted being raped.' He indicated that Government of Sudan soldiers then took some of the women to Khartoum as a form of 'booty' and that the Governor and Deputy Governor of Mukjar were present during the attacks. The account of the rapes and the removal of women to Khartoum is widely enough known that the al Bashir government, in a rare intervention, authorized a court inquiry into the abduction of women and girls from the villages of Wadi Saleh in 2005 (Winter 2007).

Death, survival, and rebellion

The killing, abductions and the enslavement of children has long been a part of the conflict in southern Sudan, as noted in the account of the Lost Boys of Sudan above. Abductions are a smaller but still very significant part of the Darfur conflict in western Sudan. To get a measure of the magnitude of the direct impact of these crimes on young males and females in Darfur, we developed a data file from the State Department survey with the age and gender of every nuclear family member identified as killed or missing in the Chad refugee sample. We then constructed the population pyramids presented in Figure 5.

This figure makes it clear that two groups are most likely to be dead and missing from the families of refugee families: the 'fighting-age' population of African males between 15 and 29 years of age, and younger pubescent females between 5 and 14 years of age. About a third of the former young adult males as well as the latter preadolescent girls are dead or missing. This is consistent with a policy of killing the fighting-age males while raping and killing younger females. This is also consistent with an exclusionary policy that is likely to intensify rebellion among victimized groups.

Note that the policy of killing fighting-age males parallels in demographic terms the earlier pattern we observed of incarcerating the young adult leaders of drug gangs in the United States. The effect of both is to create a vacancy chain for the recruitment of remaining younger replacements. The potential pool of recruits is identified in the population pyramids presented in Figure 6 from three internal displacement camps in West Darfur. This figure displays what demographers call a 'population bulge' of adolescent males.

The German demographer Gunnar Heinsohn (2003) indicates 68 of the most populous nations of the world have

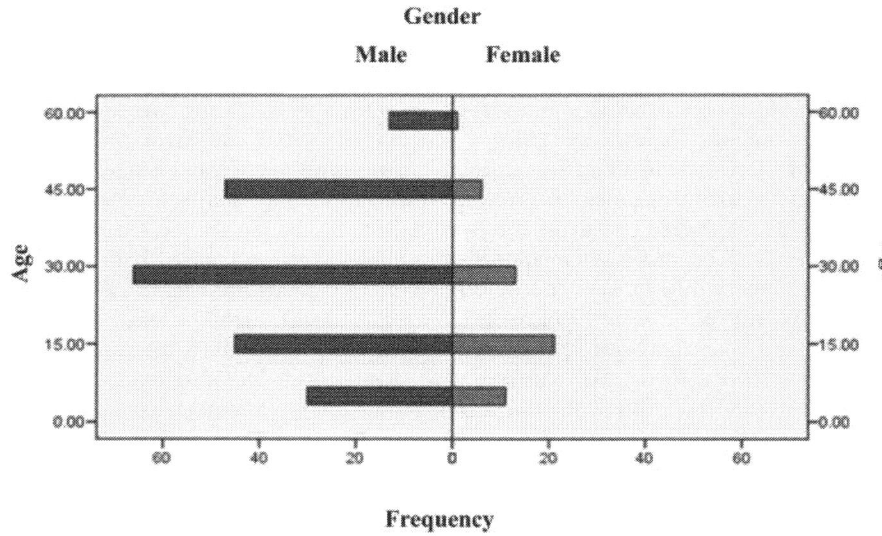

Figure 5. *Age and sex distribution of killed and missing household members (Atrocities Documentation Survey, Darfur 2004).*

adolescent bulges that will mature into 'fighting-age' bulges, and that 62 of these 68 nations are—or recently have been—characterized by high levels of violent mortality. As a result of its high birth-rate, Sudan is already among these nations. In Darfur, this pattern is intensified by the killing of fighting-age males. Criminologists, among all others, are perhaps most sensitive to the violent potential of these population dynamics. In the Global North as well as the

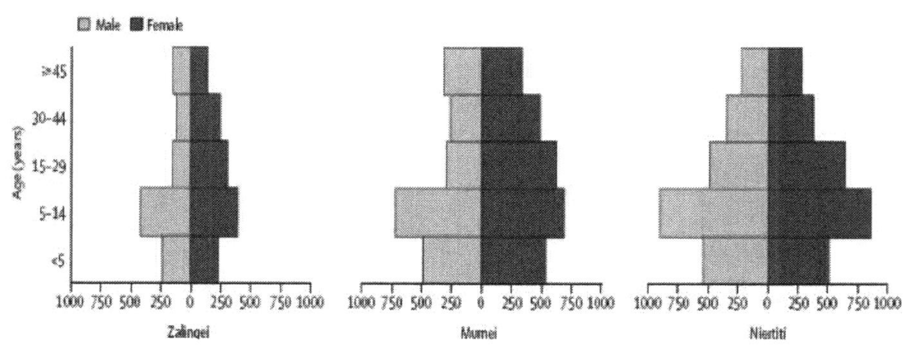

Figure 6. *Age and sex distribution of surviving household members. Reprinted from* The Lancet, *Vol. 364 No. 9442, E. Depoortere et al., Violence and Mortality in West Darfur, Sudan (2003–04): Epidemiological Evidence from Four Survey, p. 1315–1320, Copyright (2004), with permission from Elsevier.*

Global South, it is the young who are most violent and aggressive. However, they are also sensitive to further aggravating factors we have been describing, most notably, of course, the killing of parents and siblings, and the raping of pubescent girls of approximately the same ages as the surviving males. These factors combine to make an intensified rebellion predictable, with age-graded networks of recruitment and subcultural resentments playing leading roles in focusing the group-based defiance.

The International Criminal Court (2007:76) also makes clear that the raping and killing reflected in these figures was explicitly linked to issues of rebels and the demonization of the Tora Bora. This point is illustrated by the following witness report described in the Court Brief:

> DFR-023... witnessed a separate incident of rape in which Militia/ Janjaweed and members of the Armed Forces selected and led away at least ten females between 15 and 18 years of age. She watched as the girls were raped in a field nearby... While carrying out the rapes, the attackers were saying 'we have taken Tora Bora's wives, praise be to God'. At least one woman who was raped bled in the course of the assault. When this happened the rapists shot their guns into the air and announced 'I have found a virgin woman' (International Criminal Court 2007).

Despite the references to Tora Bora, the Court (78) explicitly indicates that 'no defense was mounted by the residents, and there was no rebel presence in the town when it was attacked'. The patterns we have described predict intensification of a more organized and youth-fueled rebellion.

Some residents of Bendesi and Mukjar and other settlements stayed in the general area in the following months, hoping that they could salvage some of their crops and survive this period of violent collective punishment. Kushayb and Harun were seen frequently with their troops in the area. In the fall of 2003, the Arab nomadic groups brought huge herds of their camels and other livestock into the area to graze on the newly available farmlands. This further undermined the African groups' hopes to resettle and reclaim these lands.

Ali Kushayb also undertook a program to systematically eliminate the leadership of the African groups in the fall of 2003 and winter of 2004. The 'educated persons' and Umdhas and Sheiks of these groups were taken into custody and executed. A refugee in Chad explained that 'they were told they were being taken to Garsila but we found them in a wadi about one half hour between Mukjar and Garsila. The bodies were in long lines of 20 to 50.... They had been shot—in the head, back, and waist'.

The limited number of SLA rebel forces in the area had by this time withdrawn into the nearby Sindu Hills. In February of 2004, the SLA were able to mount some successful attacks on government troops and installations. The government struck back with an unprecedented show of force:

> The SLA's presence and attacks prompted a massive response by Sudanese government forces and militias that targeted civilians and civilian

villages. By mid-March, the government's scorched earth campaign of ground and air attacks around the Sindu Hills had removed almost all existing or perceived support base for the rebellion by forcibly displacing, looting, and burning almost every Fur village near the hills and then extending 'mopping up operations' to villages and towns farther away (Human Rights Watch 2005:11).

At this point, the villages had been destroyed, and the African groups who had lived there were gone—either as a result of being killed or displaced, in large part to the refugee camps in Chad.

Before and after the government offensives

We have already presented evidence that in Bendesi and the surrounding area families lost on average one to two members. We have also seen that these losses disproportionately involved young adult men and teenage girls. This loss of life occurred in an intensely racial atmosphere that included both the shouting of racial epithets during the attacks and claims about membership and support of the Tora Bora or rebels in the area. A study of the Bendesi and surrounding area by ITERSOS (2005), for the United Humanitarian High Commissioner for Refugees, provides some final insights on the impact on families of the attacks.

Of the total number of 245 villages and towns considered in this research, about 100 were found to have been destroyed, with 8 more abandoned but not destroyed. Furthermore, in most of the destroyed or abandoned villages, nomad Arab groups had moved on to the sites and started to put the land to use for farming or grazing. This was especially true in the Mukjar area (de Montesquiou 2007).

The families and children displaced by the government offensives tend to be living in highly problematic conditions. Less than 20% of the children who have survived their ordeal are attending school. Girls are even less likely to be doing so than boys. It is estimated that about 10% of the families are very conservatively classifiable as 'vulnerable' in the whole population of this region. This figure is estimated at 25%–30% among the internally displaced. Single parenthood is the most common vulnerability, with the greater number of these families headed by a female caring alone for her children. A social norm known as 'zaka' fostered the reintegration of vulnerable children and families before the recent conflict in Darfur. This norm has lost much of its force and protective capacity in the current circumstances. These are among the many and most disturbing collateral consequences of the exclusionary armed conflict in Darfur.

The streets of the global village

Is it surprising that there are similarities as well as differences in the patterns of legal and criminal exclusion we see in the streets of the Global North and South? As distant and foreign as the streets of Bendesi in West Darfur may seem, they bear similarities and connections to the everyday world of the Global North. In revealing ways, they are as close as the contrasting images of *The Lost Boys of Sudan* and the defiant rebels of Tora Bora. It is not a coincidence that the faces of the rebel youth hiding out in the Sindu Hills nearby Bendesi—with their dreadlocks, wraparound sunglasses, and their menacing weapons—look very much like the indigenous and immigrant youth increasingly seen on the streets of the Global North. In the high-speed warp of late modern electronic technology, the mean streets of the global village overlap more closely than we often imagine.

The challenge of joining late modern domestic and foreign policies is to see common themes as well as differences. The domestic policies of exclusion in the Global North—with their legal forms of arrest, due process, conviction, and incarceration—are a world apart from the policies of criminal exclusion in the Global South—with their criminal forms of death squads, militias, disappearances, and displacements. The individualized punishments of the North offer some protection against the collective punishments of the South. One important hope is that the institutions of international criminal law can narrow the distance between these worlds. Yet both are based on punishment rather than restoration. They have notable features in common: the impulses to exclude and repress. The alternative impulses, to include and support, are elusive notwithstanding the contrasting faces of the abundance the Global North and the scarcity of the Global South. Mass incarceration and genocidal death and displacement display an awkward symmetry along the mean streets of the global village.

The fragile and disrupted families of the North parallel the destroyed and displaced families of the South. They are parallel faces of vulnerability. The mean streets of Vancouver and Bendesi are not the same, but their risks and vulnerabilities are joined by parallel and failed policies of punishment and exclusion. Their fates are joined by the shrinking distances between them. The hopeful faces of *The Lost Boys of Sudan* are reassuring but misleading alternatives to the defiant faces of the rebel youth of Tora Bora.

References

Ali-Dinar A (2004). Darfur: The Next Afghanistan? London: Darfur Information, The European-Sudanese Public Affairs Council.

Allam A, Slackman M (2005). Egypt Disperses Migrants' Camp: 23 Sudanese Die. New York Times December 31, 2005: 1.

Blumstein A (2006). The Crime Drop in America: An Exploration of Some Recent Crime Trends. Journal of Scandinavian Studies in Criminology and Crime Prevention 7(Suppl 1): 17–35.

Braithwaite J (1987). Crime, Shame and Reintegration. Cambridge: Cambridge University Press.

Braithwaite J (2002). Restorative Justice and Responsive Regulation. New York: Oxford University Press.

Cheadle D, Prendergast J (2007). Not on Our Watch: The Mission to End Genocide in Darfur and Beyond. New York: Hyperion.

de Montesquiou A (2007). Darfur Graves Unearth Evidence of Atrocities. The Moscow Times, May 28, 2007: issue 3685.

de Waal A (2006). Who Are the Darfurians? Arab and African Identities, Violence and External Engagement. Contemporary Conflicts, Social Science Research Council. New York.

El Talib H (2004). Definition and Historical Background of the Janjaweed. Sudan

Embassy in South Africa, August 21, 2004.

Fitzpatrick S (2000). Young Homeless People. New York: St. Martin's Press.

Flint J, de Waal A (2005). Darfur: A Short History of a Long War. London: Zed Books.

Foster H, Hagan J (2007). Incarceration and Intergenerational Exclusion. Social Problems 54(4): 399–433.

Gamson W (1995). Hiroshima, the Holocaust, and the Politics of Exclusion. American Sociological Review 60:1–20.

Garland D (2001). The Culture of Control. New York: Oxford University Press.

Gettleman J (2007). The Perfect Weapon for the Meanest Wars. New York Times, April 29, 2007, section 4, P.

Hagan J (1993). The Social Embeddedness of Crime and Unemployment. Criminology 31:465–91.

Hagan J, Dinovitzer R (1999). Children of the Prison Generation: Collateral Consequences of Imprisonment for Children and Communities. Crime and Justice 26:121–62.

Hagan J, McCarthy B (1997). Mean Streets: Youth Crime and Homelessness. Cambridge: Cambridge University Press.

Hagan J, Rymond-Richmond W, Parker P (2005). The Criminology of Genocide: The Death and Rape of Darfur. Criminology 43:525–62.

Heinsohn G (2003). Söhne und Weltmacht. [Sons and World Power]. Zurich: Orell Fuessli Verlag.

Herbert B (2007). Arrested While Grieving. The New York Times, May 26, 2007.

Human Rights Watch (2004). Darfur Destroyed: Ethnic Cleansing by Government and Militia Forces in Western Sudan. New York: Human Rights Watch.

Human Rights Watch (2005). Targeting the Fur: Mass Killings in Darfur. A Human Rights Watch Briefing Paper, January 21, 2005, New York.

International Criminal Court (2007). Situation in Darfur, The Sudan. 27 February 2007.

ITERSOS (2005). Return-Oriented Profiling in the Southern Part of West Darfur and Corresponding Chadian Border Area. Geneva: United Nations High Commissioner for Refugees, July, 2005.

Lemert E (1967). Human Deviance, Social Problems and Social Control. Englewood Cliffs: Prentice-Hall.

Liu Institute for Global Issues (2006). Human Security Brief 2006. Human Security Centre, Liu Institute for Global Issues, Vancouver, Canada: The University of British Columbia.

Losel F, Schumucker M (2005). The Effectiveness of Treatment of Sex Offenders: A Comprehensive Meta-Analysis. Journal of Experimental Criminology 1:117–46.

Moffit T (1993). Adolescence-Limited and Life Course Persistent Anti-Social Behavior: A Developmental Taxonomy. Psychological Review 100:674–701.

Osgood W, Foster EM, Flanagan C, Ruth G (2005). On Your Own Without a Net: The Transition to Adulthood for Vulnerable Populations. Chicago: University of Chicago Press.

Petersen A, Tullin L-L (2006). The Scorched Earth of Darfur: Patterns in Death and Destruction Reported by the People of Darfur, January 2001–September 2005. Copenhagen: Bloodhound.

Physicians For Human Rights (2006). Darfur: Assault on Survival. Cambridge: Massachusetts.

Sherman L (1993). Defiance, Deterrence, and Irrelevance: A Theory of the Criminal Sanction. Journal of Research in Crime and Delinquency 30:445–73.

Winter J (2007). Probe of Darfur 'Slavery' Starts. BBC News, March 21, 2007.

PROFESSOR JOHN HAGAN
Northwestern University American Bar Foundation
Department of Sociology
1810 Chicago Avenue
Evanston
Illinois 60201
USA
Tel: +1-847 491-5688
Fax: +1-847 491-9907
Email: j-hagan@northwestern.edu

Part II
Power, Harm and Crime: Global Actors and Crimes of Globalization

[6]

Crimes of Globalization: Health Care, HIV and the Poverty of Neoliberalism in Sub-Saharan Africa*

*Ifeanyi EZEONU***

ABSTRACT

This paper contributes to the growing body of literature on crimes of globalization. Following a broader conceptualization of crime which goes beyond the proscriptions of the criminal law, it argues that the dynamics of market economics has criminogenic (social harm) effects, especially in economically-challenged regions like the sub-Saharan Africa. The paper challenges the hegemony of law in the criminalization process by locating social harm at the epicentre of criminological inquiry.

Keywords: Crimes of globalization, neoliberalism, heterodox criminology, social harm, sub-Saharan Africa

---

* I am grateful to Professors Andrew Okolie (Columbia University, New York), Emmanuel Koku (Drexel University, Philadelphia) and Jonah Butovsky (Brock University, St. Catharines, Canada) for critiquing the earlier drafts of this paper.

** Brock University

Introduction

Studies in "crimes of globalization" are part of the growing heterodoxies of contemporary criminology (see, Friedrichs, 2007; Friedrichs and Friedrichs, 2002; Rothe et al 2006; Wright and Muzzatti, 2007). Driven by the epistemological framework of critical criminology, these studies are rooted on the argument that many of the policies of the Bretton Woods institutions (and the World Trade Organization) cause enormous harm to people in different parts of the world and that these harms could be classified as crime "whether or not specific violations of international or state law are involved" (Friedrichs and Friedrichs, 2002: 16). This position follows the suggestion by scholars who believe that the violation of laws should not constitute the nucleus of criminological inquiry (see, Ezeonu, 2007; Kauzlarich and Friedrichs, 2003; Friedrichs and Friedrichs, 2002; Barak, 1991).

Sociological criminology often treats the powers of the state to criminalize behaviours as sacrosanct. Thus, criminologists of this school and criminal justice bureaucrats have exerted scholarly and policy energies on studying and trying to address the commission of those acts criminalized by the state, and the omission of those obligations demanded by it through its criminal law. A corollary of this legalistic definition of crime is that offences such as murder, rape, burglary, assault, and the likes as well as the lawless individuals who commit these offences often come to mind when most people think about crime. However, the increasing heterodoxies of the contemporary criminological literature challenge the orthodox meta-narratives which tie criminal behaviours strictly to the letters of a state's domestic criminal law or the legislative activities of the state (Ezeonu, 2007). One of the nascent areas of these heterodoxies emerged under the canopy of "crimes of globalization".

Although crimes of the state and corporations have largely been studied over the years (Sutherland, 1940, 1961; Barak, 1991; Friedrichs, 1998; Reiman, 1996), crimes committed under the direction, instigation, and/or supervision of international financial institutions such as the IMF, the World Bank and the WTO are often discussed largely as economic policy failures (Ezeonu, 2000, 2003; Ezeonu and Okolie, 2001) even though they sometimes result in the loss of millions of lives and cause physical and psychological harm. Borrowing Galtung's (1969) and Farmer's (2004) concept of "structural violence", this paper contributes to the growing body of literature which treats the devastating social harms caused by particular forms of domestic and global capitalist arrangements as criminal. Although the works of Galtung (1969) and Farmer (2004) are relatively unknown in criminological literature, an emerging heterodoxy in the discipline evokes their argument and calls for the broadening of the criminological imagination to include economic-driven social harms (Kauzlarich and Friedrichs, 2003; Friedrichs and Friedrichs, 2002, Hillyard and Tombs, 2004; Tombs and Hillyard, 2004). This paper looks at how neoliberal policies contribute to the crises of poverty, health care provisions and the HIV/AIDS pandemic in sub-Saharan Africa.

The paper is divided into three principal sections. The first section discusses neoliberalism as the bedrock of the contemporary global economic practice, while the second section challenges the hegemony of the criminal law in defining criminal behaviours and suggests an elastic definition of crime that incorporates issues of social harm and justice. The third section reviews the operation of neoliberal economic policies in sub-Saharan Africa and argues that the complicities of these policies in the victimisation of vulnerable population, especially the poor, bring the policies and the institutions that enforce them within the interrogative lens of critical criminology.

Neoliberalism and the Age of Globalization

Since the Europeans set out to "discover", conquer and dominate the world some 500 years ago, capitalism has brought ideas, capital, labour and other resources across nations and cultures together. So, what is today known as globalization is not entirely new (Peet, 2003). However, "the intensification" of this global social relations (Giddens, 1990: 64) and the "overwhelming sense of *compression* of our spatial and temporal worlds" (Harvey, 1989: 240) seem to create "a new sense of globalism" (Peet, 2003: 1). Although there are competing definitions of the concept of globalization, I focus on its economic or market form - i.e., the imposition of neoliberal economic policies and priorities on the world principally through the organizational frameworks and activities of the economic tripod: the International Monetary Fund (IMF), the International Bank for Reconstruction and Development (otherwise known as the World Bank), and the General Agreement on Tariffs and Trade, GATT (and its successor institution, the World Trade Organization). Thus, this paper is couched on the contextualization of globalization "in terms of world trade, capital flows, FDI[1], integration of national economies, the expansion of multinational and transnational corporations or the expansion of capitalism" (Smith, 2003: xviii). The tool for achieving these objectives is the economic policy known as neoliberalism.

---

1 FDI is an acronym for Foreign Direct Investment

This policy is aimed at breaking down political borders on behalf of the market, pulling back the state from economic activities and creating the enabling environment for the forces of the market to regulate economic activities.

Neoliberalism is predicated on the belief that economic behaviour, across time and space, follows the strictures of economic rationality (Marshall, 1996; Ezeonu, 2000, 2003; Ezeonu and Okolie, 2001). It is a modern version of Adam Smith's classical economics. Adam Smith and the 19th century classical economists believed that economic growth could only be stimulated and sustained if private individuals were allowed to pursue their self-interests unhindered by the state. In his highly-acclaimed book, *The Wealth of Nations*, Smith (1937) suggested that left on its own, capitalism would operate on a rationality which makes possible the transformation of individual selfish interests into public virtue. "Virtue" in this context is "interpreted as an efficiently organized, growing economy capable of providing benefits for everyone" (Peet, 2003: 4).

However, the claims of classical economists were weakened by the economic devastations of the post-World War I period which resulted in the Great Depression. The social chaos created by this global economic depression exposed the weakness of the type of untrammelled capitalism advocated by Adam Smith and created the background for the emergence of a social economics known as Keynesianism. Unlike classical economics which emphasized economic growth and the creation of private wealth with the belief that it would improve public good, Keynesianism focused on human welfare and argued for the intervention of the state in economic activities in order to achieve this objective. The Keynesian economics stressed the crucial role of the state as a moderating institution in economic development, especially through its investments in public infrastructure and the development of human capital. However, pro-market economists and political leaders have since undermined the social economics of Keynesianism and revived the classical economic thinking which is now repackaged as neoliberalism.

The emergence of neoliberal economic thinking was particularly aided by the growth in influence of market-friendly economists such as Milton Friedman and Friedrich von Hayek, and the assumption of office of such pro-market politicians as Margaret Thatcher in the United Kingdom and Ronald Reagan in the United States. As an undergraduate at Oxford, Margaret Thatcher had read and been influenced by the economic ideas of Friedrich von Hayek. Similarly, Ronald Reagan was a strong believer in market economics and in an address to the World Bank in 1983, he had claimed that the "belief in the magic of the marketplace" was the most common factor among "all societies that achieved the most spectacular, broad-based economic progress in the shortest possible time" (Peet, 2003: 13). With the degree of political and economic power commanded by these two politicians in the late 1970s and the 1980s and the influence of their countries over the Bretton Woods institutions, the globalization of neoliberal policies became almost inevitable. This was greatly aided by the liberal reforms of the Soviet politics under Mikhail Gorbachev and the eventual collapse of the country.

Neoliberal economists believe that underdevelopment in poor countries is a factor of poor resource allocation due to unnecessary state intervention in economic activities and improper pricing policies. They claim that for a country to stimulate economic efficiency and growth, it has to encourage free market competition, privatise state-owned enterprises, promote free trade and export expansion, welcome foreign capital investments, and eliminate several government regulations and price distortions in factor, product, and financial markets. They posit that the straight and narrow path to economic efficiency and growth is, in fact, to dismantle the benevolent and interventionist roles of the state (see, Todaro, 1997; Ezeonu, 2000, 2003).

Crimes of Globalization: Challenging the Hegemony of the Criminal Law

The nascent area of criminology broadly described as the "crimes of globalization" developed from the belief by some critical criminologists that a scholarly focus on social harm is crucial in broadening the frontiers of criminological inquiry (Friedrichs and Friedrichs, 2002; Friedrichs, 2007; Wright and Muzzati, 2007). A major trend in traditional criminological literature is the contextualization of crime in terms of the violation of a country's criminal law. Such a violation may involve the commission of an act prohibited by the criminal code of a state or a failure to perform an obligation demanded by the criminal code. In other words, for an act or an omission to be a crime, its definition and punishment must be clearly stated in the criminal code. Even the much-celebrated introduction of white-collar crime to the criminological literature by Sutherland (1961) was hinged on "violations of law by persons in the upper socio-economic class" in the course of performing their occupational duties (Sutherland, 1961: 9). Such laws mentioned by Sutherland include "laws regarding restraint of trade, misrepresentation in advertising, infringement of patents and analogous rights…unfair labour practices" as well as "those relating to rebates or adulteration of food and drugs" (Sutherland, 1961: 29-30). So, although

Sutherland expanded the scope of criminological inquiry beyond the traditional focus on street crimes and criminals, and brought attention to the illegal activities of powerful individuals pursuing organizational goals, his analysis was equally hinged on legalistic framework.

Over the years, the legal definition of crime has featured prominently in the literature of traditional sociological criminology. However, one issue commonly neglected by traditional criminologists and policy makers is that most laws (including criminal laws) are political instruments embodying the values of the dominant class, race, gender, and other social groups in society. Despite the celebration of laws as equalitarian instruments enacted for the benefits of all members of society, history has shown that laws have sometimes served as instruments of repression, exclusion and domination, and that some legislations prohibiting or legalising certain behaviours may sometimes be intended to serve the interests of particular groups or to undermine other groups. This truism is exemplified in the Jim Crow laws of the United States, the Nazi laws of Hitler's Germany, the apartheid laws of South Africa, the laws of colonial and military occupations and the androcentric laws of most states. For instance, Hitler's Germany used a set of state laws to galvanize the people to commit some of the most-publicized crimes of the 20th Century and the Jim Crow segregationist social structure in the United States and the atrocities of apartheid in South Africa were encouraged and defended through state laws. Even in today's criminological literature, homicide scholarship substantially fails to acknowledge the criminality of murderers in the United States who lynched many African Americans for violating the Jim Crow laws or for challenging the social psychology of the American racial hierarchy of the pre-1970s. As Quinney (1978: 40) puts it, "the role of law in society is vastly different from what we have been led to believe in our mythology".

In their scholarly focus on the behaviours prohibited or demanded by the criminal code, some traditional criminologists often ignore, underemphasize or trivialize the role of power relations in the emergence of laws and the definitions of crime. However, their fundamental assumptions and scholarships are increasingly challenged by critical criminologists who reject the hegemony of the criminal code as the sole parameter for determining criminal behaviours and emphasize issues of power and social inequality in the criminalization and criminal justice processes (Schwartz and Hatty, 2003;

Lynch and Groves, 1989; Kauzlarich and Friedrichs, 2003).[2] Other scholars (see, Hillyard and Tombs, 2004; Tombs and Hillyard, 2004) have even called for the disbandment of academic criminology and the establishment of a new discipline around the broader problem of "social harm" as one way of addressing the limitations of traditional criminology.

Tombs and Hillyard (2004: 44) observe that the neoliberal market dynamics produce perhaps "the most extensive and far-reaching harms", a fact which traditional criminology has, over the years, failed to address. However, criminologists of globalization have since the early 2000 focused attention on social harms emanating from the global domination of market forces. For instance, Friedrichs and Friedrichs (2002: 16) hinged their study on the understanding that,

> *If the policies and practices of an international institution such as the World Bank result in avoidable, unnecessary harm to an identifiable population…then crime in a meaningful sense has occurred, whether or not specific violations of international or state law are involved.*

This argument is in line with those espoused by theorists of "structural violence" (Galtung, 1969; Farmer, 2004) whose works are relatively unknown in criminology. These scholars contextualize structural violence as insidious ways in which a particular social structure decimates vulnerable populations by systematically denying them access to the most basic human needs. Arguing that "the arrangements are *structural* because they are embedded in the political and economic organization of our social world", Farmer and his colleagues argue that this inequitable social structure puts the poor in harms' way by constraining their agency in trying to survive the limitations imposed by the social structure (Farmer, 2004; Farmer et al, 2006: 1686). He uses this theory to explain the epidemiology of HIV and tuberculosis in Haiti, and names other fatal effects of the violence as death, injury, illness, subjugation, and stigmatization, among others (see, Farmer 2004).

The critical criminology literature has since expanded to accommodate this line of thinking (see, Rothe et al, 2004; Wright and Muzzatti, 2007; Friedrichs, 2007). So, it has become acceptable among a growing number of criminologists that neoliberalism could have criminogenic effects. Friedrichs

---

2 One critical deficiency of the legal definition of crime is that an atrocious behaviour cannot be called a crime unless it is expressly prohibited by the state. Yet many of such behaviours are very rarely outlawed

(2007: 149), therefore, conceptualizes crimes of globalization as harmful "consequences of policy decisions of high-level officials of major financial institutions and government agencies who are attempting to realize positive outcomes (or avoid losses)" in the advancement of a global market-based economy. He argues that, "although *it is not typically their specific intent to cause harm,* their policy decisions can have devastating financial and human consequences for large numbers of especially vulnerable people" (Friedrichs, 2007: 149, emphasis mine). This definition deviates radically from the purely legalistic conception of crime, because apart from focusing on the problem of social harm (a deviation first introduced by Sutherland, 1940), it gives little weight to criminal intent (*mens rea*) as an intrinsic quality of a criminal behaviour. Crimes of globalization, therefore, do not necessarily require a violation of a law or the establishment of an offender's guilty mind. In this sense, criminologists of globalization have moved criminological discourse increasingly away from law and legalism in pursuit of the objective problems of market-generated social harms and injustice. Crimes of globalization are, therefore, contextualized as the harmful consequences to vulnerable populations of the economic policies of the international financial institutions such as the IMF, World Bank, and the WTO. These consequences often result from massive deregulation of economic activities and the withdrawal of states from participating actively in such activities (*see the formula below*):

$$C_g = \sum(c[{}_mD + {}_mS])$$

where,

C_g = *crimes of globalization*

c = *harmful consequences to vulnerable populations*

${}_mD$ = *massive deregulation*

${}_mS$ = *minimal state*

The Poverty of Neoliberalism in Sub-Saharan Africa

The IMF, World Bank, GATT (and its successor institution, WTO) have historically been used to advance and sustain the neoliberal experiment, especially in developing economies. This is particularly true of sub-Saharan Africa, where continuing economic crisis and increasing poverty have supported the desire for alternative economic policies to the state-led ones. Although neoliberal policies, as currently packaged, are not the sole cause of economic woes in sub-Saharan Africa, the desire to open up the African market and resources for Western exploitation (which earlier manifested in trans-Atlantic slave trade and colonialism) was foundational to the economic crisis confronting the continent. This foundation of exploitation has historically been aided by some home-grown crises such as corrupt and inept leadership, dictatorships, ethnic crises, civil wars and analogous conflicts, political instability, among others. In other words, African leaders have contributed to the problems of the continent through their greed, ineptitude and political rascality. However, the activities of the IMF, World Bank and GATT/WTO have particularly been devastating for the continent commonly seen as the poorest in the world. Often working in tandem with corrupt leadership in many African countries, these international financial institutions have failed to deliver the promised economic "El Dorado" to the long-suffering people of the continent. It has, in fact, been documented that the policies promoted by these institutions have actually worsened the social conditions of many Africans (see, Ezeonu, 2003, 2000; Okolie, 2003; Ezeonu and Okolie, 2001).

The IMF and the World Bank (jointly referred to as the Bretton Woods institutions) came into being in 1944 as part of the multilateral agreements entered into at Bretton Woods, New Hampshire, to regulate international trade and economic relations, and to help rebuild post-World War II global economies. The IMF was established to regulate international exchange rates among currencies and to maintain international financial stability by offering loans to member states undergoing balance of payment crisis. The World Bank, on the other hand, was set up to help eradicate global poverty, by aiding the rebuilding of those industrialized economies ravaged by World War II and strengthening the economies of poorer countries. This mission is succinctly captured in its motto: "Our dream is a world without poverty" (Kawachi and Wamala, 2007: 11, quoting Stiglitz, 2002; see also, Evans and Newnham, 1992). The mission of the World Bank could be said to have been realized in respect of the first objective, i.e., the facilitation of the post-war reconstruction of industrialized economies. However, in respect of developing economies, its mission has achieved minimal results - a fact demonstrated by the lingering poverty in sub-Saharan Africa where it (alongside the IMF) has dominated economic policies for more than two decades.

The structural adjustment programme was the common policy used by the IMF and the World Bank to "reform" the economies of most African countries in the 1980s and the 1990s (Engberg-Pedersen et al, 1996). This policy was aimed at creating a friendly environment for private enterprises by reducing state involvement in economic activities. Structural adjustment was, therefore, a policy framework for trade, financial and market liberalization. Trade liberalization entails such policies as the promotion of international trade through the elimination of government subsidies to export goods, the removal of import controls and currency devaluation. Financial liberalization involves the removal of restrictions or regulations of foreign capital moving in and out of the country, as well as, the liberalization of the domestic financial markets (such as the removal of government controls on interest rates and the privatization of the banking sector). Market liberalization includes the liberalization of prices that affect labour and capital (such as wages and interest rates), the elimination of price controls through the abolition of institutions as state marketing boards, and the removal of government subsidies to indigenous farmers and manufacturers. Other policies promoted by structural adjustment programmes include the privatization of state-run enterprises, the reduction in the size of the civil service (usually through massive retrenchment of workers) and the introduction of user fees in key sectors, including education and healthcare (Ezeonu, 2003: 2000).

Similarly, following the Uruguay Round Agreements of the last GATT trade negotiations which require greater liberalization of international trade, sub-Saharan African countries have become unequal partners in a global economy driven by market forces and imposed by the world's biggest economies, especially the United States and the European Union. The institutional framework for enforcing the Uruguay Round agreements is the World Trade Organization (WTO). This institution has replaced GATT as a forum for multilateral trade negotiations. In its relatively short existence, the WTO, especially the philosophy behind its establishment, has become a subject of controversy, derision, praise and protests. Its secretive, unrepresentative, undemocratic and unfair methods of conducting its business and its double-standard approach to free trade have been sources of tensions among states and non-state actors. One of the most criticized policies initiated under the Uruguay Round of trade agreements is the TRIPS agreement. Though originally intended to encourage innovation, the TRIP agreement favours powerful multinational corporations (especially, pharmaceutical companies) at the expense of poor people in the developing world, whose access to life-saving drugs has become increasingly restricted (Kawachi and Wamala, 2007; Ezeonu and Okolie, 2003).

The conditions created by the neoliberal agenda to which African countries have been subjected over the years often have devastating effects on the vulnerable population of the region, especially the poor, women and children. For instance, one criticism commonly levied against structural adjustment programmes in the region is that they were insensitive to local circumstances and that in rolling back state expenditure in such an important sector as the health care, the few health care options available to the poor have become even more limited (see, Engberg-Pederson, 1996). This situation has been exacerbated by the requirements of the Uruguay Round's Trade-Related Investment Measures (TRIMS) which even advances the neoliberal agenda further, and the Trade-Related Intellectual Property Rights (TRIPS) agreements which limit the access of many Africans to drug curtails needed to manage health crisis, especially the HIV/AIDS. O'Manique (2004: 79) argues that the HIV/AIDS pandemic in sub-Saharan Africa, "graphically illustrates not only the fallacy of the market mechanism as the most efficient, beneficent arbiter of wealth and life chances, but also the hypocrisy of those who stand behind the ideology of free market". He observes that the extension of the neoliberal paradigm to the developing world, such as sub-Saharan Africa, has contributed to the "deeper problem of the commodification of basic human necessities" which he argues "has life-and-death implications" for vulnerable populations.

In fact, the implementation of neoliberal policies in sub-Saharan Africa has had some worrisome criminogenic (social harm) effects. Firstly, neoliberalism encourages massive retrenchment of workers from the public service and the pauperization of those who survive the retrenchment. Most of the retrenched workers have families and dependents to support. They, therefore, often desperately seek alternative employments to meet their financial obligations. Many of them, especially the men, sometimes migrate farther away from their families in search of work opportunities. While living away from their spouses, they sometimes patronize commercial sex workers, many of whom are HIV positive. On occasional visits to their families, their spouses potentially become exposed to the virus (see, O'Manique, 2004). Also, the spouses left behind may engage in extra-marital affairs themselves for material or emotional support, and where these sexual relationships are unsafe, they (and eventually their husbands) may also become exposed to HIV infection. Thus, studies have established a close association between labour migration and HIV infection (Becker, 1990; Hunter, 1989; Brummer, 2002). In this case, such labour migration may be motivated by loss of jobs, a condition made possible by the implementation of neoliberal policy.

Similarly some female workers retrenched from the public service, in desperation for survival, resort to commercial sex work. Hunter (2003) calls this type of sexual liaison "survival sex" (27), and suggests that "sex is a major part of the economy for poor women" (28). She argues that some poor women "form steady, sometimes clandestine, relationships with relatively wealthy men in the hope that it will bring them some material benefits" such as their children's school fees. Sometimes "sex is the only currency these poor women have" to confront their destitute situation (Hunter, 2003: 28 quoting Epstein, 2002: 43; see also, O'Manique, 2004). In the light of their squalid economic conditions, many of the women who engage in survival sex often find themselves in positions of disadvantage in negotiating protective sex with their clients or financial patrons. This has enormous implications for HIV transmission considering the vast population of men served by these women, and the fact that some of the men concerned are married. Krieger (2007: 658) emphasizes the effect of poverty on public health, warning that "epidemiologists cannot afford to ignore poverty" in trying to understand the etiology and distribution of diseases.

Perhaps no single issue has attracted more controversy in the discourse of neoliberalism in sub-Saharan Africa than the debates over access to health care. Firstly, neoliberal policies, such as the structural adjustment programmes, require states to download the cost of medical care to individual citizens, so as to free up government funds for debt servicing. The implementation of these policies results in budget cuts to the health sector, and the introduction of user-fees for medical services. With high level of poverty and redundancies in the public sector, citizens often find it difficult to access health care. Individuals with life-threatening diseases become the victims of this experimental economics of health commodification. With respect to the HIV pandemic, access to drugs becomes particularly problematic since "drug therapies costing $10,000 to $20,000 per year are essentially irrelevant in countries where the total per capita spending on health care is perhaps $2 or $3" (Brigham, 1997: 48-49). For instance, it is documented that in Tanzania where more than a million children have been orphaned as a result of AIDS, the government expenditure on health care stands merely at around US$3.20 per person per annum. Meanwhile, under increasing pressure from the International Monetary Fund (IMF), this same government "spends in excess of three times more on debt servicing than it does on health care" (World Development Movement, 2006). Also, as part of the adjustment conditionality in such countries as Zimbabwe, Tanzania, Uganda, and Ghana user fees were introduced in the health sectors, thereby pushing a great percentage of medical expenditures to individuals, irrespective of their employment or income statuses. One obvious outcome of this policy, for instance in Zimbabwe, was the tendency for the poor not to access treatment (Engberg-Pedersen et al, 1996).

Adjustment conditionality also encourages mass retrenchment and salary freeze in the public health sector, thereby exacerbating the public health crisis in many parts of Africa. Health professionals, who are retrenched or have poor salaries and uncertain future, often migrate in great numbers to the more economically viable countries of the West in search of greener pastures. Hogstedt et al (2007) observe that health care professionals represent an essential part of economic migrants in many Western countries, especially as the aging population in these countries creates the need for increasing health care and services. This need has led to massive recruitments of health care professionals from developing countries, including Africa. Statistics show that foreign-trained nurses constitute 23% of the entire nursing workforce in New Zealand in 2002; 6% in Canada in 2001; 8% in Ireland in 2002; and 4% in the United States in 2000. Between 1998 and 2003, the population of newly registered foreign-trained nurses grew rapidly in the United States. Many of these nurses came from sub-Saharan Africa, where conditions created by the neoliberal experiment, among other factors, have made economic migration irresistible. In 1998/1999, the population of newly registered foreign-trained nurses in the United Kingdom were 179 (from Nigeria), 52 (Zimbabwe), 40 (Ghana), 19 (Kenya), 15 (Zambia), 6 (Mauritius) and 4 (Botswana). However, by 2002/2003, the numbers have risen to 509 (Nigeria), 485 (Zimbabwe), 251 (Ghana), 152 (Kenya), 133 (Zambia), 59 (Mauritius), 57 (Malawi) and 39 (Botswana) (see, Batata, 2005: 1, 5; Aiken et al, 2004). Perhaps, there are more African-trained nurses and midwives working in the United States and Western Europe today than those working in the continent and many of those still "trapped" in sub-Saharan Africa are determined to join the economic exodus to the West.

All the countries mentioned above have experimented with structural adjustment programmes, and are today unequal partners in a global market economy supervised by powerful Western countries through their institutional surrogate, the World Trade Organization. A keen observer of the African political scene may argue that the migration of African nurses and other public health professionals to the West can be accounted for by political instability in most African countries, such as Zimbabwe (under Robert Mugabe) and Nigeria (where public service was made unattractive by decades of military dictatorships, and where crime rate has gone up astronomically). However, such an argument cannot hold of Mauritius, Zambia, Ghana and Botswana, where national politics has been relatively stable.

Similarly, sub-Saharan Africa experiences rapid depletion of physicians, many of whom immigrate to Western countries in search of better working conditions. Studies show that many English-speaking OECD countries[3] have benefited from the migration of foreign-trained physicians. For instance, the Southern African Migration Project (2006) reports that the number of sub-Saharan African-trained physicians (especially from South Africa and Nigeria) practising in Canada has increased between 1993 and 2003. According to this report, within this period, South African-trained physicians working in Canada have increased by more than 60%, while the number from Nigeria has more than tripled. Again, one may argue that other factors, such as the post-apartheid politics or high crime rate in South Africa or political instability, high crime rate or corruption in Nigeria, explain this migration. However, one common reason given in this report is economic survival, since these physicians "do not earn enough in their countries" of origin (see, p.21). In fact, Chikanda (2006) traces the migration of African public health professionals to low salaries and poor working conditions resulting from the disastrous implementation of Structural Adjustment Programmes (SAPs) in many of these countries. Nevertheless, not all health professionals from Africa are lucky to find jobs in their chosen professions. African physicians who work as taxi drivers and private security guards are becoming common sights in Western countries. This shows a pragmatism to survive at the lowest edges of Western economies rather than work as poorly-remunerated physicians in their countries of origin.

The increasing migration of African health professionals has worsened the already severe shortage of health workers in the continent. Apart from the economic loss of training these professionals, these migrations also affect health promotion, disease prevention and diagnoses, as well as, treatment and rehabilitation of sick people (Kirigia, et al, 2006). In a continent suffering a number of health epidemics and devastated by the HIV/AIDS pandemic, the depletion in the population of health workers contributes to high mortality rates. The World Health Organization's 2006 annual report documents that of the 57 countries that have the most critical shortage of health service providers, 36 are in sub-Saharan Africa (World Health Organization, 2006: 12-13). In this market dynamic, the ultimate loser is the average poor African whose options in respect of health care are increasingly limited.

---

[3] OECD is the short form for the Organization of Economic Co-operation and Development. It is made up of 30 mostly wealthy countries operating market economies. The current membership includes Australia, Austria, Belgium, Canada, Czech Republic, Denmark, Finland, France, Germany, Greece, Hungary, Iceland, Ireland, Italy, Japan, Korea, Luxembourg, Mexico, Netherlands, New Zealand, Norway, Poland, Portugal, Slovak republic, Spain, Sweden, Switzerland, Turkey, United Kingdom, and the United States.

Chikanda (2006) observes that the depletion of African health professionals through economic migration has worsened the management of HIV/AIDS pandemic in the continent, especially in the light of the increased workload of health personnel who remain behind. He argues that the increasing migration of these professionals to the West has also largely affected the overall quality of health care available to African people, especially those who rely on public health services. This falling standard of health care is "largely attributed to low morale resulting from... excessive workload associated with the stress of dealing with so many dying patients" (Chikanda, 2006: 675). In fact, the deregulation of the health sector in many poor African states, no doubt, contributes to the high mortality rates in the continent.

Another area of concern regarding the harmful consequences of neoliberalism in Africa is in respect of Trade-Related Intellectual Property Rights (TRIPS) agreed upon at the Uruguay Round of the General Agreements on Tariffs and Trade (GATT). Intellectual property rights are exclusive rights granted to inventors or innovators to prevent others from appropriating their inventions, designs, innovations, or creations without permission and/or compensation (see, World Trade Organization, 1998). At the GATT Uruguay Round of trade negotiations, intellectual properties (i.e., all creations of the mind that have monetary values) became internationally recognised as private commodities, which deserve the same level of protection accorded private property, and member states were enjoined to formulate or amend their domestic laws in accordance with this objective.

However, the implementation of the intellectual property rights in poor African countries has shown clearly the oft-harmful nature of free market economics. Confronted with an escalating increase in HIV infection and the high cost of drugs needed to manage this disease, South Africa produced generic versions of these drugs to provide cheaper access to medication to its teeming population of HIV patients. One of these drugs is Azidothymidine (AZT), an antiretroviral drug which helps to prevent the transmission of HIV from a mother to her unborn child. However, this action was challenged by US-based pharmaceutical companies which accused South Africa of patent rights violations. These companies were supported by the United States government which claimed that the country was losing more than $2.5 million per annum in royalties not paid to its pharmaceutical companies (O'Manique, 2004: 84). It threatened economic sanctions against South Africa for using these "home-made generic versions" of the drugs to reduce the cost of treatment from $10,000 to $300 per individual, per year. A number of U.S.-based pharmaceutical companies actually went to court to block the South African government from making these cheaper versions of the drugs available to its population. The legal challenge attracted public indignation, and facing massive opposition from the international civil society, the pharmaceutical companies dropped the lawsuits.

In all of these litigations, the interest of the United States government and pharmaceutical companies was profit maximization, as dictated by free market economics. It did not matter that this objective would be achieved at the expense of millions of lives and monumental misery in South Africa and other countries which benefit from the cheaper versions of the medications. It was even more disheartening considering the fact that poor people, especially in sub-Saharan Africa, were often used as guinea pigs in testing the potency of most of these drugs. For example, 160 South Africans were among the 3,500 AIDS patients on whom Hoffman La Roche tested its HIV drug, Seuinivir (Johnston and Nicoll, 1997).

The United States government and pharmaceutical companies based their opposition to South Africa's production of generic versions of HIV drugs on the argument that South Africa violated the TRIPS agreements negotiated under the Uruguay Round. However, the TRIPS agreements were largely imposed by powerful industrialised countries (the US, the EU, Japan and Canada) on the rest of the world to promote and protect their economic interests. Equally, multinational corporations such as the U.S.-based firms, Pfizer and IBM, played crucial roles in bringing up and influencing the issue of intellectual property rights at the Uruguay Round of trade negotiations (O'Manique, 2004). These agreements are, therefore, akin to unjust laws imposed by one powerful social group over another, and as Zinn (1997) would argue, there is no moral justification to obey them.

Moreover, the United Nations Commission on Human Rights (2004) has declared access to essential medicine as a fundamental human right, and enjoins member states "to do all it reasonably can to make an essential medicine available in its jurisdiction". The right to health specified by this Commission requires that "health facilities, goods and services shall be *available, accessible* and of *good quality*" and that "whether publicly or privately provided, the essential medicine must be affordable to all, not just the well-off". It also enjoins states to take every necessary measure to prevent third parties from interfering with this fundamental right (UNCHR, 2004: 10-11). These important human rights provisions no doubt overshadow the logic of patent rights protection in the health sector, especially in an economically-challenged region like sub-Saharan Africa.

Although the TRIPS agreements made some provisions which authorize member states to "adopt measures necessary to protect public health" (World Trade Organization, 2006, see Article 8[1]), these provisions, until the WTO's Fourth Ministerial Conference held in Doha, Qatar in November 2001, have been subject to ambiguous and controversial interpretations. The Doha Declaration has given greater impetus to addressing the public health concerns associated with the TRIPS agreement in the developing world; however, much work is required in balancing the desire for private profit (which advocates of the TRIPS agreements argue is necessary for greater innovation) and the protection of public good as it affects the health and life chances of the most vulnerable populations in many parts of the world.

In any case, it suffices to say that the duty of a state to protect its population from preventable harm justifies the need for the state to intervene in the globalization process. The use of cheaper generic drugs for HIV treatment in poor countries comes to mind in this regard. In denying the social obligations of the state in respect of public health, neoliberalism creates the enabling environment for millions of avoidable deaths in sub-Saharan Africa and the other poor areas of the world. It is estimated that of about 28 million people who have died of AIDS by the end of 2002, 26 million came from sub-Saharan Africa and that 18 million more people will die of the disease by 2010 (Hunter, 2003: 21 and 45). Similarly, an epidemic update released by the Joint United Nations Programme on HIV/AIDS (UNAIDS) in December 2002 indicates that of the 42 million people currently living with HIV around the world, 29.4 million are from this part of the world (O'Manique, 2004: 1). Comparing the HIV/AIDS mortality rates with those of some deadly conflicts of the 20th Century (such as the two world wars, the Vietnam and Korean wars, the U.S. Civil War, the Bolshevik Revolution, among others), Hunter (2003) concludes that if the rate of HIV infection continues unabated, the mortality rate will take as many lives as those of the above conflicts put together. Yet in a continent where such a horrendous disaster is taking place, international financial institutions have been pressuring governments to refrain from intervening for the social good of their citizens and Western-based drug companies have been fighting governments' attempts to provide cheaper drugs to the victims, in the name of respecting international patent laws.

Studies have consistently established that the ecology of extreme poverty, often created, sustained and perpetuated by market-friendly policies, lies at the root of the HIV pandemic in sub-Saharan Africa (see, Stillwaggon, 2006; Hunter, 2003; Sachs, 2005). In the words of Susan George, the politics of neoliberalism has become about "who has the right to live or does not?" (quoted in Giroux, 2004: xxii). If corporate abuses which are purely of economic nature could attract the scholarly attention of criminologists, there is no reason why the activities of the international financial institutions, which are often responsible for even greater social harm, should not come under interrogation by criminologists. The implications of neoliberalism should go beyond the concerns of economists and development experts; after all, like colonialism, which emerged in pursuit of cross-border capital and profit, neoliberal policies ravage the vulnerable population across the world.

Although the numerous genocides and atrocities committed under colonialism have often been treated as historical rather than criminological events (see, Agozino, 2003; Elkins, 2005; Rodney, 1972; Fanon, 1963), it will be dangerous for contemporary criminology to repeat this mistake in respect of the insurgent force of the global market in the developing world. The acerbic Occidentalism of traditional criminology which romanticizes law and legalism clogs the discipline's potential for growth. To expand the intellectual circumference of criminology, the discipline should take seriously the issue of social harms, like the ones generated by the neoliberal experiment in sub-Saharan Africa.

As Friedrichs and Friedrichs (2002: 16) put it, "a criminology of the 21st century must address immensely consequential forms of crime being committed in an evolving new global order". These forms of crime go beyond the proscriptions of the criminal law and are often even committed in accordance with the spirit and letters of the law. But they have lethal consequences for the vulnerable population, especially the poor. Pfohl (2003: xi), therefore, warns against "criminology's blindness to… the victimization" caused by the "global system of power".

Conclusion

For years, the criminological imagination has been predominantly driven by Occidental epistemology and has been anchored on the belief in the supremacy (and sometimes the presumed infallibility) of the law. To the traditional criminologists, the ubiquity of the criminal law protects our society from regress to the brutish state of nature. Their focus on the "law and the lawlessness of individual offenders" (Pfohl, 2003: xiv) has historically been presented as the sacred scroll of criminological inquiry. However, counter-hegemonic narratives, which often find shelter under the broader canopy of critical criminology, are increasingly challenging the essentialist conclusions of traditional criminology, especially with respect to the definition of crime. Many of these schools of critical criminology rather see the legal definition of crime as inadequate and limiting. The criminologists of globalization, in putting social harm at the epicentre of criminological inquiry, participate in this challenge to the hegemony of the law in the criminalization process.

This paper reviews the operation of neoliberal economics in sub-Saharan Africa and shows how poverty, the migration of health professionals, and the epidemiology and management of diseases (especially the HIV/AIDS pandemic), among other factors, are strongly associated with untrammelled capitalism in the region. It concludes that the ecology of poverty created by neoliberalism in sub-Saharan Africa produces enormous social harm which criminologists are encouraged to embrace as criminal. This is in line with a certain level of acceptance that the legal definition of crime does not adequately address the vital problem of social harm, which affects a wider population than the traditional street crime.

REFERENCES

Agozino, B. (2003). *Counter-Colonial Criminology: A Critique of Imperialist Reason*. London: Pluto Press.

Aiken, L. H. et al (2004). "Trends in International Nurse Migration". *Health Affairs*. 23: 69-77.

Barak, G. (ed.) (1991). *Crimes by the Capitalist State*. Albany: State University of New York Press.

Batata, A. (2005). "International Nurse Recruitment and NHS Vacancies: A Cross-Sectional Analysis". *Globalization and Health*. 1 (7): 1-10.

Becker, C. M. (1990). "The Demo-Economic Impact of the AIDS Pandemic in Sub-Saharan Africa". *World Development*. 18(12): 1599-1619.

Brigham, T. (1997). "Most people with AIDS can't even get an aspirin". *Africa Today* (January/February): 48-49.

Brummer, D. (2002). *Labour Migration and HIV/AIDS in Southern Africa*. IOM: International Organization for Migration Regional Office for Southern Africa.

Chikanda, A. (2006). "Skilled Health Professionals' Migration and Its Impact on Health Care Delivery in Zimbabwe". *Journal of Ethnic and Migration Studies*. 32(4): 667-680.

Elkins, C. (2005). *Imperial Reckoning: The Untold Story of Britain's Gulag in Kenya*. 1st ed. New York: H. Holt.

Engberg-Pedersen, P. (eds.) (1996). *Limits of Adjustment in Africa: The Effects of Economic Liberalization, 1986-1994*. Copenhagen: Centre for Development Research.

Epstein, H. (2002). "The Hidden Cause of AIDS". *The New York Review*. (May 9): 43-49.

Evans, G. and J. Newnham (1992). *The Dictionary of World Politics: A Reference Guide to Concepts, Ideas and Institutions*. (Revised Edition). New York: Harvester Wheatsheaf.

Ezeonu, I. (2007). "State Crime Control" in Gregg Barak (ed.). *Battleground: Criminal Justice. Vol. 2*. Westport, CN: Greenwood Press.

Ezeonu, I. C. (2003). "Structural Adjustment and Stabilization in sub-Saharan Africa" in Malinda S. Smith (ed.). *Globalizing Africa*. Trenton, NJ: Africa World Press, Inc.

Ezeonu, I. C. (2000). "Ghana and Uganda: A Reappraisal of the 'success story' of market-led Development Strategy". *Africa Quarterly*. 40(4): 77-118.

Ezeonu, I. C. and A. C. Okolie (2001). "The GATT Uruguay Round Agreements and their implications for sub-Saharan Africa". *Africa Quarterly*. 41(3): 33-75.

Fanon, F. (1963). *The Wretched of the Earth*. New York: Grove Press.

Farmer, P. (2004). "An Anthropology of Violence". *Current Anthropology*. 45 (2): 305-325.

Farmer, P. E. et al (2006). "Structural Violence and Clinical Medicine". *Policy Forum*. 3 (10): 1686-1691.

Friedrichs, D. O. (1998). *State Crime: Volumes I and II*. Aldershot, U.K.: Ashgate/Dartmouth.

Friedrichs, D. O. (2007). *Trusted Criminals: White Collar Crime in ContemporarySociety. Third Ed*. Belmont, CA: Thomson Higher Education.

Friedrichs, D. O. and J. Friedrichs (2002). "The World Bank and Crimes of Globalization: A Case Study". *Social Justice*. 29: (1-2): 13-36.

Galtung, J. (1969). "Violence, Peace, and Peace Research". *Journal of Peace Research*. 6: 167-91.

Giddens, A. (1990). *The Consequences of Modernity*. Cambridge: Polity Press.

Giroux, H. A. (2004). *The Terror of Neoliberalism*. Boulder: Paradigm Publishers.

Harvey, D. (1989). *The Condition of Postmodernity*. Oxford: Basil Blackwell.

Hillyard, P. and S. Tombs (2004). "Beyond criminology?" in Paddy Hillyard et al (eds.). *Beyond Criminology: Taking Harm Seriously*. London: Pluto Press.

Hogstedt, C. et al (2007). "The Consequences of Economic Globalization on Working Conditions, Labor Relations, and Workers' Health" in Ichiro Kawachi and Sarah Wamala (eds.). *Globalization and Health*. Oxford: Oxford University Press.

Hunter, C. W. (1989). "Migrant labor and sexually transmitted disease: AIDS in Africa". *Journal of Health and Social Behavior*. 30: 353-373.

Hunter, S. S. (2003). *Black Death: AIDS in Africa*. New York: Palgrave Macmillian.

Johnston, L. and R. Nicoll (1997). "AIDS Drugs Cut to 'Guniea Pigs'". *Review of African Political Economy*. 73(24):388-389.

Kauzlarich, D. and D. O. Friedrichs (2003). "Crimes of the State" in M. D. Schwartz and Suzanne E. Hatty (eds.). *Controversies in Critical Criminology*. Cincinnati, OH: Anderson Publishing Co.

Kawachi, I. and S. Wamala (2007). "Globalization and Health: Challenges and Prospects" in Ichiro Kawachi and Sarah Wamala (eds.). *Globalization and Health*. Oxford: Oxford University Press.

Kirigia, J. M. et al (2006). "The Cost of Health Professionals' Brain Drain in Kenya". *BMC Health Services Research*. 6(89): 1-10.

Krieger, N. (2007). "Why Epidemiologists Cannot Afford to Ignore Poverty". *Epidemiology*. 18(6): 658-663.

Lynch, M. J. and W. B. Groves (1989). *A Primer in Radical Criminology. 2nd ed*. New York: Harrow and Heston Publishers.

Marshall, D. D. (1996). "National Development and the Globalization Discourse: Confronting 'Imperative' and 'Convergence' Notions". *Third World Quarterly*. 17 (5): 838-889.

Okolie, A. C. (2003). "Development Hegemony and the Development Crisis in Africa: The Importance of Indigenous Knowledges and Practices in the Making of Food Policy". *Journal of African American History*. 88(4): 429-448.

O'Manique, C. (2004). *Neoliberalism and AIDS Crisis in sub-Saharan Africa: Globalization's Pandemic*. New York, NY: Palgrave Macmillan.

Peet, R. (2003). *Unholy Trinity: The IMF, World Bank and WTO*. London and New York: Zed Books.

Pfohl, S. (2003). "Foreword". Biko Agozino. *Counter-Colonialism Criminology: A Critique of Imperialist Reason*. London: Pluto Press.

Quinney, R. (1978). "The Ideology of Law: Notes for a Radical Alternative to Legal Oppression" in Charles E. Reasons and Robert M. Rich (eds.). *The Sociology of Law: A Conflict Perspective*. Toronto: Butterworths and Co. (Canada) Ltd.

Reiman, J. (1996). *...And the Poor Get Prison: Economic Bias in American Criminal Justice*. Boston: Allyn and Bacon.

Rodney, W. (1972). *How Europe Underdeveloped Africa*. London: Bogle-L'Ouverture.

Rothe, D. et al (2006). "Crime on the High Seas: Crimes of Globalization and the Sinking of the Senegalese Ferry Le Joola". *Critical Criminology*. 14: 159-180.

Todaro, M. P. (1997). *Economic Development*. 6th ed. London: Addison Wesley Longman Ltd.

Tombs, S. and P. Hillyard (2004). "Towards a Political Economy of Harm: States, Corporations and the Production of Inequality" in P. Hillyard et al (eds.). *Beyond Criminology: Taking Harm Seriously*. London: Pluto Press.

Sachs, J. (2005). *The End of Poverty: Economic Possibilities for Our Time*. New York: Penguin Press.

Schwartz, M. D. and S. E. Hatty (2003). *Controversies in Critical Criminology*. Cincinnati, OH: Anderson Publishing Co.

Smith, A. (ed.) (1937). *The Wealth of Nations*. New York: The Modern Library.

Smith, M. (ed.) (2003). *Globalizing Africa*. Trenton, NJ: Africa World Press, Inc.

Southern African Migration Project (2006). *The Brain Drain of Health Professionals from Sub-Saharan Africa to Canada*. Cape Town: Idasa.

Stiglitz, J. E. (2002). Globalization and Its Discontents. New York: W. W. Norton and Co.

Stillwaggon, E. (2006). *AIDS and the Ecology of Poverty*. Oxford: Oxford University Press.

Sutherland, E. H. (1961). *White Collar Crime*. New York: Holt, Rinehart and Winston.

Sutherland, E. H. (1940). "White-Collar Criminality". *American Sociological Review*. 5(1): 1-12.

United Nations Commission on Human Rights (2004). *Economic, Social and Cultural Rights: The right of everyone to the enjoyment of the highest attainable standard of physical and mental health (Report of the Special Rapporteur, Paul Hunt)*. Geneva: United Nations Commission on Human Rights.

World Development Movement (2006). "Briefing on Debt and AIDS: Deadly conditions? Examining the relationship between debt relief policies and HIV/AIDS". http://www.wdm.org.uk/campaigns/cambriefs/debt/ (*Sourced*: October 15, 2007).

World Health Organization (2006). *Working Together for Health*. Geneva: The World Health Organization.

World Trade Organization (2006). *Uruguay Round Agreement: Trade-Related Aspect of Intellectual Property Rights*. (http://www.wto.org/english/docs_e/legal_e/27-trips_01_e.htm. (*Sourced*: November 15, 2007).

World Trade Organization (1998). *Trading into the Future. 2nd ed.* Geneva: World Trade Organization.

Wright, W. and S. L. Muzzatti (2007). "Not in my port: The "death ship" of sheep and crimes of agri-food globalization". *Agriculture and Human Values*. 24:133-145.

Zinn, H. (1997). "Law and Justice". *The Zinn Reader: Writings on Disobedience and Democracy*. New York: Seven Stories Press.

[7]

Facilitating corruption and human rights violations: the role of international financial institutions

Dawn L. Rothe

Published online: 19 March 2010

Abstract The connection between corruption and the suppression of human rights has been recognized by scholars of human rights, state and state-corporate crime, non-governmental organizations, the United Nations as well as various governments. Scrutiny of governmental and/or regime corruption has been a primary focus, in relation to barriers and/or violations of human rights. Additionally, multinational companies' complicity in corruptive policies and practices has raised concerns, in particular in the arms and natural resources sector. Glaringly absent, however, within the criminological literature are discussions of, and research on, the role of international financial institutions (IFIs) in relation to high levels of state corruption, save for the relatively little criminological research that has explored how cooperative endeavors between international financial institutions, transnational corporations, and states often result in demonstrably harmful activities as a result of structural adjustment policies. As such, it seems appropriate to consider how certain components and/or policies of IFIs facilitate rather than constrain corruptive practices by regimes, militias, paramilitaries, and transnational corporations. Such an exercise is not only important for its etiological contributions, but also to draw criminological attention to this phenomenon and because these organizations have stated a commitment to reducing state level corruption. I hope to extend the focus and insights of criminological analysis of crimes of globalization herein.

> "Donor governments and multilateral agencies such as the World Bank and International Monetary Fund frequently put forward anti-poverty and "good governance" agendas, but their other actions send a different signal about where their priorities lie." (Hawley [25], p. 1)

Introduction

Over the last 20 years researchers of globalization have linked International Financial Institutions (IFIs) policies to the production of grave human rights

D. L. Rothe (✉)
Old Dominion University, Norfolk, VA, USA
e-mail: Drothe@odu.edu

violations; however, criminologists have given this topic little attention until 2002 when Friedrichs and Friedrichs [19] suggested that harms caused by the policies and practices of IFIs could be operationalized as 'crimes of globalization'. Informed by Falk's [11] observation that globalization is driven by the interests of capital over people, "crimes of globalization" refer to mass social harms—especially within developing countries—that occur as latent consequences of the development and expansion of global capital. Friedrichs and Friedrichs [19] highlight the role of international financial institutions, transnational corporations, and states in the context of crimogenic tendencies within globalization.

Similarly, scholars of human rights have been concerned with the role of IFIs policies and human rights violations, especially within the context of development. More recently this has included an emphasis on the role of corruption and human rights violations, direct and indirectly [4, 20, 22, 24, 29, 50], including the relationship between bilateral assistance and corruption. It has been argued that general or widespread corruption and/or institutionalized corruption lends to non-compliance with human rights obligations (e.g., [30, 59, 60]).

Recently the International Council on Human Rights (ICHR) [30], p. 2 noted the importance of dealing with corruption associated with aid programs in relation to development assistance. In particular, the ICHR [30] suggests that several factors may act as a catalyst of corruption and hinder or violate economic, social, and cultural rights: privatization processes of healthcare, education, water sector, and other previously public services; redirection of funds used for social programs, accessibility, hindered delivery of public services (e.g., health care and education); land sales, and/or use of land sales and natural resources that restrict use for food, shelter, and general sustainability or without attention to human rights; social exclusion, and the discriminate distribution of resources. However, the Council only suggests that donor and recipient countries are in need of tackling such corruption.

Absent from the ICHR report, the human rights and corruption literature, and from the criminological research in general, including those works focused on crimes of globalization, is the connection with the policies and practices of international finance institutions and corruption (IFIs) (i.e., the World Bank Group and the International Monetary Fund) (save for the rare exceptions of [22, 29]). After all, corruption is not merely a practice for which state or corporate actors are to blame: IFIs' policies play a role in facilitating corruption. After all, both the International Monetary Fund (IMF) and World Bank Group (WB) have stated a commitment to 'constraining corruption' in debtor countries. For example, the IMF's "approach to combating corruption emphasizes prevention, concentrating on measures to strengthen governance and limiting the scope for corruption by promoting *good governance*" (IMF [31], p. 1). The World Bank [68], p. 1 also proclaims to have a vested interest in controlling corruption, suggesting it is "the greatest obstacle to economic development" and "weakening the institutional foundation on which economic growth depends".

Undoubtedly, levels of corruption exist that are separate from or not linked to IFI policies. However, the focus here is not on causal mechanisms of corporate or state corruption per se, but corruption that is or has been linked to IFI policies as this connection remains largely ignored by the IFIs themselves, the larger international political community (e.g., the Organization for Economic Cooperation and

Development, the United Nations and the United Nations Office on Drugs and Crime) criminologists in general, and scholars of crimes of globalization.

As such, I hope to extend the focus and insights of criminological analysis of crimes of globalization herein. In this paper, I frame the role of and facilitation of corruption by IFIs as a form of 'crimes of globalization' [10, 18, 19, 48, 53], beginning with a short overview of the crimes of globalization literature. This is followed by a brief discussion of IFIs and their policies that have been linked to the facilitation of corruption and human rights violations. Several examples of these connections are then offered. From this, in an effort of theory generation, criminological theoretical concepts are used in an effort to build the explanatory power of this phenomenon.

Crimes of globalization

The concept of Crimes of Globalization was first introduced by Friedrichs and Friedrichs [19]. According to Friedrichs and Friedrichs [19], p. 18 crimes of globalization have characteristics of "state crime, political crime, white-collar crime, state-corporate crime, and finance crime," but do not fit neatly into any of these categories. Specifically, these crimes "involve cooperative endeavors between international financial institutions, transnational corporations, and state or political entities that engage in demonstrably harmful activities in violation of international law or international human rights convention."[1]

Friedrichs' approach highlights the role of international financial institutions, transnational corporations, and states in the context of crimogenic tendencies within globalization. Friedrichs and Friedrichs [19] examined the role of policies implemented by the WB, the IMF, and the World Trade Organization (WTO) in developing states that result in socially harmful practices and human rights violations. The privileging of transnational corporate interests and the interests of powerful states, coupled with the arrogance with which these institutions implement a "top down" form of globalization, results in immensely harmful consequences that conflict with the ideology and promotion of human rights. The policies and practices of these international finance institutions can have dramatic societal effects, as reflected in the "structural adjustments" imposed on countries such as Argentina, Senegal, and Rwanda which destroyed the way of life of large numbers of indigenous peoples [44]. The political economy of development and IFIs 'builds a process in which poverty is, in a counterintuitive sense, not reduced but embedded and reproduced' (Bracking [5], p. xiii).

Following Friedrichs and Friedrichs [19] and Friedrichs's [17] call to criminologists to engage with the literature of globalization, Rothe et al. [47] conducted research that explored the interrelations between international institutions such as the IMF and WB, legacies of colonialism, and foreign policies that set the stage leading to the sinking of the ferry *Le Joola*, September 26, 2002. Rothe et al. [47] suggest

[1] For a more complete discussion of the typology see Friedrichs [17].

that in response to imposed Structural Adjustment Programs (SAPs)[2], the Senegalese government was forced to cut spending in many areas, including its ferry programs which were central to transportation in the country, especially in light of the geographic location, governmental cuts mandated by the IFIs, and lack of alternative travel. This had a direct impact on the upkeep and return of the *Le Joola* to open waters with only one of the two functioning engines when it capsized, resulting in 1863 passengers deaths. Most crucially, Rothe et al. demonstrated why scholars need to examine the domination of western capitalism and international finance lenders and institutions and their criminogenic effect on 'developing' states. They suggest that focused attention to the economic contexts generated by the pro-capital, non-human emphasis of the IMF and WB are essential to understand such crimes.

In 2008, Ezeonu and Koku framed the neo-liberal policies of IFIs in sub-Saharan Africa as factors that contributed to, rather than constrained, their vulnerability to HIV infection. They suggest that there are lethal consequences to the policies associated with "untrammeled capitalism" and that criminologists needed to pay more attention to the "structural and institutionalized victimization of the people by the market in an increasingly globalizing world" [10], p. 1.

Crimes of globalization have also been conceptualized as facilitating conditions that led to the Rwandan genocide of 1994 [48]. In this case, the authors' propose that IFIs policies set the stage for the political and economic disaster preceding the civil war and subsequent genocide. They also suggest that the IMF and WB violated international human rights principles; through imposing rigid conditions tied to aid packages, IFIs actions served to facilitate rather than constrain criminal activities of regimes.

Given that the subfield of crimes of globalization is relatively new within criminology, the case studies to date are rather limited. However, there are an abundance of case examples from scholars of globalization, non-governmental organizations, and regional experts that share basic premises behind 'crimes of globalization'. This includes scrutinizing the assumption that privately-owned industries are more efficient and economically beneficial than their state-run counterparts. Demanded privatization and decentralization as a condition of loans can result in a downward spiral of social conditions versus the progression and poverty reduction claimed. Instead, the "benefits" of privatization are realized primarily by local elites and foreign investors who can purchase ownership interest cheaply within established utility grids and the like. Additionally, structural adjustment policies that demand a reduction in social program spending in target countries have significant social consequences [5, 26, 36, 41]. While the IMF and WB presume that lower social expenditure is economically beneficial, the reduction of spending on welfare, health care, education and other elements of necessary infrastructure development has drastic effects on the population of developing countries, especially disempowered groups plagued by illness, poverty, and militia-based violence [64].

What has not been included in the literature in general, and specifically within criminological research including crimes of globalization, is a specific focus on the

[2] SAPs mandates included: currency devaluation, decreased funds for government and civil employees, decreased spending on social services, and cuts in infrastructure funds including transportation.

connection between IFI policies with corruptive practices by states, state-corporate endeavors, militias and/or paramilitaries. I hope to extend the focus and insights of criminological analysis of crimes of globalization herein. First, the following provides a brief overview of IFIs.

International finance institutions

From the onset, international financial institutions were designed to maintain growth of the world economies and provide currency stabilization loans to alleviate any major economic crisis, as well as development loans to foster and promote a neo-liberal laissez-faire economic system. For example, since the IMF was first established, its stated purposes have remained largely unchanged, but its operations such as surveillance, financial assistance, and technical assistance have changed in focus somewhat throughout its history. The IMF continues to 'encourage' countries to adopt what it believes to be 'sound economic policies,' or what most commentators refer to as neo-liberal economics. In addition to providing financing, the World Bank Group offers advice and assistance to developing countries on almost every aspect of economic development. Since the mid- to late 1990s, the World Bank Group utilizes the Private Sector Development (PSD) as its strategy to promote privatization in developing countries wherein other strategies must be coordinated with the push towards privatization.

Such economic reforms are often a component of mandated structural adjustment policies (SAPs). SAPs (now often referred to as Poverty Reduction Strategy Papers under the HIPC Initiative), are imposed on borrowing states supposedly to create socio-economic conditions more conducive to economic health and growth. These can include, but are not limited to, opening government owned industries to privatization, removal of tariffs, health care fees, acceptance of currency re-(d)evaluations and reductions in social or other governmental spending programs in ways determined by the lenders. In most cases, there has been "a strong focus on fiscal thrift to which most other concerns are subordinated" (Torrance and Lochery [57], p. 3).

More recently, IFIs have stated a commitment to suppressing corruption associated with not only international aid, but within debtor states. The realizations of the need to address such acts are situated in the belief that corruption lowers investment and 'retards economic growth'. Absent from the IFI corruption campaigns is awareness of or interest in how their own policies may facilitate corruption.

The following section draws from criminological theory in an effort to understand why these IFIs continue to promote policies that directly and indirectly facilitate corruptive practices. As such, the theory development is not meant to explain motivating forces of corruption per se, but of the policies that undergird IFIs and their subsequent actions that contribute to the crimes of corruption and human rights violations.

Theory generation

Criminological inquiry has, for the most part, produced theories addressing one specific level of analysis (e.g., interactional, meso or community, and/or structural level). However, due to the complexities of 'crimes of globalization', and in particular crimes of IFIs (complicit and implicit) utilizing theories that explain only the individual level processes or even that of organizations is bound to overlook the complexities of such cases. Consequentially, an integrated theoretical approach is necessary.

There have been attempts to provide integrated theories to explain traditional street crime. Likewise there are integrated theories that have been applied to explain organizational offending including corporate crime [6, 13] state-corporate crime [34, 37], and state crime-'an integrated theory of international criminal law violations' [40, 43, 45, 46]. The latter group of integrated theories that address organizational crimes are drawn from and expanded on here to help illuminate IFI actions. Here, Rothe and Mullins built explicitly off of the theoretical frame by Kauzlarich and Kramer [34], which itself built off earlier work by Kramer and Michalowski [37], to present an integrated model of offending that explored motivation, opportunities, controls and constraints at four levels of analysis (interactional, organizational, state/structural, and international). In doing so, the integrated theory combines insights from criminological theories and other disciplines to explain the multiple levels at play within each specific case (see Appendix A).

For example, from the criminological literature, social learning theories (e.g., differential association), anomie, strain, rational choice, routine activities, techniques of neutralization, and control theories have been brought together within an integrated approach to address specific components of organizational offending. Additionally, criminologists have drawn from sociological organizational analysis (e.g., network and/or system analysis, and isomorphism); and from political economy models to explain driving forces at the state and international levels. This integrated approach recognizes that organizations (be they corporate or states) are neither monolithic entities nor do they operate within a vacuum. Instead, it recognizes agency at the interactional level, while simultaneously noting the impact of organizational culture and the broader structure on the individual agency level of decision-making.

In the case of corruption, it is the individual decision-making to partake in corruptive practices that result in a crime. However, the focus presented here is on the role of IFIs in facilitating the criminogenic conditions (directly and indirectly) as case examples have shown. As such, I draw from the insights of the integrated theory by Kauzlarich and Kramer [34]; Mullins and Rothe [40]; and Rothe and Mullins [45, 46], paying particular attention to the organizational level (e.g., organizational culture, sub-units, role specialization, and task segregation, reward structures, goal attainment, networks, and isomorphism). However, as with any theory refinement, I find it necessary to also consider theoretical models of power, discourse, regimes of truth (e.g., [15]), hegemony [21], and ideology, [23] as well as neo-realism to explain the interconnections.

For example, from a Foucauldian standpoint, IFIs can be said to be a site where capitalistic hegemonic power is exercised (Welch [65], p. 10). After all, according to Foucault [14] power extends beyond states' apparatuses, as do politics. Additionally, soft power provides the realm wherein political persuasion could be used to advance the "virtues" of neoliberalism [12, 65]. The Foucauldian notion of a 'regime of truth' can serve as a next step to operationalize the authority of 'truth' of the concept of development. Included within this is the idea of discourse, which includes a needed statements of, in this case-development, a defining of it, followed by the rules guiding the ways it is discussed, and how this then frames the authority of 'truth' about the subject (development) and finally how the 'regime of truth' [15] then guides the practice within the institution for dealing with the subject (development).

With Foucault, it is not the statement of 'truth' that decides about the functionality, acceptance and/or effectiveness of definitorial powers, it is the 'material reality' of a societal 'regime of truth', in this case the international financial community (Foucault [15], p. 131). This 'material reality' can be said to be represented by the interactions of international players [9]: in particular the network of institutions involved within the global finance/banking processes. This 'regime of truth' then serves to undergird the operational practice of IFIs. It also serves as *the* political discourse designed to legitimate policies of IFIs. The following figure provides a visual schematic of this process (Fig. 1).

This political discourse is also reflected in the major stakeholders (notably the G7) policies where select interests mandate decision-making for foreign policy, aid, and support. The idea of state-self interests dictating policy is not new, as it is associated with not only classical realism, but neo-realism. As such, neo-realism can

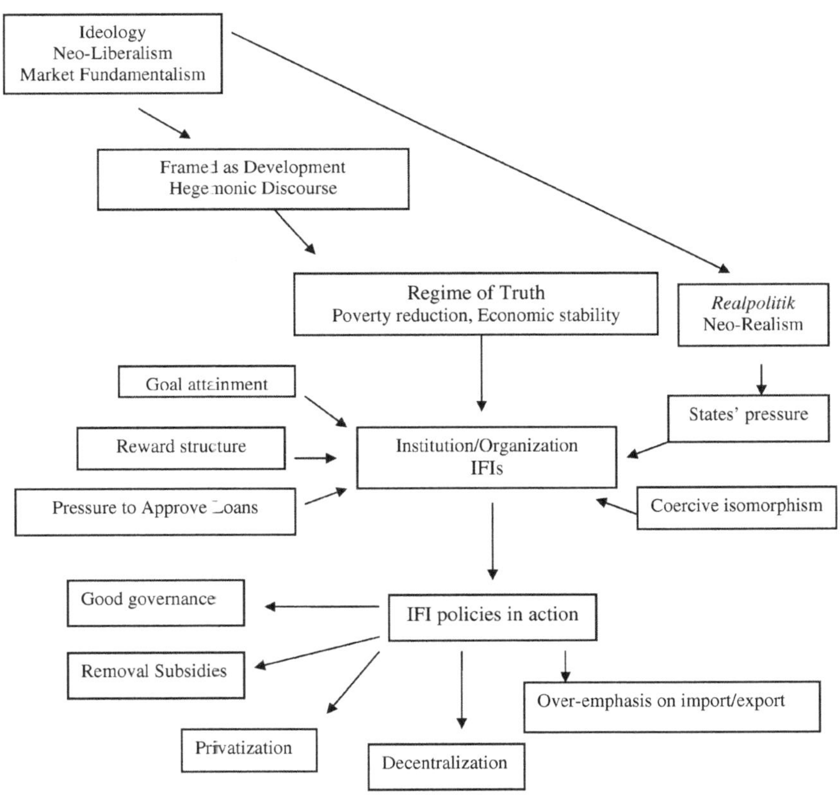

Fig. 1 Pathways of facilitating factors

also contribute to theory generation for the case at hand as it recognizes that the international arena is composed of states acting in their own vested interests, thus, foreign policy is dictated first and primarily in accordance with states' self-interests (economical and political interests). This is in essence, what some have called the theory of *realpolitik*, a framework that guides states' foreign policy based on self-interest. This model also takes into account politics, with a focus on power and states' self-interest. While there is recognition that morality and responsibility are components of state decision-making, these too are often interpreted through the lens of self-interest and/or short term pragmatism.

Theoretical relevance

There is undoubtedly, a genuine belief in the neo-liberal policies that guide mandated restructuring policies. As such, this ideology serves to undergird the ways in which development is portrayed and understood (e.g., means to achieve economic stability and poverty reduction). This then becomes the 'regime of truth', the authoritative correctness to which discussions of development occur and subsequent measures of implementing policy become institutionalized within the organizational culture.

When an organization truly believes in its cause, it is indeed difficult to see the negative ramifications that may be associated with the actions that are guided by a deep seated belief system which becomes the 'regime of truth' that defines discussions, actions, and policy. In other words, the processes by which regimes of truth that support the status quo are instilled within the institution/organization, appearing as common sense and as if consensually accepted. This 'regime of truth' can also be viewed as, in a Gramscian sense, hegemony and subsequent hegemonic discourse (Gramsci [21]). Discourse is discussed then as a social moral language, informing all "modes of thought and behavior" (Green and Ward [22], p. 3). Once institutionalized, it becomes far more difficult to alter given the highly complex bureaucratic structure, save for a major institutional shake-up.

To understand how deeply ingrained this can become, consider that in 2002[3], a 4 year assessment and report was completed by the World Bank, seven countries, and a multitude of NGOs showing that the Bank's policies and SAP practices had done more harm than good, increasing inequality, unemployment, states' debts, higher costs of education and healthcare and environmental degradation. Yet, there were no changes in general policy or procedure, and more importantly, no change in the underlying belief that such economic policies were sound advice for debtor states. This of course does not imply the organization is monolithic, however, as organizational theorists point out, there are overarching cultures and goals that remain in tact as interchangeable employees and appointees change. Furthermore, as Green and Ward [22] note, corruption can be "tolerated for organizational goals". In this case, goals of development, coupled with the need to remain profitable can be viewed as factors of IFIs facilitation of conditions conducive to corruption.

[3] See, The Role and Effectiveness of Development Assistance: Lessons from World Bank Experience. March 18, 2002.

IFIs are for profit organizations. As such, profit remains a highly motivating factor, for the organizations themselves, as well as for the major 'donors' and their multinational, transnational corporations. This becomes an important factor in the pressures and pulls for goal attainment. Consider that in 2002, the World Bank profits were 2.8 billion USD [67]. For 2008, the WB gave figures that totaled 37 billion USD in shareholder's equity and 178.3 billion USD in callable capital. Liquid assets are listed as 26 billion with a net income for 2008 of 1,491,000.00 USD. On June 22, 2009 the IMF reported that it expects to post a net profit of 126 million USD for the fiscal year of 2009 (Barklay [1], p. 1). Further, for the past 2008 fiscal year, IMF's net income was far above the estimated 11 million USD that the organization reaped the year before. Given the significant rise in loans with the global economic session, that figure has been estimated to jump to 1.14 billion USD. Increased levels of income provide motivation to continue lending practices as it is profitable and with little to no risk for the stakeholders. Additionally, the application of harsh and ineffective measures promoted by IFIs (i.e., structural adjustments) and a general refusal to modify these economic policies that contribute to corruption are analogous to "western governments' response to street crime: it applies harsh but ineffective law and order measures… but refuses to modify the economic policies that give rise to the problem" (Green and Ward [22], p. 15). This reinforces the status quo, having a positive effect on the stability of the organizations.

The World Bank also operates under the marked political influence of certain countries, the holders of the majority votes, most notably the United States. These entities profit from advancing their access to additional markets as well as specific resources available in less economically, politically, and militarily empowered states, such as cheap labor, gold and diamond mining, peanuts, and electric industries. Moreover, having a notable political influence on IFIs policies of restructuring, the G7 states' priorities are directed toward private ownership policies for companies within their own territory. As previously pointed out, "[p]olitics has always influenced the advice offered by the IMF and World Bank…. World Bank projects are sometimes covertly shaped by pre-existing agreements for contracts between large companies backed by powerful governments and borrowers" [66]. After all, nearly one-half of the monies the WB lends is dispersed directly to corporations through its 'international competitive bidding', with the majority going to companies out of the G7.

An April 2009 report, *Corporate Misgovernance at the World Bank*, confirms this as it notes that "serving on the board of directors at the International Bank for Reconstruction and Development (IBRD) doubles funding opportunities for the board members' home countries by about $60 million"(Kaja and Werker [33], p. 2). Thus, corporate favoritism is a component of the decision-making for projects [5], or as Green and Ward [22], p. 21 note, clientelism-"a pattern of social exchange between patrons, normally the holders" of administrative offices and "clients who may be businesses".

Here the role of *realpolitik*, neo-realism, is of importance as states pressure IFIs to approve loans for specific contractors and/or regimes that are questionable, have negative track records, or would otherwise not qualify—due to their own self-interests (economic, military, and political) whether that be for their ally or against their foe (economic strangulation). The World Bank in particular often fails to investigate and bar companies that are found guilty of corrupt practices such as bribery, fraud or malpractice. However, the pressures by states to promote their corporations can outweigh any leanings towards non-issuance of contracts.

Additionally, *realpolitik* plays a role in motivating IFIs to extend loans and/or aid to highly corrupt regimes. Major donors pressure the institutions to support country B as country A has a vested economic, political, or military interest (e.g., the Suharto regime and Indonesia). The opposite is true is as well (e.g., the US economic strangulation of Nicaragua). Given the dialectic and mutual relationship between the major powers and IFIs, such political pressure can easily translate into decision-making not in the interest of human rights or ending corruption. Here international relations, power, and the practice of *realpolitik* at the structural level filters down to the organizational and interactional level, creating a culture wherein donor desires, political interests, and economic profits take primacy over what may well have been 'true' intentions to aid countries in devastating situations. As such, IFIs become complicit in the corruption of the corporations as well as the regimes.

Additionally, as Shah [51], p. 2 noted, the "World Bank's 'pressure to lend' culture where staff are rewarded for the volume of the portfolio they manage" adds additional pressure to approve aid and/or loans that may have been flagged or seen as to risky. This translates then to the organizational level where a 'culture of approval' and a reward structure is reified into decisions not necessarily in line with established lending criteria, human rights, or the doctrine of ending corruption.

Factors noted above then come into contradiction with external pressures (coercive isomorphism) for the institutions to pay particular attention to and join in the campaign to end corruption. This then results in both real and symbolic efforts to combat corruption, while simultaneously safeguarding the organizational goals and ideologies that undergird its actions. Consequentially, we see sporadic applications of regulation of corruption. On the other hand, due to the many other influences, including the 'regime of truth' that is embedded with the organizational structure, policies that have been shown to facilitate the 'crime' they are to be tackling, remain intact. The following section provides a few examples of this facilitation.

Cases of complicity, facilitation, corruption, and IFI policies

During the past decade or so, there have been many instances of IFI complicity in corruption that have been well documented and researched by a variety of scholars. One such example was the knowing acceptance of Rwanda and Uganda's illegal expropriation of the Democratic Republic of Congo's (DRC) gold and diamonds [40]. Focusing specifically on Uganda, IFI policies reinforced corruptive practices, thus, magnifying and exacerbating the already tumultuous conditions and human rights violations in Uganda and the DRC.

One of the widespread criminal actions within the DRC has been the wholesale looting of the country's rich mineral resources (e.g., large deposits of diamonds, copper, gold, coltan, zinc, and silver among others) by foreign powers and regional ethnic militias. This has included various forms of corruption from the local and state levels in the DRC to foreign states including Uganda and Rwanda. During the

Second Congolese War, 1998–2004, Uganda occupied gold rich lands in the north, establishing control over the Gorumbwa, Dubra and Agbarabo mines. Without the resources to engage in industrial mining practices, they forced miners to engage in artisanal labor practices [40]. At the Gorumbwa mine, these practices led to the collapse of the mine in late 1999. Ugandan soldiers frequently beat and extorted the local miners by requiring monetary payment to enter the mines and taking a percentage of the ore which they mined [27, 28].

Consider that in 1995, 3.09 t of gold was exported from Uganda totaling $23 million (USD)[4] while only .0015 t were produced within the legal borders of the state. In 1996, exports increased to $60 million; exports were later valued at $105 million in 1997. Ugandan gold production peaked at .0092 t in 1998 and its export of gold peaked in 1999 at 11.45 t. According to Human Rights Watch [28], almost a ton of gold was extracted during a four-year period (1998–2002) worth approximately $9 million. In 2007, Uganda produced about $500 worth of gold within its domestic territory, but in the same year, it exported $75 million in gold. Almost all of that is coming from the DRC war zone. Similar gaps between production and export were noted in diamonds as well. Uganda has no indigenous diamond production. According to the Diamond High Council in 1997 Uganda exported $120,000 in diamonds; $1,440,000 in 1998; $1,810,000 in 1999; and $1,260,000 in 2000.

With the discrepancies of Ugandan exports and their native production and/or actual resources, Mullins and Rothe [40] note that the government of Uganda acknowledged to the IMF that the volume of gold exports does not mirror production levels and may indicate some exports are 'leaking over the borders' from the DRC. Yet, the IMF proclaimed the increase in exports as a strengthening of the Ugandan economy, upgrading its assessment grade for balance of payments status. Due to these revenues, the WB lauded Uganda as a success story for what its SAPs could accomplish. The irony is that the SAPs did nothing to increase Ugandan economic health and can be seen as providing motivation for the government's corruption and illegal mineral expropriation actions. In fact, the United Nations Security Council cites internal memos establishing that the World Bank was well aware of this, yet didn't seem to care. In fact, the World Bank "not only encouraged Uganda and Rwanda indirectly by defending their case, but equally gave the impression of rewarding them by proposing these countries for the Highly Indebted Poor Countries debt relief initiative" (UNSC s/[61]/357, p. 39). Thus, not only did they profit from their organized criminal activity, but were rewarded by the IFIs for doing so [40].

Similar patterns have been established with Rwanda's exporting of minerals. For example, as with Uganda, Rwandan readily acknowledges it has no indigenous diamond production. The UNSC, the WTO and the Diamond High Council have established that starting in 1997 Rwanda began a major export enterprise of bringing rough diamonds to the international markets. Rwanda exported approximately $720,000 in diamonds in 1997; $20,000 in 1998; $440,000 in 1999 and; $1,790,000 in 2000 (as of October). Between 1997 and 2000, the Diamond High Council estimates that Rwanda exported a total value of $2,964.414 (UNSC S/[61]/357, p. 25). As with Uganda, in 1999 and

[4] All future amounts will be in U.S. dollars (USD).

2000, Rwanda had entered into agreements with local militias to smuggle diamonds over the border.[5] By comparison, the value of DRC diamond exports were $752,800,000 in 1997; $879,000,000 in 1998; $520,100,000 in 1999 and; $210,500,000 in 2000 (UNSC S/[61]/357). Thus in a 2 year period the country's diamond exportation fell by almost three-fourths [40].

The same processes have occurred with niobium, coltan, coffee, timber and cassiterite have been noted by international agencies. Coltan, an essential ingredient in portable electronics, became the focus of smuggling across the border into the eastern part of Rwanda and the northern region of Angola [40]. During 1999 and 2000 world prices of coltan exploded; increasing nearly ten-fold [32, 49]. Rwanda reaped massive benefits from this, exporting 250 million USD in that period, again with little-to-no indigenous sources of the mineral.

Another example of the linkages between IFI policies and rampant corruption can be seen with the liberalization and privatizations that occurred in Pakistan. Consider that during the late 1990s, twenty-one Western power companies were investigated for corruption, alleged kickbacks, and for over-pricing. The levels of corruption led to inflated prices. As British Member of Parliament, Hugh Bayley [3][6], stated in a speech to the House of Commons:

> The cost of bribes falls primarily on the poor. When a corrupt contractor from this or some other rich country pays a 15% bribe, he adds that to the price of his contract. His power station or irrigation scheme will cost more, and the little people—those who buy the electricity or the water to irrigate their crops—will pay the price of that bribe. Bribery is a direct transfer of money from the poor to the rich.

While the companies filed statements denying corruption, six of the twenty-one later confessed [25]. The World Bank (WB), on the other hand, initially sent in a team of investigators, yet, the International Monetary Fund "went so far as to make a new package of loans at the end of 1998 conditional on the government's dropping the charges against the companies"(Hawley [25], p. 15).

More recently, June 2009, The National Accountability Bureau (NAB) submitted to the Justice Bhagwandas Commission, a report on corruption, between 2001 and 2006, involving government functionaries and the oil industry including the pricing of petroleum products which caused a loss of 83 billion Rupees (converted to1,794,596,037.60 USD) over a period of 5 years. According to former deputy chairman of NAB, Maj-Gen Muhammad Siddique, "Pakistan State Oil Company Limited (PSO) and others are involved in massive misappropriation/misuse of authority and forgery in the import of HSD (high speed diesel) and its subsequent sale in the country and … committed the offence of corruption and corrupt practices"

[5] The UN Panel of Experts [62] named over 100 corporations with problematic or suspect dealings within the DRC during the chaos of the past 8 years (see the UNSC [62] report for a full accounting of those involved). While the majority of these were African-based companies (most based in neighboring countries), major transnational organizations, like DeBeers, were also named. Belgium, Canada, Germany, Israel, the Netherlands, Switzerland, the United Kingdom, and the United States all have multiple companies on the list.

[6] See the House of Commons, Hansard, Column 374, February 25, 1998.

(Dawn [8], p. 2). Nonetheless, the profits of "Shell Pakistan, Caltex and PSO" increased by 232% between 2001 and 2002, 281% 2003 and 2004, and 252% between 2004 and 2005. "Likewise, the profits of Attock Refinery, National Refinery, Pak Refinery and Parco jumped" by 4,331% between 2001 and 2002, 3,578% between 2002 and 2003, and 1,717% between 2004 and 2005 (Dawn [8], p. 5). Additionally, the Oil Companies Advisory Committee charged commissions on government taxes. Major multi-national oil companies operating in Pakistan include BP, Eni, and Orient Petroleum Inc. As has been noted, these large private oil industries have long been cited for corruptive practices and lack of transparency including revenue shares [58]. To further complicate matters, Pakistan's Minister of Petroleum and Natural Resources regulates the private and public sectors which has included granting oil concessions through private negotiations [7].[7] The report continues by concluding that "it is sufficiently evident that (functionaries in the) ministry of petroleum in collusion with the Oil Companies Advisory Committee (OCAC), oil industry and Oil Marketing Companies (OMCs) have engaged themselves in corrupt practices for generating colossal undue financial gains for refineries and OMCs at the cost of public and economy as a whole" (Dawn [8], p. 8).

Additionally, electric subsidies in Pakistan, following rounds of privatization and high levels of corruption, are to be cut, raising another basic service for the general population. With the removal of the subsidies, the increase in oil and electric prices, Pakistan's carbon tax[8] will also increase, thus fueling inflation (Khan [35], p. 1). The processes of privatization of the banking industry also have been riddled with corruption in Pakistan:

> A record 700 billion Rupees ($10.76 billion[USD]) of corruption has taken place during the privatization of financial institutions. When Habib Bank Limited (HBL) 51% shares were sold out to Agha Khan Fund For Economic Development in December 2004 for only 22 Billions Rupees, its total assets were more than 570 billion Rupees ($8.76 billion). While another large bank, United Bank Limited (UBL) was sold out only for 13 billion Rupees. HBL had 1437 branches and another 40 branches abroad in 26 countries with ownership of the buildings that the branches are functioning (Tariq [56], p. 1).

The IMF failed to disapprove these sales, regardless of the corruption and extreme low prices given their pre-sale value.

As previously discussed, IFIs major infrastructure projects have led to serious undermining of human rights as well as direct violation of those rights, most notably in building large dam projects. While corporate corruption has been cited in some cases (generally the bidding stage), corruptive practices can also be pervasive at the local level as these projects are initiated. Such is the ongoing case in Pakistan. According to Transparency International, Pakistan officials reap roughly eight times their salaries from bribes paid by the local population to obtain irrigation water (i.e., corruption tax). Yet, as noted by the Peter Basshard [2], p. 2,

[7] International oil companies operating in Pakistan include BP (UK), Eni (Italy), OMV (Austria), Orient Petroleum Inc. (OPI, Canada), Petronas (Malaysia) and Tullow (Ireland) [7].

[8] The carbon tax is a surcharge attached to the price of petroleum products.

> The World Bank has played a major role in promoting and financing Pakistan's misguided and unsustainable water policy… Since the country's creation in 1947, the financial institution has spent almost $20 billion on Pakistan's water sector (in 2005 prices)...Paradoxically, while financing these mega-dams and canals, the World Bank has also pointed out the wastefulness of Pakistan's irrigation system, the corruption plaguing the allocation of water, and the need for reform…When the country's water bureaucracy resisted change and misused the loans, the World Bank looked the other way. As an internal evaluation found, 'the Bank did not insist on the implementation of the agreed strategy against the pressures of special interests,' and 'the Bank's concern to keep disbursement flowing reinforced this focus.'

The examples listed above are by far not exhaustive. However, they do serve to illustrate how IFIs can be complicit in corruption as well as how their mandated policy reforms can facilitate extant conditions or those ripe for corruptive practices. As stated in the report of the US Joint Economic Committee Study [63],

> The conditions placed on IMF loans to these countries often may (perhaps unwittingly) foster circumstances spawning further corruption. Conditions promoting increases in taxation, government spending, and subsidies to the bureaucracy, for example, may be counterproductive. IMF lending may also more directly promote corruption through the "voracity effect:" i.e., by increasing the conflict among powerful special interest groups and factions, their power and influence is strengthened and corruption thereby promoted. (Tanzi [55], p. 3)

Their complicity can be associated with not only their inaction against highly corrupt regimes but also in their ignoring of and or rewarding of corruption directly and indirectly [42]. As an example of direct complicity, consider the situation in Timor-Leste which involved IFI support of roughly 30 billion USD which was channeled to the Suharto regime despite massive known corruption, false accounting, and the 'militaristic appropriation of funds' (Stanley [52], p. 5). As the World Bank's focus was on Indonesia, the state was able to use the funds against the Timorese civilians which included the misuse of the poverty allocation funds that were used for Indonesia's 'socialization' program which has been called a campaign of terror-deterring people from voting for independence [38, 53]. In this case, IFIs were directly impacting/funding the massive human rights violations and the institutionalized corruption within the Indonesian government.

The following section draws together these common conditions associated with indirect complicities and those direct correlated situations.

Contextual conditions and IFI interventions

A common thread between IFI policies and corruption at the state and local level is grounded in neo-liberalism and the belief in free markets. This is then framed within the discourse of development with the espoused regime of truth: poverty reduction and economic stability. These are then crystallized by structural adjustments such as the push to privatize state owned entities without consideration of the conditions of the extant infrastructure within a given country. These "conditionalities are then based" on "the notion that free trade is the route to development" (MacKenzie [39], p. 172).

As Stigletz [54] has noted, a one-size-fits-all economic policy used by IFIs can damage rather than help countries with unique financial, governmental and social institutions.

Additionally, the push to privatize state-owned businesses such as the banking, oil, electric industries have been done without, 1) requiring a solid regulatory system or framework be put in place; 2) requiring reforms within agencies already embedded with corruption versus privatizing a highly corrupt system where the corruption then becomes heightened and involves the private sector; 3) considering how the privatization will impact the current situation with subsidies (which has resulted in additional levels of corruption at the local level). Where governments or regimes are embedded with systems of favoritism and payoffs, the forced introduction of privatization, without self-directed domestic change, becomes another venue of corruption: one that is heavily financed by foreign investment. Likewise, in countries where heavy centralization of government have long been established, decentralization can in effect result in weakening of the internal infrastructure, leading to a breakdown of regulation (as was the case in Pakistan).

Furthermore, in conflict ridden regions, promotion of privatization and/or mega-infrastructure projects facilitate conditions that are already heavily embedded with high levels of corruption, violence, and more often than not, massive violations of human rights. Here, the levels of complicity are only broadened to include the multi-nationals and put additional motivating forces at play within the broader violence (e.g., access to resources, economic empowerment) in highly tumultuous regions. Corruption has also been linked with IFIs over-focus on debt repayment, debt status, and a country's levels of exports [22]. This was the case with the looting of the DRC's resources by Uganda and Rwanda.

Additionally, the broader organizational culture premised on profit and goal attainment and the internal 'pressure to lend' has been factors in the promotion of policies that have then linked IFIs to corruption, directly and indirectly through the facilitation of a criminogenic environment as the previously mentioned cases highlight. Simply "the prioritization of these interests is diffused in the organizational sociology of the routines of the institutions" (MacKenzie [39], p. 168). The role of corporate lobbyists and the preference of select states' corporate interests and contractual preference cannot be ignored within this process. As noted by [39], p. 168,

> the relationship between favorable outcomes for financiers and corporations in developed nations is not a case of simple string pulling in respect of puppet institutions. There is some level of influence that may be characterized as fairly direct: corporate lobbying, the bare threats and other less obvious coercive political tactics employed by developed nations in negotiations, and at root the power of veto given to the U.S. in relation to the IMF and the World Bank.

I am not suggesting the above as policies to address the identified catalysts. Specifically, I am not implying a need for careful privatization, slower deregulation, or additional contingencies on loans, as this in of itself would do little to damper the overall harms and/or crimes of globalization associated with IFIs and their development models as they have been linked to increased levels of poverty and unemployment. Likewise, I am not suggesting a mere restructuring of the organizational culture to ending corporate lobbying or the influence of select states on lending practices as the underlying ideology embedded within development would still remain and the regime of truth would continue to be played out in policies that are not only socially harmful to the recipient countries, but fuel corruption. Instead, these points are to highlight some of the contextual factors where IFI policies have facilitated criminogenic conditions.

Concluding thoughts

The aim of this paper was threefold: 1) to situate the linkage between IFI policies and practices with corruption and the literature on crimes of globalization; 2) to add to the extant literature on the linkages between IFI policies, development, human rights, and corruption and; 3) theory generation, drawing from criminology, the integrated theories for corporate, state-corporate, and state crime by adding neo-realism and by drawing from Foucault's concepts of power, discourse, and the regime of truth. Additionally, it is important to note that cases of corruption have and will continue to occur regardless of IFI policies (those tackling corruption as well as those mandating reform policies). However, the point being made here is that while these forms of corruption are important to tackle, it is as vital to deal with the interventionist policies of IFIs and their role in facilitating criminogenic conditions and/or directly involved in corruption. After all, "trying to make corrupt and inefficient states retrench through structural adjustment and economic liberalization stands a good chance of making corruption and misgovernment worse" (Green and Ward [22], p. 27).

Additionally, as the dogma of development and economic reform are concepts that have come to be seen as 'truths' for policies to reduce poverty in this international political field, it should be noted that, as with the concept of globalization or a 'global economy', development is not a natural or unstoppable phenomenon. There are measures that extend beyond reformatting IFIs, as recommended by Stiglitz [54], that could have a beneficial outcome, including empowering those highly indebted countries to rebuild their own economic system in accordance with their own needs versus those of the global power holders. On a concluding note, I return once again to Foucault and his insistence that critique should "be an instrument for those who fight, those who resist, and refuse what is" [16], p. 84.

Acknowledgement I wish to thank Jeffrey Ian Ross, Christopher W. Mullins, and the reviewers for their insightful comments and suggestions on an earlier draft.

Appendix A: An integrated theory for international criminal law violations

	Motivation	Opportunity	Constraints	Controls
International Level	Political interests	International relations	International reaction	International law
	Economic interests	Economic supremacy	Political pressure	International sanctions
	Resources	Military supremacy	Public opinion social movements	
	Ideological interests	Complementary legal systems	NGOs and INGO	
			Oversight/ economic institutions	
Macro Level	Structural transformations	Availability of illegal means	Political pressure	Legal sanctions
	Economic pressure or goals	Control of information	Media scrutiny	Domestic law
	Political goals	Propaganda	Public opinion	
	Ethnogenses	Ideology/ nationalism	Social movements	
	Anomie	Military capabilities	Rebellion	
Meso Level	Organizational culture and goals	Communication structures	Internal oversight	Codes of conduct
	Authoritarian pressures	Means availability	Communication structures	
	Reward structures	Role specialization	Traditional authority structures	
Micro Level	Strain	Obedience to authority	Personal morality	Legitimacy of law
	Socialization	Group think	Socialization	
	Individual goals and ideologies	Diffusion of responsibility	Obedience to authority	Perception of reality of law application
	Normalization of deviance	Perceived illegal means	Informal social controls	
	Definition of the situation			

References

1. Barklay, T. (2009). IMF Sees $126 million net profit in FY09 amid higher demand for loans. Dow Jones Newswires; 202-862-9275. Retrieved, June 24, 2009. http://news.morningstar.com/newsnet/ViewNews.aspx?article=/DJ/200906221615DOWJONESDJONLINE000500_univ.xml.
2. Basshard, P. (2006). *The World Bank's conflicted corruption fight.* Berkley: International Rivers.
3. Bayley, H. (1998). Public speech. House of commons, Hansard, Column 374. February 25, 1998.

4. Boersma, M. (2009). Corruption as a violation of economic, social and cultural rights. Presented at Maastricht Centre for Human Rights conference on Corruption and Human Rights. Maastricht October 22, 2009.
5. Bracking, S. (2009). *Money and power.* London: Pluto.
6. Braithwaite, J. (2002). *Restorative justice and responsive regulation.* New York: Oxford University Press.
7. Clough, L. (2008). *Energy profile of Pakistan.* Retrieved, June 25, 2009. http://www.eoearth.org/article/Energy_profile_of_Pakistan.
8. Dawn (2009). Pakistan corruption report. June 25, 2009. Retrieved November 28, 2009. http://iaoj.wordpress.com/2009/06/29/pakistan-corruption-report/.
9. Ewald, U. (2008). Reason and truth in international criminal justice. In R. Haveman & A. Smeulers (Eds.), *Supranational criminology: Towards a criminology of international crimes* (pp. 399–434). Intersentia.
10. Ezeonu, I., & Koku, E. (2008). Crimes of globalization: the feminization of HIV pandemic in sub-Saharan Africa. *The Global South, 2*(2), 112–129.
11. Falk, P. (1993). *Global visions: Beyond the new world order.* Boston: South End.
12. Ferguson, N. (2005). *Colossus: The rise and fall of the American empire.* New York: Penguin Books.
13. Fisse, B., & Braithwaite, J. (1993). *Corporations, crime and accountability.* Cambridge: Cambridge University Press.
14. Foucault, M. (1977). *Discipline and punish: The birth of the prison.* Translated by Alan Sheridan. New York: Vintage.
15. Foucault, M. (1980). In C. Gordon (Ed.), *Power/knowledge. Selected interviews and other writings 1972–1977.* Brighton: Wheatsheaf.
16. Foucault, M. (1991). Governmentality. In G. Burchell, C. Gordon, & P. Miller (Eds.), *The foucault effect: Studies of governmentality.* Chicago: University of Chicago Press.
17. Friedrichs, D. (2004). White-collar crime in a globalized world. Presentation at. Western Michigan University.
18. Friedrichs, D. (2007). White-collar crime in a postmodern, globalized world. In H. N. Pontell & G. Geis (Eds.), *International handbook of white-collar and corporate crime* (pp. 163–184). New York: Springer.
19. Friedrichs, D. O., & Friedrichs, J. (2002). The World Bank and crimes of globalization: a case study. *Social Justice, 29*(1–2), 1–12.
20. Goodwin, M., & Sender, K. (2009). The human right to be free of corruption? A dangerous addition to the developmental discourse. Presented at Maastricht Centre for Human Rights conference on Corruption and Human Rights. Maastricht October 23, 2009.
21. Gramsci, A. (1971). *Selections from the prison notebooks.* London: Penguin.
22. Green, P., & Ward, T. (2004). *State crime: Governments, violence and corruption.* London: Pluto.
23. Hall, S. (1996). Gramsci's relevance for the study of race and ethnicity. In T. A. Van Dijk (Ed.), *Ideology: A multidisciplinary approach, 1998* (pp. 277–312). Newbury Park: Sage.
24. Harrington, A. (2009). Corrupting natural rights. Presented at Maastricht Centre for Human Rights conference on Corruption and Human Rights. Maastricht October 22, 2009.
25. Hawley, S. (2000). *Exporting corruption, privatisation, multinationals and bribery.* Retrieved, June 21, 2009. http://www.thecornerhouse.org.uk/item.shtml?x=51975.
26. Hiatt, S. (Ed.). (2007). *A game as old as empire: The secret world of economic hit men and the web of global corruption.* San Francisco: Berrett-Koehler.
27. Human Rights Watch. (2003). *Ituri: "covered in blood": Ethnically targeted violence in Northeastern Democratic Republic of Congo.* New York: Human Rights Watch.
28. Human Rights Watch. (2005). *The curse of gold: Democratic Republic of Congo.* New York: Human Rights Watch.
29. Hunt, S. (2009). Corruption in the oil trading industry. Presented at Maastricht Centre for Human Rights conference on Corruption and Human Rights. Maastricht October 23, 2009.
30. International Council on Human Rights. (2009). *Corruption and human rights: Making the connection.* International Council on Human Rights Policy. Versoix: ATAR Roto.
31. International Monetary Fund. (2008). The IMF and good governance: Fact sheet. September 2008. Retrieved, June 3, 2009. http://www.imf.org/external/np/exr/facts/gov.htm.
32. Jackson, S. (2002). Making a killing: criminality and coping in the Kivu war economy. *Review of African Political Economy, 93/94*, 517–536.
33. Kaja, A., & Werker, E. (2009). Corporate misgovernance at the World Bank. Working paper 09-108, April 20, 2009, Harvard Business School.
34. Kauzlarich, D., & Kramer, R. C. (1998). *Crimes of the American nuclear state: At home and abroad.* Boston: Northeastern University Press.

35. Khan, M. Z. (2009). Pakistan asks IMF for $4bn to plug budget deficit. Retrieved, June 26, 2009. http://www.dawn.com/wps/wcm/connect/dawn-content-library/dawn/news/business/11-pakistan-asks-imf-for-4bn-to-plug-budget-deficit-il-07.
36. Klein, N. (2008). *Shock doctrine: The rise of disaster capitalism*. New York: Metropolitan Books.
37. Kramer, R., & Michalowski, R. (1990). *Toward an integrated theory of state*-corporate crime. Presented at the American Society of Criminology, Baltimore, MD.
38. La'o Hamutuk. (2000). Justice for Timor-Leste remains an unfulfilled international obligation. Timor-Leste institute for development monitoring and analysis. Retrieved August 2008. http://www.laohamutuk.org/reports/09bgnd/JusticeEn.pdf.
39. MacKenzie, S. (2006). Systematic crimes of the powerful: criminal aspects of the global economy. *Social Justice, 33*(1), 162–182.
40. Mullins, C. W., & Rothe, D. L. (2008). Gold, diamonds and blood: international state-corporate crime in the Democratic Republic of the Congo. *Contemporary Justice Review, 11*(2), 81–99.
41. Perkins, J. (2005). *Confessions of an economic hit man*. London: Ebury.
42. Pieterse, J. N. (2002). Global inequality: bringing politics back in'. *Third World Quarterly, 23*(6), 1023–1046.
43. Rothe, D. L. (2009). *State criminality, the crime of all crimes*. Lanham MD: Lexington/Roman and Littlefield Publishers.
44. Rothe, D. L., & Friedrichs, D. (2006). The state of the criminology of state crime. *Social Justice, 33*(1), 147–161.
45. Rothe, D. L., & Mullins, C. W. (2008). Genocide, war crimes and crimes against humanity in Central Africa: a criminological exploration. In R. Haveman & A. Smeulers (Eds.), *Towards a criminology of international crimes*. Antwerp: Intersentia.
46. Rothe, D. L., & Mullins, C. W. (2009). Toward a criminology for international criminal law: an integrated theory of international criminal violations. *International Journal of Comparative and Applied Criminal Justice, 3*(1), 97–118.
47. Rothe, D. L., Mullins, C., & Muzzatti, S. (2006). Crime on the high seas: crimes of globalization and the sinking of the Senegalese Ferry Le Joola. *Critical Criminology: An International Journal, 14*(2), 159–180.
48. Rothe, D. L., Mullins, C., & Sandstrom, K. (2009). The Rwandan genocide: international finance policies and human rights. *Social Justice, 35*(3), 66–86.
49. Samset, I. (2002). Conflict of interests or interests in conflict? Diamonds and war in the DRC. *Review of African Political Economy, 93/94*, 463–480.
50. Selpulveda, M., & Terracino, J. (2009). Corruption and human rights: Making the connection. Presented at Maastricht Centre for Human Rights conference on Corruption and Human Rights. Maastricht October 22, 2009.
51. Shah, A. (2008). Corruption. *Global issues*. Retrieved, June 26, 2009. http://www.globalissues.org/article/590/corruption#.
52. Stanley, E. (2007). Transnational crime and state-building: the case of Timor-Leste. *Social Justice, 34* (2), 124–137.
53. Stanley, E. (2009). *Torture, truth and justice: The case of Timor-Leste*. Abingdom: Routledge, Taylor & Francis Group.
54. Stigletz, J. (2002). *Globalization and its discontents*. New York: Norton and Company.
55. Tanzi, V. (1998). Corruption around the world: causes, consequences, scope, and cures. IMF Working Paper, WP/98/63, May 1998; 3, 6, 10–16.
56. Tariq, F. (2009). *Facing the Musharraf dictatorship*. Lahore: Good Books.
57. Torrance, M., & Lochery, E. (2008). An analysis of the IFIs' fiscal policy Recommendations. *The Oxford Council on Good Governance*. Retrieved. June 27, 2009. http://ocgg.org/fileadmin/Publications/EY008.pdf.
58. Transparency International. (2008). Widespread corruption in oil industry. Retrieved. June 3, 2009. http://www.transparency.org/news_room/corruption_news/ti_in_the_news/2008.
59. United Nations Committee on the Rights of the Child. (2006). *Session/Annual report of committee A/61/41 (SUPP)*. Published by United Nations High Office Human Rights.
60. United Nations Convention against Transnational Organized Crime. (2004). Published by United Nations Office on Drugs. Online http://www.unodc.org/documents/treaties/UNTOC/Publications/TOC%20Convention/TOCebook-e.pdf.
61. United Nations Security Council. (2001). *Report of the panel of experts on the illegal exploitation of natural resources and other forms of wealth of the Democratic Republic of Congo*. S/2001/357.

62. United Nations Security Council. (2003). *Report of the panel of experts on the illegal exploitation of natural resources and other forms of wealth of the Democratic Republic of Congo*. S/2003/1027.
63. United States Joint Economic Committee Study. (1999). Retrieved. June 1, 2009. http://www.house.gov/jec/imf/corrupt.htm.
64. Weisbrot, M. (2007). What the IMF doesn't see IMF-World Bank meeting. *International Herald Tribune*, October 19, 2007 Retrieved. June 5, 2009. http://www.unpan.org/directory/worldNews/include/displayIssueDetail.asp?issueID=3.
65. Welch, M. (2008). Foucault in a Post-9/11World: excursions into security, territory, population. In *Discipline, security, and beyond: Rethinking Michael Foucault*. College of France de'Lectures. Carcel Notebooks.
66. Woods, N. (2006). Quoted in Guttall, S. (2006). "Fuelling discontent: The World Bank and International Monetary Fund in Singapore". (pp. 5). Retrieved. May 1, 2009. (http://alainet.org/active/13945).
67. World Bank Annual Report. (2003). *Financial statements and appendixes* (Vol. II). Published by World Bank. ISBN Number: 0-8213-5595-3.
68. World Bank Annual Report. (2009). Statement on corruption. Retrieved. June 2, 2009. http://web.worldbank.org/WBSITE/EXTERNAL/EXTSITETOOLS/0,contentMDK:20147620~menuPK:344192~pagePK:98400~piPK:98424~theSitePK:95474,00.html.

[8]

Good guys, bad guys: transnational corporations, rational choice theory and power crime

Leslie Holmes

Published online: 18 November 2008

Abstract While its scope and scale can be exaggerated, the power transnational corporations (TNCs) exert in the contemporary world is considerable. This is often at the expense of states, or at least is exercised in a way that can undermine states. Some interactions between corporations and states or their officers constitute prime examples of power crime. A blatant form is where corporations either offer or else agree to pay bribes to state officials in order to secure a major contract. This capacity to corrupt state officials via large scale bribes gives corporations significant potential power. This article begins by citing allegations of active corruption of state officials by TNCs, as well as counter-examples (i.e. where TNCs have taken a stand against rent-seeking officials). It then argues that active corruption by corporations constitutes a major dimension of power crime, and seeks to explain apparently contradictory behaviours by TNCs, relating these to rational choice theories and neo-liberalism. It is argued that recent changes in corporate governance and behaviour have made rational-choice models and simplistic neo-liberalism either questionable or redundant. Bu at the same time, globalisation and its stable mate neo-liberalism encourage improper behaviour–various forms of power crime-by corporations.

Growing awareness of the problem of rogue Transnational Corporations (TNCs) can be demonstrated by the fact that, in 2000, the world's leading NGO for combating corruption, Transparency International (TI), amended its definition of corruption to include B2B (business to business) improprieties. While it can be confusing to use the term corruption to refer to what are exclusively private sector activities, the change of definition testified to two facts of direct relevance to the present article. The first is precisely that corporate crime has assumed a far higher public profile since the late-1990s than it has ever had, with scandals such as Worldcom, Enron, Parmalat, AWB

I am indebted to the Melbourne Research and Innovation Office at the University of Melbourne for a grant that enabled me to conduct preliminary research into this topic in 2008.

L. Holmes (✉)
School of Social and Political Sciences, University of Melbourne, Level 4, John Medley Building, Grattan Street, Victoria 3010, Australia
e-mail: leslieth@unimelb.edu.au

and BAE highlighting just how criminally all too many private corporations operate or are alleged to operate.[1] The second, intimately connected to the first, relates to the apparent rise in corporate crime; this is the impact of neo-liberalism, in which the boundaries between the state and the private sector become increasingly blurred.

This article begins by providing examples of both allegations and proven cases of active corruption of state officials by TNCs ('bad guys'), as well as counter-examples (i.e. where TNCs have taken a stand against rent-seeking officials—'good guys'). It then argues that active corruption by corporations constitutes a major dimension of power crime, and seeks to explain the apparently contradictory behaviours by TNCs, relating these to rational choice theories and neo-liberalism. Following this is an explicit consideration of the ways in which corporate crime constitutes power crime, and why it matters if it does. A brief section on the ways in which corporate crime is being and can be addressed precedes the conclusions, in which it is argued that the power crimes of TNCs are often part of an even more significant form of power crime involving *complicity* between TNCs and state elites.

Bad guys

In recent years, there have been numerous cases of corporations being accused of acting improperly in various ways. One is consciously to deceive, or at least seriously mislead, their shareholders about the state of the company; well known examples include the Italian food corporation Parmalat and the US energy corporation Enron. But in this article, the focus will be on another aspect of corporate impropriety and illegality: offering and/or paying bribes to officials.

Siemens

Siemens has been subject to numerous accusations of offering bribes over the past 10–15 years, at least two of which—Singapore 1996, Italy 2004—resulted in the corporation being temporarily banned from tendering in the respective countries. The public appears to have been only vaguely aware of Siemens' misbehaviour until 2006, when the media widely reported the existence of a 'global slush fund', from which an estimated €1.3bn had been paid in overseas bribes over recent years. The revelation was described in the German media as the 'biggest bribery scandal in German history' [13]. The situation became so serious that the Chief Executive Officer of Siemens, Klaus Kleinfeld, felt obliged to resign in 2007; though Kleinfeld himself was not personally accused of any impropriety, the Board of Directors apparently considered it necessary to send a loud and clear message to both shareholders and employees that Siemens had learned a lesson from its past misdemeanours.

Daimler–Chrysler

There have been numerous allegations in the 2000s that the Euro–American corporation Daimler–Chrysler has been paying bribes in at least three continents.

[1] It could be objected that all the scandals cited post-dated the TI change. The reason for their inclusion here is that these cases 'enjoyed' even higher profiles than those in the 1990s.

The most significant were claims made by former Chrysler accountant David Bazzetta in 2004, as part of his case against Chrysler for wrongful dismissal (though his claims related primarily to Mercedes Benz). These allegations resulted in an official investigation into the company by the US Securities and Exchange Commission, commencing in 2004, while the US Department of Justice launched its own investigation in 2005, following the suicide of Daimler–Chrysler's managing director for Nigeria. In March 2006, it was publicly announced that German authorities were now also commencing investigations into allegations that this major vehicle manufacturer had been paying bribes worth up to US$10m in various parts of the world; the German authorities were focusing mainly on Belgium, Ghana and Poland (*Frankfurter Allgemeine Zeitung*, 8 March 2006, Wirtschaft: 19). At about the same time, it was revealed that, following internal investigations, the corporation had itself either dismissed or suspended a number of employees for having made 'improper payments', primarily in Africa, Asia and Eastern Europe (especially in Poland), over the previous 12 years.

While there is still relatively little publicly available information on this scandal, it was announced in December 2006 that Daimler–Chrysler had hired Louis Freeh, former Head of the FBI, as an external consultant to investigate the allegations in more depth. Another aspect of the case is that, according to media reports, a number of senior managers at Mercedes had made the point to employees in the early-2000s that offering bribes had been a normal way of conducting business in less developed countries for decades; since Germany had indeed *permitted* such bribery until the late-1990s, their comments were on one level understandable. However, they also revealed that senior executives had not kept abreast of major changes in German law and international norms on such a serious matter [12, 18].

Statoil

Although Nordic states, along with New Zealand, always top the TI Corruption Perceptions Index—i.e. they are perceived to be the least corrupt countries in the world—this does not mean that they never experience serious corruption scandals. One of the most prominent in recent years involved the Norwegian State Oil Company, Statoil. A Norwegian newspaper published allegations in September 2003 that Statoil had paid bribes to influence senior Iranian officials to grant the company oil and gas contracts. The case was investigated, and the company charged by both Norwegian and US authorities with corrupting foreign officials. A Norwegian court found Statoil guilty, and fined it some US$3m, while a US court found it guilty of violating the Foreign Corrupt Practices Act (FCPA) and fined it US$21m. Moreover, a number of senior executives were forced to resign ([15]: 30).

BAE

One of the most disturbing accusations of corporate malfeasance in recent years relates to the leading British defence equipment manufacturer, and Europe's largest single defence contractor, BAE (formerly British Aerospace). According to the very public allegations, BAE paid Saudi government officials—in particular Prince Bandar—more than £1bn between 1985 and some time in the 2000s to secure a major Saudi contract (eventually worth £43bn—the biggest export contract in British history) for fighter aircraft and other weaponry, under the al-Yamamah arms deal. The allegations led the Serious Fraud Office (SFO) to establish an investigation team in 2004.[2] But the British government, apparently on instructions from Prime Minister Blair, terminated this investigation in December 2006 on the grounds that it could negatively impact upon the UK's security. This decision was challenged in 2007 and was considered by the British High Court in early-2008. The High Court found in April that the British government had broken the law by terminating the SFO investigation—although it stopped short of insisting that it be re-opened [1, 20, 21, 26]. However, the UK's ultimate court, the Law Lords, ruled at the end of July 2008 that the SFO had had no choice but to terminate the investigation when it did, thus essentially closing the whole issue from the British legal perspective. This said, the US Department of Justice was still considering whether or not the al-Yamamah contract broke US anti-bribery laws, so that the case cannot be considered definitively closed [23].

As with Siemens, allegations against BAE of offering bribes are not limited to one high profile case. There have been allegations that BAE was involved in offering bribes to Czech politicians in 2002 in an attempt to persuade them to vote in favour of Czech purchase of Gripen fighter aircraft. An investigation by Czechia's anti-corruption police concluded that there had been an attempt to bribe Czech politicians from various parties, but was unable to identify the source of the bribe offers. As with the al-Yamamah case, the whole affair apparently led to tensions between the US and British governments, as the former accused the latter of corrupt practices over the aircraft deal.[3] In the event, the Czech government declared that it could not afford the aircraft anyway—at which point BAE offered to lease second-hand Tornado aircraft at a much lower price. Finally, in 2004, Czechia agreed to lease 14 Gripen fighters ([10] *Czech Business Weekly* 21 July 2007). But this case cannot be considered closed either, since the SFO was still investigating it as of mid-2008 [23, 33].

AWB

Like Norway, Australia has generally performed well in surveys about perceived levels of corruption. While it does not score quite as well in the Transparency International Corruption Perceptions Index (CPI) as either the Nordic states or its trans-Tasman neighbour, Australia came 2nd in the first ever Bribe Payers Index (BPI) in 1999, and actually topped the 2002 BPI. In other words, its companies were seen as the least likely to offer bribes in developing states. Unfortunately, this squeaky clean image has now been severely tarnished by the scandal that emerged

---

[2] This investigation covered BAE activities in six countries, two of which were Saudi Arabia and Czechia—*Czech Business Weekly*, 21 July 2007.

[3] It is interesting to note that, soon after the US criticisms of shady UK arms dealing practices, the British authorities accused the US of using improper means to secure a major Polish order for fighter aircraft, which BAE had also hoped to secure. To an outside observer, this all looks like a case of pots and kettles calling each other black! For the record, it emerged in July 2007 that the US Department of Justice was investigating American connections to possible BAE bribery.

around AWB in late-2005.[4] AWB is Australia's privatised wheat board, and was, when state-run (until 1999), known as the Australian Wheat Board. It appears that, at the end of the 1990s, employees of AWB began to offer 'kickbacks' to officials of the Iraqi state and agreed to pay exorbitant inland transportation fees to secure wheat sales. This was at a time when the UN had imposed sanctions on the Saddam Hussein regime, so that AWB was clearly breaking UN sanctions.

The AWB scandal broke when Canadian (in 2000) and then US (in 2003) farmers lodged a formal complaint with the UN that AWB had been ignoring sanctions and engaging in activities that contravened notions of fair, competitive trading. The kickbacks paid were eventually assessed at almost €180m, so that AWB appears to have been the worst culprit in the UN's 'oil-for-food' scandal that related to the Saddam regime in Iraq. Under pressure from the UN, the Australian government established a public enquiry, the Cole Commission of Inquiry, which found that AWB had deceived the Australian government in making payments to the Saddam regime and had consciously broken UN sanctions (Resolution 661). It also recommended that there was sufficient evidence for a number of AWB executives to be prosecuted for their role in the affair [6]. By almost any criteria, these conclusions would indicate serious misdeeds on the part of AWB. Yet not everyone saw the Commission's findings in this light. One of the most surprising—and disturbing—aspects of the AWB affair is that, in December 2006, the Australian Tax Office (ATO) ruled that, since the Cole Commission did not label the secret payments actual bribes, but rather abnormally high transportation fees and 'kickbacks', AWB had acted perfectly legally in claiming (and being granted) tax deductions on the payments.[5] Quite what either the Cole Commission or the ATO sees as the difference between a bribe and a kickback remains unclear.[6] One practical ramification of the ATO's ruling was that, contrary to what many had hoped and expected, AWB was not required to pay up to €270m in back taxes and fines. The price of shares in the company rose markedly (more than 15%) immediately following the ATO ruling. (*The Australian*, 20 December 2006; *ABC Online*, 20 December 2006—accessed 8 June 2008; [17]: 2)

[4] The tarnishing was not clearly reflected in the 2006 BPI, however, in which Australia emerged as the 3rd cleanest country out of 30 assessed. This might be because the news had not yet spread widely by the time of the surveys for the 2006 BPI (early-2006) and/or because the Australian government had soon demonstrated a willingness to investigate the accusations—and perhaps even because some did not believe the allegations at that stage. The eventual outcomes of the inquiry (see below), however, could yet result in a further deterioration in Australia's corporate image.

[5] The Cole Commission was extremely circumspect in its conclusions, arguing that, 'what the IIC [Independent Inquiry Committee – LTH] described as 'kickbacks' did not necessarily carry with it any implication of illegality' ([6]: 126). The word 'bribe' does not appear in the 346 pages (total) of Vol. 1 of the Commission's findings, the sub-title of which is *Summary, Recommendations and Background*.

[6] One view is that bribes are offered *before* an improper action is taken by a corrupt official, whereas kickbacks are given *afterwards*. However, recipients of kickbacks have usually been *promised* a 'fee', in return for a favour, *before* that improper favour has been granted. In this sense, the difference between a bribe and a kickback is minimal, and both the Cole Commission and the ATO can be argued to have been playing semantic games.

Good guys

While there is considerably more evidence of corporations either offering or being accused of offering bribes to state officials than there is of corporations resisting demands from 'meat-eating' officials,[7] a few corporations have been identified in the media as having stood up to such demands. Just two examples will be cited here.

Motorola

The US mobile-telephone company Motorola decided in 1997 to cancel a planned investment of some $500m in Ukraine after it lost a bid to a little-known company—Kyivstar—that was headed by President Kuchma's brother-in-law, and on the board of which sat the president's daughter. The risks associated with such an apparently corrupt economy appear to have outweighed the possible benefits, and Motorola made it clear it was unwilling to invest in such a system [19, 27, 34].[8]

IKEA

The Swedish—and Dutch-based TNC IKEA has apparently lodged formal complaints with the Russian government concerning demands for bribes when the company established itself in Moscow. Such complaints date from at least 2000, when IKEA opened its first Moscow store and articles appeared in the *Economist* (1 April 2000), the *New York Times* and elsewhere about demands for bribes made to it by Moscow officials [14]. But the case became more widely known in 2006 (*Newsweek*, 23 October 2006).

One of the surprising findings at this early stage of research into this topic has been the reluctance of even 'good guy' corporations to respond to requests for further information and their views on these cases. Unfortunately, this reluctance or indifference raises the question of whether some corporations might only be masquerading as good guys!

Rational choice theory and corporate crime

Both 'good guy' and 'bad guy' behaviour can be explained in terms of rational choice theory (RCT). Several versions of this theory have been developed in the social sciences since the publication of what is usually taken to be the seminal work on the subject, Kenneth Arrow's *Social Choice and Individual Values* (1951). However, a commonly accepted classification is provided by John Ferejohn [11], who distinguished between 'thick' and 'thin' theories. The former refers to goals or

---

[7] The term 'meat-eating' in this context refers to officials who actively solicit bribes, as distinct from less predatory 'grass-eating' officials, who will accept bribes offered to them. The terms derive from the Knapp Commission's 1973 report on corruption in the New York Police Department.

[8] It is worth noting here that the Russian company RussGPS accused Motorola in 2006 of violating patent rights, in connection with the alleged use of RussGPS technology in Motorola products—following which Motorola accused RussGPS of defamation. The defamation case was heard in Moscow in September 2006, and found in favour of the Russian defendant.

motives, such as power or profit maximisation, while the latter pertains to the means used to attain goals.

Thick RCT's assumption that profit maximisation is the ultimate objective of businesses is unexceptionable but trite, and will not be interrogated further. The focus, here, will therefore be on thin RCT; this assumes only one basic motivator to action, anticipated utility maximisation, and rationality is reflected not in the choice of goal but in the adoption of what are perceived to be the most efficient means or procedures to achieve that utility maximisation. However, it is necessary to modify one of the key assumptions of most rational choice theories, namely that the concept of utility maximisation can only apply to individual *persons* [2, 25]. The concept can in fact apply to individual *agents*, including a single corporation, which typically works individually, very much in competition with other firms. It is precisely this competition that encourages the firm to operate individually, and to seek improper advantage over its competitors in order to secure contracts.

The old English adage 'let the best man win'—here meaning that the most attractive and proper corporate bid should secure the contract—is often too naïve a concept for the realities of business. For instance, it implicitly assumes both that there are clear criteria for determining the best, and that there is a single best. In the real world of business, it is often difficult to determine the best offer, since so many variables (price, quality, delivery dates, product support, etc.) enter the equation; even nationalistic (protectionist) issues can play a role in a decision. Moreover, two or more players—firms—may be seen as equal; in terms of choosing between their bids, it does not matter whether they are perceived as equal and similar or equal and different. This fuzziness creates an opportunity or space for one or more competitors to offer bribes; were the choice between tenders a very obvious one, potentially corruptible state officers involved in making the final decision would normally—if acting rationally—think twice about accepting bribes and awarding a contract to a clearly inferior bidder. This is not to suggest that state officers never accept bribes in such a situation and never award contracts to inferior bidders; a 'rational' cost-benefit calculation, including their knowledge of their own country's track-record in dealing with corruption, might lead them to conclude that they run a low risk of being accused of corruption, and a far lower risk of being punished in any serious way even if they were to be prosecuted for and convicted of corruption. This said, the focus here is on the notion of rationality from the corporation's perspective, not that of the corrupt or potentially corrupt official. How, then, can thin RCT explain two opposing positions—the approaches of both the good guys and the bad guys?

The simple answer to this conundrum is that both the good guys and the bad guys can be seen to be working to the same basic rationale, utility (here, profit) maximisation. This is in line with thick RCT, but, as noted above, is a trivial argument; it is hardly a major theoretical insight to argue that companies exist primarily to make profit. Turning to thin RCT, firms interpret their best *means* to achieve profit in different ways. Firm X might be more focused on short-term outcomes, and hence less interested in overall reputation. Its argument may be that public opinion is fickle anyway, and that the public's memory is short. When 'push comes to shove', firm X believes, the vast majority of consumers will buy a company's products if they decide that these products best meet their needs, even if, in an opinion survey, these same consumers have indicated disapproval of firm X's improper behaviour. Firm Y, on the other hand, may be more concerned with its longer-term prospects, and notices that ethical investment is rapidly gaining in popularity. It is also aware that the country in which it is bidding has been internationally branded as highly corrupt, which might suggest there will shortly be a serious clampdown by state authorities. Whether or not there is such a clampdown, readily available survey results indicate that the public in this country are angry about corruption levels, so that firm Y expects long-term benefits from its reputation as a 'clean' corporation.

In short, both firm X (bad guy) and firm Y (good guy) are acting 'rationally' in terms of their perceived utility maximisation and choice of means, so that rational choice theory can explain their actions. The only—rather significant—problem is that the two companies reach opposite conclusions, since they have focused on different criteria in reaching their 'rational' decisions. Given this, even though thin RCT *can* be used to explain both good guy and bad guy behaviour, it is ultimately of little value.[9] Not only can it not predict how particular corporations will act in future situations, but it can be used to explain diametrically opposite outcomes.[10] It thus becomes banal.[11] Moreover, while thin RCT *can* explain our two corporations' perspectives, the principal explanatory factors might actually lie somewhere else altogether. For example, corporate culture and the ethics of individual senior managers might explain particular corporations' behaviour better than—or at least as well as—rather crude notions of utility maximisation.

Why corporate crime is power crime

For the purposes of this analysis, we adopt two versions of what are probably the most widely-cited definitions of power, those by Robert Dahl. The first is that 'A has power over B to the extent that he can get B to do something that B would not otherwise do' [8]. A second, which overlaps with the first but is subtly different, is that A has power if it can act 'in such a manner as to control B's responses' ([7]: 13). Both of these definitions are appropriate for our purposes. In the situations being considered here, we *initially* assume that A represents a TNC, while B is a state or its officers.

In the 1960s and 1970s, several analysts began to argue that the state was in decline. Many factors were cited to explain this apparent phenomenon, including the development of macro-regionalism (notably what is now the EU) and concomitant decline of sovereignty, the rise of 'new' politics and social movements—and the increasing power of the TNCs [3, 5, 31, 32]. By the 1990s, with globalisation becoming a household word, the potential of TNCs to exercise at least influence, and often power, over states became increasingly obvious. Often, this power has been

[9] One of the better known advocates of RCT has acknowledged that using what he calls substantive and procedural forms of rationality (which appear largely to correspond to thick and thin notions of rationality) can result in very different conclusions about the rationality of a given action or actor—see [25]: 174. Once again, the usefulness of RCT must be questioned.

[10] The future behaviour of a given corporation might reasonably be predicted on the basis of past and present behaviour. But such prediction is based on knowledge and experience, and the application of RCT would be superfluous.

[11] For an example of a former advocate of RCT renouncing his faith in it see [30].

transparent. Perhaps the most common example is when a corporation 'threatens' a state that it will close one or more plants and transfer its activities offshore unless the state agrees to meet a number of conditions set by the corporation itself (e.g. a lower corporate tax rate, no taxes, a state subsidy, import tariffs, etc.) While this may well be perceived by outside observers as a highly undesirable action on the part of the corporation, and unquestionably demonstrates an attempt to exercise power, such behaviour, assuming it is successful, cannot reasonably be described as power *crime*. But what of the situation in which corporations offer bribes to state officials?

Unfortunately, the assumption that a corporation is committing an actual *crime* if it offers a bribe to a state official is not invariably correct, at least from a narrow legalistic perspective. Below, it will become clear how and why many TNCs were, until the late-1990s, acting fully within the laws of their own states when offering bribes to state officials in other countries. While most Western states have now changed their laws on this, it is less than a decade since such legislative amendments were introduced. Thus, many Western corporations that offered bribes in the 1990s to overseas officials were not, technically, committing crimes. Yet, while survey data on this are scarce, it is reasonable to assume that many citizens in many countries would have been both surprised and concerned to learn in the 1990s that some of the corporations that produced the household brands they purchased were both paying bribes overseas to secure contracts *and* were being granted tax allowances for doing so. In any case, it is now formally illegal for Western corporations to offer bribes to foreign officials, as will be outlined in the following section.

Whether or not such acts are formally legal, the use of a company's economic clout to secure concessions, rent or contracts from the state and its officials unquestionably constitutes a form of political power. And this power is very unevenly distributed. There is no shortage of hard evidence to show that large corporations, especially TNCs, are far less likely to suffer in any meaningful sense from improper behaviour, including paying or offering bribes, than smaller companies (SMEs). In fact, given the empirical fact that blacklisting (debarment) of firms is far more likely to be directed towards SMEs than TNCs, it emerges that there is one law for the rich and another for the poor when it comes to company misbehaviour and debarment. Thus, of the US's top ten repeat offenders ('recidivist corporations'!) in the period 1990–2002, only one—General Electric—had actually been debarred as of the early-2000s [9], while numerous small firms have been.[12]

One of the reasons for this differential track-record is that larger corporations generally have far better resources than SMEs for defending themselves in legal processes. Thus, with reference to the approach adopted by Ruggiero and Welch in this collection, this point highlights the fact that not all white collar crimes are equal, and that access to better resources helps to explain not only greater power, but also greater freedom, including the freedom to 'get away with it'. Another reason for the difference is that governments are sometimes highly dependent on large corporations. Thus, of the ten most recidivist corporations in the USA (1990–2002), all are major suppliers to the US Government. Moreover, the first five (GE; Lockheed Martin; Boeing; Raytheon; Northrop Grumman), plus the 7th and 8th (United

[12] As of 2004, GE had been accused of misconduct (of various kinds) 63 times, and had had to pay fines, restitutions, costs etc. totalling almost US$1 billion [9].

Technologies; Thompson Rado Wooldridge), are directly involved in the defence industry[13]. Many Western states would not dare to upset these manufacturers too much—as the BAE scandal illustrates.[14]

However, it would be incomplete and potentially misleading to argue only that corporations exercise power over states. Framing the argument in such a way can make the state look almost like an innocent victim, being coerced by big business and cheated by its own officers. The issue of *complicity* needs to be introduced at this juncture. While some states do adopt a relatively tough stance on misbehaving corporations—Singapore, for example—others have been either weak (Germany and Italy in terms of debarment), or else actually work with corporations against what many analysts would see as the public interest. The Howard regime's position on the AWB scandal is a prime example. In such cases, the power crime is being committed jointly by state and corporate elites, who share responsibility.

Thus the earlier assumption that A represents a TNC and B a state or its officers clearly needs to be refined in some instances. A might in fact be more than one agent—a corporation and a part of the state. In the BAE case, for instance, A can be seen to comprise BAE and the British Cabinet, while B could be another part of the state. From another perspective, A can be seen to comprise a corporation *and* a foreign state, both exercising power over B, the British state. The possibility that, in the 'real world', it can sometimes be difficult clearly to identify A and B in a power crime relationship is an example of the blurring of roles that privatisation, deregulation and in general neo-liberalism intensify.

We have not yet completed our exploration of the ways in which a corrupting corporation might exert power. Another may be in relation to other corporations, those with which the miscreant is competing. Even if it is only recently in most countries other than the USA that such behaviour has actually been labelled criminal, the fact that other corporations may suffer as a result of bribery by an unethical corporation makes them potential victims. Thus, the actions of the bribe-paying corporation can be described as power crime, in that they may deprive other corporations of some of their control (Dahl's second definition) over their own destiny, and in a sense create victims, even if they do not come into direct contact with them.

Reasons for the apparent rise in corporate crime and corruption

Anyone who has attempted to measure corruption knows that, ultimately, we are forced to work primarily with guesstimates. To a large extent, the same can be said about corporate crime; what is publicly reported is but the tip of an iceberg. Moreover, many analysts of both corruption and corporate crime accept that the apparent rise in both *might* be an illusion; it is not necessarily that both have

[13] Project on Government Oversight, http://www.pogo.org/p/contracts/co-020505-contractors.html, accessed 13 May 2008.

[14] This is not to overlook the fact that the British government's decision in December 2006 to terminate the SFO's investigation was largely due to pressure from Saudi Arabia. But the British Ministry of Defence had also supported BAE's position, and the British government can be seen to have been defending the interests of one of the UK's most significant companies, in many ways against its better judgement.

significantly increased in recent years, but merely that our awareness of them has dramatically increased. The truth probably lies somewhere in between these two positions; both corruption and corporate crime *have* increased in recent years, but by less than our perceptions suggest. But how and why has our awareness of these phenomena been heightened?

In the case of corruption, this is often linked to the end of the Cold War. Until the beginning of the 1990s, the West often considered it more important to keep developing (in those days often called Third World) states on their side than to criticise them for corruption and risk losing them to the Soviet bloc. Once the Cold War was over, there was no such incentive to turn a blind eye. By the mid-1990s, the fight against corruption, as well as related activities such as money laundering [29], had begun to reach the agendas of both Western states and (Western-dominated) international organisations. To a limited extent, the same could be said of corporate crime—at least the sort being considered here (i.e. bribing officials)—by TNCs. If Western governments and agencies had started criticising developing states too much for corruption, this would almost inevitably have led to many revelations about Western companies operating in those states. But if the end of the Cold War meant that Western states could be more critical of corruption in other states, it also increased the likelihood that more of the improprieties committed by TNCs, especially overseas, would come to light. And indeed, the fact that TI felt compelled by the late-1990s to produce a Bribe Payers' Index (BPI), as a way of demonstrating a more even-handed approach to both developed and developing states (i.e. as a counterweight to its CPI that had been published annually since 1995), was one clear indication of this linkage.

During the Cold War, it was not only the corruption and other forms of questionable behaviour of developing states to which the US opted to turn a blind eye; in general, Washington also chose not to embarrass its First World allies. This is not to deny that there were scandals involving corporate crime and corruption in the West until the 1990s; the Flick scandal in West Germany is a prime example that disproves such an assumption. But such cases were relatively rare—certainly in comparison with the flood of cases that have been reported since the late-1990s. Once the Cold War imperative had been removed, however, the US changed its position and began to push hard for the international criminalisation of corporate bribery of state officials. It was apparently this US pressure, above all, that led the OECD to adopt first 'Recommendations' (May 1994) and then a 'Convention' (adopted 1997, effective February 1999) to combat the bribery of foreign public officials. As states signed up to and then ratified this convention, many—including Australia, Germany and the Netherlands—were required to change their legislation so as to outlaw tax deductions for bribery.

Does it matter?

Former Chief Economist of the World Bank and Nobel Prizewinner for Economics, Joseph Stiglitz, argued in a recent (best-seller) book on globalisation that, 'For many people, multinational corporations have come to symbolize what is wrong with globalization; many would say they are a primary cause of its problems' ([28]: 187). While Stiglitz is referring to a broader range of corporate misbehaviour than the bribery of state officials—for instance, he is concerned with the lack of concern so many display towards the environment—he is also highly critical of their role in corrupting state officials.[15] There is thus a serious legitimacy issue for advocates of globalisation. If the concept is associated with corporate malfeasance, then the public negativity towards it that radical anti-globalisation activists have already displayed could spread among publics more generally. But do such negative attitudes matter if they do not manifest themselves in public outrage?

The simple answer to this question is that negative public attitudes do matter to anyone who claims to favour the rule of law, which is supposed to be a bedrock of democracy. Indeed, negative public attitudes matter to anyone seriously committed to the very concept of democracy; both public opinion and transparency should be significant parts of the democratic equation. But in an era when democracy and the rule of law appear to be becoming lower priorities for many Western governments, and perhaps even publics, there are less idealistic and abstract reasons for arguing that corporate bribery of state officials matters.

One important factor relates to the point just made about democracy. Ever since 9/11, a number of Western states—primarily in the Anglophone world—have argued that national security is ultimately more important than human rights or civil liberties. This has led in many instances to a reduction in transparency. Ironically, this reduced transparency can *increase* security risks. If corporate crime, in the form of the corruption of public officials, contributes to a *general* increase in corruption—to what Miller, Grødeland and Koshechkina [22] have called a 'culture of corruption'—the likelihood that corruption will spread to and within the security branches of the state increases. If this happens, there is a growing danger that corrupt security officials will cooperate with organised crime gangs, who in turn can have links to terrorist organisations. If this all appears to be fanciful, it is worth noting that the British High Court accepted secret documents in February 2008, in connection with the BAE scandal outlined above, that indicated that the head of the Saudi National Security Council and other Saudi leaders had threatened to terminate their cooperation with British anti-terrorist intelligence agencies if the investigation of the al-Yamamah scandal proceeded and implicated Saudi officials [21].

It is not only democracy, the rule of law and public security that can suffer as a result of corporate malfeasance. Other corporations can suffer financially if they lose contracts to TNCs that have won them through paying bribes.[16] But, in an era when corporate reputation appears to be of increasing importance, being accused of offering or paying bribes, let alone being found guilty of these crimes, can negatively impact upon a TNC. This relates in part to ethical consumers; but their numbers, while apparently growing, are still not sufficient for us to be confident that their indignation will have much impact on a corporation's conduct. However, states' actions can have a real impact. Thus Siemens was one of five Western

---

[15] The underlying theme in Stiglitz's comment is not new. Thus, Clinard and Yeager ([4]: 155) observed almost three decades ago that 'Probably nothing has tarnished the image of corporations within recent years more than the public revelation of the widespread illegal payments made to attain certain corporate objectives'. For an early analysis of one form of questionable corporate payment (that to political elites to secure advantage) see [16].

[16] Or, in some cases, *higher* bribes than those offered by companies not awarded contracts.

corporations that were blacklisted by Singapore in 1995 for allegedly paying bribes to Singaporean officials; Siemens was forbidden to tender for any Singaporean government project for a period of five years.[17]

Signs of improvement? or 'what is to be done?' (with apologies to Lenin)

What has happened to the various corporations identified above since the allegations of bribery? As already noted, Siemens' CEO resigned in 2007 because of the major bribery scandals; his successor, Peter Löscher, has vowed to clean up the company. When Daimler–Chrysler published its annual report in March 2006, it acknowledged that internal investigations had revealed the company had been paying bribes, and substantially revised downwards its earning statements to reflect the fact that it had been making improper payments. It also announced that it was restructuring its internal control mechanisms to ensure that there would be no future payments of bribes [12]. Statoil has been required to pay substantial fines. BAE was, at the time of writing, still being investigated by the OECD, the US Department of Justice, and Swiss authorities, even if the Law Lords had determined that the termination of the SFO enquiry in December 2006 was lawful. And while the corporation itself appeared to have returned to 'business as usual', a number of senior AWB executives were facing trial at the time of writing.

International organisations are also beginning to take TNC malfeasance more seriously. Thus the World Bank engaged in its first ever debarment of a large (Canadian) corporation in July 2004, while in February 2004 the EU adopted a policy on public procurement that permits debarment ([9]: 3).

Pressure to reform can also come from civil society. The role of the media in exposing corporate malpractice has been crucial in many of the case-studies referred to in this article. Groups of concerned citizens can form lobby groups. Shareholders can also play an important role; again citing the BAE case, a group of shareholders brought a lawsuit against the corporation in 2007 for making 'illegal bribe payments' at precisely the same time as it was presenting itself as a 'highly ethical, law-abiding corporation' [21].

The bribery of foreign public officials has at last been recognised as a crime by most Western states and an increasing number of international organisations. This represents an improvement, but as I will show in the concluding section of this article, problems remain—and the situation could deteriorate again.

Conclusions

I have argued that corporations that offer bribes to win contracts and that secure those contracts are committing a form of power crime. Inasmuch as the punishments meted out to corporations found guilty of such crimes are, relative to the pecuniary value of the gains, typically minor, the inequity of sentencing regimes reflects another aspect of power crime—the ability of the rich (here, corporations) to be treated far more leniently than the poor. If one compares the likely sentence for a

[17] The four other firms were BICC Cables, Marubeni Corporation, Pirelli Cables and Tomen Corporation.

burglar who may have stolen from one family with that for a corporation whose misdeeds have negatively impacted on thousands of people, the power imbalance becomes highly visible. This inequity typically relates to resource inequality; TNCs can afford the best solicitors and barristers, whereas many individuals accused of burglary are dependent on legal aid, if they have any legal assistance at all. I have also argued that, while rational choice theory can help to explain the form of power crime considered here, its value is limited; common sense would arrive at similar explanations as a complex theory.

States can to some extent counter corporate power crime. Given the possibility that misbehaving corporations that are threatened or punished in some way by a particular state have until now usually been able simply to shift to other countries, it is only if states collaborate with each other—engage in collective action—that their role in curbing the overall power of big business to commit power crimes might become significant. But the question arises as to whether states really have a vested interest in doing this. While they might pay lip service to such collective action, the fact remains that states, like corporations, frequently place their own vested interests ahead of those of either the collective or their own publics. This will sometimes result in collusion with miscreant big business in various forms of power crime. Neo-liberalism, with its emphasis on markets' unfettered freedom, deregulation, and the blurring of the boundaries between the state and the market, greatly increases the likelihood of such collusive power crime.[18] It is worth noting that while some states that have signed up to the OECD Convention—notably the USA, and to a lesser extent Germany—have been taking their responsibilities for investigating alleged bribery of foreign officials seriously, other states—including the UK and Australia—did not prosecute any firms at all for this crime in either 2006 or 2007 [15]. Unfortunately, if countries such as Australia and the UK do not prosecute miscreant firms, other countries that *have* been prosecuting could soon conclude that it is against their interests to continue doing so if others do not, especially if a global recession increases the pressure on both companies and states to outperform rivals. And if *collusive* power crime increases, there is precious little that either international organisations or civil society can do. In short, power crime is not going to disappear any time soon, and could actually become more salient in the coming years.

References

1. BBC (2008). Q and A: the BAE-Saudi allegations, BBC news online, 10 April (accessed 6 June 2008).
2. Buchanan, J., & Tullock, G. (1962). *The calculus of consent: Logical foundations of constitutional democracy.* Ann Arbor: University of Michigan.
3. Camilleri, J., & Falk, J. (1992). *The end of sovereignty?.* Cheltenham: Elgar.
4. Clinard, M., & Yeager, C. (1980). *Corporate crime.* New York: Free.
5. Cohen, J. (1983). Rethinking social movements. *Berkeley Journal of Sociology, 28*, 97–113.

[18] See O'Brien ([24]: 3–4 and 101–2) for an argument that deregulation, in the form of the repeal of the Glass-Steagall Act in 1999, played an important role in the increase of corporate malfeasance in the USA in the 2000s.

6. Cole, T. (2006). *Report of the inquiry into certain Australian companies in relation to the UN Oil-for-food programme—Vol.1*. Canberra: Commonwealth of Australia.
7. Dahl, R. (1956). *A preface to democratic theory*. Chicago: Chicago University.
8. Dahl, R. (1957). The concept of power. *Behavioural Science*, *2*(3), 201–15.
9. Drew, K. (2004). Compliance with anti-corruption laws through access to public procurement: sanctioning or voluntary self-regulation, background paper for workshop 4, OECD global forum on governance—fighting corruption and promoting public integrity in public procurement, 29–30 November.
10. Evans, R., Traynor, I. Harding, L., & Carroll, R. (2003). Politicians claims put BAE in firing line', *The Guardian*, 12 June.
11. Ferejohn, J. (1991). Rationality and interpretation: Parliamentary elections in early Stuart England. In K. Monroe (Ed.), *The economic approach to politics: A critical reassessment of the theory of rational action*. New York: Harper Collins.
12. Foley, S. (2006). Daimler employees fired over bribery scandal, *The Independent*, 7 March
13. Fong, D. (2008). German firms not affected by siemens scandal, experts say, deutsche welle world online, 7 May (accessed 6 June 2008).
14. Goldman, M. (2005). Political Graft: The Russian way, *Current History*, October: 313–18.
15. Heimann, F., & Dell, G. (2007). *Progress report 07: Enforcement of the OECD convention on combating bribery of foreign public officials*. Berlin: Transparency International.
16. Jacoby, N., Nehemkis, P., & Eells, R. (1977). *Bribery and extortion in world business: A study of corporate political payments abroad*. New York: Macmillan.
17. KordaMentha (2006). Agribusiness industry roundup. Australia: KordaMentha research unit, December, No.618.
18. Krust, M., Scannell, K. and Power, S. (2006). Daimler, U.S. discuss a deal to end bribe case, wall street journal, 14 September: A11.
19. Kuzio, T. (2003). Ukraine's international image suffers as Kuchma threatens agricultural reform, *Ukrainian Weekly*, 71/17 (27 April).
20. Leigh, D., & Evans, R. (2007). BAE accused of secretly paying £1bn to Saudi prince, *The Guardian*, 7 June.
21. Leigh, D., & Evans, R. (2008). BAE: secret papers reveal threats from Saudi prince, *The Guardian*, 15 February.
22. Miller, W., Grødeland, Å., & Koshechkina, T. (2001). *A culture of corruption: Coping with government in post-communist europe*. Budapest: Central European.
23. Murphy, M. and Peel, M. (2008). Fraud officers vow to pursue BAE, *Financial Times* online, 30 July (accessed 6 August 2008).
24. O'Brien, J. (2003). *Wall street on trial: A corrupted state?*. Chichester: Wiley.
25. Riker, W. (1990). Political science and rational choice. In J. Alt, & K. Schepsle (Eds.), *Perspectives on positive political economy*. Cambridge: Cambridge University.
26. Robertson, D. (2007). Former law lord is asked to head inquiry into BAE's ethics, *The Times*, 12 June.
27. Shelley, L. (1998). Organized crime and corruption in Ukraine: impediments to the development of a free market economy. *Demokratizatsiya*, *6*(4), 648–63.
28. Stiglitz, J. (2006). *Making globalization work*. Camberwell, Vic: Penguin.
29. Tanzi, V. (2004). Foreword. In D. Masciandaro (Ed.), *Global financial crime: Terrorism, money laundering and offshore centres* (pp. ix-x). Aldershot: Ashgate.
30. Taylor, M. (2006). *Rationality and the ideology of disconnection*. New York: Cambridge University.
31. Touraine, A. (1981) *The voice and the eye*. Cambridge: Cambridge University.
32. Walker, R. B. J., & Mendlovitz, S. (eds.) (1990), *Contending sovereignties* (Boulder: Rienner).
33. Wardell, J. (2008). UK law lords uphold decision to halt BAE enquiry, *Washington Post* online, 30 July (accessed 6 August 2008).
34. Woronowycz, R. (1997). Justice ministry announces program to fight corruption. *Ukrainian Weekly*, *65*(16), 20 April.

[9]

Narcophobia: drugs prohibition and the generation of human rights abuses

Fernanda Mena · Dick Hobbs

Published online: 22 December 2009

Abstract This paper is concerned with the negative aspects of global drugs prohibition. The paper argues that prohibition, which is driven by moralism rather than empirical research, creates a black market that is regulated by violent entrepreneurs, and particular in developing countries where there is a lack of economic opportunities for the poor, offers the only feasible employment options. The paper suggests that the results of experimental legislation should be taken seriously. The militarisation of prohibition enforcement has hindered the advancement of democracy and led to violence and increases in human rights abuses. In conclusion it is argued that the current system of global prohibition creates more problems than it solves, and that issues of drug production and trade need to be dealt with by regulation from within a development perspective.

Introduction: an old/new debate

In 1909 the first international effort to ban the drugs trade took place in Shanghai, creating a system of drug control based on prohibition, and establishing worldwide a principle bound by international law to forbid drugs production, trade, and consumption. Although the aspiration to eliminate both supply and demand is contentious, it has been reiterated by the United Nations periodic reviews of international drug policy, in spite of the negative outcomes that are highlighted both by scholars (Friedman 1989; Nadelmann 1990; Levine 2003; Miron 2004; Bancroft 2009; Barrett and Nowak 2009) and civil society (Transnational Institute 2008; Latin American Commission on Drugs and Democracy 2009).

F. Mena
Centre for Human Rights, Department of Sociology, London School of Economics, London, UK
e-mail: mena.fe@gmail.com

D. Hobbs (✉)
Department of Sociology, London School of Economics, London, UK
e-mail: R.Hobbs@lse.ac.uk

The prohibitionists' main claim is that criminalization deters drug use, and therefore reduces harm to health, which would exponentially increase under legalization. However, once we cut through the liberal façade, authors such as Wilson and Bennett ultimately argue that fundamentally "drugs use is wrong" (Bennett 1991: 339), and that drugs "illegality rests in part on their immorality" (Wilson 1990: 26). Conversely, we argue that drug prohibition harms society in several ways, in particular creating a black market that has little concern for human rights, as participants do not have access to the legal and judicial system in order to resolve disputes, and as a consequence seek other methods of reaching a resolution, in particular violence (Miron 2004: 12; Hobbs forthcoming).

In addition, "illegality creates obscene profits that finance the murderous tactics of the drug lords; illegality leads to the corruption of law enforcement officials; illegality monopolizes the efforts of honest law forces so that they are starved for resources to fight the simpler crimes of robbery, theft and assault" (Friedman 1989: 2). However, the *status quo* argument denies direct connection between prohibition and the advent of organized crime, a form of "interpretative denial" (Cohen 2001), in which the abuse of human rights is acknowledged but not its exact causes. The orthodoxy of the drugs debate hides the problems caused by the prohibition of illicit drugs, distorting the damage that it causes often to the most vulnerable in society. "At worst, it actually contributes to the generation of harm" (Bancroft 2009: 72).

The first section of this paper will draw on a review of drug policy developments, from free trade to bans, focusing on its relation to commercial interests, and suggesting that moral discourses have been key in raising support for the "war on drugs". Secondly, we will examine UN drug treaties currently in force and interrogate the harms that they generate by imposing burdensome goals on governments without assuring human rights accountability. We will then look into Portuguese drug decriminalization, since 2001, and finally we will analyse the case of Brazil, demonstrating that prohibitions pernicious outcomes are worsened by features common to new democracies.

We then conclude that drug prohibition is increasingly costly, harmful to health and welfare, and counterproductive for the establishment of an international order that aims for development, security and the protection of human rights.

From commodities to evildoers

Historically drugs have comprised an important commodity for global trade, and were an important source of revenue for governments with overseas empires; for instance the Dutch, English and Portuguese trafficked opium in the seventeenth and eighteenth centuries (Mcallister 2000: 10). The first step towards prohibition emanated from a change in the way that drugs were perceived, and the shift from economic liberalism, based on the free market, to a prohibitionist stance, based on images of moral degeneration and deviance, laid the groundwork for contemporary prohibitionism.

By 1900 the idea of "instituting controls reinforced the authority of the medical profession, government agencies and moral entrepreneurs" (Mcallister 2000: 17-18), and the drugs debate combined apparently paradoxical approaches: physicians' unionising efforts, governments' commercial interests and churches' moral pleas concerning obstacles to new conversions (Ibid: 14). The role of religious movements in the anti-drugs crusade was crucial. Taylor described the international campaign for drugs prohibition as "missionary diplomacy" (1969: 29), and in Britain various Church groups, in particular the Quakers, founded anti-opium societies, and gathered Parliamentary allies to their cause (Nadelmann 1990: 503). In the US, Episcopal bishop Charles Henry Brent became an international leader of the anti-drugs movement. A former missionary in the Far East, Brent released a report in 1904 in which he argued for total prohibition of opium, based on his observations of the natives' moral degeneration (Musto 1987: 28).

The notion of opium as an "evil" was also emphasized both by the Chinese and the North American governments. The former needed a scapegoat to heighten nationalism and sovereignty (Dikotter 2003: 2), and while the latter had no significant interest in the opium trade, the burgeoning Chinese market held an allure for the American government that was sufficient for them to curry favour with the Chinese government (Mcallister 2000: 27–30). The ultimate motor for narcotic controls was, therefore, the product of the combined endeavours of moral entrepreneurs, nationalist politicians and the economic aspirations of the US.[1]

Bishop Brent was the chairman of the first international meeting aiming to regulate the opium trade, the Shanghai Opium Commission of 1909, which took place just a few decades after the last of Britain's Opium Wars (1856–1860) against China, the purpose of which was to assure the import of opium to China (Hanes and Sanello 2003). One of the Shanghai Commission's recommendations was that opium could not be exported to nations which prohibited it by domestic legislation. After the Shanghai meeting, however, opium was still entering China, mostly through Portuguese traders, and the US presented a supply oriented vision of international drug control through measures such as limiting cultivation, controlling manufacturing and distribution, equalizing national controls and instituting reciprocal rights to search suspected vessels (Taylor 1969: 83-4).

Various states responded by requesting amendments. Italy wanted marijuana and hashish to be included in the draft, and Portugal asserted that it would not change its opium trade policy unless all other governments involved in the business agreed to do so. France opposed the requirement of domestic legislation review, and Britain insisted that the treaty must include manufactured drugs such as morphine, heroin and cocaine. Germany, the main exporter of manufactured drugs, objected to this proposition, while Turkey, a major player in the opium trade, simply refused to attend the meeting (Mcallister 2000: 31-32). The next step in the history of global anti-drugs efforts took place via the Hague Opium Conferences (1912–1914), which established the first international drug control treaty. Forty-four countries signed the Convention but just a few ratified it (Willoughby 1976).

After the First World War, the League of Nations became a central forum for transnational affairs, and as this global arena was occupied by representatives of states, the role of moral entrepreneurs, such as the Church, became less obvious. The

[1] Coincidence or not, it is interesting to note that in China, according to Dikotter (2003), "the commodity that most benefited from prohibition was the ready-made cigarette", a market dominated by the US and the UK.

League's covenant explicitly mentioned the control of "dangerous drugs" as an objective, and the Hague Opium Convention was included in the peace agreements of the Treaty of Versailles (Levine 2003: 146). However, the lack of support from the US, which never took part in the League, weakened considerably initiatives attempting to create a permanent system of global drug control.

The advent of the United Nations in 1945, and the establishment of drug control as one of its priorities, paved the way for the 1961 Single Convention on Narcotic Drugs, which was ratified by 98% of the world's nations. Combined with the 1971 Convention on Psychotropic Substances and the 1988 Convention against Illicit Traffic in Narcotic Drugs and Psychotropic Substances, it created the current system of drugs prohibition (Chatterjee 1981). It had taken over half a century of international meetings, intense diplomatic leverage and insistent demonization discourses for anti-drugs actors to achieve consensus on global drug prohibition.

The 1961 Convention focused on plant-based drugs such as opium, heroin, coca, cocaine and cannabis, limiting its production, trade and use exclusively to medical and scientific purposes. It also created the International Narcotics Control Board (INCB), which monitors the implementation of UN Conventions on drugs, "operating like a World Trade Organisation in reverse", ensuring that signatories may not permit narcotic drugs to be produced, traded or sold (Bancroft 2009: 117).

Ten years later, the 1971 Convention was settled as a result of growing concerns over synthetic drugs (amphetamines, barbiturates and LSD), and in 1988 another convention tackled drug trafficking, introducing the requirement that each signatory to the Convention make the possession of drugs for personal consumption a criminal offense under domestic law (Bewley-Taylor 2003: 173). In 1998 a United Nations General Assembly Special Session (UNGASS) on drugs released a Political Declaration[2] which reiterated the UN previous commitment to a "drug free world" by 2008.

The politics of fear: aliens and anti-drugs discourses

Until the late nineteenth century, substances like cocaine, cannabis or heroin, were not placed under one single category of "drugs" and, according to Bancroft, the mere categorization of "drug" is a function of power, "inebriety becomes deviance, anti-social, an addiction, requiring surveillance and possible coercive intervention" (2009: 17–20). This "politics of fear", launched at the end of the 19th century in order to tackle trade and consumption of substances capable of altering states of consciousness, marks a diversion from a commercial to a moral discourse, and was marked by the way that drugs were defined, labelled, stigmatized and, therefore, controlled (Best 1989).

In 1902, the main British argument in defence of the opium trade was that "if we did not supply the Chinese with opium, they would supply themselves with it, and that if someone was to supply them, we should have the profit of doing so" (The Times 1902: 5). Just 20 years later, drug traders, were presented as "purveyors of

[2] A/RES/S-20/2, "Political Declaration", General Assembly 20th Special Session, 9th Plenary Meeting. June 10 1998.

debauchery" (The Times 1922: 13) and "enemies of society" (The Times 1922: 19). From 1851 to 1900 (not inclusive), there was only one piece of news published by "The Times" that combined the terms "drug" and "evil". Between 1900 and 1940, when the first international anti-drugs agreements came into force, the occurrence of this association increased to thirteen citations. Between 1940 and 1985, they decreased to nine news pieces. And, finally, between 1985 and 2009, 1,504 articles mentioned "drug" and "evil" side by side (Mena 2009).

This strategy of stigmatization and control was also applied to the increasing immigration of Chinese labourers entering the US by the early twentieth century, and their association with opium created the illusion of indigenous virtue and outsider "evil", legitimising the government's agency against "threat" (Silverstone 2006: 57-58). The American Pharmaceutical Association (APhA) and its Committee on the Acquirement of the Drug Habit, that was active between 1898 and 1902, reinforced the stereotyping of the Chinese by writing that, "if the Chinaman cannot get along without his 'dope', we can get along without him" (Reinarman 1979; Musto 1987). The demonisation of the Chinese culminated with the USA's permanent exclusion of Chinese labourers from the US in 1902 (Musto 1987:30).

The emergent popularity of cocaine in the 1900s enabled this process of othering to be extended to the already oppressed black American population. Newspapers published by the New York Times in 1914 asserted that cocaine caused "negroes" to commit "violent crimes", and made them more resistant to police bullets (The New York Times, 8/2/1914). The stigmatization of blacks through drugs sustained racist policies and violent remedies, "the fear of the cocainized black coincided with the peak of lynching, legal segregation and voting laws all designed to remove political and social power from him" (Musto 1987: 7). The articulation of moral judgements of "good" and "evil" applied towards certain ethnic groups defined "agendas of public culture" (Silverstone 2006: 57), creating not only support but actual demands for punitive action.

After the Second World War, international conspiracies were frequent in the Western world, and the head of the US Federal Bureau of Narcotics (FBN), Harry J. Anslinger, was not only responsible for drug-enforcement policies, but was also involved in the US post-war foreign policy, and in the 1950s, Anslinger provided journalists with conspiratorial stories claiming that the People's Republic of China provided drugs to the US in order to fund a future war, while simultaneously weakening the "health and moral fibre of its enemies" (Woodiwiss 1993: 3). In sum, the association of drugs with notions of "evil" that labelled Chinese, black Americans and communism, constitutes an exercise of power that culminates in the constitution of a moral and political ideology —a framed version of reality that established barriers to full interaction and understanding, underpinning social exclusion and legitimising hostility and violence (Picketing 2001: 48-49).

Declaration of war

In 1971, President Nixon identified drugs as the US "public enemy number 1" and declared a "war on drugs", proclaiming that "every son and daughter" in the US was "at risk" because of drugs (Woodiwiss 1988: 221-2). The invocation of the American family unit alongside a "war" was appealing to the media, and articulated discourses that created an "infrastructure in the engineering of consent to the war on drugs" (Elwood 1994: 11-12).

The Reagan Presidency that commenced in 1981 saw First Lady Nancy Reagan create pressure for international prohibition at a meeting of the UN General Assembly in 1988, in particular by offering support for the treaty that would become the Vienna Convention against Narcotic Drugs and Psychotropic Substances (National First Ladies Library 2008; Woodiwiss and Hobbs 2009). President Reagan also used metaphors of war in his anti-drug speeches, contributing to a moral panic (Hawdon 2001: 419–445) that demanded action based on an eight-point plan aiming to "cripple organized crime" (Woodiwiss 1988: 200), expanding the anti-drug budget, and shifting responsibility for drug enforcement from the DEA to the FBI.

In 1987 the United Nations announced a new international treaty against drug trafficking, and in 1988 a G-7 task force flagged up international action against money laundering to confiscate drug profits. In December of the same year, the G-7 countries incorporated these proposals into the 1988 U.N. Convention Against Illicit Traffic in Narcotic Drugs and Psychotropic Substances (Friman 1991: 880-2; Woodiwiss and Bewley-Taylor 2005: 17–21). By 2005, 173 countries had signed up to the convention (Bewley-Taylor 1999: 171-4).

For geographic reasons as well as for being the main producer of coca leaves, Latin America was at the forefront of the US "war on drugs". In 1989, "Operation Just Cause" marked the invasion of Panama by US troops to depose General Manuel Noriega, citing his alleged links to drug trafficking. In Bolivia, security forces were trained by the US, and human rights groups reported summary executions of coca farmers and unlawful detentions (Ledebur 2005, p. 144). In 1998, a forced-eradication operation named "Plan Dignidad" (Plan Dignity), that aimed to eliminate "illicit" crops within 5 years, turned into a series of confrontations between "cocaleros" (coca farmers) and Bolivian military and police forces, during which Evo Morales emerged as a leader, before being elected president in 2005.

In the early 2000s, "Plan Colombia" inaugurated a US$ 1.3 billion military aid package, although Colombia's long and complex guerrilla warfare, and the army's poor record on human rights (Sweig 2002: 130) posed an additional threat to the success of the initiative. According to the United Nations High Commissioner for Refugees, 2008, today Colombia has a similar amount of internally displaced people (IDPs) to Iraq, and more than 374,000 refugees.

The militarization of anti-drugs efforts was spawned by the US throughout the region exactly when Latin America was undergoing a "third wave of democratization" (Huntington 1991) that attempted to overcome decades of military coups and dictatorships, and strengthening the military presented a setback to fragile democracies, their institutions and accountability processes (Youngers and Rosin 2005: 343). Moreover, crop eradication and substitution programmes tended to be effective in the short-term, but worthless and harmful in the long run. Worthless because substitutive crops proved to be less profitable, pulling peasant farmers back to coca plantations afterwards. Harmful because many eradication strategies involved the spray of toxic herbicides, causing birth defects, diseases and environmental damage (del Olmo 1987, cited in Johns 1992: 52). The long-term effects on the environment is particularly serious because the "poorest segment of the population is totally dependent on the land" (Johns 1992: 54).

An additional "war on drugs" strategy was to "certify" countries for cooperation in US anti-drugs efforts, and those who failed to meet US standards faced economic sanctions, such as a withdrawal of aid or trade benefits (Bullington 1993: 49; Youngers and Rosin 2005: 22). However, it must be stressed that although the US "war on drugs" presented an extra pressure on Latin America drug policies, its goals coincided with those established by the UN drug conventions.

UN drug policies: inconsistency and human rights

This paper has elucidated the series of stigmatizations supporting the advent and advance of a prohibitionist system of drug control, its enforcement practices and some pernicious consequences. Yet it is necessary to illuminate how those outcomes are intertwined with the neglect of human rights principles within UN drug policies (Bewley-Taylor 2005: 423). The UN Charter, the foundational document of the UN, has supremacy over other treaties (UNODC 2008: 218). Its article 1 states in paragraph 1 that the purpose of the UN is to "take effective collective measures…for the suppression of acts of aggression or other breaches of peace". Paragraph 3 in the same article, states that the UN must promote and encourage "respect for human rights and for fundamental freedoms for all without distinction". Following this reasoning, UN bodies should have "suppression of acts of aggression" and "respect for human rights" as overarching principles. Moreover, the primacy of human rights was enshrined in another foundational UN document: the Universal Declaration of Human Rights (1948). However, as detailed above, the prohibitionism that is at the core of international law on drugs sustains a black market and a whole network of illegality and crime, inspiring progressively abrasive enforcement strategies and social exclusion. This cause-effect link was noted by the UNODC (2009) as the "unintended effects of drug control" in the preamble of the World Drug Report 2009, and a previous UN report, "making drug control 'fit for purpose'", has enumerated five "unintended" and "unexpected" consequences of drug control.

First, it acknowledged the rise of "a huge criminal black market" as a drug prohibition outcome. Secondly, a "policy displacement", in which resources are withdrawn from areas such as public health in favour of public security. Thirdly, "geographical displacement" pushes drugs production away from places with harsher enforcement. The fourth consequence was "substance displacement", as both users and suppliers move from controlled substances to others that are subjected to flawed or weak control, although they may be more harmful (as in the case of crack-cocaine or crystal meth). Finally, it recognizes the marginalization and social exclusion suffered by drugs users (UNODC 2008: 10-11).

The UN's acknowledgment of the consequences of drug prohibition suggests that international drug policies have been undertaken with little regard to their potential consequences, and with lack of accountability. It could be argued that those "unintended and unexpected" consequences entail breaches of fundamental human rights (namely articles 3, 5, 13 paragraph 1, and article 28). Death (art.3), torture (art.5) and displacement forced by guerrilla warfare (art. 13 paragraph 1) all seem to be generated, in one way or another, by the black market nature of current global and local drug flows. Therefore, it can be contended that the present drugs control system exacerbates conditions for a "social and international order in which the rights and freedoms set forth" in the UDHR cannot be "fully realized" (art. 28).

Chinkin (1998) articulates the unevenness between international and human rights law when arguing that, "effective human rights law must be fully integrated into the substance and procedures of other branches of international law, both for determining the causes of human rights violations and for ensuring that they are taken into account in the decision making of all types. This is not currently the case" (Chinkin 1998: 117). At the drugs treaties level, international drug policies have been developed and interpreted "in a vacuum from human rights law, with little reference to human rights norms, and little regard for their own human rights obligations" (Barrett and Nowak 2009: 451). Barrett and Nowak provide myriad examples of such inconsistencies, for instance the use of virulent herbicides in crop eradication policies, beatings and death threats in order to obtain information and confessions from drug suspects in Indonesia (Nowak 2008), and the death penalty for drug offences still being retained by over thirty countries. Ostensive police raids into poor communities, often involving reckless shootings and the execution of alleged criminals, are also mentioned by the authors. In Rio de Janeiro, the Security Secretary stated that violent conflicts were a "bitter pill" that slum residents would have to swallow if they wished to get rid of drug gangs in their communities (see Phillips 2007). Because drug policy success is measured in terms of tons of drugs seized, and number of drug offenders imprisoned, "there is no human rights scrutiny of processes" and "nothing in the way of human rights outcome evaluation for drug control projects" (Barrett and Nowak 2009: 471). While it is important to emphasize that UN agencies do not endorse poisonous spraying, torture, the death penalty or the deliberate use of violence to achieve its drug related goals, it is extremely relevant to bring those consequences to the centre of the drugs debate: are they intrinsic to a prohibitionist regime? How to minimize those harms?

Certain goals such as "eradicating" cultivation, and eliminating "the root causes" of drugs abuse —apart from contention in terms of feasibility *per se*— were determined by the 1988 Convention to be achieved through "appropriate measures" at the domestic level, and it is the responsibility of individual states to choose how to achieve them. Can the UN be held accountable for the repercussion of its policies inside a sovereign state border? Some scholars and organizations argue that it can. They point to "UN complicity in those violations", an approach made possible after the Officer of the High Commissioner for Human Rights (OHCHR) noted in 2004 that an organisation may be complicit in violations of human rights if it "tolerates, or knowingly ignores" abuses (Beckley Foundation 2008: 6, Barrett and Nowak 2009: 474). After Kofi Annan ascertained that human rights are one of the pillars of the UN (Annan 2005), it seems clear that international drug policy is at odds with this provision.

Civil society: claims for a pragmatic approach

At the end of June 2009, a group of fourteen international organizations, including the Latin American Commission on Drugs and Democracy—co-chaired by former presidents of Brazil, Colombia and Mexico, released a call to action named "Support

Global Drug Policy Reform". The document stated that the "war on drugs" has become a war on people, and proposed actions based on the "given overwhelming evidence" that criminalizing drugs is "both counterproductive and highly destructive" (Latin American Commission on Drugs and Democracy 2009).

The Commission also stated that "violence and the organized crime associated with the narcotics trade are critical problems in Latin America today" (Latin American Commission on Drugs and Democracy 2009: 5), and pushed for an "urgent" in-depth revision of current drug policies "in the light of their enormous human and social costs and threats to democratic institutions" (ibid, 2009: 5).

The report states that over the past decade, Latin America has witnessed "a rise in organized crime caused both by the international narcotics trade and the growing control exercised by criminal groups over domestic markets and territories; a growth in unacceptable levels of drug-related violence affecting the whole of society and, in particular, the poor and the young"; the criminalization of politics and the politicization of crime, as well as the proliferation of linkages between them, as reflected in the infiltration of democratic institutions by organized crimes" and "the corruption of public servants, the judicial system, governments, the political system and especially the police forces in charge of enforcing law and order" (Latin American Commission on Drugs and Democracy 2009: 5)

The Commission states that prohibition has been disastrous, and indicates that human rights violations have particularly harmed vulnerable populations in the region, especially peasant farmers and poor communities living in areas controlled by drug trafficking organizations. The document proposes a new paradigm in drugs policy which would involve a change of status for drug addicts from criminals to patients in the public health system, an evaluation of the decriminalization of cannabis for personal use, and a redirection of resources to "fighting the most harmful effects of organized crime on society such as violence, institutional corruption, money laundering, arms trafficking and the control over territories and populations" (Latin American Commission on Drugs and Democracy 2009: 10)—the exact features which are central to the prohibitionist regime on drugs.

The effects of decriminalization: Portugal

The Dutch experience on drugs policy has until recently been the best source of evidence on alternative approaches to orthodox prohibition based drug policy. In the Netherlands the purchase, possession and consumption of cannabis, although still a crime, is *de facto* decriminalized (Cohen et al. 2004: 836). Cohen et al. compared cannabis usage rates in Amsterdam to those in San Francisco where drug use remains criminalised, and found that drug usage in the North American city was higher than in the Dutch capital, therefore suggesting that there was no evidence that criminalization deters use (Ibid: 838–841).

However, Portugal has emerged as a more complete case study as it is the first European Union country to have decriminalized the purchase, possession and consumption for personal use (defined as an average quantity for 10 days of use) of all drugs, although drug trafficking remains criminalized. The Portuguese policy was implemented in 2001 in the light of a deteriorating drug problem in the 1990s, especially with regard to heroin. In his investigation into the Portuguese case, Greenwald (2009) states that the political impetus for decriminalization was driven by the perception that the principal obstacles to effective policies to manage drug problems were the treatment barriers and resource drain imposed by the criminalization regime. Greenwald acknowledges that decriminalization "has had no adverse effect on drug usage rates in Portugal, which, in numerous categories, are now among the lowest in the EU" (Greenwald 2009: 12). Particularly when compared with states that have stringent criminalization regimes, usage decreased among teenagers and mildly increased among young adults. The number of newly reported cases of HIV/AIDS among drug users also decreased significantly, along with drug-related mortality, and decriminalization freed up resources that were channelled into treatment and other harm reduction programs (Ibid).

Brazil: poverty, violence and human rights

Brazil is not a main producer of opium or cocaine, but it does take part in the global drug market as a cannabis producer, and it shares borders with the three main cocaine producers: Colombia, Peru and Bolivia. As a result, 15% of South America's cocaine exports pass through Brazil. Crucially, Brazil has developed as a major consumer market for all drugs.[3]

Brazil has one of the most unequal income distributions in the world, with around 34% of its population under the poverty line.[4] This is relevant to the drug trade as "it configures a perverse social and economic integration for those who suffer exclusion… poor people work perilously at the retail trade in order to assure enormous profits at superior nodes" (Zaluar 2001: 370). In rural areas, cannabis is cultivated in plantations, and according to the Labour Prosecution Office of Pernambuco region (the main cannabis producing area in Brazil), there are around 40,000 marijuana workers, and among them 10,000 are estimated to be young people, and "many are forced to work by criminal gangs" (Iulianelli 2004: 9–11).

In the urban centres of major cities like São Paulo and Rio de Janeiro this situation is far more complex. Drug gangs dominate entire territories; the most vulnerable of these are *favelas* (shanty towns), which lack state presence and basic services. A study conducted in Rio followed 230 young people working for drug traffic 'organizations', and concluded that economic motivation was the main push factor for them to be involved in the drug trade, an involvement that is enforced via coercion and violent practices sustained by the widespread possession of military standard weaponry: rifles, machine guns and grenades (Favela Watch 2006; see also Phillips 2009).

As mentioned above, in black markets violence is often used because the justice and legal systems are not viable resources for solving drug related business conflicts, and drug gangs tend to use their arsenal to "threaten possible competitors, violently

[3] Brazil has the larger population of opioid (635,000) and cocaine users (890,000) in South America as well as the third highest rate of amphetamines' consumption in the world, according to the 2009 World Drug Report (UNODC 2009).

[4] Analysis of data from National Household Survey (PNAD, 1999 cited by Paes de Barros et al. 2001).

coerce debtors, make fragile agreements with the policemen who extort them, and intimidate witnesses" (Zaluar 2001: 375). As a result, the drug business is embedded in violent practices, such as coercion, torture and executions. The general homicide rate in Europe is 1.2 deaths per 100,000 inhabitants, while in Brazil it is 26.1. In the population of 15 to 24 years old, the European homicide rate is still 1.2, while the Brazilian rate increases to 51.6 (Waisenlfisz 2008). In Rio the homicide rate rises to 104.4, and if we concentrate upon homicides among the population of Rio de Janeiro's blacks and dark skinned (highly concentrated among *favelas* inhabitants), from 22 to 23 years old, the rate achieves a staggering 370 deaths per 100,000 inhabitants (Ramos 2009: 3).

As Zaluar states (2001), one cannot look at the "tremendous" rates of homicide in Brazil without linking them to drug trafficking, and points to the fact that studies suggest that a high proportion of homicides are related to narcotraffic (Adorno 1990; Soares et al. 1996; Beato and Assunção 2000): an estimated 25% to 52% of the total. Calculating drug-related homicides on the basis of the minimum estimate (25%), Rio's drug-related deaths would still be ahead of the terror inflicted by Uganda's infamous Lord's Resistance Army. Using the maximum rate of 52% this places Rio's deaths above those generated by major conflicts in Sierra Leone and Afghanistan. Between 1991 and 1999, Sierra Leone's civil war produced around 11,000 deaths among young people, while during the same period in Rio, 23,480 teenagers died due to firearm injuries; in the Uganda conflict, from 1994 to 1998, about 3,000 youngsters died, while in Rio 12,404 boys died from gunshots (Dowdney 2003: 114–116).

The Police also contribute significantly to these Brazilian death statistics via extrajudicial killings, especially in *favelas* dominated by drug gangs.[5] According to the Human Rights Watch World Report 2009, "police are responsible for one out of every five intentional killings". Not included in these figures are bystanders killed by stray bullets during police raids, during which "indiscriminate shootings" occur (HRW 2009: 160). According to another report from the Beckley Foundation (2008), in Brazil, "police are engaged in an increasingly violent and frequently lethal war on drugs" in which "children recruited into drug trafficking gangs are considered legitimate targets for armed police and are shot at without hesitation" (2008: 6-7).

Despite extensive reports on human rights violations during these police operations, the government still tends to support certain high-profile militarized police operations (AI 2008: 74). This data suggests that the "war on drugs" produces more casualties than in many "official" conflicts, and the violence that emanates from drugs prohibition also entails abuses of human rights in terms of life, torture and security.

Concerning Brazilian drug consumption deaths, although potentially under-reported, overdoses constitute a minor harm compared to deaths associated with drug-related violence. In 2007, 3,866 people were hospitalized due to drug abuse and 64 died of overdose (UNODC estimates drug abuse-related deaths are 200,000

[5] Reports from Human Rights Watch (1996) and Amnesty International (2005) have well documented evidence of police practices such as torture and extrajudicial executions in areas of social exclusion.

per year worldwide). On the other hand, in Brazil 34,028 people were hospitalized due to intoxication from legal medication and 91 died.[6]

This might be because licit drug consumption in Brazil is much higher than illicit drug consumption, and the first six most consumed drugs are, respectively, alcohol, tobacco, marijuana, solvents, tranquillizers and amphetamines (Brazilian Information Centre for Psychotropic Drugs 2005). This could be related to the phenomenon named by UNODC as "substance displacement" —a consequence of the policy of criminalizing the use of certain drugs, pushing users towards other substances that are subjected to less stringent controls.

Another important outcome of drugs prohibition is "policy displacement". Because the police and the criminal justice system tend to focus on drug offenders rather than other criminals, nondrug-related crimes may be encouraged (Miron 2004: 12), and Adorno and Pazinato's (2009) research in São Paulo suggests that drug related offences are far more vigorously investigated and punished than murders. Other types of "policy displacement", however, might be especially harmful in developing countries, which already suffer a lack of resources to accomplish rights enshrined at the International Covenant of Economic, Social and Cultural Rights (ICESC 1966). According to the Ministry of Justice (2008), Brazil has a prison population of 440,013, a number that has increased fourfold in the last 12 years. Of these, 69,049 were arrested for national or international drug trafficking. As an example of the unbalanced prioritization entailed in "policy displacement", it is interesting to look at very basic services for human dignity as sanitation, which relates to "adequate living standards" as entrenched in Article 11 of ICESC. In Brazil, 48% of the population does not have access to sanitation, and the government's annual investment in providing sanitation is US$ 375 million, or 63% of its expenditure on imprisoned drug offenders.

After exploring aspects of the relationship between drugs, poverty, and violence, it is difficult to avoid the fact that the prohibitionist regime exacerbates structural and situational conditions for the abuse of human rights.

Conclusion: towards regulation and development

This paper has explored the notion that the prohibitionist approach to drugs promotes harm, and suggests that prohibition generates a narcotraffic that relies on violence to solve disputes, promotes corruption, resource displacement and social insecurity, all of which tend to be especially harmful to the most vulnerable members of society.

By unveiling the role of moral entrepreneurs and the weight of economic interests in discourses that shaped the drugs shift from commodities to evildoers, this paper has evidenced how rising claims for control and stringent law enforcement have culminated with the so-called "war on drugs", irrespective of the human rights violations that it creates. Strategies for fighting drugs targeted the supply side of the drug market, and are especially disadvantageous to producing countries, which tend

[6] Official data from the National System of Toxic Pharmacology Information (Ministry of Health)

also to be developing countries with less leverage than consuming countries (United States and Europe, according to UNODC) at global decision-making fora.

Brazilian estimates on drug-related homicide provide a glimpse into how developing countries tied to the global drug market are burdened with drug-related harm, such as high drug-related homicide rates, and a distinct lack of resources for the basic provision of human dignity. Analysis of those features suggests that UNODC policies have been overly concerned with crop eradication and drugs seizure. It also suggests that, certainly in human rights terms, the prohibitionist approach is not evidence-based, and on the contrary, creates conditions for abuses by denying their cause-effect relationship with prohibition itself.

We contend, therefore, that a change in the prohibitionist paradigm is required for it to engage with human rights beyond mere rhetoric. Alternatives to prohibition, however, will also need to heed these findings. For instance, legalization might not be appropriate because the free-trade nature of the drugs business is oblivious to the concerns raised by this paper, especially the gaping void between suppliers and consumers, which is, broadly speaking, a gap between developing and developed countries. Further, legalization would probably leave drug supplying developing countries, which are already experiencing the most harmful effects of prohibition, at a disadvantage by placing the drugs business under the control of transnational corporations, leaving the poor who are engaged in the most risky tasks in vulnerable situations that could lead to a migration from the drug market to other types of criminal activities. Hence, a development perspective is required in order to withdraw from prohibition's harm without creating further damage and injustice. Regulation, therefore, seems to be the key, for it could combine an alternative to prohibition with development and a new emphasis on education, harm reduction, treatment and social inclusion. For if we continue to afford a higher priority to moral arguments concerning drug consumption than to the human rights violations that prohibition causes, it is hard not to repeat Milton Friedman's question: "Can it still be considered moral?"

References

Adorno S (1990) Violencia urbana, justica criminal e organização social do crime, (urban violence, criminal justice and crime social organization). Núcleo de Estudos da Violência (USP), São Paulo

Adorno S, Pazinato W (2009) Estudo da impunidade penal no município de São Paulo, 1991–1997 (Study on legal impunity in São Paulo 1991–1997). São Paulo University (USP), São Paulo

Bancroft A (2009) Drugs, intoxication and society. Polity, Cambridge

Barrett D, Nowak M (2009) The United Nations and drug policy: towards a human rights-based approach. In: Constantinides A, Zaikos N (eds) The diversity of international law: essay in honour of professor Kalliopi Koufa, Martinus Nijhoff, pp 449–477

Beato C, Assuncao R (2000) Homicide clusters and drug traffic in Belo Horizonte from 1995 to 1999. Anais da 24 Reuniao da ANPOCS, Sao Paulo

Bennett W (1991) The plea to legalize drugs is a siren call to surrender. In: Lyman M, Potter G (eds) Drugs in society. Anderson, Cincinatti

Best J (1989) Images of issues: typifying contemporary social issues. De Gruyter, New York

Bewley-Taylor D (1999) The United States and International Drug Control, 1909–1997, London

Bewley-Taylor D (2003) Challenging the UN drug control concentions: Problems and possibilities. Int J Drug Pol 14:171–179

Bewley-Taylor D (2005) Emerging policy contradictions between the United Nations drug control system and the core values of the United Nations. Int J Drug Pol 16:423–431
Bullington B (1993) All about eve: the many faces of United States drug policy. In: Pearce F, Woodiwiss M (eds) Global crime connections. University of Toronto, Toronto, pp 32–71
Chatterjee SK (1981) Legal aspects of international drug control. Nijhoff, The Hague
Chinkin C (1998) International law and human rights. In: Evans T (ed) Human rights 50 years on: a reppraisal. Manchester University, Manchester, pp 105–129
Cohen S (2001) States of denial: knowing about atrocities and suffering. Polity, Cambridge
Cohen P, Reinarman C, Kaal H (2004) The limited relevance of drug policy: cannabis in Amsterdam and in San Francisco. Am J Public Health 94(5):836–842
Dikotter F (2003) Patient zero': China and the myth of the opium plague. School of oriental and African studies (SOAS), http://web.mac.com/dikotter
Dowdney L (2003) Children of the drug trade: a case study of children in organised armed violence in Rio de Janeiro, Brazil: 7 Letras
Elwood W (1994) Rhetoric in the war on drugs: the triumphs and tragedies of public relations. Praeger, Westport
Friedman M (1989) An open letter to Bill Bennett. Wall Street Journal, September 7
Friman H (1991) The United States, Japan, and the international drug trade: troubled partnership. Asian Surv 31(9):875–890
Greenwald G (2009) Drug decriminalization in Portugal: lessons for creating fair and successful drug policies. Cato, Washington
Hanes WF, Sanello F (2002) Opium wars: the addiction of one empire and the corruption of another. Sourcebooks, Chicago
Hawdon J (2001) The role of presidential rhetoric in the creation of a moral panic: Reagan, Bush and the war on drugs. Deviant Behav 22:419–445
Hobbs D (forthcoming) Populating the underworld. Polity, Cambridge
Huntington S (1991) The third wave: democratization in the late twentieth century. University of Oklahoma, Norman
Iulianelli JAS (2004) Rural Brazil: cannabis and violence. Drugs and Conflict No. 11
Johns CJ (1992) Power, ideology and the war on drugs: nothing succeeds like failure. Praeger, New York
Ledebur K (2005) Bolivia: clear consequences. In: Youngers CA, Rosin E (eds) Drugs and democracy in Latin America: the impact of US policy. Rienner, Boulder, pp 143–184
Levine HG (2003) Global drug prohibition: its uses and crises. Int J Drug Pol 14:145–153
Mcallister W (2000) Drug diplomacy in the twentieth century: an international history. Routledge, London
Mena F (2009) From commodities to evildoers: moral discourses towards drugs trade, prohibition and war. LSE. Department of Sociology, London
Miron JA (2004) Drug war crime. Independent, Washington
Musto DF (1987) The American disease: origins of narcotic control. Oxford University, Oxford
Nadelmann E (1990) Global prohibition regimes: the evolution of norms in international society. Int Organ 44(4):479–526
Paes de Barros R, Henrique R, Mendonça R (2001) A estabilidade inaceitável: desigualdade e pobreza no Brasil. Texto para Discussão, n. 800. Rio de Janeiro: IPEA
Picketing M (2001) Stereotyping and politics of representation. Macmillan, Houndmills
Ramos S (2009) Meninos do Rio: Jovens, violência armada e polícia nas favelas cariocas. UNICEF
Reinarman C (1979) Moral entrepreneurs and political economy: historical and ethnographic notes on the construction of the cocaine menace. Contemp Crises 3:225–254
Said E (1978) Orientalism. Penguin, London
Silverstone R (2006) Media and morality: on the rise of the Mediapolis. Polity, Cambridge
Soares LE, Se JTS, Rodrigues JAS, Piquet Carneiro L (1996) Violência e política no Rio de Janeiro (violence and politics in Rio de Janeiro). Relume Dumara, Rio de Janeiro
Sweig J (2002) What kind of war for Colombia? Foreign Aff 81:122–141
Taylor AH (1969) American diplomacy and the narcotics traffic, 1900–1939: a study in international humanitarian reform. Duke University, Durham
Willoughby W (1976) Opium as an international problem. John Hopkins, Baltimore
Wilson JQ (1990) Against the legalization of drugs. Commentary 89(2):21–28
Woodiwiss M (1988) Crime, crusades and corruption: prohibitions in the United States, 1900–1987. Pinter, London
Woodiwiss M (1993) Crime's global reach. In: Pearce F, Woodiwiss M (eds) Global crime connections. University of Toronto, Toronto, pp 1–32

Woodiwiss M, Bewley-Taylor D (2005) The global fix: the construction of a global enforcement regime. Amsterdam: Transnational Institute, available at http://www.tni.org/detail_pub.phtml?&know_id=68.
Woodiwiss M, Hobbs D (2009) Organized evil and the atlantic alliance. Br J Criminol 49(1):106–128
Youngers CA, Rosin E (2005) Drugs and democracy in Latin America: the impact of US policy. Rienner, Boulder
Zaluar A (2001) Violence in Rio de Janeiro: styles of leisure, drug use and trafficking. Int Soc Sci J 63 (169):369–378

UN documents, NGO/civil society organization's reports and newspaper articles

AI (Amnesty International) (2005) They come in shooting: policing socially excluded communities', available online at: http://www.amnesty.org/en/library/info/AMR19/025/2005
AI (Amnesty International) (2008) Amnesty international report 2008, available at: http://archive.amnesty.org/air2008/eng/Homepage.html
Annan K (2005) In larger freedom: toward development, security and human rights for all. United Nations, New York Report of the Secretary-General, document A/59/2005
Beckley Foundation Drug Policy Programme (2008) Recalibrating the regime: the need for a human rights based approach to international drug policy. Report No. 13, available online at: http://www.beckleyfoundation.org/pdf/report_13.pdf
Brazilian Information Centre for Psychotropic Use (2005) II home survey on the use of psychotropic use in Brazil 2005. Federal University of Sao Paolo, Sao Paolo
Convention on Psychotropic Substances (1971) 32 U.S.T. 543, T.I.A.S. 9725, 1019 U.N.T.S. 17
Convention Against the Illicit Traffic in Narcotic Drugs and Psychotropic Substances (1988) U.N. Doc. E/CONF.82/15
Favela Watch (Observatorio de Favelas) (2006) The journey of children, teenagers and young adults in retail drug trafficking in Rio de Janeiro: 2004–2006. Available online at: http://www.observatoriodefavelas.org.br
Human Rights Watch (1996) Fighting violence with violence: human rights abuses and criminality in Rio de Janeiro. Hum Rights Watch/Am 8(2):1–29
Human Rights Watch (2009) World report 2009. Human Rights Watch, New York
ICESC (International Covenant for Economic, Social and Cultural Rights) (1966) General assembly resolution A/RES/21/2200 A
Latin American Commission on Drugs and Democracy (2009) Towards a paradigm shift, available online at: http://www.drogasedemocracia.org/Arquivos/declaracao_ingles_site.pdf
Nowak M (2008) Report of the special rapporteur on torture and other cruel. Inhuman or degrading treatment or punishment', UN Doc. No. A/HRC/7/3/Add.7, 10 March 2008
OHCHR (2004) The global compact and human rights: understanding the sphere of influence and complicity. OHCHR briefing paper. December 2004, available online at: http://www.unglobalcompact.org/docs/issues_doc/human_rights/Resources/OHCHR_briefing_paper_Dec_04.pdf
Phillips T (2007) Blood on the streets as drug gang and police fight for control of Rio favelas. The Guardian, June 27
Phillips T (2009) Twelve dead and helicopter downed as Rio de Janeiro drug gangs go to war. The Guardian, October 17
Single Convention on Narcotic Drugs (1961) March 30, 1961, 520 U.N.T.S. 204
The Times (1902) The primate on the opium traffic. October 9th, p. 5
The Times (1922) Cocaine. April 25th, p. 13
The Times (1922) Cocaine debauchery. May 1st, p. 19
Transnational Institute (2008) Rewriting history: a response to the 2008 world drug report. Drug policy briefing No 26, available online at: http://www.tni.org/detail_page.phtml?act_id=18438
United Nations High Commissioner for Refugees (UNHCR) (2008) Global trends 2008. Available online at: http://www.unhcr.org
UNODC (2008) Making drug control fit for purpose: building on the UNGASS decade. UN Doc. No. E/CN.7/2008/CRP.17
UNODC (2009) World drug report 2009. UNODC, Vienna
Waisenlfisz JJ (2008) Mapa da Violência: os Jovens da América Latina 2008. Unesco Brasil
Williams EH (1914) Negro cocaine 'fiends' are a new southern menace. The New York Times. February 8th

Part III
Localizing the Global: Cities, Markets and Crime

[10]

The Global City: Strategic Site/New Frontier

Saskia Sassen

The master images in the currently dominant account about economic globalization emphasize hypermobility, global communications, the neutralization of place and distance. There is a tendency in that account to take the existence of a global economic system as a given, a function of the power of transnational corporations and global communications.

But the capabilities for global operation, coordination and control contained in the new information technologies and in the power of transnational corporations need to be produced. By focusing on the production of these capabilities we add a neglected dimension to the familiar issue of the power of large corporations and the new technologies. The emphasis shifts to the *practices* that constitute what we call economic globalization and global control: the work of producing and reproducing the organization and management of a global production system and a global marketplace for finance, both under conditions of economic concentration.

A focus on practices draws the categories of place and production process into the analysis of economic globalization. These are two categories easily overlooked in accounts centered on the hypermobility of capital and the power of transnationals. Developing categories such as place and production process does not negate the centrality of hypermobility and power. Rather, it brings to the fore the reality that many of the resources necessary for global economic activities are not hypermobile and are, indeed, deeply embedded in place, notably places such as global cities and export processing zones.

Why does it matter to recover place and production in analyses of the global economy, particularly as these are constituted in major cities? Because it allows us to see the multiplicity of economies and work cultures in which the global information economy is embedded. It also allows us to recover the concrete, localized processes through which globalization exists and to argue that much of the multiculturalism in large cities is as much a part of globalization as is international finance. Finally, focusing on cities allows us to specify a geography of strategic places at the global scale, places bound to each other by the dynamics of economic globalization. I refer to this as a new geography of centrality, and one of the questions it engenders is whether this new transnational geography also is the space for a new transnational politics. Insofar as my economic analysis of the global city recovers the broad array of jobs and work cultures that are part of the global economy though typically not marked as such, it allows me to examine the possibility of a new politics of traditionally disadvantaged actors operating in this new transnational economic geography. This is a politics that lies at the intersection of economic participation in the global economy and the politics of the disadvantaged, and in that sense would add an economic dimension, specifically through those who hold the other jobs in the global economy—whether factory workers in export processing zones in Asia, garment sweatshop workers in Los Angeles, or janitors on Wall Street.

These are the subjects addressed in this paper. The first section examines the role of production and place in analyses of the global economy. The second section posits the formation of new geographies of centrality and marginality constituted by these processes of globalization. The third section discusses some of the elements that suggest the formation of a new socio-spatial order in global cities. The fourth section discusses some of the localizations of the global by focusing particularly on immigrant women in global cities. In the final section I discuss the global city as a nexus where these various trends come together and produce new political alignments.

Place and Production in the Global Economy

Globalization can be deconstructed in terms of the strategic sites where global processes materialize and the linkages that bind them. Among these sites are export processing zones, off-shore banking centers, and, on a far more complex level, global cities. This produces a specific geography of globalization and underlines the extent to which it is not a planetary event encompassing all of the world.[1] It is, furthermore, a changing geography, one that has changed over the last few centuries and over the last few decades.[2] Most recently, this changing geography has come to include electronic space.

The geography of globalization contains both a dynamic of dispersal and of centralization, a condition that is only now beginning to receive recognition.[3] The massive trends towards the spatial dispersal of economic activities at the metropolitan, national, and global levels that we associate with globalization have contributed to a demand for new forms of territorial centralization of top-level management and control operations. The spatial dispersal of economic activity made possible by telematics[4] contributes to an expansion of central functions *if* this dispersal is to take place under the continuing concentration in control, ownership, and profit appropriation that characterizes the current economic system.[5]

National and global markets as well as globally integrated organizations require central places where the work of globalization gets done.[6] Further, information industries also require a vast physical infrastructure containing strategic nodes with hyperconcentration of facilities; we need to distinguish between the capacity for global transmission/communication and the material conditions that make this possible. Finally, even the most advanced information industries have a production process that is at least partly place-bound because of the combination of resources it requires even when the outputs are hypermobile.

Further, the vast new economic topography that is being implemented through electronic space is one moment, one fragment, of an even more vast economic chain that is in good part embedded in non-electronic spaces. There is no fully dematerialized firm or industry. Even the most advanced information industries, such as finance, are installed only partly in electronic space. And so are industries that produce digital products, such as software designers. The growing digitalization of economic activities has not eliminated the need for major international business and financial centers and all the material resources they concentrate, from state of the art telematics infrastructure to brain talent (Castells 1989; Graham and Marvin 1996; Sassen 1998, chapter 9).[7]

In my research I have conceptualized cities as production sites for the leading information industries of our time in order to emphasize the infrastructure of activities, firms, and jobs that is necessary to run the advanced corporate economy, including its globalized sectors.[8] These industries are typically conceptualized in terms of the hypermobility of their outputs and the high levels of expertise of their professionals rather than in terms of the production process involved and the requisite infrastructure of facilities and non-expert jobs that are also part of these industries. A detailed analysis of service-based urban economies shows that there is considerable articulation of firms, sectors, and workers who may appear as though they have little connection to an urban economy dominated by finance and specialized services, but in fact fulfill a series of functions that are an integral part of that economy. They do so, however, under conditions of sharp social, earnings, and often racial/ethnic segmentation (Sassen 2000a, chapters 8 and 9).

In the day-to-day work of the leading services complex dominated by finance, a large share of the jobs involved are lowly paid and manual, many held by women and immigrants. Although these types of workers and jobs are never represented as part of the global economy, they are in fact part of the infrastructure of jobs involved in running and implementing the global economic system, including such an advanced form of it as international finance.[9] The top end of the corporate economy—the corporate towers that project engineering expertise, precision, "techne"—is far easier to mark as necessary for an advanced economic system than are truckers and other industrial service workers, even though these are a necessary ingredient.[10] We see here at work a dynamic of valorization that has sharply increased the distance between the devalorized and the valorized, indeed overvalorized, sectors of the economy.[11]

A New Geography of Centers and Margins

The ascendance of information industries and the growth of a global economy, both inextricably linked, have contributed to a new geography of centrality and marginality. This new geography partly reproduces existing inequalities but also is the outcome of a dynamic specific to current forms of economic growth. It assumes many forms and operates in many arenas, from the distribution of telecommunications facilities to the structure of the economy and of employment. Global cities accumulate immense concentrations of economic power while cities that were once major manufacturing centers suffer inordinate declines; the downtowns of cities and business centers in metropolitan areas receive massive investments in real estate and telecommunications while low-income urban and metropolitan areas are starved for resources; highly educated workers in the corporate sector see their incomes rise to unusually high levels while low- or medium-skilled workers see theirs sink. Financial services produce superprofits while industrial services barely survive.[12]

The most powerful of these new geographies of centrality at the global level bind the major international financial and business centers: New York, London, Tokyo, Paris, Frankfurt, Zurich, Amsterdam, Los Angeles, Sydney, Hong Kong, among others. But this geography now also includes cities such as Bangkok, Taipei, Sao Paulo, and Mexico City (Sassen 2000). The intensity of transactions among these cities, particularly through the financial markets, trade in services, and investment has increased sharply, and so have the orders of magnitude involved (e.g., Noyelle and Dutka 1988; Knox 1995).[13] At the same time, there has been a sharpening inequality in the concentration of strategic resources and activities between each of these cities and others in the same country.[14]

Alongside these new global and regional hierarchies of cities is a vast territory that has become increasingly peripheral, increasingly excluded from the major economic processes that are seen as fueling economic growth in the new global economy. Formerly important manufacturing centers and port cities have lost functions and are in decline, not only in the less developed countries but also in the most advanced economies. Similarly in the valuation of labor inputs: the overvalorization of specialized services and professional workers has marked many of the "other" types of economic activities and workers as unnecessary or irrelevant to an advanced economy.

There are other forms of this segmented marking of what is and what is not an instance of the new global economy. For instance, the mainstream account about globalization recognizes that there is an international professional class of workers and highly internationalized business environments due to the presence of foreign firms and personnel. What has not been recognized is the possibility that we are seeing an internationalized labor market for low-wage manual and service workers; or that there is an internationalized business environment in many immigrant communities. These processes continue to be couched simply in terms of immigration, a narrative rooted in an earlier historical period.

This signals that there are representations of the global or the transnational that have not been recognized as such or are contested representations. Among these is the question of immigration, as well as the multiplicity of work environments it contributes in large cities, often subsumed under the notion of the ethnic economy and the informal economy. Much of what we still narrate in the language of immigration and ethnicity I contend is actually a series of processes having to do with (a) the globalization of economic activity, of cultural activity, of identity formation, and (b) the increasingly marked racialization of labor market segmentation so that the components of the production process in the advanced global information economy taking place in immigrant work environments are components not recognized as part of that global information economy. Immigration and ethnicity are constituted as otherness. Understanding them as a set of processes whereby global elements are *localized*, international labor markets are constituted, and cultures from all over the world are de- and reterritorialized, puts them right there at the center along with the internationalization of capital as a fundamental aspect of globalization.

How have these new processes of valorization and devalorization and the inequalities they produce come about? This is the subject addressed in the next section.

Elements of a New Socio-Spatial Order

The implantation of global processes and markets in major cities has meant that the internationalized sector of the urban economy has expanded sharply and has imposed a new set of criteria for valuing or pricing various economic activities and outcomes. This has had devastating effects on large sectors of the urban economy. It is not simply a quantitative transformation; we see here the elements for a new economic regime.

These tendencies towards polarization assume distinct forms in (a) the spatial organization of the urban economy, (b) the structures for social reproduction, and (c) the organization of the labor process. In these trends towards multiple forms of polarization lie conditions for the creation of employment-centered urban poverty and marginality, and for new class formations.

The ascendance of the specialized services-led economy, particularly the new finance and services complex, engenders what may be regarded as a new economic regime because, although this sector may account for only a fraction of the economy of a city, it imposes itself on that larger economy. One of these pressures is towards polarization, as is the case with the possibility for superprofits in finance, which contributes to devalorize manufacturing and low-value added services insofar as these sectors cannot generate the super-profits typical in much financial activity.

The super-profit-making capacity of many of the leading industries is embedded in a complex combination of new trends: technologies that make possible the hypermobility of capital at a global scale and the deregulation of multiple markets that allows for implementing that hypermobility; financial inventions such as securitization that liquify hitherto unliquid capital and allow it to circulate and hence make additional profits; the growing demand for services in all industries along with the increasing complexity and specialization of many of these inputs, which has contributed to their valorization and often overvalorization, as illustrated in the unusually high salary increases beginning in the 1980s for top level professionals and CEOs. Globalization further adds to the complexity of these services, their strategic character, their glamour, and therewith to their overvalorization.

The presence of a critical mass of firms with extremely high profit-making capabilities contributes to bid up the prices of commercial space, industrial services, and other business needs, and thereby makes survival for firms with moderate profit-making capabilities increasingly precarious. And while the latter are essential to the operation of the urban economy and the daily needs of residents, their economic viability is threatened in a situation where finance and specialized services can earn super-profits. High prices and profit levels in the internationalized sector and its ancillary activities, such as top-of-the-line restaurants and hotels, make it increasingly difficult for other sectors to compete for space and investments. Many of these other sectors have experienced considerable downgrading and/or displacement—for example, the replacement of neighborhood shops tailored to local needs by upscale boutiques and restaurants catering to new high-income urban elites.

Inequality in the profit-making capabilities of different sectors of the economy has always existed. But what we see happening today takes place on another order of magnitude and is engendering massive distortions in the operations of various markets, from housing to labor. For instance, the polarization among firms and households and in the spatial organization of the economy contribute, in my reading, towards the informalization of a growing array of economic activities in advanced urban economies. When firms with low or modest profit-making capacities experience an ongoing if not increasing demand for their goods and services from households and other firms in a context where a significant sector of the economy makes super-profits, they often cannot compete even though there is an effective demand for what they produce. Operating informally is often one of the few ways in which such firms can survive: for example, using spaces not zoned for commercial or manufacturing uses, such as basements in residential areas, or space that is not up to code in terms of health, fire, and other such standards. Similarly, new firms in low-profit industries entering a strong market for their goods and services may only be able to do so informally. Another option for firms with limited profit-making capabilities is to subcontract part of their work to informal operations.[15]

The recomposition of the sources of growth and of profit-making entailed by these transformations also contributes to a reorganization of some components of social reproduction or consumption. While the middle strata still constitute the majority, the conditions that contributed to their expansion and politico-economic power in the post-war decades—the centrality of mass production and mass consumption in economic growth and profit realization—have been displaced by new sources of growth.

The rapid growth of industries with strong concentration of high and low income jobs has assumed distinct forms in the consumption structure, which in turn has a feedback effect on the organization of work and the types of jobs being created. The expansion of the high-income work force in conjunction with the emergence of new cultural forms have led to a process of high-income gentrification that rests, in the last analysis, on the availability of a vast supply of low-wage workers.

In good part the consumption needs of the low-income population in large cities are met by manufacturing and retail establishments that are small, rely on family labor, and often fall below minimum safety and health standards. Cheap, locally produced sweatshop garments, for example, can compete with low-cost Asian imports. A growing range of products and services, from low-cost furniture made in basements to "gypsy cabs" and family daycare is available to meet the demand for the growing low-income population.

One way of conceptualizing informalization in advanced urban economies today is to posit it as the systemic equivalent of what we call deregulation at the top of the economy (See Sassen 1998, chapter 8). Both the deregulation of a growing number of leading information industries and the informalization of a growing number of sectors with low profit-making capacities can be conceptualized as adjustments under conditions where new economic developments and old regulations enter into growing tension.[16] "Regulatory fractures" is one concept I have used to capture this condition.

We can think of these development as constituting new geographies of centrality and marginality that cut across the old divide of poor/rich countries, and new geographies of marginality that have become increasingly evident not only in the less developed world but inside highly developed countries. Inside major cities in both the developed and developing world we see a new geography of centers and margins that not only strengthens existing inequalities but sets in motion a whole series of new dynamics of inequality.

The Localizations of the Global

Economic globalization, then, needs to be understood also in its multiple localizations, rather than only in terms of the broad, overarching macro level processes that dominate the mainstream account. Further, we need to see that some of these localizations are not generally acknowledged as having anything to do with the global economy. The global city can be seen as one strategic instantiation of such multiple localizations.

Here I want to focus on localizations of the global that are marked by those two features. Many of these localizations are embedded in the demographic transition evident in such cities, where a majority of resident workers are today immigrants and women, often women of color. These cities are experiencing an expansion of low-wage jobs that do not fit the master images about globalization yet are part of it. Their embeddedness in the demographic transition evident in all these cities, and their consequent invisibility, contribute to the devalorization of these types of workers and work cultures and to the "legitimacy" of that devalorization.

This can be read as a rupture of the traditional dynamic whereby membership in leading economic sectors contributes conditions towards the formation of a labor aristocracy—a process long evident in western industrialized economies. "Women and immigrants" come to replace the Fordist/family wage category of "women and children" (Sassen 1998, chapter 5).[17] One of the localizations of the dynamics of globalization is the process of economic restructuring in global cities. The associated socio-economic polarization has generated large growth in the demand for low-wage workers and for jobs that offer few advancement possibilities. This has occurred amidst an explosion in the wealth and power concentrated in these cities—that is to say, in conditions where there is also a visible expansion in high-income jobs and high-priced urban space.

"Women and immigrants" emerge as the labor supply that facilitates the imposition of low wages and powerlessness under conditions of high demand for those workers and the location of those jobs in high-growth sectors. It breaks the historic nexus that would have led to empowering workers and legitimates this break culturally.

Another localization that is rarely associated with globalization—informalization—re-introduces the community and the household as an important economic space in global cities. I see informalization in this setting as the low-cost (and often feminized) equivalent of deregulation at the top of the system. As with deregulation (e.g., as in financial deregulation), informalization introduces flexibility, reduces the "burdens" of regulation, and lowers costs, in this case especially the costs of labor. Informalization in major cities of highly developed countries—whether New York, London, Paris or Berlin—can be seen as a downgrading of a variety of activities for which there is an effective demand in these cities—but also a devaluing and enormous competition given low entry costs and few alternative forms of employment. Going informal is one way of producing and distributing goods and services at a lower cost and with greater flexibility. This further devalues these types of activities. Thus, immigrants and women are important actors in the new informal economies of these cities who absorb the costs of informalizing these activities (See Sassen 1998, chapter 8).

The reconfiguration of economic spaces associated with globalization in major cities has had differential impacts on women and men, on male-typed and female-typed work cultures, on male and female centered forms of power and empowerment. The restructuring of the labor market brings with it a shift of labor market functions to the household or community. Women and households emerge as sites that should be part of the theorization of the particular forms that these elements in labor market dynamics assume today.

These transformations contain possibilities, even if limited, for women's autonomy and empowerment. For instance, we might ask whether the growth of informalization in advanced urban economies reconfigures some types of economic relations between men and women. With informalization, the neighborhood and the household re-emerge as sites for economic activity. This condition has its own dynamic possibilities for women. Economic downgrading through informalization creates "opportunities" for low-income women entrepreneurs and workers, and therewith reconfigures some of the work and household hierarchies in which women find themselves. This becomes particularly clear in the case of immigrant women who come from countries with traditional male-centered cultures

There is a literature showing that immigrant women's regular wage work and improved access to other public realms has an impact on their gender relations (Grasmuck and Pessar 1991; Pessar 1995; Mahler 1995; Castro 1987; Hondagneu-Sotelo 1994; Boyd 1989; Bose and Acosta-Belen 1995; but for a different set of findings see Prieto 1992; Fernandez Kelly and Garcia 1992). Women gain greater personal autonomy and independence while men lose ground. Women gain more control over budgeting and other domestic decisions, and greater leverage in requesting help from men in domestic chores. Also, their access to public services and other public resources gives them a chance to become more fully incorporated into the mainstream society—they are often the ones in the household who mediate in this process. It is likely that some women benefit more than others from these circumstances; we need more research to establish the impact of class, education, and income on these gendered outcomes. Besides the relatively greater empowerment of women in the household associated with waged employment, there is a second important outcome: their greater participation in the public sphere and their possible emergence as public actors.

There are two arenas where immigrant women are active: institutions for public and private assistance, and the immigrant/ethnic community. The incorporation of women into the migration process strengthens the settlement likelihood and contributes to greater immigrant participation in their communities and vis-a-vis the state. For instance, Hondagneu-Sotelo (1995) found immigrant women come to assume more active public and social roles, which further reinforces their status in the household and the settlement process. Women are more active in community building and community activism and they are positioned differently from men regarding the broader economy and the state. They are the ones that are likely to have to handle the legal vulnerability of their families in the process of seeking public and social services for their families. This greater participation by women suggests the possibility that they may emerge as more forceful and visible actors and make their role in the labor market more visible as well.

There is, to some extent, a joining of two different dynamics in the condition of women in global cities described above. On the one hand they are constituted as an invisible and disempowered class of workers in the service of the strategic sectors constituting the global economy. This invisibility keeps them from emerging as whatever would be the contemporary equivalent of the "labor aristocracy" of earlier forms of economic organization, when a low-wage worker position in leading sectors had the effect of empowering that worker—i.e., by enhancing the possibility of unionizing. On the other hand, the access to (albeit low) wages and salaries, the growing feminization of the job supply, and the growing feminization of business opportunities brought about with informalization do alter the gender hierachies in which they find themselves.[18]

The Global City: A Nexus for New Politico-Economic Alignments

What makes the localization of the above described processes strategic, even though they involve powerless and often invisible workers, and potentially constitutive of a new kind of transnational politics is that these same cities are also the strategic sites for the valorization of the new forms of global corporate capital as described in the first section of this article.

Typically the analysis about the globalization of the economy privileges the reconstitution of capital as an internationalized presence; it emphasizes the vanguard character of this reconstitution. At the same time it remains absolutely silent about another crucial element of this transnationalization, one that some, like myself, see as the counterpart of that of capital: this is the transnationalization of labor. As I suggested above, we are still using the language of immigration to describe this process.[19] Second, that analysis overlooks the transnationalization in the formation of identities and loyalties among various population segments that explicitly reject the imagined community of the nation. With this come new solidarities and notions of membership. Major cities have emerged as a strategic site for both the transnationalization of labor and the formation of transnational identities. In this regard they are a site for new types of political operations.

Cities are the terrain where people from many different countries are most likely to meet and a multiplicity of cultures come together. The international character of major cities lies not only in their telecommunication infrastructure and international firms; it lies also in the many different cultural environments in which these workers exist. One can no longer think of centers for international business and finance simply in terms of the corporate towers and corporate culture at its center. Today's global cities are in part the spaces of post-colonialism and indeed contain conditions for the formation of a postcolonialist discourse (See Hall 1991; King 1990).[20]

The large Western city of today concentrates diversity. Its spaces are inscribed with the dominant corporate culture but also with a multiplicity of other cultures and identities. The slippage is evident: the dominant culture can encompass only part of the city.[21] And while corporate power inscribes these cultures and identities with "otherness," thereby devaluing them, they are present everywhere. For instance, through immigration a proliferation of originally highly localized cultures now have become presences in many large cities, cities whose elites think of themselves as cosmopolitan—that is, transcending any locality. An immense array of cultures from around the world, each rooted in a particular country or village, now are reterritorialized in a few single places, places such as New York, Los Angeles, Paris, London, and most recently Tokyo.[22]

Immigration and ethnicity are too often constituted as "otherness." Understanding them as a set of processes whereby global elements are localized, international labor markets are constituted, and cultures from all over the world are deterritorialized, puts them right there at the center of the stage along with the internationalization of capital as a fundamental aspect of globalization today.

The specific forms of the internationalization of capital we see over the last twenty years have contributed to mobilize people into migration streams—regional, national, transnational (Sassen 1998, Part One). They have done so principally through the implantation of western development strategies, from the replacement of small-holder agriculture with export-oriented commercial agriculture and export manufacturing, to the westernization of educational systems. At the same time, the administrative, commercial, and development networks of the former European empires and the newer forms these networks assumed under the Pax Americana (international direct foreign investment, export processing zones, wars for democracy) have not only created bridges for the flow of capital, information, and high level personnel from the center to the periphery, but, I argue, also for the flow of migrants from the periphery to the center. See, for example, Hall's account of the post-war influx of people from the Commonwealth into Britain and his description of how England and Englishmen were so present in his native Jamaica as to make people feel that London was the capital where they were all headed to sooner or later (1997).

Similarly, the renewal of mass immigration into the United States in the 1960s, after five decades of little or no immigration, took place in a context of expanded U.S. economic and military activity in Asia and the Caribbean Basin. Today, the United States is at the heart of an international system of investment and production that has incorporated not only Mexico but areas in the Caribbean and Southeast Asia. In the 1960s and 1970s, the United States played a crucial role in the development of a world economic system. It passed legislation aimed at opening its own and other countries' economies to the flow of capital, goods, services, and information. The central military, political, and economic role the United States played in the emergence of a global economy contributed, I argue, both to the creation of conditions that mobilized people into migrations, whether local or international, and to the formation of links between the United States and other countries that subsequently were to serve as bridges for international migration. Measures commonly thought to deter emigration—foreign investment and the promotion of export-oriented growth in developing countries—seem to have had precisely the opposite effect. Among the leading senders of immigrants to the United States in the 1970s and 1980s have been several of the newly industrialized countries of South and Southeast Asia whose extremely high growth rates are generally recognized to be a result of foreign direct investment in export manufacturing.

This way of narrating the migration events of the post-war era captures the ongoing weight of colonialism and post-colonial forms of empire on major processes of globalization today, and specifically those binding emigration and immigration countries. While the specific genesis and contents of their responsibility will vary from case to case and period to period, none of the major immigration countries are innocent bystanders.

The centrality of place in a context of global processes engenders a transnational economic and political opening in the formation of new claims and hence in the constitution of entitlements, notably rights to place, and, at the limit, in the constitution of "citizenship." The city has indeed emerged as a site for new claims: by global capital, which uses the city as an "organizational commodity," but also by disadvantaged sectors of the urban population, frequently as internationalized a presence in large cities as capital.

I see this as a type of political opening that contains unifying capacities across national boundaries and sharpening conflicts within such boundaries. Global capital and the new immigrant workforce are two major instances of transnationalized categories that have unifying properties internally and find themselves in contestation with each other inside global cities. Global cities are the sites for the over-valorization of corporate capital and the devalorization of disadvantaged workers. The leading sectors of corporate capital are now global, in both their organization and operations. And many of the disadvantaged workers in global cities are women, immigrants, people of color. Both find in the global city a strategic site for their economic and political operations.

The linkage of people to territory as constituted in global cities is far less likely to be intermediated by the national state or "national culture." We are seeing a loosening of identities from what have been traditional sources of identity, such as the nation or the village (Yaeger 1996). This unmooring in the process of identity formation engenders new notions of community, of membership, and of entitlement.

Yet another way of thinking about the political implications of this strategic transnational space is the notion of the formation of new claims on that space. Has economic globalization at least partly shaped the formation of claims?[23] There are indeed major new actors making claims on these cities, notably foreign firms that have been increasingly entitled to do business through progressive deregulation of national economies, and the large increase over the last decade in international businesspeople. These are among the new city users. They have profoundly marked the urban landscape. Perhaps at the other extreme are those who use urban political violence to make their claims on the city, claims that lack the *de facto* legitimacy enjoyed by the new "city users." These are claims made by actors struggling for recognition and entitlement, claiming their rights to the city.[24]

There is something to be captured here—a distinction between powerlessness and a condition of being an actor or political subject even though lacking power. I use the term presence to name this condition. In the context of a strategic space such as the global city, the types of disadvantaged people described here are not simply marginal; they acquire presence in a broader political process that escapes the boundaries of the formal polity. This presence signals the possibility of a politics. What this politics will be will depend on the specific projects and practices of various communities. Insofar as the sense of membership of these communities is not subsumed under the national, it may well signal the possibility of a transnational politics centered in concrete localities.

Conclusion

Large cities around the world are the terrain where a multiplicity of globalization processes assume concrete, localized forms. These localized forms are, in good part, what globalization is about. If we consider, further, that large cities also concentrate a growing share of disadvantaged populations—immigrants in Europe and the United States, African-Americans and Latinos in the United States, masses of shanty dwellers in the megacities of the developing world—then we can see that cities have become a strategic terrain for a whole series of conflicts and contradictions.

We can then think of cities also as one of the sites for the contradictions of the globalization of capital. On the one hand they concentrate a disproportionate share of corporate power and are one of the key sites for the overvalorization of the corporate economy; on the other, they concentrate a disproportionate share of the disadvantaged and are one of the key sites for their devalorization. This joint presence happens in a context where (1) the transnationalization of economies has grown sharply and cities have become increasingly strategic for global capital; and (2) marginalized people have increasingly found their voice and are making claims on the city as well. This joint presence is further brought into focus by the sharpening of the distance between the two.

These joint presences have made cities a contested terrain. The global city concentrates diversity. Its spaces are inscribed with the dominant corporate culture but also with a multiplicity of other cultures and identities, notably through immigration. The slippage is evident: the dominant culture can encompass only part of the city. And while corporate power inscribes noncorporate cultures and identities with "otherness," thereby devaluing them, they are present everywhere. The immigrant communities and informal economy in cities such as New York and Los Angeles are only two instances.

The space constituted by the global grid of global cities, a space with new economic and political potentialities, is perhaps one of the most strategic spaces for the formation of new types, including transnational, of identities and communities. This is a space that is both place-centered in that it is embedded in particular and strategic sites; and it is transterritorial because it connects sites that are not geographically proximate yet intensely connected to each other. It is not only the transmigration of capital that takes place in this global grid, but also that of people, both rich—i.e., the new transnational professional workforce—and poor—i.e., most migrant workers; it is also a space for the transmigration of cultural forms, for the reterritorialization of "local" subcultures. An important question is whether it is also a space for a new politics, one going beyond the politics of culture and identity, though at least partly likely to be embedded in these. The analysis presented in this article suggests that it is.

The centrality of place in a context of global processes engenders a transnational economic and political opening in the formation of new claims and hence in the constitution of entitlements, notably rights to place, and, at the limit, in the constitution of new forms of "citizenship" and a diversity of citizenship practices. The global city has emerged as a site for new claims: by global capital, which uses the city as an "organizational commodity," but also by disadvantaged sectors of the urban population, frequently as internationalized a presence in large cities as capital. The de-nationalizing of urban space and the formation of new claims centered in transnational actors and involving contestation constitute the global city as a frontier zone for a new type of engagement.

Notes

1. Globalization is also a process that produces differentiation, but the alignment of differences is of a very different kind from that associated with such differentiating notions as national character, national culture, national society. For example, the corporate world today has a global geography, but it isn't everywhere in the world: in fact it has highly defined and structured spaces; second, it also is increasingly sharply differentiated from non-corporate segments in the economies of the particular locations (a city such as New York) or countries where it operates. There is homogenization along certain lines that cross national boundaries and sharp differentiation inside these boundaries.

2. We need to recognize the specific historical conditions for different conceptions of the international or the global. There is a tendency to see the internationalization of the economy as a process operating at the center, embedded in the power of the multinational corporations today and colonial enterprises in the past. One could note that the economies of many peripheral countries are thoroughly internationalized due to high levels of foreign investments in all economic sectors, and of heavy dependence on world markets for "hard" currency. What center countries have is strategic concentrations of firms and markets that operate globally, the capability for global control and coordination, and power. This is a very different form of the international from that which we find in peripheral countries.

3. This proposition lies at the heart of my model of the global city (See Sassen 2000a, chapter 1).

4. By telematics I refer to telecommunications and computer technologies that allow for instantaneous transmission of information over short and long distances.

5. More conceptually, we can ask whether an economic system with strong tendencies towards such concentration can have a space economy that lacks points of physical agglomeration. That is to say, does power, in this case economic power, have spatial correlates?

6. I see the producer services, and most especially finance and advanced corporate services, as industries producing the organizational commodities necessary for the implementation and management of global economic systems (Sassen 2000, chapters 2-5). Producer services are intermediate outputs, that is, services bought by firms. They cover financial, legal, and general management matters, innovation, development, design, administration, personnel, production technology, maintenance, transport, communications, wholesale distribution, advertising, cleaning services for firms, security, and storage. Central components of the producer services category are a range of industries with mixed business and consumer markets; they are insurance, banking, financial services, real estate, legal services, accounting, and professional associations.

7. Telematics and globalization have emerged as fundamental forces reshaping the organization of economic space This reshaping ranges from the spatial virtualization of a growing number of economic activities to the reconfiguration of the geography of the built environment for economic activity. Whether in electronic space or in the geography of the built environment, this reshaping involves organizational and structural changes.

8. Methodologically speaking, this is one way of addressing the question of the unit of analysis in studies of contemporary economic processes. "National economy" is a problematic category when there are high levels of internationalization. And "world economy" is a problematic category because of the impossibility of engaging in detailed empirical study at that scale. Highly internationalized cities such as New York or London offer the possibility of examining globalization processes in great detail, within a bounded setting, and with all their multiple, often contradictory aspects. King (1990) notes the need to differentiate the international and the global. In many ways the concept of the global city does that.

9. A methodological tool I find useful for this type of examination is what I call circuits for the distribution and installation of economic operations. These circuits allow me to follow economic activities into terrains that escape the increasingly narrow borders of mainstream representations of "the advanced economy" and to negotiate the crossing of socioculturally discontinuous spaces.

10. This is illustrated by the following event. When the first acute stock market crisis happened in 1987 after years of enormous growth, there were numerous press reports about the sudden and massive unemployment crisis among high-income professionals on Wall Street. The other unemployment crisis on Wall Street, affecting secretaries and blue collar workers, was never noticed nor reported upon. And yet, the stock market crash created a very concentrated unemployment crisis, for instance, in the Dominican immigrant community in northern Manhattan where a lot of the Wall Street janitors live.

11. For me as a political economist, addressing these issues has meant working in several systems of representation and constructing spaces of intersection. There are analytic moments when two systems of representation intersect. Such analytic moments are easily experienced as spaces of silence, of absence. One challenge is to see what happens in those spaces, what operations (analytic, of power, of meaning) take place there. One version of these spaces of intersection is what I have called analytic borderlands (Sassen 1998, chapter 1). Why borderlands? Because they are spaces that are constituted in terms of discontinuities; in them discontinuities are given a terrain rather than reduced to a dividing line (see Sassen 2000b).

12. There is by now a vast literature documenting one or another of these various aspects. (See generally, Fainstein et al. 1993; see Abu-Lughod 1999 on New York, Chicago, and Los Angeles, which she defines as the three U.S. global cities.)

13. Whether this has contributed to the formation of transnational urban systems is subject to debate. The growth of global markets for finance and specialized services, the need for transnational servicing networks due to sharp increases in international investment, the reduced role of the government in the regulation of international economic activity, and the corresponding ascendance of other institutional arenas, notably global markets and corporate headquarters—all these point to the existence of transnational economic arrangements with locations in more than one country. These cities are not merely competing with each other for market share, as is often asserted or assumed; there is a division of labor that incorporates cities of multiple countries, and in this regard we can speak of a global system (e.g., in finance) as opposed to simply an international system (See Sassen 2000a, chapters 1-4, 7). We can see here the formation, at least incipient, of a transnational urban system.

14. Further, the pronounced orientation to the world markets evident in such cities raises questions about the articulation with their nation-states, their regions, and the larger economic and social structure in such cities. Cities have typically been deeply embedded in the economies of their region, indeed often reflecting the characteristics of the latter; and they still do. But cities that are strategic sites in the global economy tend, in part, to disconnect from their region. This conflicts with a key proposition in traditional scholarship about urban systems, namely, that these systems promote the territorial integration of regional and national economies.

15. More generally, we are seeing the formation of new types of labor market segmentation. Two characteristics stand out. One is the weakening role of the firm in structuring the employment relation. More is left to the market. A second form in this restructuring of the labor market is what could be described as the shift of labor market functions to the household or community.

16. Linking informalization and growth takes the analysis beyond the notion that the emergence of informal sectors in cities like New York and Los Angeles is caused by the presence of immigrants and their propensities to replicate survival strategies typical of Third World countries. Linking informalization and growth also takes the analysis beyond the notion that unemployment and recession generally may be the key factors promoting informalization in the current phase of highly industrialized economies. It may point to characteristics of advanced capitalism that are not typically noted. For an excellent collection of recent work focusing on the informal economy in many different countries, see Parnreiter et al. (1997).

17. This newer case brings out more brutally than did the Fordist contract, the economic significance of these types of actors, a significance veiled or softened in the case of the Fordist contract through the provision of the family wage.

18. Another important localization of the dynamics of globalization is that of the new professional women stratum. Elsewhere I have examined the impact of the growth of top level professional women in high income gentrification in these cities—both residential and commercial—as well as in the re-urbanization of middle class family life (See Sassen 1998, chapter 9).

19. This language is increasingly constructing immigration as a devalued process insofar as it describes the entry of people from generally poorer, disadvantaged countries, in search of the better lives that the receiving country can offer; it contains an implicit valorization of the receiving country and a devalorization of the sending country.

20. An interesting question concerns the nature of internationalization today in ex-colonial cities. King's (1990b, 78) analysis of the distinctive historical and unequal conditions in which the notion of the "international" was constructed is extremely important. King shows us how during the time of empire, some of the major old colonial centers were far more internationalized than the metropolitan centers. Internationalization as used today is assumed to be rooted in the experience of the center. This brings up a parallel contemporary blindspot well captured in Hall's (1997) observation that contemporary post-colonial and post-imperialist critiques have emerged in the former centers of empires and they are silent about a range of conditions evident today in ex-colonial cities or countries. Yet another such blindspot is the idea that the international migrations now directed largely to the center from former colonial territories, and neo-colonial territories in the case of the United States, and most recently Japan, might be the correlate of the internationalization of capital that began with colonialism.

21. There are many different forms that such contestation and "slippage" can assume. Global mass culture homogenizes and is capable of absorbing an immense variety of local cultural elements. But this process is never complete. The opposite is the case in my analysis of data on electronic manufacturing, which shows that employment in lead sectors no longer inevitably constitutes membership in a labor aristocracy. Thus Third World women working in export processing zones are not empowered: capitalism can work through difference. Yet another case is that of "illegal" immigrants; here we see that national boundaries have the effect of creating and criminalizing difference. These kinds of differentiations are central to the formation of a world economic system (Wallerstein 1990).

22. Tokyo now has several, mostly working-class, concentrations of legal and illegal immigrants coming from China, Bangladesh, Pakistan, Philippines. This is quite remarkable in view of Japan's legal and cultural closure to immigrants. Is this simply a function of poverty in those countries? By itself it is not enough of an explanation, as they have long had poverty. I posit that the internationalization of the Japanese economy, including specific forms of investment in those countries and Japan's growing cultural influence there have created bridges between those countries and Japan, and have reduced the subjective distance with Japan (See Sassen 2000, 307-315).

23. For a different combination of these elements see e.g., Dunn (1994).

24. Body-Gendrot (1999) shows how the city remains a terrain for contest, characterized by the emergence of new actors, often younger and younger. It is a terrain where the constraints placed upon, and the institutional limitations of, governments to address the demands for equity engenders social disorders. She argues that urban political violence should not be interpreted as a coherent ideology but rather as an element of temporary political tactics, which permits vulnerable actors to enter into interaction with the holders of power on terms that will be somewhat more favorable to the weak.

References

Abu-Lughod, Janet L. 1999. *New York, Los Angeles, Chicago: America's Global Cities.* Minneapolis.
Bose, Christine E. and Edna Acosta-Belen, eds. 1995. *Women in the Latin American Development Process.* Philadelphia.
Boyd, Monica. 1989. "Family and Personal Networks in International Migration: Recent Developments and New Agendas." *International Migration Review* 23.
Castells, Manuel. *The Informational City.* London.
Castro, Mary Garcia. 1986. "Work Versus Life: Colombian Women in New York." In June Nash and Helen Safa, eds. *Women and Change in Latin America.* South Hadley.
Dunn, Seamus, ed. 1994. *Managing Divided Cities.* Staffs, U.K.
Fainstein, Susan S., Ian Gordon, and Michael Harloe, eds., 1993. *Divided City: Economic Restructuring and Social Change in London and New York.* New York.
Fernandez Kelly, Maria Patricia and Ana Garcia. 1990. "Power Surrendered, Power Restored: The Politics of Home and Work among Hispanic Women in Southern California and Southern Florida." In Louise Tilly and P. Guerin, eds. *Women and Politics in America.* New York.
Graham, Stephen and Simon Marvin. 1996. *Telecommunications and the City: Electronic Spaces, Urban Places.* London.
Grasmuck, Sherri and Patricia Pessar. 1991. *Between Two Islands: Dominican International Migration.* Berkeley.
Hall, Stuart. 1997. "The Local and the Global: Globalization and Ethnicity." In Anthony D. King, ed., *Culture, Globalization and the World-System: Contemporary Conditions for the Representation of Identity.* Minneapolis.
Hondagneu-Sotelo, Pierrette. 1994. *Gendered Transitions.* Berkeley.
The Journal of Urban Technology. 1995. Special Issue: *Information Technologies and Inner-City Communities.* 3:1 (Fall).
King, Anthony D. 1990. *Urbanism, Colonialism, and the World Economy. Culture and Spatial Foundations of the World Urban System.* London and New York.
__________. ed. 1996. *Representing the City. Ethnicity, Capital and Culture in the 21st Century.* London.
Mahler, Sarah. 1995. *American Dreaming: Immigrant Life on the Margins.* Princeton.
Noyelle, Thierry, and Anna B. Dutka. 1988. *International Trade in Business Services: Accounting, Advertising, Law and Management Consulting.* Cambridge, Mass.
Paul L. Knox and Peter J. Taylor, eds. 1995. *World Cities in a World-System.* Cambridge.
Pessar, Patricia. 1995. "On the Homefront and in the Workplace: Integrating Immigrant Women into Feminist Discourse." *Anthropological Quarterly* 68:1.
Prieto, Yolanda. 1992. "Cuban Women in New Jersey: Gender Relations and Change." In Donna Gabaccia, ed. *Seeking Common Ground.* Westport, Conn.
Richard T. LeGates and Frederic Stout, eds. 1996. *The City Reader.* London and New York.
Sassen, Saskia, 1995. *Losing Control? Sovereignty in an Age of Globalization.* New York.
__________. 1998. *Globalization and its Discontents.* New York.
__________. 2000 *The Global City: New York, London, Tokyo.* (New Updated Edition) Princeton.
__________. 2000a. *Cities in a World Economy* (New Updated Edition). Thousand Oaks, Calif.
__________. 2000b. "Spatialities and Temporalities of the Global," *Public Culture.* Millenial issue. Forthcoming.
Short, John R. and Y. Kim. 1999. Globalization *and the City.* Essex.
Taylor, Peter J. "World Cities and Territorial States: the Rise and Fall of their Mutuality." In Knox and Taylor, eds., *World Cities in a World-System.*
Wallerstein, Immanuel. 1990. "Culture as the Ideological Battleground of the Modern World-System" in Mike Featherstone, ed. *Global Culture: Nationalism, Globalization and Modernity,* London, Newbury Park, and Delhi.
Yaeger, Patricia. 1996. *The Geography of Identity.* Ann Arbor, Mich.

[11]

Going Down the Glocal: The Local Context of Organised Crime

DICK HOBBS

Professor of Sociology, University of Durham

Abstract: Transnational organised crime is currently regarded as a threat to contemporary political and economic regimes. This paper will query the use of the term transnational, and suggest that a better understanding of organised crime can be gained from interrogating its local manifestation.

'For the moment we are not only without an adequate cartography of global capitalism, we lack political maps of our own backyards'. (Cooke 1988, p. 489)

'And sometimes a person from the underworld?'
'Yes' said the witness, 'some might drop in'.
'Pimps and thieves and things?' queried the judge.
'Possibly so' replied the gambler. (Landesco 1968, p. 72)

The destruction of national boundaries, and in particular the redundancy of cold war narratives, have resulted in an enormous growth in concern regarding transnational organised crime (see Godson and Olson 1993; Labrousse and Wallon 1993; Williams 1993, 1994; Williams and Savona 1995; Sterling 1994; Calvi 1993). 'Transnational' is especially problematic in referring to organised crime, as it is a term that normally relates to cross border activity involving the explicit exclusion of the State (Hobsbawm 1994). The relationship between the State and serious crime is now established as so varied and indeed ambiguous that the term 'transnational organised crime' only has some meaning when situated within the political science inspired moral panics that have emerged as a response to the fragmentation of the Eastern bloc and found a home within the budget wars of declining western states (Naylor 1995). This paper, while not seeking to engage with the new apocalypse, will highlight a complementary conceptual trend, that of localisation.

Current trends in the study of organised crime express both the concept's global nature and the redundancy of any perception of organised crime that does not embrace the centrality of transnationality. Yet this trend persists without the hindrance of empirical evidence. For instance at a conference on organised crime in Aix en Provence during the mid-1990s, the Chinese representative explained that organised crime had been eliminated in 1949, and blamed the slackening of social controls and the infiltration of outsiders on its recent manifestation in Chinese society. The French blamed the Russians, and the Interpol representative spoke mysteriously of the threat from the

East. Only the Italians saw the phenomenon as a home-grown phenomenon, and for them the Italian experience was the sole authentic one (Borricand 1997). As Potter (1994) expertly explains: 'To suggest that righteous citizens are being perverted, intimidated, and forced into vice by alien forces is far more palatable than suggesting that "native" demands for illicit drugs, sex, and gambling invite the creation of organised crime groups' (p. 10).

The persistence of Alien Conspiracy theories has not been limited to academic debate (cf. Cressey 1972). Threat assessments contrived by the National Criminal Investigation Service (NCIS) have concentrated upon Triads, Yardies, Russians, Colombians, Italians and Turks (NCIS 1993a, 1993b). The identification of Aliens as the principal organised crime threat to British society, is a device that conveniently excludes British society from taking responsibility for its own maladies, conforming to a mythological version of globalisation (Ferguson 1992). An overriding of the particular, that is little more than a reworking of 'mass society' rhetorics crossed with a jingoistic belief that this sceptred isle's crime, like its beef products, is perfectly harmless if only meddling foreigners would desist from dipping their toxic bread in our gravy.

As indicated by Robertson (1992, 1995), globalisation has intensified the distinctiveness and viability of locality as a context for a distinct social order, and as Hobbs (1997) and Ruggiero (1995) argue, the organisation of criminal labour mirrors trends in the organisation of legitimate labour. Local criminal organisation was always deeply entrenched in the cultures of the urban working class, and de-industrialisation and the consequent fragmentation of traditional communities has resulted in their transformation into disordered mutations of traditional proletarian culture (Hobbs 1995). Transactions within the new criminal market, in common with its legitimate counterpart, are within networks of small flexible firms featuring short-term contracts and lack of tenure.

As the dialectic between the local and the global substantiates, the indirect nature of the power wielded by large multinationals confirms elements of flexibility, autonomy and independence that were absent during previous eras dominated by increasingly arcane institutions such as the mob, the firm or the gang. Trading relationships between coalitions of criminals of different national origins involves a coagulation of local interests. It is at the local level that organised crime manifests itself as a tangible process of activity. However, research indicates that there also exist enormous variations in local crime groups (Hobbs and Dunnighan 1997). It is possible to draw close parallels between local patterns of immigration and emigration, local employment and subsequent work and leisure cultures with variations in organised crime groups. In this article I will concentrate upon two aspects of organised crime at opposite ends of the serious crime spectrum. In the first section I will summarise preliminary findings from Hobbs and Dunnighan that relate to traditional local neighbourhood organised crime in two areas of England. In the second section I will refer to organised crime personnel and suggest that for a contemporary understanding of organised crime the career trajectories suggested by life histories emphasise characteristics of the current serious crime market that require a very different reading from that required of the traditional model.

The Local Firm

1. Downton

The Downton scene reflects the diversity of both the legitimate economy and the ethnic mix of its population. Since the 1960s the fragmentation of working-class populations and disintegration of extended family networks have been extensive (see Beck 1992). When the material base for such communities is removed, crime becomes located within loose collectivities of *ad hoc* groupings. All that is left behind from the family firms of the 1960s are remnants, some of whom can be found wandering around the public bar in a shiny suit with inappropriate lapels mumbling 'they only hurt their own' into a glass of flat beer. Others however, often trading under the family name operate successfully as individuals, while other family firms have mutated into all-purpose disorganised deviant scavengers operating at the edge of any coherent society criminal or otherwise; the kind of family recently described as 'Steptoe and Son written by Tarrantino' (Campbell 1996). What is suggested here is not a denial of the importance of families in nurturing and generating deviant collaborations, rather than the fragmentation of both the traditional working-class neighbourhood and of the local labour market has made it difficult for family-based units to establish the parochial dominance previously enjoyed by the feudal warlords of the 1950s and 1960s. 'The dissolution of the traditional working class milieu with its particular domestic arrangements, organisation of leisure time, neighbourhood patterns and oral networks' (Pakulski and Waters 1996, p. 110) has led to the dissolution of those traditional forms of organised crime that were so reliant upon this milieu, and upon traditional family structures in particular. The new entrepreneurial based arenas are supportive of networks that function as fertile terrain for an abundance of entrepreneurial options, both legal and illegal (Ruggiero and South forthcoming). As Potter (1994) explains, these networks are: '. . . flexible, adaptive networks that readily expand and contract to deal with the uncertainties of the criminal enterprise' (p. 12).

The new rhythms of consumption and circulation which are bound by new configurations of bureaucratic and technological capital determine social incorporation, and are a direct consequence of the emergence of the market-place as the primary societal dynamic. Any analysis of contemporary society that is harnessed to the boundaries of traditional cultures and subcultures (Horne and Hall 1995) is meaningless, and in the case of organised crime it is apparent that the serious crime community has followed the same trajectory as that of communities based upon traditional industries (Soja 1989). It should be stressed that unlike traditional heavily localised criminal groups, with their overt adherence to the formal relations inherited and adapted from the indigenous socio-economic sphere (Block 1983, ch. 2), the contemporary serious crime community is the 'arch enemy of uniformity' (Bauman 1992, p. 52).

A fine example of the new hybrid form of criminal governance, concerned with market, as opposed to territorial domination, can be found in the case of Patrick Tate, Tony Tucker, and Craig Rolph. Not the first group of criminals to name themselves 'the firm' these three men captured part of the lucrative ecstasy market of south Essex, and were involved in the importation of cannabis. A small disintegrated firm, located amongst a mixed, but largely working-class population relocated some way removed from the traditional inner city alcoves, which along with the neighbourhood and the extended family serve to nurture the traditional family firm. This alliance made vast sums of money in a very short time without having any significant influence upon the local social order. For instance, a near neighbour of Tate, aggravated by the constant barking of the body-building heroin addict's dog, was unaware of Tate's criminal status, or the fact that he often carried a handgun. Until a couple of days before Tate's death the neighbour was threatening to 'go around and sort him out'. In December 1995 Tate, Tucker, and Rolph were shot dead while parked in a Land Rover in a remote country lane. While all three men had violent criminal careers, only one had any significant lineage, retaining close links with his native East London. Their influence was upon local trade, their territory defined by the whims of a predominantly youthful market; the normative local order of south Essex remaining unaffected.

2. Upton

Despite the destruction of its industrial base, Upton's cultural inheritance is one of a static population grounded in traditional notions of family and neighbourhood, both of which remain coherent and relatively intact. The principal crime groups reflect this traditional profile by being family based and territorially orientated and are persistent features of the local landscape across generations. Their focus is the drug trade and the protection business generated by the city's highly concentrated leisure industry, and they represent in both style and content an overt, identifiable and heavily localised image of organised criminality that is totally in accord with the city's cultural inheritance (Ianni 1971). The form of protection that is referred to here, is as specific and particular as that considered by Gambetta (1988, 1993), as being central to the development and persistence of the Sicilian Mafia. The creation of an illegal drug market centred on amphetamines and Ecstasy generated a necessity to police the trade in and around the point of consumption; youth orientated pubs and clubs. Unable to turn to more conventional methods of regulating trade and protecting market share, club owners and managers rely heavily upon the violence and violent potential that is central to the existence of the traditional neighbourhood crime groups that are so prominent in Upton. Their reputation and longevity inspire a sense of trust that is crucial to the continued prosperity of any old established firm (Hobbs 1995, chs. 3, 6), while simultaneously enhancing its future prospects by expanding its operations beyond the confines of the old neighbourhood into the newly defined leisure ghettos of the post industrial city (Hollands 1995). The spectacle of physically imposing, frequently uniformed security staff policing both the interiors and public exteriors of pubs and clubs, afford an elevated and highly marketable profile for criminal entrepreneurs seeking to establish a monopoly via the image of super competency implicit to the working of any market that leans heavily upon the marketing of trust (Gambetta 1988, 1993). Unlike the now dated form of protection described by Schelling (1984), the protection that is provided within the context of Upton is extremely ambiguous, in that the entity being protected is essentially a mutant of both market and territorial domains. The ambiguity lies in the question whose market? and whose territory? For although the premises are seldom owned by the crime groups concerned, and their services have been purchased to discourage disorder, when the market is manifested as contested space it can become an arena for old feuds between families and individuals, as well as more innovative conflicts concerning market dominance.

Their primary concern is to translate territorial priorities into market prerogatives, and this is reflected in the essentially conflictual relationships that exist between the groups. The style of organised crime in Upton represents an ideal synergy with the past, and internal order and identity is maintained by 'lifting out' (Giddens 1991, p. 18) and rearticulating those routine traditional strategies that retain coherent market potential, and shift them to the forefront of pragmatic consciousness (see Horne and Hall 1995; Davis 1990, ch. 5; Hobbs 1988). The dilution and eventual disappearance of the legitimate employment market redefines criminality in the context of the new decentered, unpredictable trading economies created by the harsh post-industrial thrust that has laid waste to traditional communities, 'emptied out' of marketable labour and traditional forms of governance (Wilson 1987).

Overt organised crime in Upton is firmly entrenched in the locations, working practices, occupational cultures and oppositional strategies of the industrial working class, which was in itself a pragmatic response to the demands of the craft and artisan based market-place that became valorised as a distinct life form in the configuration of a material community (Samuel 1981). There are, no doubt, bigger money-makers operating locally, but in terms of their effect on the local order of this city, the impact is made by these traditional neighbourhood firms who provide a form of spatial governance that fits with the immobility of the working-class population, and the continuity of neighbourhood boundaries and the relevance of familial ties. We consider Upton to be an exception. The fact that it is possible to conduct mapping exercises indicating the origins and operations of the city's organised crime groups suggests that compared to Downton where such mapping exercises have been futile for a quarter of a century, Upton's mode of organisation is very simple.

New networks of criminal entrepreneurs, some with ancient affiliations, have no need to limit themselves to the parameters of specific neighbourhoods, and operate across locales, while local thieves and dealers no longer require the benefaction of the local lord of the manor to make a fast Ecu. The Downton scene is diverse, fragmentary and temporaneous: the ancient feuds that mark much of the violence to be found on Upton are largely missing. With so few traditions or reputations to protect, violence at this level in

Downton is far more likely to be either economically instrumental or purely recreational[1]. The important issue here is to stress that this is not a wholly 'culturally constituted world' (McCracken 1988). Material success is dependant upon performance within the constraints of the structural dynamics of a local class milieu that is realigned in negotiation with global markets. Consequently the ever evolving ecology of late 20th century urban Britain is as influential upon structures of criminality as it was in the writings of Mayhew (1861) or Booths (1889; cf. Chesney 1968). The east ends and the west ends of our cities, and their signature deviant coalitions were created by the 'ecological communities' (Burgess 1929; cf. Thrasher 1927; Landesco 1968; Morris 1957, chs. 2, 4, 11), of both pre-industrial and industrial worlds, which in turn were framed by the economic exploitation of particular topographies (Hobbs 1988, ch. 5) as well as the municipal strategists of the 19th century (Stedman-Jones 1971, ch. 8) and their contemporary heirs. This is the backcloth upon which contemporary serious crime networks operate.

Hubs

During our, at times, vain search for structure amongst the plethora of deviant identities that inhabit the urban landscape, we became all too aware of the biographies and career trajectories of individuals who were free to seek out money-making opportunities as sole traders, yet will often collaborate with established criminal firms. These individuals operate within multiple cross-cutting networks of criminal and legitimate opportunity: they are not 'gang members', nor have they pledged allegiance to some permanent structure, but constitute hubs of action and information linking networks featuring webs of varying densities. In some cases these individuals are better money-makers than the household names who make up the criminal firms that will be recognisable to any local cab driver.[2]

Bill and Ben

Bill and Ben's criminal careers began separately as local teenage burglars. They started working together in their late teens, robbing offices and factories, operating within various amorphous coalitions of part-time thieves. In his early twenties Bill received two years imprisonment for theft and receiving stolen goods, and on his release he teamed up with Ben and an associate from prison in order to plunder building sites. They worked in collaboration with building workers and contractors to steal large quantities of builders supplies, and then switched to equipment and light plant machinery. With the close collaboration of contractors, in particular, they became over a five-year period wealthy men, and both were able to invest in property. Ben bought a suit and moved into property development funded by mortgage frauds, using family members on his wife's side as a front. During the property boom Ben had invested in the importation of cannabis and by the time his business went bust he was borrowing money to invest in dope. The property market collapsed, his marriage failed, and the familial fallout of the mortgage scam intensified the chaotic divorce proceedings. Ben's lack of funds and an unrelated dispute with his partners assured the decline of the dope importation business which had been located within a legitimate transport company, and Ben joined the massed ranks of small-time local dealers.

Bill meantime had prospered, buying a share in a thriving pub. He teamed up with Ben as part of a loose collectivity of men who plundered lorries in all night car parks. They would borrow a lorry, put false plates on, enter the lorry park, pay the fee to the security guard, park the lorry and the driver would leave. During the night the thieves, who had been playing cards in the back of the lorry, would exit, locate a target or targets and load up their own lorry. At dawn the driver would return and drive thieves and plunder to the goods yard of Ben's dope partner, change the plates back to the original and distribute the goods via a network of outlets constituted mainly of legitimate businesses.

Bill struck up an association with a group of men importing and dealing in amphetamines. The myriad of connections that this led to in the pub and club fraternity proved more profitable than robbing lorries, an activity from which he gladly retired and opened a secondhand furniture business, using his contacts in the clubs to move large quantities of stolen CDs and designer clothes. Bill, lost in drink, remarried and left the area, and Ben's business partners have become 'heavier' as his wealth has increased.

There are no key players in this network, no ring leaders, bosses or godfathers. It is a co-operative, a series of temporary social arrangements that enables a constantly changing group of actors to make money from predominantly criminal opportunities.

Dave Peters

Dave Peters was an all-purpose thief who by the late 1970s regularly collaborated with various criminal coalitions to import and wholesale cannabis. His criminal career has featured a long-term relationship with Gary Smith. He was involved during the early 1980s with the administration of a team of burglars who were working freelance with Gary Smith, and later went on to assist in the management of a number of prominent pubs that now form a chain across Downton. In the early 1990s, Dave moved to Spain and set up a business as a shipping agent: he deals primarily with consignments to Ibiza and owns both commercial and residential property on the Costa Del Sol. Gary Smith owns clubs on Ibiza and has for at least eight years been importing and distributing Ecstasy and amphetamines, and for about five years he has been involved in importing cocaine. Dave also owns warehouses on the periphery of Downton, which apart from their legitimate use, are also used by thieves as a 'slaughter', a venue for the 'cutting up' of loads and distribution of stolen goods.

Ned

In many respects, Ned is not dissimilar to other successful 50-year-old businessmen. He lives with his second wife and their two children in a £100,000 house; he drives a new Mercedes car, is being pursued by the Inland Revenue for unpaid tax, is a member of his local sports-health club and has a mistress. Where he differs, however, is in the diversity of legal and illegal income-generating activities in which he has been, and is, involved.

Born into a family who had for three generations been successfully involved (both legally and illegally) in taking bets on horse races, he had, as a young man, been accustomed to having access to large sums of ready cash. However, on leaving school with a handful of GCEs and CSEs, he found the small fixed wage he received as a trainee shop manager insufficient to satisfy his developing fondness for women, gambling, drinking bourbon and smoking cannabis. With requests for cash rebuffed by his father, who told him that 'you've to stand on your own two feet', Ned sought additional sources of income. He became a regular visitor to greyhound racing 'flapping' tracks where he quickly became involved in the doping of dogs and the fixing of races. Using pseudonyms and travelling widely, his betting on fixed races started to generate the income he desired. However, he sought greater rewards. Using the proceeds of a win on a fixed race, he bought enough cannabis to set himself up as a small dealer in the predominantly rural clubs and pubs that he regularly visited to listen to folk music. Initially dealing to friends and close acquaintances, within months he had established a small distribution network, directly employed three others and was able to leave his paid employment. Through that drug network, Ned met Angus who was part of an active burglary team targeting 'good quality houses'. Over the next two years he bought stolen property from Angus and others who had learned of his abilities to sell-on virtually any item through the extensive network of contacts he had built up by his drug trading and his gambling at dog and horse race tracks throughout the UK and Ireland.

The good luck ran out when someone whom the police had caught in possession of ten crates of stolen whisky, bought from Ned, informed on him. Ned was sentenced to nine months for handling stolen goods. On release, he set himself up as a jobbing plumber (having learned the basics from a family friend) and quickly became reasonably prosperous. Within two years he was employing a dozen or so men and, by paying backhanders to 'oil the wheels', successfully tendering for large plumbing contracts. At the same time, Angus introduced him to a wider circle of criminal contacts – some of who were part of a gang involved in armed robberies at sub-post offices.

Having found prison a 'devastating experience', Ned believed it might be useful, if he was arrested again, to have a bargaining tool with which to alleviate the consequences of the situation. He decided therefore, to inform on the robbery team. He approached a police detective he had met at a social event and, over a period of months, provided information that eventually led to the arrest of a number of gang members. Although money was not his motivation for doing so, he found the rewards that the police paid for information a useful addition to his income. Ned has maintained relationships with police officers since that time – informing 'as and when necessary'. His informing activities went undetected by his criminal acquaintances, and throughout the 1970s and 1980s Ned continued to dispose of stolen property – anything from an industrial generator to a lorry-load of toys. During this period his legitimate business activities had their ups and downs and, while continuing to run the plumbing business, he briefly diversified into the hire of plant and the selling of upholstery. Neither proved viable and, after selling them at a loss, he concentrated on consolidating his plumbing business.

With the awarding of plumbing contracts within the UK and Europe, his network of contacts grew. Many of those he met through legitimate activities were wealthy and it was not unusual for Ned to be invited to their homes. Sometimes, if he thought he could make a reasonable amount of money, he later arranged for their homes to be broken into and have items he specified stolen. Believing dealing in drugs to be 'too risky' and likely to get him a substantial prison sentence if caught, Ned had not resumed dealing on his release from prison. However, during the 1980s while working on a contract in Holland he was approached by a group of criminals whom he knew by reputation only. 'You could not refuse these people unless you wanted to end up badly beaten or worse' and on two occasions he allowed a work van to be driven into the UK from Europe by a third party. Although never directly told what was being smuggled he had little doubt and was 'well rewarded' for his 'assistance'.

By the end of the 1980s Ned was relatively well off. Nevertheless, during the 1990s, while continuing with his flourishing legitimate business activities, he is persistently on the look out for supplementary sources of income. Provided he assesses the activity to have a low risk factor, he will still buy and sell stolen property, dabble in selling counterfeit currency or any other commodity that will return a profit. However, most days of the week Ned can be found at his health club where he is considered by the staff as a businessman reaping the rewards of a successful career.

Discussion

The flexibility that is apparent within the contemporary serious crime 'community' assures that there is considerable scope for innovative engagements with the market. These engagements create disintegrated criminal firms unfettered by 'nostalgic paradigms' (Robertson 1995), or the shackles of arcane practices, and are typified by their flexible nature and increasingly unpredictable temperament. They are operating within multiple, interwoven networks of legitimate and illegitimate opportunity constituting both personal criminal networks and specific activity networks, and as Potter (1994) notes, these networks are: 'small, fragmented, and ephemeral enterprises (which) tend to populate illegal markets – not large corporate syndicates' (p. 13). Within the drug market in particular, trade is carried out between networks of these small flexible firms, for disorganised crime mirrors disorganised capitalism, in that the indirect nature of the power exercised by large transnationals confirms elements of flexibility and adaptability amongst smaller structures (Lash and Urry 1994).

The heritage of locales such as in Upton, that are steeped in traditional notions of criminality established by the precedents of indigenous markets, yet succeed in simultaneously engaging with contemporaneous criminal opportunities, is an explicit acknowledgement of the distinct characteristics inherent in local demographics, of variations in demand, of the indigenous utility of space, and of the power inherent in the notion of a distinct homogeneous and identifiable enacted environment of local serious criminal activity. Cumulatively, this empowers organised crime with the capacity to summon some retrospective order, and inject it into a lifeworld that is prone to chaotic, apparently incoherent interludes (Reuter 1984). By blending their experiences of the enacted environments of contemporary serious crime markets with this sense of 'retrospective unity' (Bauman 1992, p. 138), a generalised recipe of locality (Robertson 1995, p. 26) relying heavily upon an invented tradition (Anderson 1983) is created.

However, in Downton, the territory that defined and shaped organised crime groups has disintegrated, and serious crime become removed from the territories that spawned its most prominent practitioners and their elementary forms of organisation (King 1991, p. 6). As Morris (1957, ch. 11) has so clearly indicated, the specificities of local housing policies are crucial in understanding the distribution of delinquency (cf. Baldwin and Bottoms 1976). In the case of organised crime groups, both Downton's municipal housing policy, and the region's private housing market has succeeded in distributing the serious crime community and its progeny over a wide, amorphous territory. This instability along with the globalisation of legitimate markets, has speeded the disintegration of traditional cultures (Bursik 1986), and the fact of global drug markets has contributed significantly to the elimination of traditional criminal territories and their accompanying historic practices, feuds, and alliances. Consequently organised crime groups as social systems have been stretched across time and space, their practitioners residing upon a socio-economic terrain indistinct from that occupied by civilians, and contrasting with all prior forms of criminality: '. . . in respect of their dynamism, the degree to which they undercut traditional habits and customs, and their global impact' (Giddens 1991, p. 1). In Downton with the exception of entrepreneurial youth gangs, it is quite simply impossible to exchange territorial superiority for market domination, and the drug market is an essentially disintegrated sector. The paradox is that the alleged emergence of transnational crime federations has created markets best served by 'vertically disintegrated networks of small firms engaged in transaction rich linkages of market exchanges' (Lash and Urry 1994, p. 23).

The dialectic between the local and the global (Giddens 1990, p. 64, 1991, p. 22) epitomises and underlines markets in both the legitimate and illegitimate spheres where complex affinities between global and local spaces are negotiated, creating an enacted environment consisting of indigenous renditions of global markets (Robins 1991). This environment is where:

> . . . the business of crime is planned, contacts are made, some crimes are carried out, the fruits of crime are often enjoyed, and the methodologies for the integration of organised criminals into civil society are established. (Block 1991, p. 15; cf. Hobbs and Dunnighan 1997)

Contemporary organised criminality is expressed through local trading networks (Dorn *et al.* 1992, pp. 3–59; cf. Piore and Sabel 1984), and appropriate commercial viability is assured (cf. Hobbs 1995, ch. 7) by the continual realignment of local precedents in the context of global markets (Giddens 1991, pp. 21–2; cf. Hobbs 1995, ch. 5). In order to co-ordinate relations between individuals and groups (Giddens 1979, pp. 65–6), both organised crime and its legitimate counterpart is involved in 'constant mediations and re-negotiations that are duplicated as perpetually mutating social systems of culturally indeterminate extraction and eclectic commercial destination' (Hobbs 1997, p. 67).

The scope and extent of this activity depends upon the degree of connectivity between sets, and it is this connectedness rather than corporate identity that forms the structural connotation inherent in 'organised crime'. The connections between sets, the relationships that lie at the core of serious crime groups, can be based upon familial, interpersonal, geographic or commercial sets, and often some combination of some or all of the above. These combinations with their multi-dimensional faces, 'form stars connected by hubs made up of shared vertices' (Gould 1991, p. 25; cf. Johnson 1986). For the purpose of our ongoing study of serious crime networks (Hobbs and Dunnighan 1997), hubs are represented by individuals who by virtue of their interconnectedness with these multidimensional sets combine flexibility and mobility with crucial qualities of relationality. The power of these individuals that I have dubbed hubs should not be underestimated. Even within environments that feature established traditional family based crime groups, network hubs are licensed to operate in an infinite variety of deviant collaborations. Dave, Bill and Ben, and Ned are associated with a whole gamut of criminal entrepreneurship and with numerous combinations of networked interactions. These interactions consist of infinite mutations based on socio-economic, spatial, familial and interpersonal sources which serve as the springboard for negotiated career trajectories featuring pecuniary arrangements of varying breadth, depth and intensity. The temporary nature of most of these arrangements is due to their degree of embeddedness, and their parallel, simultaneous, and incidental engagements with legitimate opportunities (Smith 1980), in no way diminish their potency. Indeed their elusiveness is considerably enhanced by these upperworld associations, and the ensuing anonymity that indirectly follows serves to make them less vulnerable to the kind of informant inspired corporate collapse that can occur within more formal structures (Iamnuzzi 1993).

It is vital to emphasise that within networked crime, careers do not necessarily follow a relentless ascent. Ben's criminal life at the time of writing is all but over, while Bill's has yet to peak. Dave's entrepreneurial activities are so well spread across Europe and so entwined with legitimate commercial activity as to make it impossible to weed out the good notes from the bad money, while Ned's past collaborators are rather more exotic and indeed venomous than the punters to whom he sells training shoes from the back of his car. Peaks and troughs, expansion and retraction all inform the density, strength, and spread of networks that must be understood as much for their flexibility and subsequent interactive qualities as for their criminal content.

The local neighbourhood firm is essentially a local social system: '. . . patterns of relationship among individuals, which have the force of kinship, and which can be changed only by drastic, often fatal action' (Ianni 1971, p. 35). Its strength and longevity stems from its proximity and therefore continued identification with a locale that retains a well of historical sentiment. It becomes possible to translate the conventions and procedures of previous eras, and place them in the present, involving what Douglas (1995) has termed: 'selective remembering, misremembering and disremembering' (p. 13). In Downton however where the material base for such communities is removed, and crime becomes located overwhelmingly within loose collectivities of *ad hoc* groupings, the construction of enduring monuments to obscure and redundant practices is reliant upon the deification of key individuals as functional touchstones of competence and honour (Hobbs 1997) whose task is: '. . . recycling old trade names, refurbishing old properties, and laying claim to the production of classics . . . their image is intensively marketed on the strength of an aestheticized version of the past' (Samuel 1994, p. 78; cf. Sinclair 1995).

The eternal recurrences of ancient underworld themes constitute a quest for order (Bauman 1993, pp. 1–17) that is a retort to the ambiguous quality of contemporary serious crime, with entrepreneurially orientated commercialism which stands in contrast to the harsh proletarianism of the past. These 'cultural chaperones from previous eras' (Hobbs 1997) perform in Downton the function of informing the practices of contemporary criminals, and providing reference points both for their activities and for those civilians for whom the notion of a distinct homogeneous and identifiable proletarian based milieu is no longer part of their enacted environment. Any touchstone with the past, with a social order that resonates of traditional working-class community empowers those that constitute the debris of the de-industrialised emptied-out locales with the ability to derive a sense of order, albeit retrospective, and implant it into a culture that is disordered, inchoate and episodic (Pilleggi 1987): 'where there were no rules, where cheating, lying, and stealing were accepted, even expected' (Anastasia 1991, p. 279). As Wilk (1995) has noted: 'The same processes that destroy autonomy are now creating new kinds of locality and identity' (p. 130), and the recurrence of sacred myths related to traditional strategies and iconic individuals, preserves an illusion of an enduring expert system. In Upton, where both the traditional community and its serious crime prodigy remain relatively intact, it is possible, to blend their experiences of the enacted environments of contemporary serious crime markets with a sense of 'retrospective unity' (Bauman 1992, p. 138), and create an imaginary community that although it may rely heavily upon an invented tradition (Anderson 1983), retains market potency as a spatially defined local order within a post-industrial milieu imbued with essentially extraterritorial organisation.

It is crucial therefore to be sceptical of models of organised or serious crime that rely heavily upon transnationality, cross border, international or other metaphors of globalisation at one end of a spectrum and 'local street gangs' (Rider 1990) at the other. Such a model fails to embrace the complexity of 'local contextualities' (Giddens 1991, p. 22), and although the essential connectedness of contemporary organised crime which is necessitated by trading relationships that stretch across the globe (Harvey 1989) is a major feature, this does not indicate either a local/global action/reaction polarity, or a cultural homogeneity that will override difference. As Robertson (1995) notes: 'it makes no good sense to define the global as if the global excludes the local . . . defining the global in such a way suggests that the global lies beyond all localities, as having systematic properties over and beyond the attributes of units within a global system' (p. 34). Current research indicates that even the classic 'international' criminal organisations function as interdependent local units (Dunnighan and Hobbs 1996), and the more recent activities of Bill for instance, suggests that the incorporation of locales into overlapping networks of legal and illegal commerce more accurately describes his activities than the compression of criminal action into a world order of transnational corporations.

Organised crime is, to paraphrase Latour (1993): 'Local at all points'. Unlike previous eras, contemporary organised crime with its emphasis upon drugs, fraud and counterfeiting, simultaneously occupies both the local and global. Further, these criminal activities offer the possibility of moving from one sphere to another. For as my examples indicate criminal career trajectories no longer are limited to specific, often stereotyped geographic locations of some urban 'underworld' (Hobbs 1997). Drug networks in particular constitute: '. . . continuous paths that lead from the local to the global, from the circumstantial to the universal, from the contingent to the necessary' (Latour 1993, p. 117). Networks are the media through which individuals and groups move between the local and the global, but this does not indicate the kind of structural determinism suggested by many writers on organised crime. Networks here refer to metaphors for relationality (Strathern 1995, p. 179), and as can be seen from the previous examples relations between individuals vary according to differentiation in demographic dispersion, familial composition, ethnic distribution and integration, commercial practice, trading patterns, the economic backcloth of the legitimate culture and the particular use of space (King 1991, p. 111; Soja 1989). Organised crime is not experienced globally or transnationally, for these are abstract fields devoid of relations (Strathern 1995, p. 179). We experience crime as a local phenomenon, and our cumulative experiences constitute a global way of seeing which afford us a sense of scale that allows us the capacity to measure and compare (Strathern 1995). It is this capacity to measure, to transcend the local and create scales that lends licence to the kind of universalist discourse that empowers the creation of scenarios of global expert systems.

The notion of organised crime, particularly in the current vogue form of 'transnationality' needs to be reconsidered in the light of empirical research, which indicates that ever mutating interlocking networks of locally-based serious criminality typifies the current situation.

Notes

1 For a discussion of the complex relationship between instrumental and non-instrumental violence within serious crime networks, see Hobbs (1995, ch. 3 and pp. 121–4).

2 The following case studies are taken from Hobbs and Dunnighan (1997).

References

Anastasia, G. (1991) *Blood and Honor*, New York: Zebra Books.

Anderson, B. (1983) *Imagined Communities*, London: Verso.

Baldwin, J. and Bottoms, A. E. (1976) *The Urban Criminal*, London: Tavistock.

Bauman, Z. (1992) *Intimations of Modernity*, London: Routledge.

Bauman, Z. (1993) *Modernity and Ambivalence*, Polity: Cambridge.

Beck, U. (1992) *Risk Society*, London: Sage.

Block, A. (1983) *East Side-West Side: Organizing Crime in New York, 1930–1950*, Newark, NJ: Transaction.

Block, A. (1991) *Masters of Paradise*, New Brunswick: Transaction.

Booth, C. (1889) *Labour and Life of the People*, London: Williams and Norgate.

Borricand, J. (Ed.) (1997) 'Organised crime and the social order in the UK', in: J. Borricand (Ed.), *Les Incidences de la Criminalité sur L'Ordère dans Societé*, ISPEC.

Burgess, R. (1929) 'Urban areas', in: T. V. Smith and L. D. White (Eds.), *Chicago: An Experiment in Social Science*, Chicago: University of Chicago Press.

Bursik, R. J. (1986) 'Ecological stability and the dynamics of delinquency', in: A. J. Reiss and M. Tonry (Eds.), *Communities and Crime*, Chicago: University of Chicago Press.

Calvi, F. (1993) *Het Europa Van de Peetvaders. De Mafia Verovert een Continent*, Leuven: Kritak Balans.

Campbell, D. (1996) 'Wayne on a warm day', Review of *Bad Business*, by D. Hobbs, *London Review of Books*, *18* (12), 21–2.

Chesney, K. (1968) *The Victorian Underworld*, Harmondsworth: Penguin.

Cooke, P. (1988) 'Modernity, postmodernity and the city', *Theory, Culture and Society*, *5* (2–3).

Cressey, D. (1972) *Criminal Organisation*, London: Heinemann.

Davis, M. (1990) *City of Quartz*, London: Verso.

Dorn, N. *et al.* (1992) *Traffickers*, London: Routledge.

Douglas, M. (1995) 'Forgotten knowledge', in M. Strathern (Ed.), *Shifting Contexts: Transformations in Anthropological Knowledge*, London: Routledge.

Dunnighan, C. and Hobbs, D. (1996) *A Confidential Report on the NCIS Pilot Organised Crime Notification Survey*, London: PRG, Home Office.

Ferguson, M. (1992) 'The mythology about globalisation', *European Journal of Communication.*

Gambetta, D. (1988) 'Fragments of an economic theory of the mafia', *Archives Europeennes de Sociologie*, *29*, 127–45.

Gambetta, D. (1993) *The Sicilian Mafia: The Business of Private Protection*, Cambridge, Mass: Harvard University Press.

Giddens, A. (1979) *Central Problems in Social Theory*, London: Macmillan.

Giddens, A. (1990) *The Consequences of Modernity*, Cambridge: Polity.

Giddens, A. (1991) *Modernity and Self-Identity*, Cambridge: Polity.

Godson, R. and Olson, W. (1993) *International Organised Crime: Emerging Threat to U.S. Security*, Washington: National Strategy Information Center.

Gould, P. (1991) 'Dynamic structures of geographic space', in: S. D. Brunn and T. R. Leinbach (Eds.), *Collapsing Space and Time*, London: Harper Collins.

Harvey, D. (1989) *The Condition of Postmodernity*, Oxford: Blackwell.

Hobbs, D. (1988) *Doing the Business: Entrepreneurship, Detectives and the Working Class in the East End of London*, Oxford: Clarendon Press.

Hobbs, D. (1995) *Bad Business*, Oxford: Oxford University Press.

Hobbs, D. (1997) 'Professional crime: change, continuity and the enduring myth of the underworld', *Sociology*, *131*, 1.

Hobbs, D. and Dunnighan, C. (1997) *Serious Crime Networks* (Final Report to the ESRC), London: ESRC.

Hobsbawm, E. (1994) *The Age of Extremes*, Harmondsworth: Penguin.
Hollands, B. (1995) *Friday Night, Saturday Night: Youth Cultural Identification in the Post Industrial City* (Working Paper No. 2), Newcastle: Department of Social Policy, Newcastle University.
Horne, R. and Hall, S. (1995) 'Anelpis: a preliminary expedition into a world without hope or potential', *Parallex, 1*, 81–92.
Iamnuzzi, J. (1993) *Joe Dogs*, New York: Simon and Schuster.
Ianni, F. (1971) 'Formal and social organisation in an organised crime "Family": case study', *University of Florida Law Review, 24*, 31–41.
Johnson, R. (1986) *On Human Geography*, Oxford: Blackwell.
King, A .D. (1991) 'Introduction', in: A. D. King (Ed.), *Culture Globalisation and the World System*, London: Macmillan.
Labrousse, A. and Wallon, A. (Eds.) (1993) *La Planete des Drogues*, Paris: Seuil.
Landesco, J. (1968) *Organised Crime in Chicago*, 2nd ed., Chicago: University of Chicago Press.
Lash, S. and Urry, J. (1994) *Economies of Signs and Space*, London: Sage.
Latour, B. (1993) *We Have Never Been Modern*, London: Harvester Wheatsheaf.
McCracken, G. (1988) *Culture and Consumption*, Bloomington: Indiana UP.
Mayhew, H. (1861) *London Labour and the London Poor*, 4 vols, London: Dover (facsimile edition 1968).
Morris, T. P. (1957) *The Criminal Area*, London: Routledge and Kegan Paul.
Naylor, R. T. (1995) 'From cold war to crime war', *Transnational Organised Crime, 1* (4), 37–56.
NCIS (1993a) *An Outline Assessment of the Threat and Impact by Organised/Enterprise Crime Upon United Kingdom Interests*, London: NCIS.
NCIS (1993b) *Organised Crime Conference: A Threat Assessment*, London: NCIS.
Pakulski, J. and Waters, M. (1996) *The Death of Class*, London: Sage.
Pileggi, N. (1987) *Wise Guy*, London: Corgi.
Piore, M. and Sabel, C. (1984) *The Second Industrial Divide*, New York: Basic Books.
Potter, G. W. (1994) *Criminal Organisation*, Illinois: Waveland Press.
Reuter, P. (1984) *Disorganised Crime*, Cambridge, Mass.: MIT Press.
Rider, B. (1990) *Organised Economic Crime* (Working Paper), Cambridge: University of Cambridge.
Robertson, R. (1992) 'Globality and modernity', *Theory Culture and Society, 9* (2).
Robertson, R. (1995) 'Glocalisation: time-space and homogeneity-heterogeneity', in: M. Featherstone, S. Lash and R. Robertson (Eds.), *Global Modernities*, London: Sage.
Robins, K. (1991) Tradition and translation: national culture in its global context', in: J. Corner and S. Harvey (Eds.), *Enterprise and Heritage*, London: Routledge.
Ruggiero, V. (1995) 'Drug economics: a Fordist model of criminal capital', *Capital and Class, 55*, 131–50.
Ruggiero, V. and South, N. (forthcoming) 'The late modern city as a bazaar', *British Journal of Sociology.*
Samuel, R. (1981) *East End Underworld: The Life and Times of Arthur Harding*, London: Routledge and Kegan Paul.
Samuel, R. (1994) *Theatres of Memory*, London: Verso.
Schelling, T. (1984) *Choice and Consequences*, Harvard: Harvard University Press.
Sinclair, I. (1995) 'Ronnie Kray bows out', *The London Review of Books, 8 June, 17* (11).
Smith, D.C. (1980) 'Paragons, pariahs, and pirates: a spectrum based theory of enterprise', *Crime and Delinquency, 26*, 358–86.
Soja, E.W. (1989) *Postmodern Geographies*, London: Verso.
Stedman-Jones, G. (1971) *Outcast London*, Oxford: Oxford University Press.
Sterling, C. (1994) *Crime Without Frontiers*, London: Little Brown.

Strathern, M. (1995) 'Afterword: relocations', in: M. Strathern (Ed.), *Shifting Contexts: Transformations in Anthropological Knowledge*, London: Routledge.

Thrasher, F. (1927) *The Gang*, Chicago: University of Chicago Press.

Wilk, R. (1995) 'Learning to be local in Belize: global systems of common difference', in: D. Miller (Ed.), *Worlds Apart: Modernity Through the Prism of the Local*, London: Routledge.

Williams, P. (1994) *The International Drug Trade: An Industry Analysis*, Pittsburgh: Ridgway Center for International Security Studies.

Williams, P. (1993) 'Transnational criminal organisations and national security', *Survival*, *36*, 96–113.

Williams, P. and Savona, R. (Eds.) (1995) 'The United Nations and transnational organised crime', *Transnational Organised Crime*, *1* (3).

Wilson, W.J. (1987) *The Truly Disadvantaged*, Chicago: University of Chicago Press.

[12]

Mumbai's Development Mafias: Globalization, Organized Crime and Land Development

LIZA WEINSTEIN

Abstract

For over a decade, researchers have analyzed the effects of liberalization and globalization on urban development, considering the local political implications of shifts at the national and global scales. Taking the case of Mumbai, this article examines how the past 15 years of political reforms in India have reshaped property markets and the politics of land development. Among the newly empowered actors, local criminal syndicates, often with global connections, have seized political opportunities created by these shifts to gain influence over land development. The rise of Mumbai's organized criminal activity in the 1950s was closely linked to India's macroeconomic policies, with strict regulation of imports fuelling the growth of black market smuggling. Liberalization and deregulation since the early 1990s have diminished demand for smuggled consumer goods and criminal syndicates have since diversified their operations. With skyrocketing real estate prices in the 1990s, bolstered by global land speculation, the mafia began investing in property development. Supported by an illicit nexus of politicians, bureaucrats and the police, the mafia has emerged as a central figure in Mumbai's land development politics. The article examines the structural shifts that facilitated the criminalization of land development and the implications of mafia involvement in local politics.

Introduction

In the mid-1990s, property prices in Mumbai's business districts reached record levels, becoming, for a brief period in 1996, the most expensive real estate in the world (Nijman, 2000; Mukhija, 2003). Unleashed by a series of national-level industrial and monetary reforms, demand for residential and commercial property intensified among both local investors and global speculators. Yet because increased demand was met with constrained supply — due both to geographic limitations (Mumbai is an island city with few transit linkages to the mainland) and a regulatory context posing restrictions or disincentives on certain types of development — prices rose dramatically (Nijman, 2000; 2002; Bertaud, 2002). Responding to these market pressures, the local state began making certain highly valued lands available for development through a series of industrial land conversions, slum clearance schemes, and the de-reservation of certain public lands. Construction activities in Mumbai's island city and northern suburbs

I would like to thank Saskia Sassen, Diane Davis, Solomon Benjamin, Navtej Kaur Bhutani, Andrew Papachristos, Kathleen Fernicola, Jennifer Buntin, Rachel Harvey, and the anonymous IJURR reviewers for their helpful comments on earlier drafts of this article.

expanded, further bolstered by the growth of the finance industry, access to new sources of capital, and both funding and pressure from multilateral aid agencies. Although activity slowed somewhat after the mid-1990s peak, when some speculators left and real estate prices began to 'correct', both prices and demand have remained high and property development has emerged as one of India's and Mumbai's fastest growing industries (*Business Week*, 2005).

With construction crews becoming a common sight throughout the city in the late 1990s, two new shopping centres drew little attention when constructed in the Crawford Market area of South Mumbai, opposite the city's police headquarters. The Sara and Sahara Shopping Centres opened in 2000, joining a myriad of new shopping centres and retail establishments that had appeared in the area in the previous five years. It was soon learned, however, that the Sara and Sahara Shopping Centres had been built illegally by the D-Company, the city's largest and most notorious mafia organization, on land belonging to the state government's public works department. As the details of the case came to light in mid-2003, it was learned that representatives of the D-Company had purchased the property from a small-scale businessman who had been illegally squatting on the public land. The D-Company then acquired the requisite building permits from the municipal building department, with the payment of hefty bribes, and constructed the buildings with few obstacles. As more information about the D-Company's involvement in the shopping centre project surfaced, it became apparent that the mafia organization had been running a highly profitable property development business since the mid-1990s, constructing retail and residential buildings in other parts of Mumbai, as well as in Dubai and Karachi. Further investigation revealed that the D-Company was not the only criminal organization involved in such activities at the time, but that all of the city's major organized crime groups had involved themselves in real estate and property development.

This article examines the conditions that enabled Mumbai's large, well-financed mafia organizations to move into land development, joining the throngs of financiers and developers who have invested in the city's lucrative property markets and construction industry since the mid-1990s. With Mumbai's large organized crime groups (OCGs)[1] previously focused on 'traditional' illicit activities, such as gold and consumer goods smuggling, narcotics distribution, and extortion and contract killings, this article follows their movement into the newly profitable field of land and property development. Tracing the rise and transformation of Mumbai's major OCGs since the 1950s, this article argues that their recent entrance into land and property development is a product of the liberalization and globalization of the Indian economy — including the increasingly global reach of Mumbai-based organized criminal activity; the national-level adoption of structural adjustment reforms; and efforts to position Mumbai as a regional, if not global, financial hub. These multiscalar political and economic shifts, this article illustrates, facilitated the movement of Mumbai's major OCGs into this growth sector. Yet certain characteristics of the OCGs themselves have also been essential to this shift, including their increased access to large sums of capital, their embeddedness in local communities, and their formal and informal linkages to political party organizations. As Mumbai's criminal organizations transformed from paternalistic local crime bosses, referred to in India as *goondas* or *dadas*, into well-financed, globally reaching organizations, they

1 It should be acknowledged that there is a large literature in criminology on the distinctions between mafias, mobs, gangs and organized crime syndicates (see Ball and Curry, 1995, for further discussion of this literature and distinctions in the terminology). Gangs generally refer to less organized groups of youth, while mafias, mobs and syndicates typically describe various organizations with older members and more formal structures. I use these terms practically interchangeably here, due to their rather loose usage in the Mumbai context. However, to avoid definitional pitfalls, I generally use the term OCGs to describe the various types of criminal actors who comprise some sort of organized unit engaged in illegal activities.

were positioned to seize the political and economic opportunities associated with liberalization and globalization and emerge as an influential force in Mumbai's land development sector.

This analysis addresses a void in the research on the governance practices that both emerge from and contribute to global urban restructuring. Although recent research on urban property relations has made significant contributions to understanding the political processes that shape land markets, it has tended to limit its focus to the role of institutional actors and local elites, neglecting the influence of informal, or illicit, governance practices. Meanwhile, the literature on informal governance has identified many of these practices, but has generally failed to situate them in the broader context of urban restructuring. This article seeks to address both omissions by examining the influence of informal governance and criminal activity on the urban property markets of a globalizing city.

The informal governance of urban property relations

This research seeks to contribute to Logan and Molotch's (1987: 13) efforts to 'construct a sociology of cities on the basis of a sociology of urban property relations'. Illustrating that land markets are not determined by value-neutral preferences, but rather by political machinations, Logan and Molotch's classic work brought attention to 'the specific processes, the *sociological* processes, through which the pursuit of use and exchange values fixes property prices, responds to prices, and in so doing determines land uses and the distribution of fortunes' (*ibid.*: 17, emphasis in original text). Building upon this contribution, Susan Fainstein's examination of property relations in New York and London in the 1980s and 1990s identified the specific strategies employed by each city's 'development industry' to promote property development at the expense of other objectives of local government. Drawing heavily from Saskia Sassen's global city thesis and situating changes in New York's and London's property markets in the increasing dispersal of production activities and concentration of producer services, Fainstein makes the important connection between local political action and the strategic management of global economic activity. Her analysis illustrates that it was not merely transformations at the global and national scales that produced the contemporary character of the global economy, but also strategic decisions at the urban scale, particularly those related to property development, that facilitated the concentration of global city functions in these particular locations during this period.

Sassen's research itself helps illuminate some of the local political actions that shape land use in these locations, including the informal political actions and illicit activities that affect the appropriation of urban space. Although not central to her argument, Sassen's analysis of the conditions of Tokyo's inner city identifies the influence of 'the Japanese version of Western-style gangsters or Mafia, the "yaksuka" ' in the maintenance of Tokyo's blighted districts, within which they manage labor pools of informal, largely immigrant workers (Sassen, 2001: 303, 282). Yet other than this brief mention of the influence of local criminal actors on the social geography of Tokyo's inner city, the sociological study of property relations in the context of global restructuring had tended to neglect analysis of informal and illegal activities, focusing instead on the activities of growth coalitions, local elites and transnational institutions.

Meanwhile, the literature on informal governance, primarily in cities on the global periphery, has failed to connect analyses of these informal, but essential, practices to broader economic and political shifts. Such studies, appearing in anthropology and political science in the early 1970s, made an important contribution by identifying alternative sources of power that exist among the urban poor and rural peasantry of highly stratified societies who have limited access to formal mechanisms of power (Lemarchand and Legg, 1972; Scott, 1972; 1976; Handelman, 1975; Frankel, 1980).

Rooting their analyses in classic sociological theories of exchange, this research identified the petty criminals who act as brokers between the poor and these formal mechanisms, providing land, services, information and security in exchange for money and political patronage. Quoting from Jeremy Boissevain's study of patronage in Sicily, Lemarchand and Legg (1972: 153–4) explain: 'The social broker places persons in touch with each other directly or indirectly for profit. He bridges gaps in communication between persons, group structures, and even cultures. A broker is then a professional manipulator of people and information to bring about communication'. Howard Handelman's (1975) study of political mobilization in Santiago's squatter settlements elaborates on some of these activities. 'Because the campamento is somewhat removed from the existing sociopolitical order and lacks basic municipal services, its inhabitants develop their own civic institutions to deal with a variety of daily problems — maintenance of law and order, criminal justice, housing, local administration and the like' (*ibid.*: 40). Existing on the boundaries of legality, these civic institutions are often embedded in broader criminal structures. As Diane Singerman (1995: 213) notes, those in the sha'bi communities of Cairo 'are not always successful in negotiating the fine lines between pragmatism, necessity, opportunism and crime. Men and women suffer the consequences of being caught between vicissitudes of government regulation and the unwritten rules of the informal system'. While they have revealed the informal arrangements that define urban governance, such studies have generally failed to identify the interactions between these arrangements and the broader property transformations underway in these cities.

This article argues that the process of urban restructuring underway in Mumbai since the early 1990s has facilitated the movement of Mumbai-based OCGs into land and property development, resulting in their increased influence over urban governance and local property relations. As economic liberalization and the globalization of consumer markets suddenly reduced demand for illicit consumer goods, OCGs began abandoning the smuggling activities that had defined their organizations for the previous four decades. Opportunities for illicit land development, being created, in part, by the same set of political and economic reforms, enabled Mumbai's large criminal organizations to establish property development branches and construct shopping centres, commercial establishments and residential buildings. Aided by their connections to local criminal organizations, embeddedness in political party organizations, and participation in increasingly global organized crime networks, OCGs had the access to the financial and political resources necessary to compete in this increasingly lucrative sector. Although OCGs were not the only set of actors to have seized the opportunities created by these shifts, they have come to represent a particularly significant force, helping to shape the city's land use practices and development context.

Criminal origins: land, liquor and gold

Although it appears that well financed mafia organizations only recently began investing in Mumbai's property markets, most of the city's major OCGs actually have their origins in land development activities, particularly in the development of slums and squatter settlements. Squatters have been taking up residence in Mumbai's open spaces and on public lands, building homes from found objects and discarded building materials, since well before independence. But slums and shantytowns only began proliferating in the late 1950s and early 1960s, with the help of 'slumlords' and local goondas. During this period, several paternalistic community leaders acquired local power by providing housing and basic services within the city's densely populated squatter settlements. Meanwhile, they were able to establish large criminal enterprises by engaging in the production and distribution of certain illicit or cost-prohibitive items, including alcohol, gold and luxury consumer goods, due to a highly restrictive regulatory context at the national level and access to the city's ports and local shipping industry.

With the central government pursuing a strategy of state-supported industrial development in the decades following independence, Mumbai's population grew rapidly, as the city's textile mills and other expanding industries were attracting workers from all over India. The worker housing built by factory owners and public authorities before independence ultimately proved inadequate, yet no new housing was being constructed by either the public or private sectors (K. Sharma, 2000; D'Monte, 2002). In addition to limited public resources, the failure to provide adequate housing in this period was a deliberate decision made by 'rational' planners to limit the city's size. These decisions did not curb migration, however, but resulted in the proliferation of slum housing and squatter settlements. In the decade between 1971 and 1981, for example, Mumbai's population grew by 2.27 million people and the population residing in slums increased by 2.25 million (Sharma, 2004).

Recognizing an opportunity, enterprising slumlords divided unused public and privately owned land and sold or rented out plots to new migrants. One entrepreneur who engaged in land development in this period was Varadarajan Mudaliar, known locally as Vardhabhai. By the early 1960s, Vardhabhai had built a powerful criminal organization based on the illicit production and sale of alcohol in the industrial squatter settlement of Dharavi.[2] Dharavi emerged as the centre of illicit alcohol production and distribution soon after the state of Bombay prohibited alcohol production in the late 1940s. Before this time, alcohol had been produced legally in Mumbai, both manufactured commercially and brewed traditionally by members of the Koli Caste in the marshy lands of Dharavi. Once prohibition was declared, commercial alcohol production ceased and the Kolis soon faced competition in the production of illicit liquor from migrants from the southern state of Tamil Nadu, many of whom had come to work in Dharavi's leather tanneries (K. Sharma, 2000). By the early 1960s, this group of Tamil liquor producers had emerged as a powerful criminal force under the leadership of Vardhabhai. For over 20 years, Vardhabhai ran the city's first and most powerful mafia organization out of Dharavi, which diversified through land dealings and the establishment of gambling dens and brothels throughout the city. Reportedly a paternalistic community leader, Vardhabhai sponsored religious festivals and established informal governance institutions in Dharavi (K. Sharma, 2000; IPCS, 2005).[3]

Because the state had no other policy in place in this period to house this growing population, public officials chose to ignore the proliferation of squatters on public lands. Furthermore, Vardhabhai and other local goondas worked closely with local administrators to ensure this policy vacuum by registering the new residents to vote for local politicians and paying bribes to police and officials in the Bombay Municipal Corporation (BMC) to protect the liquor business and growing squatter settlements. Describing the role of Vardhabhai's organization in slum development and the growth of Dharavi, a Dharavi-based social worker explained:

> In Mukund Nagar [a settlement in Dharavi] Vardhabhai's right hand man, SK Ramaswamy was in charge . . . He and his men were in charge of land grabbing and selling plots in this area. They would 'catch' the plots and build huts with gunny bags. They would sell huts for 5,000 to 10,000 rupees. The BMC made a lot in hafta [bribe] payments and worked closely with the goondas.

In this manner, squatter settlements proliferated through the city.

As Dharavi expanded, so did Vardhabhai's organization, as it helped residents gain access to utilities and basic services. Not only in Dharavi, but throughout the city,

2 Today Dharavi is a 535-acre residential and industrial squatter settlement, commonly referred to as 'Asia's largest slum'. Much of the primary research for this piece focuses on Dharavi.

3 Vardhabhai is also the subject of several *Godfather*-like Hindi and Tamil-language films and has attained mythical status in the Tamil community.

goondas worked closely with municipal officials to establish illegal water and power connections, acquire ration cards for food and cooking gas, and get people out of jail and fines erased (SPARC, 1998; Benjamin, 2005). A long-time activist explains how water was accessed in Dharavi at this time:

> They had to pay for water even though it was being given for free by the BMC. Goondas had a water tap in Kings Circle [an area two kilometers from Dharavi] and women would get up at four in the morning to get the water and carry it back. Getting water took five or six hours and they had to pay money for it.

Aware that the municipality had not set up a tap in Dharavi, Vardhabhai's men appropriated the closest tap in King Circle and charged residents for this basic service. Neglected by formal governance institutions, Dharavi residents would not have had access to water without these enterprising, though hardly altruistic, goondas.

As has been well documented by researchers identifying similar patron–client networks in other locations, the ambiguity resulting from a neglectful state, corrupt enforcement, and otherwise powerless urban residents makes it less useful to consider these illegal acts in moral terms (Singerman, 1995; Benjamin, 2000). Rather, such acts are situated within a broader set of survival strategies that depend — due to their dangerous and high-risk nature — on deep embeddedness in family and community networks. Although the relationships between patrons and clients are often inequitable and exploitative, goondas provide essential services in the absence of other, 'legitimate' alternatives. In exchange for these services, the criminal organizations strengthen their ties to both community networks and formal governance and political institutions. Without Vardhabhai's deep connections in Dharavi, he would not have been able to transform his bootlegging business into a wide-reaching, diversified criminal organization.

Changes at the national scale also facilitated this shift. The passage of the Gold Control Act and other import barriers in the early 1960s soon led Vardhabhai's organizations into new enterprises and resulted in the emergence of new OCGs. After back-to-back wars with China and Pakistan, the Indian government introduced limitations on gold imports in an effort to preserve valuable foreign exchange in the midst of economic stagnation (Naylor, 1996). Additionally, in order to protect India's fledgling electronics industries, a 300% tax was levied on imported electronic goods, along with other taxes and tariffs imposed to support a broader strategy of import substitution (Rudolph and Rudolph, 1987; Charles, 2001). These changes occurred during a gradual decriminalization of alcohol, and Vardhabhai and other bootleggers simply shifted their operations to satiate the ever-present demands for gold and imported consumer goods.

New syndicates, organized under the leadership of Haji Mastan and Yusuf Patel, also arose to supply these items (Najmi and Jathar, 2003). With bribes paid to customs officers, illicit cargo, primarily from Dubai (nicknamed the 'smugglers' supermarket'), easily passed through Mumbai's ports (Charles, 2001). Government corruption and illicit networks with elected officials and bureaucrats were required to facilitate these massive smuggling operations. Vardhabhai's gang reportedly had strong backing from the Congress Party until his arrest in the mid-1980s (K. Sharma, 2000; Charles, 2001). Meanwhile, Mastan, who reportedly made over $25 million, in gold smuggling, launched his own political party in the mid-1970s (Mehta, 2005).

As Vardhabhai's, Mastan's, and Patel's organizations arose or shifted operations to exploit the altered regulatory context and engage in more profitable smuggling activities, they typically abandoned the less profitable slum development and service delivery activities. Although they generally retained their connections to local communities and political networks, the basic service delivery activities that had defined their initial operations were gradually taken over by others. As these OCGs established elaborate criminal operations by the 1970s, they began to split from more localized crime bosses.

Although linkages likely remained between the two sets of actors, their organizations and activities eventually became functionally distinct.

Political embeddedness and the emergence of global crime networks

In the late 1970s and 1980s, Mumbai's now powerful OCGs strengthened their ties to the city's political parties. As the political context became fragmented, with the Congress Party losing its single party dominance in this period, OCGs fortified their power by forming close associations with these new, predominantly ethnic, political movements. Meanwhile, due to police crackdowns in this period, the heads of the largest OCGs moved their base of operations out of India and, in doing so, expanded the geographic reach of their criminal enterprises. Linking now to increasingly global organized crime networks, Mumbai's OCGs had access to new sources of power and new forms of capital.

After a brief period of instability in the mid-1970s, following the 21-month suspension of democracy and police crackdowns by Prime Minister Indira Gandhi, referred to as the Emergency, Mumbai's smuggling operations came to be run by Afghan immigrants known as the Pathan Gang (Mehta, 2005). Climbing the ranks of the Pathan Gang in this period was Dawood Ibrahim, a petty criminal whose father was a constable in the Bombay Crime Branch. Dawood broke with the Pathan Gang in 1981, however, and began building a separate criminal organization, which he called the D-Company (Sharma, 1999; Mehta, 2005). Soon the D-Company surpassed the size and strength of both the Pathan gang and Vardhabhai's organization. Continued police crackdowns in the mid-1980s, however, led Dawood to move his operations to Dubai, which was attractive both because of its central role in smuggling networks and absence (until recently) of an extradition treaty with India (Charles, 2001).

With the D-Company no longer in Mumbai, two new groups emerged to fill the void, including one led by Amar Naik and another by former D-Company member Arun Gawali (Sharma, 1999; Singh, 2002). Amar Naik's gang was established in the early 1980s, starting out as a group of local goondas, collecting protection money from street vendors, small-time bootleggers and smugglers. Around the same time, D-Company associate Arun Gawali split from Dawood and, together with other former-D-Company members, began building a powerful organization around extortion and contract killings. As alcohol had been largely decriminalized by this time, the city's OCGs had moved out of alcohol-related activities and more deeply into narcotics smuggling and contract killings. Organized crime activity in the 1980s was marked by turf battles and bitter gang rivalries between Naik's and Gawali's gangs and the D-Company, resulting in considerable inter-gang activity and street-level violence (Sharma, 1999; Singh, 2002).

The links between the political parties and the OCGs also grew stronger in this period, with the right-wing Shiv Sena accumulating power through local neighborhood and criminal networks (Lele, 1995; Hansen, 2001). Although Vardabhai and Mastan had well-known connections to political parties, the growing power of the right-wing Shiv Sena and other non-Congress factions in the mid-1980s raised the stakes of local politics and political leaders increasingly sought power and resources from OCGs (Hansen, 2001). The connections between organized crime and the Shiv Sena were particularly strong in the mid-1980s, as 'several well-established gangsters, major slumlords, and dadas ran on a Shiv Sena ticket' (Hansen, 2001: 99).

By the late 1980s, the Shiv Sena had seized the growing popularity of Hindu fundamentalism and began building a strong *Hindutva* movement through 'an efficient machine of cadres spread across Bombay's segmented underworld' (Lele, 1995: 2002). Meanwhile, mass layoffs in the city's textile mills supplied both the movement and the underworld with a seemingly endless supply of angry young men (Sharma, 1995). The movement's deep entrenchment in Mumbai's neighbourhoods and slums became apparent when the city erupted in communal riots in December 1992 and January 1993. The first set of riots were initiated by Muslim youth on the night of 6 December 1992, just hours after Hindu fundamentalists destroyed the Babri Masjid, a north Indian mosque on land believed to have deep Hindu significance. A month later, rival gangs, with the support of political parties and the local police, carried out a more orchestrated series of attacks, disproportionately targeting Muslim homes and businesses (Sharma, 1995; Hansen, 2001; Mehta, 2005). The riots were an extremely significant event, reshaping much of Mumbai's social and political landscape, including the composition and activities of the city's major OCGs.

Three months later, in what was seen as a retaliation for the January riots, a group of primarily Muslim men, most associated with the D-Company, carried out a series of 15 coordinated bomb blasts in hotels, corporate offices, and public spaces across Mumbai, killing more than 300 people. The ammunition and arms used in the attacks were smuggled into India through the D-Company's smuggling networks, allegedly assisted by a Pakistani intelligence unit (Hansen, 2001; Varma, 2004). In the intervening years, several high-ranking D-Company members would be extradited and convicted for the bombings, although Dawood Ibrahim, the alleged perpetrator, was never arrested. The blasts were viewed as a show of Muslim force in the city, a response to years of growing Hindu militancy. As historian Thomas Blom Hansen (2001: 125) writes ' "Don't mess with us" was the message allegedly sent by the legendary Dawood Ibrahim, now elevated to the status of stern godfather, along with his gang, on behalf of the Muslim community'.

Around this time, Chhota Rajan, a chief Hindu lieutenant of the D-Company, split with Dawood and started a new criminal organization, based out of Kuala Lumpur (Raghavan, 2003). Although Rajan announced that his departure reflected his opposition, as a Hindu, to the March bombings, the D-Company attributed the split to older intra-gang rivalries (Mehta, 2005). Emerging as the city's fourth major OCG — alongside the D-Company, Amar Naik's and Arun Gawali's gangs — Rajan's organization spread from Southeast Asia into South India and Mumbai, focused primarily on drug smuggling and contract killings (Singh, 2002).

Extended now from the Persian Gulf to Malaysia, and with linkages identified in London, Johannesburg, and New York, the strength of the city's large OCGs resulted not only from their ties to political parties and embeddedness in antagonistic religious communities, but also in their increasingly global reach (Varma, 2004). As has been documented by scholars of organized crime and street gangs, criminal networks, like many enterprises, are becoming transnational, as the institutions established to facilitate the globalization of the formal economy have been appropriated by purveyors of the informal economy (Singh, 2002; Papachristos, 2005). Supported, in part, by systems to ease financial transfers and goods shipments by foreign investors and non-resident Indians, Dawood has been able to carry out Mumbai-based activities from Karachi, while Chhota Rajan can run his Mumbai operations from Kuala Lumpur (Charles, 2001; Varma, 2004).[4] Meanwhile, by spreading their operations over a broad geographic area and diverse activities, Dawood and Rajan have acquired the resources to build even stronger organizations. Mumbai's OCGs have long had connections outside of India, including the use of smuggling trade networks with Dubai since the 1970s, the involvement of local gangs from Afghanistan in the 1980s, and the alleged involvement of Pakistani security in the 1993 bomb blasts. But the city's OCGs have built increasingly global organizations since the early 1990s, with the support of digital technologies and a more sophisticated global financial infrastructure.

4 At the time of the 1993 bomb blasts, Dawood Ibrahim was living in Dubai. But due to changes in UAE's extradition laws and other difficulties Dawood faced in Dubai, he is believed to have since moved to Karachi. The Pakistani government, however, denies this claim and his whereabouts remain officially unknown.

Economic liberalization and the criminalization of land development

By maintaining deep ties to local communities and political party organizations, and building new linkages to global criminal networks, Mumbai's large OCGs were poised to exploit the opportunities created by the economic reforms of the 1990s to invest in the city's burgeoning property development sector. Squeezed out of smuggling activities by a newly liberalized trade context, opportunities for land development were emerging just as they were seeking new areas for investment. With the use of violence and payment of bribes, OCGs became implicated in the development of certain high-profile properties and established highly profitable property development operations.

Although most political economists date the first phase of India's gradual and inconsistent economic liberalization and integration in the world economy to around 1975, when the central government began deviating from its long-held import-substitution strategy, the reformed regulatory context did not begin to affect the activities of Mumbai's OCGs until the early 1990s. Market reforms could be discerned in the 1970s, but foreign imports remained restricted and domestic industry remained highly regulated throughout the 1980s (Denoon, 1998; Corbridge and Harriss, 2000; Nayar, 2001; 2006). More deliberate reforms were enacted in the mid-1980s, initiating modest industrial deregulation and allowing some technology imports. Most significant in this period, however, was an *ideological* shift regarding national development, signalled by the young, cosmopolitan Prime Minister Rajiv Gandhi 'proclaim[ing] his faith in a new India that would "seek to do a Korea" ' (Corbridge and Harriss, 2000: 150–1; Nayar, 2006). Despite a greater openness to capitalist growth, regulations remained largely intact throughout the 1980s and Mumbai-based illicit smuggling operations continued, facilitated by Dawood's base in the 'smugglers' supermarket' of Dubai.

In the early 1990s, the central government succumbed to pressure from the International Monetary Fund and initiated its most deliberate deregulation strategy yet, devaluing the rupee, reducing restrictions on imported consumer goods, and, most significantly from the perspective of organized crime, repealing the Gold Control Act (Bhagwati, 1995; Corbridge and Harriss, 2000; Nayar, 2006). As OCGs now faced competition from legal importers of consumer goods, they responded by further diversifying their activities, becoming involved in narcotics smuggling, film financing, and, most recently, property development. Although the D-Company began narcotics smuggling in the early 1980s, the participation of Mumbai's criminal syndicates in this area grew considerably in the early 1990s (Charles, 2001; Mehta, 2005). The deeper involvement of Mumbai's OCGs in narcotics resulted, in part, from political conflict in adjacent regions, including Afghanistan, Pakistan and Myanmar, which created porous borders and an endless supply of willing 'mules' in border regions (Charles, 2001). In addition to smuggling, OCGs took a more active role in the street-level distribution of narcotics, but the connections between the larger syndicates involved in smuggling and local goondas, who often employ children and family members to distribute narcotics, are likely weak (Charles, 2001). Drug use increased in Mumbai in this period, as did the incidence of contract killings and street-level violence (Mehta, 2005).

Film financing became another activity undertaken by OCGs in the early 1990s, particularly as OCGs sought 'white' ventures within which to launder illicitly acquired money (Appadurai, 2000; Gangar, 2003; Raghavan, 2003; Varma, 2004; Mehta, 2005). As mafia money entered Bollywood in the mid-1990s, organized crime bosses reportedly acquired influence over film scripts, musical scores, casting decisions and production schedules. Such influence, it has been noted, can be recognized in the content of films of this period, many of which focused explicitly on gangster themes (Gangar, 2003; Pendse, 2003). Several producers and financers were arrested in this period for alleged links to D-Company lieutenant Chhota Shakeel and other mafia figures. Meanwhile, several high-profile murders took place in Bollywood, including those of producer Mukesh

Duggal and cassette maker Gulshan Kumar, both allegedly killed by members of the D-Company (Raghavan, 2003).

Yet with dramatically rising land prices in the mid-1990s, one of the mafia's most significant growth activities became real estate and property development. High land prices and a strict regulatory context, particularly open to corruption, helped create an opening for OCG investment in this area. The opening was seized in the mid-1990s when, after decades of industrial decline, the government began to allow the sale of hundreds of acres of former textile mill lands in the virtual centre of the city. As Darryl D'Monte describes (2002: 153), 'the loss of industrial jobs was a grim reality; prices of real estate were going through the roof; and the ugly face of the underworld was emerging. All three ingredients of this deadly brew were on the boil when it came to the sale of mill land in the notorious Khatau case'. In this case, Sunit Khatau, chairman of one of the city's oldest textile mills, wanted to sell a factory on prime real estate and relocate to a lower-value plot to the north of the city.[5] Taking his case to the government, the sale was approved, provided that the labor union gave its consent. Recognizing that the union president would not agree to the sale, Khatau employed the help of mafia leader Arun Gawali to engineer a union coup and install a more 'sympathetic' president. With a new union president in power, Gawali helped gather the requisite worker support to approve the sale. For his part, Gawali was allegedly promised 5% of the sale price of the land — estimated to fetch as much as $100 million due to the timing of the sale at the height of Mumbai's land boom (D'Monte, 2002).

Once the land was approved for sale, Dawood reportedly struck a deal with Khatau to purchase the land for $90 million. Before the sale was finalized, however, Sunit Khatau was shot while sitting in the backseat of his car. The assassins managed to escape, while Khatau died on the way to the hospital. It is widely believed that the murder was ordered by Amar Naik, anticipating the power Gawali's gang would acquire if the sale went through and he received his cut of $4.5 million. Although Naik was never arrested for the murder, he was killed in a police 'encounter' in 1996.[6] An editorial in the *Times of India* three days after Khatau's murder mused:

> At one level, the Khatau murder can be viewed as a fall out of the continuing war between Bombay's two main ganglords . . . At a deeper level, the incidents reflect the lack of a rational land use policy in a city where archaic laws have pushed up real estate prices to unrealistic heights. The contentious issue of the sale of mill lands is linked to the absence of such a policy . . . In the current climate of economic liberalization, which calls for the upgrading and modernization of the ailing textile industry, millowners desirous of raising funds for this purpose must provide adequate compensation to workers. The tragic murder of Sunit Khatau demonstrates that relying on dubious elements to achieve such aims carries too heavy a price (quoted in D'Monte, 2002: 160).

An unsuccessful assassination attempt was also made on the union president who worked with Khatau and Gawali to secure union support for the sale. A longtime worker advocate who had fought against the sale of Khatau and other mill lands was assassinated in January 1997. Three assassins associated with Chhota Rajan were eventually convicted for the advocate's murder (D'Monte, 2002). Because of the murders and alleged mafia involvement, the government eventually nullified the sale of the Khatau Mill. The union, mill owners and government are still fighting the case in court.

5 Khatau's efforts to relocate the textile operations were representative of many mill owners in this period that shifted from the weakening textile industry to the more lucrative land development sector. This shift was facilitated by the particularities of Mumbai's political regimes, comparable in certain ways to New York's property development industry discussed by Fainstein (2001).

6 The term 'encounter' is widely understood to be a euphemism for assassinations carried out by police officers against violent criminals for whom convictions are unlikely (see Mehta, 2005, for further discussion of this issue).

The implication of the D-Company, Chhota Rajan, Arun Gawali and Amar Naik — all of the city's major OCGs — in the Khatau case, illustrates the breadth of mafia involvement in the preparation, sale and development of potentially valuable lands in Mumbai. While financial records and other systematic data on their involvement are difficult to collect, anecdotal evidence suggests that the development activities of Mumbai's OCGs include the payment of bribes and permit fees, the use of violence and threats, as well as the use of 'black' money to finance land acquisition and property developments, including the construction of shopping malls, residential buildings and hotels (Raghavan, 2003; Kumar, 2005; Sen, 2005).

Although it is similarly difficult to quantify the power OCGs have acquired over the city's property relations, it is apparent that they have garnered considerable influence in this industry. When details about the D-Company's involvement in the Sara and Sahara Shopping Centres began to surface in 2003, it became clear that the OCG had acquired ownership in dozens of properties throughout the city through the 'banami' method, by which land is purchased in the name of a third party (*Daily Excelsior*, 2004; Sen, 2005). This method of acquisition has made it difficult to catalogue the D-Company's property investments, or prosecute in the case of suspected criminal involvement. Chhota Rajan, however, has acquired properties in the name of family members, making it relatively easier to trace his organization's landholdings. Rajan's gang reportedly owns three construction companies in and around Mumbai, controlled by his wife, his brother, and brother-in-law (Sen, 2005).

Along with the increased participation of OCGs in this area has come the greater use of violence. Since the mid-1990s, there have been several high-profile murders in the construction industry implicating members of all of the major OCGs. In a high-profile case in the mid-1990s, local developer Pradeep Jain was killed in his north Mumbai office after he allegedly refused to sell a plot for the quarter of a million dollars demanded by Dawood's brother Anees Ibrahim (Vora, 2006). As the wealthiest and most global of the city's major OCGs, the D-Company and Chhota Rajan appear to have become more directly involved in property development activities than the others. The organizations of Arun Gawali and Amar Naik, however, have also established close associations with builders since the mid-1990s, assisting in extortion and contract killings and pressuring tenants and builders to support development schemes (D'Monte, 2002; Raghavan, 2003; *Chennai Online*, 2006). According to crime researchers, property development has been one of the most profitable activities for each of these organizations, and profits acquired through Mumbai's lucrative real estate markets have been used to finance many of these organizations' other activities (Sharma, 1999; Singh, 2002).

Discussion: the implications of Mumbai's development mafias

In the mid-1990s, Mumbai's large, increasingly global OCGs emerged alongside a broader set of actors to gain greater influence in the property development industry. Relying on deep connections to political party organizations and other local elites, including Bollywood producers and actors, they built powerful organizations able to overcome regulatory barriers and prohibitively high land prices. Their activities were supported by Mumbai's strict regulatory context, which limited opportunities to develop property through purely legal means. But rather than being passively affected by regulations, Mumbai's OCGs appear to be shaping this context, pressing for the continuance of certain restrictive barriers on legal development. Meanwhile, the involvement of both OCGs and local goondas in land politics has helped support the state's efforts to clear land and pursue its own development objectives. Amidst a slew of state-sponsored urban renewal schemes, initiated to bolster Mumbai's global standing, newly supportive relations between the state and OCGs appear to be reshaping the city's development context.

Justified on the grounds of turning Mumbai into a clean, efficient, 'world class' city on the model of Asia's other commercial capitals, a spate of infrastructure and development projects have been launched in Mumbai since the mid-1990s. To support these efforts, the central government initiated the $11 billion Urban Renewal Mission in 2005, sending an as yet undetermined amount of funding for redevelopment in the commercial capital. Meanwhile, the World Bank has made significant investments in roads and railway construction over the past decade, while the state government has financed the construction of office space, facilitated the sale and development of converted industrial lands, and carried out slum redevelopment schemes and transportation projects. In an effort to intensify such efforts, the state government assembled a taskforce of local elites and civil society leaders to prioritize and plan for land development, housing, and economic development activities to improve the city's global standing and 'make Mumbai a world class city by 2013' (State of Maharashtra, 2004).

Endorsing certain infrastructural, commercial and residential projects as necessary to improve the city's competitive position, the Taskforce, along with representatives from the World Bank and numerous economists, has identified the local regulatory context as a barrier to development (Bertaud, 2002; Nijman, 2002; State of Maharashtra, 2004). With the enforcement of regulations and the granting of exemptions concentrated in the hands of government bureaucrats, local regulations, it is widely acknowledged, have become open to abuses of power (Mahalingam, 1998; Narayanan, 2003; Prabhu, 2005). According to housing activist Chandhrashekhar Prabhu (2005: 25), 'The placing [of land] under reservation and the removal of the same became a major source for the politician to make money. Any favor to any individual or group could be doled out across the table, for a hefty amount of bribe'. High land prices, paired with the government's non-transparent land use laws and opportunities for corruption, have helped facilitate the entrance of OCGs into this area of investment. Consequently, despite mounting pressure to reform or repeal certain regulations, the regulations most open to abuses of power have been maintained.[7] In a context dependent upon close relations between political parties and the city's major OCGs, the legal development of land remains remarkably arduous or, in some cases, impossible. The city's major OCGs have effectively utilized violence, threats and bribes to secure permits and overcome regulatory barriers, where non-criminal developers may otherwise be halted. Just as restrictions on alcohol production facilitated the emergence of Mumbai's 'liquor mafias', and tariffs and regulations on imported gold and consumer items supported their transition to 'smuggling mafias', land use regulations have helped create Mumbai's 'development mafias'. As they have grown powerful in part because of their formal political connections, these groups have sought to retain the regulatory structure on which much of their economic activity depends.

The association of regulatory change and organized crime has been well documented. In some cases, the reduction or elimination of regulations, resulting in 'so-called self-regulating markets', can facilitate the rise or transformation of organized criminal activities (Skaperdas, 2001; Stiglitz, 2001: xv). The origins of the Sicilian mafia, for example, have been traced to the land reform policies that broke up feudal estates in the nineteenth century. After the existing political structure was dismantled, mafia groups arose to meet demands for new forms of land protection and property dispute mediation (Bandiera, 2000). More recently, the collapse of governance institutions with the end of Soviet communism has brought about a transformation in Russian organized criminal activity (Anderson, 1995; Shelley, 1995). Although under communism, the 'red mafia' managed an extensive underground economy, supported by corrupt bureaucracies and heavily regulated markets, organized crime has hardly disappeared as these institutions

7 This is particularly true with respect to the Urban Land Ceiling and Reclamation Act (ULCRA) and the city's rent control laws. The Central Government has put considerable pressure on the state to repeal or reform these laws, and has tied release of the central government funds to the reform of these regulations. By spring 2007, both laws are on the verge of repeal, but political party opposition has stalled legislative approval.

have crumbled. Rather, it has grown more powerful as law enforcement mechanisms have been weakened and distribution systems have failed to provide basic services (Anderson, 1995; Shelley, 1995; Stiglitz, 2001). Moreover, Russian mafias — like Mumbai's OCGs — have bolstered their economic might by joining global criminal networks, which has improved their access to financial resources and the global trade in oil, arms, and narcotics (Shelley, 1995).

Meanwhile, as OCGs have been able to enter into Mumbai's lucrative land and property markets only through their close associations with bureaucrats and political parties, the state has become dependent on OCGs and goondas to carry out its own development objectives. Goondas have become instrumental to state-sponsored schemes, particularly the state's efforts to dismantle squatter settlement and hawker collectivities. In order to fulfil a campaign promise to provide housing for more than four million slum dwellers, the state launched the ambitious Slum Rehabilitation Scheme (SRS) in the mid-1990s (Banerjee-Guha, 2002). Although the program has moved slowly, thousands of families have been moved into tenements in seven-story buildings throughout the city. According to the scheme, a community of slum dwellers is supposed to seek out a builder to construct a mid-rise building on the site of the original slum settlement. Once arrangements are made, the builder is obligated to construct the building and pay maintenance fees for 10 years. In exchange, the builder receives additional land on which to build market-rate properties. Given that the program was first launched during the height of Mumbai's real estate boom in the mid-1990s, there was initially considerable interest from the builders to participate in the scheme (Mukhija, 2003; Risbud, 2003). As prices declined in the late 1990s, many builders withdrew from the scheme, leaving many buildings unfinished. But in parts of the city in which land prices have remained high, builders have been eager to construct housing for slum dwellers in exchange for market-rate land. Although the SRS stipulates that the scheme be initiated by residents, builders frequently approach slum dwellers to propose rehabilitation projects. In some cases, residents have to be 'persuaded' into accepting the plan and many builders employ goondas to help coerce residents with the threat of violence.

In one such resettlement project currently underway in Dharavi, an SRS construction was left unfinished in the late 1990s. Although the residents moved into the building, they had to temporarily share flats because the upper floors were still uninhabitable. After this 'temporary' situation went on for more than seven years, the residents began to work with activists and government officials to pressure the builder to complete construction. A resident explains:

> This is when Babu began coming around. He is the builder's right hand man. Once we started complaining, the builder started using *goondagiri*. We haven't seen the builder; he is nowhere to be found. But Babu has been threatening to evict us and use violence against us if we don't stop complaining.

In this case, the use of goondagiri has proved an effective strategy for some of the residents, who now patiently waiting for the builder to complete construction. But other residents claim that they do not fear the goondas and are continuing to press for completion of the building.

Goondagiri has reportedly become a standard mode of operation within the SRS. Under this program, goondas appear to be assuming new roles vis à vis the state, private developers, and residents. With the state now taking an active role to clear slum lands and work with builders to construct slum housing and market rate properties, goondas — still operating in a patron role, yet now serving a different set of clients — have begun working with the state to help implement the scheme.

These changing relations can also be identified in recent efforts to clear public lands of street vendors and establish designated 'hawking zones'. As part of these efforts, the BMC recently commissioned a study to document the activities of the hawkers on municipal land, thereby revealing established networks between street vendors, municipal administrators and local goondas. The study, conducted in the late 1990s, counted more than a 100,000 vendors working on BMC land, finding that vendors were often forced to pay the police weekly graft, or *hafta*, to avoid fines (R.N. Sharma, 2000). Working through goondas, however, helped hawkers avoid these payments. Researcher R.N. Sharma (2000: 50) explains:

> The mafia owned several handcarts, which were rented to the hawkers on a daily payment for selling specific goods. The owners were influential goons of the area who made a sizable profit by renting out the carts (and supplying the goods). The handcarts carried a distinct identification mark known to the police and BMC staff. Hawkers using such carts were not harassed by government staff since a part of the profits appropriated by the local goons were transferred as hafta.

With the BMC now clearing public lands of hawkers, both as part of 'beautification' efforts and to prepare the lands for sale and development, the networks are being exposed and are undergoing transformation.[8] Similar efforts to clear public land of vendors in Kolkata in 1996, under the notorious Operation Sunshine which forcibly removed more than a hundred thousand street venders from Kolkata's streets in a single night, were recognized to employ the strong arm tactics of goondagiri (Bhowmik, 2006). Justified by moral statements, asserting the need to combat the growing power of the land mafias and goondas, the implementation of such schemes ironically appears to be carried out with the help of the very same land mafias.

Identifying some of these ambiguities, researcher Solomon Benjamin (2005: 251) writes:

> For the Master Planners, these are the 'illegal' operatives catering to the Ghost that haunts the image of the planned and orderly city; for the elite, these are touts, the land encroachers and builders, and land mafia of unauthorised construction, the slums staining the imaginary of the grand plan and thus to be cleared away.

Yet with OCGs increasingly working with government administrators to acquire land and permits to construct high-end developments and goondas acquiring a new role in the context of SRS and land clearance initiatives, the boundaries between 'master planners' and 'illegal operatives' appear to be breaking down (Dhareshwar and Srivatsan, 1996). Amidst these shifting boundaries between formal and informal governance, OCGs and goondas have assumed new roles within Mumbai's development industry. Exploiting and helping to define the city's regulatory context, those actors who grew powerful outside of regulatory frameworks are now helping to define them.

Conclusion

Mumbai's development mafias and smaller scale goondas grew powerful in the context of this city's strict regulatory context. While development regulations and land reservations — paired with government inactivity and misguided strategies to curb rapid urbanization — prevented the construction of adequate housing for the growing number of workers, enterprising goondas constructed low-cost housing. Although they garnered state support with the payment of bribes and use of goondagiri, the state also chose to 'supportively neglect' these activities because they addressed the city's housing shortage

8 The designated 'hawking zones' that the BMC seeks to create will contain the activities of vendors to designated plots, out of the way of formal commercial establishments and, as vendors fear, pedestrian traffic. A powerful group of business owners and elite civic organizations are backing these efforts, while a comparatively weaker resistance is being mounted by vendors and local goondas (Bhowmik, 2006).

with minimal public expenditure. As development schemes are now being promoted to leverage Mumbai's competitive position, the state has similarly chosen to 'supportively neglect' the large-scale construction activities of the city's development mafias, including the shopping centres being built under the noses of local politicians and police officials. Most of the development activity currently underway in Mumbai is not mafia backed, however, and represents the growth of a legitimate property development industry, strengthened by regulatory reforms and the expansion of the finance sector of the past 15 years. But OCG property development activities have emerged alongside and intertwined with the growth of the industry as a whole.[9] As the stakes of urban development in Mumbai have increased, the state has not only allowed OCGs to acquire and develop prime properties, but development authorities have increasingly employed both major OCGs and more local goondas to help clear lands and promote redevelopment schemes. With both the stakes and pace showing no signs of abating, amidst a more concerted effort to use urban development to bolster the city's competitive position, it is likely that OCGs will build on the power they have acquired in this domain and concentrate more resources on these activities.

The globally oriented developments underway in Mumbai — designed to clear informal settlements and develop urban land to meet the commercial, residential and consumptive demands of the financial services sector and its employees — are growing increasingly common in cities throughout the world. Although the discussion in this article has been limited to Mumbai, parallels can certainly be drawn to other cities, in which altered regulatory contexts, and heightened development activity have facilitated the criminality of land and property development. While particular social and economic histories and distinct political institutions and regulatory contexts facilitated the integration of OCGs within Mumbai's development industry, this phenomenon is not unique to this context. Further research and comparative case studies would be required before generalizations can be made, but this article represents an attempt to document an instantiation of the informal governance practices shaping property relations in one particular globalizing city.

Liza Weinstein (lizaw@uchicago.edu), Department of Sociology, University of Chicago, Pick Hall, Room 320, 5828 S. University Street, Chicago, IL 60637, USA.

References

Anderson, A. (1995) The red mafia: a legacy of communism. In E.P. Lazear (ed.), *Economic transition in Eastern Europe and Russia: realities of reform*. The Hoover Institution Press, Stanford.

Appadurai, A. (2000) Spectral housing and urban cleansing: notes on millennial Mumbai. *Public Culture* 12.3, 627–51.

Ball, R. and G.D. Curry (1995) The logic of definition in criminology: purposes and method for defining 'gangs'. *Criminology* 33.2, 225–45.

Bandiera, O. (2000) Land reform and the origins of the Sicilian mafia: a model and a test. In *The Latin American and Caribbean Economic Association (LACEA) 2000 Annual Meeting*, Rio de Janeiro, 12 October 2000.

Banerjee-Guha, S. (2002) Shifting cities: urban restructuring in Mumbai. *Economic and Political Weekly* 37.1, 121–8.

Benjamin, S. (2000) Governance, economic settings and poverty in Bangalore. *Environment and Urbanization* 12.1, 35–56.

9 It is worth mentioning that the majority of Mumbai's major property developers do not have connections to OCGs. Although allegations periodically surface of such connections — arising because of the rather flippant use of the term 'land mafia' by media and housing rights advocates — such claims have not been substantiated. While it has been suggested that a majority of the financing for Bollywood now comes from OCGs or other illicit sources, the same thing cannot be said of Mumbai's real estate and construction industries.

Benjamin, S. (2005) Touts, pirates and ghosts. In S. Reader (ed.), *Bare acts*, Sarai Centre for the Study of Culture, New Delhi.

Bertaud, A. (2002) The economic impact of land and urban planning regulations in India. Unpublished White Paper.

Bhagwati, J. (1995) *India in transition: freeing the economy*. Clarendon Press, Oxford.

Bhowmik, S. (2006) Social security for street vendors. In *Seminar: Securing the insecure: a symposium on extending social security to unprotected workers*, v. 568, December 2006.

Business Week (2005) Indian land grab. 19 September.

Chennai Online (2006) Dawood drops investment plans in Mumbai. 31 January.

Corbridge, S. and J. Harriss (2000) *Reinventing India: liberalization, Hindu nationalism, and popular democracy*. Polity Press, Malden, MA.

Charles, M. (2001) The growth and activities of organised crime in Bombay. *International Social Science Journal* 53, 359–67.

D'Monte, D. (2002) *Ripping the fabric: decline of Mumbai and its mills*. Oxford University Press, New Delhi.

Daily Excelsior (2004) Police target property business of Dawood. 3 June.

Denoon, D.B.H. (1998) Cycles in Indian economic liberalization, 1966–1996. *Comparative Politics* 31.1, 43–60.

Dhareshwar, V. and R. Srivatsan (1996) 'Rowdy-sheeters': an essay on subalternity and politics. In S. Amin and D. Chakrabarty (eds.), *Subaltern studies IX*, Oxford University Press, New Delhi.

Fainstein, S. (2001) *The city builders: property development in New York City and London, 1980–2000*. University of Kansas Press, Kansas.

Frankel, P. (1980) The politics of poverty: political competition in Soweto. *Canadian Journal of African Studies* 14.2, 201–20.

Gangar, A. (2003) Tinseltown: from studios to industry. In S. Patel and J. Masselos (eds.), *Bombay and Mumbai: a city in transition*, Oxford University Press, New Delhi.

Handelman, H. (1975) The political mobilization of urban squatter settlements: Santiago's recent experience and its implications for urban research. *Latin American Research Review* 10.2, 35–72.

Hansen, T.B. (2001) *Wages of violence: naming and identity on postcolonial Bombay*. Princeton University Press, Princeton, NJ.

IPCS (2005) *Non-traditional security issues: evolution of criminal gangs in Mumbai*. Institute of Peace and Conflict Studies, New Delhi.

Kumar, S. (2005) Dawood shifts to retail and tourism: the gang owns top gutkha brands: police. *The Chandigarh Tribune* 22 February.

Lele, J. (1995) Saffronization of the Shiv Sena. In S. Patel and A. Thorner (eds.), *Bombay: metaphor for modern India*, Oxford University Press, New Delhi.

Lemarchand, R. and K. Legg (1972) Political clientelism and development: a preliminary analysis. *Comparative Politics* 4.2, 149–78.

Logan, J. and H. Molotch (1987) *Urban fortunes: the political economy of place*. University of California Press, Berkeley.

Mahalingam, S. (1998) The false ceiling. *Frontline* 1 August.

Mehta, S. (2005) *Maximum city: Bombay lost and found*. Knopf Publishers, New York.

Mukhija, V. (2003) *Squatters as developers: slum redevelopment in Mumbai*. Ashgate, Burlington.

Najmi, Q. and D. Jathar (2003) Don in twilight zone: ten years after he triggered the Mumbai blasts, Dawood Ibrahim's empire is crumbling. *The Week* 9 March.

Narayanan, H. (2003) In search of shelter: the politics and implementation of the Urban Land (Ceiling and Reservation) Act 1976 in Greater Mumbai. In S. Patel and J. Masselos (eds.), *Bombay and Mumbai: a city in transition*, Oxford University Press, New Delhi.

Nayar, B.R. (2001) *Globalization and nationalism: the changing balance of India's economic policy*. Sage, Thousand Oaks.

Nayar, B.R. (2006) India's globalization: evaluating the economic consequences. *Policy Studies 2*, East–West Center, Washington.

Naylor, R.T. (1996) The underworld of gold. Crime, *Law & Social Change* 25, 191–241.

Nijman, J. (2000) Mumbai's real estate market in the 1990s: de-regulation, global money, and casino capitalism. *Economic and Political Weekly* 12 February.

Nijman, J. (2002) The effects of economic globalization: land use and land values in Mumbai, India. In R. Grant and J.R. Short (eds.), *Globalization and the margins*, Palgrave McMillan, New York.

Papachristos, A.V. (2005) Gang world. *Foreign Policy* March/April.

Pendse, S. (2003) Satya's Mumbai, Mumbai's Satya. In S. Patel and J. Masselos (eds.), *Bombay and Mumbai: a city in transition*, Oxford University Press, New Delhi.

Prabhu, C. (2005) Revitalization of Mumbai — XXV: amenity spaces and de-reservation. *Monthly Economic Digest* April.

Raghavan, R.K. (2003) D-Company on the run. *Frontline* 2.4.

Risbud, N. (2003) The case of Mumbai, India. In *Understanding slums: case studies for the global report on human settlements*. UN-Habitat, Nairobi.

Rudolph, L. and S.H. Rudolph (1987) *In pursuit of Lakshmi: the political economy of the Indian state*. University of Chicago Press, Chicago.

Sassen, S. (2001) *The global city: New York, London, Tokyo*. Princeton University Press, Princeton, NJ.

Scott, J.C. (1972) Patron–client politics and political change in Southeast Asia. *The American Political Science Review* 66.1, 91–113.

Scott, J.C. (1976) *The moral economy of the peasant: rebellion and subsistence in Southeast Asia*. Yale University Press, New Haven.

Sen, S. (2005) Rajan's properties to be attached. *Times of India* 24 December.

Sharma, K. (1995) Chronicle of a riot foretold. In S. Patel and A. Thorner (eds.), *Bombay: metaphor for modern India*, Oxford University Press, New Delhi.

Sharma, K. (2000) *Rediscovering Dharavi: stories from Asia's largest slum*. Penguin Books, New Delhi.

Sharma, M.L. (1999) Organized crime in India: problems and perspectives. *Resource Material Series* No. 54. The United Nations Asia and Far East Institute for the Prevention of Crime and the Treatment of Offenders (UNAFEI), Tokyo.

Sharma, R.N. (2000) The politics of urban space. *Seminar* 491, 49–54.

Sharma, R.N. (2004) Housing market in metropolitan Mumbai and its irrelevance to average citizens. Unpublished White Paper.

Shelley, L.I. (1995) Post-Soviet organized crime: problem and response. *European Journal on Criminal Policy and Research* 3.4, 7–25.

Singerman, D. (1995) *Avenues of participation: family, politics, and networks in urban quarters of Cairo*. Princeton University Press, Princeton, NJ.

Singh, S.P. (2002) Transnational organized crime: the Indian perspective. *Resource Material Series* No. 59. The United Nations Asia and Far East Institute for the Prevention of Crime and the Treatment of Offenders (UNAFEI), Tokyo.

Skaperdas, S. (2001) The political economy of organized crime: providing protection when the state does not. *Economic Governance* 2.3, 173–202.

SPARC (1998) Enumeration as a tool for mobilization: the community census of structures in Dharavi. Society for the Preservation of Area Resources, Mumbai.

State of Maharashtra (2004) *Transforming Mumbai into a world-class city*. Chief Minister's Taskforce.

Stiglitz, J. (2001) Forward. In K. Polyani, *The great transformation: the political and economic origins of our time*, Beacon Press, Boston.

Varma, R. (2004) Provincializing the global city: from Bombay to Mumbai. *Social Text* 22.4, 65–89.

Vora, J. (2006) Two accused turn approver in Pradeep Jain murder case. *Mumbai Mirror* 23 July.

[13]

DANGEROUS SPACES OF CITIZENSHIP: GANG TALK, RIGHTS TALK AND RULE OF LAW IN BRAZIL

James Holston
University of California, Berkeley, USA

Abstract This article considers an apparently perplexing aspect of democratization in Brazil: the use by notorious criminal gangs (*comandos*) from the poor urban peripheries and prisons of the discourses of democratic citizenship, justice, and rule of law to represent their own organizations and intentions. I situate this use within an unsettling development in Latin America generally during the last 30 years: the coincidence of increasing political democracy and increasing everyday violence and injustice against citizens. My discussion considers these new territorializations of power and violence and their consequences for citizenship, democracy, and urbanization. To bring them to light, I focus on public pronouncements by Brazilian criminal gangs that typically combine rationalities of crime with those of democracy, citizen rights, rule of law, and revolution. I also compare them with public declarations made by the police. I analyze both in relation to the historically dominant paradigm of Brazilian citizenship that democratization destabilizes. I then evaluate this destabilization with regard to the new kinds of violence and paradigms of insurgent citizenship that have emerged as characteristics of urbanization and democratization worldwide.

Keywords Brazil, criminal gangs, democracy, insurgent citizenship, rule of law, urban peripheries

Brazilian democracy has advanced significantly in the last two decades. Indeed, it has pioneered innovations that place it at the forefront of democratic development worldwide. Yet precisely as democracy has taken root, new kinds of violence, injustice, corruption, and impunity have increased dramatically. This coincidence is the perverse paradox of Brazil's democratization. As a result, many Brazilians feel less secure under the political democracy they achieved, their bodies more threatened by its everyday violence than by the repressions of dictatorship (1964–85). At the same time, moreover, that a generation of insurgent citizens democratized urban space and key aspects of its planning, creating unprecedented access to resources, a climate of fear and incivility also came to permeate public encounters. These new estrangements produce an abandonment of public space, fortification of residence, criminalization of the poor, and support for police violence.

These conditions debilitate democracy. They erode a public sphere undeniably broadened by novel popular participation. In the domains of law and urban planning, for example, traditionally arenas of humiliation and oppression for the poor, popular mobilizations of national scale profoundly shaped the 1988 Citizen Constitution and its innovative principles of citizen participation and social justice. These innovations are particularly evident in its sections on righting the inequalities of urban life in Brazil. Nevertheless, the institutions of justice – particularly the courts and the police – have become even more discredited with democratization. Instead of its anticipated glories, Brazilians experience a democratic citizenship that seems simultaneously to erode as it expands, a democracy at times capable and at other times tragically incapable of protecting the citizen body and producing a just society.[1]

Researchers have now examined many of these contradictions as they twist and turn through Brazilian society, taking shape in violence, police abuse, corruption, misrule of law, land conflicts, segregation, fortification, privatization, racism, and illness, often in studies that link these conditions.[2] However, providing a theoretical account of their relation to the process of democratization remains problematic. The difficulty is to account for them from within this process without dismissing them as aberrations and externalities, disrespecting democratic intentions, or predetermining antidotes on the basis of a convergence to ideal types modeled on particular and usually North Atlantic democracies. Given that the extraordinary global democratization of the last 35 years is overwhelmingly non-North Atlantic, occurring in societies of vastly different cultures and histories, such convergence of models seems as unconvincing theoretically as it is unlikely empirically. Even its suggestion strikes many proponents of democracy in Latin America and elsewhere as a new North Atlantic imperialism. If, as I think, neither convergence nor dismissal constitute adequate accounts, then democratic theory must be rethought in terms of the new conditions that characterize the current worldwide insurgence of democratic citizenships. As I argue below, planning theory and urban studies must be similarly reconceived to address the new spatializations of power inherent in these processes.

Democracy, linguistics, and the rationalities of gang violence

Of the new conditions, it is especially the widespread concurrence of democratic politics with systematic violence and injustice against citizens that reveals these limitations of theory and method. In many regions of the world, not only in Brazil and Latin America, increasing everyday violations of *civil* citizenship in the form of urban violence and discredited judiciaries appear to accompany increasing political democracy. Indeed, their entanglement has become an intractable problem of emerging democracies worldwide.[3] For Brazilian democracy, it is a particularly bitter development. The victories of President Luiz Inácio Lula da Silva and his Workers' Party (PT) at all levels of government in the elections of 2002 seemed a resounding triumph for democratic politics and an insurgent citizenship of social justice. Those who pioneered new models of participatory planning achieved prominence in a new Ministry of Cities and elsewhere throughout national and local government. But after just three years, both his administration and party are beset by corruption scandals of unprecedented magnitude. To date, more than 20 percent of congress and many others at all levels of government have been implicated. Yet none of these officials is on trial or in jail. Although congress opened impeachment proceedings against more than 75 members, it has managed to revoke the political rights of only four. Two more resigned. Others have already been acquitted by secret congressional ballot, despite hard evidence of their guilt.[4]

At the same time that the political system of Brazil's democracy appears bankrupt, and both the public and the judiciary numb to its unending and unpunished corruptions, urban violence has mutated into the terror of organized crime. First in Rio de Janeiro and São Paulo and then elsewhere, gang-cartels (*comandos*) organized massive prison rebellions, during which they denounced the hell-hole conditions of state imprisonment, demanded justice, and killed their rivals. Their organizations spread to the poorest urban neighborhoods where they both run the drug trade and supply social services the state neglects. Beginning in May 2006, the Primeiro Comando da Capital, repeatedly paralyzed the city of São Paulo, attacking police stations, government buildings, banks, buses, and prisons. Almost 200 police, guards, suspected gang members, and innocents have been killed, many summarily executed. These insurrections reveal gross failures of the state and its justice system to enforce the law, protect citizens, respect the rights of prisoners, and develop policies of security beyond truculence. Not surprisingly, paramilitary gangs have arisen in some places to combat the criminal gangs, exercise vigilantism, and – of course – take over their lucrative criminal enterprises. The irony is not lost on Brazilians that the congress, the comandos, and the police sustain organized crime. All use the language of rights. All discredit democratization. This delegitimation shows Brazilians, to their enormous frustration, that political democracy does not necessarily generate a rule of law that is democratic and that without democratic justice, democracy corrodes.

Thus Brazilian democratization is at a critical point. It has not been able to overcome the violence and impunity that lacerate all social groups, discredit the judiciary and the police, and undermine the democratic rule of law. At the same time, however, these counter-configurations of democracy have not prevented its consolidation in significant measures of insurgent citizenship that subvert still-dominant paradigms of rule. By insurgent, I mean a counter-politics that destabilizes the dominant regime of citizenship, renders it vulnerable, and defamiliarizes the coherence with which it usually presents itself to us. Brazil's violence has not prevented the extensive legitimation of this insurgent democratic citizenship and its adoption as the language in which the most diverse sectors of society, including organized crime, frame their interests. For the time being, neither democracy nor its counters prevail in Brazil. Rooted yet rotted, they remain entangled, unexpectedly surviving each other.

In this article, I analyze one of the most perplexing examples of this entanglement. It offers strange proof of the generalized legitimacy of democratic discourse throughout Brazilian society. I refer to the use by notorious criminal gangs of the language of democratic citizenship, rights, and justice to represent their own organizations and intentions.[5] These criminal *comandos* originated during the early 1990s as gangs within the state prisons of Rio and São Paulo. They initially formed in large measure to defend the rights of prisoners in the horrifically abusive prison systems. This defense was central to their recruitment and organization of members. Today, however, they command vast operations in drug trafficking, extortion, and other criminal enterprises, both inside and outside prisons. To the chronic embarrassment of officialdom, these activities are coordinated from within the prisons via an underground network of cellphones. Ensconced as well in some of the poorest neighborhoods of the urban peripheries, they dominate a certain amount of territory in major cities with a rule that distributes summary execution along with diapers, milk, medication, and employment, combining terror and public works. In this combination, they are not unlike the state itself.[6]

Regularly, these criminal cartels also launch surprisingly well-coordinated attacks against entities of government they claim commit crimes against prisoners. They consider themselves at war with the security apparatus of the state. They target especially the persons and property of the justice system, assassinating police, prison staff, prosecutors, and judges and sponsoring 'mega-rebellions' in the prisons. In São Paulo, the PCC has also attacked public transportation, burning empty buses in campaigns of violence that paralyzed the city repeatedly in 2006. Their violence against rival and apostate gang members is exceptionally brutal. They do not merely kill. They torture and mutilate, decapitating, disemboweling, and burning the bodies of their enemies.

The *comandos* occasionally make public pronouncements, typically during a prison rebellion, city assault, or police operation. Curiously, this gang talk takes the form of rights talk. It justifies crime and terror with the rationalities of citizenship. Thus, on 24 February 2003, the Comando Vermelho issued a proclamation to the city of Rio imposing a shutdown of commerce in the name of justice. It ended with the following:

> So ENOUGH, we only want our rights, and we are not going to give them up, so shops had better keep their doors closed until midnight on Tuesday [25 February 2003], and the one who dares to open his doors will be punished in one form or

> another [;] it's no use, we are not joking, those who joke are in politics with this total abuse of power and with this generalized robbery [;] the judiciary must begin to empty the prisons and act within the law before it is too late. If the laws were made to be followed, why this abuse? [7]

What can we make of such appeals to rights, justice, and the democratic rule of law by organized crime? What do they suggest about Brazilian democracy, its trajectory, and the social transformations it induces? Should they be taken as indicating anything about such matters? Or should we view them with skepticism, as nothing more than cynical attempts to dissimulate and mock? I confess that I have no certain answers to these questions, at least none regarding the deeper views of gang members. Moreover, I can only discuss the public discourse, as sustained ethnographic research inside these gangs is practically impossible and formal interviews notoriously unreliable. What is certain, however, is that the criminal gangs are crucial elements of both the new territorializations of power and violence and the new paradigms of citizenship in urban peripheries throughout Brazil and, indeed, throughout the global South that have taken shape during the extraordinarily intense processes of worldwide democratization and urbanization of the last 50 years. Efforts to actualize this democracy in the context of gargantuan cities and their metropolitan societies – efforts in planning, law, and administration – will likely encounter these gangs in control of or disputing significant extensions of urban territory. Thus to ignore the new territorializations of power and genealogies of citizenship the gangs instantiate is not only to perpetuate the errors of negligent, repressive, and incompetent states with regard to urban poverty and inequality. It is also to disable new conceptualizations of democracy and planning that must engage an urbanized planet and its globalized demands for democratic citizenships.

The public discourses of the gangs offer distinct opportunities to probe this new urban cartography of democracy. As I do not have access to the inner deliberations of the gangs, I propose that a productive way to analyze this gang talk is by means of a triangulation: I can locate it in relation to the historically dominant paradigm of Brazilian citizenship that democratization destabilizes and evaluate this destabilization with regard to violence. My objective in this mapping is not to give a history of these criminal cartels or to attribute their growth solely to the injustices of this dominant paradigm of citizenship, though they are an important factor. Nor do I think that addressing these problems will end gang criminality and violence, though respecting prisoner rights will eliminate an important motivation for joining prison gangs.

Rather, my mapping will show that Brazil's democracy has thus far produced a dangerous, hybrid space of citizenship as a sphere of social change in which the legal and illegal, legitimate and criminal, just and unjust, and civil and uncivil claim the same moral ground of citizen rights and respect by way of contradictory social practices. This conjunction of opposites is certainly perverse. Nevertheless, it also indicates a fundamental characteristic of democratization in Brazil and elsewhere: the equalities of democratic citizenship always produce new inequalities, vulnerabilities, and destabilizations, as well as the means to contest them. For example, the right of citizens to associate freely, considered a fundamental equality, nevertheless generates organizations of unequal capacities and powers – such as the *comandos* themselves (criminal and paramilitary), neighborhood associations, and real estate lobbies. As citizens advance their interests, these groups are set against each other in the arena of citizenship. In this way, equality predictably becomes the foundation on which new inequality is built and challenged.[8] If that is so, then it follows that citizenship's contradictions are internal and not incidental or extraneous to democracy's theory. It must also be the case, therefore, that significant contradiction, paradox, and disjunction are inevitable in the development of all democracies, established and emergent. Hence, if we cannot consider Brazil's democratic development abnormal for being disjunctive, the problem to investigate is the specificities of its contradictions.

With regard to Brazil, my example suggests that even at the perverse outer bounds of Brazilian society – in prison-based gangs and police-based death squads – it has become common practice to use the language of democracy to explain murderous violence. This slippage between the legal and the illegal is a deeply paradoxical development for political democracy. But as I have shown in my study of Brazilian citizenship (Holston, 2008), the productions of the illegal and the legal have long been reciprocating processes in Brazil, a symbiosis key to the perpetuation of the dominant regime of citizenship. Should we be surprised that they now share the legitimation of rights talk? That is, my example of gang talk indicates the consolidation of a common language of democratic measure, a new commensurability we might call it, that destabilizes, challenges, and unevenly replaces an older public sphere of citizenship grounded in very different values and justifications. It suggests, moreover, the limitations of democratic theory that focuses on narrow yet totalizing conceptions of the political and the advantages of the anthropological view that considers the lived and contingent conditions of citizenship – however messy and disjunctive – as a better means of understanding contemporary forms of democratic development in insurgent citizenships and disjunctive democracies.

Thus I suggest that democratization destabilizes in specific ways that often entail specific kinds of violence. Democratization does not account for all destabilization and violence in contemporary Brazil. Other important processes of social change – such as urbanization and neoliberalization – also destabilize entrenched social, spatial, and economic regimes. Each of these processes brings its own kinds of disruption, and each gets entangled with the others. Therefore, I stress that there are many causes for the increase in violence and injustice in Brazil and that my objective is not to provide either a sufficient or global explanation. Nor do I suggest that Brazil has become both more democratic and more violent primarily because of a clash between entrenched elites and insurgent citizens. There are many contributing factors. Rather, my aim is to identify some of those associated with democratization and to avoid reducing my analysis to any one factor. To map the incendiary mix of the legal and the illegal that marks my example of gang talk, I must therefore begin with the historic paradigm of citizenship that establishes the terms of democracy's destabilizations.

Differentiated citizenship

I ask you to consider this paradigm because its formulation of citizenship is still current and in many ways dominant in Brazil. Thus, the history I outline is ever-present. It turns contemporary citizenship into a hybrid mix of the entrenched and the insurgent. The history of citizenship is important precisely because insurgence bubbles up from the past in places where present circumstances seem propitious for an irruption, destabilizing the present and rendering it fragile. In this view, the present is like a bog, with history leaking through; it is full of holes, gaps, contradictions and misunderstandings, right alongside all the taken-for-granted assumptions that give the present its apparent coherence. The ethnographic present is something to be acted upon by historical investigation because we realize that the past always leaks through, disturbing the present and breaking it up into heterogeneous elements that are recomposed and transformed. In the case at hand, as history haunts the present, it provides possible sites for the destabilization of the older paradigm of citizenship. Such destabilization provokes the kind of violent reactions we find under democracy. Thus, my objective is not to give a complete historical account of Brazilian citizenship, either in the brief discussion here or in the larger work from which it is drawn. Rather, I use history as an argument about the present.

I analyze the historical trajectory of Brazilian citizenship as a combination of two considerations: one is formal membership, based on principles of incorporation into the nation-state. The other is the substantive distribution of the rights, meanings, institutions, and practices that membership entails to those considered citizens. This combination produced a distinctive formulation of citizenship in Brazil, one distinguished from its competitors on the world stage of nation-states through the deliberate constructions of 18th and 19th-century Brazilians: a national citizenship that was, from the start, universally inclusive in membership and massively inegalitarian in distribution. This inclusively inegalitarian citizenship has been remarkably consistent in maintaining its principles of both incorporation and distribution since the inception of the Brazilian nation-state 200 years ago. Indeed, membership became more inclusive with independence in 1822 and differentiation more severe with the foundation of the Republic at the end of the century. When Vargas introduced social citizenship based on urban labor in the 1930s, he (and the military dictatorship later) perpetuated this differentiated citizenship by modernizing it, that is, by adapting it to the new circumstances of a modern, urban, industrial economy and society. To distribute rights differentially, the Brazilian formulation of citizenship requires the use of social differences that are not the basis of national membership, but prior or other to it. It uses social differences of education, property, race, gender, occupation, and the like to create legal and extralegal inequalities, generating a gradation of differential rights among citizens, and it focuses its energies on the distribution and maintenance of such privileges. I describe it, therefore, as a differentiated citizenship in which such social qualifications organize its various political, civil, and social dimensions and regulate its distribution of powers. Thus, most rights have been available only to particular kinds of citizens and exercised as the privilege of particular social categories.

When elites sought to consolidate this conceptualization of differentiated citizenship in response to the great 19th-century changes of independence and the abolition of slavery, their solution was twofold.[9] To control political citizenship, they made suffrage direct and voluntary but restricted it to the literate. This restriction denied most Brazilians their political rights for a century, from 1881 to 1985. To dominate civil and economic matters, they created a real estate market to legitimate the ownership of private property and finance the immigration of free labor. But, adapting the English theorist of colonialism E.G. Wakefield, they kept land prices high and wages low so that the working masses would have practically no legal access to property and independent production and would be forced, as a result, to remain a source of semi-servile cheap labor. Thus, political and civil citizenship developed in step: both became more restrictive as Brazil changed from an imperial nation based on slave labor to a republican nation based on wage labor over the course of the 19th century. Moreover, both restrictions remained in force until the urbanization of Brazil, beginning in the 1940s, resulted in the construction by the poor of the massive peripheries around Brazil's major cities. In these peripheries, a new formulation of citizenship emerged.

As a result of the distribution of inequality that organizes this difference-specific citizenship, therefore, most Brazilians have been denied political rights, excluded from property ownership, forced into segregated and often illegal conditions of residence, refused access to justice, and estranged from the law. This historic paradigm of citizenship is not an archaic embodiment of backland Brazil. It is a still dominant aspect of its modernity.

The exclusion from property had a number of profound consequences for Brazilian law and law's relation to citizenship. It had the effect of forcing most Brazilians to reside illegally, making illegality if not the norm, then the predominant condition of settlement. For most citizens, the effect was overwhelming. Their status as illegal residents subverted their civil citizenship. It did so in two ways: first, by placing them on the other side of the law, the condition of having to live illegally alienated citizens from law generally, diminishing their access to its rights and justice, undermining it as an institution of and for citizenship, and rendering it 'for enemies'; second, their exclusion from the legal ownership of land also denied them the civil standing that legitimate property ownership is conventionally understood to create.[10] This estrangement from law is precisely the meaning of the classic Brazilian adage, 'for friends, everything; for enemies, the law'.

Particularly in relation to property, law became estranged from citizenship in the new 19th century nation as it became a system of stratagem and bureaucratic entanglement, deployed by state and subject alike to create invincible complication, obfuscate problems, neutralize opponents, and, above all, legalize usurpations. This misrule of law, as I call it, emerged from its colonial and imperial circumstances as a brilliantly constructed scheme of alibis for the absence of effective social regulation, a form of social management in which more law was the corrective for the ineffective application of previous law and meant more opportunity for entanglement and usurpation. In this context, obeying the law had low status, because to do so signified weakness. Compliance was therefore a means of humiliation, directed at opponents and the poor. Conversely, manipulating, breaking, or choosing when to obey the law signified power and became a habit of wealth. Most Brazilians, however, did not have the resources to use the law in these ways. Overwhelmingly, their exclusion from political rights denied them participation in making laws, and their exclusion from property made illegality the norm of their residence.

These denials of citizenship rights, alienations from the legal system, and entrenched conditions of illegality meant, moreover, that many Brazilians regularly suffered repression, violence, and injustice. The regime of differentiated citizenship has always accommodated high levels of public and private violence, corruption, police abuse, impunity, judicial discredit, scofflawism, and privatizations of justice and security, in addition to the structural violence of malnutrition, abysmal health care, and all the reduced life chances of massive poverty. We have only to think of the alliance between public powers and private forces, of the appropriation of the public by the private that characterizes *coronelismo* to realize that much of the privatization of justice and security that we denounce today follows an old pattern. In other words, the current violence has many elements that derive from and are sustained by the differentiated formulation of citizenship that disempowers most Brazilian citizens and increases their inequality. Indeed, the systematic violence inherent in this citizenship has never been in doubt, and its hostility to equal rights and social justice has always been evident – as Washington Luís, governor of the state of São Paulo and future president (1926–30) confirmed on the campaign trail in 1920 with his famous remark: 'The social question is a question of the police.'

Although urban Brazil is surely violent today, and violent in different ways than before, analysts regularly present the violence and terror under which the poor live as new. They are not. Thus, the commonly heard nostalgia for the civility of Brazilian public space before current democratization – to the aesthetic pleasures of its social heterogeneity and its race-mixing – misses the crucial point Often advanced by democracy's critics, it ignores that this 'peace of the street' was only possible because it was maintained by a discriminatory and repressive regime of citizenship that made certain that everyone knew their place and responded severely to threats of displacement.

Democratic destabilizations

The paradigm of differentiated citizenship remains contemporary, having survived – indeed nourished – every political regime over the last 200 years, thriving under monarchy, military dictatorship, and electoral democracy. However, some of its conditions – exclusion from property, denial of political rights, misrule of law – changed as the majority of Brazilians became urban citizens. After the 1940s, they moved massively to cities, built the peripheries, and engaged in a different formulation of citizenship. In the context of these autoconstructed peripheries, the very same historical sites of differentiation – political rights, landed property, residential illegality, misrule of law, servility – fueled the irruption of an insurgent citizenship that destabilized the differentiated. Although these elements continue to sustain the regime of differentiated citizenship, they are also the conditions of its subversion as the urban poor gained political rights, became property owners, made law an asset, became modern consumers, and achieved personal competence through their experience of the city.

In such ways, the lived experience of the periphery became both the context and the substance of an urban citizenship – one that has generated significant democratic innovation in law, government, and practice. By urban citizenship, I mean a citizenship that refers to the city as its public sphere and to right-claims addressing urban practices as its substance – claims concerning residence, neighborhood life, infrastructure, transportation, consumption, and so forth. This insurgence has cracked open the principles of differentiation that for centuries legitimated a particularly inegalitarian formulation of citizenship. It turned the poor resident of the periphery into a new citizen and launched a citizenship that has transformed Brazil.

We would hardly expect, however, this insurgent urban citizenship to be stable and coherent in its expansions. It too has holes into which it collapses. Exactly because the old formulas of differentiated citizenship persist, new incivilities and injustices have arisen with democratization. Even though Brazilians successfully institutionalized mass political citizenship, democratized urban space, and pioneered new practices of law, many basic aspects of democratic citizenship remain unrealized. Hence, the intertwining of the differentiated and the insurgent is unstable and has contradictory effects. It erodes the coherence of taken-for-granted categories of domination that gave daily life its sense of order and security. If it did not, it would be inconsequential.

But this entanglement also provokes violent reactions that undermine the new democratic practices and institutions, some with the objective of restoring the old paradigms of order. These reactions are articulated precisely around the historic sites of citizen differentiation, and they shape the conditions that characterize this contradictory period of Brazil's democratization, including criminal and police violence, incivility in public encounters, criminalization of the poor, indignation at impunity, massive property conflicts, new privatizations of justice and security, and popular support for violent measures of social control. The attempts to restore the old paradigms do not generate these attributes alone, as there are other factors and types of destabilization. But insofar as this engagement of citizenships provokes democratic change, democracy brings its own kinds of violence that irrupt where it destabilizes older formulations of order and repression.

Emblematic of this unstable mix of old and new formulations of citizenship is the high level of everyday street violence perpetrated by both criminals and police. So much has now been written about this violence that I only need observe that violent criminality increased continuously in Brazil since the early 1980s to the point that by the mid-1990s, the rates of homicide in most of the country's metropolitan regions ranked among the highest in the world.[11] In São Paulo during this period, it was around 65 per 100,000 inhabitants or more than 6500 homicides per year. However, among young men, ages 15–24, the homicide rate in 2002 was an extraordinary 247 per 100,000! Moreover, the police have committed about 10 percent of the homicides in São Paulo's metropolitan region in the past 15 years. They are therefore co-responsible for the high levels of violence.[12] Furthermore, most murders remain uninvestigated and unpunished. Indeed, the same is true for crimes of all types. Rather, impunity reigns. Hence, the population's distrust of the police as well as the courts is based on good evidence.

Nevertheless, these increases in everyday violence in the context of discredited institutions of law and order have not prevented significant expansions of either formal or substantive democracy in Brazil. They have not hindered the widespread diffusion of its values of citizen rights and dignity. This combination of democracy, violence, and injustice generates an overwhelming sense of perversity and instability in contemporary experience. Moreover, it is at the heart of the outrage that the key agents of everyday violence – police and criminals – both voice in reaction to the destabilizations of the present, which to the police threaten their taken-for-granted social order and to the criminals expose the egregious failures of that same order. Both sorts of violence appear in reaction to its perceived unraveling. Police violence appears as a recourse to re-establish that order; criminal violence appears as a consequence of its being undone.

Let us look at several public proclamations by police and *comandos*, made in reaction to their perceptions of the present, to substantiate this argument. We will see that they both refer to democracy's rights and the rule of law and, moreover, that both resignify them to justify violence. However, they do so in opposite ways and perhaps with opposite ends at stake.

During the transition to electoral democracy in the mid-1980s, the human rights movement that had originated in the demand for amnesty for political prisoners shifted its focus to defend the human rights of common prisoners. It vigorously denounced police abuse and exposed the degradations of Brazilian prisons, condemning, in other words, the historic regime of citizenship that was business-as-usual for the police. As many have analyzed – none more astutely than Caldeira (2000) – police reaction against the human rights campaign was swift and violent. Here is a passage from the Manifesto of the Association of Police Chiefs of São Paulo, directed to the city's population on 4 October 1985, and widely distributed among police units. The chiefs made this declaration at a crucial moment in the process of democratization. They released it at the peak of the campaign for the first direct popular elections for mayor since the dictatorship. Moreover, it was during a period when the first directly elected state governor, Franco Montoro (1983–7), was trying to reform police use of lethal force. Predictably, the police chiefs attacked this initiative, savaging the human rights project and its supporters:

> The situation today is one of total anxiety for you and total tranquility for those who kill, rob, and rape. Your family is destroyed and your patrimony, acquired with a lot of sacrifice, is calmly being reduced. Why does this happen? You know the answer. Believing in promises, we chose the wrong governor, the wrong political party: the PMDB. How many crimes have occurred in your neighborhood and how many criminals were found responsible for them? You also know this answer. They, the bandits, are protected by so-called human rights, something that the government considers that you, an honest and hardworking citizen, do not deserve.

In this argument, the police evoke human rights according to the historic paradigm of differentiated citizenship, in which rights and justice are privileges of certain social categories, essentially privileges of those who have the power and resources to manipulate the legal system. According to this logic, human rights for criminals are nothing more than 'privileges for bandits' – as the expression popularized during this period puts it and as Caldeira (2000) analyzes. If justice and its rights are privileges and if the majority of Brazilian citizens are denied them by a state that is indifferent or incompetent in protecting their right to security, it is clearly an outrage to provide them to criminals. In terms of my analysis of citizenship, therefore, the police chiefs use the differentiated order of citizenship to undermine the insurgent. Their 'solution' is not to condemn the traditional order by demanding that human rights become available to all Brazilians as absolute attributes of their citizenship. Rather, they use the historic order to condemn democracy and its human rights for abetting criminal violence and to justify their violent repression of civilian criminal suspects – a repression that escalated progressively during this period from just over 500 killings in 1989 to 1470 in 1992.

This same logic is also evident in the policies of the next two governors of São Paulo, Orestes Quércia (1987–91) and Luiz Antonio Fleury Filho (1991–5). When the number of police killings started to rise considerably in 1989 as a result of these policies, Fleury, at that point Quércia's secretary of public security, declared:

> The fact that this year there were more deaths caused by the military police means that they are more active. The more police in the streets, the more chances of confrontations between criminals and policemen. . . From my point of view, what the population wants is for the police to act boldly.[13]

Both the police chiefs and the governors evoke the moral ground of citizen rights and dignity as a means, perversely, of denying it. They portray rights and dignity as unavailable to the majority to justify their continued negation. Because they are unavailable to the majority, they should be unavailable to criminals. But who are the criminals? Before they are convicted, they are suspects. As the police generally view the poor as criminally suspect, the majority are suspects and should be denied human rights as a matter of security. This logic of security evokes citizenship, therefore, to undermine democracy, to disarticulate its language of insurgent values and common measures. If we may take as evidence the countless accusations of police abuse and corruption throughout Brazil – documented since the beginning of democratization by international human rights organizations and Brazilian citizens – these efforts to encourage police violence and to limit police and prison reform have been largely successful.[14]

Nevertheless, the police have not remained entirely immune to democracy. Within a decade after the manifesto just cited, the Military Police of the State of São Paulo felt compelled to change its public image. Adopting new initiatives, such as community policing, it tried to counter its reputation as an institution that abused citizens on a daily basis. It developed a new website in 2001 that framed the institutions and actions of the police in terms of democratic citizenship:

> The 1988 Constitution brought a new concept that became strong in our society: *citizenship*. People became more aware of their rights, more demanding in relation to the Institutions, and this was an invitation to those willing to serve well to revise their posture. The question was not only to expand services, but also one of attitude . . . With the new established order, something more was necessary than just placing ourselves in the clients' position and imagining new products. It was necessary to listen to them . . . It was an invitation to a cultural change . . . It was necessary to shift from a bureaucratic model . . . to a new model, the managerial, which was introduced at the Military Police of the State of São Paulo through a Program of Quality Improvement. Its goal is to get closer to the population via the improvement of the services rendered to the population.[15]

In this statement, the police announce a new model of operations and institutional identity, governed by the constitutional rules of an insurgent democratic citizenship. The passage indicates the legitimacy that this citizenship has acquired in contemporary Brazil. I also note in passing a peculiarity that catches the reader's attention. In the new model, citizens are presented as demanding clients and public security as a product the police offer. The organizing logic of this presentation mixes legal and market rationalities, unified by a notion of management. This packaging suggests that the military police are also following the neoliberal twist that global democratization took in the 1990s.

Yet if there has been a change in the discourse and even in the organization of the military police, the same cannot be said about their practice. In spite of efforts to reform the police by unifying some of their operations, instituting an ombudsman, creating community policing, and requiring that officers receive training in human rights, the police of São Paulo continue to kill civilians in very high numbers: 807 in the year 2000 and 703 in 2001. As investigations done by the police ombudsman reveal, the majority of those killed had no criminal history (Cunha, 2000). That these violations continue despite good intentions to control them indicates the resilience of these limits to Brazil's democratization. It suggests, moreover, another perversity: As my interviews with Brazilians of all social classes make clear, and as Caldeira (2000, 2002) has analyzed, police killings often correspond to the expectations of citizens who are frustrated with the inefficacy of the justice system and who do not believe in the likelihood of security in a social system with immense inequality. In this context, many citizens view police killing as necessary to their right to security.

Let me return in conclusion to the other indication of limit with which I began, to the public proclamations of the prison-based gangs that combine rationalities of crime, justice, and revolution. In spite of their barbarity, even these criminal comandos cannot do without the language of insurgent democratic citizenship. They talk about justice, rights, and the rule of law in ways similar to human rights reports, portraying themselves as the victims of entrenched social inequalities, abuses, and violence, in which they, Brazilian citizens, are victims of their own historic system of national citizenship. When asked in a 2001 congressional hearing if he were the leader of the PCC, Marcola replied:

> I am a person who fights for his rights. I have read the Penal Code and the Law of Penal Procedures, and I know that I am violated in all of my rights . . . So, [I ask you], where is the state? . . . In this context, what is society for me? . . . The PCC revolts against this hypocrisy.

The statute of the PCC (1993) – for these gangs have founding statutes – joins this discourse of rights to that of revolution and crime and ends with a battle cry:

> In coalition with the Comando Vermelho – CV and PCC – we will revolutionize the country inside the prisons and our armed fist will be the 'Terror of the Powerful,' oppressors, and tyrants who use the [prisons] as instruments of society's vengeance . . . Liberty, Justice, and Peace!!![16]

The declaration of the Comando Vermelho to the city of Rio that I cited at the outset uses an explicit talk of rights, citizenship, and rule of law to frame its demands. After denouncing the 'terror [that the government] practices in poor communities . . . causing the death of many innocent people' and expressing outrage that 'all this abuse ends in impunity as if nothing had happened', it proclaims:

> So now is the time to react firmly and with determination and to show this repulsive and oppressive politics that we deserve to be treated with respect, dignity, and equality, because if this doesn't come to pass, we will no longer stop causing chaos in this city, because it is absurd that all of this keeps happening and always remains unpunished.
>
> The judiciary also continues doing whatever it wants with its power . . . because it is violating with a total abuse of power all the established and legal laws and even the Lawyers are targets of hypocrisy and of abuse, and they can do nothing, so if someone has to put a stop to this violence that someone will have to be us because the people don't have how to fight for their rights, but clearly they know who is robbing and massacring them and this is what is important, because the time has passed when the bandit was from the favelas and behind prison bars, well, these days, those one finds living in a favela or behind prison bars are nothing more nothing less than humble and poor people, and, our President Luiz Inácio Lula da Silva, the country only counts on you to get us out of this mud, because does there exist a violence greater than robbing the public's money and killing the people with bad food, without a decent minimum salary, without hospitals, without work, and without food[?] Will this violence succeed in ending the violence, for violence generates violence[?] Is it possible that there exists among the prisoners of this country one

> who has committed a crime more heinous than killing a nation with hunger and misery[?] . . . So ENOUGH, we only want our rights . . . If the laws were made to be followed, why this abuse?

I do not intend to romanticize these statements. They are made by criminals whose lives have spiraled into the personal insanity of an especially cruel and terrorizing violence. They are made, moreover, to justify violence. Even though the *comandos* must be credited with introducing some protection within prisons – in particular, reducing rape – and educating prisoners about their rights, their dominion is based on other kinds of violence inside and outside jail. Furthermore, although they demand a democratic rule of law, there is nothing democratic about their own military-like organization, which 'admits no disputes of power in the leadership' (Art. 12). In that aspect, one might argue that they are like many other civil society groups. Yet their draconian order also requires members in liberty to make monthly contributions, on pain of 'death without pardon' (Art. 7). If the *comandos* began with the anger of revolutionaries, they are today also dedicated to the big business of narco-trafficking and racketeering outside prison They remain, in other words, violent criminal gangs.

Nevertheless, their language is striking, not only for its use of rights talk but also in its contrast with the manifesto of the police chiefs discussed earlier, who are also violent individuals justifying violence. The police manifesto undermines Brazil's new democracy by advocating violent and illegal practices. It denies democracy's legitimacy as the frame of reference for citizenship. For the chiefs, the law is still, as it has always been, 'for enemies'. In contrast, the gangs hurl their outrage at the historical abuses of this misrule of law and frame it in terms of the new democracy and its project of social justice. Their outrage is that of the Brazilian poor against the despicable quality of Brazilian citizenship. If, in the past, the oppressed found expression in millenarian religious movements, today they have a secular voice and it speaks in rights talk.

What is remarkable about this gang talk/rights talk is that even at this perverse extreme of society, insurgent democratic citizenship has become the common language of justification, the moral center of the illegal as well as the legal. This common measure, this new commensurability, refers to the city and beyond it to the nation as a public sphere to which all citizens have rights to a fair share. It refers to a public sphere of equivalencies founded on a democratic project of citizenship. The right claims of the poor – including those of the gangs – to this public constitute their understanding of a new democratic citizenship. Moreover, the new rights talk of the poor suggests that the law, which has oppressed them for centuries, has become something intimate to their sense of belonging to the public, something people want for themselves, no longer 'for enemies' but for citizens. We can only conclude that this change in the culture of law promises to be fundamental for the development of Brazilian democracy.

The perversity of this democracy continues to be that it has not yet realized significant social justice and egalitarian rule of law. However, Brazil has never had either under any regime. It is too late for the gang members to avoid an awful fate. But at least they tell us, even if they cannot show us, that Brazilians have made social justice and rule of law central aspirations of their democracy and that Brazil's citizens, even at the extremes, have found in that project of citizenship a common ground.

Criminal gang cartels like the PCC and the CV are significant elements of contemporary peripheral urbanization in cities worldwide. No one concerned with metropolitan conditions – neither theorists nor practitioners of democracy, planning, law, and government – can neglect developing an understanding of their significance if they are to engage the forces of urbanization and democratization productively. The gangs are important to these processes not only because they control territory in urban peripheries through a combination of violence and administration. They are also important when they combine, as they often do, the rationalities of crime with those of democratic rights, rule of law, social justice, and revolution. This combination articulates in an extreme way the achievements and contradictions of the movements of insurgent democratic citizenship that have become characteristic responses of the urban poor to the new inequalities and segregations of global urbanization.

The sort of gang talk I have analyzed illustrates a fundamental feature of this new urbanism, namely, that the sites of contemporary metropolitan innovation frequently emerge at the very sites of metropolitan degradation. Moreover, in using concepts that structure the dominant public sphere, like 'the rule of law', the gang talk makes clear that without democratic practice, this structuring is likely to be a means of oppression. Whereas the undemocratic rule of law (in land use planning or in impunity, for example) segregates the urban poor in the peripheries and reduces them to a 'bare life' of servility and illegality, those very same conditions of inequality incite hinterland residents to demand a life worthy of citizens and to create new formulations of citizenship to achieve it. The criminal gang members are part of this inventive response, and their mix of the illegal and the legal, insurgent and entrenched, righteous and violent, are drastic instances of its destabilizations, confusions, and entanglements.

In its extreme register, the complexity of this gang talk also demonstrates that the identification of billions of people throughout the urban world as 'slum dwellers' misses more than it identifies by homogenizing a global population. The stigma of 'slum' squashes people into totalizing characterizations and, in that reductive way, reproduces an over-determination of urban poverty that has difficulty recognizing emergent spaces of invention and agency. To grasp the significance of criminal gangs as protagonists in the new urbanization and its insurgent citizenships, urban theory needs to conceptualize citizenship, democracy, and their new spatializations in ways that do not totalize these fields of analysis by defining them in terms of singular or homogenizing conditions like 'slums', 'elections' and even 'political rights'. Such conditions are surely components of these complex fields. But they are ones that investigation needs to problematize to undermine the imperial regimes of knowledge and policy that typically ground them in formal, ideal, universalizing, and ethnocentric definitions.

By problematize I mean demonstrating the consequences that both the unexamination of taken-for-granted assumptions and their defamiliarization have for the construction of what passes for 'the real and the actual'. In the case at hand, I problematized conceptualizations of citizenship, democracy, and urbanization to show how their interaction produces a destabilizing sphere of social change, in which the gangs are among several actors – including paramilitary groups, the police, political parties, the national congress, and the judiciary – to use the legal and illegal, legitimate and criminal, and just and unjust to claim the moral ground of citizen rights. This triangulation of bedfellows and strategies makes the significance of the gangs in processes of democratization and urbanization more evident. Moreover, it historicizes and particularizes citizenship and in this way debunks it as an ideal. Thus, by investigating the substantive distribution of the rights, meanings, and practices that formal national inclusion and exclusion entails, it becomes clear that the combination of the formal and the substantive generates historically and culturally distinctive formulations of citizenship in every case. None is ideal, though some are advocated and imposed as such.

Furthermore, by understanding democracy as a field of destabilization as well as of electoral competition, I argued that all democracies, emergent and established, simultaneously expand and erode citizen rights. This conceptualization makes it difficult to assume that electoral democracy automatically produces a democratic rule of law or to construe some democracies as ideal and others as pathological. Similarly, I argued that contemporary mobilizations of the urban poor for citizenship develop not primarily through struggles of labor, as so much European social theory proposed, but through those of illegal residence, house building, and land conflict. This shift in theoretical perspective makes it possible to appreciate the city itself not only as the context but also as the text of emerging paradigms of citizen power and vulnerability.

The kind of historical, ethnographic, and conceptual investigation that I emphasize, the kind that problematizes and defamiliarizes, is apt to detect new sites of creativity in the vastness of the contemporary metropolis. And what, after all, is the point of urban theory with respect to democracy and planning if not to bring to the surface the possibilities for alternative futures among the many conditions that exist as potentials in the city?

Notes

1. An expanded version of this article appears as part of chapter 8 in my book *Insurgent Citizenship: Disjunctions of Democracy and Modernity in Brazil* (Princeton University Press, 2008). For an analysis of the new paradigm of urban planning that developed from the 1988 Constitution, see also Caldeira and Holston (2005).
2. Some of the work on these topics includes Adorno (1995), Arantes (2000), Caldeira (2000), Chevigny (1995), Fix (2001), Holston (1991), Holston and Caldeira (1998), Paixão (1988), Paoli (1982), Pinheiro (1983), Scheper-Hughes (1992) and Zaluar (1985, 2004).
3. By civil, I refer not to the classic liberal separations of state and non-state, political society and civil society, public and private, or to any dichotomies that typically derive from the state/non-state divide. Rather, I use civil to specify the aspect of citizenship that concerns liberty and security and establishes justice as the means to

all other rights. Thus civil citizenship relates society and state ambiguously, not dichotomously: it differentiates society from the political system by defending the former from the abuses of the latter; however, it also integrates the two by utilizing state power to confront relations of inequality and domination within society itself and to shape people into certain kinds of citizens.

4. See Holston (2008), pp. 272–3 and 353, nn. 3, 4. for details of these corruptions scandals.
5. Teresa Caldeira and I developed the following analysis of violence and the perverse use of democratic discourses of rights together. See Caldeira (2006) for her interpretation of some of these issues.
6. The most important *comandos* are the PCC of São Paulo and the CV (Comando Vermelho) of Rio. In São Paulo, others include the Seta Satânica, CRBC (Comando Revolucionário Brasileiro da Criminalidade), and TCC (Terceiro Comando da Capital).
7. This and the other manifestoes I discuss were published in the major Brazilian newspapers (such as the *Estado de São Paulo*, the *Folha de São Paulo*, and the *Jornal do Brasil*) and may be consulted in their online archives. In my translation, I have retained original syntax as much as possible. The most useful work in the history and organization of the PCC I have found is a collection of articles and interviews published in an 'extra edition' of the monthly magazine *Caros Amigos* (28 May 2006).
8. This type of citizen conflict is especially apparent in democracies (often labeled liberal) where the state is committed to a constitution that provides citizens with formally equal rights but far less committed to providing them with equal means to realize those rights. As a result, the inequalities of class transform the formal equalities of citizenship into substantive differences, as those who have the social and economic means to take advantage of their formal rights outperform those who do not. See Bendix (1977) for more on this point. Thus, the unorganized poor in these democracies are typically formal citizens without much substantive citizenship. Democracies become disjunctive, therefore, because the development of democratic citizenship intrinsically generates both equality, inequality, and the terms of conflict that engage the two.
9. For a discussion of the term 'elites', see Holston (2008), pp. 18–19, 316n.6. With regard to citizenship, I use it to specify those who established and perpetuate the regime of differentiated citizenship to benefit themselves with rights exercised as privileges.
10. By that, I refer to the relation between property and personality, as political philosophy has called it, in which property ownership is the means to establish such fundamental qualifications of citizenship as independence, respect, responsibility, and capacity.
11. See note 1, above, for a sample of research.
12. For a discussion of police violence, popular support of it, and the failure of various government initiatives to control it, see Caldeira (2002) and Caldeira and Holston (1999). I would note that the most lethal year of police action in São Paulo was 1992, when they killed 1359 *suspected* criminals, in addition to the 111 at Casa de Detenção! In the same year, the Los Angeles police killed 25 and the New York 24 (Chevigny, 1995).
13. Luiz Antonio Fleury Filho, *Folha de São Paulo*, 28 November 1989. Fleury was subsequently elected governor (1991–5). See Caldeira (2000) for a fuller discussion of this period and its security policies.

14. Comaroff and Comaroff (2004) describe a different but related spectacle of re-ordering in postcolonial South Africa: not actual police violence, but dramatic enactments of crime and punishment by police, which aim to (re)establish plausible representations of social order and law in a world where the state seem incapable of ensuring either.
15. 'Qualidade na Policia Militar do Estado de São Paulo', Policia Militar do *Estado de São Paulo* [http://www.polmil.sp.gov.br/qtotal/evolucao.asp].
16. In 1995, a founder of the PCC, Misael Aparecido da Silva, drafted a manifesto (the 'Party of Crime') articulating the gang's identity. It became, along with the Statute, required reading for gang initiation. The manifesto combines the rationalities of crime and revolution under the banner of justice, demonstrating a fusion of criminal gangs, anti-capitalist politics, terrorist actions, and revolutionary parties found in subversive organizations worldwide – for example, the ANC, IRA, Black Panthers, FARC, and *jihad* groups – though, as the PCC acknowledges, members joined as and remain criminals. The manifesto states:

> The cowardly capitalist, and corrupt . . . system itself created the Party [the PCC]. The Party is part of a dream of struggle; today we are strong where the enemy is weak. Our revolution . . began in the penitentiary system and its objective is greater: to revolutionize the governmental system, to end this capitalist regime in which the rich grow and survive massacring the poorer class. As long as children die of hunger, sleep in the streets, have no opportunity for education and a dignified life, the violence will only increase. Today's children who humiliate themselves begging will tomorrow, through crime, transform their dreams into reality, with all hatred, all revolt, for the oppressed of today will be the oppressor of tomorrow. What is not won with words will be won with violence and a gun in hand. Our goal is to affect the powerful, the owners of the world, and the unequal justice; we are not criminals by choice and yes we are subversives and idealists. (reproduced in *Caros Amigos*, 28 May 2006: 12)

References

Adorno, S. (1995) 'Discriminação Racial e Justiça Criminal em São Paulo', *Novos Estudos* 43: 45–63.

Arantes, R.B. (2000) 'Ministério Público e Corrupção Política em São Paulo', in M.T. Sadek (ed.) *Justiça e Cidadania no Brasil*, pp. 39–156. São Paulo: Editora Sumaré/Idesp.

Bendix, R. (1977) *Nation-Building and Citizenship*. Berkeley: University of California Press.

Caldeira, T.P.R. (2000) *City of Walls: Crime, Segregation, and Citizenship in São Paulo*. Berkeley: University of California Press.

Caldeira, T.P.R. (2002) 'The Paradox of Police Violence in Democratic Brazil', *Ethnography* 3(3): 235–63.

Caldeira, T.P.R. (2006) '"I Came to Sabotage Your Reasoning!": Violence and Resignifications of Justice in Brazil', in J. Comaroff and J.L. Comaroff (eds) *Law and Disorder in the Postcolony*, pp. 102–49. Chicago, IL: University of Chicago Press.

Caldeira, T.P.R. and Holston, J. (1999) 'Democracy and Violence in Brazil', *Comparative Studies in Society and History* 41(4): 691–729.

Caldeira, T.P.R. and Holston, J. (2005) 'State and Urban Space in Brazil: From Modernist Planning to Democratic Interventions', in A. Ong and S.J. Collier (eds) *Global Assemblages: Technology, Politics, and Ethics as Anthropological Problems*, pp. 393–416. Malden, MA: Blackwell.

Chevigny, P. (1995) *The Edge of the Knife: Police Violence and Accountability in Six Cities of the Americas*. New York: New Press.

Comaroff, J. and Comaroff, J.L. (2004) 'Criminal Obsessions, after Foucault: Postcoloniality, Policing, and the Metaphysics of Disorder', *Critical Inquiry* 30: 800–24.

Cunha, L.G. (2000) 'Ouvidoria de Polícia em São Paulo', in M.T. Sadek (ed.) *Justiça e Cidadania no Brasil*, pp. 259–304. São Paulo: Editora Sumaré/Idesp.

Fix, M. (2001) *Parceiros da Exclusão*. São Paulo: Boitempo Editorial.

Holston, J. (1991) 'The Misrule of Law: Land and Usurpation in Brazil', *Comparative Studies in Society and History* 33(4): 695–725.

Holston, J. (2008) *Insurgent Citizenship: Disjunctions of Democracy and Modernity in Brazil*. Princeton, NJ: Princeton University Press.

Holston, J. and Caldeira, T.P.R. (1998) 'Democracy, Law, and Violence: Disjunctions of Brazilian Citizenship', in F. Agüero and J. Stark (eds) *Fault Lines of Democracy in Post-Transition Latin America*, pp. 263–96. Miami, FL: University of Miami North-South Center Press.

Paixão, A.L. (1988) 'Crime, Controle Social e Consolidação da Democracia', in F.W. Reis and G. O'Donnell (eds) *A Democracia no Brasil: Dilemas e Perspectivas*, pp. 168–99. São Paulo: Vértice.

Paoli, M.C. (1982) 'Violência e Espaço Civil', in R. DaMatta et al. (eds) *Violência Brasileira*, pp. 45–55. São Paulo: Brasiliense.

Pinheiro, P.S. (1983) 'Violencia sem Controle e Militarização da polícia', *Novos Estudos Cebrap* 2(1): 8–12.

Scheper-Hughes, N. (1992) *Death without Weeping: The Violence of Everyday Life in Brazil*. Berkeley: University of California Press.

Zaluar, A. (1985) *A Máquina e a Revolta*. São Paulo: Editora Brasiliense.

Zaluar, A. (2004) *Integração Perversa: Pobreza e Tráfico de Drogas*. Rio de Janeiro: Editora FGV.

ERRATUM

Holston, J. 2009: Dangerous Spaces of Citizenship: Gang Talk, Rights Talk, and Rule of Law in Brazil. *Planning Theory* 8, 12–31. (Original DOI: 10.1177/1473095208099296)

On page 14, the heading should read:

Democracy, injustice, and the rationalities of gang violence

Part IV
Crossing Borders: Global Movements, Crime and Control

[14]

Without Borders? Notes on Globalization as a Mobility Regime*

RONEN SHAMIR
Tel Aviv University

While globalization is largely theorized in terms of trans-border flows, this article suggests an exploratory sociological framework for analyzing globalization as consisting of systemic processes of closure and containment. The suggested framework points at the emergence of a global mobility regime that actively seeks to contain social movement both within and across borders. The mobility regime is theorized as premised upon a pervasive "paradigm of suspicion" that conflates the perceived threats of crime, immigration, and terrorism, thus constituting a conceptual blueprint for the organization of global risk-management strategies. The article draws on multiple examples, singling out some elementary forms of the mobility regime, emphasizing the sociological affinity between guarded borders on the one hand and gated communities on the other. In particular, the article aims at theorizing the translation of the paradigm of suspicion into actual technologies of social screening designed to police the mobility of those social elements that are deemed to belong to suspect social categories. Specifically, the article points at biosocial profiling as an increasingly dominant technology of intervention. Biosocial profiling, in turn, is theorized in juxtaposition to other modalities of power, namely, legal and disciplinary measures.

> Iddy Kaoungou, from the Democratic Republic of the Congo, told me that four of his friends had drowned trying to swim around the fence to Ceuta ... For Europeans, crossing from Morocco to Ceuta means just a five minute walk in the sun—the Spanish immigration officer didn't even ask to open my passport once I had flashed the cover at him.[1]

A significant body of literature indicates that the era of globalization is simultaneously an era of growing restrictions on movement (Blomley, Delaney, and Ford 2001; Sassen 1991, 1988). This scholarship reminds us that while globalization is a lived reality of hypermobility for a small social stratum of "cosmocrats" (Adams 1999), mobility is still a scarce resource and the overwhelming majority of the world's population is more or less permanently immobilized (Bauman 2002; Doyle and Nathan 2001).[2] Yet, regardless of the attention given to the widening mobility gap in the present era, globalization is predominantly theorized in terms of social openness and social fluidity.[3] In fact, the very concept of "globalization" connotes and

*I thank the anonymous reviewers for their useful and challenging comments. I also deeply thank Dicle Kogacioglu for her insights. Address correspondence to: Ronen Shamir, Department of Sociology and Anthropology, Tel-Aviv University, Tel-Aviv 69978, Israel. E-mail: shamirr@post.tauac.il

[1]"Attacking Europe's Border Fences," a report by Joseph Winter for the BBC News Online Service, April 13, 2004, available at http://news.bbc.co.uk/.

[2]Bauman (2002) writes that 98 percent of the world's population never moves to another place to settle, while even in the United Kingdom, 50 percent of the population live within five miles of the place where they were born.

[3]See, for example, a special issue of *European Studies*, subtitled "Culture and Cooperation in Europe's Borderlands," where almost all articles focus on cross-border cooperation and integration (Anderson et al. 2003).

presupposes some transcendental imagination and, accordingly, the typical notions that social scientists use to define, characterize, and theorize globalization are those of "networks," "flows," and "trans-nationalism" (or other types of "trans-" thereof). The imagery of the trans-national, in particular, regardless of whether the subject matter is confrontational activism, regulatory schemes, or corporate practices, seems to dominate the sociological imagination and to shape the visions of both the proponents of Trade-Without-Borders and the promoters of Doctors-Without-Borders. Thus, some theorists (Held et al. 1999; Castells 1996) discuss globalization in terms of a network society, others analyze globalization as trans-national capitalism (Sklair 1997; Gottdiener 1995; Harvey 1989; Soja 1989), still others (Lechner and Boli 2000; Appadurai 1996) describe globalization as a seamless flow of goods, services, ideas, technologies, cultural forms, organizational forms, and people, all more or less in agreement that globalization is largely about "free movement across national boundaries" and cross-border interdependencies (Anderson, O'Dowd, and Wilson 2003; Held 1995; Giddens 1990).[4]

This is not to say that globalization is theorized as a unidirectional and homogenous process. Furthermore, I do not mean to suggest that globalization is theorized only in formal terms, as a set of transactions and cross-border flows. To the contrary, the meaning and consequences of globalization are highly contested and, moreover, globalization is now routinely theorized as a highly contradictory set of cultural and normative pressures, involving tensions between capitalism and democracy, the north and the south, the haves and have-nots, empire and multitude (Hardt and Negri 2000), McWorld and Jihad (Barber 1996), as well as between "globalizers" and a variety of so-called anti-globalization movements (Kellner 2002, 1999; de Sousa Santos 2002).

Of specific interest for present purposes is the juxtaposition of the "old" principles of national sovereignty and citizenship rights on the one hand and the emergence of a global regime of human rights on the other. Soysal (1994), for example, suggests that two institutionalized principles are at work in regard to immigration: national sovereignty and universal human rights. She finds that it is the latter, a new globalizing principle, which has become "a pervasive element of world culture" (1994:6), in fact announcing a postnational era that undermines the national order of citizenship. Soysal bases her theoretical postulates on studies of guest-workers in Europe. She shows that guest-workers with no formal citizenship rights managed to establish both local and cross-border social networks, thereby creating an on-the-ground necessity to develop a variety of new "patterns of incorporation" (1994:4) that transcend and bypass formal citizenship rights. Hence, she finds that under the new conditions of global migration and an emergent global regime of human rights, "the logic of personhood supersedes the logic of national citizenship" (1994:164) and that "citizenship is losing ground to a more universal model of membership anchored in transcendent and de-territorialized notions of personal rights" (1994:3).

Studying illegal immigration and guest-workers in both Europe and the United States, and with different normative concerns than those of Soysal in mind, Jacobson nonetheless seems to share with Soysal some core theoretical observations. In his

[4]An example of this deeply rooted meaning of globalization may be derived from Kellner's (2002) comments on the events of September 11. In his *Theorizing Globalization*, Kellner suggests that terrorism elicits "policing measures to stem the flow of movements of people and goods both across borders and internally." Kellner criticizes this state of affairs, arguing that "the U.S. Patriot Act has led to repressive measures that are replacing the spaces of the open and free information society with new forms of surveillance, policing, and repression" (2002:291). However, Kellner also seems to believe that this latest development may only be "an anomalous paroxysm" (2002:291).

Rights Across Borders: Immigration and the Decline of Citizenship, Jacobson (1996) argues that the combined effect of trans-national migration and the emergence of a sweeping trans-national regime of human rights brings about the erosion of the traditional basis of nation-state membership, namely, citizenship. Under the emergent global human rights regime, he argues, the notion of "universal personhood" comes to dominate the social and political imagination. Subsequently, rights are increasingly predicated on residency rather than on citizen status, eroding the very distinction between citizen and alien and compromising the link between territorially bounded national sovereignty and citizenship.

Both Soysal and Jacobson, therefore, seem to share the view that normative or cultural globalization—here conceptualized in terms of an emergent global human rights regime—is a process that profoundly challenges the heretofore sacred notion of bounded territoriality and its bundle of associated citizenship rights. The perceived tension is thus between the trans-national ("open") principle and the national ("close") principle. In other words, to the extent that some states or political blocs try to halt or slow the process of conferring rights on immigrants in the name of sovereignty and social integrity, the assumed implication is that we have to theorize these attempts as running against the sweeping pressure of globalization-qua-openness. Moreover, both Soysal and Jacobson focus on noncitizens who are already residing within the borders of some affluent countries. Both theorize the ability of immigrants to create webs of ties and to induce new patterns of inclusion but do not theorize concomitant patterns of exclusion that generally, but not exclusively, apply to people outside those borders.

In contrast, the theoretical contribution I propose in this article is to conceive processes of globalization as also producing "their own," so to speak, principles of closure. I posit that above and beyond tensions such as between national sovereignty and human rights, we are witnessing the emergence of a new cultural/normative global principle that operates as a counterbalance to the normative principle of global human rights. We are witnessing the emergence of a global mobility regime, oriented to closure and to the blocking of access, premised not only on "old" national or local grounds but on a principle of perceived universal dangerous personhoods (hereinafter referred to as "a paradigm of suspicion"). The analytical framework of this article is that the mobility regime is constructed to maintain high levels of inequality in a relatively normatively homogenized world.[5] In practice, this means that local, national, and regional boundaries are now being rebuilt and consolidated under the increased normative pressure of, and as a counterbalance to, the universal human rights regime.

Thus, in contrast to the tendency to announce the "death of distance" (Cairncross 1997) and to declare a "mobility turn" (Urry 2003), in this article, I seek to conceptualize and theorize globalization in terms of processes of closure, entrapment, and containment. Specifically, I emphasize the extent to which processes of globalization are also concerned with the prevention of movement and the blocking of access. I posit that such processes should neither be theorized as a systemic malfunction nor as the unintended consequences of globalization. Rather, following the terminology of Simmel ([1908] 1950), I argue that the social nearness that globalization allows for is also constitutive of simultaneous processes of social distance. To wit, the technological platforms that carry all that we recognize as globalization reduce the distance

[5]I thank one of the anonymous reviewers of this article for pointing out this framework and for suggesting a lucid way for articulating it.

among people and at the same time amplify a perceived experience of dangerous social proximity between those who have and those who have not, between what is perceived as safe and familiar and that which is perceived as dangerous and contaminating (Coutin, Maurer, and Yngvesson 2002). Black directly applies this geometrical-sociology logic to terrorism, writing that "because social distance historically corresponded to physical distance, terrorism often lacked the physical geometry necessary for its occurrence: physical closeness to civilians socially distant enough to attract terrorism. New technology has made physical distance increasingly irrelevant, however, and terrorism has proliferated" (2004:14). In this article, however, I add an epistemological dimension to this perspective, emphasizing the perceived sense of threat emanating from this sociospatial dialectic. Specifically, I posit that as a result of the growing disjuncture between physical distance and social distance, globalization actually announces an unprecedented agenda of "integrated risk management" as a prominent feature of social organization. This emergent integrated risk-management system, in turn, is a central feature of the global mobility regime.

The fundamental elements of the mobility regime are analytically distinguished in this article. For this analysis to take place, the point of departure is that the differential ability to move in space—and even more so to have access to opportunities for movement—has become a major stratifying force in the global social hierarchy. The so-called mobility gap covers a wide continuum of social possibilities, stretching from the differential ability of farmers to deliver their products to nearby towns, to the differential ability to enter a corporate compound in a third-world country; from the severely restricted ability of an unemployed inner-city woman to find work and to shop, to the severely restricted ability of Pakistani citizens to visit family members in London.

The mobility gap, in and of itself, is an expression of the conditions of the possibilities of movement, such as socioeconomic factors, geographical locations, cultural imperatives, and political circumstances. However, all of these variables operate in relation to a trans-national political economy of movement. "The blatant inequality of access to mobility," writes Bauman, "is not just the expectable, since 'natural', effect of income differentiation, casting the costs of transport beyond the reach of the poor. Differentiation of mobility chances is one of the few strategies avidly and consistently pursued by the governments of more affluent areas in their dealings with the population of less affluent ones" (2002:83). The epistemological, technical, and institutional expression of this political economy is that which I hereby designate as a global mobility regime. Thought of as a modality that works at local, regional, and global levels, we may thus begin to theorize the mobility regime as an important feature of globalization. A series of questions ensue. How does the mobility regime develop and how is it maintained? What are the social technologies that facilitate it? What sorts of social imageries sustain it?

In this article, I offer an exploratory sociological framework for addressing these questions. I posit that the global mobility regime is predicated, first, on the classification of individuals and groups according to principles of perceived threats and risks, and second, on an emergent technology of intervention that provides the technical/statistical means for creating elaborate forms of such social distinctions. Concretely, I posit that the engine of the contemporary mobility regime is a "paradigm of suspicion" that conflates the perceived threats of crime, immigration, and terrorism (hence the notion of "integrated risk management"), and that the technology of intervention that enables it is biosocial profiling.

In the first section of the article, I explain and describe the contours of the above-mentioned paradigm of suspicion. In the second and third sections, I introduce some of the elementary forms of the mobility regime. In the fourth and fifth sections of the article, I discuss the logic of operation characteristic of the mobility regime and elaborate on the practice of biosocial profiling. In the final section, I discuss profiling as a modality of power and distinguish it from other mechanisms of social control. I conclude by returning to Simmel's portrayal of the Stranger.

THE PARADIGM OF SUSPICION

In speaking about a paradigm of suspicion, I mean that the primary principle for determining the "license to move," both across borders and in public spaces within borders, has to do with the degree to which the agents of mobility are suspected of representing the threats of crime, undesired immigration, and terrorism, either independently or, increasingly, interchangeably. Apart from terrorism, being a newly articulated form of organized trans-national violence (Tilly 2004),[6] the perceived threats of crime and immigration, and particularly their mutually constitutive interplay, are part of the history of modernity. The residents of the modern cities that absorbed Europe's new urban proletariat in the 19th century retained a profound mistrust of people without established connections. This mistrust has been an important engine in the increasing formal criminalization of mobility itself, from the concept of "criminal vagabondage" in France, where mobility was the crime, through a series of vagrancy panics in Britain, to increasing legal hostility to vagrants and anxiety about "crimes of mobility" in the United States (Cole 2001:9). It is also no coincidence, therefore, that early efforts to create reliable identification systems were based on the simultaneous development of police records, photographic methods, and the perfection of the passport system (Deflem 2002).

The conceptual link between immigration and social vices such as crime, disease, and moral contamination has gripped the public mind long before the present era and continually shapes immigration policies and border-control measures. Mobility is perceived as a suspicious activity especially when it relates to those without property. Immigration seekers aside, consider the policy that guides the grant of nonimmigrant visas to the United States. The standard reason for refusing to issue a visa, when such a reason is given, is that the applicant did not qualify under Section 214(b) of the Immigration and Nationality Act. This section is premised upon a paradigm of suspicion that stipulates that every foreigner seeking to enter the United States is considered an immigrant as long as he or she did not convince the immigration officer that at the time of the application he or she was eligible for a nonimmigrant status. To convince the immigration officer, one has to show proof of "strong ties" to the country of origin, such as a permanent job or ownership of property, in fact identical in nature to the old need to establish "settled connections."

Both the European and American media are flooded with reports and studies that link immigration and crime, often mediated through indicators of poverty. In the Netherlands, for example, reports abound about such links, citing scientific evidence that illegal immigrants are by far more likely to be involved with crime and singling

[6]In the 1970s, although terrorist groups operated internationally and struck across the globe, such did not trigger responses of the type we witness today. It is only with the development of a global imagery of trans-national entities, whether multinational corporations or terrorist organizations, that solutions are offered on this basis and coupled with other cross-border concerns.

out Moslem "culture of religious extremism" as a factor. While crime records are not kept according to ethnicity, Dutch police and government officials have publicly linked a rise in crime to immigrants, and according to criminologist Chris Rutenfrans, 63 percent of those convicted of homicide are immigrants—Moroccans, Antilleans, and sub-Saharan Africans being the chief culprits.[7] In the United States, a senior policy analyst at the Center for Immigration Studies published a study showing that immigrants and their minor children now account for almost one in four persons living in poverty. The proportion of immigrant-headed households using at least one major welfare program is 24.5 percent compared to 16.3 percent for native households and the poverty rate for immigrants and their U.S.-born children (under 18) is two-thirds higher than that of natives and their children, 17.6 percent versus 10.6 percent (Vaughan 2004a).

Alongside the more familiar link between immigration and crime, often mediated through indicators of poverty, there also seems to emerge a new conceptual link, associating poverty with the threat of terrorism. "In the era of the War against Terror," writes Roy, "poverty is being slyly conflated with terrorism" (2004:12). Yet, even without the mediation of poverty, the link between immigration and terrorism increasingly shapes public consciousness and public policy. Here, again, the conceptual link between immigration and terrorism may be traced to earlier similar links. At the height of the Cold War, writes Jacobson (1996), the legal category of "alien" in the U.S. Immigration and Nationality Act of 1952 had assumed a new meaning. Whereas prior immigration policies focused on setting numerical and ethnic-based limits on immigration, newly conceived concerns translated into a focus on the ideological profile of new entrants. Hence, the legal category of "alien" assumed an ideological association (i.e., the threat of incoming subversives) as opposed to an ethnic one (1996:48–49). In the aftermath of the September 11 attack, with the growing association of Islam with global terrorism, ideological and ethnic concerns are woven together to create an even more potent and irresistible paradigm of suspicion.

Sometimes, the link between immigration and terrorism is especially intricate. In a case involving a detained undocumented Haitian immigrant, the U.S. Department of Justice argued that although the individual in question had no links to terrorism, his release could prompt an influx of illegal Haitian refugees that, in turn, could jeopardize national security because it would have diverted immigration resources currently allocated to the fight against terrorism (Jachimowicz and McKay 2003). In general, it is argued that the immigration system plays a crucial role in the war against terrorism and that the best way to prevent the entry of terrorists into the United States is to have a well-functioning immigration system that deters, detects, and promptly removes those who lack a legitimate purpose for entering or staying in the country. However, reporting on the successes of immigration schemes such as SEVIS (a foreign students tracking system) and USVISIT (Visitor and Immigrant Status Indicator Technology, a nonimmigrant visitor tracking project) in the war on terrorism, one study revealed that achievements so far included the exposure of a smuggling ring and the discovery of 30 wanted criminals, thus illustrating the growing conflation of the perceived concerns about immigration, terrorism, and crime (Vaughan 2004b).

Explicit links between immigration from Moslem countries and terrorism are rapidly emerging. One recent report shows that the number of Middle Eastern

[7]See, for example, the December 19, 2003 electronic edition of the *Christian Science Monitor* (http://www.csmonitor.com) and the July 15, 2002 electronic edition of the *National Review* (http://www.nationalreview.com).

immigrants (including Morocco and Pakistan) in the United States has grown nearly eightfold from 1970 to 2000, reached 1.5 million people in 2000, and is expected to double again by 2010. The report stated that this growth can have "significant repercussions for our homeland security" and that the presence of a large Middle Eastern immigrant population on American soil made it easier for Islamic extremists to operate within the United States (Camarota 2002). Ethnic profiling, discussed below within the context of biosocial profiling, is thus rapidly emerging. Accordingly, Levy (2001) reports that 60 percent of Americans want Arabs to undergo more intensive screening at airports. He also reports that the Federal Motor Carrier Administration, which inspects trucks carrying hazardous materials, has announced that it "will be looking closely at the drivers, and if the person looks to be of Arab descent that would be enough" for stepped-up scrutiny. It is also on the basis of an identical logic that Israel recently introduced an amendment to its Citizenship and Entry to Israel Law, barring Palestinian spouses of Israeli citizens from entering the country on grounds that these spouses may engage in terrorist activities. Beyond studies, reports, and cover stories that shape public discourse in this direction, the conflation of the perceived threats of terror, crime, and immigration into a unitary paradigm of suspicion now routinely guides policy making, institution building, and regulation. Thus, for example, the 1998 Cairo summit of the Interpol launched a joint international policy for handling crime, immigration, and terrorism, and the United States explicitly designed its USVISIT program—regulating nonimmigrant entry to the United States—to identify travelers who violate immigration controls, have criminal records, or belong to groups listed as terrorist organizations.

Once we identify a conflated paradigm of suspicion that brings together the perceived threats of terrorism, crime, and immigration, we may appreciate the strong sociological affinity between metal detectors in American public schools and airport X-ray machines, between passports burnt with the sociobiological profile of their bearers and Interpol records of tissues and retinas, or between armed guards in restaurants, guarded gated communities, and the strengthening of immigration and border police. In all these instances, although located in different spatial settings, and although often formally established to address different types of social threats, a paradigm of suspicion is an overarching framework that sets these diverse practices in motion. In the next two sections, I therefore introduce some of the elementary forms that constitute some of the physical features of the emerging mobility regime.

ELEMENTARY FORMS OF THE MOBILITY REGIME: BORDERS, FENCES, AND HYPER-GHETTOES

The first principle of division that governs the mobility regime is that which separates privileged countries and regions from most other regions of the world, in effect turning the latter into suspect countries. It is typically within these suspect countries that we find large concentrations of dispossessed groups, located in lesser regulated areas such as slums or in the more regulated confines of refugee camps. Concurrently, such countries are perceived as social spaces that have the potential of exporting criminal elements, terrorists, and undocumented immigrants into the more privileged social spaces of the globe. Thus, while the traditional function of guarded borders was conceived in terms of the need to defend sovereignty (physically against organized violent invasion and symbolically as an affirmation of national identity), the mobility potential that globalization processes facilitate simultaneously produces the conceptualization of borders in terms of the need to protect a perceived stable and secure social fabric from unwarranted infiltration by suspect populations.

Of course, borders are not a new invention. Yet, it is noteworthy that the rational and systematic closure of national borders in general and the use of border controls to prevent immigration in particular are a modern phenomenon. Tilly (1992), theorizing the history of state-building in Europe, pays only cursory attention to borders despite the fact that control over bounded territories is inseparable from his very definition of a state. Rather than using the concept of borders, Tilly (1992) finds that rulers normally tried to establish both a secured area within which they could enjoy the returns from coercion and a fortified buffer zone to protect the secured area. However, once such buffer zones could be turned into secured areas in and of themselves, rulers initiated drives for creating newly expanded buffer zones (1992:184). Borders acquired a more significant meaning only in tandem with the consolidation of the modern national state, when governments began to "control movement across frontiers, to use tariffs and customs as instruments of economic policy, and to treat foreigners as distinctive kinds of people deserving limited rights and close surveillance" (1992:116).

However, the regime of movement in the present era is not unlike previous regimes in its primary reliance on physical barriers as means of blocking and containing mobility. These elementary practices, in turn, are based on the quite conventional methods of constructing fences. Accordingly, and in tandem with free trade agreements, an eight-foot fence stretches along the 2,000 miles border between Mexico and the United States, from Brownsville, Texas to San Diego, California. As it ends in the Pacific Ocean, between San Diego and Tihuana, the fence is 15 feet high. Hundreds of names are scribbled on the Mexican side of the fence, a kind of unofficial memorial to those killed while trying to outsmart the U.S. Operation Gatekeeper. Before it stretches a few 100 feet into the ocean, the fence also cuts across Friendship Park (Parque de la Amistad), so titled in 1971 as a gesture to the Mexican people (Nevins 2001; Andreas 2000).

Similarly, at the 2003 Tsaloniki Summit, the European Union discussed new measures for preventing entry to its territory and to consolidate what is already referred to as Fortress Europe.[8] In recent years, Germany dramatically increased the budget of its border police and stationed on its eastern borders more police officers than the number of guards patrolling the Mexican-U.S. border. Spain built Europe's most formidable and sophisticated system for border surveillance, relying on electronic fences, radar, and infrared cameras. And the European Union provides millions of Euros annually to countries at its periphery to enhance their border-control capacities.

A concrete fence, at times turned into barbed wire and deep trenches, also stretches between much of Israel and the Palestinian territories it occupies. At some points, it functions as a border line. At other points, it cuts right through villages and neighborhoods, sometimes encircling whole communities, sometimes isolating one or two families from the rest. Indeed, the Israeli fence is unique in that it simultaneously tries

[8]It is difficult to know the exact number of people who died while trying to enter Fortress Europe. Various sources differ in their reporting; also many deaths are by drowning and therefore unaccounted for. United for Intercultural Action, a Dutch-based European network organization that supports migrants and refugees, has documented 5,017 deaths between January 1993 and June 2004 (see its report at http://www.united.non-profit.nl/pdfs/listofdeaths.pdf under Refugee Campaigns at http://www.unitedagainstracism.org). Apart from drowning, reports in Europe collect data on deaths caused by suicides, institutional neglect, border and immigration police, death following deportation, and as a result of human trade (http://www.carf.demon.co.uk/deaths98/table.html).

to establish a border and to concentrate the Palestinian suspect population in highly guarded enclaves that look like a mixture of medieval ghettoes and gigantic gulags (Wacquant 2004).

While the spatial confinement of Palestinians may be regarded as exceptionally harsh, mass containment of refugees, internally displaced communities, internal migrants, and impoverished populations in general is an elementary form of the mobility regime. It may be useful to think of ghetto and ethnic cluster, writes Loic Wacquant, as two ideal-type configurations at opposite ends of a continuum along which different groups are located depending on the intensity with which forces such as stigma and spatial confinement impinge upon them (Wacquant 2004).[9] Conceived in line with these analytic criteria, many suspect countries may be analyzed as hyper-ghettoes. The hyper-ghetto is, first and foremost, an extension of scale. Unlike the ghetto, which in sociological literature marks an urban setting, the hyper-ghetto refers to both urban and rural areas, at times covering an entire "sovereign" national territory to whose boundaries the population is more or less permanently confined. The hyper-ghetto is also distinct in that it may stigmatize the national population as a whole (apart from thin layers of elite and middle-class groups) as one or more ethnic clusters whose mobility must be closely guarded and, to the extent possible, restricted to the confines of the "sovereign" territory. As at least part of the population is formally allowed to move within the territorial state-container, and as the suspect state does have institutions that at least formally resemble the global model of how states "should look like" (Meyer et al. 1997), the hyper-ghetto is closer, in terms of Wacquant's analytic terms, to the ethnic cluster end of the continuum.

However, suspect states are often also prime hosts of refugees and of increasing numbers of displaced groups who are concentrated in refugee camps and shanty towns. Refugees and internally displaced people are therefore often doubly immobilized, coerced into designated and stigmatized areas, and located at the very bottom of the social mobility hierarchy of an already suspect country. The overwhelming majority of refugees and internally displaced people reside in impoverished countries at the global periphery, as refugees typically flow in from other impoverished and war-stricken suspect countries. Asia hosts half of the world's refugees, Africa 22 percent, Europe 21 percent, and 10 percent are located in South and North America. Among the leading host countries of refugees in the world are Pakistan, Tanzania, the Democratic Republic of Congo, Sudan, and Armenia. Iran was until recently the world's number one host of refugees, hosting nearly 2 million Afghan people.[10] Moreover, the population of suspect countries as a whole tends to be located at the lower end of the mobility gap. In general, its mobility constraints reflect lack of access to the resources required for mobility (e.g., money, information, and travel documents) and, moreover, this population often serves as a source of cheap labor, directly and indirectly catering to the needs of multinational corporations. From this perspective, the hyper-ghettoes of suspect countries look closer, in terms of Wacquant's analytic terms, to the ghetto end of the continuum.

[9] In general, Waquant (2004) offers four criteria for articulating the sociological analytical concept of the ghetto. The ghetto is treated as an urban space subjected to forces of stigma, constraint, spatial confinement, and institutional duplication.

[10] See *UNHCR 2003 Global Refugee Trends* at http://www.unhcr.ch/cgi-bin/texis/vtx/home. The report refers to over 20 million mobility-challenged people, of whom 51 percent are refugees, 5 percent seek political asylum, 12 percent are deported immigrants, and 28 percent are internally displaced. Also see accounts and personal interviews in *Human Rights Watch Annual Report 2002 on Refugees, Asylum Seekers, Migrants and Internally Displaced Persons* at http://www.hrw.org.

Typically, most attention has been given to the increasing difficulties of residents of suspect countries to obtain immigration permits and political asylum. Yet not less indicative for sorting out the elementary forms of the mobility regime, when it comes to the effective constitution of stigmatized suspect countries and stigmatized suspect populations, is the fact that the ability to leave them is increasingly difficult for nonimmigrants as well. Holding a Turkish or a Russian or a Nigerian passport does not so much indicate one's identity as a bearer of rights as much as it marks one as a potential unwanted immigrant. Accordingly, the mobility regime is increasingly based on limiting the travel opportunities of such citizens en masse, putting enormous difficulties on the ability to get ordinary tourist visas, often using basic tactics such as long waits, high application fees, and a variety of bureaucratic hurdles.[11]

ELEMENTARY FORMS OF THE MOBILITY REGIME: QUARANTINES AND GATED COMMUNITIES

The mobility regime also operates within the perimeters of privileged localities, countries, and economic and political blocs. It is useful to distinguish between those elementary forms that work through the prevention of exit (e.g., prisons) and those elementary forms that work through the prevention of entry (e.g., gated communities). While these two forms of social isolation address and manage different social strata, and while they operate on the basis of almost diametrically opposite logics, they may be sociologically located along a continuum of practices designed to consolidate a mobility regime in general and to strategically distance suspect social elements in particular. Indeed, while there are strong sociological reasons not to collapse such distinct phenomena as prisons and gated communities into a single category, there are also other sociological reasons to treat them both as products of distinct strategies of group power; in the former case, the power of dominant groups to stigmatize, isolate, and immobilize suspect groups by controlling their exit rights, and in the latter case, the power of dominant groups to isolate themselves from suspect groups by controlling their rights of entry into certain designated social spaces. Specifically, we may thus see the integrated risk-management system of the mobility regime as predicated upon two pillars: segregating suspect social elements in prisons, urban ghettoes, and quarantines on the one hand, and sheltering privileged groups in gated communities, secured work places, and guarded shopping malls on the other (Davis 1990).

In this section, the concept of quarantines refers to multiple forms of containment and imprisonment. Quarantine, in general, operates by identifying and distancing people perceived as dangerous by subjecting them to particular treatment protocols. Foucault (1980)—while not specifically discussing a mobility regime—theorized the development of modern governance in relation to various forms of quarantine. Medieval cities, wrote Foucault, already relied on two types of measures to deal with perceived threats such as leprosy and plague: exclusion and quarantine (Curtis 2002). Urban authorities in later times, pressured by the bourgeoisie, dealt with the politicosanitary menace by perfecting the instrument of quarantine. Yet what started

[11]British families of Asian decent, for example, complain that their family members in Asia encounter growing difficulties in obtaining permission to visit them in the United Kingdom. Indeed, there was a dramatic increase in the British rate of refusal for nonimmigrant visa applicants in 2002: in India, the rate of refusal climbed from 29 to 59 percent, in Bangladesh it reached 85 percent, in Iran it tripled, and the rate of refusal for Russian citizens increased by 124 percent compared to the previous year. See Jenny Bourn, "Step Up in Family Visitor Visa Denial," November 27, 2003, *Independent Race and Refugee News Network*, available at http://www.irr.org.uk/2003/november/ha000016.html.

as urban politics of health later converged with other forms of containment to become an important element of modern "governmentality" (Foucault 1991, 1980).

Also on the privileged side of border fences, the mobility regime still relies on the old methods of using prisons, penitentiaries, detention camps, and a host of other types of quarantines to isolate social elements perceived to be dangerous. With the world's largest prison population, the United States imprisons at a far greater rate than both rich and many impoverished and authoritarian countries. On a per capita basis, the United States has three times more prisoners than Iran, four times more than Poland, five times more than Tanzania, and seven times more than Germany[12] (Garland 2001; Wacquant 2001). Affirming a no-compromise approach to jailing, as well as a conceptual fusion between immigration and terrorism, the U.S. Department of Justice also announced that undocumented immigrants could be detained indefinitely, without bond, if the government provided evidence that their release might threaten national security.

To inhibit, contain, and control unauthorized immigration, countries such as the Netherlands, the United Kingdom, Sweden, and Australia created large detention camps for asylum seekers and undocumented immigrants. In recent years, changing geopolitics and numerous national crises led to dramatic increases in the number of people seeking asylum in Europe. Whereas in 1987, 57,400 individuals applied for asylum in Germany alone, between 1988 and 1992 a total of 1.1 million asylum applications were lodged. A peak was reached in 1992, when nearly 440,000 asylum seekers filed applications. In the much smaller Netherlands, there were 43,900 asylum requests in 2000, mostly submitted by citizens of the former Yugoslavia, Afghanistan, and Iraq.[13] In the United Kingdom, private contractors run sites such as the Oakington Detention Centre for asylum seekers and the Campsfield Prison for refugees, holding a few hundred detainees at a time. On the other side of the English Channel, the Red-Cross-run Sangatte refugee camp near the Eurotunnel transport terminal in Calais accommodates more than 1,500 asylum seekers, most of them Afghans and Kurds. Australia has put in place a mandatory detention policy for asylum seekers who arrive without entry visas, many of them by boat from countries such as Indonesia. The detainees are held in sites such as the Womera camp, where thousands are detained in the Australian desert. All across Europe, detention camps and prisons also serve as a transit port for undocumented immigrants targeted for deportation. The current deportation rate from Europe is 350,000 people annually, in addition to another 150,000 people who participate in various European "voluntary" programs of return. These deportees sooner or later join the immobilized suspect populations who inhabit the hyper-ghettoes in suspect countries.[14]

Not least important, if less visibly harsh in its consequences, is the way privileged populations shield themselves against risks by using methods of self-enclosure. Self-enclosure has become an intensive process in poor and rich countries alike, involving a host of market entities specializing in providing the needed equipment, personnel, and infrastructure. Multinational corporations doing business in impoverished countries are leaders in this art. Consider the following description of ChevronTexaco's compound in Angola: "Built in the 1960s, Malongo is a campus of ranch houses,

[12] "U.S. Prison Population Largest in the World," *Baltimore Sun*, June 1, 2003, citing Bruce Western, a sociologist at Princeton University; see http://www.charleston.net/stories/060103/wor_01jailbirds.shtml.

[13] Source: http://www.migrationinformation.org/feature/display.cfm?id = 123.

[14] The European Union allocates 250 million Euros annually for deporting unwanted newcomers. The budget currently includes the cost of leasing airplanes, because regular commercial airlines, under public protest, are increasingly reluctant to transport deportees.

manicured green lawns and smooth paved roads. ChevronTexaco's own well and private filtration system supplies drinkable tap water—a rare luxury in Africa. Spacious dining halls offer a stunning array of fresh seafood, imported meats, salad and dessert bars. The vegetables are all grown in an organic greenhouse on the compound, set up by Norwegians, and bright green Granny Smith apples are flown in from South Africa . . . ChevronTexaco does everything it can to keep it that way. No one enters or leaves the compound without special permission. And there's no way to avoid the tightly guarded security gates, because the entire compound is surrounded by a double fence of barbed wire that encloses a ring of anti-personnel land mines" (Eviatar 2004:13).

Whether we consider policies and practices that are based on the logic of defense against the threat of terrorism, the threat of immigration, or the threat of crime, the sociological common denominator is a dramatic social effort to perfect mechanisms of self-enclosure. Those in Brazil who can afford it spend $4.5 billion annually on private security. The proportion between the number of private security guards and the Brazilian police is 3:1, and private policing has become one of the most prosperous activities in Brazil in recent years (Beato 2003). In South Africa, the annual spending on private home security is $1.3 billion, tripling the governmental annual spending on public housing (Masuku 2003).

Spreading fast is that residential spatial arrangement known as the gated community. Blakely and Snyder (1997), documenting the proliferation of gated communities in the United States, estimate that as many as 8 million Americans live in as many as 20,000 gated communities, often citing fear of crime as the reason behind gating. In a sense, the gated community is a microcosm of the global mobility regime, predicated as it is on a combination of governmental and market forces. While governments contract with construction companies to build fences and border barriers, private security firms sell private police forces, armed vehicles, cameras, sensors, alarm systems, and fences that surround whole middle-class and even working-class communities (Salcedo and Torres 2004; Low 2003).

In many U.S. schools, metal detectors screen all boys and girls who come in, while armed guards ensure that no student will escape the compound during the school day. North-American inner-city schools, already located within distinct boundaries deemed dangerous to cross use technological surveillance, security personnel, metal detectors, and paramilitary control tactics to maintain order and safety (Devine 1996). In affluent urban areas, on the other hand, shopping malls are restricted zones designated to accommodate only certain classes of consumers (Crawford 1992). Thus, the guards of one strictly gated mall in Rhode Island, for example, bar the entry of people who wear T-shirts that bear what the guards consider to be inappropriate language. Visitors who form groups of more than five people are subjected to deportation back to the street. All in all, self-enclosure thus denotes not only a relentless process of privatizing the public sphere but also a not less relentless process of "militarizing" it, subjecting it to a highly regulated mobility regime (Davis 1990).

THE OSMOTIC PROPERTIES OF THE MOBILITY REGIME

The deployment of the mobility regime, precisely because it must facilitate global cross-border flows, depends upon the creation of screening mechanisms. Thought of in spatial terms, globalization is a process constitutive of a global mobility regime that aspires to screen those substances (viruses, people, and hazardous materials) that may cross the boundaries of some designated social containers (e.g., national borders and gated communities) from those that may not. In the present era, writes Bauman, "the state tends to be reduced to the status of an enlarged and ennobled police precinct," whose function is "to guard the selectivity of osmosis" (2002:82). Again not unlike the elementary forms discussed above, there is nothing substantively new about the regulation of movement through the creation of osmotic mechanisms. Practices of enclosure, even in extreme cases of sealed total institutions, must always rely on some selection procedures that distinguish that which may come across from that which cannot.

During the feudal era, most people could not leave their communities without written consent, and those who did risked imprisonment and death. Feudal estates closely watched their boundaries, deriving revenue from fees of passage and multitude types of tariffs and excise duties. In the 18th century, with the birth of the modern bureaucratic sovereign state, the regulation of movement reached new levels of precision. From then on, governments increasingly saw it as their business to generate and archive knowledge about individuals and ordinary people, among other things, to regulate mobility. Primary among the measures developed for facilitating an osmotic regime of movement had been the introduction of passports, first in France in 1792 and soon after in many other European countries. Passports, also needed for domestic travel, came coupled with regulation designed to control vagrancy, crime, and foreign infiltration, thus turning the 19th century into a hotbed for developing the paradigm of the modern mobility regime (Cole 2001; Torpey 2000).

The current global mobility regime, writes Bauman, is based on a distinctive principle of osmosis: "traveling for profit is encouraged; traveling for survival is condemned" (2002:84). To maintain this osmotic system, new technologies of social intervention are developed and perfected in tandem with the physical development of fences, prisons, and gated enclaves. One instance of this osmotic fine-tuning concerns infinite administrative classificatory expansion. A basic illustration of this is the classificatory scheme of American nonimmigrant visas. As of 2004, there have been 48 different categories of nonimmigrant visas to the United States. Thus, for example, the H-2A type of nonimmigrant visa is applicable to "temporary agricultural workers coming to the United States to fill positions for which a temporary shortage of American workers has been recognized by the U.S. Department of Agriculture," while the L-1 type of nonimmigrant visa is applicable to "intracompany transferees who work in positions as managers, executives or persons with specialized knowledge." Thus, classes of people who are typically barred entry, namely, unskilled laborers, may be granted mobility rights for designated tasks, while people who become valuable citizens of multinational corporations, namely, corporate executives, are granted special mobility privileges. In both cases, the visa system allows for the fine-tuning of movement, carefully sorting out individual identities. In particular, the osmotic system is now geared toward sorting out those who are deemed necessary to enhance the quality of the labor market from those who are considered redundant or, worse, a burden. Thus, the continued mobility of high-skilled workers is considered a vital issue for many rich countries. Accordingly, around 1.1 million people considered high skilled came to work in the United States in 2000 on temporary stay visas, more than the roughly 850,000 immigrants admitted for legal permanent residence (Jachimowicz and Meyers 2002). Similarly, Germany introduced a "green card" system to help satisfy the demand for highly-qualified information technology experts. Through this new immigration program, about 9,200 highly-skilled workers have entered Germany through August 2001, with 1,935 Indians accounting for the largest group (http://www.migrationinformation.org). At the same time, millions are barred entry, whether as immigrants or visitors, on various grounds of perceived threats. In sum, the osmotic system developed under the guidelines of the global mobility regime must rely not simply on fences but on finely-tuned screening mechanisms that provide it with its necessary social elasticity. Screening, in turn, relies on that technology of intervention that I designate as biosocial profiling.

PROFILING: BEYOND LAW AND DISCIPLINE

Profiling, and specifically racial and ethnic profiling, attracts significant attention from sociologists, public policymakers, and legal experts.[15] In the United States, racial profiling commonly refers to any police-initiated action that relies on race, ethnicity, or national origin rather than on particular individual behavior as criteria for selecting whom to stop or arrest (Ramirez, McDevitt, and Farrell 2000). Here, I would like to expand the notion of profiling to cover a whole range of practices aimed at both one's physical and social identity that are undertaken by a host of mobility regime market and governmental agents. I treat profiling and more precisely, biosocial profiling, as an emergent technology of social intervention that objectifies whole strata of people by assigning them into suspect categories, thereby enabling the paradigm of suspicion to be translated into elaborate practices of containment. In contrast to the modality of law, which punishes and locks away through a binary guilty/innocent distinction, and in contrast to the modality of the disciplines, which corrects behavior and occasionally quarantines through bell-curve matrices of normalization (Hunt 1992; Foucault 1977), profiling predicts behavior and regulates mobility by situating subjects in categories of risk.

Now two qualifications of the above formulation must be immediately introduced. First, laws and disciplines are not substituted for profiling. Legal regulation and disciplinary procedures are widely applied and certainly play a central role in facilitating imprisonments, deportations, and a host of other types of containment. Rather, it would be more accurate to say that profiling emerges as a more discrete technology of intervention that facilitates and complements the regulation of mobility by legal and disciplinary means. Moreover, while laws and regulations may formally enable governance through profiling, they nonetheless lack the instruments and the type of gaze that allows profiling to function as a mode of spatial containment that is able—on the ground—to maintain the selectivity of boundary-crossing and to effectively distinguish those who are licensed to move from those who are not.

Second, profiling does not operate exclusively at the service of the mobility regime, nor is it a technology specifically designed to contain mobility. Profiling is also widely used as a technology for screening, hiring, and controlling employees, as a technology for the monitoring and channeling of consumption, as a technology for establishing insurance premiums, and as a technology of sentencing. In these latter functions, profiling works through actuarial practices: techniques that "use statistics to represent the distribution of variables in a population," treat individuals "as locations in actuarial tables of variation," and seek to predict behavior and situate subjects "according to the risk they pose" (Simon 1988:771–72). Indeed, profiling—in its

[15]For example, the 2002 annual meeting of the American Sociological Association devoted a special plenary to discuss racial profiling and offered attendees a short course about racial profiling and organizations. A special issue on "Ethnic and Racial Profiling" is also forthcoming in the *Canadian Journal of Law and Society* (Vol. 18(3), 2004).

actuarial manifestation—has long been used by insurance companies as a risk-management strategy for evaluating the monetary threat different categories of individuals posed for insurers (thus young drivers pay higher premiums than veteran drivers, reflecting statistics showing that they are more vulnerable to traffic accidents). Actuarial practices also migrated from the insurance market and began to shape criminal sentencing. The logic of risk management has become a central theme of criminal justice policy and a new paradigm of "actuarial justice"—namely, the management of crime opportunities and risk distribution rather than the management of individual offenders—now drives and shapes sentencing policies (Kemshall 2003; Feeley and Simon 1992). In recent years, profiling has not simply become a major technique of screening and licensing but has emerged as a constitutive feature of the entire mobility regime. Absorbing and internalizing the methods developed by both market entities and state policing apparatuses, the profiling of the mobility regime represents a fusion between insurance-oriented risk-management strategies and a criminal-justice-oriented sentencing paradigm. In the process, profiling shifted from being a method for assigning specific individuals into various categories of risk into an all-encompassing method that targets society as a whole and treats mobility per se as a suspect practice. In this sense, as Agamben (2004) aptly observed, humanity itself has become a dangerous class.

As a global technology that creates social barriers by designating a status of suspects to an ever-growing number of individuals, biosocial profiling is concerned with establishing degrees of threat and corresponding rated rights of movement. Profiling is therefore the technology of intervention that underwrites the possibility of maintaining the global osmotic system. It works by assigning individuals into an ever-expanding list of suspect categories, each based on intricate internal sublevels of suspicion, and each cross-examined in relation to other categories. Accordingly, profiling is based on endless series of observations, data gathering, and classificatory procedures that allow for the creation of highly complex profiling models. In general, profiling is based on the creation and inscription of a holistic personal profile into electronic databases in ways that allow the classification of individuals into various categories of suspicion. It operates at two analytically distinct levels that are coupled and subsequently jointly inscribed. At one level, profiling is based on the systematic ("actuarial") collection of demographic, ethnic, and socioeconomic data. At another level, profiling is based on the collection of data that directly refers to the individual body, such as color of skin, facial characteristics, tissues, irises, fingerprints, and DNA. Combined, these collections converge into an identity that is, "outside the physical body, in the files and paper records of some government bureaucracy" (Cole 2001:10) to a degree unimaginable by previous generations.

As an operational technology, profiling is interchangeably formal, quasi-formal, and informal. At times, it is executed through unmediated human contact. Such is the case when the category of DWB (Driving While Black) is intuitively produced as a category of suspicion that licenses a potentially violent arrest. This display of "mundane" racial profiling is extremely important, as it becomes an intuitive routine of everyday life. Thus, analyzing the work of insurance underwriters, Glenn challenges the "myth of the actuary," namely, the "general belief that insurance practices are predicated on objective statistics" (2003:132, 2000). The insurance underwriter, writes Glenn, does not simply and scientifically compare "applicants to a matrix, and if they fit into it they are accepted" (2003:133). Rather, many property/casualty insurance companies perform what is called "character underwriting," which is a holistic assessment of the applicant as having a "mature, stable, and responsible" character. In the 19th century, writes Glenn, immigrants were considered a risk because their character traits were "indefinite, incapable of analysis, separation, or estimation" and, as a result, entire categories of individuals were excluded on the basis of race or nationality (2003:133). In present times, writes Glenn, insurance agents complement formal actuary practices with a "risk report" that includes observations on issues such as an excessive number of liquor bottles spotted in the house, unusual hobbies, or other evidence of an unconventional lifestyle. In fact, such profiling is performed in one way or another each time we enter a guarded restaurant, let alone when we answer the inquiries of security "selectors" at airports. In this latter case, profiling is based on a series of questions that are carefully designed—based on preexisting models of risk with which such "selectors" are equipped—to determine one's suspicion rating and hence one's freedom to board a plane or to cross a border. Similarly, consular officers and immigration police officers are trained in the art of interviewing, believed to provide essential personal data that formal questionnaires fail to capture. The interview, then, becomes a vital profiling technique, as much as the test is a vital disciplinary method.

Profiling also benefits from information sharing between governmental and market entities. Profiling serves credit companies, banks, and insurance companies to determine the risks and threats that individuals represent to their normal commercial operations. Profiling technologies that are developed in the market for commercial purposes allow for unprecedented projects of detecting and regulating mobility. Such projects are based on the perfection of databases that facilitate a close watch over the movements of individuals as they are tracked and recorded by the use of cellular phones, credit cards, and Internet-based consumption. Both governments and market players, therefore, contribute to the transformation of the public sphere into an arena of surveillance and screening, thereby enabling the osmotic mobility regime of the present era. Thus, for example, European leaders agreed in March 2004 on a range of security measures, including monitoring data from mobile phone calls, a practice that inevitably implicates private phone companies in the overall monitoring scheme. To the extent that many of the immobilized and spatially contained populations of the world do not have access to digital devices such as credit cards and cellular phones, this very lack may suffice for high-risk classification in the profiling matrix.

Profiling, the higher we climb the institutional ladder, refers not only to dress, accent, and color of skin, not even solely to religious, ethnic, or national identity (although these are of course critical), but rather to a dense web of biological, demographic, consumerist, and economic data.[16] When it comes to attempts to acquire a visa and to cross borders, profiling is becoming particularly penetrating and is increasingly based on technologies of examination that are by far more sophisticated than the impressionist judgments of police officers and security guards. Thus, for example, the 1998 Cairo summit of the Interpol created a new unit whose mandate is "to provide strategic and technical support to enhance member states' DNA profiling capacity and to promote its widespread use in the international law enforcement environment." Following post-September 11 regulations, most of those who enter the United States are face-scanned and fingerprinted prior to entry under the provisions of the USVISIT program. The program is designed to expand both profiling capabilities and detection possibilities by enhancing spatial monitoring

[16]For example, immigrants arriving in the United States may be subjected—beyond interviews, biometric tests, and inspection of documents—to detention for physical and mental examination under Section 232 of the Code of Federal Regulations issued by the Department of Homeland Security (8 U.S.C. §1252).

beyond the port of entry. It mandates information sharing among mobility regime agencies such as the Bureau of Immigration and Custom's Enforcement (ICE), the National Crime Information Center (NCIC), the Student and Exchange Visitor Information System (SEVIS), and the Interagency Border Inspection System (IBIS). Also, the data generated by USVISIT are designed to assist the Department of Homeland Security (DHS) in generating and updating social categories of suspicion. The European Union as well, along with its decision to establish a joint border police by 2005, decided upon a joint visa system that will enable detection and information sharing through an electronic system that would burn biometric data of visa applicants onto their passports. European countries also prepare to issue new passports, burnt with biometric data such as fingerprints and iris patterns.

Bioprofiling, however, is not simply a more accurate and efficient way to validate one's identity and to cross it with relevant data on illegal immigration, crime, or terrorism. Bioprofiling inscribes a designated category of suspicion on human bodies, facilitating a situation in which one's fingerprints testify to one's travel log and consumption patterns along with one's place of origin, ethnic background, or religious affiliation. In this way, biosocial profiling transforms mobility into a public performance, both in the sense of treating the human individual as a mobile unit located within collective categories of suspicion and in the sense of subjecting a relatively discreet social action to public scrutiny. Perhaps ironically, however, the transformation of mobility into a moment of utmost exposure does not enhance social proximity but rather maintains and facilitates a regime of social distance.

Profiling represents a distinct modality of power, in this case the power to immobilize, to create social distances, and in general to police and regulate spatial behavior. Profiling has to be distinguished from other modalities of power. Foucault characterized late modernity by arguing that an intricate web of nonegalitarian distinctions—enabled by technologies of normalization—underwrites the package of egalitarian and universal rights promised to individuals in liberal constitutions. Normalization, as Foucault called it, announced an era of lesser reliance on physical punishment in general and on the life-taking powers of law in particular. Rather, normalization uses disciplinary techniques that manage life by subjecting individuals to an ever-expanding list of standards to which they are expected to conform. Perceiving people as "moral and rational actors" (Simon 1988), normalization aspires to "change" people and to correct behavior. In guiding sentencing policies, write Feeley and Simon (1992), this meant concerns with rehabilitation and reform. However, the new penology, they argue, relies on actuarial techniques rather than individual characteristics to determine punishment, aiming more at efficient risk management than at rehabilitation (Feeley and Simon 1994, 1992). Because this actuarial justice does not seek to change people but rather "to manage them in place" (Simon 1988:773), its logic seems to be in perfect fit with the mobility-curbing and mobility-confining tasks of biosocial profiling as well. Biosocial profiling, activated at the service of a mobility regime, is not concerned with correction (whether through education, persuasion, or sanctions), but rather with fixing individuals into given categories of suspicion. If various tests serve the disciplines in their attempt to normalize individual behavior, then the classifications of profiling serve the mobility regime in its attempt to block or contain individuals. Thus, paraphrasing Foucault, we may argue that a dense web of nonegalitarian distinctions—establishing a system of highly differential movement licenses—underwrites the universal declarations of human rights that are so strongly associated with globalization.

CONCLUSION

Globalization has been intensively theorized in terms of cross-border flows connoting imageries of openness. Of specific interest to this article has been the way that issues such as citizenship and personhood-based entitlements have been theorized in terms of the diminishing or eroding capacities of states to confer rights on the basis of sovereignty and in terms of the ascent of global principles of human rights as a newly found basis of trans-national governance (eliciting certain perceptions about the normative dimension of globalization as well as concrete organized social action such as humanitarian intervention). In this article, I suggested that globalization is overtheorized in terms of social openness and undertheorized in terms of social closure. I further argued that the normative dimension of globalization should be theorized not only in terms of the ascent of the global principle of universal human rights and its impact on individual and collective entitlements but also in terms of another ascending principle, namely, a global mobility regime that works in the opposite direction, limiting and preventing access to certain rights and entitlements through the regulation of social space (relying not only on individual states but also on multistate cooperation, regional blocs, and international organizations.

I argued that the regulation of movement that evolves under the new cultural and normative conditions brought about by globalization is predicated on a paradigm of suspicion, one that constructs individuals and often whole social groups as having suspect identities related to the risks of immigration, crime, and terrorism. I suggested that immigration, crime, and terrorism, each on its own account and often coupled with one another, have been more or less intensely conceived as social problems throughout the 20th century. Hence, the "newness" in speaking about a paradigm of suspicion does not lie at the level of absence or presence of historical precedents. Rather, the newness lies in the normative and structural global conditions that turn the paradigm of suspicion into a potent cultural force in the regulation of movement. First, cross-border movements are not only coupled with both crime and terrorism, but crime and terrorism are also conceived in terms of trans-national activities on their own account. Second, it is only in recent years that a technology of social screening has fully ripened, allowing for new forms of risk management that are geared toward "fixing" people in their place. And third, arguably above all, the mobility regime is theorized as a global principle precisely because it represents a structural response to the problem of maintaining high levels of inequality in a relatively normatively homogenized world. In this sense, the already familiar legal and constitutional debates concerning the adequate balance between human rights and, say, national security, are not mere replications of the tension between the global and the local. Rather, they should be understood as increasingly representing the tension between universal rights and universal fears, both operating at the global level, albeit materializing at concrete localities.

In his classic article on the Stranger, Georg Simmel argued that the unity of nearness and remoteness involved in every human relation is organized, in the phenomenon of the stranger, in a way that makes the one who is close by to be perceived as far, and the one who is perceived to be far, to be perceived as actually near ([1908] 1950). Globalization, among other things, means that we now fully live in such a society of strangers. However, Simmel treated the sociological phenomenon of the Stranger not simply as a specific form of interaction but also as "a very positive relation" (1950:402). For Simmel, the Stranger represented and embodied a freedom of mobility unavailable to others, thus allowing for novel forms of what he called social participation. In this article, I tried to show that under a newly articulated paradigm of suspicion, new forms of social participation and association are conditioned by the emergence of a mobility regime that aims at curbing the movement of strangers precisely at a historical moment when it is becoming harder to establish who is a stranger. The "stranger," in this sense, has become the one who is constituted as a suspect, facing an expansive set of physical, psychological, and sociological fences, a subject of a mobility regime that operates not only through visible presence on borders and the policing of bounded spaces but also through multilayered gestures of closure that operate at the most minute aspects of social interaction. The stranger is now fully recognized, simultaneously as a universal rights-bearer and a universal threat.

REFERENCES

Adams, J. 1999. *The Social Implication of Hypermobility*. OECD Project on Environmentally Sustainable Transport. Paris: OECD.

Agamben, G. 2004. "No to Bio-Political Tattooing." *Le Monde* January 10, p. 3.

Anderson, J., L. O'Dowd, and T. M. Wilson, eds. 2003. "Culture and Cooperation in Europe's Borderland." *European Studies: An Interdisciplinary Series in European Culture, History and Politics*, Vol. 19 (special issue).

Andreas, P. 2000. *Border Games: Policing the U.S.-Mexico Divide*. Ithaca, NY: Cornell University Press.

Appadurai, A. 1996. *Modernity at Large: Cultural Dimensions of Globalization*. Minneapolis, MN: University of Minnesota Press.

Barber, B. 1996. *Jihad vs. McWorld: How the World Is Both Falling Apart and Coming Together and What This Means for Democracy*. New York: Ballantine.

Bauman, Z. 2002. *Society Under Siege*. Cambridge: Polity Press.

Beato, C. 2003. "Public Safety in Brazil." Paper delivered at the Living Law Forum: Policing and Security Around the World, February 19–22 2003, Montreal, Canada.

Black, D. 2004. "The Geometry of Terrorism." *Sociological Theory* 22(1):14.

Blakely, E. and M. G. Snyder. 1997. *Fortress America: Gated Communities in the United States*. Washington, DC: Brookings Institute Press/Lincoln Institute of Land.

Blomley, N., D. Delaney, and R. T. Ford, eds. 2001. *The Legal Geographies Reader*. Oxford: Blackwell.

Cairncross, F. 1997. *The Death of Distance*. Cambridge: Harvard Business School Press.

Camarota, S. A. 2002. "The Muslim Wave—Dealing with Immigration from the Middle East." *National Review* August 30. Available at http://www.nationalreview.com/advance/advance091602.asp#title4.

Castells, M. 1996. *The Rise of the Network Society*. Oxford: Blackwell.

Cole, S. A. 2001. *Suspect Identities: A History of Fingerprinting and Criminal Identification*. Cambridge: Harvard University Press.

Coutin, S. B., B. Maurer, and B. Yngvesson. 2002. "In the Mirror: The Legitimation Work of Globalization." *Law and Social Inquiry* 27(4):801–43.

Crawford, M. 1992. "The World in a Shopping Mall." Pp. 3–30 in *Variations on a Theme Park: The New American City and the End of Public Space*, edited by M. Sorkin. New York: Hill and Wang.

Curtis, B. 2002. "Foucault on Governmentality and Population: The Impossible Discovery." *Canadian Journal of Sociology* 27(4):505–33.

Davis, M. 1990. "Fortress Los Angeles: The Militarization of Urban Space." Pp. 223–63 in *City of Quartz: Excavating the Future of Los Angeles*, edited by M. Davis. New York: Verso.

Deflem, M. 2002. *Policing World Society: Historical Foundations of International Police Cooperation*. New York: Oxford University Press.

de Sousa Santos, B. 2002. *Toward a New Legal Common Sense: Law, Globalization and Emancipation*. London: Butterworths.

Devine, J. 1996. *Maximum Security: The Culture of Violence in Inner-City Schools*. Chicago, IL: University of Chicago Press.

Doyle, J. and M. Nathan. 2001. *Wherever Next: Work in a Mobile World*. London: Industrial Society.

Eviatar, D. 2004. "Africa's Oil Tycoons." *Nation* April 12, 13.

Feeley, M. and J. Simon. 1992. "The New Penology: Notes on the Emerging Strategy of Corrections and its Implications." *British Journal of Criminology* 30:449–74.

———. 1994. "Actuarial Justice: The Emerging New Criminal Law." Pp. 173–201 in *The Futures of Criminology*, edited by D. Nelken. London: Sage.

Foucault, M. 1977. *Discipline and Punish. The Birth of the Prison*. London: Penguin Books.

———. 1980. "The Politics of Health in the Eighteenth Century." Pp. 166–82 in *Power/Knowledge: Selected Interviews & Other Writings, 1972–1977*, edited by C. Gordon. New York: Pantheon.

———. 1991. "Governmentality." Pp. 87–104 in *The Foucault Effect: Studies in Governmentality*, edited by G. Bruchell et al. Chicago, IL: University of Chicago Press.

Garland, D. 2001. *The Culture of Control: Crimes and Social Order in Contemporary Society*. New York: Oxford University Press.

Giddens, A. 1990. *The Consequences of Modernity*. Cambridge: Polity Press.

Glenn, B. J. 2000. "The Shifting Rhetoric of Insurance Denial." *Law and Society Review* 34(3):779–808.

———. 2003. "Postmodernism: The Basis of Insurance." *Risk Management and Insurance Review* 6(2):131–44.

Gottdiener, M. 1995. *Postmodern Semiotics: Material Culture and the Forms of Postmodern Life*. Oxford: Blackwell.

Hardt, M. and A. Negri. 2000. *Empire*. Cambridge: Harvard University Press.

Harvey, D. 1989. *The Conditions of Postmodernity*. Cambridge: Blackwell.

Held, D. 1995. *Democracy and the Global Order: From the Modern State to Cosmopolitan Governance*. Cambridge: Polity Press.

Held, D., A. McGrew, D. Goldblatt, and J. Perraton, eds. 1999. *Global Transformations: Politics, Economics and Culture*. Cambridge: Polity Press.

Hunt, A. 1992. "Foucault's Expulsion of Law: Toward a Retrieval." *Law and Social Inquiry* 17(1):1–38.

Jachimowicz, M. and R. McKay. 2003. *Justice, Homeland Security Departments Announce Changes*. Migration Policy Institute, May 1, 2003 (http://www.migrationinformation.org/Feature/display.cfm?ID = 120).

Jachimowicz, M. and D. W. Meyers. 2002. *Temporary High-Skilled Migration*. Migration Policy Institute. Available at http://www.migrationinformation.org/Feature/display.cfm? ID=69.

Jacobson, D. 1996. *Rights Across Borders: Immigration and the Decline of Citizenship*. Baltimore, MD: Johns Hopkins University Press.

Kellner, D. 1999. "Globalization from Below? Toward a Radical Democratic Technopolitics." *Angelaki* 4(2):101–13.

———. 2002. "Theorizing Globalization." *Sociological Theory* 20(3):285–305.

Kemshall, H. 2003. *Understanding Risk in Criminal Justice*. New York: Open University Press.

Lechner, F. J. and J. Boli, eds. 2000. *The Globalization Reader*. London: Blackwell.

Levy, R. A. 2001. *Ethnic Profiling: A Rational and Moral Framework*. Cato Institute (http://www.cato.org/index.html).

Low, S. 2003. *Behind the Gates: Life, Security and the Pursuit of Happiness in Fortress America*. New York: Routledge.

Masuku, S. 2003. "For Better and for Worse: South African Crime Rates in 2002." *South Africa Crime Quarterly* 3:17–24.

Meyer, J. W., J. Boli, G. M. Thomas, and F. Ramirez. 1997. "World Society and the Nation-State." *American Journal of Sociology* 103:144–81.

Nevins, J. 2001. *Operation Gatekeeper: The Rise of the Illegal Alien and the Making of the U.S.-Mexico Boundary*. New York: Routledge.

Ramirez, D., J. McDevitt, and A. Farrell. 2000. *A Resource Guide on Racial Profiling Data Collection Systems*. U.S. Department of Justice, November 2000.

Roy, A. 2004. "The New American Century." *Nation* February 9:11–14.

Salcedo, R. and A. Torres. 2004. "Gated Communities in Santiago: Wall or Frontier?" *International Journal of Urban and Regional Research* 28(1):27–45.

Sassen, S. 1988. *The Mobility of Labor and Capital: A Study in International Investment and Labor Flow*. New York: Cambridge University Press.

———. 1991. *The Global City*. Princeton, NJ: Princeton University Press.

Simmel, G. [1908] 1950. "The Stranger." In *The Sociology of Georg Simmel*, edited by K. H. Wolff. New York: Free Press.

Simon, J. 1988. "The Ideological Effects of Actuarial Practices." *Law and Society Review* 22:771–800.

Sklair, L. 1997. "Social Movements for Global Capitalism: The Transnational Capitalist Class in Action." *Review of International Political Economy* 4(3):514–38.

Soja, E. 1989. *Postmodern Geographies*. London: Verso.

Soysal, Y. N. 1994. *Limits of Citizenship: Migrants and Postnational Membership in Europe*. Chicago, IL: University of Chicago Press.

Tilly, C. 1992. *Coercion, Capital, and European States, AD 990–1992*. Cambridge, MA: Blackwell.

———. 2004. "Terror, Terrorism, Terrorists." *Sociological Theory* 22(1):5.

Torpey, J. 2000. *The Invention of the Passport: Surveillance, Citizenship and the State*. Cambridge: Cambridge University Press.

Urry, J. 2003. "Social Networks, Travel and Talk." *British Journal of Sociology* 54(2):155.

Vaughan, J. M. 2004a. "America's New Welcome Mat: A Look at the Goals and Challenges of the US-VISIT Program." Testimony before the U.S. House of Representatives, Committee on Government Reform, March 4, 2004.

———. 2004b. "Preventing the Entry of Terrorists into the United States." Testimony before the U.S. House of Representatives, Committee on International Relations, Subcommittee on International Terrorism, Nonproliferation and Human Rights. February 13, 2004.

Wacquant, L. 2001. "Deadly Symbiosis: When Ghetto and Prison Meet and Mesh." *Punishment and Society* 3:95–133.

———. 2004. "What is a Ghetto? Constructing a Sociological Concept." In *International Encyclopedia of the Social and Behavioral Sciences (Revised Ed.)*, edited by N. Smelser and P. Bates. London: Pergamon.

[15]

Analysing a world in motion

Global flows meet 'criminology of the other'

KATJA FRANKO AAS
University of Oslo, Norway

Abstract

The globalizing world has been described as a 'world in motion', permeated by transnational networks and flows of goods, capital, information and cultural symbols, as well as potentially risky individuals and substances. This article examines the implications of the various global mobilities for criminological theory, method and policy. The world of global networks and flows introduces new notions of social ordering and exclusion, as well as challenging the prevailing conceptions of society, community, culture and social belonging, while growing demands for control of global mobilities create a complex dynamics between the nation-state and the emerging 'world risk society'.

Key Words

borders • criminology of the other • globalization • migration • world risk society

'Siamo tutti Londinesi' ('We are all Londoners'), said the posters, hanging in the streets of Rome the day after the 7 July London attacks. The message was similar to the one displayed on the cover of the French *LeMonde*, in the aftermath of the 11 September attacks, proclaiming that 'We are all Americans now'. Other than expressing solidarity, the messages also revealed shared feelings of fear and vulnerability between the western capitals. They were a sign of the emerging 'world risk society', a society connected by its shared awareness and fear of 'de-bounded' global risks (Beck, 2002). The issue clearly has a certain western bias, and the proclamations of global solidarity in the western media tend to be primarily reserved for affluent global capitals and tourist resorts rather than third world cities and countries. Nevertheless, the melting of global threats and local fears seems to have become a daily occurrence, through milder and stronger forms of moral panics about terrorism, crime by immigrants and asylum seekers, global paedophile and trafficking networks, cyber crime, etc. The so-far privileged position of the State and the national as the primary field of criminological reference is increasingly overshadowed by various transnational and sub-national configurations. 'In the post-9/11 world, threats are defined more by the fault lines *within* societies than by the territorial boundaries *between* them. From terrorism to global disease or environmental degradation, the challenges have become *transnational* rather than *international*' (National Commission on Terrorist Attacks Upon the United States, 2004: 517, emphases added). However, if these phenomena are to provide criminological relevance, we need to turn our attention to the underlying social transformations, caused by the emerging, deeply stratifying global ordering. The globalizing world has been described as a 'world in motion' (Inda and Rosaldo, 2002). Various transnational flows and connections are shaping contemporary life more than ever, influencing our perceptions of community, identity and culture. From issues of organized crime, transnational policing, transfer of penal knowledge and policies, to a variety of trans-border sex industries (cyber and corporeal)—to name just a few—the criminological world is in motion. While these mobilities are becoming a frequent empirical object of criminological inquiry, their implications are less frequently addressed on the theoretical level. The purpose of this article is therefore to explore the possible impact of these 'transformative mobilities' (Valier, 2003) on criminological theory and method. In what follows, I first offer a brief description of the emerging world of transnational flows and then examine the implications of these phenomena for studies of punishment and social control.

Towards a criminology of mobilities

Although a constant in the world of modernity, mobility has acquired new dimensions in the late modern context (Lash and Urry, 1994). Many of the most potent concepts and metaphors of the late-modern condition have been built around notions of movement, flow and transformations of time and space (Harvey, 1989; Castells, 1996; Bauman, 2000). Castells (1996) outlines the emergence of the so-called network society and a new notion of space, the 'space of flows', rather than a 'space of places'. This socio-economic model is marked by great productive dynamism and by the way it excludes, or 'switches off', large territorial and social sectors. Globally connected and locally disconnected, global networks and flows introduce qualitatively different experiences of social ordering and exclusion.

Mobility and travel take many forms, physical and virtual. Although migration and movement of people have been a constant aspect of modern life, today there are more people living outside their homeland than at any previous time in history (Papastergiadis, 2000: 10). The movement of people has become such a pervasive aspect of contemporary life, be it related to work, pleasure or migration, that 'it can no longer be considered as the exceptional event in the otherwise long historical process of settlement' (Papastergiadis, 2000: 24).[1] Paraphrasing Hall (1995), individuals' *routes* rather than *roots* have become a defining feature of social life, identity-making and cultural belonging. Consequently, Urry (2000), in line with other authors, argues that social sciences need to take account of these multiple and diverse mobilities. Sociology needs to go 'beyond societies'; beyond the static notion of a society and nation-state in a 'pre-global' order, and examine the various mobilities of people, images, capital, objects, information and risks: 'This new mobility paradigm has moved beyond static idealizations of society towards theories that are marked by terms such as nomadism, displacement, speed and movement' (Adey, 2004: 501).

These transformations tend to be categorized under the broadly defined and burgeoning field of globalization studies. However, criminologists have been, with some exceptions,[2] somewhat careful to join the debate. Many have noted a discomfort with using the word, due to the highly generalized, polarized and divisive nature of the debates in the past decades. Sheptycki prefers to talk of transnationalization in order to avoid over-generalization and to 'suggest that transnational practices impact on human relationships in diverse ways in different places' (2005: 79). Robertson's (1995) highly influential term 'glocalization' may be a useful pointer here, in order to denote the immanent intertwining of the global and the local. Nevertheless, even though globalization may not be an attractive term, one can hardly avoid the impact of the growing interconnectedness of the world on the nature of our sociality. Within criminology, Hogg poses a vital question:

> What happens to the conceptual apparatus of criminology and how salient are its taken-for-granted terms—crime, law, justice, state, sovereignty—at a time when global change and conflict may be eroding some elements at least of the international framework of states it has taken for granted ...?
>
> (2002: 195)

In line with Hogg's argument, studies of transnational flows and mobilities have much to offer to criminological inquiry, particularly through their potential to reach beyond the nation-state framework and open alternative fields of inquiry, as well as shed light on the emerging new dynamics of social control and exclusion.

However, rather than seeing the global as the new structure—an assumption frequently made by eager globalization analysts—Urry's more modest suggestion envisions it as an unfinished process, 'which problematises the fixed, given and static notions of social order' (2002a: 59). Furthermore, it should be noted that this trans-border interconnectedness does not primarily presume homogenization (Chan, 2005) but has, as I shall proceed to suggest, far more complex, diverse and less predictable effects.

'AlieNation is my Nation'

The shift of focus towards the global questions the notion of society that has been, in the past two centuries, the natural unit of criminological inquiry. 'Society here meant that which was ordered through a nation-state, with clear territorial and citizenship boundaries and a system of governance over its particular citizens' (Law and Urry, 2004: 398). In the emerging global (dis)order, the notion of 'society' is transformed beyond recognition by the growing transborder flows, and can no longer preserve the illusion of being a discrete and separate entity. Consequently, one can no longer study, for example, Italy simply by looking at what happens inside its territory, but rather one needs to acknowledge the effects that distant conflicts and developments have on national crime and security concerns, and vice versa. Through the immediate impact of a 24/7 global newsmedia, many forms of local offences no longer remain local, but have an impact far beyond their locality. At the same time, one 'cannot ignore the broader political economies of labour, capital and communications which are closely connected to the construction of apparently "localised" cultural expressions' (Cunnen and Stubbs, 2005: 97).

These local transformations are, as Giddens (1990) points out, as much part of globalization as the extension of social relations across time and space. The meanings of home, community, nation and the local become transformed beyond recognition by the global, creating hybrid identities and 'glocal' belongings. Furthermore, as the new channels of communication establish possibilities of having conversations across borders, new forms of cultural, political and religious belonging, as well as displacement, can occur without the physical movement of people (Appadurai, 1996). We are thus witnessing new forms of cultural expression and de-territorialization which are marked, as Castells points out, by their ability to mix cultural impulses from across the globe—'from the rap culture of American ghettoes, mimicked a few months later in the pop groups of Taipei or Tokyo, to Buddhist spiritualism transformed in electronic music' (1996: 463). 'The ghetto' is therefore not only an experience connected to physical space (the 'space of places'), but also a cultural one which, through global travel of images, music and discourses, transcends spatial limits (the 'space of flows').

It has been argued that the nation-state has been to some extent outrivalled as the primary locus of belonging and identity-making (Appadurai, 1996; Bauman, 2000). The sentiment is beautifully expressed in the title of Ove Sernhede's (2002) book *AlieNation is my Nation*, depicting how Swedish immigrant youth, due to their national marginalization, create alternative identities and belongings through hip hop and other global cultural connections. Furthermore, religions 'that were in the past resolutely national now pursue global missions and diasporic clienteles with vigor' (Appadurai, 1996: 22), and the elites' sense of belonging may be as much with people of similar life style in other global capitals as with the fellow members of the nation-state (Castells, 1996; Bauman, 2000). For them, Ulf Hannerz remarks, 'the big question would be, what can your nation do for you that a good credit card cannot do?' (2005: 215).

However, it would seem that at this moment, the nation still has a number of tasks. The 'sovereign state strategy' (Garland, 2001) also appears to be relevant for controlling the 'darker sides of globalization' (Colin Powel in Urry, 2002a: 57), and providing protection from the threatening and undesirable mobilities. We have been witnessing a renewed exhibition of the State's muscle power through the 'war on terror', visible in the intensification of border controls, and the expansion of state surveillance and bureaucracy. The 'seemingly irrefutable tenets of neoliberalism—that economics will supersede politics, that the role of the state will diminish—lose their force in a world of global risks' (Beck, 2002: 47). Regulating the various forms of transnational mobilities is becoming one of the vital tasks of contemporary governance. Furthermore, as Loader and Sparks observe, it is precisely in times of global transformations 'that people's *sense of place*—and of *differences* between 'here/there', 'inside/outside', 'us/them'—takes on renewed force as a structuring feature of social relations and culture' (2002: 104, emphases in original). The longing 'for a lost (if mythical) world of secure and settled identities' (Morley, 2000: 152) seems to be at the forefront of contemporary, particularly European, political and media debates, and the role of the national is therefore far from eclipsed by transnational connections and solidarities. Globalization is far from being a singular development leading to an integrated world system, even though it may appear so at times, and one needs to keep in mind not only the intensity of the transnational connections, but also the disconnections, the paradoxes, concrete modalities and resistance.

At the same time, transnational connections crucially transform governance of what was previously designed as nation-state's 'internal' security. Policing thus in important ways moves to the transnational stage (Mawby, 1999; Sheptycki, 2000, 2002; Deflem, 2002), and Findlay even suggests that, in cases such as terrorism, the 'state as the definer of crime and the monopolist of punishment gives way to global declarations of collective (cultural) deviance' (2003: 236). Similarly, we are witnessing a development towards globalized legal and control systems with increasingly diluted ties to state institutions (Mathiesen, 2005). Looking at the role of the national and the nation-state, we are faced with complex developments that defy clear categorizations.

'Defending our way of life'

Mobility has been, inevitably, connected to insecurity. The issue was already deeply acknowledged by the Chicago school, who 'believed that modern mobilities could be disorienting, as well as destructive of locally based social control' (Valier, 2003: 5). The immigrant and the asylum seeker represent the classical examples of Simmel's figure of the stranger, marking and accentuating the 'us' and 'them' divisions within the society and serving to crystallize the symbolic and cultural limits of community (Bauman, 2000; Melossi, 2003; Valier, 2003; Hughes, 2006). The discourse about the 'deviant immigrant' plays a central role in political and media debates in most western countries: '[T]he otherness of the stranger and the otherness of the deviant are collapsed in the social portrayal of the criminal immigrant' (Melossi, 2003: 376).

However, punishment of immigrant crime (and the debates surrounding it) seems to perform not only the classical Durkheimian function of strengthening social bonds and social solidarity. It also functions as a sort of 'purifying filter' protecting the local and the national from threatening foreign elements. The law and order discourse is thus intertwined with demands for the reinstatement of the nation-state with clear assumptions about national identity and strong cultural and moral boundaries. The drawing of moral boundaries, a traditional concern of criminal law, is today performed not only through punishment, but also through practices of banishment and expulsion. The classical model of the panopticon and its disciplinary control is, as Bigo (2006) suggests, gradually being reframed as a ban-opticon. The discourse about the deviant immigrant therefore needs to be situated within a broader context of the growing global divisions and insecurities. The deviant immigrant represents the polluting element, the quintessential Other, which accompanies global transformations.[3] According to Bourdieu (1999), the opposition between 'natives' and 'immigrants' is gradually obscuring traditional class divisions within societies. The inequalities produced by the neoliberal economic order are translated into political struggles about 'who has the right to claim all the advantages attached to membership in the national community' (Bourdieu, 1999: 188).

Wacquant goes as far as asking whether today we are witnessing a parallel development in Europe as we have seen in the United States in the past three decades with the explosive growth of black and Latino prison populations: '[f]rom this point of view, foreigners and quasi-foreigners would be "the blacks" of Europe' (1999: 216; see also Albrecht, 2000). The recent images of the burning French *banlieues* clearly bear a resemblance to the 1992 Los Angeles riots, ignited by a similar combustive mixture of controversial police action and pervasive racialized social exclusion. Foreign nationals and ethnic minority members constitute a growing proportion of the swelling prison populations across Europe and account for much of the European prison population surge since the 1990s (Albrecht, 2000; Melossi, 2003). To that, add a wide net of detention centres for asylum seekers, 'waiting areas' and the like, to get a clearer picture of the growing 'carceral archipelago' of foreign populations. Although legally detention is only an administrative measure, its application often takes on characteristics of de facto penal incarceration, resulting in physical and mental health problems for the detainees (Weber, 2002).

The discourse about refugees and asylum seekers can be situated within the context of Garland's often cited 'criminology of the other' (Welch and Schuster, 2005; Hughes, 2006). The media portrayals of asylum seekers as 'bogus', 'fraudulent', 'benefit scroungers' are further compounded by the heightened security concerns in the post-9/11 world (Welch and Schuster,

2005). The diffuse and exterritorial nature of the terrorist threat brings up allusions to an 'enemy within' or a 'fifth column', thus creating innumerable points of insecurity and suspicion of foreign populations. Immigration and asylum have therefore become issues defined as matters of justice and domestic security and we have been witnessing a simultaneous 'securization' and 'criminalization' of migration (Hughes, 2006). Asylum seekers have in many aspects become populations one needs to be protected *from*, rather than people who need protection.

Asylum takes up a number of central criminological concerns such as the relationship between liberty and security, construction of moral panics, the negative effects of imprisonments and the role of private security firms such as Group 4 Securicor and Wakenhut in running detention facilities. However, despite the fact that there is a growing body of research addressing the issues of asylum and criminalization, one could hardly claim that the issue has reached the criminological mainstream (Weber, 2002; Hughes, 2006). Mainstream criminology remains preoccupied with 'outsiders' who, at the same time, in many ways still are the 'insiders' of the privileged club of western citizens. If we live in 'fortress continents' whose borders are heavily militarized, and almost daily claim human lives, we seldom seem to be aware of the fact that the objects of our research—often referred to as the 'British society', 'American society', the EU, etc.—are results of intense and strict social control and exclusion.

The current preoccupation with the protection of borders is an intrinsic aspect of the present, deeply stratified global condition. Borders establish the limits of community by selecting those who are allowed to enter and those who are to remain outside. The defence of the border, on the practical and on the symbolic level, is conducted through what Simon (1997) terms 'governance through crime' (Walters, 2004; Aas, 2005a). For example, the morally charged discourse about 'sexual slavery' seeks to establish distinctions between 'innocent' and 'guilty' migrants, and therefore, while protecting the former, also aims to justify stricter controls of the latter (Chapkis, 2005). The discourses about terrorism, about honour killings and unscrupulous trafficking networks, play a central role in everyday police work, as well as, on the broader level, in the resurgence of the politics of xenophobia and the renewed debates about the fate of multiculturalism. Melossi therefore suggests that the 'deviant immigrant' plays a role of a 'suitable enemy' (Christie, 1986), and thereby serves as 'a vehicle for intra-European debate about the existence, nature and essential characteristics of a European identity' (Melossi, 2003: 376).

Similarly, Hudson sees the terrorist as a paradigmatic image of the 'monstrous other', whose 'grievance warrants no explanation; he or she is pre sumed immune to normal human emotions such as compassion, and is oblivious to such reasonable objections as the innocence of victims' (2003: 204). One could also suggest that, in the figure of the terrorist, Garland's 'criminology of the dangerous other' meets Said's (1978/1985) 'Oriental other'—a mirror image of the West and a prototype of all that is inferior, irrational and alien. The 'monstrous others' challenge the limits of the traditional, liberal and communitarian, notions of justice (Hudson, 2003). Contemporary societies face the challenge of 'dealing with people who are so different that they really do seem to be beyond inclusion in the liberal community' (Hudson, 2003: 204). One of the vital challenges of criminal justice today is therefore 'to find ways of doing justice to these "outsiders" as well as readmitting some of these we presently classify as outsiders to the status of insiders' (Hudson, 2003: 204).

Tony Blair's statement, in the aftermath of the London 7 July attacks, about 'the determination to defend our values and our way of life',[4] clearly expresses not only the wish to 'defend the sanctity of home' (Walters, 2004), but also the view of the enemy as the cultural other (Johnson, 2002). However, the notion of 'defending our way of life' obtains a somewhat incongruous meaning in the time of 'liquid modernity'. What constitutes a society and a community is changing and sometimes unclear. The notions of home, 'home territories' and 'imagined communities', to borrow Benedict Anderson's popular term, become increasingly destabilized (Appadurai, 1996; Morley, 2000; Papastergiadis, 2000). Where is 'home' for immigrants, building large houses in their countries of origin, yet almost never living in them (Morley, 2000)? Similarly, one can wonder where the home of the British 'home-grown terrorist' is? The extraterritoriality of contemporary technologies and cultural transfers puts into question a number of presuppositions about life and where it is lived. In the space of flows, physical reality may be just one of the 'windows' we have opened at a particular point in life while other windows may be open to our cyber lives or satellite-mediated realities. Globalization, and the various mobilities traversing national boundaries, disrupt before seemingly stable notions of culture and national identity (Appadurai, 1996). Ferrell et al. therefore conclude that 'neither criminality nor the cultures that construct it can any longer be conceptualized as phenomena contained within the legal borders of the nation state' (2005: 7). The destabilizing tendencies of contemporary (physical and imaginary) mobilities force us to abandon even the last attempts at holding essentialist notions of culture and cultural identity.

Not surprisingly, for many groups, global transformations in the forms of migration, cultural hybridity and neoliberal ideology, are seen to be threatening the integrity of their local communities and the survival of their cultural traditions. Consequently, we are seeing a revival of ethnicity through 'the attempt to restore strong, closed definitions of what constitutes a culture' (Hall, 1995: 200). Essentialism, present in the depictions of the 'deviant immigrant', is according to Young, a 'response to the precariousness of identity which is in itself fragile' (1999: 163). The figure of the immigrant stranger gains particular salience precisely in a society permeated by the fluidity of social bonds. The revival of cultural essentialism has been, according to Hall (1995), one of the surprising responses to global transformations in a variety of cultural settings across the world; in what are usually thought of as both modern and traditional societies. Obvious examples are the revival of nationalism, the resurgence of racist and neo-fascist violence across Europe as well as the massive resistance to migration. Furthermore, the rise of religious fundamentalism is marked by an equally exclusive definition of 'culture', in this case with the focus on religion, rather than on race and ethnicity (Hall, 1995). In this perspective, some observers have argued that religious fundamentalism can be seen as a form of cultural essentialism emerging as a reaction and a contradiction to the colonizing nature of global flows (Castells, 1996).

Controlling the mobile subject

Contemporary mobilities represent an enormous challenge for the state apparatuses trying to control them. The speed and distance of communication and movement, and their exterritorial and elusive nature, make them both difficult to spatialize, and impossible to build a wall around (Bauman, 2002). Morley thus notes the absurdity and the symbolism, in the case of Albania, where the Hoxha regime installed hundreds of thousands of concrete bunkers 'to defend the country against invasion by its foreign enemies, and the concave satellite dishes through which foreign culture invaded Albanian airwaves' (2000: 155). The informational and mediated nature of social relations transcends the old notions of panopticon as the paradigmatic image of modern social control (Bauman, 2000; Aas, 2005b; Bigo, 2006).

In his observations on 11 September, Bauman sees the fallen Manhattan towers as a potent symbolic reminder of the end of the 'era of space' and the annihilation of the protective capacity of space, where 'no one can hide from blows, and nowhere is so far away that blows cannot be plotted and delivered from that distance' (2002: 88). Power is therefore about speed, lightness and distance, which is true both for the global elites as well as those trying to resist them, such as anti-globalization protesters and terror networks (Urry, 2002a: 60). In the world of global media and information flows, 'the camera may be the most effective weapon with which to retaliate, bring violence of an extraordinary intensity into the living rooms of global audiences' (Ferrell et al., 2005: 8). As in the case of Albania, also today, protecting the homeland from the 'preachers of hate' (to borrow Tony Blair's expression) by building walls, by expulsion and protection of physical borders, may be futile in light of the extraterritorial flows of information, ideas and images. And as much as radical Muslim identities are described as primitive and uncivilized within the various 'clash of civilizations' theses, they are sustained by distinctly global networks of communications (Internet, mobile phones, global television networks, etc.) and patterns of living (immigrant diasporas and global travel).[5] In the era of time–space compression, 'safe' and the 'wild zones' are highly proximate, only a plane-ride or an Internet connection apart (Urry, 2002a: 63). The highly publicized threat of the deviant immigrant serves as a constant and potent reminder that 'the domestic populations and ways of life of Western nations in the "zones of prosperity" are no longer effectively sealed off from contemporary global disorders' (Hogg, 2002: 200).

It was argued—optimistically—particularly before the present hype of 'the war on terror', that the globalizing process would eventually lead to a borderless world. The rise of the so-called 'fortress continents', as Europe, Australia and North America have been called (Klein, 2003), might therefore seem strangely at odds with the spirit of transnational flows of capital, goods and information. Yet, border controls became stricter even before the paradigmatic shifts of 9/11. The list of countries requiring a visa to enter the EU, the so-called 'black list', expanded from 70 in 1985 to over 126 in 1995 (Bigo and Guild, 2004). The militarization of the border represents an intrinsic aspect of the globalizing condition (Bauman, 1998). Freedom of movement is available only to a relatively small number of highly privileged individuals, while others are doomed to various forms of clandestine and imaginary travel. Consequently, clandestine migration has risen as third world migrants are forced to choose other, more dangerous routes. While the fall of the Berlin Wall once appeared to be the defining moment of a new, 'free' world, it clearly no longer captures the spirit of the day; new, expensive and technologically advanced walls are being erected across the western world (Aas, 2005a). Within western states, curbing immigration and protecting the border from a perceived flood of foreign populations have become important measures of symbolic politics. The emerging strategies for defending the border constitute, according to Walters, a new type of governance and politics—'domopolitics'—'a will to domesticate the forces which threaten the sanctity of home' (2004: 242). Like being tough on crime, defending the border and protecting the nation from a contamination by foreign elements also carries an enormous political and symbolic capital.

An essential part of the globalizing condition is precisely the creation of mechanism for distinguishing between 'good' and 'bad' mobilities, between what Bauman (1998) terms tourists and vagabonds. Contemporary governments seem to be caught between two contradicting impulses: on the one hand, the urge towards increasing securitization of borders, and on the other hand, the awareness of the importance of global flows for sustaining the present world economic order (Aas, 2005a). Borders have the function of a membrane, which allows the flows to get through, but keeps the unwanted 'residue' out. The passport, the nation-state's traditional instrument for controlling mobile identities, has gained a renewed salience as an instrument of social control and exclusion (Adey, 2004; Lyon, 2005). As a result of new global threats, the quest to control the mobile subject and fix him/her with a stable identity has resulted in a series of new technologies, such as machine-readable and biometric passports, biometric visas, residence permits and ID cards, and various information systems such as Schengen and US-VISIT program (Mathiesen, 2003; Zureik and Salter, 2005). Lyon (2005) points out that the practices of identifying the 'other' have proliferated and have been built into a number of automated bureaucratic systems—'the border is everywhere'. Furthermore, airports—the symbol of contemporary mobility—are becoming an intensified focus of contemporary security strategies, and an important locus for screening out the 'treacherous' traveller (Adey, 2004; Curry, 2004).

Vastly stratified patterns of mobility mirror the immense inequalities of the global order. The slogan, 'Wherever it takes you, the future takes VISA', painfully juxtaposes with images of desperate African migrants trying to climb the wired fences of Ceuta and Melilla, and images of dead bodies on the shores of Southern Europe or in the Mexican desert. The globalizing condition divides the world into those who are constantly on the move, and those who are locally tied and for whom 'the world is moving by' (Bauman, 1998: 89). Nowhere was this more visible than in the recent disastrous ravaging of Hurricane Katrina. Left in the flooded New Orleans were those who were socially most marginalized, and therefore, *unable to move*. The helicopter, elites' preferred mode of transport, is not only a status symbol, but also a ticket to safety from urban chaos and natural disasters (Johnston and Shearing, 2003). Controlling and securing mobility becomes an integral part of city life, and 'fortress continents' are replicated, in a number of countries and global cities, in the form of gated communities, which guard their borders from strangers with similar fervour and technological savvy as affluent states do (Blakely and Snyder, 1997; Johnston and Shearing, 2003).

The globalizing condition is full of paradoxes 'in the way it unifies and delineates, internationalizes and localizes' (Findlay, 2003: 235). While the demise of the old Soviet bloc and colonial laws removed restrictions of movement in numerous developing countries (Findlay, 2003: 235), new mechanisms for regulating mobility across the world grow. In spite of the proclaimed salience of the 'space of flows', space continues to matter. Restriction of movement becomes a central mechanism of social stratification and exclusion and '[e]nforced localization guards the natural selectivity of the globalizing effects' (Bauman, 1998: 93). However, one does not need prisons to be, or feel, incarcerated in the locality. Electronic monitoring and satellite tracking are some of the new modes of 'punishment in the community', centred on control of movement and spatial exclusion (Nellis, 2005). Furthermore, the inability to move can be a result not only of technological surveillance, permits and passes, security checkpoints and border controls, but also a result of public transport prices and public transport design, city planning and residential segregation. One can also feel 'incarcerated' in the local community, like the residents of the French *banlieues*, for whom the centre of Paris may feel as far as Mauritius for the privileged residents of the city (Morley, 2000).

The local takes on a variety of meanings, which cannot be addressed in detail in this article. It can be seen as a site of optimistic potential for new forms of sociality built on what might be called 'globalization from below', where a multi-ethnic, multi-cultural reality becomes the normal form of the local (Hall, 2006). However, while bearing a great potential for empowerment and democracy, as well as protection from the world of speed, the local is also marked by marginalization due to its exclusion from the world of global flows, and therefore, power. The stress on local self-reliance in some governmental strategies may be a denial of state responsibility for these areas. Amin, for example, argues for the need to challenge the perception of some disadvantaged places as deserving 'only local community while other are allowed to enjoy cosmopolitan society' (2005: 630).

The 'tourist gaze'

The figure of the tourist rarely finds its way into a criminological text, yet it can be seen as a prime metaphor for the contemporary mobile subject (Bauman in Franklin, 2003). The 'looseness of attachment—being *in* but not *of* the place—makes tourism a well-aimed and pertinent metaphor for contemporary life' (Bauman in Franklin, 2003: 208, emphases in original). Drawing on Foucault's concept of the gaze, Urry (2002b) develops the notion of the 'tourist gaze'. Aided by guidebooks, cameras and various other practices, the tourist gaze is a certain way of relating to places, which affects not only the tourists themselves, but also the places that are its object, and their economies. The criminological significance of the 'tourist gaze' is yet to be properly established. However, the desire of the tourist to escape the dreary routines of everyday life and seek the 'four Ss'—sun, sand, sea and sex—has had a profound impact on the growth of sex tourism, or so-called 'prostiturismo', across the globe (Cohen and Kennedy, 2000: 218; Altman, 2001). And although travel has a long history of being associated with a quest for sexual experience with 'exotic Others', today, commercial sex and sexual entertainment have become regular features of numerous tourist destinations all over the world (Davidson, 2005: 124).

Tourist flows carry important implications for the governance of security at the places of their destination. Some of the recent, highly publicized, terrorist attacks can be seen as symbolically targeting the contemporary mobile subject, by attacking tourist destinations (Egypt, Bali, Turkey), public transport systems (Madrid, London) and centres of the 'footloose economy' (World Trade Center in New York). Egypt established its 'tourist police' force in 1997, after the tragic and economically devastating massacre of 60 tourists at the Hatsheptsut temple in Luxor. Similarly, the Olympic Games have been turned into megalomaniac media and tourist events, supported by an extensive security infrastructure.[6] Security is of vital importance since it is those states, companies and destinations with the most powerful 'commercial brands' that have 'most to lose if they cannot guarantee the safety of their own citizens, companies or visitors' (Urry, 2002a: 66).

Creating sanitized environments, free of unwanted risks, can be seen as one of the steps necessary to please the tourist gaze. Striking 'the right balance between security of the familiar and the adventure of the strange' (Bauman in Franklin, 2003: 213) is a project wrought with difficulties and contradictions. The results are often tourist enclaves of themed environments with 'staged authenticity', geared towards entertainment and consumption (Urry, 2002b). Tourism increasingly shapes contemporary landscapes, exemplified best by the so-called 'nowherevilles' such as Holiday Inns, shopping malls, airports and Disneylands, designed to provide reassuring familiarity for the global traveller anywhere in the world (Bauman in Franklin, 2003). This adjusting of our environments to the sensibilities of the tourist gaze has been described as part of a broader trend towards 'disneyization of society' (Bryman, 2004) and de-territorialization of culture. However, the tourist also subverts traditional notions of the 'other'. Despite being 'outsiders' in terms of membership of the nation-state, tourists clearly enjoy the protection of numerous security strategies due to their power as consumers. Not only are contemporary societies making themselves 'authentic', they are also making themselves secure, for the benefit of the tourist. The position of the tourist can be contrasted with that of some other groups of global nomads—third world migrants, asylum seekers, political dissidents, etc.—who due to their lack of purchasing power clearly cannot claim any such protections.

The figures of the 'immigrant other' and the tourist reveal a new dynamics of social belonging and exclusion emerging at an intersection between the global and the local, which in many ways defies traditional categorizations. The examples of gated communities, fortress continents, tourist enclaves and the like, reveal that the retreat into the locality may be not only a destiny to which some are 'doomed', but also a choice, a form of escapism of the affluent (Bauman, 1998). Diken and Laustsen (2005) go as far as suggesting that gated communities and tourist enclaves bear an essential similarity to refugee camps, Guantanamo Bay and favelas, as they all represent a new cultural *logic of exception* (from the 'normal' and the 'social'). An important task for criminological inquiry may therefore be to explore further the implications of living in a society, in which exception is increasingly becoming the rule (Diken and Laustsen, 2005: 6), for the nature of law, state sovereignty and governance.

Conclusion

Throughout most of its history, criminology has 'assumed the Hobbesian conception of political community: of sovereign states securing within their own borders the conditions of domestic peace by monopolising the means of internal violence' (Hogg, 2002: 212). Issues of law, justice, community, safety, social justice, etc. have been implicitly built on the notion of a bounded territory and state sovereignty. Global flows, networks and mobilities, discussed in this article, disrupt this seemingly organized and state-centred system. They bring into question the centrality of the nation-state—a theme which by no means is a stranger to criminology. There exists a large body of criminological research about governance of crime and security which is transcending the static notions of nation-states and nation-state societies: from the various Foucauldian accounts of the dispersal of governance and security (Rose, 1999; Garland, 2001; Johnston and Shearing, 2003), to the communitarian critiques of the state-centred criminal justice (Christie, 2004), and the accounts about transnationalization of crime and crime control strategies (Sheptycki, 2000, 2002; Newburn and Sparks, 2004; Mathiesen, 2005), to name just a few. These perspectives also clearly have much to offer when analysing the contemporary dynamics of global risks.

None the less, and in spite of the increasingly international habitus of criminal justice practitioners and academics (Chan, 2005), a considerable part of criminological research still seems to be in many ways guilty of what Beck (2002) terms '*methodological nationalism*'—equating social boundaries with state boundaries, and having a nation-state outlook on society, law and justice. This may be partly due to the traditional connection between criminological knowledge and the nation-state apparatus (Foucault, 1977; Christie, 1997). Consequently, criminology seems to be, theoretically and methodologically, somewhat ill-equipped for analysing and researching the relevance of the emerging 'space of flows'. There is therefore a need to develop concepts and methodologies that are sensitive to the complexities of the global. As Law and Urry point out, method 'needs to be sensitive to the complex and the elusive. It needs to be more mobile. It needs to find ways of knowing the slipperiness of "units that are not" as they move in and beyond old categories' (2004: 403–4).

How are we to address appropriately phenomena such as police ICT networks, cyber crime, smuggling and trafficking, which by their nature call for a global, rather than simply a comparative inter-*national* standpoint? Taking my own research about border controls as an example, I was faced with a similar difficulty. How does one grapple, empirically, with the concept of a 'border', when a border is no longer simply a 'wall' around a nation-state territory, but rather a distributed network of myriad checkpoints, technologies and actors, which can be situated inside or outside a given state territory (Aas, 2005a)? The transnational and the distributed is by its nature elusive and harder to grasp, thus making the spatialized and the local(ly marginalized) a seemingly easier object of enquiry.

As boundaries between the inside and the outside become blurred, as it becomes difficult to distinguish between inter-state and intra-state conflicts, it is less clear than ever what is to be the subject and scope of criminological research and discourse. Ruggiero (2005: 240), for example, notes that war has miraculously escaped the attention of conventional criminology.[7] The omission gains particular importance in light of the recent claims about 'asymetric warfare' where '[c]onventional resolutions of global conflict such as war state-against-state have been replaced ... by crime as warfare, and warfare as crime control' (Findlay, 2003: 234). Morrison (2005) furthermore argues that criminological texts are foremost meant as conversations within a particular community, where terms such as 'contemporary society', 'modern crime control' and 'late-modern society' automatically refer to a small group of western (primarily US and UK) audiences (see also Agozino, 2003). Crimes committed outside these bounded nation-state territories, although enormous by comparison, tend not to penetrate the criminological discourse (Morrison, 2006). A vital question is therefore whether we can continue to limit our research to the phenomena that are allowed to penetrate the heavily guarded boundaries (physical and virtual) of the western states?

If criminological inquiry is not only descriptive, but also constitutive of the phenomena it addresses, then a question can be asked about the political implication of such choice of research phenomena. Beck, for example, points out that 'fragmentation of the world into nation-states removes accountability for global inequalities' (2003: 50). Paraphrasing Cohen (2001), nation-states are to that extent also 'states of denial' about the enormous social inequalities and suffering on the global scale. Similarly, Law and Urry suggest that the choice of object and method of social enquiry are questions of 'ontological politics':

> [T]o the extent social science conceals its performativity from itself it is pretending to an innocence that it cannot have. And to the extent that it enacts methods that look for or assume certain structural stabilities, it enacts those stabilities while interfering with other realities mentioned above.
>
> (2004: 404)

The global perspective may open our eyes for a variety of actors and activities that tend to be neglected by traditional criminology such as, for example, detention centres for illegal immigrants (Weber, 2002). Although in many cases de facto prisons, these institutions tend to be overlooked in most penological studies, partly due to the unclear legal status of their inmates and access difficulties.

The point here is that sharp distinctions between the domestic and the international matters are in themselves becoming a major source of injustice. An important dilemma for critical criminology is therefore whether, in the face of global transformations, to defend the embattled territorial nation-state, or whether to transcend the nation-state order and to include in its repertoire of outsider also the 'global others'. The question of framing and boundary setting is of crucial importance as it can exclude large groups of individuals from participating in a political community and designate them as non-persons with respect to justice. If we are to grasp, and challenge, the major sources of social injustice today, we need to move beyond the state-territorial principle (Benhabib, 2004; Fraser, 2005; Morrison, 2006). When the major sources of injustice belong to the 'space of flows', 'they cannot be made answerable to claims of justice that are framed in terms of the state- territorial principle' (Fraser, 2005: 81). This should apply to a variety of issues, many of which tend to be mentioned as criminological blind spots, such as the global criminal economy, corporate crime, state crime, corruption, environmental crime, as well as the so-called 'secret renditions' and the use of torture in the war on terror, cyber crime and genocide, to name just a few. The global has already emerged as a facilitator of new forms of empowerment and resistance in several issues, such as the global anti-domestic violence campaigns, anti-death penalty activism, international human rights discourse, etc. It therefore remains to be seen whether the heavily guarded boundaries of the 'fortress continents' are to be the boundaries of criminological imagination.

Notes

I would like to thank N. Christie, H.O. Gundhus, C. Høigård, H.M. Lomell, T. Mathiesesn, L. Scherdin, W. Morrison and the editors and referees for their valuable comments.

1. About half of world migrants are women, often living and working in conditions of what is sometimes described as 'modern day slavery' (as nannies, maids, sex workers, 'imported' wives, etc.), concealed from public view and vulnerable to exploitation. This 'female underside of globalization' has also profound effects on the migrants' local communities through the enormous 'care drain', affecting particularly the children of female migrants (Ehrenreich and Hochschild, 2003).
2. See, for example, Findlay (1999); Loader and Sparks (2002); Mathiesen (2003); Baker and Roberts (2005); Chan (2005); Muncie (2005); Morrison (2006).
3. As the British ex-prime minister Mrs Thatcher once bluntly put it, 'we joined Europe to have free movement of goods ... I did not join Europe to have free movement of terrorists, criminals, drugs, plant and animal diseases and rabies and illegal immigrants' (cited in Morley, 2000: 226).
4. Source: http://news.bbc.co.uk/1/hi/uk/4659953.stm
5. Al-Qaida has been described as 'McDonald's of terrorism' (Murdoch, 2004)—being a 'global brand', using the media to its advantage and assuming a franchise form not unlike the ones used in the contemporary business world.
6. Securing the Olympics in the post-9/11 world is certainly not inexpensive. The cost of the latest Olympics in Greece rose to over $1.2 billion, more than three times the amount spent in Sidney in 2000. Source: www.economist.com/agenda/displayStory.cfm?story_id=3082670
7. However, see McLaughlin (2001) and Jamieson (2003).

References

Aas, K.F. (2005a) '"Getting Ahead of the Game": Border Technologies and the Changing Space of Governance', in E. Zureik and M. Salter (eds) *Global Surveillance and Policing: Borders, Security, Identity*, pp. 194–214. Cullompton: Willan Publishing.

Aas, K.F. (2005b) *Sentencing in the Age of Information: From Faust to Macintosh*. London: Glasshouse Press.

Adey, P. (2004) 'Secure and Sorted Mobilities: Examples from the Airport', *Surveillance and Society* 1(4): 500–19.

Agozino, B. (2003) *Counter-Colonial Criminology: A Critique of Imperialist Reason*. London: Pluto Press.

Albrecht, H.-J. (2000) 'Foreigners, Migration, Immigration and the Development of Criminal Justice in Europe', in P. Green and A. Rutherford (eds) *Criminal Policy in Transition*, pp. 131–50. Oxford, Portland, OR: Hart Publishing.

Altman, D. (2001) *Global Sex*. Chicago, IL & London: University of Chicago Press.
Amin, A. (2005) 'Local Community on Trial', *Economy and Society* 34(4): 612–33.
Appadurai, A. (1996) *Modernity at Large: Cultural Dimensions of Globalization*. Minneapolis, MN: University of Minneapolis Press.
Baker, E. and J. Roberts (2005) 'Globalization and the New Punitiveness', in J. Pratt, D. Brown, M. Brown, S. Hallsworth and W. Morrison (eds) *The New Punitiveness: Trends, Theories, Perspectives*, pp. 121–38. Cullompton: Willan Publishing.
Bauman, Z. (1998) *Globalization: The Human Consequences*. Cambridge, UK: Polity Press.
Bauman, Z. (2000) *Liquid Modernity*. Cambridge, UK: Polity Press.
Bauman, Z. (2002) *Society under Siege*. Cambridge, UK: Polity.
Beck, U. (2002) 'The Terrorist Threat: World Risk Society Revisited', *Theory, Culture and Society* 19(4): 39–55.
Beck, U. (2003) 'The Analysis of Global Inequality: From National to Cosmopolitan Perspective', in M. Kaldor, H. Anheier and M. Glasius (eds) *Global Civil Society*, pp. 45–55. London: The Centre for the Study of Global Governance, Yearbook 2003.
Benhabib, S. (2004) *The Rights of Others: Aliens, Residents and Citizens*. Cambridge: Cambridge University Press.
Bigo, D. (2006) 'Security, Exception, Ban and Surveillance', in D. Lyon (ed.) *Theorizing Surveillance: The Panopticon and Beyond*, pp. 46–68. Cullompton: Willan Publishing.
Bigo, D. and E. Guild (2004) 'Distancering af de Fremmede—Logikken i Schengenvisumet', *Tidsskriftet Politikk* 7(3): 23–33.
Blakely, E.J. and M.G. Snyder (1997) *Fortress America: Gated Communities in the United States*. Washington, DC: Brookings Institution Press.
Bourdieu, P. (1999) 'The Abdication of the State', in P. Bourdieu et al. (eds) *The Weight of the World: Social Suffering in Contemporary Society*, pp. 181–8. Cambridge: Polity Press.
Bryman, A. (2004) *The Disneyization of Society*. London, Thousand Oaks, CA & New Delhi: Sage.
Castells, M. (1996) *The Rise of the Network Society*. Oxford: Blackwell Publishers.
Chan, J. (2005) 'Globalisation, Reflexivity and the Practice of Criminology', in J. Sheptycki and A. Wardak (eds) *Transnational and Comparative Criminology*, pp. 337–55. London: Glasshouse Press.
Chapkis, V.W. (2005) 'Soft Glove, Punishing Fist: The Trafficking Victims Protection Act of 2000', in E. Bernstein and L. Schaffner (eds) *Regulating Sex: The Politics of Intimacy and Identity*, pp. 51–66. New York & London: Routledge.
Christie, N. (1986) 'Suitable Enemy', in H. Bianchi and R. van Swaaningen (eds) *Abolitionism: Toward a Non-Repressive Approach to Crime*, pp. 42–54. Amsterdam: Free University Press.
Christie, N. (1997) 'Four Blocks against Insight: Notes on the Oversocialization of Criminologists', *Theoretical Criminology* 1(1): 13–24.

Christie, N. (2004) *A Suitable Amount of Crime*. London: Routledge.

Cohen, R. and P. Kennedy (2000) *Global Sociology*. New York: Palgrave Macmillan.

Cohen, S. (2001) *Folk Devils and Moral Panics: The Creation of the Mods and Rockers*. London: Routledge.

Cunnen, C. and J. Stubbs (2005) 'Cultural Criminology and Engagement with Race, Gender, and Post-colonial Identities', in J. Ferrell, K. Hayward, W. Morrison and M. Presdee (eds) *Cultural Criminology Unleashed*, pp. 97–108. London: Glasshouse Press.

Curry, M. (2004) 'The Profiler's Question and the Treacherous Traveler: Narratives of Belonging in Commercial Aviation', *Surveillance and Society* 1(4): 475–99.

Davidson, J. O'Connell (2005) *Children in the Global Sex Trade*. Cambridge: Polity.

Diken, B. and C.B. Laustsen (2005) *The Culture of Exception: Sociology Facing the Camp*. London & New York. Routledge.

Ehrenreich, B. and A.R. Hochschild (2003) *Global Woman: Nannies, Maids, and Sex Workers in the New Economy*. London: Granta Books.

Ferrell, J., C. Greer and Y. Jewkes (2005) 'Hip Hop Graffiti, Mexican Murals and the War on Terror', *Crime Media Culture* 1(1): 5–9.

Findlay, M. (1999) *The Globalization of Crime*. Cambridge: Cambridge University Press.

Findlay, M. (2003) 'Crime, Terror and Transitional Cultures in a Contracting Globe', in C. Dauvergne (ed.) *Jurisprudence for an Interconnected Globe*, pp. 231–48. Aldershot: Ashgate.

Foucault, M. (1977) *Discipline and Punish: The Birth of the Prison*. New York: Vintage Books.

Franklin, A. (2003) 'The Tourist Syndrome: An Interview with Zygmunt Bauman', *Tourist Studies* 3(2): 205–17.

Fraser, N. (2005) 'Reframing Justice in a Globalizing World', *New Left Review* (November–December): 69–88.

Garland, D. (2001) *The Culture of Control*. Oxford: Oxford University Press.

Giddens, A. (1990) *The Consequences of Modernity*. Cambridge: Polity.

Hall, S. (1995) 'New Cultures for Old', in D. Massey and P. Jess (eds) *A Place in the World? Places, Cultures and Globalization*, pp. 175–239. Milton Keynes: The Open University Press

Hall, S. (2006) 'Cosmopolitan Promises, Multicultural Realities', in R. Scholar (ed.) *Divided Cities*, pp. 20–51. Oxford: Oxford University Press.

Hannerz, U. (2005) 'The Withering Away of the Nation?', in B. Mazkish and A. Iriye (eds) *The Global History Reader*, pp. 209–20. New York & London: Routledge.

Harvey, D. (1989) *The Condition of Postmodernity*. Oxford: Blackwell.

Hogg, R. (2002) 'Criminology beyond the Nation State: Global Conflict, Human Rights and the "New World Disorder"', in K. Carrington and R. Hogg (eds) *Critical Criminology: Issues, Debates, Challenges*, pp. 185–217. Cullompton: Willan Publishing.

Hudson, B. (2003) *Justice in the Risk Society*. London: Sage.

Hughes, G. (2006) *The Politics of Crime and Community*. Basingstoke: Palgrave Macmillan.

Inda, J.X. and R. Rosaldo (2002) 'Introduction: A World in Motion', in J.X. Inda and R. Rosaldo (eds) *The Anthropology of Globalization: A Reader*, pp. 1–34. Oxford: Blackwell.

Jamieson, R. (ed.) (2003) 'War, Crime and Human Rights', Special Issue of *Theoretical Criminology* 7(3).

Johnson, R. (2002) 'Defending Ways of Life: The (Anti-)Terrorist Rhetorics of Bush and Blair', *Theory, Culture and Society* 19(4): 211–31.

Johnston, L. and C. Shearing (2003) *Governing Security: Explorations in Policing and Justice*. London & New York: Routledge.

Klein, N. (2003) 'Fotress Continents: The US and Europe Are Both Creating Multi-Tiered Regional Strongholds', *Guardian*, 16 January. Available at http://www.guardian.co.uk/usa/story/0,12271,875703,00.html

Lash, S. and J. Urry (1994) *Economies of Signs and Space*. London: Sage.

Law, J. and J. Urry (2004) 'Enacting the Social', *Economy and Society* 33(3): 340–410.

Loader, I. and R. Sparks (2002) 'Contemporary Landscapes of Crime, Order and Control', in M. Maguire, R. Morgan and R. Reiner (eds) *The Oxford Handbook of Criminology*, pp. 83–111. Oxford: Oxford University Press.

Lyon, D. (2005) 'The Border Is Everywhere: ID Cards, Surveillance and the Other', in E. Zureik and M. Salter (eds) *Global Surveillance and Policing: Borders, Security, Identity*, pp. 66–82. Cullompton: Willan Publishing.

McLaughlin, E. (2001) 'Political Violence, Terrorism and States of Fear', in J. Muncie and E. McLaughlin (eds) *The Problem of Crime*, 2nd edn, pp. 283–330. London: Sage.

Mathiesen, T. (2003) 'The Rise of the Surveillant State in Times of Globalisation', in C. Sumner (ed.) *The Blackwell Companion to Criminology*, pp. 437–51. Maiden, Oxford, Victoria & Berlin: Blackwell Publishing.

Mathiesen, T. (2005) '"Lex Vigilatoria"—Towards a Control System without a State?', in The European Civil Liberties Network *Essays for Civil Liberties and Democratic Standards in Europe*. Available at http://www.ecln.org/essays.html

Mawby, R.I. (ed.) (1999) *Policing across the World: Issues for the Twenty-First Century*. London: UCL Press.

Melossi, D. (2003) '"In a Peaceful Life": Migration and the Crime of Modernity in Europe/Italy', *Punishment and Society* 5(4): 371–97.

Morley, D. (2000) *Home Territories: Media, Mobility and Identity*. London: Routledge.

Morrison, W. (2005) 'Rethinking Narratives of Penal Change in Global Context', in J. Pratt, D. Brown, M. Brown, S. Hallsworth and W. Morrison (eds) *The New Punitiveness: Trends, Theories, Perspectives*, pp. 290–307. Cullompton: Willan Publishing.

Morrison, W. (2006) *Criminology, Civilisation and the New World Order: Rethinking Criminology in a Global Context*. London: Glasshouse Press.

Muncie, J. (2005) 'The Globalization of Crime Control: The Case of Youth and Juvenile Justice', *Theoretical Criminology* 9(1): 5–33.

Murdoch, G. (2004) 'Democracy in Digital Times', paper presented at the Materiality of Mediated Communication Conference, Bergen, Norway, 17–18 May.

National Commission on Terrorist Attacks Upon the United States (2004) *The 9/11 Report*. New York: St Martin's Press.

Nellis, M. (2005) 'Electronic Monitoring, Satellite Tracking, and the New Punitiveness in England and Wales', in J. Pratt, D. Brown, M. Brown, S. Hallsworth and W. Morrison (eds) *The New Punitiveness: Trends, Theories, Perspectives*, pp. 167–88. Cullompton: Willan Publishing.

Newburn, T. and R. Sparks (eds) (2004) *Criminal Justice and Political Cultures: National and International Dimensions of Crime Control*. Cullompton: Willan Publishing.

Papastergiadis, N. (2000) *The Turbulence of Migration*. Cambridge: Polity Press.

Robertson, R. (1995) 'Glocalization: Time–Space and Homogeneity–Heterogeneity?', in M. Featherstone, S. Lash and R. Robertson (eds) *Global Modernities*, pp. 25–44. London: Sage.

Rose, N. (1999) *Powers of Freedom*. Cambridge: Cambridge University Press.

Ruggiero, V. (2005) 'Criminalizing War: Criminology as Ceasefire', *Social and Legal Studies* 14(2): 239–57.

Said, E. (1978/1985) *Orientalism*. London: Penguin Books.

Sernhede, O. (2002) *AlieNation is my Nation: Hiphop och unga mans utanforskap I Det Nya Sverige*. Stockholm: Ordfront forlag.

Sheptycki, J.W.E. (2000) *Issues in Transnational Policing*. London & New York: Routledge.

Sheptycki, J. (2002) *In Search of Transnational Policing: Towards a Sociology of Global Policing*. Aldershot: Ashgate.

Sheptycki, J. (2005) 'Relativism, Transnationalisation and Comparative Criminology', in J. Sheptycki and A. Wardak (eds) *Transnational and Comparative Criminology*, pp. 69–88. London: Glasshouse Press.

Simon, J. (1997) 'Governing through Crime', in L. Friedman and G. Fisher (eds) *The Crime Conundrum: Essays in Criminal Justice*, pp. 171–89. Boulder, CO: Westview Press.

Urry, J. (2000) *Sociology beyond Societies: Mobilities for the Twenty-First Century*. London: Routledge.

Urry, J. (2002a) 'The Global Complexities of September 11th', *Theory, Culture and Society* 19(4): 57–69.

Urry, J. (2002b) *The Tourist Gaze* (2nd edn). London: Sage.

Valier, C. (2003) 'Foreigners, Crime and Changing Mobilities', *British Journal of Criminology* 43(1): 1–21.

Wacquant, L. (1999) 'Suitable Enemies', *Punishment and Society* 1(2): 215–22.

Walters, W. (2004) 'Secure Borders, Safe Haven, Domopolitics', *Citizenship Studies* 8(3): 237–60.

Weber, L. (2002) 'The Detention of Asylum Seekers—20 Reasons Why Criminologists Should Care', *Current Issues in Criminal Justice: Special Issue—Refugee Issues and Criminology* 14(1): 9–30.

Welch, M. and L. Schuster (2005) 'Detention of Asylum Seekers in the UK and USA: Deciphering Noisy and Quiet Constructions', *Punishment and Society* 7(4): 397–417.

Young, J. (1999) *The Exclusive Society*. London: Sage.

Zureik, E. and M. Salter (eds) (2005) *Global Surveillance and Policing: Borders, Security, Identity*. Cullompton: Willan Publishing.

KATJA FRANKO AAS is Senior Researcher at the Institute of Criminology and Sociology of Law, University of Oslo. She has written extensively on the use of information and communication technologies in contemporary penal systems, including *Sentencing in the Age of Information: From Faust to Macintosh* (Glasshouse Press, 2005). She is currently completing a book entitled *Globalization and Crime* (Sage Publications).

[16]

Human trafficking:

Sketchy data and policy responses

JO GOODEY
European Union Agency for Fundamental Rights (FRA), Austria

Abstract

This article looks at the phenomenon of trafficking in human beings, with examples drawn from intergovernmental organizations, the European Union and the UK. It begins by outlining legal recognition of and current responses to trafficking, and goes on to present an overview of what we currently know and don't know about the extent and nature of this crime in relation to its various manifestations. The article critically examines policy responses to trafficking in the light of what are often, at best, sketchy data. The existence of a trafficking 'industry', both as an organized crime 'industry' and as an IGO and NGO 'industry', is introduced in the arcicle through legal and policy responses that set out to identify, map and counter trafficking. The article concludes by asking where the focus on trafficking is heading, and if it will be supported in future by more robust evidence for policy development.

Key Words

data • human trafficking • legalsation •policy responses • victim-centred

Legal recognition of and responses to human trafficking

Human trafficking encompasses labour and sexual exploitation, and its victims can include men and women, adults and children. Trafficking can manifest itself both within and between countries, and therefore should not only be thought of as a transnational crime but one that can also take place within a country's borders. Exploitation—using means such as fraud, force, threat and deception— lies at the heart of trafficking; as such, human trafficking is often described as 'modern day slavery'.

International legislative developments

The abolitionist movement against slavery has a history dating back hundreds of years, with 2007 marking the 200th anniversary of the abolition of the slave trade in Britain's colonies[1]. In the 20th century, notable legal developments against slavery include the League of Nations 1926 Slavery Convention and the United Nations 1956 Supplementary Convention on the Abolition of Slavery, the Slave Trade, and Institutions and Practices Similar to Slavery. The UN's first convention dealing specifically with trafficking was the 1949 Convention on the Suppression of Trafficking in Women and the Exploitation of Prostitution of Others. The association of slavery with prostitution, and particularly with concerns related to the 'white slave trade' in women, came to a fore at the beginning of the 20th century. Since this time, the specific crime of trafficking has been linked with prostitution of women and, more recently, children, and less so with other areas of 'slave-like' exploitation in the labour market.

Renewed international interest in human trafficking emerged in the late 1980s and 1990s in response to increased population movements in the wake of war, civil conflict and, in Central and Eastern Europe, the fall of communism; events which were often accompanied by the illegal movement of people and exploitation of vulnerable populations at the hands of organized crime. In Europe, the European Parliament adopted its first resolution on the exploitation of prostitution and trafficking in human beings in 1989, which was followed in 1993 by a parliamentary resolution calling for international co-operation to combat trafficking in women and to improve the situation of victims. Currently, the United Nations Protocol to 'Prevent, Suppress and Punish Trafficking in Persons, Especially Women and Children', which supplements the 2000 UN Convention against Transnational Organized Crime (TOC), provides the legal reference point for an international definition of human trafficking[2]. While the protocol encompasses forced labour or services, the removal of organs, and prostitution, the onus of the international community's attention in practice, as evidenced by the UN's Global Programme Against Trafficking (GPAT), lies disproportionately with sex trafficking.

The UN Convention against TOC also has a supplementary protocol against the Smuggling of Migrants by Land, Sea and Air, which includes a separate definition of smuggling[3]. In legal terms, smuggling becomes trafficking once a person who is being smuggled experiences exploitation at any point from recruitment through to arrival at their destination. Yet, media reporting and political debates on illegal immigration have often conflated human trafficking with human smuggling; with the terms used interchangeably. Legal distinctions between smuggling and trafficking are not so easy to apply in reality, as smugglers also exploit those who want to move from one country to another by, for example, charging exorbitant fees for their services. This overlap is reflected in many policy responses that place illegal immigration, human smuggling and human trafficking together under the 'migration–crime–security' nexus (Goodey, 2003a). In this regard, the 1997 joint action by the Council of the European Union to Combat Trafficking in Human Beings and the Sexual Exploitation of Children is illustrative of this mixed response, with its objective being to:

> ... establish common rules for action to combat trafficking in human beings and sexual exploitation of children in order to contribute to the fight against certain forms of unauthorised immigration and to improve judicial cooperation in criminal matters [4]

In the same way as this joint action muddies concerns about victimization within the framework of criminality, illegal immigration and judicial co-operation, the UN trafficking protocol can be critiqued as an adjunct to a convention that seeks primarily to combat organized crime (Reilly, 2006). In this regard the convention's focus rests with crime against state parties rather than on individual victims of trafficking. As an illustration: where the trafficking protocol provides for assistance to and protection of victims it does so in the language of 'soft law'; for example, with the use of phrases such as 'in appropriate cases and to the extent possible under its domestic law, each State Party shall ...'[5], and 'each State Party shall consider'[6] (van Liempt, 2006). However, these kinds of compromises are common to a lot of legislation dealing both with conventional and organized crime, and reflect the fact that the law is traditionally constructed with a definition of and response to crime as, first, against the state, and, sometimes a distant second, against the individual.

EU and UK legislative developments

In the 10 years following the 1997 joint action by the Council of the European Union, European legislators have been busy in the anti-trafficking field. For example, in 2002, the Council of the European Union adopted its own framework decision on combating trafficking in human beings; in 2003, the framework decision on combating the sexual exploitation of children and child pornography was adopted, which addresses child trafficking. And, in 2004, the Justice and Home Affairs Council adopted the directive on residence permits issued to third-country nationals, *who co-operate with the authorities*, who are victims of trafficking or who have been the subject of an action to facilitate illegal immigration; so serving to remind us that legislation that purports to be 'for' trafficking victims is sometimes more focused on the needs of law enforcement in acquiring victim testimonies. More encouragingly, as 'victim-centred' legislation, the

Charter of Fundamental Rights of the European Union specifically prohibits trafficking in human beings under one article, and, in so doing, serves to emphasize trafficking as a human rights violation.

The UK, as an EU Member State coming under certain European legislative obligations and as a signatory to the UN Convention and its trafficking protocol, has, since 2000, been actively incorporating anti-trafficking measures into domestic law. In 2002, a specific offence of trafficking in relation to prostitution was introduced for the first time into UK legislation as part of the Nationality, Immigration and Asylum Act 2002. This was followed by the Sexual Offences Act 2003, which went further than the UN Protocol by not requiring traffickers to use coercion, deception or force during recruitment of trafficking victims. Further, in 2004, legislation covering trafficking for labour exploitation was introduced under the Asylum and Immigration Act 2004. In the same year, and in response to one particular tragedy in Morecambe Bay, England, when over 20 Chinese illegal workers drowned as they were cut off by rising tides when cockle-picking, the Gangmaster (Licensing) Act 2004 was adopted in an attempt to undermine the grey world of illegal workers and the gangmasters who control them. Although this Act was not directly addressed to trafficking, it presented a landmark in recognition of the plight of illegal immigrant workers who are often victims of exploitative practices at the hands of organized crime.

These legislative developments in the UK have not been received without criticism from some quarters, and in particular from human rights NGOs, for failing to incorporate provisions addressing victims' needs and rights, and for continuing to focus on trafficking as a problem of organized illegal immigration/organized crime rather than a human rights abuse (Goodey, 2003b; Craig et al, 2007). In response to growing criticism about its lack of a victim-centred response to trafficking, and to coincide with the 200th anniversary of the UK's abolition of slavery, the government launched its Action Plan on Tackling Human Trafficking in March 2007 and, at the same time, signed the Council of Europe Convention on Action against Trafficking in Human Beings, which includes a recovery period and assistance for victims of trafficking of at least 30 days.

The above only begins to outline the various pieces of legislation at the international, EU and UK level that recognize and address the crime of human trafficking. It is clear that there has been a great deal of activity in recent years in recognition of and legal responses to human trafficking; in particular to trafficking in relation to the sex industry. However, the question is—what information has served to inform these legal developments? In other words, what do we know about the extent and nature of human trafficking?

The scale of the trafficking problem

Accurate data on the extent of trafficking in human beings does not exist. General figures are often given by inter-governmental and non-governmental organizations whose sources and reliability can be difficult to verify. This situation is not unique to data on human trafficking, but is typical of criminal justice data in the area of serious and organized crime, which remains under-reported, under-detected and, therefore, under-prosecuted. The problem in the case of human trafficking is that its human victims are often unaware of how to report their abuse or are unable to do so, particularly when they are minors. It is also typically the case that victims are scared to report their abusers for fear of reprisals against themselves or their families. In addition, victims are often distrustful of the police and criminal justice authorities as being able or willing to assist them should they report their victimization. These factors, combined with the problems of corrupt policing and criminal justice personnel, serve to undermine criminal justice responses to the crime of human trafficking and make accurate estimates of its scale difficult.

In the introduction to a UN publication, as part of the UN Global Initiative to Fight Human Trafficking (UN.GIFT), the following sentence typifies how the scale of trafficking is presented – *'Billions of dollars are being made at the expense of millions of victims of trafficking*[7]. Rather than critique this sentence as inaccurate, it is symptomatic of international efforts that have been around for some years now to try to highlight the problem of what is largely an undocumented crime. In Europe, the same 'guesstimates' have been used to map the scale of the trafficking phenomenon since it came increasingly to the attention of NGOs and EU Member State governments from the early 1990s on. As noted by Aromaa and Lehti (2007) with respect to Europe, the highest figure used by a variety of NGOs—of 500,000 women and children trafficked annually for prostitution into the 'old' EU Member States—probably came from a 'common unmentioned source' (which is often given as the IOM).

The United Nations, particularly through the UN Office on Drugs and Crime (UNODC) and the International Labour Organisation (ILO), has developed a range of global estimates of the extent of human trafficking.

The 2006 UNODC report 'Trafficking in Persons: Global Patterns' used content analysis of print material from a range of international and national sources to map how often certain countries are cited as origin, transit and destination countries for trafficking, and to map the characteristics of trafficking, its offenders and victims, according to how often certain characteristics are cited. A simple citation index was established on the basis of the number of times a country or trafficking characteristic was referred to in print material, ranging from very low to very high. On this basis, the citation index report indicates the following for Europe: Belgium, Germany, Greece, Italy and the Netherlands are ranked *very high* as destination countries, while Austria, Bosnia and Herzegovina, the Czech Republic, Denmark, France, Kosovo, Poland, Spain, Switzerland and the UK are ranked *high* as destination countries.

Although the UNODC report makes it clear that it does not set out to provide an estimate of the extent of trafficking, the real problem is that its findings are easily interpreted as reflecting a 'count', rather than a citation count, of the extent and nature of trafficking. To this end, a country having a *very high* citation index as a destination for trafficking victims is perhaps as much a reflection of its active policies to combat trafficking and put information in the public domain as it is of the country's position as a main destination for victims. The results of the report also make it clear that the subject of *sex* trafficking tends to dominate publications, while trafficking for *labour* exploitation receives less attention. To this end, the patterns of trafficking reported in the citation index appear to underestimate the global extent of labour trafficking. This critique was also levelled at the UN's Global Programme against Trafficking in Human Beings by an internal evaluation report, which concludes that the programme had placed too little emphasis on trafficking for labour exploitation and on trafficking in human organs[8].

In contrast with UNODC, the UN's ILO office has undertaken various pieces of research in recent years that attempt to critically assess different methodologies for estimating the extent and nature of global trafficking, and which place equal emphasis on labour exploitation as well as sexual exploitation (Kutnick et al., 2007; De Cock, 2007; Ghinararu and van der Linden, 2004). In a 2007 report on 'Methodologies for global and national estimation of human trafficking victims', ILO contrasts its method for estimating the global scale of trafficking with that of the US government. Based on their different approaches, the ILO calculates that between 275,068–508,931 people are actively being trafficked both within and between countries at any given point in time, and that at least 2.45 million people are caught by trafficking across the world. In comparison, the US government estimates that between 600,000–800,000 people are trafficked across international borders each year.[9] These numbers are markedly lower than the 500,000 figure used by NGOs in the late 1990s and early 2000s to describe the annual extent of sex trafficking into the old EU-15 Member States alone. More recently, after some criticism of figures being presented that are difficult to substantiate, estimates about the scale of trafficking are more modest and are usually accompanied with a word of warning concerning the figures. As an example of a more cautious shift in the presentation of numbers, the International Organisation for Migration (the IOM) states the following on its internet counter-trafficking pages:

> 'Although the global scale of human trafficking is difficult to quantify, as many as 800,000 people may be trafficked across international borders annually, with many more trafficked within the borders of their own countries'.[10]

The nature of the trafficking problem

What we know about the detailed nature of trafficking is largely based on qualitative victims' accounts gathered by NGOs and some IGOs, such as the IOM, which actively assist victims. As official criminal justice statistics on trafficking are either non-existent or inadequate in many countries and regions throughout the world[11], NGO and IGO reports, together with the media and researchers, present the richest sources of information on the nature of trafficking, and in particular on victims' experiences.

The situation in Europe: from the Balkans to the 'old' EU

In Europe, some of the most detailed reports on trafficking are focused on sex trafficking in the countries of Central and Eastern Europe, and the south-eastern European region; namely the Balkans (Velkoska, 2007). This reflects the fact that these regions include origin, transit and destination countries for sex trafficking, with some engaged in two or all three practices—particularly in the case of the Balkans. The role that the transition from communist to capitalist market economies has played in both the creation of poverty, in particular female poverty, and opportunities for (legal/illegal) migration from east to west, and for organized crime to exploit this situation, is now well documented (Nikolic-Ristanovic, 2000, 2002). At the same time, civil war in the Balkans has served to exacerbate the negative economic situation of women, and has provided a ready market for organized crime and prostitution[12]. A combination of economic and social push and pull factors, including a thriving sex industry, has meant that there is a steady supply and demand for women and girls. The entry in 2004 of 10 new countries into the EU, and in 2007 of a further two, Bulgaria and Romania, which are typically countries of origin for sex trafficking, has meant that the job of trafficking has become easier for traffickers.

Various NGOs—such as La Strada[13], the Coalition Against Trafficking in Women (CATW)[14], and The Global Alliance Against Trafficking in Women (GAATW)[15]—are active in prevention, advocacy and victim assistance, and have published information about the nature of sex trafficking in Europe. The IOM[16], as the largest international organization working in the field of migration, is also very active in Europe in providing assistance to trafficking victims, as part of its migrant return programme, and in the process has collected a significant volume of information on trafficking. In 2003 the IOM established its Regional Clearing Point (RCP) in the Balkans, which resulted in co-ordinated data collection on trafficking cases gathered by the IOM shelters through which trafficking victims pass prior to being returned 'home'. In the mid 2000s, the RCP data indicated a drop in trafficking cases in the Balkans. This drop was variously attributed by different parties to successes in combating trafficking, or as an indication that traffickers were becoming more successful in hiding their activities from law enforcement, or as a consequence of the IOM's policy of repatriation (with the suggestion that victims were no longer turning to the IOM for assistance and, therefore, were not being registered through the RCP (Lindstrom, 2007).

Among EU Member States, which represent destination countries for trafficking, a handful of government bodies and criminal justice agencies collect data and publish reports on the extent and nature of trafficking. In 'western' Europe, two of the most comprehensive reports come from the German Federal Police (the Bundeskriminalamt (BKA)) and the Dutch National Rapporteur on Trafficking.

The 2005 BKA situation report[17], which refers to police data from 2004, indicates that there were 370 investigations involving 972 victims, of whom 845 were non-Germans; in other words, 127 were German. In comparison, the recorded figures for 2003 were higher, with 431 investigations involving 1235 victims, of whom 1108 were non-Germans; again, 127 were German. The situation report, which is focused on sex trafficking, characterizes victims as female, aged between 18–25 years, and as originating in the main from Bulgaria, Romania, Russia and the Ukraine. The BKA also indicates that, on average, 40 per cent of suspects are German nationals; in 2004, of the 297 German suspects recorded, 55 were not born in Germany. Other dominant suspect nationalities are Bulgarian and Russian. It is also noteworthy that 182 of the 370 investigations recorded in 2004 only involved a single suspect per investigation. This could indicate a number of factors—including the loose 'organization' of sex trafficking networks that allows only for the identification of individual suspects rather than criminal groups. Alternatively (or in parallel to loose networks), the fact that there was a lone suspect could reflect the nature of sex trafficking, particularly where there is some relationship between trafficker and victim, such as a relative or 'boyfriend', which facilitates close relationships of abuse and dependency.

The 2007 report by the Dutch National Rapporteur on Trafficking, which refers to 2005 figures collected by the Foundation against Trafficking in Women (STV), the police, and the prosecutor's office, indicates a similar pattern to Germany with respect to the nature of trafficking in the Netherlands.[18] Of the 424 (possible) victims registered in 2005, the main countries of origin, after internal cases of Dutch victims of trafficking, were Bulgaria, Russia and Nigeria. In previous years, Bulgarian, Romanian and Nigerian victims also dominated the figures, and Dutch nationals to a lesser extent; which may reflect an increased focus on internal trafficking in recent years. Of the 135 suspects who were registered in 2005, the largest group comprised people born in the Netherlands, with the next largest being Moroccans and Turkish suspects. In previous years Romanian and Bulgarian suspects tended to dominate numbers of known suspects. And, as with the BKA report, the Dutch National Rapporteur also notes that trafficking tends to involve individuals who might not be working as part of what we would traditionally consider as 'organized crime'. In this regard, the Rapporteur indicates that there are few registrations of trafficking offences in combination with the offence of 'participation in a criminal organization', which might show that traffickers work alone as 'loverboys' to exploit victims, and that 'quick hit' cases, rather than organized crime operations, may be the norm.

In the UK, Kelly and Regan's 2000 report for the Home Office was the first major publication to try to map the extent and nature of the sex trafficking industry in the UK. Based on 1998 figures received from 36 of the 43 police forces in England and Wales, the report indicates that only five police forces handled trafficking cases in 1998, which resulted in a total of 18 trafficking cases involving 71 victims who were most likely trafficked to the UK from Central and Eastern European countries and Thailand. However, as Kelly and Regan note, this low official figure can be contrasted with two large trafficking cases in England and Wales, prior to 1998, each of which involved upwards of 100 women from Thailand and Brazil. In acknowledging that official figures can grossly underestimate the scale of sex trafficking, Kelly and Regan calculate that the 'true' number of trafficked women in the UK in 1998 could have been anywhere between two and 20 times greater—that is, involving between 142 and 1420 victims. However, what their report does not describe is the characteristics of trafficking suspects or convicted traffickers.

The same is true for publicly available information concerning the UK's largest police raid on brothels and massage parlours, which was undertaken under Operation Pentameter in 2006 and Pentameter II in 2007. Once again, the information made available tells us the gender (all female), age (majority between 18–25 years) and countries of origin of the victims (ranging from Brazil and India through to the 'new' EU Member States), but provides no details about the suspects apart from the numbers arrested and charged.[19] Critiquing Operation Pentameter, O'Connell Davidson, writing in *The Guardian*[20], refers to the 'hyperbole and emotive rhetoric about sex slaves' in Britain, which she states is fuelled by inaccurate and exaggerated information concerning the extent of the problem, and a lack of focus on the actual circumstances and needs of prostitutes. She sees police operations such as Pentameter as serving primarily the 'migration–crime–security' focus, with many raids leading to the deportation of trafficking victims.

What we (don't) know about the traffickers

In comparison with the volume and range of information available from both NGO and IGO sources on victims of trafficking, information centred on suspects and perpetrators, such as that supplied by the BKA and the Dutch rapporteur, is comparatively sparse. While it can be argued that sensitive data cannot be put in the public domain that might jeopardize ongoing and future convictions, it remains the case that research attention has not been focused on traffickers. Admittedly any area of organized crime is difficult, and dangerous, to research, but it appears that there is a gap in criminological research concerning traffickers themselves. The typical route to find out about traffickers' modus operandi is to interview trafficking victims about their stories. These accounts reveal a great deal about victims' circumstances prior to recruitment and what made them vulnerable to trafficking, and also provide invaluable detail about victims' experiences of exploitation during the trafficking process and afterwards—but these accounts are victim rather than offender-centred.

Surtees (2005, 2008), who has interviewed trafficking victims in south-eastern Europe, notes that traffickers, according to victims' accounts, appear far more diverse in their profiles than the representation of (typically) male traffickers would suggest. Surtees' research indicates that female traffickers are as numerous as male traffickers in some countries (such as Moldova). She also suggests that traffickers, or rather recruiters, might not always be aware that they are recruiting people to be trafficked. In other words, some recruiters, unlike traffickers, may believe they are finding legitimate jobs for family members and acquaintances. Also, the extent to which male/female trafficking pairs work together, and the extent to which transnational co-operation exists between traffickers is difficult to verify in the absence of primary research with traffickers. As Surtees comments (2008: 44): 'Future research on traffickers should, where possible, also include alternative data collection methodologies, such as interviews with traffickers or a secondary analysis of court cases'. Less reliance on victims' testimonies and more research with traffickers could reveal a great deal about traffickers' personal life histories and the operation of trafficking as 'organized' crime.

A rare example of primary research with non-convicted traffickers concerns interviews conducted in 2003 by Troshynski and Blank (2008); however, unfortunately, these researchers' accounts tell us more about the research methodology and ethics of interviewing traffickers than they do about the business of trafficking as seen through traffickers' eyes. Given the difficulties of interviewing convicted let alone non-convicted traffickers, perhaps the most valuable untapped source of information is court cases. To this end, an online database provided by the Office for Democratic Institutions and Human Rights (ODIHR)[21] the Office for Security and Cooperation in Europe (OSCE's) Office for Democratic Institutions and Human Rights) offers a handful of detailed accounts of trafficking cases. These cases are rich sources of information about the recruitment process and the nature of exploitation, and also provide details about traffickers' personal histories and the nature of trafficking networks.

To a large extent, the focus on victims in publicly available reports on trafficking reflects the fact that NGOs, such as La Strada and the Coalition against Trafficking in Women, have been primary movers in highlighting the crime of human trafficking. In their efforts to identify and support victims of trafficking, NGOs have sought to inform people about the victims' experiences. Where NGOs do refer to perpetrators it is typically to describe the means by which they recruit and exploit victims. The same approach can be noted in reports that emanate from inter-governmental organizations, such as the UN and the IOM. Arguably, though many NGOs and researchers would beg to disagree (Apap, 2002), these IGOs' trafficking programmes have gradually shifted from an organized crime and illegal immigration focus to one that is victim-centred. One could speculate that this shift has echoes in how all victims of crime were gradually placed centrestage in the 1980s and 1990s in countries that were experiencing high levels of crime—

such as the United States and the UK (Crawford and Goodey, 2000; Goodey, 2005b). By placing the victim centrestage, the spotlight of attention turns away from the more difficult problem of trying to stop crime (or illegal immigration for that matter) by focusing, instead, on the relatively 'easy' issues of victim assistance and crime prevention based on potential victims. With this in mind, and given the focus of trafficking data collection on victims, the next section critically explores policy responses to human trafficking in the context of the European Union and the UK.

Policy responses

A victim-centred response?

A three-pronged response to human trafficking is now well established in inter-governmental and NGO circles, from which policy and practical initiatives variously emanate. The three approaches are: prevention of trafficking, protection and support of victims, and prosecution of traffickers—in other words, the three 'Ps' of trafficking. Two of the three—prevention, and protection and support, are firmly rooted in a victim-centred response to trafficking (Goodey, 2004a, 2005a; Gallagher, 2006).

A victim-centred focus has become an established way of addressing crime *indirectly* by addressing victims (Goodey, 2005b). In this regard, the increasing attention that has been given throughout the 1990s and 2000s to victims of trafficking is, in part, a response to the real problem that the causes of trafficking, rather than the symptoms, are much harder to treat. If we can agree that human trafficking is fuelled by inequality in global markets, and by conflict and war, then these are problems that are obviously difficult to respond to in comparison with more immediate and tangible initiatives that offer assistance to victims of these inequalities—in this case, trafficking victims.

Lindstrom (2007), referring to the Balkans, classifies the different responses to trafficking by the international community as follows: the migration approach—exemplified by the IOM; the law enforcement approach—exemplified by Europol; the human rights approach—exemplified by NGOs, which is essentially victim-centred; and the economic approach—which is close to the human rights approach, but which emphasizes the economic causes of trafficking and looks at alternative routes out of poverty for potential victims and those who have been trafficked. Lindstrom, along with other commentators, argues that the migration and law enforcement approaches dominate current responses to trafficking in Europe, and are embedded in the construction of the 'migration–crime–security' nexus that forms the backbone of EU responses to trafficking. However, it is apparent too, as evidenced by the focus on prevention and protection, that the victim's place in trafficking policy and practice has become increasingly important over recent years.

In the EU, some notable European Commission-funded programmes since the mid 1990s have supported anti-trafficking initiatives. These include the DAPHNE programme, which specifically concerns violence against women and children, as well as programmes that have focused on police and judicial co-operation, such as STOP and, more recently, AGIS. For example, in 2002, a European Conference on Preventing and Combating Trafficking in Human Beings was organized under the framework of the European Commission's STOP programme, and took place in the European Parliament with the co-operation of the IOM, the European Commission, the Parliament and EU Member States. The conference resulted in the so-called 'Brussels Declaration' on Preventing and Combating Trafficking in Human Beings, which, in turn, resulted in the Commission establishing an expert group on trafficking in human beings; with the remit to write a report containing concrete proposals for implementing the Brussels Declaration[22].

Alongside the European Commission, the Council of Europe and, in particular, the OSCE, through its ODIHR office, have put human trafficking centre-stage in their policies. As a reflection of the centrality of their human rights mandate, the Council of Europe and ODIHR have stressed the human rights approach to combating trafficking. To this end, the OSCE has convened a number of high-level conferences to enhance co-operation between IGOs, NGOs and OSCE Member States in the area of trafficking, and has assigned a Special Representative for Combating Trafficking in Human Beings. The OSCE's output is centred on both policy development and practical responses to trafficking, ranging from the production of a practical handbook for national referral mechanisms to protect the rights of trafficked persons (OSCE, 2004), through to a publication on compensation for trafficking victims (OSCE, 2008b).

The US Department of State, through its office to monitor and combat trafficking in persons, also plays an important global role in forming policy responses on and allocating resources to trafficking; though it is less influential in the EU, which is governed and funded by its own stakeholders. In its annual report on trafficking in persons the Department of State assigns a 'Tier' to each country, which indicates the extent to which it is considered to be in compliance with *US* anti-trafficking policies (rather than taking the UN Convention against TOC and its accompanying Trafficking Protocol as the sole basis for compliance): Tier 1 indicates compliance with US anti-trafficking policies, through to Tier 3 indicating the lowest level of compliance. For many countries in the developing world, their placement in this tier ranking is significant, as a Tier 3 placement can mean that the government will have sanctions imposed on it by the US government; such as withholding non-humanitarian and non-trade-related foreign assistance. For this reason, the placement of countries within a particular Tier is not without its critics. According to the 2007 report[23], no EU Member State falls under a Tier 3 classification, but Cyprus is put on a Tier 2 'watch list' to indicate that it is in danger of falling under a Tier 3 category. Although the

US Department of States report differs from other approaches by classifying countries and threatening sanctions, it does follow the established approach of looking at each country's compliance with anti-trafficking policies with respect to the 'three Ps' of prevention, protection and prosecution.

Rather than see approaches to trafficking as distinct, as suggested by Lindstrom (2007), with each actor playing its separate part, one can argue that there is increasing evidence of a crossover in roles and approaches to trafficking, as well as examples of co-operation between different actors; for example, law enforcement manuals on combating trafficking now contain sections on treatment of victims and victim assistance. At the beginning of the 1990s these kinds of developments would have been unthinkable, with the relationship between law enforcement and anti-trafficking NGOs typically hostile. As a reflection of these changes, no policy paper on trafficking can be written now without reference to victims and acknowledgement of their needs, though not necessarily their concrete 'rights'. The UK government's March 2007 'Action Plan on Tackling Human Trafficking' is illustrative of this trend, with the first page of the executive summary stressing the need for a 'human rights' approach to trafficking.

In their edited book on transnational organized crime, Edwards and Gill (2003: p. 275) refer to the need to move towards a 'socialization of criminal policy', away from the current focus on the 'criminalization of social policy', with the argument that the latter has served the needs, primarily, of the crime and security industry rather than the societies in which crime occurs. Policy responses to human trafficking, unlike many other areas of organized crime, do focus on victims through programmes that address prevention and protection. However, it is debatable whether the current focus of trafficking has yet reached a 'socialisation of criminal policy'. Rather, one could argue that the move towards a 'victim-centred' focus is well on its way—with reference to the needs of individual victims of trafficking incorporated into policy and practical papers; in this regard the latest European Commission tender for a feasibility study on a European 'hotline' for victims of trafficking is evidence of a growing victim-centred response.[24]

However, a comprehensive human rights approach—which would force us not only to look at the individual but also at questions of economic, social and gender inequality that lie at the heart of trafficking—is some way off yet. Herein, Lindstrom's point—that the migration and crime response to trafficking still holds sway—*is* valid if one considers human rights as incorporating economic and social rights. Yet, it is clear that a shift towards a victim-centred response to trafficking has developed over recent years, as increasing emphasis and resources are being placed on victim assistance. The real test of how far these initiatives are 'for' victims is whether they exist separate to conditions that stipulate that the victim should co-operate with the authorities in order to receive certain services. To this end, the continued absence of open residence permits for trafficked victims, regardless of whether they co-operate with the authorities[25], is still some way off *in practice*.

In Italy, which has long been praised for having residence permits for trafficking victims that do not require co-operation with the criminal justice authorities, there is criticism that these rights exist on paper but are not meted out to those in need *in practice* (Goodey, 2004b: 38). A recent proposal by the chair of the Justice and Constitutional Affairs Committee of the Italian Senate, on 5 June 2008, to amend the Security Decree Law to include prostitutes as a category of 'dangerous persons to the security and public morality'—alongside traffickers—resulted in an intense debate in Italy and an outcry from NGOs.[26] As a result, the proposed amendment concerning prostitutes was removed five days later. However, the debate illustrates the extent to which the tide can quickly turn to lump illegal trafficked prostitutes into the same category as traffickers and other criminals when the political climate is right in consideration of concerns (real or imagined) about migration–crime–security.

A changing international focus?

The international community's collective response to human trafficking, and in particular sex trafficking, has gained momentum since the mid 1990s and does not appear to be slowing down. At the same time as we are told that the trafficking industry is growing, so the international anti-trafficking industry has grown in response to it. Not a month goes by without some conference or meeting being convened to address trafficking. Writing in May 2008 from Vienna, the international community has witnessed a number of major anti-trafficking events in this city alone since the beginning of the year: the February 2008 Vienna Forum to Fight Human Trafficking, which was organized as part of UN.GIFT (the United Nations Global Initiative to Fight Trafficking[27]), a meeting in April 2008 of the OSCE's anti-trafficking focal points, and the 26–27 May 2008 OSCE conference on Child Trafficking.[28]

As evidenced by the 2008 Vienna Forum to Fight Human Trafficking, which attracted thousands of delegates from around the world, the resources currently devoted to trafficking are phenomenal. While the continued international focus on trafficking is to be welcomed, the absence of reliable data on many aspects of trafficking would suggest that careful consideration needs to be given to policy developments and funding to ensure attention is allocated to all areas of trafficking, including those not usually in the spotlight–such as trafficking for labour exploitation of men.

As an example, the degree to which anti-trafficking resources can be too focused on one aspect of trafficking is perhaps illustrated by the attention that was devoted to sex trafficking in the run up to the 2006 World Football Cup in Germany. In the same way that Germany comes out very high on the UN citation index, as a reflection of intense NGO and government attention on the problem of trafficking, the country was inundated with media and NGO reports of a predicted explosion in women being trafficked into the country to work as prostitutes during the World Cup. As the Presidency of the Council of Europe stated:

> Taking into account the European Parliament's resolution of 15 March 2006 on forced prostitution in the context of world sports events, the Presidency emphasises the fact that major international events, including sports events, have shown to pose the risk to contribute to a temporary increase in trafficking in human beings.[29]

However, as the IOM notes in a March 2008 bulletin on trafficking that refers to sporting events and human trafficking, the actual extent of sex trafficking for the German World Cup 'was unrealistic and unfounded hype'. The IOM's own report on the 2006 World Cup (Hennig et al., 2007) shows that a mere five investigated cases concerned sex trafficking and were assumed to have a direct link to this sporting event. In comparison, as the report documents, over 300 German online articles were published in the period surrounding the World Cup that made reference to sex trafficking in connection with the event.

It could be argued that the increased attention given to the potential for trafficking during the World Cup worked as a crime deterrent. Or, it could be argued that all trafficking cases did not come to light, which would suggest that the resources devoted to anti-trafficking surrounding the 2006 World Cup were misspent, as they failed to identify more cases. Whichever way one looks at it—it appears that the resources devoted to counter-trafficking activities and media attention surrounding the World Cup were out of proportion to the scale of the problem. Critically, whether the same conclusion can be reached with respect to the resources currently devoted to other areas of trafficking is debatable. However, as the IOM March bulletin goes on to note:

> 'Regardless of the limited existing evidence on the link between such large-scale sporting events and increased incidences of human trafficking, it seems countries hosting recent and upcoming international sporting events are taking the issue seriously'.[30]

This is not to suggest that too much attention and too many resources are devoted to the specific area of sex trafficking, but rather that the focus also needs to pay attention to those areas that have been relatively neglected. At the same time, policy attention and resource allocation needs to be supported by better evidence of the scale and nature of the trafficking problem.

Developments in the past couple of years suggest that the focus of trafficking *is* turning more to areas that have traditionally received less attention than sex trafficking, which has tended to dominate debates.[31] To this end, a 2006 OSCE publication on legal responses to human trafficking for labour exploitation[32], together with a 2008 OSCE publication on human trafficking for labour exploitation, forced and bonded labour',[33] are illustrative of a trend towards mainstreaming other areas of trafficking in parallel to the continued focus on sex trafficking. At the same time, attention is increasingly turning to the need for better data on the phenomenon of trafficking.

Of particular note is the European Commission's creation in April 2007 of a 'new' expert sub-group on 'trafficking in human beings', which is in addition to the earlier expert group established after the Brussels Declaration of 2002. The new expert sub-group on trafficking has emerged from the Commission's establishment of an expert group on the policy needs for data on crime and criminal justice, which was set up in response to the Commission's long-term goals to develop harmonized and comparable EU crime and criminal justice statistics.[34] Recognizing that existing criminal justice data on trafficking is not comparable and cannot provide an accurate estimate of the scale and nature of the crime, a steering group was formed within the trafficking sub-group to develop a methodology for building consensus from a range of external experts on a list of operational indicators that can characterize different trafficking situations. The work of the expert sub-group places equal emphasis on sexual and labour exploitation in the development of indicators, with experts identified for consultation through labour inspectorates, as well as NGOs and criminal justice personnel who have traditionally focused on sex trafficking. To this end, the group's work combines a balanced focus on different areas of trafficking, together with the need for improved indicators to be able to practically identify the phenomenon of trafficking in its diverse guises.

At the same time as more attention appears to be paid to labour exploitation as part of trafficking, the focus of sex trafficking appears to be turning more towards sexual exploitation of children. This attention reflects increased concerns to address and tackle the crime of paedophilia that have emerged in recent years, and would also seem to reflect a real concern about the under-documented area of child trafficking for sexual abuse. In the UK a number of key publications have highlighted that child trafficking is under-documented (CEOP, 2007; Sillen and Beddoe, 2007), and have brought to public attention the particular problem of unaccompanied minors 'disappearing' from care while in the UK; with the implication that these children are vulnerable to trafficking rings. The 2007 report 'Missing Out' by the UK branch of ECPAT (End Child Prostitution, Child Pornography and the Trafficking of Children for Sexual Exploitation) presents the following stark figures as a result of interviews conducted with social services, statutory agencies and the voluntary sector in different regions of the UK (focusing on Manchester, Newcastle, Birmingham, Solihull and Coventry):

> Across three regions there were 80 reported cases of known or suspected child victims of trafficking. Even more disturbing is that 48 (60%) of these children have gone missing from social services care and have never been found.[35]

The UK government's 2007 Action Plan on Human Trafficking also devotes one of four main chapters to the subject of child victims of trafficking. This attention to child trafficking in the Action Plan is acknowledged, in part, as a response to calls by NGOs such as ECPAT to more fully engage with child trafficking (Home Office, 2006).

The UN Protocol to 'Prevent, Suppress and Punish Trafficking in Persons, Especially Women and Children' illustrates the fact that trafficking in children is often mentioned in the same breath as trafficking in women. However, the real development recently has been the promotion of separate data collection and policy responses specifically on child trafficking; for example, the 2007 Annual Report of the OSCE Special Representative and Co-ordinator for Combating Trafficking in Human Beings highlights 'action against child trafficking' as one of six priority areas in 2007, and indicates that child trafficking will be a priority area in 2008.[36] In parallel, there are calls to look at child trafficking as both sexual and labour exploitation (Dottridge, 2007). As an illustration of how this very specific area of child abuse is receiving increasing attention, the European Union Agency for Fundamental Rights (FRA) commissioned research in 2007 on 'The Rights of the Child', which focuses on the development of indicators in three areas—child poverty, children's family relationships, and child trafficking. This focus on the child would seem to exemplify the increased attention that is being paid to trafficking as a human rights abuse or victim-centred crime; one in which the child cannot be seen as anything other than a victim.

Conclusion

This article has presented an overview of where legislative and policy responses to trafficking have come from and where they are currently going with respect to developments at the international, European and UK level. With increased recognition of the problem of inadequate data on trafficking, as with so many areas of organized crime, there appears to be a renewed focus on the need for better data on which to build policy responses. This development reflects a general trend at the level of governments and IGOs to collect more robust data for policy development; particularly in the area of crime and criminal justice.

The focus of trafficking has, since the late 1980s, predominantly been on sex trafficking, with less attention paid to other areas that are arguably equally significant in terms of their magnitude and impact—though the data cannot 'prove' this assertion one way or another. At present, trafficking appears to be witnessing a subtle shift with respect to its focus of attention: trafficking for labour exploitation and child trafficking are increasingly receiving more attention. While many NGOs and academic commentators would dispute the idea that trafficking is being responded to as a victim-centred crime, this article suggests that a shift can be noted in this direction, at the same time as trafficking continues to be responded to as part of the 'migration–crime–security' nexus.

Finally, where perhaps too little attention is paid at present is with respect to knowledge concerning traffickers themselves; who they are and how they operate. While researchers, the international community and NGOs have built up a wealth of data on victims' experiences of trafficking, there is a real paucity of data and detailed information concerning traffickers. Another area that also remains under-researched is work on the demand side of trafficking. Although abolitionists call for the criminalization of all aspects of prostitution, and Sweden has gone so far to become the first country in the EU to criminalize the buying of prostitution, there is still a great deal we don't know about the demand side of prostitution that could provide some insights for policy responses in the area of trafficking prevention, and particularly in consideration of localized trafficking markets; although research on this theme is growing too[37]. The list of areas yet to be researched could be extended, but the message here is that the research onus in the field of criminology, and in non-criminological research in general, rests with victims. To this end there is much that the discipline of criminology could add to knowledge on trafficking that could be used for policy responses to address this crime.

Notes

The opinions of the author expressed in this article do not represent those of the European Union Agency for Fundamental Rights.

1 See Anti-Slavery International: http://www.antislavery.org/homepage/antislavery/history.htm

2 Article 3(a) of the UN Protocol to Prevent, Suppress and Punish Trafficking in Persons, Especially Women and Children, which supplements the 2000 UN Convention against Transnational Organised Crime, defines trafficking as: 'the recruitment, transportation, transfer, harbouring or receipt of persons, by means of the threat or use of force or other forms of coercion, of abduction, of fraud, of deception, of the abuse of power or of a position of vulnerability or of the giving or receiving of payments or benefits to achieve the consent of a person having control over another person, for the purpose of exploitation. Exploitation shall include, at a minimum, the exploitation of the prostitution of others or other forms of sexual exploitation, forced labour or services, slavery or practices similar to slavery, servitude or the removal of organs'.

3 Article 3(a) of the Protocol against the Smuggling of Migrants by Land, Sea and Air, which supplements the 2000 UN Convention against Transnational Organized Crime, defines smuggling as: 'the procurement, in order to obtain, directly or indirectly, a financial or other material benefit, of the illegal entry of a person into a State Party of which the person is not a national or a permanent resident'.

4 Joint Action 97/154/JHA of 24 February 1997 adopted by the Council on the basis of Article K.3 of the Treaty on European Union concerning action to combat trafficking in human beings and sexual exploitation of children

[Official Journal L 63 of 04.03.1997]; http://europa.eu/scadp lus/leg/en/lvb/l33072.htm
5 For example: II Article 6 of the Protocol against the Smuggling of Migrants by Land, Sea and Air.
6 For example: II Article 7 of the Protocol against the Smuggling of Migrants by Land, Sea and Air.
7 http://www.ungift.org/docs/ungift/pdf/knowledge/ebook.pdf
8 Williams, P. (2005) Evaluation of the Global Programme against Trafficking in Human Beings, United Nations Office on Drugs and Crime, Independent Evaluation Unit Report; http://www.unodc.org/pdf/Evaluation_04-Trafficking.pdf
9 Kutnick, B., Belser, P. and Danailova-Trainor, G. (2007) Methodologies for global and national estimation of human trafficking victims: current and future approaches, ILO publication, p. 1, 11.
10 The IOM counter-trafficking internet pages; http://www.the IOM.int/jahia/Jahia/pid/748 (accessed 23 May 2008).
11 As an illustration: The US Department of State '2007 Trafficking in Persons Report' indicates that in 2006 for the whole of 'Europe', which encompasses Ireland in the west through to Russia in the east and Turkey in the south, there were only 2950 prosecutions and 1821 convictions for trafficking—which includes all forms of trafficking; http://www.state.gov/documents/organization/82902.pdf
12 Including exploitation of prostitution by the very people that were supposed to be acting as peacekeepers in this region; according to a Council of Europe publication on the 'Octopus Programme' (2004), which partly explores the issue of trafficking, the list of bars that was classified as 'off limits' to UNMIK and KFOR staff because of these establishments' suspected involvement in trafficking went from 18 in late 1999, to 75 in January 2001 and 200+ in January 2004.
13 http://www.lastradainternational.org/?main=home
14 http://www.catwinternational.org/
15 http://www.gaatw.net/
16 http://www.the IOM.int/jahia/Jahia/pid/748
17 http://www.bka.de/lageberichte/mh/2004/lagebildmh_en.pdf
18 http://english.bnrm.nl/reports/fifth/—The Netherlands is currently the only EU Member State that formally regulates prostitution through licensing permits, which is the result of 2000 legislation that legalized some forms of voluntary prostitution of adults (Rijken and van Krimpen, 2008).
19 http://www.pentameter.police.uk/docs/pentameter.pdf
20 O'Connell Davidson 'Sex slaves and the reality of prostitution', *The Guardian*, Friday, 28 December 2007.
21 See: www.legislationonline.org
22 Report of the Experts Group on Trafficking in Human Beings (2004); http://ec.europa.eu/justice_home/doc_centre/crime/trafficking/doc/report_expert_group_1204_en.pdf
23 http://www.state.gov/documents/organization/82902.pdf
24 European Commission tender JLS/2008/D2/004

25 The EC Temporary Residence Permit Directive (Directive 2004/81/EC, 29 April 2004), which is on the residence permit issued to third country nationals who are victims of trafficking in human beings or who have been the subject of an action to facilitate illegal immigration, *who co-operate with the authorities*, is indicative of the limited rights afforded to victims.
26 Based on the article Clandestini, norma anti prostitute Soggetti pericolosi da allontanare, *Repubblica* (5 June 2008). Available at: http://www.repubblica.it/2008/06/sezioni/cronaca/sicurezza-politica-7/maroni-immigrazione/maroni-immigrazione.html [accessed on 20 June 2008].
27 http://www.ungift.org/
28 For a list of some past and coming events on trafficking see: http://www.humantrafficking.org/events
29 Council of the European Union, 2725th Justice and Home Affairs Council meeting, Luxembourg, 27–28 April 2006, Council conclusions on 'Trafficking in Human Beings'.
30 http://www.theIOM.int/jahia/webdav/site/myjahiasite/shared/shared/mainsite/projects/showcase_pdf/global_eye_2nd_issue.pdf
31 See report by Craig et al. (2007) for the Joseph Rowntree Foundation, which highlights the plight of migrant workers in different sectors in the UK.
32 http://www.osce.org/publications/cthb/2008/01/ 23622_811_en.pdf
33 http://www.osce.org/publications/cthb/2008/05/ 31148_1143_en.pdf
34 EC 2006/581/EC
35 Beddoe, C. (2007), p. 5.
36 OSCE (2007) Annual Report of the OSCE Special Representative and Co-ordinator for Combating Trafficking in Human Beings presented at the Permanent Council Meeting, 22 November 2007; http://www.osce.org/publications/cthb/2007/12/28676_1001_en.pdf
37 O'Connell Davidson, J. 'Men, middlemen, and migrants: the demand side of trafficking' at: http://www.eurozine.com/articles/2006–07–27-davidson-en.html (accessed 20 June 2008).

References

Apap, J. (2002) 'Countering human trafficking—protecting victims of trafficking.' Paper by the centre for European policy studies for the European Conference on preventing and combating trafficking in Human Beings: Global Challenge for the 21st Century, 18–20 September, Brussels: European Parliaments.

Aromaa, K. and M. Lehti (2007) 'Trafficking in Human Beings: Policy Problems and Recommendations', in P.C. van Duyne, A. Maljevic, M. van Dijck, K. van Lampe and J. Harvey (eds) *Crime Business and Crime Money in Europe: The Dirty Linen of Illicit Enterprise*, pp. 97–199. Nijmegen: Wolf Legal Publishers.

Beddoe, C. (2007) *Missing Out: A Study of Child Trafficking in the North-West, North-East and West Midlands*. UK: ECPAT UK.

CEOP (2007) *A Scoping Project on Child Trafficking in the UK*. London: CEOP.

Craig, G., A. Gaus, M. Wilkinson, K. Skrivankova and A. McQuade (2007) *Contemporary Slavery in the UK*. York: Joseph Rowntree Foundation.
Crawford, A. and J. Goodey (2000) (eds) *Integrating a Victim Perspective within Criminal Justice: International Perspectives*. Dartmouth: Ashgate.
De Cock, M. (2007) Directions for national and international data collection on forced labour, Geneva: International Labour Office (ILO).
Dottridge, M. (2007) *A Handbook on Planning Projects to Prevent Child Trafficking*. Lausanne: Terre des Hommes Foundation.
ECPAT (2007) *Missing Out: A Study of Child Trafficking in the North-West, North-East and West Midlands*. ECPAT UK.
Edwards, A. and Gill, P. (2003) *Transnational Organised Crime: Perspectives on global security*. London: Routledge.
Ghinararu, C. and van der Linden, M.N.J. (2004) Trafficking of migrant workers from Romania: Issues of labour and sexual exploitation, Geneva: International Labour Office (ILO).
Gallagher, A.M. (2006) 'Triply Exploited: Female Victims of Trafficking Networks, Strategies for Pursuing Protection and Legal Status in Countries of Destination', pp. 152–81 in C.L. van den Anker and J. Doomernik (eds) *Trafficking and Women's Rights*. Basingstoke: Palgrave.
Goodey, J. (2003a) 'Migration, Crime and Victimhood: Responses to Sex Trafficking in the EU', *Journal of Punishment and Society*. 5(4): 415–31.
Goodey, J. (2003b) 'Recognising Organised Crime's Victims: The Case of Sex Trafficking in the EU,' in A. Edwards and P. Gill (eds), *Transnational Organised Crime: Perspectives on Global Security*, pp. 157–73. London: Routledge.
Goodey, J. (2004a) 'Promoting Good Practice in Sex Trafficking Cases', *Special Issue of International Review of Victimology on Trafficking* 11(1): 89–110.
Goodey, J. (2004b) 'Sex Trafficking in Women from Central and East European Countries: Promoting a "Victim-Centred" and "Woman-Centred" Approach to Criminal Justice Intervention', pp. 26–45. *Feminist Review, Special Issue No.76 on 'Post-Communisim: Women's Lives in Transition'*.
Goodey, J. (2005a) 'Sex Trafficking in the European Union', in J. Sheptycki and A. Wardak (eds) *Transnational and Comparative Criminology*, pp. 269–85 London: Cavendish.
Goodey, J. (2005b) *Victims and Victimology: Research, Policy and Practice*. Harlow: Pearson.
Henning, J., Craggs, S., Laczko, F. and Larsson, F. (2007) Trafficking in Human Beings and the 2006 World Cup in Germany, Geneva: International Organization for Migration (IOM).
Home Office (2006) *Tackling Human Trafficking: Summary of Responses to the Consultation on Proposals for a UK Action Plan*. London: Home Office.
Home Office (2007) *UK Action Plan on Tackling Human Trafficking*. London: Home Office.
Kutnick, B., Belser, P. and Danailova-Trainor G. (2007) *Methodologies for global and national estimation of human trafficking victims: current and future approaches*. Geneva: International Labour Office (ILO).
Lindstrom, N. (2007) 'Translational Responses to Human Trafficking: The Politics of Anti-Trafficking in the Balkans', in H. Richard Friman and Simon

Reich (eds) *Human Trafficking, Human Security and the Balkans*. University of Pittsburgh Press. Online: http://www.maxwell.syr.edu/moynihan/programs/ces/pcconfpdfs/lindstrom.pdf (accessed).

Nikolic-Ristanovic, V. (ed.) (2000) *Women, Violence and War*. Budapest: Central European University Press.

Nikolic-Ristanovic, V. (2002) 'War and Post-War Victimization of Women', pp. 138–45. *European Journal of Crime, Criminal Law and Criminal Justice* 10: 2–3.

O'Connell Davidson, J. and B. Anderson (2006) 'The Trouble with Trafficking', in C.L. van den Anker and J. Doomernik (eds) *Trafficking and Women's Rights*, pp. 11–26. Basingstoke: Palgrave.

OSCE (2004) *National Referral Mechanisms: Joining Efforts to Protect the Rights of Trafficked Persons—A Practical Handbook*. Warsaw: OSCE/ODIHR.

OSCE (2006) *A Summary of Challenges Facing Legal Responses to Human Trafficking for Labour Exploitation in the OSCE Region*. Warsaw: OSCE/ODIHR.

OSCE (2008a) *Human Trafficking for Labour Exploitation/Forced and Bonded Labour: Identification, Prevention and Prosecution; Human Trafficking for Labour Exploitation/Forced and Bonded Labour: Prosecution of Offenders, Justice for Victims*. Vienna: OSCE.

OSCE (2008b) *Compensation for Trafficked and Exploited Persons in the OSCE Region*. Warsaw: OSCE.

Reilly, A.A. (2006) '...' in C.L. van den Anker and J. Doomernik (eds) *Trafficking and Women's Rights*, pp. 89–117. Basingstoke: Palgrave.

Rijken, C. and L. van Krimpen (2008) 'The introduction of Quality Labels in the Prostitution Sector as a Means to Combat Trafficking in Human Beings', *European Journal of Crime, Criminal Law and Criminal Justice* 16: 59–88.

Sillen, J. and C. Beddoe (2007) *Rights Here, Rights Now: Recommendations for Protecting Trafficked Children*. UNICEF and ECPAT UK.

Surtees, R. (2008) 'Traffickers and Trafficking in Southern and Eastern Europe: Considering the Other Side of Human Trafficking', *European Journal of Criminology* 5(1): 39–68.

Troshynski, E.I. and J.K. Blank (2008) 'Sex Trafficking: an Explanatory Study Interviewing Traffickers', *Trends in Organised Crime* 11(1): 30–41.

Van Liempt, I. (2006) 'Trafficking in Human Beings: Conceptual Dilemmas', in C.L. van den Anker and J. Doomernik (eds) *Trafficking and Women's Rights*, pp. 27–42. Basingstoke: Palgrave.

Velkoska, V. (2007) Criminal Justice Responses to Organized Crime—Macedonia. OSCE: Monitoring Mission to Skopje.

JO GOODEY is Programme Manager for Research at the European Union Agency for Fundamental Rights (FRA) in Vienna.

---

[17]

POLICING HOUSEMAIDS

The Criminalization of Domestic Workers in Bahrain

STACI STROBL*

This research stems from ethnographic observations in 2005 and 2006 of the women's sections of police stations in Bahrain. It uncovered details of a larger social and economic problem in the Arabian Gulf countries involving the unique legal status of the female expatriate guest workers. Housemaids or former housemaids formed the majority of female defendants who were ethnographically observed at Bahrain's local police stations. Observations revealed that this reflected an overall trend of criminalization of domestic worker-related labour disputes. This research presents the types of cases observed and discusses the women police as agents of social control whose job involves handling a larger socio-economic problem at the backend, through policing.

Introduction

In the Middle East, as well as in many countries around the world, domestic workers, or housemaids (*khaddamah*), who have migrated from their primarily South Asian home countries for work have become increasingly vulnerable to human rights abuses such as physical and sexual abuse at the hands of their employers. In the Arabian Gulf in particular, the situation is exacerbated by the lack of labour laws protecting these foreign workers, as well as popular attitudes that reinforce this legal imbalance.

This research stems from a larger ethnographic project exploring policewomen's roles in Bahrain (Strobl 2008). It focuses on the prevalence of housemaid-related cases in the women's section of Bahraini police stations. The use of local police stations to handle labour-related disputes represents a criminalization of housemaids even when their behaviour is not criminal. Furthermore, policewomen in general may have been able to enter, and maintain themselves as necessary to, the criminal justice system because of the criminalization of housemaids. Their willingness to enforce laws that are arguably detrimental to expatriate women in their society has contributed to their growth in numbers within policing. Today, they make up approximately 10 per cent of the total police force (Strobl 2008).

The term 'housemaids' is used in this research because it is employed by the press in the Gulf when these cases are reported. Furthermore, 'housemaid' is a better translation of the Arabic term (Modern Standard Arabic: *khaddamah*; Gulf Arabic: *khidamah*), which implies servitude and connects the phenomenon to the discourse of modern-day slavery. Historically, in the Middle East, this term was used for female slaves in Arabian Gulf tribes (Lienhardt 2001) who were attained as the spoils of war (Ehrenreich and Hochschild 2002). In traditional Bedouin contexts, slaves formed the outer ring of the tribal clan, spatially delineated by the arrangement of their tents; the inner tent rings

*Dr, Johh Jay College of Criminal Justice, 899 Tenth Ave, New York, NY 10019, USA; stacistrobl@gmail.com. Coinmill.com—currency conversion. Conversions from BD to USD on 21 May 2008. All conversions have been rounded.

were the *shaykhs*, their immediate families and unrelated Bedouin families who had joined the clan (Abu-Lughod 1986/1999).

Two recent studies of housemaids in Lebanon, for example, connect them directly to slavery because the following conditions are present in their employment: abuse or violence (or the threats of abuse and violence), denial of freedom and exploitative work conditions (Beydoun 2006; Jureidini and Moukarbel 2004). One Sri Lankan former housemaid documents repeated beatings at the hand of her Lebanese sponsor in a recent book centring on modern-day slave narratives (Fernando 2006).

Criminalization

Recent work theorizing about the forces that contribute to criminalization views it as a process involving the decentring and diffusion of legal forms and practices across agencies and jurisdictions. This discourse brings criminalization into a global context in which international norms and capitalist system pressures influence criminalization within a particular state (Jenness 2004). Young (1999) highlights the irony of the discourse of meritocracy in global capitalism with the cementing of inequalities. This global system 'promises self-actualization but it relegates a large portion of its members to service providers to the egos of the super-rich and the successful' (Young 1999: 196). In a neo-liberal global economy, the pressure to modernize drives policy making (Garland 2001) and potentially directs punishment at those who become obstacles in this regard, as a back-end means of regulation (Pickering 2007; Fitzpatrick 2001). Migrant workers are then constructed as deviant and undeserving of state protection (Pickering 2007).

Many have documented that globalization has given rise to a particular dependency on female labour as individual women attempt to survive within the global context of World Bank structural reforms and other neo-liberal programmes (Willman-Navarro 2006; Boyle 2002). The same policies also increased the demand for female domestic work in receiving countries that need cheap labour for modernization endeavours (Misra *et al.* 2006; Willman-Navarro 2006). In addition, labour migration, both legal and illegal, means profits for those who control the migration networks (Sassen 2002). As such, many international migration flows today are arranged by contract and driven by a migration industry in which the women themselves become commodities on an open market (Boyle 2002), and private households employing these migrants become microcosms of social inequality (Lan 2003).

Criminalization also bolsters expanding criminal justice systems in modernizing countries, providing jobs (Pickering 2007). In the case of Bahrain, I argue that the expansion of women in policing can be attributed to housemaid-related caseload in local police stations—a situation that criminalizes housemaid-related conflicts in general. This inquiry fits into the larger discourse on post-colonial feminism in which the use of 'women' as a category of analysis is viewed through particular social contexts that illuminate the micro-politics of work, home or family (Mohanty 2003). Post-colonially, many former colonies have created a space for women's work as part of a modernizing mission, initiating new relations of social production. On a superficial level, the representation of Bahraini women in their national police force appears to point to progressive gender relations, but, ironically, they are necessary precisely because they are deemed the appropriate state actors who can manage women, including foreign women, while still preserving traditional gender segregation (Strobl 2008). Where once women, including foreign housemaids, related to family or tribe, post-colonially, they must relate to the state and its bureaucracy for managing their contract labour. According to Spivak (2008), it is the post-colonial 'managerial' state that exhibits poor gender values and ultimately is not held accountable, as it fails to protect the vulnerable. The promise of the post-colonial nation-state to better protect women from injustice has not been achieved in a way that protects all women, regardless of class, national origin or ethnicity.

The Scope of the Housemaid Problem

Although there are no official statistics kept as to the number of housemaids being processed in Bahrain for either committing criminal offences or being processed pursuant to deportation, housemaids or former housemaids formed the majority of female defendants who were observed at local police stations (Strobl 2008). Some high-ranking male police informants, when asked about the prevalence of housemaid cases, denied that these cases were significant in number, even at stations where this was clearly observable. However, policewomen unanimously acknowledged the high workload generated by housemaid-related complaints.

The Ministry of Labor has reported that, in 2005, there were 40,000 housemaids working in Bahrain, and, in 2006, as many as 50,000 (*Bahrain Tribune* 2005; Filio 2006). According to Gulf Cooperation Council (GCC) data, at the end of 2003, there were 30,000 foreign housemaids in Bahrain, 95 per cent of whom are female, among approximately two million in the Gulf countries overall. On average, there is one housemaid for each household in Bahrain. The average is the same in Saudi Arabia and Oman. The United Arab Emirates (UAE) and Kuwait report a higher rate, having one housemaid for every two citizens. Qatar declined to report its figures (*Gulf Daily News* 2004*b*: 1). According to the Ministry of Labor in Bahrain, sponsors spend approximately 25 million Bahraini dinar ($66.5 million USD) on employing housemaids, 90 per cent of which gets sent home to the housemaid's native country, thereby 'draining' the Bahraini economy (*Gulf Daily News* 2003*b*). Indians and Sri Lankans each compose 20 per cent of total housemaids in Bahrain; Indonesians are 12 per cent; Bangladeshis and Nepalis make up 10 per cent each; Ethiopians are 7 per cent; and expatriate Arabs compose 3 per cent (Al-Tawashi 2003). Based on all accounts and personal observation, nearly every Bahraini household employs a housemaid. Unlike in Western countries, live-in housemaids are not the mark of upper socio-economic class status, but rather they are found in even lower, working-class homes. As such, 'domestic helpers have become a major part of family life' (Al-Tawashi 2003, no page number). South Asian embassy officials report that a majority of the labour complaints they receive stem from housemaid-sponsor problems. For example, a representative of the Philippines embassy indicated that 95 per cent of the labour conflicts they confront involve housemaids (Rosario 2005*b*).

Legal gap

The number of housemaid-related cases being processed at the local police stations is a consequence of the unique legal position of domestic workers in Bahrain and the Gulf countries. Unlike other guest workers, housemaids (and 'houseboys', who exist, but are far fewer in number) are not covered under the labour laws in Bahrain. Article 2 of The Labor Law for the Private Sector (Ministry of Labour and Social Affairs 1976) lists 'domestic servants and persons regarded as such' as exceptions to the labour laws. By default, domestic servants are treated as part of the family for which they work (Smith 2005); however, their cases are never processed in the *shari'ah* courts, where all other family-related matters are litigated. According to Hondagneu-Sotelo (2002), who studied Latina housemaids in Los Angeles, the notion of housemaids as family members is common rhetoric in these employer–employee situations: 'Indeed this attitude has a long history in paid domestic work, and, as many analysts have noted, it helps blur the boundaries between paid work and unpaid favors, which in turn often leads to exploitation' (Hondagneu-Sotelo 2002: 67).

There has only been one case in Bahraini history in which a sponsor was ever successfully convicted of abusing a housemaid in a criminal court. A Bahraini woman was found guilty in June of 2005 of assaulting her housemaid, Anita Devi Verma. The incident took place in October 2003 and she was subsequently sentenced to three months' imprisonment by the Lower Criminal Court (*Gulf Daily News* 2005). According to Verma, she was beaten daily by her sponsor. The final beating she received was so violent that neighbours phoned the police because they could hear Verma screaming. After this beating, Verma required 22 stitches on her head (*Gulf Daily News* 2003*a*).

Because housemaids do not fall under the labour laws, there is no legal regulation of the number of hours they work, the amount of money they are paid and the conditions of their live-in accommodation. For example, when pressed by housemaid recruiters and the Philippine embassy to interfere over whether the embassy has a right to set a minimum wage for housemaids, one Ministry of Labor official declared that the ministry has a 'hands-off policy':

> A minimum wage for housemaids is an issue for employers, recruiters and sending countries to resolve. The governments of the countries from where the housemaids arrive have the prerogative to set wages. We are hands off because the maids sector is not under the labor law. (Filio 2005: 3)

Recruiters arguably take advantage of the demand for low-cost housemaids in the Gulf, the vulnerability and lack of education of the housemaids, and the social attitudes that turn a blind eye to the abuses within the system. Because of the lack of legal protection for housemaids, they are able to operate with little oversight. Recruitment agencies are organized under the umbrella of a professional group, the Bahrain Recruiters Society (BRS). There are 85 recruiting agencies in Bahrain, approximately 60 of which belong to the BRS. According to the Ministry of Labor, labour regulators monitor the activities of these agencies and, if three genuine complaints against an agency are registered, the agency's license to operate will be revoked. According to the ministry, 64 agencies were closed during 2004 for 'various irregularities' (Baby 2005).

For other guest workers, like the multitudes of South Asian male construction workers, minimal regulations are provided by the labour laws and Memorandums of Understanding between the government and specific embassies (Singh 2008), though they are often deemed inefficient by human rights workers (personal communications: Marietta Dias, President of the Migrant Workers Society; personal communication, 6 December 2005; Nabeel Rajab, President of the Bahrain Center for Human Rights, 1 March 2006).

Individual sponsorship

The immigration sponsorship laws that apply to all expatriate guest workers in general, often referred to as a *kafala* (sponsorship) system of individual sponsorship (Longva 1999), create additional hardships for housemaids and for foreign workers in general. All foreign housemaids must be recruited through a recruiting agency. Direct hiring is illegal. Any sponsor bringing in a foreign housemaid must first obtain a work permit from the Ministry of Labor, which costs 30 Bahraini dinar ($80 USD). The sponsor then must arrange an exit visa for the housemaid at the relevant embassy, followed by arranging a work visa from the Directorate of Immigration, Nationality and Passports—a police function within the Ministry of the Interior (Smith 2005). Sponsors who earn less than 1,000 Bahraini dinar ($2,660 USD) per month are entitled to only one housemaid. Those earning more can receive visas for additional housemaids. Unique to Gulf systems of individual sponsorship—and contrary to international immigration standards—each domestic worker recruited is contractually bonded to the employer as her sponsor, usually for a period of two years. If the sponsor withdraws sponsorship at any time, for any reason, stated or unstated, the housemaid no longer has legal immigration status.

In some cases, workers are hired by Bahraini employers illegally. In this situation, workers arrive in Bahrain on a tourist visa despite laws that state that all foreign workers must be hired by licensed recruiting agencies. Often, the worker has agreed to pay back the cost of the free visa through their eventual salary, but end up earning too little in order to pay it back. Based on information received from Indian male construction workers, who refused to be named out of fear of losing their employment, the illegal 'free visa' scheme is not perpetrated by local organized crime figures. Rather, they implicated two members of the royal family who make additional income simply by signing off on sponsorship paperwork for workers who are working for someone else, in a direct violation of the sponsorship laws. One informant indicated that one of these members of the royal family is his sponsor whom he has never met and for whom he does not actually work (personal communication, 15 March 2006). In addition, a Bahraini sales manager revealed that he takes money from three guest workers to whom he provides sponsorship through phoney employment in a shell company he created. One Filipina 'free visa' worker he sponsors was listed as a 'physical metallurgist' in her visa paperwork to the government, despite having less than a secondary school education and working as a housemaid once she arrived in Bahrain. He stated that 'everyone' participates in schemes like this in order to make extra money, and that his behaviour was not deviant, though technically illegal (personal communication, 12 April 2006).

Moreover, embassy bans on housemaids from their countries have been implemented in order to send a message to recruiters as well as to buy time so that embassies can study the labour issues and implement their own solutions. Bangladesh and Indonesia have banned the recruiting of housemaids from their countries for a period of time during the past two years and the Philippines embassy has been contemplating such a ban (Al-Qahtani 2005; Rosario 2005*a*; 2005*e*). Blacklists are also kept by Indonesia (Rosario 2005*a*), India (R. Raghunathan, under-secretary to the Indian Ambassador to Bahrain, personal communication, 8 January 2006), and the Philippines; exit visa permission to work as housemaids for blacklisted employers is not given by these embassies.

Recruiters have been known to mistreat housemaids, as aforementioned, often illegally demanding money from housemaids in order to arrange their passage to Bahrain (Ravi 2005). Although cases of violence by recruiters are rarely reported, advocates believe that it often occurs (personal communication, Marietta Dias, 6 December 2005).

Criminal justice connection

Of particular importance to this study is the central role police play in handling housemaids entering and exiting the country. Because immigration is a police function in Bahrain, all changes in sponsorship status come immediately to the attention of police authorities. The local police station is the site at which sponsors register complaints against their housemaids in order to initiate a revocation of sponsorship at the General Directorate of Nationality, Passports and Residence. Despite registering housemaids with a work permit at the Ministry of Labor, as aforementioned, no subsequent regulation or oversight is provided by that ministry with regard to housemaids.

Deportation of housemaids occurs when (1) a sponsor decides to revoke sponsorship for any reason; (2) the housemaid has been convicted of a criminal offence; or (3) the housemaid wishes to leave and she has the funds to buy herself out of her contract (giving the employer money equivalent to her outstanding labour owed by the contract) and pay her way home. Housemaids rarely have the funds to leave the country without their sponsors' support. Although some funds are available from private charities such as the Migrant Workers Protection Society (MWPS), there is not enough money to meet the demand for stranded housemaids. As such, they swell the numbers of women in prison as they wait for the financial means to leave. To date, no sponsor has ever been held formally accountable for refusing to pay for their former housemaid's return ticket. In many instances, however, policewomen attempt to apply informal pressure on sponsors, in the form of shaming them in the police stations, to provide return tickets.

Washing one's hands of housemaids

Early terminations of housemaid–sponsor relationships are rarely amicable. Housemaids and sponsors' families reside in the same household. Housemaids come to know sponsors intimately because they are cleaning up after them and taking care of their children; they are privy to the private lives of their sponsors. Because there are no regulations or oversight over the work environment for the housemaid, the nature of the work experience is at the whim of the particular sponsor. Although there are many sponsors who treat their housemaids with respect and care, numerous reports have been documented in the last decade of exploitation and abuse, ranging from physical punishments for allegedly doing the job poorly to sexual abuse and rape by male members of the household.

Even in situations that are problematic, but do not rise to the level of abuse or exploitation, the close nature of the housemaid–sponsor relationship itself makes these situations dramatic and emotional. The women's section of the police station becomes the forum for sponsors' passionate re-telling of how they have been wronged by their housemaids and the housemaids' subsequent emotional rebuttal, laced with their fear of a criminal justice system they may not necessarily understand. Disputes quickly rise to the level of a criminal investigation as accusations of theft, assault and other criminal behaviour on the part of the housemaid are alleged to the police.

Hondagneu-Sotelo (2002), in her analysis of interviews with Latina domestic workers in Los Angeles, referred to these pressured domestic situations that suddenly turn emotional and ugly as 'blowups':

> It's a dramatic way to end a job, but not an uncommon one for domestic workers who often spend months or years in daily contact with the most intimate aspects of their employers' lives. (Hondagneu-Sotelo 2002: 55)

Intimacy in the employer–employee relationship was also highlighted as a source of conflict in Constable's (2002) study of Filipina housemaids in Hong Kong:

> The relationship between a household worker and her employer is potentially intense and complicated. Working in her employer's private domain she often observes behaviors to which only the closest family members are otherwise privy. (Constable 2002: 118)

Hondagneu-Sotelo (2002) further found that most of her interviewees had experienced a blow-up style termination, which became the norm, in her study of how these employment situations come to an end:

> Domestic work ... produces relationships that fall somewhere between family and employment yet are often regarded as neither. Caught betwixt and between, the domestic worker also finds herself on the losing end of a highly asymmetrical balance of power and privilege between employer and employee. Taken together, these conditions comprise a recipe for abuse and abrupt job endings. (Hondagneu-Sotelo 2002: 67)

The largely dramatic and emotional cases in Bahrain that featured housemaids were observed daily during the ethnographic period in local police stations.

Human rights activists have denounced the current system in Bahrain and other Gulf countries as criminalizing victims. Housemaids who report harassment, abuse and ill treatment are still expected to work for the sponsor for the rest of a contracted two-year period. According to the MWPS, judges deciding about runaway cases in Bahrain's courts rarely consider the housemaids' reasons for running away, focusing narrowly on the running away and ordering jail time followed by deportation (Fakhri 2005).

Methodology

The ethnographic data here were collected as part of a larger inquiry that sought to understand Bahraini female police officers as they performed their duties and included semi-structured interviews about their attitudes toward their work and toward gender segregation (Strobl 2008). It consists of unanticipated, but important, findings that warranted further investigation.

The researcher shadowed Bahraini policewomen for approximately eight months in 2005 and 2006. Twenty-two policewomen were shadowed for three or more days, respectively (and many more were observed within the workplace during the course of shadowing a particular officer) in the gender-segregated Women's Police Directorate, the women s prison, juvenile detention centre, social care unit and child protection units. Additional women were observed in the General Directorate of Traffic, National Directorate of Passports, Citizenship and Residency and the Criminal Investigation Division (CID). Approximately five of the eight months spent with policewomen in Bahrain involved observation in the kingdom's local police stations. Eleven police stations were visited, each over the course of several days. In Manama, the capital, policewomen were observed at Nabih Saleh, Hoora and Naim police stations. In addition, the researcher spent time at stations in Muharraq, Hidd, Khamis, Madinat Isa, Madinat Hamad, Riffa' and Budaiyah.

Semi-structured interviews were conducted about the policewomen's attitudes toward housemaids and housemaid-related cases. Eighty-four of the 368 policewomen on the force in May of 2006 were interviewed over the course of the research. The research involved both the English and Arabic languages. The researcher, though not fluent in Arabic, is able to read daily newspapers, converse and understand what policewomen are saying as they are observed. All data derived from oral Arabic were double-checked with policewomen for comprehension. Often, interaction with policewomen and other research subjects involved code-switching between English and Arabic—a common means of communication in Bahrain.

Criminal Complaints against Housemaids

There were five major typologies identifiable in cases observed at local police stations that involved housemaids: the amicably departing housemaid, the thieving housemaid, the runaway housemaid, the indiscrete housemaid, and the violent housemaid. Because the Ministry of the Interior did not permit the researcher to examine case files or any other written documents, the typologies described below were based on observations of interviews, interrogations and investigations of housemaids being performed by policewomen during the observation period. Because the criminalization of housemaid-related cases is a new academic frontier, the researcher developed the below typology after reviewing field-notes and grouping the cases into categories related to the housemaid's alleged behaviour as described by the complainant. Over the course of the observation period, the investigation into 150 cases against housemaids was viewed at some point in the policewomen's involvement in the matter. Most often, the researcher observed interviews with the housemaid and the housemaid's sponsor about the criminal complaint. In more rare instances, the researcher shadowed a policewoman to court, where a housemaid-related case was being adjudicated.

The first typology identified is an amicable dissolution of the housemaid–sponsor relationship. Even in cases in which the housemaid and sponsor agree to end their contract and sponsorship early, and the agreement has not been prefaced by any alleged criminal behaviour, both must appear at the local police station and/or the Directorate of Immigration, Nationality and Passports—a division of the police.

The remaining four typologies represent cases in which the housemaid's conduct is allegedly criminal, at least at the stage at which the situation is brought to the attention of police. The second typology identified is the thieving housemaid who stands accused of stealing from her sponsor. Under the third typology, the runaway housemaid, she is found by police having run away from her sponsor and is supporting herself through illegal employment, sometimes as a prostitute (although, at other times, she is found illegally employed by a legitimate employer). The fourth category, the indiscrete housemaid, represents situations in which a housemaid is caught in the sponsor's home with a man. The fifth typology is the rarest, but has occurred. This type of case, the violent housemaid, involves housemaids believed to have assaulted their sponsors. In some cases, a combination of the criminal typologies is found; for example, in one case in Riffa' police station, a housemaid was found to have run away from her sponsor after allegedly stealing from the home to finance her escape.

An example of each typology is presented below.

The thieving housemaid

A common complaint by sponsors is that their housemaids have stolen money or possessions from their home. According to the president of the Migrant Workers Protection Society (MWPS), although this is sometimes a legitimate complaint, it is often used as a means for the sponsor to quickly rid themselves of legal sponsorship of a housemaid that they no longer want for other reasons (personal communication, Marietta Dias, 6 December 2005). Based on ethnographic observation, many accusations of theft were adamantly denied by the housemaids. Often, there was no hard evidence, particularly with the theft of money, to determine who was most likely telling the truth. However, discerning whether the housemaid is guilty ends up being irrelevant to the outcome in most cases. Under the law, once a sponsor would like to revoke sponsorship of a housemaid, the housemaid has no right to contest this. Once the sponsor cancels the sponsorship, deportation proceedings begin.

Numerous accusations and investigations of housemaid theft were witnessed during the course of the ethnographic observation. In one case, an Indian housemaid, Swati,[1] was accused of stealing 1,500 Qatari riyal ($412 USD) and 220 Bahraini dinar ($585 USD) from her male sponsor's bedroom. According to him, she gave the money to a Filipino guest worker, whose name he provided, in order to wire it to her husband and family in India. Swati had only been in Bahrain working for the sponsor for 10 days prior to the accusation. The sponsor dropped the housemaid off at the local police station in the middle of the night and she was subsequently taken to the women's prison for holding until being returned to the local police station for interrogation the next morning. At this time, the sponsor and the labour recruiter who placed Swati in the sponsor's home were summoned to the women's section of the police station. The sponsor, a Bahraini man in a traditional robe (*thaūb*) and wearing an expensive watch and shoes, and the recruiter, a well dressed Indian expatriate, were each interviewed and their statements taken by the policewomen. Additional details were revealed by the sponsor, including that the Qatari riyal was found tucked in the housemaid's sari after the theft and that she had admitted to him that she had stolen the money. The recruiter provided little insight into the ordeal, but vouched for the credibility and good character of the sponsor.

Subsequently, Swati was brought into the interview process, but the sponsor and recruiter were not dismissed. Her interview and statement-taking were conducted in the presence of her accusers. Swati spoke in broken Arabic, but was not provided a translator in order for her to speak in her native language of Malayalam. She denied stealing and said that she never placed any money in her sari and that she never confessed to the sponsor as to the crime. She began to cry and to repeat over and over again that she was a good person. The sponsor and recruiter then began to argue with her in Arabic and Malayalam—an argument that escalated to yelling and screaming. The policewoman interviewing Swati tried to re-establish control by yelling even louder. Eventually, the housemaid became silent, tears streaming down her face, no longer participating in the argument. The policewoman explained that she could be prosecuted for the theft, which is punishable by imprisonment. Swati agreed that in exchange for agreeing to be deported at her sponsor's financial expense, she would not contest the allegations

[1] Name has been changed.

against her. The solution, however, was not agreeable to the sponsor and he began to argue with the recruiter, saying that the recruiter should pay for the deportation and pay him back the stolen money. A fight between the sponsor and recruiter ensued. Meanwhile, the housemaid signed a statement written in Arabic, which she could not read. In fact, because she was illiterate, she was unable to sign her name and was simply instructed to mark an 'X' as her signature. The policewoman then had her make an ink imprint of her right index finger beside the 'X'.

Dramatic arguments, crying, screaming and other emotional outbursts by sponsors, housemaids, recruiters and policewomen were common throughout the ethnographic observation of housemaid-related cases, re-enforcing Hondagneu-Sotelo's (2002) findings that such drama is common in the termination of the housemaid–employer relationship.

The runaway housemaid

Housemaids often run away from their homes in order to escape abuse. In other situations, employers find that the easiest way to rid themselves of workers whom they don't want to pay for is by going to the police and reporting the worker missing (Horton 2005). According to ethnographic observation, police do not independently investigate the credibility of reports of runaway workers, but rather wait until the worker is found to make any inquiries.

Housemaids on the run often support themselves by taking illegal work at local hotels. In one situation, two Indonesian women, Farida and Devi,[2] were reported to the police by an anonymous tipster of working as waitresses in a hotel bar without the proper work visa and sponsorship. Subsequent interviews by policewomen revealed that the women had originally entered the country as housemaids, but had both left their mutual sponsor, reportedly because the sponsor had not paid them in many months. The policewomen contacted the sponsor to let him know his housemaids were found. When inquiring about their salaries, the sponsor said that he had paid them; this response was satisfactory to the policewomen. Once the housemaids were away from their sponsor's home, their immigration status automatically became illegal during the three months they had been working at the hotel bar. As such, they had criminally violated the statutes against running away from one's sponsors and overstaying a residency visa.

A policewoman from the local station accompanied them to their appearance before a judge in the Lower Criminal Court in Manama, where they admitted that they ran away from their sponsor. They indicated that they wanted to return to Indonesia rather than continuing to work for the sponsor; however, they lacked the funds to make the trip. They explained that the sponsor had not paid them their salaries for several months when they were working for him. Like the police, the judge did not choose to follow up on this allegation of non-payment. The judge sentenced them each to ten days' imprisonment. According to the judge, the only way he can compel the sponsor to finance Farida and Devi's trip home is if the sponsor agrees to terminate their outstanding two-year contract. Alternatively, the sponsor has the right to request them back to the home to finish their two-year work contract, in which case Farida and Devi could only return home if they could find the financial means to do so. The judge ruled that a decision about deportation was pending further information as to the sponsor's desires.

[2] Names have been changed.

Just as often as seeking illegal work in legitimate businesses, runaway housemaids turn to prostitution rings to support themselves. In one such case, Ratna[3] was arrested for prostitution after neighbours complained of the heavy traffic of men coming in and out of her apartment in Muharraq. When interviewed by policewomen, Ratna stated that she originally had been a housemaid, but had run away from her sponsor after he accused her of beating his child. According to the housemaid, she never hurt the child, but rather was a victim herself of the sponsor's wife's regular beatings. Ratna wept as she described the blows she took whenever the wife was dissatisfied with the food she prepared or the way she cleaned the house. One time, she was beaten for putting the baby in front of the television when it was on an Indonesian station instead of a station that shows cartoons in Arabic. After enduring the abuse for seven months, the housemaid ran away after being promised a job at a hotel by an Indonesian man. Instead of being taken to her new job at a hotel, she was reportedly locked in the Muharraq flat and forced into prostitution to earn her keep. Ratna could not identify her pimp beyond a first name, so police were unable to capture him. Despite the horrific details alleged by the housemaid, the interview with her was approximately 20 minutes long with few follow-up questions. Later that morning, when the housemaid's sponsor and his wife were brought into the station, their interview with policewomen lasted well over an hour and their denials of any abusive treatment of the housemaid appeared to be believed. At the end of the fieldwork period, this case remained pending.

The indiscrete housemaid

Complaints that a housemaid is acting inappropriately in the home also are lodged at the local police station. In particular, many cases observed featured housemaids found being intimate with a man in the sponsor's home without the sponsor's permission. In one such case, which was prosecuted in the Lower Criminal Court, a Bengali housemaid, Madhu,[4] was allegedly found by her sponsor's son in an embrace with an Indian man in the middle of the night in the sponsor's garage. Both were prosecuted for the offence. During court proceedings, the offenders appeared at the same time before the judge and were questioned in Arabic despite the fact that they were not capable of fully expressing themselves in the language and often misunderstood questions.

According to Madhu, her brother, who is employed in the same house, had been causing her problems four months previously. Her brother gave her a letter from the male defendant by way of introduction. He requested a meeting with Madhu, who explained that she did not reply to the request. Her brother, however, arranged for the two to meet in the middle of the night and, from there, the two began a relationship. However, Madhu and her boyfriend adamantly denied having sex during the relationship. Ultimately, the judge sentenced both to one month in prison followed by deportation. Neither would be permitted to return to Bahrain for three years.

In another case, a housemaid arrived at a local hospital suffering from excessive bleeding. After medical tests, it was determined that the housemaid was pregnant. By law, the hospital is mandated to report to police that she was in violation of the statute against pregnancy out of wedlock. The police then contacted her sponsor, who had been

[3] Name has been changed.

[4] Name has been changed.

unaware that she was pregnant. Although she had lived and worked with her sponsor's family for a year and a half without any problems, her sponsor decided to fire her from her employment. Once pregnant, explained one policewoman, it becomes clear to the sponsor that the housemaid had violated the household and shamed them. As a consequence, she must be let go. But, because the sponsor agreed to forego any criminal prosecution for the pregnancy and agreed to cancel the housemaid's visa (a 'no objection letter'), and pay for her plane ticket home, the case was resolved without prosecution.

The violent housemaid

This category represents a rare situation in which the housemaid stands accused of violent behaviour. The most notorious housemaid-related case remains that of Ethiopian Youshirik Dhafta Zodi, who, on 1 December 1998, beat to death her Filipina employer, Sadiya Beltar, with a hammer and then hacked up the body with a machete and boiled the body parts. Her Bahraini husband found the body parts in the laundry machine and called the police. According to trial testimony reported in the press, the housemaid alleged chronic physical abuse by the employer, which led to the killing. Despite pleading insanity, the maid was found to be sane by the High Criminal Court and sentenced to the death penalty (*Gulf Daily News* 2000). However, her life was later spared when the Supreme Court of Appeals commuted her death sentence to life imprisonment after external pressure from human rights groups (*Gulf Daily News* 2004*a*).

During the ethnographic observation period, only one case out of about 150 witnessed involved charging a housemaid with a violent offence as a result of an episode with her sponsor. In one case, Rosa,[5] a Filipino housemaid, engaged in a physical fight with her sponsor after nine years of service. According to the medical report, the sponsor's wife suffered scratch marks and bruising over her face, chest and breast and trauma to her neck muscles. The sponsor's wife told policewomen how 'shocked' and 'surprised' she was that, after such a long relationship, Rosa would attack her. However, according to Rosa, she had been overworked during Ramadan, a religious month in Islam during which Muslims fast during the day but break their fast with a large feast (*ifṭār*) each evening. During the month, households find themselves overburdened with feast preparations for extended family members and guests. The incident occurred when, according to Rosa, she had been working several days for 18 hours straight with no breaks and only approximately five or six hours per night to take care of herself and sleep. She said that she was required to cook and prepare the house for numerous guests, plus take care of the children in the household—a job that was too much for just one person. Although the sponsor initially wanted to seek prosecution for assault, the policewomen managed to convince her to seek a quick resolution by agreeing to terminate the housemaid's employment, cancel her visa and pay for her deportation plane ticket.

According to the Philippine's embassy, reports of housemaid abuse spike each year during Ramadan. In the first ten days of Ramadan 2005, there were 100 cases of housemaid abuse reported to the embassy—approximately ten per day. The number of housemaids sheltered by the embassy swelled from approximately 30 on average to 44 (Rosario 2005*d*; Filio 2006). Housemaids reported that the reason they left

[5] Name has been changed.

their workplace was that they were overworked during Ramadan, physically and sexually abused and were not being paid (Rosario 2005*c*). The Indonesian embassy reports an average of three runaway housemaids a day during Ramadan (Rosario 2005*a*).

Policewomen's Attitudes toward Housemaids

Policewomen exhibited similar attitudes regarding housemaids as could be found in the larger society. As such, housemaids who found themselves at the local police stations were often looked down upon. Policewomen made little effort to comprehensively investigate their claims, and often more readily believed a Bahraini sponsor's side of the story over the foreign housemaid. Many policewomen stated, over the course of the observation, that housemaids usually had ill intentions. As one explained:

> The fault in these cases is usually with the housemaid wanting either sex or money. People in Bahrain have good hearts. They give their housemaids everything, but they always want more. The housemaids always claim they are mistreated, but if that is so, why do the run away and work illegally in hotels or become prostitutes? If they are so mistreated they should go to their embassies. Here we have no solution other than making a case against them.

Another policewoman said:

> The housemaids who have problems with the police have something wrong in their hearts. They have stolen money or run away because their own character is weak. What can we [policewomen] do? We cannot change them.

It should be noted that Bahraini policewomen identify more with sponsors rather than housemaids, likely due to their own social position in society. The vast majority of policewomen were raised in households that heavily relied on housemaids for their daily functioning. Known as the 'nanny state', labour watchdogs have explained that Bahrainis find that jobs involving manual labour or domestic work are not theirs to undertake, but rather are perceived as the exclusive domain of foreign workers (Horton 2004). This is common across countries that experience female labour migration as a 'global transfer of services associated with a wife's traditional role' (Ehrenreich and Hochschild 2002: 4).

In addition, the notion that impoverished conditions from which housemaids come justify abuse and exploitation in Bahrain (the 'it could be worse' argument) is widespread among policewomen. This was echoed by one policewoman when she said:

> It may seem like housemaids here are treated badly, but it's so much better than their lives at home. There they have absolutely nothing. At least here we give them a job, food and a place to live.

In addition, policewomen's careers have benefited from housemaids who are able to handle the cooking, cleaning and childcare while the women work outside the home. In essence, the forward trajectory of Bahraini women in the workplace has been made more possible by the cheap availability of housemaids:

> Women in [rich] countries have increasingly taken on paid work, and hence need others—paid domestics and caretakers for children and elderly people—to replace them. (Ehrenreich and Hochschild 2002: 6)

Ehrenreich and Hochschild (2002) attribute the insatiable demand for housemaids as a consequence of wealthier countries' unwillingness to provide public childcare for working mothers. In addition, men in most households failed to increase their contributions to domestic chores as women entered paid employment.

According to a survey of policewomen undertaken in February 2005, pursuant to this research, 25 per cent of respondents who have children indicated that their children were in the care of housemaids while they were working. The number jumps to approximately a half when considering only respondents who have children below the age of 12. The other half of the policewomen put their children in the care of their mother or sister.

Of the handful of policewomen known socially outside the workplace during this research, all employed a live-in housemaid to assist them with cooking, cleaning and raising children. It should be noted that all these policewomen appeared to treat their housemaids with respect and care—and, in some cases, had a strong friendship with their housemaid. Nonetheless, it is apparent that the policewomen would be unable to go to work and devote the hours required of their police careers without the housemaid's labour filling in the gap at home. In no Bahraini households visited were male family members ever primarily involved in child rearing, cleaning or cooking. Only one household featured a Bahraini father, a policeman, assisting in this regard on a regular basis (though the housemaid took primary responsibility).

In another example of the social attitudes prevalent in Bahrain, the following headline appeared in the *Bahrain Tribune* on 17 January 2006: 'Indian Maid Unlucky for Second Time' (*Bahrain Tribune* 2006: 4). The story describes the plight of Stella Mary, who left her first employer after being overworked to exhaustion and made to sleep outside on a mattress without any blankets. When she returned to Bahrain to work for a second employer, she was beaten by the sponsor's wife with kitchen appliances and high-heeled shoes and was kept prisoner in the children's nursery, having to ask permission to use the bathroom. In a final showdown before Stella left the household, the sponsor's wife accused her of not feeding the children and began tearing off her clothes in a fit of rage—in front of the housemaid's male sponsor. The headline stating that the housemaid was 'unlucky', when coupled with this story, implies that the fate of this particular housemaid is a fluke—part of some terrible streak of luck—rather than being an all-too-common situation. This is a typical framing of the female labour migrant's situation in Bahraini discourse, where employment and migration are viewed as a 'personal choice' and its consequences are seen as 'personal problems' (Hochschild 2002: 27). Although the end of the newspaper article quotes Marietta Dias, President of the MWPS, who defends the housemaid and attempts to place the situation in its larger context, her statement pales in comparison to the headline's message.

'Dumping' Housemaids in the Criminal Justice System

The problem with housemaids transcends the authority of local police stations, yet local police stations, and particularly the policewomen, have been tasked as the primary responders. Police are unable to directly confront the larger socio-political, economic and legal issues surrounding the problem and instead must utilize the tools at their disposal to handle the influx of housemaids. Because of this, housemaids tend to be criminalized and incarcerated even in cases in which this is not appropriate. Police cannot operate in a manner not provided for by law; they have only the procedures of criminal investigation at their disposal. Furthermore, policewomen are at the back-end of the problem, being made aware of situations only after they have reached the point of crisis. As such, they cannot make up for the lax regulation of the housemaid industry, the unethical recruitment practices and the cruelty of sponsors, nor do they have the information, means or mandate to prevent these problems before they happen. Coupled with their own aforementioned identification with sponsors and employers over housemaids, the dumping of housemaids into the criminal justice system often creates further trauma for housemaids. The result is that the housemaids are punished for the exploitation and abuse of their sponsors; as aforementioned, there is only one example in Bahrain of a sponsor being convicted of a crime against a housemaid.

According to a high-ranking female police officer, the Ministry of Labor refuses to accept responsibility for housemaid–sponsor conflicts and, by default, all these cases are 'dumped' into the Women's Police Directorate (WPD). Once the police have responsibility for a housemaid who has been cut loose by her sponsor, who has run away or who refuses to return to her sponsor's home, she is incarcerated, even if she has not committed a criminal violation. Approximately 70 per cent of all detainees in the women's prison in 2004 came from South Asian nations, the majority of which were housemaids (Strobl 2008).

The high-ranking female police officer further opined that the hands-off policy on the part of the labour ministry has consequences for policewomen. She stated 'No one wants to take responsibility for the problem and so we are stuck with it'. She suggested that housemaid cases that do not involve allegations of violence should be dealt with by the Ministry of Labor in a special sub-agency devoted to housemaid issues. She believes the ministry should also be responsible for housing runaway workers in order to relieve the women's prison of overcrowding. However, the government continues to move in a direction that would maintain the status quo, despite public statements to the contrary. The Ministry of the Interior is currently working on converting a dry dock in Hidd to incarcerate housemaids in order to separate them from the general population of women detainees.

Housemaids and Policewomen's Careers

The role of housemaids in the development of policewomen in Bahrain represents an important shifting of the original policewomen's mission of helping women with problems such as domestic abuse. Because of the social attitudes and discriminatory legal code in Bahrain, this original mission does not extend to poor, mostly South Asian women working as housemaids. Instead, these victims are criminalized, treated as people who do not deserve the special treatment that the female police are said to offer. This indicates that economic class and nationality are significant barriers to the care policewomen provide. Because policewomen do not identify with housemaids as fellow women, but feel that they are an identifiable 'other', there is a lack of what many Western scholars would call feminist consciousness apparent in the police stations. Ironically, the rise in the number of policewomen in the last decade occurs contemporaneously with the rise in housemaid cases. From 2004 to 2006, the number of policewomen in Bahrain nearly doubled (Strobl 2008). Although this does not prove that policewomen owe their sustained and increasing presence to the criminalization of housemaids, one can't help but wonder whether the amount of female personnel in local police stations, immigration and the women's prison would be required if these cases were properly diverted to another agency.

In the historical development of Bahraini policewomen, opportunities were shown to originate from the need to keep customary gender segregation intact within police stations and the criminal justice system in general. Policewomen found themselves in the liminal space between genders, empowered to act as authorities, but in a capacity designed to keep men and women's roles in society delineated. As policewomen were becoming symbols of progressive female roles in Bahrain, they were simultaneously re-enforcing social customs that perceived women as suitable for quite opposite roles within private domestic spheres. Likewise, the policewomen today are deployed to maintain the complicated boundaries of employer and housemaid in the realm of the family. The continued exploitation and criminalization of housemaids make policewomen the indirect, back-end agents maintaining Bahrain's patriarchal social and economic fabric, which relies so heavily on cheap, female foreign labour. As such, policewomen find themselves as agents of social control in ways that are not necessarily compatible with women's best interests in a general sense, whether conceived of in the Western, Arab or Muslim feminist literature.

Most stakeholders agree that solutions to the housemaid problem do not rest within the Women's Police Directorate, the police or the Ministry of the Interior. All critics emphasize larger political and social reform as the best hope for housemaids, involving a revamping of labour laws—a response that must occur at the top levels of government and have the support of parliament, the consultative (*shura*) council and the royal family.

The deployment of women police is often a reification of patriarchal social control because policewomen are largely used in order to control the behavior of women and to enforce laws that are patriarchal in nature. As one sees in Bahrain, policewomen can be both markers of liberalizing policies designed to win over the hearts and minds of the global, capitalist community, yet be deployed in ways that further reinforce customary patriarchal notion about the role of women, such as being used to handling housemaids (Strobl 2008). The overwhelming extent to which policewomen's daily work involves responding to the larger, socio-economic problem of housemaids draws into question whether the interests of women globally and collectively are met by the existence of policewomen in some national forces.

Notions of feminism that privilege particular cultures, identities and other essentialisms problematize the imagining of a police system that empowers the diverse members of a given society, per the general framework of community policing and policing in democratic countries. Feminisms with nationalist, secularist or Islamic orientations, though useful as a means of resistance, ultimately fall short and displace ontological anxieties on yet another group. As such, these forms of feminism have a theoretical limitation in imagining women and the criminal justice system in diverse societies. At the same time, as An-Naim (1992) has persuasively argued, any transcendent human-based approaches to justice must nurture cultural rethinking and reinterpretation from within a local milieu in order to be authentically created and maintained. Therefore, feminist thinking must begin to work within cultural spaces while simultaneously imagining a transcendence of identity politics and discriminatory policing that fuels the 'devastating rhetoric of "us vs. them"' (Suleri 1992: 756).

Instead, the notion of 'planetary' feminism could be employed—a framework that includes all human women (Spivak 2006: 107) and can be approached through Spivak's 'politics of the imagination' (Sharpe and Spivak 2002). Because the link between capitalism, patriarchy and criminal justice is part of the imaginative power of the politics of corporate globalization, 'it requires an equally forceful appeal to the imagination for contestation' (Sharpe and Spivak 2002: 610).

Funding

Funding was provided by a grant from the U.S. Fulbright program administered by the U.S. Dept of State.

References

Abu-Lughod, L. (1986/1999), *Veiled Sentiments: Honor and Poetry in a Bedouin Society*, 2nd edn. Berkeley: University of California Press.

Al-Qahtani, R. (2005), 'Countries Draw Line over Maids', *Gulf Daily News*, 22 October, retrieved from archives at *Gulf Daily News* in Madinat Isa, Bahrain.

Al-Tawashi, E. (2003), 'Maids Jobs to Be Slashed', *Gulf Daily News*, 26 June, retrieved from archives located in Isa Town, Bahrain.

An-Naim, A. (1992), 'Towards a Cross-Cultural Approach to Defining International Standards of Human Rights: The Meaning of Cruel, Inhuman, or Degrading Treatment or Punishment', in A. An-Naim, ed., *Human Rights in Cross-Cultural Perspective*, 19–43. Philadelphia, PA: University of Pennsylvania Press.

Baby, S. (2005), 'Labour Watchdog', *Gulf Daily News*, 20 November, retrieved from *Gulf Daily News* archives in Madinat Isa, Bahrain.

Bahrain Tribune (2005), 'Housemaids Seek Some Respect', 10 December: 2.

Bahrain Tribune (2006), 'Indian Maid Unlucky for Second Time'.

Beydoun, K. A. (2006), 'The Trafficking of Ethiopian Domestic Workers into Lebanon: Navigating through a Novel Passage of the International Maid Trade', *Berkeley Journal of International Law*, 24: 1009–45.

Boyle, P. (2002), 'Population Geography: Transnational Women on the Move', *Progress in Human Geography*, 26: 531–43.

Constable, N. (2002), 'Filipina Workers in Hong Kong Homes: Household Rules and Relations', in B. Ehrenreich and A. R. Hochschild, eds, *Global Woman: Nannies, Maids and Sexworkers in the New Economy*, 115–41. New York: Henry Holt.

Ehrenreich B. and Hochschild A,, eds. (2002), *Global Woman: Nannies, Maids and Sex Workers in the New Economy*. New York: Henry Holt.

Fakhri, A. (2005), '"Change System of Sponsorship" Plea', *Gulf Daily News*, 19 September, retrieved from archives located in Isa Town, Bahrain.

Gulf Daily News (2000), 'Death for Maid who Butchered Employer', 29 November, retrieved from *Gulf Daily News* archives in Madinat Isa, Bahrain.

——(2003*a*), 'Abuse of Maids "Will Not Be Tolerated"', 2 November, retrieved from *Gulf Daily News* archives in Madinat Isa, Bahrain.

——(2003*b*), 'Maids "Draining the Economy"', 26 June 26, retrieved from archives located in Isa Town, Bahrain.

——(2004*a*), 'Court Spares Killer Maid's Life', 28 January: 1.

——(2004*b*), 'Number of Maids in Gulf on the Rise'19 October: 1.

——(2005), '"Fast-Track Abuse Cases" Appeal', 23 October, retrieved from *Gulf Daily News* archives in Isa Town, Bahrain.

FERNANDO, B. (2006), 'Trapped on the Balcony: A Tale of a Sri Lankan Held Hostage in Lebanon', in J. Sage and L. Kasten, eds, *Enslaved: True Stories of Modern Day Slavery*, 81–111. New York: Palgrave MacMillan.

FILIO, T. (2005), 'Without Powers, Ministry Keeps Hands Off Minimum Wage for Maids', *Bahrain Tribune*, 16 October: 3.

——(2006), 'No Break for Housemaids', *Bahrain Tribune*, 1 May: 3.

FITZPATRICK, T. (2001), 'New Agendas for Social Policy and Criminology: Globalization, Urbanism and the Emerging Post-Security State', *Social Policy & Administration*, 35: 212–29.

GARLAND, D. (2001), *The Culture of Control: Crime and Social Order in Contemporary Society*. Chicago: University of Chicago Press.

HOCHSCHILD, A. R. (2002), 'Love and Gold', in B. Ehrenreich and A. R. Hochschild, eds, *Global Woman: Nannies, Maids and Sexworkers in the New Economy*, 15–30. New York: Henry Holt.

HONDAGNEU-SOTELO, P. (2002), 'Blowups and Other Unhappy Endings', in B. Ehrenreich and A. R. Hochschild, eds, *Global Woman: Nannies, Maids and Sexworkers in the New Economy*, 55–69. New York: Henry Holt.

HORTON, S. (2004), '"Even in Death these People Are Not Free"', *Gulf Daily News*, 20 November, retrieved from *Gulf Daily News* archives in Madinat Isa, Bahrain.

JENNESS, V. (2004), 'Explaining Criminality: From Demography and Status Politics to Globalization and Modernization', *Annual Review of Sociology*, 30: 147–71.

JUREIDINI, R. and MOUKARBEL, N. (2004), 'Female Sri Lankan Domestic Workers in Lebanon: A Case of "Contract Slavery"?', *Journal of Ethnic and Migration Studies*, 30: 581–607.

LAN, P. (2003), 'Negotiating Social Boundaries and Private Zones: The Micropolitics of Employing Migrant Domestic Workers', *Social Problems*, 50: 525–49.

LIENHARDT, P. (2001), *Shaikhdoms of Eastern Arabia*. New York: Palgrave.

LONGVA, A. N. (1999), 'Keeping Migrant Workers in Check: The Kafala System in the Gulf', *Middle East Report*, 211: 20–2.

Ministry of Labour and Social Affairs, Bahrain (1976), 'Labor Law for the Private Sector', retrieved 3 April 2006 from www.bah-molsa.com/english/chap1.htm.

MISRA, J., WOODING, J. and MERZ, S. (2006), 'The Globalization of Care Work: Neoliberal Economic Restructuring and Migration Policy', *Globalizations*, 3: 317–32.

MOHANTY, C. (2003), *Feminism without Borders: Decolonizing Theory, Practicing Solidarity*. Durham, NC: Duke University Press.

PICKERING, S. (2007), 'Transnational Crime and Refugee Protection', *Social Justice*, 2: 47–61.

RAVI, M. (2005), 'Dumped Maids Given a Break', *Bahrain Tribune*, 20 October: 1.

ROSARIO, E. (2005*a*), 'Jobs Pact Plan to Curb Maid Abuse', *Gulf Daily News*, 15 November, retrieved from archives located in Isa Town, Bahrain.

——(2005*b*), 'New Clamp on Worker Abuse', *Gulf Daily News*, 7 July, retrieved from archives located in Isa Town, Bahrain.

——(2005*c*), 'Philippines to Ban Housemaids', *Gulf Daily News*, 4 April, retrieved from archives located in Isa Town, Bahrain.

——(2005*d*), 'Runaway Maid Cases on the Rise', *Gulf Daily News*, 15 October: 5.

——(2005*e*). 'Warning to Recruiters', *Gulf Daily News*, 23 November, retrieved from archives located in Isa Town, Bahrain.

SASSEN, S. (2002), 'Counter-Geographies of Globalization', in K. Saunders, ed., *Feminist Post-Development Thought*, 255–6. London: Zed Books.

SHARPE, J. and SPIVAK, G. C. (2002), 'A Conversation with Gayatri Chakravorty Spivak: Politics and the Imagination', *Signs: Journal of Women in Culture and Society*, 28: 609–24.

SINGH, M. (2008), 'Welfare of Maids to be Highlighted', *Gulf Daily News*, 6 May, retrieved 9 May 2008 from www.gulf-daily-news.com.

SMITH, R. (2005), 'Workers' Rights for Housemaids', *Gulf Daily News*, 29 March, retrieved from archives at *Gulf Daily News* in Madinat Isa, Bahrain.

SPIVAK, G. C. (2006), 'World Systems and the Creole', *Narrative*, 14: 102–12.

——(2008), 'Gayatri Spivak and Peter Hitchcock in Conversation', presentation at the Center for the Humanities, The Graduate Center, City University of New York, 7 February.

STROBL, S. (2008), 'The Women's Police Directorate in Bahrain: An Ethnographic Exploration of Gender Segregation and the Likelihood of Future Integration', *International Criminal Justice Review*, 18: 39–58.

SULERI, S. (1992), 'Woman Skin Deep: Feminism and the Postcolonial Condition', *Critical Inquiry*, 18: 756–69.

WILLMAN-NAVARRO, A. (2006), 'Making It at the Margins: The Criminalization of Nicaraguan Women's Labor under Structural Reform', *International Feminist Journal of Politics*, 8: 243–66.

YOUNG, J. (1999), *The Exclusive Society*. Thousand Oaks, CA: Sage Publications.

Part V
Global Trades: At the Intersection of Legal and Illegal Business Transactions

[18]

Global Anomie, Dysnomie, and Economic Crime: Hidden Consequences of Neoliberalism and Globalization in Russia and Around the World

Nikos Passas

Introduction

TRANSNATIONAL CRIME HAS RECENTLY ACQUIRED A PROMINENT PLACE IN PUBLIC debates. It is commonly presented as the most significant crime problem at the turn of the millennium (Myers, 1995–1996; Shelley, 1995). Many have even suggested that it represents a serious domestic and international security threat (Paine and Cillufo, 1994; Williams, 1994). The argument is also made that a wave of transnational crime undermines neoliberal policies and the functioning of an increasing number of market economies around the globe (Handelman, 1995; Shelley, 1994). As a consequence, the proposed remedies are often quite drastic and involve undercover operations, privacy-piercing approaches, and the participation of intelligence services in the fight against global crime (Andreas, 1997; Naylor, 1999; Passas and Blum, 1998; Passas and Groskin, 1995).

Yet, little attention and virtually no systematic research has been devoted to understanding the causes, structure, extent, and effects of serious cross-border misconduct (Passas, 1998). The risks it poses may be grossly exaggerated (Naylor, 1995; Lee, 1999). The draconian measures being contemplated and implemented in different countries, therefore, are essentially an exercise in shooting in the dark. Chances are good that the target will be missed and substantial "collateral damage" may be caused by ill-conceived policies in this "war" on crime. This risk is

---

NIKOS PASSAS is Associate Professor in the Department of Criminal Justice at Temple University (529 Gladfelter Hall, Philadelphia, PA 19122; e-mail: npassas@nimbus.temple.edu). The author specializes in the study of white-collar crime, corruption, organized crime, and international crime. He is the author of *Informal Value Transfer Systems and Criminal Organizations: A Study into So-called Underground Banking Networks* (1999) and the editor of *The Future of Anomie Theory* (1997), *Transnational Crime* (1999), and *Organized Crime* (1995). Dr. Passas has authored numerous papers and research reports. He serves as Northeastern University Press series editor on transnational crime. He has acted as a consultant to various bodies, including the United Nations Centre for International Crime Prevention, the Commission of the European Union, the German Parliament, and a number of governments. The author wishes to thank warmly Bob Weiss for his constructive feedback and patience.

particularly high in countries in transition toward a market democracy. It would be much wiser, thus, to carefully study the problem before taking ineffective and possibly damaging actions.

This article seeks to make a contribution by concentrating on the causes of transnational economic crime. The main argument is that, contrary to conventional wisdom, neoliberalism and globalization contribute to processes leading to global anomie, dysnomie, and, ultimately, economic misconduct. They do so by activating the criminogenic potential of economic, political, legal, and cultural asymmetries, as well as by creating new such asymmetries (Passas, 1999). These asymmetries cause crime by furnishing opportunities for misconduct, by generating motives for actors to take advantage of such opportunities, and by weakening social controls. More specifically, means-ends disjunctions are systematically created, as neoliberal policies foster new needs and desires that are all too often left unfulfilled. Promises of more freedom, prosperity, and happiness for a larger number of people have turned out to be chimerical. Economic and power inequalities have widened within and across countries in the last two decades. The number of poor has reached unprecedented levels, while welfare programs and safety nets are reduced or abolished. Enormous populations have become more vulnerable to exploitation, criminal victimization, and recruitment in illicit enterprises or rebel and fundamentalist groups. Normative standards and control mechanisms are weak or completely absent exactly when they are needed the most.

This article begins with some basic conceptual clarifications and outlines the theoretical framework so far applied to the analysis of U.S. organizational and individual deviance. Then, the main features of globalization and neoliberalism are presented, followed by a contrast of promises made by proponents of neoliberal policies and their actual consequences. Attention then shifts to specific criminogenic effects of these outcomes and the case of Russia, which illustrates the different stages in the processes leading up to serious misconduct and anomie. The chief policy implication of this analysis is that the recently unleashed forces of neoliberalism need to be reined in and held in check, while government policies ought to better shield the least privileged from the adverse effects of globalization.

Some Conceptual Clarifications

Although there is no universally accepted definition of transnational crime, many commentators seem to think of it as a globalized form of the stereotypical "organized crime." This, however, leaves out corporate and governmental crimes, whose effects can be far more harmful than those of "professional" criminals and ethnic groups involved in the business of illegal goods and services. We therefore need a definition that is inclusive enough without becoming too relativistic and subjective. For our purposes, transnational crime refers to cross-border misconduct that entails avoidable and unnecessary harm to society, is serious enough to warrant state intervention, and is similar to other kinds of acts criminalized in the countries concerned or by international law. Crime will be viewed as transnational when the offenders or victims are located in or operate through more than one country (Passas, 1999).

Globalization is another term that is often used without clear definition. In the simplest sense, it refers to a growing interconnectedness and multilateral linkages across national borders. According to Keohane and Nye (2000: 104),

> globalism is a state of the world involving networks of interdependence at multicontinental distances. The linkages occur through flows and influences of capital and goods, information and ideas, and people and forces, as well as environmentally and biologically relevant substances (such as acid rain or pathogens).

Globalism has several dimensions, such as economic, cultural, environmental, or military, not all of which take place at the same time. So, whenever globalism increases and becomes thicker or more intense, we can speak of globalization. When globalism decreases, we can speak of de-globalization.

Finally, the term "criminogenic asymmetries" refers to structural discrepancies and inequalities in the realms of the economy, law, politics, and culture. Such asymmetries are produced in the course of interactions between unequal actors (individual or organizational) or systems with distinctive features. All asymmetries contain some criminogenic potential. Durkheim argued that crime cannot be eliminated, because we are and always will be different from each other. Even in a society of saints, minor deviations would be considered serious offenses. In modern societies, crimes are those behavioral differences (asymmetries) that have been outlawed by legislative bodies. There is always the opportunity for powerful actors to victimize less privileged ones (economic, political, and power asymmetries). This potential is not always materialized. Criminal opportunities are not necessarily taken advantage of. Mostly this is because actors do not always seek or wish to make use of illegal opportunities. They may not regard such action as appropriate (due to socialization, internalization of norms) or fear adverse consequences. The criminogenic potential is most likely to be activated when opportunities, motives, and weak controls are all present.

For example, a combination of legal/regulatory asymmetries with economic and political asymmetries has given rise to a huge illicit market for toxic waste disposal. Many Third World countries either did not regulate toxic waste or did so much less rigorously than did industrialized states. This provided an opportunity for maximum-profit-seeking companies to get rid of their hazardous waste in areas where rules were lax or nonexistent (Center for Investigative Reporting and Moyers, 1990; Critharis, 1990). Power and economic asymmetries between rich and poor countries have led waste recipients to allow this to go on because of their dependence on foreign investment, the need for cash to service external debt, or the desire to create jobs (Korten, 1995). Economic and knowledge asymmetries also shaped the motivation of local participants in this questionable trade. The decision to go along reflects an incomplete understanding of the extent or nature of the hazard, their desperate need for additional income, an effort to be competitive and attractive to foreign companies (race to the bottom), or corruption.

Anomie and Deviance

Both Durkheim (1983) and Merton (1968) have stressed how high rates of deviance should be expected when social expectations are out of balance with realistic opportunities to reach the desired goals. According to Durkheim, this means-ends discrepancy is caused by society's inability to regulate people's naturally limitless desires. This problem was particularly acute in the commercial and business sector, in which anomie was chronic during the industrial revolution, opening up new horizons and undermining society's ability to contain aspirations. A similar situation can be observed in contemporary societies, where electronic, information, and biological technologies constantly redefine what is possible and break new ground.

According to Merton, unrealistic hopes and expectations are not simply natural, but socially constructed and promoted. Structural problems are at the heart of the means-ends disjunction. The U.S. culture and the ideology of the American Dream encourage lofty expectations, while society fails to provide equal access to legal opportunities. Meanwhile, there is a cultural overemphasis on success goals at the expense of normative behavior (as further elaborated by Messner and Rosenfeld, 1994). Both of these factors make for deviance and anomie.

Without ignoring the differences between the two sociologists, it has been possible to use an elaborated version of their anomie theories to explain corporate crime in the context of capitalist economies (Passas, 1990). Regardless of whether people strive for "more" due to natural drives or because of cultural encouragement, the point is that market economies cannot perform without lofty aspirations, consumerism, emphasis on material/monetary goals, and competition. All this leads to the pursuit of constantly moving targets and systematic sources of frustration. A synthesis of anomie theory with reference group analysis made clear how means-ends discrepancies are socially generated and experienced by people in all social strata. It also showed how this theoretical framework is applicable to the analysis of crime without strain or problems (i.e., anomie theory is not a strain theory) and to "organized crime" even after discrimination or blockage of legitimate opportunities no longer affects minority groups (Passas, 1997).

In brief, the dynamic social process leading to structurally induced strain, anomie, and deviance without strain is as follows. Means-ends discrepancies are caused by a strong cultural emphasis on monetary or material success goals for all members of society, while a good number of them do not have a realistic chance to attain them. Socially distant comparative referents are constantly introduced and sustained through the school, family, politics, workplace, media, advertising, and even religion (Passas, 1994). Regardless of their social background and the social capital available to them, people are urged to desire more than they have. Success stories of going from rags to riches make the American Dream even more believable. As this cultural theme is internalized, competitive forces and consumerism foster normative referents on what is "normal" and appropriate. The widely internalized egalitarian discourse clashes in practice with widespread inequality (power and economic asymmetries). Consequently, those members who fail to meet such comparative and normative standards are likely to experience relative deprivation and frustration. This strain, combined with the culturally induced overemphasis on goals and the concomitant underemphasis on the proper methods, makes for deviance of various types (see Merton's typology). A good part of the deviance is an individual search for a solution to these structural problems. If the deviant solution is successful (i.e., perpetrators are not caught or adequately punished), this adaptation may become normative for others in a similar social context. To the extent that this solution is available to them (demand for illicit goods or services, access to illegitimate opportunity structures), they may adopt this role model — and may be expected by their significant others to follow this path — even though the original source of strain has by now been eclipsed. Unless effective control measures are taken, this process continues in a vicious circle toward higher rates of deviance and widespread anomie (for a schematic representation of this process, see Figure 1 at the end of the article).

In the literature, anomie is often conceptually confused with its causes or effects. To keep its explanatory potential, this mistake should be avoided. Anomie is a withdrawal of allegiance from conventional norms and a weakening of these norms' guiding power on behavior. This is caused by structural contradictions and affects deviance in two ways. One is associated with strain, the other is not. The former is caused by relative deprivation, frustrations, and the almost obsessive focus on goals. This makes deviance thinkable, as conventional norms are regarded as nonbinding, at least temporarily. Rationalizations enable departures from otherwise accepted/internalized social rules, as actors convince themselves that in their particular circumstances an exception is acceptable (Aubert, 1968; Sykes and Matza, 1957). Through interactive processes, techniques of neutralization and rationalizations contribute to a context in which newly socialized actors may adopt normative referents and deviant behavior as a matter of course. If "this is the way business is done around here," people may engage in price fixing or misleading advertising without experiencing any prior frustration or problem.

Globalization and Neoliberalism

These structural problems have been most prominent in the USA. However, a very similar process is now being reproduced throughout the world through globalism and neoliberalism. Promises are made that are not fulfilled. People's expectations are exalted at a time when economic and power asymmetries increase and become less justifiable and intolerable in the eyes of the people affected. The logic of the market permeates popular thinking and introduces rationalizations, making the adoption of a criminal or unethical solution more acceptable. The horizontal lines in Figure 1, rather than representing controlling influences, at the global level point to the criminogenic impact of globalization and neoliberal policies.

Nowadays, globalism and neoliberalism seem to be indistinguishable empirically or even conceptually (Cox, 1993; Stewart and Berry, 1999). Nevertheless, I think it is useful to try to separate them analytically. As noted earlier, globalism refers to the degree of interconnectedness and the increase or decrease of linkages. By contrast, neoliberalism refers to an economic and political school of thought on the relations between the state on the one hand, and citizens and the world of trade and commerce on the other. Because it espouses minimal or no state interference in the market and promotes the lifting of barriers to trade and business transactions across regional and national borders, it certainly becomes a motor of globalization.

Globalization in the last two decades shows clear signs of deeper and thicker interconnections that affect many more people than ever before. The effects are now much faster, as shown by the financial crisis in Thailand in 1997. The world has shrunk and become "one place," with global communications and media, transnational corporations, supranational institutions, and integrated markets and financial systems that trade around the clock (McGrew, 1992; Sklair, 1995). The cultural landscape has changed under the influence of mass media. Through their ads, TV programs, movies, and music, they contribute to cultural globalism, target young children, and foster consumerism (e.g., "Image Is Everything," "Just Do It," or "Coke Is It"). Information technology is making for "distant encounters and instant connections" (Yergin and Stanislaw, 1998). Fresh normative and comparative ideals are thus promoted, legitimated, and presented as attainable. Scholars attribute the momentum of this process to the forces of capitalism (Wallerstein, 1983), technology (Rosenau, 1990), the presence of a hegemon (Gilpin, 1987), or a combination of them all (Giddens, 1990).

Neoliberalism, in particular, has made a major contribution to the dynamic and contradictory processes of globalization since the elections of Ronald Reagan, Margaret Thatcher, and Helmut Kohl. During the 1950s and 1960s, the dominant concerns revolved around distributive justice, neocolonialism, and dependency theory. These were displaced in the 1980s and into the 1990s by discourses of "free markets," individualism, and self-help (Woods, 1999). Policies of deregulation, privatization of state assets, and removal of tariffs implemented the doctrine that the state should get out of the way of free enterprise. Unemployment, inequality, and poverty were no longer explained by structural contradictions or constraints. The problems became individualized and blamed on corrupt administrations or on the poor themselves. The proposed medicine was more liberalization of the economy, free competition, privatization of inefficiently managed government agencies, abolition of capital controls, and permitting foreign capital to enter all markets.

The ideological underpinning of globalization, thus, has been the primacy of economic growth, which is thought to be benefiting the whole planet. Consistent with that prime directive, country after country has been persuaded (or forced) to promote "free trade" and consumerism, to reduce government regulation of business, and to adopt the same economic model regardless of local specificities and differences between industrialized and developing countries (Bello, 1999; Mander, 1996).

More specifically, shifts in the North, the East, and the South have been quite remarkable. In the North, the welfare state that used to care for citizens "from cradle to grave" has been replaced by a "pay as you go" social service system. Even public utilities have been privatized and have begun to charge "economic prices," as former subsidization systems were abolished. Further, "industrial interventionism and labour protection have given way to laissez-faire; and...tax systems whose major purpose was to correct inequalities have been transformed into systems mainly intended to promote incentives and economic efficiency" (Stewart and Berry, 1999: 151).

In developing countries, similar shifts took place as a result of hegemonic influences from the North. Western-educated Third World "technocrats" returned to their home countries eager to introduce neoliberal policies (Burbach et al., 1997: 86; *Newsweek*, June 15, 1992). As the bandwagon of liberalization took off, few countries wished to be left out. As a World Bank official warned, "lagging countries risk being left farther behind.... For economies that remain inward-looking, the risk of being marginalized is greater than ever" (cited in Klak, 1998: 21).

Yet, the shifts have not always been voluntary. A host of measures and conditions consistent with the neoliberal agenda were imposed on countries through international institutions, such as the International Monetary Fund (IMF), the World Bank, the OECD, the European Union, the G7, etc. Countries drowning in external debt sought additional loans to pay off their older ones — chiefly to banks from the industrialized world. Billions of dollars were made available to them, but only if they introduced Structural Adjustment Programs (SAPs). Despite important differences among the various economies, SAPs shared the same basic elements: long-term "structural" reforms to deregulate the economy, liberalization of trade, removal of restrictions on foreign investment, promotion of an export orientation of the economy, wage reductions and controls, privatization of state enterprises, and short-term stabilization measures such as cutbacks in government spending, high interest rates, and currency devaluation (Bello, 1996; 1999).

Changes along these lines also took place in the East, where the switch from state-managed economies toward "free market" and parliamentary democracy has been quite drastic and swift (Glinkina, 1994; Woods, 1999). The problem is that the introduction of global neoliberalism has brought about enormous economic and political asymmetries, as its promises and theoretical expectations remain unfulfilled.

The Promises of Global Neoliberalism

The supporters of global neoliberalism make a series of claims. For instance, the world is shrinking following greater connectivity (IBM claims to offer "solutions for a smaller planet"). The distinction between core and periphery states is presumed to be getting fuzzier and irrelevant, as there are only winners from now on. Investment, trade, and development opportunities are more widely distributed around the world. There is a marked convergence into one world economy, in which everyone can find a market niche. Media and cultural influences are more widespread and multilateral, as foods, music, and art are imported to the North and integrated into local cultures. Finally, people are more integrated thanks to telecommunication technologies and immigration (Klak, 1998).

To economists, all these trends are positive, even if short-term hardship is deemed necessary for some parts of the population. Global welfare is expected to be enhanced, as the forces of free competition within and between countries will encourage more efficient resource allocation and bring about higher productivity (Oman, 1999). A more open, trade-creating world should, therefore, benefit everyone, if unevenly. Trickle-down effects of wealth creation would ensure that virtually everyone will participate in this welcome trend (Korten, 1996).

The objective of SAPs was to render developing economies more efficient, drive up growth rates, and provide foreign exchange that could be used to repay debt. Higher growth rates are empirically associated with comparatively more equal income distribution (Alesina and Rodrik, 1994). Hence, neoliberal policies would bring about not only more economic growth, productivity, a better division of labor (multistate production and wider participation), lower unemployment, more wealth and prosperity, but also more democracy, less poverty, and fewer inequalities. Unfortunately, in most countries, these virtuous circles did not occur.

The Consequences of Global Neoliberalism

Throughout the world, the expectations raised by neoliberal theorists have not materialized despite the extensive application of their policy recommendations. Instead, most economies "fell into a hole" of low investment, decreased social spending and consumption, low output, decline and stagnation. Both the World Bank and the IMF retreated from SAPs and acknowledged their failure (Bello, 1999; Katona, 1999; *Multinational Monitor*, June 2000; Watkins, 1997).

In the North, GDP growth was lower in the 1980 to 1990 period than in the 1950s and 1960s. We also witness a higher volatility in growth (e.g., booms and busts). Lost in all the talk about huge technological advances ushering in the computer and Internet era is the fact that productivity growth now is half that of levels in the 1950s and 1960s. Unemployment in OECD (Organization for Economic Cooperation and Development) countries has risen from eight million in 1970 to 35 million in 1994. In the midst of U.S. prosperity and economic expansion, inequalities increased. The number of people living under the officially defined poverty level grew from 11.4% of the population in 1978 to 13.5% in 1990. Almost one in four new babies in the U.S. are born into poverty, while the top one percent of Americans saw their real income shoot up by 50% (Levy, 1998; Wilterdink, 1995). Also noteworthy is that U.S. and Western European international trade relative to GDP was greater a century ago than in recent years (Hirst and Thompson, 1996).

Neoliberal dreams proved to be even more chimerical in the South. Role models, like South Korea, Malaysia, and Indonesia plunged into crises in the 1990s. Mexico and Brazil, which faced their own scary periods, experienced growth of three percent in the last two decades, whereas that rate was six percent during the *dirigiste* period of 1950 to 1980. Wage gaps widened. Even in Costa Rica and Chile, models of success in Latin America, the results have been an unmitigated disaster for the lower social classes. The number of Costa Ricans below the poverty line rose from 18.6% in 1987 to 24.4% in 1991, while 42% of all Chileans are also living in poverty (Burbach et al., 1997: 86). Half of the investment flows to developing countries went to just three countries (China, Mexico, and Argentina). In addition, some investments had negative local effects. For instance, as diverse agriculture was converted into monocultures or to export-oriented flower plantations, self-sufficiency was undermined (Clinard, 1990; Klak, 1998).

Moreover, the core-periphery distinction is as relevant as ever. Its real meaning relates to power, authority, and the accumulation of wealth, where the gaps (asymmetries) are increasing. Although production (of certain items) is more dispersed, the concentration of power, control, and benefits has become more pronounced. In 1991, 81% of the world stock of direct foreign investment was in the core triad of the USA, the European Union, and Japan — up from 69% in 1967. The appearance of integrated markets also obscures the fact that 80% of all world trade is within the core triad, in which resides less than 20% of the planet's population (Hirst and Thompson, 1996; Klak, 1998).

In Latin America, debt jumped from $230 billion in 1980 to $600 billion in 1997. Capital had been fleeing those countries up to the early 1990s, when net inflows were the result of casino capital — seeking short-term gains and likely to abandon those countries at the first hint of trouble. Consequently, new debts were created with a new round of borrowing (Robinson, 1998–1999). An important reason why developing countries cannot pay off their debt is that trade protectionism in the North has kept them from penetrating those markets. Trade liberalization has been inconsistent in that rich countries demand more open markets abroad, while continuing to subsidize their own economic sectors, such as agriculture (Andreas, 1999; UNDP, 2000; Watkins, 1997). Compounding these problems, aid to poor countries has been cut back. Whatever assistance is offered comes with strings attached, including the reduction of state intervention, which could have softened the effects for the most vulnerable (Watkins, 1997; Woods, 1999). These policies further undercut food security, cause poverty, and increase economic and power asymmetries. For instance, the cost of living in the Caribbean and the U.S. is quite comparable. In 1997, however, per capita income in Trinidad and Tobago, the richest Caribbean state, was less than half that of Mississippi, the poorest U.S. state. The gap between skilled and unskilled workers widened even more: Haitian workers made clothing with Disney logos for less than 60 cents per hour, while Disney's CEO made $9,700 per hour (Klak, 1998).

The claim of multilateral and even cultural influences also masks tremendous asymmetries. Even though we listen to reggae in the North, 95% of TV programs in St. Lucia come from the U.S. The most widely read newspaper in the Caribbean is the *Miami Herald*. Consequently,

> U.S. affluence and opportunity, often romanticized, is especially well-known, deeply ingrained, and alluring to the Caribbean... [where] people are prone to set their living standard goals in accordance with what the U.S. media ascribe to the United States. And the imbalance in media flows is increasing with the Caribbean's economic crisis and neoliberalism, as local media have been slashed (Klak, 1998: 11).

As dreams of consumption are disseminated, 86% of total private consumption expenditures is accounted for by 20% of the world's people in industrialized countries (UNDP, 1998). For the people who live outside the consumption geographical area, big banks offer credit to only 10% of the people in developing countries, whereas ads for credit cards and consumer items are omnipresent (Barnet and Cavanagh, 1994). Well over one billion people are deprived of basic consumption needs. For hundreds of millions, basic sanitation, clean water, adequate housing, and health services are unattainable luxuries. Two billion people live on less than two dollars a day and 1.3 billion on less than one dollar a day (ICFTU, 2000). Struggling to survive, some decide to sell their body parts to make ends meet, which is the ultimate symbol of commodification (Scheper-Hughes, 2000).

A negative effect of the Internet is that it alters the relationship between our place of residence and our cultural preferences, experiences, and identities. A spreading global virtual reality disconnects locality from culture, weakens the bonds to particular communities, and estranges people from each other (Minda, 2000). Ladakh, a Himalayan province that prospered for a millennium despite harsh weather conditions, illustrates how (especially cultural) globalization devastated local communities (Norberg-Hodge, 1996). In 1962, isolated Ladakh was linked to the rest of India by an army-built road. The modernization that began in 1975 took about a decade to change the pride Ladakhis felt until then into a collective inferiority complex. Tourism and the media conveyed a picture of wealth, technology, power, and work that was alien and irresistible to them. Village life by comparison began to appear "primitive, silly, and inefficient" (*Ibid.*: 35). Ladakhis felt ashamed of their culture and strove for consumer items that symbolize modern life, such as sunglasses and Walkmans. As Western educational standards penetrated Ladakh, the intergenerational learning experience that helped them provide for themselves in their rough terrain gave way to schools that used texts imitating Indian and British models that were completely irrelevant to their lives (e.g., figuring out the angle of the Tower of Pisa and learning how to keep a London-like bedroom tidy). There used to be no such thing as a "paying job"; there was no money economy. Gradually, however, unemployment — previously nonexistent — became a serious problem, because naturally available resources were abandoned, cheap imports made local farming redundant, and people flocked to the cities to compete for scarce jobs. Radios and TVs chased away the traditions of singing together and group story telling. The points of reference ceased to be real people living nearby, but geographically and socially remote ideals. Consumerism bred new "needs," which could hardly be materialized. Family and other bonds disintegrated and divisions emerged between old and young, Buddhists and Muslims. The result was unprecedented violence, community breakdown, and anomie.

Criminogenic Effects: Systemic Strains and Global Anomie

What makes the ideology of the American Dream unique is a focus on money and material goods, a strong emphasis on "winning" (often, by all means), and success for everyone in a society where many opportunities for material advancement are available and plenty of "rags to riches" stories lend legitimacy and credibility to the egalitarian discourse. Legal opportunities, however, for achieving the lofty goals are inaccessible to most Americans. In such a consumption-driven culture, which highly values competition and individualism, the means-ends disjunction has entailed a significant criminogenic risk, much greater than in the rest of the world. Crime has been the flip side of economic growth, innovation, and better living standards for certain segments of the population. What sheltered other countries from this negative potential were things absent or minimized in the USA, such as rigid social stratification, low rates of social mobility, less materialism and time spent before TV boxes, safety nets for the underprivileged, more emphasis on other priorities (e.g., solidarity), etc.

This made it possible to explain the higher crime rates in the U.S. compared to other developed or developing countries. These protective factors, however, are now being gradually lost. Disjunctions between socially induced goals and legal means are few in societies that do not encourage high social mobility. In such societies, people may not feel that they are lacking anything, even when they are "objectively" deprived. Economic or other asymmetries are unknown or not experienced and perceived as intolerable. Global neoliberalism breaks down societal barriers and encourages new needs, desires, and fashions. It promotes the adoption of nonmembership reference groups for comparisons that can be unfavorable and upsetting. New normative reference groups define what is "cool" to do. People's ideals in the South and the East may not be about getting from "a log cabin to the White House." However, they are being systematically driven to abandon old ways and values in order to consume. They do not necessarily think that they can be "like Mike," but they do fancy those pricey athletic shoes. So, fresh normative and comparative models create new "needs," together with the expectation that the fulfillment of such needs is vital and achievable.

Yet, as needs and normative models are "harmonized," people become conscious of economic and power asymmetries, and directly experience their impact. Globalization and neoliberalism heightened this awareness, further widened the asymmetries, and fostered the interpretation of them as unnecessary and changeable. In the end, most people realize that the attainment of their lofty goals and lifestyles is beyond reach, if they are to use legitimate means. The success in spreading neoliberalism has brought about a series of failures: more poverty, bigger economic asymmetries, ecosystem deterioration, slower and unsustainable growth patterns. At the time that societies most needed the shield of the state to cushion these effects, welfare programs, safety nets, and other assistance to the poor (individuals, companies, and states alike) forcibly declined or disappeared. Thus, global neoliberalism systematically causes relative deprivation as well as absolute immiseration of masses of people. In effect, it has generated new sources of criminogenesis and removed existing antidotes to it.

All this provides multiple motivations for criminality, as many would turn left and right for solutions and illicit opportunity structures become more international and accessible. At the same time, many weak states lose their autonomy, come to depend more on international organizations and transnational capital, and are unable to cope with emerging crime threats from criminal enterprises and powerful corporations. So, globalism and neoliberalism replace the "egalitarian discourse" of the American Dream in the scheme represented in Figure 1 in a process occurring in the industrialized world, developing countries, and those in transition from Communism to market democracies. Nowhere are these results more clearly visible than in the former USSR.

The Case of Russia

No one argues that there was no appetite for consumer goods in the years of the USSR or that such goods were widely available. Crime, corruption, illegal markets, and even underground factories could be found behind the official facade of the command system before *glasnost* and *perestroika*, although black marketeers were not numerous and lived modestly. The government turned a blind eye to these activities, because they served as a safety valve in an inefficient system (Gleason, 1990; Handelman, 1995; Naylor, 1999b). Discontent, enormous structural problems, and an inability to deal with them characterized the pre-transition years. This is particularly true for the 1960s, when Khrushchev pledged that the USSR would overtake the U.S. in the production of industrial goods by the 1980s. Yet, as inefficiencies precluded such progress, demands for more consumer items "from an increasingly educated, by now self-assured, population, started to put pressure on government...as a loyal expression of the citizens' request for the gradual delivery of promised well-being" (Castells, 2000: 25).

In the 1990s, however, the rates of fraud, prostitution, drug trafficking and abuse, alcoholism, smuggling, white-collar crime, violence, and corruption skyrocketed (Castells, 2000; Handelman, 1995; Holmes, 1997; Lee, 1994; Shelley, 1994). To be sure, Russia is unique in the degree of chaos and disintegration that accompanied the transition to a market economy and the implementation of neoliberal reforms. Few countries have experienced the speed and intensity of privatization, deregulation, and the lack of political leadership and administrative skills we witness in Russia. Indeed, it is the closest we can come to a social state of anomie, without a total collapse and anarchy. This does not mean that Russia is atypical. Very similar, albeit less intense, processes have occurred throughout the world (Lee, 1999; Mander and Goldsmith, 1996; van Duyne et al., 2000). Nevertheless, precisely because it is such an extreme case, it illustrates the theoretical points made here and the process toward anomie and economic crime.

Enter Neoliberalism

In the 1985 to 1989 period, reforms took place while the Communist Party was still in control. The Law on Cooperatives (1986) and the Law on Individual Labor Activity (1987) paved the way for further reforms, such as legalization of small businesses in 1989. Between 1990 and 1991, the USSR Supreme Soviet, with Yeltsin as chairman, introduced laws that made state and private enterprises equal, allowed state companies relative independence from government managers, abolished most restrictions on property bought by citizens, promoted privatization, and allowed foreign companies to operate in Russia. Such reforms did not take place at the same pace throughout the USSR. This set Russia apart from the Union and Yeltsin from Gorbachev. Legal asymmetries made the task of law enforcers impossible, as they did not know which laws to prioritize and apply (Afanasyef, 1994). Up to the 1991 coup and the collapse of the USSR, reforms were cautious and gradual, and had not challenged the core of the command economy system. Following the failed coup and under Yeltsin, however, this changed dramatically. Demagogy and erroneous judgments on the feasibility of a swift transition to a market democracy compounded the problem. The Russian government was warned of the dire consequences of a speedy transition to a market economy without previous establishment of the necessary institutions and legal infrastructure. The chairman of an international advisory committee, which repeatedly issued warnings in 1992, was told that "forces in the Kremlin" favored a less "regulatory approach that would provide greater freedom of manoeuvre. Gaidar, supported by the IMF, believed firmly in the intrinsic capacity of market forces to remove obstacles by themselves, and people could use their vouchers to acquire shares" (Castells, 2000: 188). Prices were liberalized, imports and exports became free, domestic trade restrictions were abolished, government intervention was minimized, and public property was massively privatized. By June 1994, officials were self-congratulatory over the fact that 70% of state assets had passed into private hands (Kuznetsova, 1994).

New Normative and Comparative Referents

The reforms initiated by Andropov and Gorbachev (*perestroika* and *glasnost*) allowed some freedom of speech and openness that let globalization and media influences into the USSR. The post-1991 changes, however, offered new hope out of the severe problems people were facing. Russian leaders fostered heightened aspirations by declaring that the country would soon be modernized and join the "civilized world." Authorities in the former Soviet republics made the same promise, arguing that "'since we got rid of the Russians,' all obstacles to prosperity have been removed and Western standards are within reach" (Burbach et al., 1997: 118). There were forceful and impressive presentations of consumerist lifestyles as "desirable," "modern," and feasible. Distant comparative and normative referents were thus promoted by the media and advertising. Indeed, the yearning for Western lifestyles and consumption items made the initial acceptance of neoliberalism by the population much easier (*Ibid.*). Neoliberalism strengthened that desire and made consumerist dreams appear realistic. Even young Russians now would like to be like Mike and wear the same type of shoes or eat the same breakfast. As Glinkina (1994: 385) put it, an important factor contributing to the criminalization of the economy has been "a drastic stratification of the population's standard of living with a simultaneous loss, in a considerable part (especially among the youth), of socially important goals—replacing them with consumption ideals...."

It must be noted that the normative shift was far more radical in the former USSR and Eastern Europe than it was in Third World countries. The transition from socialism to capitalism by overzealous authorities espousing the new dogma of neoliberalism has had its own direct anomic effects, as will be seen below.

The Consequence: Means-Ends Discrepancies

The worldwide consequences of neoliberal policies were replicated in Russia. However, the effects have been far more disastrous than elsewhere: lower productivity, high unemployment, much steeper inequalities, increased levels of absolute poverty, disappearance of familiar safety nets, and administrations paralyzed by ineptness and corruption. The ensuing means-ends discrepancies are far more than a theoretical construct. They are painfully experienced by large numbers of people who realize that they simply cannot attain their goals. Within one year, inflation wiped out most people's life savings, while the buying power of most wages dropped to the level of the 1950s. In the winter of 1993, funds were often insufficient to heat residential buildings (Burbach et al., 1997; Handelman, 1993).

As a new bourgeoisie emerged from the ashes of the Communist regime, one-third of the population became impoverished. The gap between the rich and the poor opened up suddenly and grew out of proportion. Official data indicate that in 1994 the difference between them was elevenfold. Researchers argue that the difference between the top 10% and the bottom 10% is 28-fold (Kuznetsova, 1994). Even the chair of the Privatization Commission admitted that the process created "pauper-proprietors" who "cannot survive without state protection" (cited in Burbach et al., 1997: 120).

Relative and Absolute Deprivation

The rising expectations of the 1960s led to disenchantment with Communism and paved the way for radical social change. The abandonment of the Soviet conservative model and very rapid implementation of neoliberal policies fueled hopes that a much better future was within reach. Russians rejected rigid stratification and strove for a socially mobile ideal. As has been noted,

> [the middle classes] believed that capitalism could offer even more. Thus, the modernization that had been promised by the neoliberals was perceived by the majority of the population as the modernization of consumption.... The Western model of consumption has finally triumphed, at least in the main cities. But for the majority of the people, the price is that even the former Soviet way of life has become an unattainable dream (Burbach et al., 1997: 124).

The aspiring yuppies have ended up as "dumpies," while a growing polarization makes them see a few of their compatriots enjoy luxuries attained by looting the remnants of the former USSR.

Thus, the post-Soviet Russian dream turned out to be a nasty nightmare (Handelman, 1995). As happened in many other countries, austerity, belt tightening, and lower (in some cases, no) salaries were imposed as consumerism took hold. The impact of these experiences on personal feelings is much more widespread, intense, and unpleasant due to the higher expectations. Even people who are not objectively deprived now feel relatively deprived. Comparisons between their present and past situations are unfavorable: "Formerly privileged sections of the Russian population, such as teachers, doctors, miners, and workers in the oil and gas industry, went on strike, for they could no longer survive on 50 to 70 dollars per month salaries" (Burbach et al., 1997: 125–126).

East-West political and administrative asymmetries, economic asymmetries, and relative deprivation in the aftermath of the collapse of the USSR and disillusionment with Western policies and capitalism have been clearly criminogenic (Handelman, 1994; Shelley, 1994). Motives for various types of crime became abundant, illegal opportunity structures multiplied, and control systems have been seriously damaged and undermined. The Mertonian category of "conformity" has almost become a rarity, as crime rates increased sharply. Even worse is the problem of economic crime. Recorded economic crimes rose almost 23% during the first seven months of 2000, compared with the same period in 1999 (Radio Free Europe/Radio Liberty, August 17, 2000). Strains and discontent have translated into a range of predatory misconduct, corruption, political violence, a variety of illegal markets, and expressive misconduct.

Search for Solutions and Anomie

In this context, many can be expected to "innovate," to employ illegal methods for survival or the satisfaction of their basic and newly acquired needs. Methods range from petty property crimes and prostitution to criminal enterprises and white-collar crime, depending on the social position of the offender. An electronics engineer, for example, could not live on his three dollars per month and moonlighted as a taxi driver. When his taxi broke down, he turned to selling poppy straw (OGD, 1996). Unpaid and depressed professionals with access to more valuable commodities, such as nuclear material, pose an even more serious threat (Lee, 1999). Consumerist teasing increased demand for goods made unavailable (e.g., cars or electronics) by the economic collapse, fueling smuggling operations, black market networks, and associated illegal enterprises. Shortages of other desired goods are artificially created by quickly adapting entrepreneurs.

Similar conditions outside Russia explain the illegal car trade between Eastern and Western Europe (van Duyne et al., 2000) and the illegal trade in various commodities between China and Hong Kong before unification (Vagg, 1992). In Russia, many took advantage of such supply-demand asymmetries, including the *vory v zakonye* (commonly described as "thieves in law"), who had been the dominant type of professional offenders in the USSR. Structural changes and globalization, however, brought about more competition from ethnic groups (Armenians, Azeris, Chechens, Georgians, etc.) in drugs and arms trafficking, as well as from loose and ad hoc associations of criminals in certain locations or industries. Unsettling reports assert a symbiotic relationship between criminal groups and active or retired intelligence officials. Deteriorating economic conditions have facilitated recruitment for employees in growing illegal markets.

Criminal enterprises, for instance, have "...invested heavily in the opium business, financing much of the new cultivation by hiring peasants and even entire villages to plant and protect the poppy crops" (Lee, 1994: 401).

Another source of criminal opportunities sprang from the disintegration of institutions and the disarray in law enforcement. Legitimate businesses are exposed to blackmail and other criminal victimization, but the authorities are unable to assist them. Consequently, many domestic and foreign companies deal with criminal groups and seek their protection, rather than rely on the government (Lee, 1994). Not surprisingly, the majority of Russian experts consider the strengthening of criminal groups to be a "very significant" social consequence of the market reforms introduced in 1992 (Afanasyef, 1994).

Other illicit opportunities were furnished by the privatization process, such as selling state assets at extremely low prices or driving down the prices of privatized companies so as to cheaply purchase vouchers owned by individuals desperate to make ends meet. Privatization in countries with an existing bourgeoisie and experienced managers and entrepreneurs facilitated certain corporate crimes and abuses of power by respected professionals. In Russia, the mix of offenders was different: former company directors, the *nomenklatura*, professional criminals, and new entrepreneurs with a black market background (Glinkina, 1994; Kuznetsova, 1994; Shelley, 1994). The attempt of former Communist officials to dominate this field did not prove lasting. Many were not competent to run private businesses and had to sell them or lose control. The main beneficiaries seem to be former black marketeers and outsiders to the old order (Naylor, 1999b). The abuse of privatization has had an anomic effect as the impunity of offenders became widely known, to the point that Russians began to refer to privatization (*privatizatsiya*) as *prikhvatizatsiya*, which means "grabbing" (Handelman, 1995: 104).

Crime and corruption in the midst of privatization fervor are not unique to Russia. (On other previously Communist states, see Popescu-Birlan, 1994; on Latin America, see Saba and Manzetti, 1996–1997.) As a former World Bank official put it, "everything we did from 1983 onward was based upon our new sense of mission to have the south privatized or die; towards this end we ignominiously created economic bedlam in Latin America and Africa" (cited in Katona, 1999). Another similarity with other parts of the world is the degree of authoritarianism that accompanied neoliberal policies. While stimulating rapid accumulation of private capital, the role of the state is reduced to implementing financial austerity. When people started to oppose such measures, "Yeltsin resorted, with Western support, to establishing a semi-authoritarian regime. Making Russian 'reformers' invincible to political and legal challenges inside the country contributed to further criminalization of the Russian State, which acquired an oligarchic character" (Beare, 2000: 6). As similar processes occurred around the world, from Pinochet's Chile to Suharto's Indonesia, one wonders if such reforms would have been possible in a democracy.

Legal organizations also "innovate" by cutting corners and breaking the law due to the environment created by unsystematic legal reforms. Unable to navigate a sea of legal gaps and inconsistencies, "...most managers of private as well as state-owned enterprises cannot run their businesses without committing crimes" (Afanasyef, 1994: 437). Many companies cannot handle the competitive challenges generated by globalism and require state protection. The subsidization of privatized companies, however, introduces further regulatory and price asymmetries that foster the smuggling of goods across newly created borders within the former USSR (see below on nonferrous materials). Enterprises that do not enjoy state intervention are at a disadvantage and may be forced into bankruptcy or crime as a last resort. This is analogous to the situation in all countries that abolish trade barriers, let transnational corporations in, and eliminate preferential treatment for domestic industries.

High-level corruption and banking crimes have become quite common, as the networks of mobsters, financiers, businessmen, and high-level officials extend beyond Eurasia (Beare, 2000). The ongoing investigations into billions of dollars (possibly IMF-provided funds) laundered through the Bank of New York have expanded to include British, Swiss, and Italian entities and actors.

Moreover, pyramid schemes and other frauds have devastated gullible investors, as is the case with other post-Communist countries. Independent Oil, Lenin Trade and Financial Corporation, Aldzher (a security corporation), and other companies defrauded more than a million depositors and investors. Just as the Lincoln Savings and Loan frauds were committed in midst of obsessive deregulation in the U.S. against "the weak, the meek, and the old," Russian pensioners have been the main fraud victims (Glinkina, 1994).

Economic asymmetries among countries produce another set of criminal opportunities, as many become strongly motivated to flee the problem and search for a better future in the West, where the "goodies" are available. However, neoliberalism has promoted the free movement of everything but labor. Quotas and restrictions in promised lands generate demand for illegal services such as the smuggling of humans (Chin, 1999). This leads to opportunities for criminal exploitation, corruption, child/cheap labor, slavery, and forced prostitution.

Women, who are increasingly breadwinners but make up two-thirds of the newly unemployed in Russia, are even more vulnerable in this respect. Economic desperation drives many of them to prostitution or high risk taking. Lack of opportunity makes Russians and East Europeans softer targets for human traffickers. They are more likely to be lured to the West with promises of well-paying, respectable jobs only to end up blackmailed, beaten up, and forced into prostitution (Bruinsma, 1999; Shelley, 1994). The same problems faced by Thai, Mexican, and other women in the U.S. have led to a public hearing before the House Subcommittee on International Operations and Human Rights (September 14, 1999).

Relative deprivation and experience of injustice have a revolutionary potential too. International communications convey the message that injustice and inequality are avoidable. Events in one corner of the earth affect feelings and encourage people elsewhere to rebel against aggression. This may inspire change and foster rebellion. Just as the ideals of the French Revolution led to rebellions in the Balkans against the Ottoman rule (Hovannisian, 1994), the independence of the Baltic states and the U.N. response to Iraq's invasion of Kuwait inspired the East Timorese to fight against the Indonesian autocratic rule (Dunn, 1994). The uprising of Zapatistas in Mexico was deliberately started on January 1, 1994, the day NAFTA went into effect, "as a highly symbolic way to protest neoliberalism and globalisation in Mexico and Latin America" (Robinson, 1998-1999: 123–124).

Repressed nationalism, globalism, and bad times have jointly contributed to several armed conflicts and rebellions in the former USSR (the Caucasus, Moldova, Crimea, Tajikistan, and Chechnya). Rebellion and illegal markets become interconnected, as armed conflicts necessitate training, weapons, intelligence, and financing. The cases of Chechnya, Tajikistan, Afghanistan, and Colombia show how political revolts are associated with corruption, money laundering, the traffic in arms, drugs, and even nuclear material and other crimes that go unpunished (Kuznetsova, 1994: 445; Lee, 1999; Naylor, 1999b; OGD, 1996). Chechnya, which survives thanks to donations from criminal organizations based in other parts of Russia, has become such a paradise for these activities that some depict the war there as "a crusade against a 'mafia republic,'" while others think of it as "a conflict between opposing criminal elites for the control of oil and the financial resources held by the government in Grozny" (Politi, 1998: 44).

Finally, "retreatism" is the only option left to those lacking access to illegal opportunities or who are unwilling to assume the associated risks of violence and arrest. Hence, expressive crimes could be expected. More important, the rates of alcohol and drug abuse (further facilitated by the decriminalization of drug use in Russia in 1991) increased geometrically, especially in the cities, and fueled the demand for things provided in illegal markets (Lee, 1994; OGD, 1996).

Anomie

The transition from a command to a market economy practically legalized large parts of the black market and made legal business dependent on criminals' protection. The dismantling of borders and increased contact among previously isolated ethnic groups contributed to the formation of new, wider networks of illegality (Politi, 1998). The result was that one could hardly tell criminals from businessmen, particularly when some outlaw groups act on instructions from government officials or the police (Handelman, 1993). Given official efforts to ensure that the transition to a market economy would occur before substantial opposition could build and that the changes would be irreversible, too many shady actors were allowed to take advantage of this official shield (Glinkina, 1994; Naylor, 1999b). In this light, common views on government-criminal interfaces and symbiosis are plausible, although difficult to prove. Surveys in 1994 showed that the concern of Russians over organized crime was second only to their fears of triple-digit inflation (Afanasyef, 1994). At the perceptual level, therefore, this interface is real and has real consequences: demoralization and anomie.

The corrupted process of privatization has generated widespread rationalizations, such as, "it is OK to steal from the state" or "everyone is doing the same thing." Taking an example pointing to international security risks, Lee (1999: 21) has noted that, "perhaps the most serious problem is the growth of a privatization mentality within the nuclear complex. Economic reform has meant a license to steal. This has resulted in broad systemic corruption and a variety of insider threats and conspiracies."

An additional sign of anomie is what has been described as a "culture of urgency" among young killers:

> For them there is no hope in society, and everything, particularly politics and politicians, is rotten. Life itself has no meaning, and their life has no future.... So, only the moment counts, immediate consumption, good clothing, good life, on the run, together with the satisfaction of inducing fear, of feeling powerful with their guns (Castells, 2000: 210).

Only effective social controls can halt the process toward further deviance and a higher degree of anomie (deviance without strain). Unfortunately, in Russia and elsewhere, a decreased level of autonomy for certain states, the increased power of international organizations and transnational corporations, and dysnomie add to the fuel.

Dependence, Deregulation, and the Race to the Bottom

> "Just between you and me, shouldn't the World Bank be encouraging more migration of the dirty industries to the LDCs (lesser developed countries)?" "I think the economic logic behind dumping a load of toxic waste in the lowest wage country is impeccable and we should face up to that.... I've always thought that underpopulated countries in Africa are vastly under-polluted; their air quality is vastly inefficiently low compared to Los Angeles or Mexico City" (1991 memo attributed to World Bank official Lawrence Summers, who later became U.S. Secretary of Treasury; it is widely believed that he did not write it, even though he has accepted responsibility for it. At any rate, this illustrates the neoliberal mindset).

The loss of autonomy and reduced sovereignty of the state relative to capital referred to earlier (Korten, 1996; Watkins, 1997) is particularly acute in the former

Communist countries. Speculative capital will quickly flee each country at the first sign trouble or wavering over neoliberal reforms. External debt grew in all former Communist countries, but especially in Russia, which bears the marks of Africa-like dependent capitalism and "colonial subjugation. The country exports fewer and fewer industrial products and more and more raw materials. Meanwhile, it imports low-quality mass consumption goods, obsolete and hence cheap technology, luxury items and radioactive waste" (Burbach et al., 1997: 120–121). An instance of the direct and blatant interference of foreign governments and transnational corporations in domestic matters was when Chase Manhattan urged the Mexican government to crush the Zapatista rebellion to calm down U.S. investors (Silverstein and Cockburn, 1995; see also Clinard, 1990).

Ironically, the higher degree of dependency in the South and East has lowered the accountability of politicians and corporations. They can now blame globalization for the loss of jobs and lower wages, and prescribe more "efficiency," deregulation, short-term austerity, and declining levels of public spending so as to keep capital in place or attract more. Thus, economic and political leaders appear to be protectors of the public interest and a stabilizing force, while they dismantle existing safety nets (economic neoliberalism has also undermined political liberalism; Klak, 1998).

The Russian government's aversion to regulation (Glinkina, 1994) is observable in other countries, where deregulation turned into competitive deregulation and a race to the bottom. Even in the U.S., the savings and loan disaster and the asymmetric regulation of hazardous wastes demonstrate how criminogenic this process has been. This made it possible to dump legally in Pennsylvania what was prohibited in New Jersey, in what has been termed "crimes without law violations" (Passas, 1999). Such crimes are most likely in the global context given the overwhelming influence of TNCs over national laws and macroeconomic policies. This has prompted some to speak of "rationalized corporate colonialism" (Mander, 1996). Such asymmetries of power make for legal norms that allow overseas that which is, for good reason, criminalized in the base country (e.g., toxic waste dumping, testing drugs on humans, bribery, tax evasion, as well as the patenting of life forms by biotechnology companies and other outrageous practices) (see King and Stabinsky, 1998–1999; Shiva, 1997). The legal asymmetries and uneven power of transnational corporations that create or perpetuate these and other asymmetries give rise to crimes without law violations. Thus, entire countries become vulnerable to victimization by TNCs, a significant problem that is often neglected in conventional discussions of transnational crime. The volatile combination of low wages, bad working conditions, tax breaks only for the rich/corporations, lower environmental standards, deregulation, and less corporate and political accountability with the government relegated to the protection of the international free trade system has predictably made for crises (e.g., Korea, Malaysia, Indonesia, Mexico, and Brazil). It also makes for dysnomie.

Dysnomie and Further (Global) Anomie

Dysnomie literally means "difficulty to govern" and obtains when the following three conditions are present: a lack of a global norm-making mechanism, inconsistent enforcement of existing international rules, and the existence of a regulatory patchwork of diverse and conflicting legal traditions and practices. Russia is in this respect a microcosm that reflects what is happening in the entire world.

Since reforms took place at an uneven pace in each Soviet Republic, an asymmetry grew wider following the collapse of the USSR. In addition, this collapse suddenly created thousands of miles of new borders that had to be policed, just as state resources were diminished. This made for porous borders that offered no resistance to smugglers. This is how Estonia became the largest exporter of nonferrous materials, even though it does not produce any (Glinkina, 1994). Extensive legal changes accelerated the transition to a market economy, but they were marked by inconsistencies and lacked the necessary legal and institutional infrastructure (Handelman, 1995). For example, the law against private entrepreneurship and commercial mediations was repealed only on December 5, 1991. The law against black market transactions, which defined them as "the buying up and reselling of goods or other items for profit-making," was first amended in February 1990 to increase penalties for certain offenses, was then officially reinterpreted to refer only to trade in commodities sold at state-fixed prices (October 1990), and was finally repealed in February 1991 (Afanasyef, 1994: 429). Lack of resources made the problem worse, as underpaid, ill-equipped, and outgunned police could not be expected to do an effective job.

Weak controls allow criminals to get away and to regard themselves as successful. Deviant "solutions" came to be seen as keys to "success." Successful deviance then becomes a normative referent, contributing to a wider normative breakdown and overemphasis on goals at the expense of normative means. In the context of massive cultural shifts — from the criminalizing of private profit and the hiring of labor outside the household to making them central values for a new social order — the sense of right and wrong became fuzzy. As the deputy minister of Internal Affairs admitted at a 1992 press conference, "even our specialists find it difficult to determine the legal from the illegal — to determine, for instance, what is profiteering and what is honest trade" (cited in Handelman, 1993). Corruption grew so much that up to 30% of illegal gains are reportedly paid to government officials (Glinkina, 1994; Lee, 1999). In the end, distinctions between white-collar crime, organized crime, corruption, and legitimate business are almost impossible to make. Lawbreaking behavior and success are fused. As a businessman told Handelman (1995: 139), "the truth is, everything you see around you, all our success, is not thanks to our wonderful economic laws. It's thanks to the fact that we do not obey them."

Dysnomic conditions also bring about anomie at the global level. As argued elsewhere (Passas, 1999), international law is more essential now than ever for the maintenance of world order and security. Yet, big powers are reluctant to contribute to the required pooling of sovereignty and have been blocking the development of an international criminal code and specific legislation to restrain their corporations. Dependent on rich countries for its operations, the U.N. has not been overly aggressive in pursuing these aims or in establishing a permanent international criminal tribunal. Globalism has thus run ahead of the creation of a desperately needed normative and enforcement infrastructure.

Existing international laws are applied selectively and never against one of the permanent members of the U.N. Security Counsel. This ad hoc approach and the extraterritorial application of national laws undermine the legitimacy of current laws and procedures. We are left with a legal patchwork of inconsistent and conflicting rules. An example of the effect of such asymmetries is the secrecy and anonymity available in certain jurisdictions that hinder investigative work by covering the tracks and proceeds of global offenders, de facto shielding them against prosecution and punishment. By exploiting the cracks between diverse state rules, companies continually commit crimes without law violation. Globalism also leads to a relativization of norms and facilitates law violations with a clear conscience (rationalizations and techniques of neutralization).

Finally, the border-policing problem in the former USSR is not unique, even if the underlying causes were specific to it and other European countries (Yugoslavia, Czechoslovakia). More generally, borders become porous, as technology and mobility enabled people, money, goods, and ideas to travel quickly and cheaply. Criminals can take advantage of this shrinking world, but law enforcement agencies are constrained by parochial laws and procedures. Though the reasons for the porousness may differ, the process and results are the same.

Conclusion

Tremendous structural strains have overwhelmed even the usually patient and submissive Russians. The economic situation deteriorated further, hopes were dashed, opportunities for criminal gain and for looting the USSR's assets multiplied, and the anomic societal context offered no assistance to anyone seeking to restore some law and order. In Russia and around the world, the neoliberal operation was successful, but the patients are being systematically frustrated, are starving, and subject to exploitation by corporations, criminal enterprises, and corrupt politicians. In short, globalization and neoliberalism spread analytically similar criminogenic processes that were once unique to the U.S. culture of the American Dream in a context of structural inequalities. Just as the world supposedly became freer, wealthier, more democratic, more enjoyable, and more equal, people find themselves poorer, more exploited, and facing increased hardships. Just as the need for strong normative guidance grows, norms break down or lose their legitimacy. Just as effective controls become necessary to slow down or stop the vicious cycle leading to higher rates of crime, a dysnomic regulatory patchwork remains in place largely because of nationalist insistence on sovereignty and states' unwillingness to allow the introduction of common principles and law enforcement mechanisms.

Two main points need to be reiterated here. First, it appears that global neoliberalism and serious crime go hand in hand. However, it would be erroneous to argue that stereotypical organized criminals are giving capitalism a bad name and undermining neoliberal policies. The implication is that, were we to rid ourselves of some very bad apples, everything would be fine. Rather, it appears that serious organizational misconduct is a consequence of such policies. Second, when we discuss transnational crime, we should bear in mind that it is not just the stereotyped ethnics who cause most problems. It may be that the biggest threat emanates from legitimate corporations and other organizations.

Detailed discussion of policy implications is beyond the scope of this article. The horizontal arrows in Figure 1 hint at the points of possible policy intervention. Myriad concrete ideas can be found in the literature, ranging from legal changes to informal controls, grass-roots movements, integration of economic growth with environmental and social protection, relocalization of production and consumption, etc. The most important ray of hope, however, is implicit in the foregoing analysis. Neoliberal policies and globalization are largely the fruit of (some) governments. They affect and are affected by governance. Therefore, governments have the ability to reverse some of these processes and to mitigate their adverse consequences. Otherwise, the current processes of globalization and neoliberalism will prove to be unsustainable and at a huge cost.

Figure 1:
Social Processes Leading to Anomie and Deviance

Egalitarian discourse, consumerism, competition
↓ ←
Socially distant comparative and normative reference groups
↓ ←
Ends-means discrepancy (power/economic asymmetries)
↓ ←
Perception of injustice, relative deprivation, strain
↓ ←
Anomie: rationalizations, deviant solution (overemphasis on goals)
↓ ←
Anomie: deviant subculture (normative referents)
↓ ←
Deviance without strain

The horizontal lines point to policy implications. This is where interventions can be attempted in order to block this process and prevent misbehavior. In the context of neoliberal globalism, they represent criminogenic influences.

REFERENCES

Afanasyef, V.
1994 "Organized Crime and Society." *Demokratizatsiya* 2,3: 426–441.

Alesina, A. and D. Rodrik
1994 "Distributive Politics and Economic Growth." *Quarterly Journal of Economics* 109,2: 465–490.

Andreas, P.
1999 "Smuggling Wars: Law Enforcement and Law Evasion in a Changing World." T. Farer (ed.), *Transnational Crime in the Americas*. London: Routledge: 85–98.
1997 "The Rise of the American Crimefare State." *World Policy Journal* 14,3: 37–45.

Aubert, V.
1968 "White-Collar Crime and Social Structure." G. Geis (ed.), *White-Collar Criminal: The Offender in Business and the Professions*. New York: Atherton Press: 173–184.

Barnet, R.J. and J. Cavanagh
1994 *Global Dreams: Imperial Corporations and the New World Order*. New York: Simon and Schuster.

Beare, M.
2000 "Russian (East European) Organized Crime Around the Globe." Paper presented at the "Transnational Crime Conference," organized by the Australian Institute of Criminology, Australian Customs Service, and Australian Federal Police, Canberra.

Bello, W.
1999 "Is the 'Structural Adjustment' Approach Really and Truly Dead?" *BusinessWorld, Internet Edition* (November 8), downloaded from Internet site http://www.bworld.com.ph/current/today.html.
1996 "Structural Adjustment Programs: 'Success' for Whom?" J. Mander and E. Goldsmith (eds.), *The Case Against the Global Economy*. San Francisco: Sierra Club Books: 285–293.

Bruinsma, G.J.N. and G. Meershoek
1999 "Organized Crime and Trafficking in Women from Eastern Europe in the Netherlands." *Transnational Organized Crime* 4: 105–118.

Burbach, R., O. Núñez, and B. Kagarlitsky
1997 *Globalization and Its Discontents*. London: Pluto Press.

Castells, M.
2000 *End of Millennium* (2nd ed.). Oxford: Blackwell.

Center for Investigative Reporting and B. Moyers
1990 *Global Dumping Ground: The International Traffic in Hazardous Waste*. Washington, D.C.: Seven Locks Press.

Chin, K.L.
1999 *Smuggled Chinese: Clandestine Immigration to the United States*. Philadelphia: Temple University Press.

Clinard, M.B.
1990 *Corporate Corruption: The Abuse of Power*. New York: Praeger.

Cox, R.W.
1993 "Structural Issues of Global Governance: Implications for Europe." S. Gill (ed.), *Gramsci, Historical Materialism, and International Relations*. Cambridge: Cambridge University Press.

Critharis, M.
1990 "Third World Nations Are Down in the Dumps: The Exportation of Hazardous Waste." *Brooklyn Journal of International Law* 6,2: 311–339.

Dunn, J.
1994 "East Timor: A Case of Cultural Genocide?" G.J. Andreopoulos (ed.), *Genocide: Conceptual and Historical Dimensions*. Philadelphia: University of Pennsylvania Press: 171–190.

Durkheim, E.
1983 *Le Suicide*. Paris: Presses Universitaires de France. (Originally published 1930.)

Gambetta, D.
1993 *The Sicilian Mafia*. Cambridge: Harvard University Press.

Giddens, A.
1990 *The Consequences of Modernity*. Cambridge: Polity.

Gilpin, R.
1987 *The Political Economy of International Relations*. Princeton: Princeton University Press.

Gleason, G.
1990 "Nationalism or Organized Crime? The Case of the 'Cotton Scandal' in the USSR." *Corruption and Reform* 5: 87–108.

Glinkina, S.P.
1994 "*Privatizatsiya* and *Kriminalizatsiya*: How Organized Crime Is Hijacking Privatization." *Demokratizatsiya* 2,3: 385–391.

Handelman, S.
1995 *Comrade Criminal*. New Haven: Yale University Press.
1994 "The Russian 'Mafiya.'" *Foreign Affairs* 73,2: 83-96.
1993 "Why Capitalism and the Mafia May Mean Business." *The New York Times* (January 24).

Hirst, P. and G. Thompson
1996 *Globalisation in Question: The International Economy and the Possibilities of Governance*. Cambridge: Polity.

Holmes, L.
1997 "Corruption and the Crisis in the Post-Communist State." *Crime, Law, and Social Change* 27: 275–297.

Hovannisian, R.G.
1994 "Etiology and Sequelae of the Armenian Genocide." G.J. Andreopoulos (ed.), *Genocide: Conceptual and Historical Dimensions*. Philadelphia: University of Pennsylvania Press: 111–140.

ICFTU (International Confederation of Free Trade Unions)
2000 *Globalising Social Justice: Trade Unionism in the 21st Century*. Durban: ICFTU.

Katona, D.
1999 "Challenging the Global Structure Through Self-Determination: An African Perspective." *American University International Law Review* 14: 1439–1472.

Keohane, R.O. and J.S. Nye
2000 "Globalization: What's New? What's Not? (And So What?)." *Foreign Policy* 118: 104–119.

King, J. and D. Stabinsky
1998-99 "Biotechnology Under Globalisation: The Corporate Expropriation of Plant, Animal, and Microbial Species." *Race and Class* 40,2–3: 73-89.

Klak, T.
1998 "Thirteen Theses on Globalization and Neoliberalism." T. Klak (ed.), *Globalization and Neoliberalism*. Lanham, MD: Rowman and Littlefield: 3–23.

Klak, T. and G. Myers
1998 "How States Sell Their Countries and Their People." T. Klak (ed.), *Globalization and Neoliberalism*. Lanham, MD: Rowman and Littlefield: 87–109.

Korten, D.C.
1996 "The Failures of Bretton Woods." J. Mander and E. Goldsmith (eds.), *The Case Against the Global Economy*. San Francisco: Sierra Club Books: 20–30.
1995 *When Corporations Rule the World*. West Hartford, CT: Kumarian Press.

Krasner, S.D.
1985 *Structural Conflict: The Third World Against Global Liberalism*. Berkeley: California University Press.

Kuznetsova, R.W.L.F.
1994 "Crime in Russia: Causes and Prevention." *Demokratizatsiya* 2,3: 442–452.

Lee, R.W.
1999 "Transnational Organized Crime: An Overview." T. Farer (ed.), *Transnational Crime in the Americas*. London: Routledge: 1–38.
1994 "The Organized Crime Morass in the Former Soviet Union." *Demokratizatsiya* 2,3: 392–411.

Levy, F.
1998 *The New Dollars and Dreams: American Incomes and Economic Change*. New York: Russell Sage Foundation.

Mander, J.
1996 "Facing the Rising Tide." J. Mander and E. Goldsmith (eds.), *The Case Against the Global Economy*. San Francisco: Sierra Club Books: 3–19.

Mander, J. and E. Goldsmith (eds.)
1996 *The Case Against the Global Economy*. San Francisco: Sierra Club Books.

McGrew, T.
1992 "A Global Society?" S. Hall, D. Held, and T. McGrew (eds.), *Modernity and Its Futures*. Cambridge: Open University Press: 62–102.

Merton, R.K.
1968 *Social Theory and Social Structure*. New York: The Free Press.

Messner, S.F. and R. Rosenfeld
1994 *Crime and the American Dream*. Belmont, CA: Wadsworth.

Minda, G.
2000 "Book Review: The Globalization of Culture." *Colorado Law Review* 71: 589–643.

Myers, W.H.
1995–1996 "The Emerging Threat of Transnational Organized Crime from the East." *Crime, Law, and Social Change* 24,3: 181–222.

Naylor, R.T.
1999a "Wash-out: A Critique of Follow-the-Money Methods in Crime Control Policy." *Crime, Law, and Social Change* 32,1: 1–57.
1999b *Patriots and Profiteers: On Economic Warfare, Embargo Busting, and State-Sponsored Crime*. Toronto: McClelland and Stewart.
1995 "From Cold War to Crime War: The Search for a New 'National Security' Threat." *Transnational Organized Crime* 1,4: 37–56.

Norberg-Hodge, H.
1996 "The Pressure to Modernize and Globalize." J. Mander and E. Goldsmith (eds.), *The Case Against the Global Economy*. San Francisco: Sierra Club Books: 33–46.

OGD, Observatoire Géopolitique des Drogues
1996 *The Geopolitics of Drugs*. Boston: Northeastern University Press.

Oman, C.
1999 "Globalization, Regionalization, and Inequality." Ngaire Woods and A. Hurrell (eds.), *Inequality, Globalization, and World Politics*. Oxford: Oxford University Press: 36–65.

Paine, L.P. and F.J. Cilluffo (eds.)
1994 *Global Organized Crime: The New Empire of Evil*. Washington, D.C.: CSIS.

Passas, N.

1999 "Globalization, Criminogenic Asymmetries, and Economic Crime." *European Journal of Law Reform* 1,4: 399–423.

1998 "Transnational Crime: The Interface Between Legal and Illegal Actors." Presented at the National Research Council Workshop on "Transnational Organized Crime." Washington, D.C.

1997 "Anomie, Reference Groups, and Relative Deprivation." N. Passas and R. Agnew (eds.), *The Future of the Anomie Tradition*. Boston: Northeastern University Press: 62–94.

1994 "The Market for Gods and Services: Religion, Commerce, and Deviance." *Religion and Social Order* 4: 217–241.

1990 "Anomie and Corporate Deviance." *Contemporary Crises* 14,3: 157–178.

Passas, N. and J. Blum

1998 "Intelligence Services and Undercover Operations: The Case of Euromac." S. Field and C. Pelser (eds.), *Invading the Private? Accountability and the New Policing in Europe*. Aldershot: Dartmouth.

Passas, N. and R.B. Groskin

1995 "International Undercover Operations." G. Marx and C. Fijnaut (eds.), *Undercover: Police Surveillance in Comparative Perspective*. Amsterdam: Kluwer: 291–312.

Politi, A.

1998 "Russian Organised Crime and European Security." E.U. Directorate-General for External Relations (ed.), *Illicit Trade and Organised Crime: New Threats to Economic Security?* Luxembourg: European Communities: 31–57.

Popescu-Birlan, L.

1994 "Privatization and Corruption in Romania." *Crime, Law, and Social Change* 21,4: 375–379.

Robinson, W.I.

1998–1999 "Latin America and Global Capitalism." *Race and Class* 40,2–3: 111–131.

Rosenau, J.

1990 *Turbulence in World Politics*. Brighton: Harvester Wheatsheaf.

Saba, R.P. and L. Manzetti

1996–1997 "Privatization in Argentina: The Implications for Corruption." *Crime, Law, and Social Change* 25,4: 353–369.

Scheper-Hughes, N.

2000 "The Global Traffic in Human Organs." *Current Anthropology* 41,2: available on the Internet at http://www.journals.uchicago.edu/CA/journal/issues/v41n2/002001/002001.html.

Shelley, L.

1995 "Transnational Crime: An Imminent Threat to the Nation-State?" *Journal of International Affairs* 48,2: 463–489.

1994 "Post-Soviet Organized Crime." *Demokratizatsiya* 2,3: 341–358.

Shiva, V.

1997 *Biopiracy: The Plunder of Nature and Knowledge*. Boston: South End Press.

Silverstein, K. and A. Cockburn

1995 "Major U.S. Bank Urges Zapatista Wipe-Out: 'A Litmus Test for Mexico's Stability.'" *Counterpunch* 2,3.

Sklair, L.

1995 *Sociology of the Global System* (2nd ed.). New York and London: Prentice Hall and Harvester Wheatsheaf.

Stewart, F. and A. Berry

1999 "Globalization, Liberalization, and Inequality: Expectations and Experience." Ngaire Woods and A. Hurrell (eds.), *Inequality, Globalization, and World Politics*. Oxford: Oxford University Press: 150–186.

Sykes, G.M. and D. Matza
1957 "Techniques of Neutralization: A Theory of Delinquency." *American Sociological Review* 22,6: 664–670.

UNDP (United Nations Development Programme)
2000 *Poverty Report*. New York: Oxford University Press.
1998 *Human Development Report: Consumption for Human Development*. New York: United Nations.

Vagg, J.
1992 "The Borders of Crime." *British Journal of Criminology* 32,3: 310–328.

van Duyne, P.C., V. Ruggiero, M. Scheinost, and W. Valkenburg (eds.).
2000 *Cross-Border Crime in a Changing Europe*. Tilburg and Prague: Tilburg University and Prague Institute of Criminology and Social Prevention.

Wallerstein, I.
1983 *Historical Capitalism*. London: Verso.

Watkins, K.
1997 *Globalisation and Liberalisation: Implications for Poverty, Distribution, and Inequality*. Occasional Paper 32: U.N. Development Program.

Williams, P.
1994 "Transnational Criminal Organisations and International Security." *Survival* 36,1: 96–113.

Wilterdink, N.
1995 "Increasing Income Inequality and Wealth Concentration in the Prosperous Societies of the West." *Studies in Comparative International Development* 30,3: 3–23.

Woods, N.
1999 "Order, Globalization, and Inequality in World Politics." Ngaire Woods and A. Hurrell (eds.), *Inequality, Globalization, and World Politics*. Oxford: Oxford University Press: 8–35.

Yergin, D. and J. Stanislaw
1998 *The Commanding Heights: The Battle Between Government and the Marketplace That Is Remaking the Modern World*. New York: Simon and Schuster.

[19]

Transnational Crime, Local Denial

Simon R.M. Mackenzie

Field and Habitus in the Antiquities Market

BOURDIEU'S HABITUS IS A FORM OF "PRACTICAL KNOWLEDGE" (BOURDIEU, 1996: 1) and an attempt to provide a model for the mediation of structure and agency; it is a method for conceptualizing:

> the way society becomes deposited in persons in the form of lasting *dispositions* or trained capacities and structured propensities to think, feel, and act in determinate ways, which then guide them in their creative responses to the constraints and solicitations of their extant milieu...individual and group history sedimented in the body, social structure turned mental structure (Wacquant, 2005: 316).

The concept of the habitus therefore brings together at once several well-rehearsed features of social existence—disposition, agency, strategy, structural reproduction, body, mind, choice, unconsciousness—without setting each off against the other in the traditional manner of polarization and antagonism. At its simplest, then, as Wacquant indicates, habitus provides a means of incorporating into our social analysis recognition that internal mental structures exist that generally are aligned with external social structures:

> Indeed there exists a correspondence between social structures and mental structures, between the objective divisions of the social world...and the principles of vision and division that agents apply to them (Bourdieu, 1996: 1).... [The habitus composes] systems of durable, transposable dispositions, structured structures predisposed to function as structuring structures... (Bourdieu, 1990: 53).

DR. SIMON MACKENZIE is Senior Research Fellow at the Scottish Centre for Crime and Justice Research, University of Glasgow (e-mail: s.mackenzie@lbss.gla.ac.uk; www.sccjr.ac.uk). His two main research interests are crimes of the powerful and community crime control. Regarding the former, he has conducted research on the illicit antiquities market, and on the global economic activities of international financial institutions. In relation to the latter, he is beginning research into community activation and the respect agenda. Spanning both research fields is an interest in the sociology of empathy and the politics of cooperation and exchange. The author gratefully acknowledges the support of the ESRC whose funding under grant number RES-00 0-2 2-1074 has made possible some elements of the research reported here.

The mental structures so "deposited" by "society" will not necessarily reflect extant social conditions or norms, if those conditions or norms have changed. Of course, the process of individual internalization of norms is not instantaneous, which suggests that at any moment the habitus may not be fully synchronized with the normative conditions of the social context with which it continues to engage. Again, it is useful to return to Wacquant, citing Bourdieu:

> [Habitus] introduces a lag, and sometimes a hiatus, between the past determinations that produced it and the current determinations that interpellate it: as "history made nature," habitus "is what confers upon practices their relative autonomy with respect to the external determinations of the immediate present. This autonomy is that of the past, enacted and acting, which, functioning as accumulated capital, produces history on the basis of history and so ensures that permanence within change that makes the individual agent a world within the world" (Wacquant, 2005: 317; citing Bourdieu, 1990: 56).

This will be particularly so in times of rapid social change. When a field changes rapidly, one effect is to remove the context within which the set of dispositions constituting the habitus would feel at home. The reflexive individual is therefore presented with the disjuncture between their dispositive impulses and the field within which those dispositions operate. This may result in: (1) on a dispositive level, an actor with a feel for a game that is not the game now being played, and (2) on a more instrumental rational level, the realization that previously effective strategies for the accumulation of capital within the field have been rendered useless or problematic, necessitating the development of new strategies more attuned to the opportunities for reward the field now offers and any new obstacles that stand in the way of the realization of those opportunities.

If the preceding analysis is correct, it implies in times of rapid social system or subsystem change an escalation in rational strategizing, informed by the habitus in terms of prior internalized dispositions ("history made nature") and the desire to preserve a trajectory of capital accumulation, symbolic and financial. This phase of strategic adjustment will result in the formation of new routines. In this way, in the evolving dialectic of habitus and field, neither is static or unitary, and during periods of "dispositional anomie," when the habitus is given drift, as it were, by the changes in the field, there may be a changing balance between routine and innovative instrumentalism, both of which compose practical logic, with innovation coming to the fore. Here, then, there is a disjuncture between mental structures and social structures that generate practice, and it is contended that in that instance practice is more likely to bear the hallmarks of rationality than when it is generated by a correspondence between the two types of structures. In the latter case, rational strategy will still obtain, but perceived strategic options will in that circumstance be more firmly framed by this very correspondence between habitus and field.

Bourdieu has set up and investigated the innovation to which structural change in a field can give rise, as well as theorizing the relationship between innovation at such times of crisis and the production of new mental structures that resolve the tension between habitus and field, a condition he calls hysteresis, by producing a new alignment between the two (Bourdieu, 1984; 1988). What becomes relevant for analysis in this model of social change is: (a) the historical development of the habitus and its internalized schemes of perception and classification as it stands at point A, prior to developments in the field that we might say characterize a "field-shift"; (b) an exposition of the nature and extent of the field-shift between point A and the present, point B; and (c) an analysis of the now somewhat strained relationship between the habitus and the field at point B.

In what follows, I shall focus on delineating and expanding upon points (b) and (c)—the nature of the field-shift I identify in the antiquities market over the last 30 to 40 years, and dealers' responses to this shift. This is not to underestimate the importance of the development of an adequate conception of the matters in point (a), but space does not permit such a full exposition; a picture of the "incipient" habitus in the antiquities market can be constructed from information available elsewhere (Mackenzie, 2005a, 2005b), and the data presented in respect of point (c) in this article will involve allusions to the habitus as is, and therefore also as was (we might feel we can assume).

In the international antiquities market the field-shift can be identified as consisting of two components of change: law and morality. Antiquities dealers have thus in recent years found themselves operating in a market characterized by increased legal regulation and by greater scrutiny of the ethical questions surrounding the collection and sale of excavated objects.

The legal element of the field-shift, as experienced by market participants, might best be conceived of in terms of the metaphor of the net of control (*cf.* Cohen, 1985). At the turn of the 20th century, there simply was no net. There were no domestic laws in source or market countries, much less international laws, to restrict the transit of, or dealing in, cultural property taken from the ground anywhere in the world. The net first appeared in the early to mid-1900s, as source countries began to pass legislation vesting title to underground antiquities in the state (Prott and O'Keefe, 1984). Further strands of control were added to the legal net with two international conventions (UNESCO, 1970; UNIDROIT, 1995). Between 1970 and the millennium, source countries continued to pass state vesting legislation and introduce export controls, and market countries made slow and tentative moves toward recognizing these laws for the purpose of their own internal prosecutions. Moreover, the introduction in the U.K. of the *Dealing in Cultural Objects (Offences) Act 2003* represented the first piece of criminal legislation worldwide that specifically targets dealing in illicit antiquities.

So the mesh of the regulatory net has become thinner. Many holes remain, however. The offense in the 2003 Act is symbolic at best, since it was drafted so so as to make a successful criminal prosecution extremely difficult to achieve (Mackenzie and Green, forthcoming). The offense it contains is of dishonestly dealing in a "tainted" cultural object (including looting, where the looting is a theft by the law of the source country), knowing or believing that the object is tainted. The Act contains no prohibition against dealing in an illegally exported object. Most important, however, it makes a prosecution unrealistic where a dealer claims "honest dealing"—that he did not know or believe the object to have been stolen. In a market where most objects, licit and illicit, are bought and sold with no systematic or reliable evidence of provenance, it will be very difficult for prosecutors to prove knowledge or belief. This is reflected in the fact that at the time of writing, three years after the introduction of the Act, there have been no concluded prosecutions in terms of the offense it creates. We have, then, a mesh-thinning of the legal net in symbolic terms, if not a practical crackdown on dealing in looted artifacts. It is symbolic in terms of the outline of a principle, a shadow of control-to-come, and a compromised compromise between the three core groups—distantly interested, distracted government, core cadre of politically active and energetically noisy moral entrepreneurs, and economically anchored dealers eager to join the regulatory circus to defuse from the inside whatever explosive possibilities may be in store.

At the same time as the legal net has appeared and its mesh thinned, the moral field has shifted. Indeed, the growth of the legal net can be quite accurately correlated to increasing moral sensitivity to the issue of the international transport, collection, and sale of antiquities. Through the writing and lobbying of moral entrepreneurs in this area, such as Clemency Coggins and Ricardo Elia (Coggins, 1969, 1970, 1971, 1998; Elia, 1991, 1993a, 1993b, 1994, 2001) in the United States and Lord Renfrew of Kaimsthorn in the U.K. (Renfrew, 1993, 1995, 1999, 2001), what was once an international business community serving a perceived moral end (the historical and cultural benefits of the preservation and diffusion of the ancient art of other cultures) has come to find itself the subject of such morally pejorative labels as "looting" and "smuggling." This moral shift has largely remained the business of this small community of moral entrepreneurs, having failed to attract much support from a generally apathetic and uninvolved public. Still, the persistence of the archaeologists and legal writers, helped by Lord Renfrew's considerable political acumen and relentless pursuit of the cause, has been influential in promoting in the U.K. the political attractions of regulatory activity. Such persistence has brought the matter into the peripheral vision of the governmental agenda as an issue where being seen, or thought, to be "doing something" is considered sensible insurance against future allegations of insular cultural nationalism that may arise if the moral climate continues to warm. The moral component of the field-shift thus provides a significant and escalating source of antagonism for the habitus of dealers, both in itself and through its legal effects.

Denial and the Antiquities Market

If the recent history of the antiquities market is one of a moral and legal field-shift, some intriguing and important empirical questions arise. Is there, as might be hoped, a straightforward translation of field-shift into (better) market action? Once the structural work is done, morally and legally, what response follows from the market? The arrogance of law and the conceit of morality both suggest that once matters are in their hands, social problems will be solved. The regulatory discourse of illicit markets—and in this respect the antiquities debate is no exception—is awash with sentiment emanating from these two poles of apparent pragmatism, suggesting the need for more and better laws, and for programs of education that will heighten sensitivity among consumers, thus reducing demand (O'Keefe, 1997; Polk, 2002). As Polk has said, setting out the apparently sensible argument for market education:

> The goal is to eliminate the demand for unprovenanced cultural heritage material, and thereby remove the basic force that drives the illicit market in antiquities, and thereby stop the plunder. How might this be accomplished? What we would propose is that market centres accept the proposition that only cultural heritage material that has documented and acceptable provenance would be offered for sale, and that consumers be educated and trained to demand such documentation before they buy such objects (Polk, 2002).

Polk is among the more reflective and balanced observers of the market, and one can find many less refined commentaries in which the ivory trade and the fur trade are put forward as popular exemplars of the obvious success of consumer consciousness-raising. Social scientists should be wary of such claims, which in many respects have achieved such unreflective currency that they approach folk-myth status. Moreover, they should pursue detailed investigation of the assumption that what may seem to have worked for one illicit market will work for another. Our empirical data collected on the antiquities market suggests that the education that has occurred so far in the market has had little impact; at present, the legal and moral interventions into the market have not produced conformity to an upgraded set of normative precepts, but denial.

Let us consider three forms of ideal-typical denial in the illicit antiquities market. Two of these are in the manner of constrained communication (Bourdieu and Wacquant, 2001: 2). Both of these are also forms of symbolic violence. These two forms of denial are silence and the entrepreneurialism of categorization, which seeks to impose a certain linguistic construction of a situation as the proper frame of reference within which to discuss the matter, and resolve any problems raised. The third category of denial we might call "career confusion," which takes the form of a more honest incapacity to grasp the new meanings attributed to one's action.

Silence

Silence in the antiquities market is the most common form of denial. It is a form of "passive" denial, as opposed to the active nature of categorical denial (see below), insofar as categorical denial must involve an argument that an act should be seen as "this"—morally, legally, culturally, etc.—rather than "that." Rather than engaging in categorical entrepreneurialism, many participants in the antiquities market choose to remain "off radar" in the debate as far as commentators and regulators are concerned. The most common, and therefore important, element of all of the research I have undertaken into the problem of illicit antiquities has been non-response, and the peculiar nature of that non-response. This is an interesting case study of the relationship between the individual and the group in respect of public appearance on the group's behalf when group interests are threatened (*cf.* Macy, 1995).

Overwhelmingly, over the course of five years of research, antiquities dealers, collectors, and even auction houses have declined the various invitations sent to them seeking their anonymous participation in our projects. Although many of these refusals have been implicit—straightforward non-response to invitation letters and follow-up e-mails—in a significant number of cases the researchers have had personal contact with non-respondents, either through "chasing" telephone calls, or in a few instances through face-to-face site visits. We therefore have some limited data on the reasons for "purposive" non-response (as opposed to those who did not respond through lack of interest, lack of time, or forgetfulness), collected ad hoc through these approaches. Targets who consciously declined to participate in the research did so for one of two reasons: denial of responsibility (Sykes and Matza, 1957) or strategic reticence.

Denial of responsibility took the form of a flat refusal to contemplate involvement in the chain of illicit supply. Here is an example, taken from an e-mail received after a follow-up invitation to participate: "I can see no point in engaging about debate on this. I do not import at all—all items I sell are sourced at public auction here in the U.K." (dealer, London).

This is nonsense, of course: there have been many cases of looted antiquities turning up in public auction sales (see, among many possible others, Lowenthal, 1994; Watson, 1997; Pomfret, 2003). Those caught in the hands of the auction house are usually withdrawn from sale, while those not caught at auction are sometimes reclaimed from unfortunate buyers. Either way, such matters are the subject of quite some publicity and cause such ripples in the community of dealers that the comment above is either a form of self-deception or a straightforward lie.

The second form of silence is strategic reticence. Predominantly, non-respondents who subsequently explained their reluctance to participate explained that they did not want to draw attention to themselves and run the risk of being singled out for law enforcement investigation, or to attract the critical rhetoric of the archaeological lobby. They were conscious that this was a difficult decision to make, in that this strategy might ultimately work against the interests of the market, but overall their immediate individual preference for relative anonymity in a difficult moral and regulatory climate dictated a discounting of their long-term interest in fighting for their moral turf:

> London dealer: [I] am no longer dealing in Asian antiquities except those with provenance and have no further comment.
>
> Bangkok dealer: I must turn down your offer of interview because traditionally we as antique dealers are not very keen on expressing our views on this sensitive issue.
>
> London dealer: considering the environment of the governments of the west as well as India, I am hesitant to put my name.... I would like to help you but at the same time do not want to come to the lime lite (*sic*).

Combined with this reluctance to put individual heads above the parapet was a perceptible hope that if a general silence were maintained, then perhaps the whole issue would just blow over. Though there are good practical reasons for silently denying one's part in a troublesome network of wrongdoing, such as the obvious attractions of obscurity in the regulatory gaze, the two categories of silent denial noted here—denial of responsibility and strategic reticence—share a foundation of literal denial (Cohen, 2001): if we do not talk about this issue, then it doesn't exist; whatever may be wrong does not trouble me; it has nothing to do with me; I am not involved in this.

Categorical Entrepreneurialism

A small proportion of the market has actively attempted to influence the construction of the issue. These individuals have been very keen to talk to researchers, with this talk being consistent with their instrumental strategy of "categorical entrepreneurialism"—a claim to authority in definition. The screen discourse of the marketers of cultural heritage rests on several philosophical pillars that present themselves as reflections of "the way the world works." In fact, they are historically constitutive of that world in the reproduction of its fashionable truths and functional in providing mechanisms for the psychosocial neutralization of wrongdoing. One of these pillars is the triumph, and therefore normalization, of neoliberal ideology, which makes many things "obvious" to (re)producers of its structures. Neoliberal thought constructs property as a right, legitimizes harm in as much as it is an essential product of any competitive strategy, and as a driver of globalization is unilaterally universalizing, imposing its thought-structures across cultural and geographical divides, judging distant agents by its own precepts and castigating them when they fail to perform as the market might hope (some of these assertions are brought out in greater depth by other contributors to this volume). It has been suggested that a property of globalization is to make a "transnational relation of economic power appear like a natural necessity" (Bourdieu and Wacquant, 2001: 3), and this is one of the tactics, linguistic and ideological, implemented by the categorical entrepreneurs in our sample:

> London dealer: I believe in the free circulation of works of art.

> London dealer: Personal ownership is a jolly good thing.

> New York dealer: We're still back to the assumption that if you have a farm in South Africa and you go dig a hole and you find a lump of gold in that hole that happened to be carved by someone a hundred years ago or a thousand years ago, it doesn't belong to you. Somehow by the divine right of archaeological something-or-other, it belongs to the archaeologists or to the State.

The ideological benefits of a global property-owning democracy are thought to weigh against any problematic issues for the market, such as looting. In some cases, the ideology is strengthened by a further screen discourse—again, that of literal denial. Although the literal denial of the phenomenon of looting is totally unsustainable in light of the evidence, the unreflective comfortable "knowledge" that looting is not a genuine phenomenon is sometimes seen in the narratives of the dealers. This literal denial is never sustained under interrogation, although sometimes the forces behind its construction are revealed:

> There's just nothing coming across (from Thailand), because it really has been stopped. And that's an amazingly good thing....

I pick him up on this, showing him pictures of looted sites in Thailand from the Cambridge "purple book" (Brodie, Doole, and Renfrew, 2001) and ask him to reflect on his denial of the issue.

> Any collector feels the same way. They don't want to see, because, you know, we have an interest in it, a passion in it... (dealer, Melbourne).

Here, the dealer seems to acknowledge the motive underlying his denial. In this respect we might ask: To what extent can an ideology be said to be a purposive, knowing work of agentic choice or, alternatively, the ineluctable and unacknowledged indoctrination of a conscience with the particular knowledge-constructs of the field? In terms of denial, then, to what extent do we instrumentally implement rationalizations for the wrong that we do, knowing it to be wrong, but choosing not to think of it as such—talking or thinking ourselves out of the wrongdoing, as it were? An alternate hypothesis would be that ideology is a strong construct, in that it may prevent us from ever knowing of the wrongful nature of our conduct, imbuing it from the start and at all times with the taint of right(eous)ness? Cohen (2001) has considered such things at length, noting that the matter presents an interesting subject of study insofar as it suggests both purpose and determinism, bad faith and an honest deficit of perspicacity. As Cohen suggests, however, and as is certainly the case with our research sample, there is no way empirically to tell through interviews whether categorical entrepreneurs are: (a) good liars who do not believe their own rhetoric, but see it as instrumental; (b) self-deceiving and persuaded by their own psycho-discursive rhetoric after a period (however short) of uncertainty; or (c) merely relaying their honest "always-held" opinion about the appropriate ethical status of their actions. This is not least because successful self-deception may begin with lying and end in sincerity, where the lie internally applied is ultimately believed.

Despite this deficit of the research method, we can ask what socio-structural factors might be responsible for generating such ideological discourse. Bourdieu gives us a conceptual framework within which to think that through. Although our conception of categorical entrepreneurialism focuses on the external indicators of "reality negotiations," this framework leaves open the question of whether these mirror parallel "ongoing internal reality negotiations" (Cohen, 2001: 38) in the minds of the interviewees. Bourdieu himself is on record as firmly behind the proposition that ideology is both internally and externally persuasive, talking of what we have called categorical entrepreneurialism as a "screen discourse...[that] deceives both those who are party to it and those who are not" (Bourdieu and Wacquant, 2001: 3).

An empirical view of ethics might bring out the importance of the linguistic and conceptual framing of a problem as instrumental in determining its resolution. The construction of a problem in certain terms rather than in others is based, in the profit-oriented world of the antiquities market (as perhaps elsewhere in societies that tend toward individualistic self-interest over communitarian duty), upon a self-serving ideology. Moreover, given a model in which the disjuncture between habitus and the moral/legal field is large, and therefore where rational strategizing becomes a more urgent priority for the actor than is normal, the creation of the ethical problem in terms that suggest a favorable outcome for the creator is transformed from a functional and largely unreflexive ideology that allows business as usual into a more vital and reflexive battle for definitional supremacy. Here we come to the symbolic violence of constrained communication: a denial of the value basis of the moral and legal field-shift and a struggle to appoint an alternative construction of the issue as sovereign. This, then, is not the ad hoc choice and implementation of an account from a pool of acceptable "reasons" to exonerate private moments of drift that have come to public attention (Sykes and Matza, 1957; Matza, 1964; Scott and Lyman, 1968), but a strategic and very public program of language-use that has as its aim the realignment of habitus and field, not by the gradual adaptation of the internal structures of the habitus to the new legal and moral structures of the field, but by dragging the field back to its original position.

Thus, a discourse emerges in the market that is calculated to achieve public effect. Acts of dealing and collecting are cast as "preservation," "cultural edification," and "private right," and regulation is perceived as a paranoid response to the performance and enjoyment of such misunderstood duties and rights. Denial for the categorical entrepreneur is therefore a vital element in sustaining the future of antiquities dealing as a business enterprise. If one can sustain the illusion that the field has not moved, its reinstatement is made considerably more "possible." Rather than attempting to unwind a process that has already begun, and gathered some momentum, denial of field-shift, or of the applicability of the various elements of field-shift to the business of the categorical entrepreneur, allows the possibility of performing a perceptual slight-of-hand in the dramaturgical suggestion that what is lost is not lost, and if recovered it was in fact never gone. Denial is in this sense a necessary component in the symbolic discourse that limits and defines the social conditions of the possible.

Career Confusion

Of the market respondents in our samples, those who did not display much of the energetic loquacity of categorical entrepreneurialism tended to present a sense of bemusement at their place in the new morally and legally charged environment of their hitherto rather quiet and civilized niche, operating with "a semi-conscious [sense] of siege," as one of our interviewees put it (dealer, London). These respondents fell conceptually halfway between the silence of non-response and the spin of the screen discourse. Aware of field-shift, their talk was not constrained or instrumental, but questioning and uncertain. While the contradictions contained in the categorical discourse were hidden beneath the veneer of a public-oriented polemic, those in career confusion engaged in a more open exploration of the contradictions of their position. Theirs was a friendly, unrehearsed conversational style, which generally acknowledged the perceived difficulties in the market that characterize the field-shift, and sought a discussion about what they meant for dealers and how they might be resolved. As Cohen has noted, and Zerubavel (2006) has further clarified, denial is often a collective activity, and this is the cause of much of the "confusion" we have identified in the market. The international dimension of the field-shift leads inevitably to inconsistencies in legal and moral climates across states, and these jurisdictional differences, although taking place under the ambit of a "global" concern with the issue, result in superficial treatment of the issue in some regions:

> You know, if you have archaeological material readily available in Hong Kong, all the shops there have fakes, real stuff, the reality is that everybody knows...its the same in Italy, it is a secret that everybody knows, is that

> basically you can export objects, nobody will bother you, but obviously everybody knows that the majority of the material has arrived, you know, last week from China. So, it is all tainted material according to the law.... So, a lot of dealers in Chinese pots, bronzes, horses, things obviously coming from underground...they still don't know now how they should behave... (dealer, London).

Such open secrets add to the confusion of dealers who are thereby exposed to mixed signals. What, after all, are they supposed to be doing? The habitus is revealed in these market actors when they freely "confess" to wrongdoing without apparent realization that their accounts are of action that has now been expressly criminalized in many parts of the world. The disjuncture between field and habitus leads them sometimes to reflect on their position in a changing moral and legal climate, and at other times to reveal a routine pattern of behavior that is entirely contradictory to the new position of the field—no doubt aided by the contradictions evident in this process of field-shift. This is most clearly illustrated in relation to a dealer from Australia who, while of the opinion that recently looting had "gone ballistic" and was "incredibly destructive," said "I haven't got many pieces with provenance" (in other words he did not know whether they were looted or not) and then proceeded to show me a pot he was selling that he thought bore the hallmarks of looting:

> Certainly, with the Chinese pieces, for example this pot (picks up pot off desk), you've got dirt in the crevices. That hasn't been out of the ground for long, so that's a recent, you know, within the last five years I'd say that one's been dug up. (He points to a striped indentation on the pot.) You can see that that's where the spade hit when they dug it (dealer, Melbourne).

Conclusion: Denial and Transnational Crime

Above all else, this study reveals the central place in regulatory problems of the generally overlooked effects of denial, myth, hearsay, routine, fuzzy logic, and constructivist ethics. These facets of the discourse-based projections of the habitus mediate the relationship of laws and agents, and obviate attempts at straightforward regulation-through-legislation.

Three types of denial found in the antiquities market are presented here as "ideal types." In practice, they are not as exclusive as they have appeared here; that is, although individual research participants tend toward one model rather than another, they resist such simple categorization, rarely displaying uniformly the characteristics of only one of our three types. Rather, various permutations of these denial-based responses were observed. Those who initially deployed silence became categorical entrepreneurs when persuaded to contribute to the project, for example, and categorical entrepreneurs would sometimes vacillate between this tactic and moments of more reflective career confusion.

Though Dick Hobbs may have been correct to observe that, to paraphrase him paraphrasing Bruno Latour (1993), "everything happens locally" (Hobbs, 1998), including denial, it does so with reference to projections of the acts and intentions of distant actors, and (legally and morally, at least) with reference to the transnational discourse-networks of laws, irritant academics, and archaeologists whose words resonate in the moral field-shift.

REFERENCES

Bourdieu, Pierre

1996 *The State Nobility*. Cambridge: Polity Press. [1989].

1990 *The Logic of Practice*. Cambridge: Polity. [1980].

1988 *Homo Academicus*. Stanford: Stanford University Press.

1984 *Distinction: A Social Critique of the Judgment of Taste*. London: Routledge.

Bourdieu, Pierre and Loïc Wacquant

2001 "NewLiberalSpeak: Notes on the New Planetary Vulgate." *Radical Philosophy* 105: 2–5.

Brodie, Neil, Jennifer Doole, and Colin Renfrew (eds.)

2001 *Trade in Illicit Antiquities: The Destruction of the World's Archaeological Heritage*. Cambridge: McDonald Institute for Archaeological Research.

Coggins, Clemency

1998 "United States Cultural Property Legislation: Observations of a Combatant." *International Journal of Cultural Property* 7: 57.

1971 "An Art Historian Speaks Out." *Auction* (January): 33.

1970 "The Maya Scandal: How Thieves Strip Sites of Past Cultures." *Smithsonian* (October): 8–16.

1969 "Illicit Traffic of Pre-Columbian Antiquities." *Art Journal* (Fall): 94–98.

Cohen, Stanley

2001 *States of Denial: Knowing About Atrocities and Suffering*. Cambridge: Polity.

1985 *Visions of Social Control*. Cambridge: Polity Press.

Elia, Ricardo J.

2001 "Analysis of the Looting, Selling and Collecting of Apulian Red-Figure Vases: A Quantitative Approach." Neil Brodie, Jennifer Doole, and Colin Renfrew (eds.), *Trade in Illicit Antiquities: The Destruction of the World's Archaeological Heritage*. Cambridge: MacDonald Institute for Archaeological Research.

1994 "The World Cannot Afford Many More Collectors with a Passion for Antiquities." *The Art Newspaper* 41 (October): 19.

1993a "A Review of Colin Renfrew's *The Cycladic Spirit: Masterpieces from the Nicholas P Goulandris Collection* (Abrams, New York, 1991)." *Archaeology* (January/February): 64.

1993b "Ricardo Elia Responds." *Archaeology* 46,3: 17.

1991 "Popular Archaeology and the Antiquities Market: A Review Essay." *Journal of Field Archaeology* 18: 95.

Hobbs, Dick

1998 "Going Down the Glocal: The Local Context of Organised Crime." *The Howard Journal of Criminal Justice* 37,4: 407–422.

Latour, Bruno

1993 *We Have Never Been Modern*. London: Harvester Wheatsheaf.

Lowenthal, Constance

1994 "Sevso Case Ended in New York." *IFAR Reports* (November): 4–5.

Mackenzie, Simon R.M.

2005a "Dig a Bit Deeper: Law, Regulation and the Illicit Antiquities Market." *British Journal of Criminology* 45: 249–268.

2005b *Going, Going, Gone: Regulating the Market in Illicit Antiquities*. Leicester: Institute of Art and Law.

Mackenzie, Simon R.M. and Penny J. Green

forthcoming "Criminalising the Market in Illicit Antiquities: An Evaluation of the Dealing in Cultural Objects (Offences) Act 2003." In *Regulating the Market in Illicit Antiquities: From Archaeology to Criminology*. Oxford: Hart.

Macy, Michael W.

1995 "Cowardly Lions: Genetic Programming or Social Learning?" *The Agora:* Newsletter of the Rational Choice Section of the American Sociological Association (December).

Matza, David

1964 *Delinquency and Drift*. New York: John Wiley.

O'Keefe, Patrick J.

1997 *Trade in Antiquities: Reducing Destruction and Theft*. London: Archetype.

Polk, Ken

2002 "Controlling the Traffic in Illicit Antiquities: Are Criminal Sanctions Appropriate?" Published as proceedings of the conference *Implementation of the UNESCO 1970 Convention*. Department for Culture Media and Sport. London: Institute of Art and Law and Art-Law Centre, Geneva.

Pomfret, John

2003 "China Uncovers Looted Buddhas: Relics Sold by Christie's in October Hong Kong Auction." *Washington Post Foreign Service* (May 28): A11.

Prott, Lyndel V. and Patrick J. O'Keefe

1984 *Law and the Cultural Heritage*. Volume 1: *Discovery and Excavation*. Abingdon: Professional Books.

Renfrew, Colin

2001 "Foreword." Neil Brodie, Jennifer Doole, and Colin Renfrew (eds.), *Trade in Illicit Antiquities: The Destruction of the World's Archaeological Heritage*. Cambridge: McDonald Institute for Archaeological Research.

1999 *Loot, Legitimacy and Ownership: The Ethical Crisis in Archaeology*. Amsterdam: Joh. Enschedé.

1995 "Introduction." Kathryn W. Tubb (ed.), *Antiquities Trade or Betrayed: Legal, Ethical and Conservation Issues*. London: Archetype.

1993 "Collectors Are the Real Looters." *Archaeology* 46,3: 16–17.

Scott, Marvin and Stanford Lyman

1968 "Accounts." *American Sociological Review* 33: 46–62.

Sykes, Gresham M. and David Matza

1957 "Techniques of Neutralization: A Theory of Delinquency." *American Sociological Review* 22: 664–670.

UNESCO

1970 *Convention on the Means of Prohibiting and Preventing the Illicit Import, Export and Transfer of Ownership of Cultural Property*. New York: UNESCO.

UNIDROIT

1995 *Convention on Stolen or Illegally Exported Cultural Objects*. UNIDROIT.

Wacquant, Loïc

2005 "Habitus." Jens Beckert and Milan Zafirovski (eds.), *International Encyclopedia of Economic Sociology*. London: Routledge.

Watson, Peter

1997 *Sotheby's: The Inside Story*. London: Bloomsbury.

Zerubavel, Eviatar

2006 *The Elephant in the Room: Silence and Denial in Everyday Life*. Oxford: Oxford University Press.

[20]

Transnational white-collar crime and risk

Lessons from the global trade in electronic waste

Carole Gibbs
Edmund F. McGarrell
Mark Axelrod
Michigan State University

Research Summary

Business transactions have increasingly been crossing national borders, thereby presenting greater opportunities for white-collar crime and for the externalization of risk. The global economic crisis, resulting in part from the subprime mortgage scandal, is a prime example of this potential. To develop theoretical perspectives and practical interventions to prevent and respond to the global financial crisis, we consider similar issues of risk and white-collar crime associated with global transactions in electronic waste (E-waste).

Policy Implications

Smart (or responsive) regulation is a promising approach for addressing both E-waste and the current economic crisis. This response includes crime prevention, third-party- and self-regulation, and the threat of strong state intervention. Future research should explore the extent to which smart regulation reduces specific forms of white-collar crime and risk, as well as whether these interventions generalize to other transnational problems.

This project was supported in part by the Michigan State University Sustainable Endowment Project and the Regulatory Network visiting scholar program. Appreciation is extended to Jennifer Melvin for her assistance with data collection. Special thanks are also extended to Neal Shover (University of Tennessee), Peter Grabosky (Australian National University), and three anonymous reviewers for their helpful comments on earlier drafts of this article. Direct correspondence to Carole Gibbs, School of Criminal Justice, Department of Fisheries and Wildlife, Michigan State University, 508 Baker Hall, East Lansing, MI 48808 (e-mail: gibbsca1@msu.edu); Edmund F. McGarrell, School of Criminal Justice 560 Baker Hall, East Lansing, MI 48808 (e-mail: mcgarrel@msu.edu); Mark Axelrod, James Madison College, Department of Fisheries and Wildlife, 362 North Case Hall, East Lansing, MI 48825 (e-mail: axelrod3@msu.edu).

Keywords
transnational crime, white-collar crime, risk, electronic waste, E-waste

Business transactions have increasingly been occurring across national borders, thereby resulting in greater opportunities for white-collar crime and the externalization of risk (Passas, 2002). In addition, the global marketplace intensifies the impact of white-collar crime and risky transactions. "When nations fail to curb emergent forms of white-collar crime the effects ripple throughout the world. This happens, for example, when unrestrained business and trading practices cause international catastrophes" (Shover and Hochstetler, 2006: 45). The global economic crisis, resulting in part from the subprime mortgage scandal, is a prime example of this potential—one that is replicated in the harm associated with the growing trade in electronic waste (E-waste).

In both cases, the harms result from white-collar crime and legal-but-risky business transactions that cross borders. Globalization has allowed these risks to be disassociated from the people accountable for them. Environmental impacts associated with E-waste, for example, have been shifted to developing nations and financial losses have been spread around the world. In other words, the risks have become externalized. In addition, trade in E-waste is fueled by a similar set of factors; namely, lure and lack of oversight. Finally, reducing the opportunities for both types of illicit and risky market transactions is a challenging regulatory and enforcement issue.

This article begins with brief comments on the global financial crisis before moving to a discussion of the problems caused by E-waste. Data are presented on the scope and destination of U.S. exports of E-waste trade and on indicators of risk and white-collar crime associated with the trade. Next considered are theoretical frameworks suitable for interpreting E-waste and the global economic crisis, which is followed by a discussion of the challenge of regulating these global business transactions. The article concludes with an overview of potential interventions to reduce the harm associated both with E-waste and with regulation and enforcement in global financial markets.

The Global Economic Crisis

Problems in the United States mortgage markets began to surface in 2007 and grew significantly thereafter, which led to historic financial failures and a credit crisis across much of the globe (Shiller, 2008). Despite disagreement about the explanation for this crisis, little doubt exists that pro-homeownership policies, global financial imbalances, and "overly aggressive" mortgage lenders were significant contributors. Inadequate oversight also played a major role (Jickling, 2009; Shiller, 2008).

During the previous decade, U.S. policy promoted the dissemination of financial tools (i.e., home ownership) to the general population (Shiller, 2008). Specifically, federal policies designed to provide assistance to lower income borrowers, such as the Community Reinvestment Act (1977), permitted banks to lend to riskier borrowers (Jickling, 2009). In addition, global financial imbalances from increasing U.S. debt and greater investment in U.S. assets by developing countries kept interest rates low (Carmassi, Gros, and Micossi, 2009; Jickling, 2009; Yifu Lin, 2008). Opportunities to profit from the housing market grew significantly. As such, home building and ownership skyrocketed, fueled by profit-seeking mortgage lenders as well as inexperienced and fraudulent appraisers and borrowers (Schmidt, 2008; Shiller, 2008). Potential homeowners, for example, were encouraged to borrow the full value of their property with little consideration of repayment risk. Financial innovation to reduce risks and increase profits among the major players followed, as the use of derivatives, securitization, and the packaging and sale of mortgages to other investors were used to hedge or transfer risks (Carmassi et al., 2009; Shiller, 2008). These financial innovations proliferated absent any significant revamping or creation of new financial institutions for oversight (Shiller, 2008). Many analysts argue that huge Wall Street profits led regulators to look the other way and to ignore the impending crisis (Frean, 2010). The Gramm-Leach-Bliley Act (1999) and the Commodity Futures Modernization Act (2000) allowed companies to continue engaging in unregulated and risky financial transactions (Faiola, Nakashima, and Drew, 2008; Jickling, 2009).

Eventually the large supply of new homes reduced overall housing prices, and borrowers began to default on loans because of higher mortgage rates after the initial low-rate period. The housing bubble burst, and financial institutions that relied on repayment of loans and continued growth in the market began to fail. This crisis quickly spread across borders and caused the failure of financial institutions in several countries. Subsequently, the problems fed back into the United States in the form of the declining value of the dollar, fluctuations in the stock market, and additional financial failures (Shiller, 2008). Discussions of how to address the problem highlighted the significant challenges for the oversight of risky and illegal international business transactions (Carmassi et al., 2009; Jickling, 2009; Shiller, 2008).

Challenges for Oversight

Although global regulation of business has increased significantly since the 1970s, most remain at the local level (Braithwaite and Drahos, 2000). Attempts at global regulation, moreover, are plagued by inconsistencies in legal requirements across jurisdictions, while international treaties designed to harmonize regulation generally are voluntary in nature (Passas, 2002). Countries can choose whether to ratify relevant treaties, and many countries choose not to do so, whereas some ratifying countries lack the requisite resources to enforce their regulations (Chayes, Chayes, and Mitchell, 1998). This variability increases the pool of potential victims and opportunities for white-collar crime and risky transactions with actors in other countries (Shover and Hochstetler, 2006).

The scale and complexity of global transactions challenge good-faith attempts at monitoring and enforcement. The quality and origin of goods, materials, and wastes easily can be misrepresented when they cross borders. The scale of trade, the number of actors, and the complexity of financial transactions make this issue difficult to detect (Elliott, 2009; Hill, 2005). The increased anonymity associated with technology and globalization also hinders the investigation of known cases of fraud, and applicable law—whether "home" or "host" country—is often unclear (Putnam, 2009). Consequently, those who are predisposed or easily tempted to violate the law can do so with the reasonable expectation of impunity (Passas, 2002; Shover and Hochstetler, 2006). As a result of the global financial crisis, the challenge of controlling international markets has come under heightened scrutiny.

The Problem of E-waste

Electronics is the world's largest and fastest growing manufacturing industry (Grossman, 2006; Puckett, et al., 2002). Yet, each year, nearly 7 million tons of high-tech electronics become obsolete, and the result is E-waste (Grossman, 2006). E-waste refers to used electronics destined for disposal, reuse, or recycling, and includes "obsolete, broken, or irreparable electronic equipment such as televisions, computers and computer monitors, laptops, printers, cell phones, VCRs, DVD players, copiers, fax machines, stereos, and video gaming systems" (Luther, 2007: 1). This technological refuse becomes a significant social problem when discarded, as electronic products contain numerous toxic substances (Jackson, Shuman, and Dayaneni, 2006; Pellow, 2007; Scanlon, 2004; Silicon Valley Toxics Coalition, 2008).

Most U.S. E-waste simply is disposed of in landfills or is incinerated, but a considerable portion of it is gathered for recycling and is exported to developing nations for remanufacture or refurbishment (Environmental Protection Agency [EPA], 2007). Many recycling facilities in developing nations, however, are not equipped to handle E-waste properly, and much of it is not processed but is instead dumped in local villages near people and water sources (Pellow, 2007). Illegal dump sites have been documented in Nigeria, Ghana, China, the Philippines, Indonesia, Pakistan, and India (Greenpeace, 2008; Iles, 2004), and they pose severe threats to both human health and the natural environment.

Computer and television displays contain an average of 4–8 pounds of lead each, which means that "the 315 million computers that came obsolete between 1997 and 2004 contained more than 1.2 billion pounds of lead" (Pellow, 2007: 187). In addition to lead, high-tech electronics contain other toxic substances such as mercury and hexavalent chromium (Jackson et al., 2006). Health and environmental impacts include developmental damage to humans, organ damage and cancer, groundwater contamination, and ozone depletion (Grossman, 2006; Huo et al., 2007; Jackson et al., 2006; Puckett et al., 2002; Scanlon, 2004; Silicon Valley Toxics Coalition, 2008). Despite the severity of the consequences, little is known about this global issue because of legal variation and ambiguity in terms of the definition of criminal behavior across states and countries, the hidden nature of the harmful or criminal behavior, and the inattention of enforcement agencies.

In response to this knowledge gap, we assembled a variety of data to describe the problem of E-waste. We began by reviewing academic, nongovernmental organization (NGO), and governmental documents, as well as data collected by the U.S. EPA. Recent legislation requires U.S. exporters to notify the EPA of their intent to export specific types of E-waste. We compiled these notifications along with several preexisting sources of data on the scope and destination of

U.S. exports. Finally, we conducted 20–25 informational interviews (ranging from 30 minutes to 2 hours in length) with business and agency personnel responsible for their organizations' electronic disposal programs, with NGO advocates familiar with E-waste, and with regulatory and law-enforcement officials involved in Interpol's Environmental Crime Program.

U.S. Trade in E-waste

The movement of E-waste across the globe generates benefits (e.g., profits for exporters and recycling of precious metals for use in developing countries). Nevertheless, it also creates harms (e.g., waste dumps and improper disposal and harvesting) and risks (e.g., health risks for recyclers and the import of toys and jewelry containing lead). However, only *some* of these harms and risks occur as the result of noncompliance. Currently, much of the global transport of E-waste is legal (although this transport varies by country and by the status of the E-waste material being shipped). Particularly, in the case of the United States, efforts to regulate domestic and international disposal and recycling of E-waste are relatively weak.

In the United States, most electronic devices (or parts of electronic devices) are either exempt or excluded from the Resource Conservation and Recovery Act (RCRA, 1976) legislation on hazardous waste and are classified as "products" or "commodities" rather than as "waste" (Tonetti, 2007a). Regulations covering the export of cathode ray tubes (CRTs)—the glass video display component in computers and televisions—represent the only explicit regulation of E-waste. U.S. firms exporting CRTs incur liability only under specific and limited conditions related to reporting requirements (e.g., failure to maintain paperwork, failure to notify the EPA, failure to wait 60 days before export of CRTs, and exporting broken, intact equipment). Enforcement of these regulations has been weak (Government Accountability Office [GAO], 2008a, 2008b).

U.S. efforts are a stark contrast to international regulation and enforcement of the trade in hazardous waste. The Basel Ban, an amendment to the Basel Convention on the Control of Transboundary Movements of Hazardous Wastes and Their Disposal, prohibits the export of hazardous waste from developed countries that belong to the Organization for Economic Cooperation and Development (OECD) to non-OECD countries. Although the Ban is not yet in force, the European Union and other developed countries have ratified it, passed domestic legislation to implement it, and extended its provisions to specific forms of E-waste (Ford, 2009; Zonneveld, 2007). Australia and the United Kingdom also have developed new methods for increasing enforcement. To date, the United States has not ratified the Basel Convention or strengthened enforcement through domestic legislation. Instead, the United States continues to generate significant amounts of E-waste and to externalize the risk by exporting it to developing nations.

Industry experts estimate that, in 2005, nearly 90% of CRT-containing products collected in the United States for recycling primarily were exported to developing countries (EPA, 2007). Nations that placed the highest number of requests to purchase U.S. E-waste on trading Web sites include China, Malaysia, India, Vietnam, Hong Kong, Taiwan, Pakistan, Egypt, and Sri Lanka (GAO, 2008a). Data on U.S. exporter notifications to the EPA of intent to export broken and used CRTs—as well as data from the California Department of Toxic Substances Control—show a similar pattern (see Table 1). In 2007, the largest *volume* of E-waste (72%) was exported to Malaysia (for additional details on estimate construction, see Gibbs, Melvin, McGarrell, and Axelrod, 2008). Malaysia also emerged as the largest export destination for California E-waste. Brazil, South Korea, China, and Mexico are the next most common sites.

TABLE 1

2007 Estimated E-waste Export by Designated Country

	California Department of Toxic Substances Control KGs (in Thousands)	EPA Notifications of Broken CRT Export KGs (in Thousands)
Malaysia	3,583	50,699
Canada	NR	11,175–11,689
Brazil	1,633	3,428–1,099
South Korea	1,588	7,103
China	1,043	NR
Mexico	816	NR
Vietnam	318	NR
India	91	NR

Note. NR = not reported. CRT = Cathode Ray Tube.
Source. California Department of Toxic Substances Control, as cited in Lee, Mike, "Some U.S. trading partners not supposed to accept it," *San Diego Union-Tribune*, June 19, 2007; EPA notification reports.

The EPA and California data likely underestimate the magnitude of E-waste exports; both rely on self-reporting, and the California data exclude E-waste that might be shipped to other U.S. states before being exported abroad. These data, moreover, probably represent exports by more compliant businesses. Because neither the EPA nor the California data include nations such as Ghana, Nigeria, and Pakistan—where exposés by journalists and NGOs have documented clearly harmful E-waste dumpsites, including E-waste originating in the United States—they assuredly underreport the volume of risky U.S. exports to developing countries (Carroll, 2008; Greenpeace, 2008; Iles, 2004; Pellow, 2007). Indications of noncompliance with minimal U.S. regulations are an additional cause for concern.

Several destinations listed in the California notification data, several countries seeking U.S. exports in the GAO investigation, and several countries with known illegal E-waste dump sites were *not* included in the EPA data. In addition, exports to China may indicate a violation of federal rules that require importers to give consent prior to shipment. China banned the import of E-waste and is therefore unlikely to have consented. More direct evidence of noncompliance also exists. In a recent GAO study, 43 businesses indicated willingness to export in response to requests for illegal exports of E-waste (e.g., export without notification and export of broken, intact electronics), often after acknowledging illegalities in the transactions. Finally, the GAO worked with the Hong Kong Environmental Department to identify 26 shipments illegally sent to Hong Kong by U.S. businesses without the former's consent (GAO, 2008a).

Theoretical Explanations

Transnational and white-collar crimes are products of choice. Recognition of this fact draws attention to conditions that encourage or permit decisions to engage in risky and criminal transactions. The distribution of lure, "arrangements or situations that turn heads," is one such condition (Shover and Hochstetler, 2006: 27). Most markets for reusable and recyclable electronics are export driven. The foreign demand for raw materials is strong, and importers profit by selling extracted metals and by selling working equipment mixed occasionally in with scrap (Tonetti, 2007b). The large pool of individuals willing to remove metals from E-waste with virtually no worker protection also creates lure for actors at lower levels of the E-waste trade. Middle men profit by exploiting these labor pools to extract metals from E-waste in exchange for extremely low pay (CBS News, 2008).

In addition, E-waste trade is appealing to exporters. Recycling a personal computer in the United States costs approximately $20, while importers will pay up to $15 for each unit, creating an estimated net gain of $35 per computer (India, the E-Wasteland, 2006). Moreover, export allows businesses to avoid the costs and the responsibility associated with health and environmental regulations governing E-waste recycling and disposal within the United States. In addition to the difference in recycling costs, the trade imbalance with China creates opportunities for inexpensive transport of E-waste overseas. Shipping lines offer lower prices on return trips to China rather than allowing cargo ships to leave the United States empty (Fuller, 2006). Thus, international trade in E-waste creates lure for many actors.

Lure includes financial profit but is not limited to profit. In the case of the harmful or illicit disposal of E-waste, one lure is the numerous impoverished villages and the vast expanse of land in developing countries, where E-waste can be dumped free from notice and from state intervention. Parties predisposed or easily tempted can do so with ease. The absence of self-restraint and credible oversight that creates another lure into criminal opportunity (Shover and Hochstetler, 2006).

In the United States, disposing of E-waste criminally is made easy by weak oversight. In other words, non-credible domestic and transnational oversight is criminogenic. Structural asymmetries and inequalities in the law (as well as in politics and culture) increase motivation and opportunity and decrease the ability to control transnational activities (Passas, 1999, 2002). More specifically, symmetries are criminogenic because "they generate or strengthen the demand for illegal goods and services; they generate incentives for particular actors to participate in illegal transactions; and they reduce the ability of authorities to control illegal activities" (Passas, 2002: 26).

Perceptional variations of lure and willingness to exploit opportunities are another consideration. Individuals and organizations—be they predisposed or tempted—have taken advantage of the criminal opportunities associated with E-waste, as evidenced by the previous description of risky transactions and white-collar crimes. In contrast, several recyclers we contacted for interview took pride in being "zero-waste stream" recyclers: They erase all memory in computers and electronics, prevent hazardous waste from moving to landfills, do not export, and do not use prison labor for disassembly. Thus, perceptions of opportunities created by lure and lack of oversight contribute to variations in white-collar criminality.

Such variations in lure, oversight, and predisposition contributed likewise to the current financial crisis. The lure of potential profits from the housing market partially drove the crisis. Indeed, profits associated with the use of derivatives, securitization, and the packaging and sale of mortgages to other investors might have led regulators to ignore the impending problem (Frean, 2010). They not only failed to address emerging risky transactions, but also regulations encouraged banks to take on riskier borrowers. Oversight did not adapt to market developments. In the presence of lure, risky and perhaps fraudulent transactions proliferated. Nevertheless, banks varied in their level of participation in the riskiest financial practices (Theil, 2009). Thus, differences in predisposition and temptation appear relevant to both forms of transnational crime and risk. In sum, E-waste trade and the business transactions leading to the financial crisis point to similar theoretical origins: lure, predisposition, and temptation and non-credible oversight. These conditions—combined with the nature of international transactions—pose significant challenges for regulation and enforcement.

The Challenge of Regulating Transnational Commerce

The nature of global business transactions is a significant barrier to effective regulation and enforcement. Technology has increased the speed and anonymity with which individuals and organizations can engage in risky and illegal transactions (Felsen and Kalaitzidis, 2005; Passas, 2002; Shover and Hochstetler, 2006). These transactions are complex and difficult to track. Business transactions, for instance, occur through multiple financial and banking systems linked across the globe (Elliott, 2009). Also, many transnational crimes occur via several smaller criminal activities, which requires intelligence analysis to disentangle the activities of internationally interconnected individuals and organizations (Hill, 2005).

The actions of nation states likewise can hamper the regulation of risky transactions. For example, asymmetries in the law that facilitate transnational crime often occur because states are unwilling to intervene to address a particular problem (Passas, 2001, 2002). Powerful nations hold more sway over the content of international treaties and can resist the criminalization of their activities or can refuse to ratify treaties that do so (Michalowski and Bitten, 2005). In addition, these countries might fail to enforce domestic legislation adequately (GAO, 2008a, 2008b). Many would argue that this kind of inaction makes countries complicit in facilitating the continued movement of illegal goods and services (Passas, 2002).

Powerful countries are not alone in their failure to act. Developing countries often lack the infrastructure and resources necessary to prevent illegal activities (Shover and Hochstetler, 2006). In some cases, government officials facilitate illegal and risky transactions to generate personal or government capital. "Grand" and "petty" corruption, for example, have fueled the illegal timber trade in Indonesia and have led to illegal exports of fish and lobster in South Africa (Hauck and Kroese, 2006; Palmer, 2001). Similarly, corruption coupled with unregulated markets and war explain nation-level variation in the effectiveness of regulations to reduce elephant poaching

(Lemieux and Clarke, 2009). In some countries banning the import of E-waste, officials have neglected its domestic dismantling and burning (CBS News, 2008).

Overall, these conditions associated with globalization create a significant incentive for individuals and organizations to engage in illicit transactions and externalize risk. The ease of these transactions and the lack of oversight make the activities appealing. It is also cheaper to externalize risks. In fact, differential compliance costs, as well as product and resource values, make illicit transactions profitable (Brack, 2004).

It is necessary to devise interventions that more adequately address transnational white-collar crimes and risks represented by E-waste and global financial transactions. Similar to the need to balance financial innovation with consumer protection, interventions are needed that encourage recycling and reuse in the name of economic development while reducing the risks and harms of E-waste. Rather than the mere promulgation of rules, the use of a "smart" or "responsive" regulation might promote more effective practices (Ayres and Braithwaite, 1992; Gunningham and Grabosky, 1998).

Prevention, Compliance Promotion, and Threat

Smart regulation is "a regulatory approach that is responsive to people's conduct rather than rigid in its response" (Foley, 2004: 2). It requires an assessment of the range of interventions and actors that might be used effectively, efficiently, and fairly to reduce environmental degradation (Gunningham and Grabosky, 1998). Flexibility is the key. Smart regulators must be willing to tailor their responses to specific groups of actors and to implement a range of interventions. Smart regulation recognizes that webs of constraint already exist and potentially are more effective than relying exclusively on government intervention. In this way, smart regulation resembles the concept of nodal governance (Wood and Shearing, 2007). Research on global business regulation supports this notion:

> The globalization of regulation never occurs on the basis of a single mechanism, no matter how powerful. . . . Dense webs of influence are needed to pull off an accomplishment as difficult as establishing a global regulatory regime that secures the compliance of relevant actors in business and the state. Such webs are dense in the sense of involving many types of actors mobilizing many types of mechanisms (Braithwaite and Drahos, 2000: 13).

The use of "webs of actors" or "third-party regulators" does not preclude the need for significant formal sanction threats. The threat of punishment serves as a constant threat to all and as a reality for violators who are unresponsive to other (less severe) interventions (Ayres and Braithwaite, 1992). Evidence of the effectiveness of criminal sanctions alone, however, is limited. Few studies have examined the effectiveness of criminal penalties in reducing white-collar and corporate crime. When legislatively available, harsh sanctions often are not used in practice either for street crime or environmental offenses (O'Hear, 2004; Tonry, 1992). The inclusion of criminal sanctions in new legislation invariably meets with resistance by industry.

NGO respondents interviewed for this study indicated that the International Scrap Recycling Institute and other powerful business interests have resisted federal E-waste legislation. (In part for these reasons, the GAO recommends that shipping codes be modified to identify clearly E-waste shipments that are currently categorized as scrap metals and mixed plastics. Such efforts would allow at least for statistical tracking, international customs cooperation, and additional insight into this largely hidden area of high-risk global trade [GAO, 2008b].)

Coupled with strong foreign demand for raw materials and the lack of recycling infrastructure in the United States for certain types of E-waste, an effective ban on U.S. exports is unlikely (Tonetti, 2007b). Furthermore, the E-waste trade might not be, in and of itself, the problem. In fact, the E-waste trade has positive effects. The trade is considered by some to be a mechanism for addressing the digital divide between developed and developing economies, and some periphery nations have developed state-of-the-art E-waste recycling as a method for economic development (GAO, 2008a; Iles, 2004; Tonetti, 2007b). Finally, even with additional legislation, shipping codes, and innovative enforcement, the detection and apprehension of illegal shipments of E-waste at ports will be extremely challenging. The scope of the problem is too large, and the number of actors is too high to rely on enforcement alone. Instead, the combined use of crime prevention, third-party- and self-regulation, and state intervention will be needed.

Prevention

Criminologists long have emphasized the importance of crime prevention, and preventive initiatives that can be used to reduce the risks associated with E-waste (Tonry and Farrington, 1995; Wood and Shearing, 2007). First, the United States is in serious need of a recycling infrastructure. To support this infrastructure, several states have passed state-, producer-, or purchaser-funded recycling programs (Luther, 2007). Although little analysis has been conducted on the costs of national versus state programs, currently the electronics industry is pushing for a national recycling management program that could be introduced via federal legislation (NCER, 2006, 2008). In addition to end-of-life strategies, the design process needs to be addressed (Iles, 2004), as the European Union requires through its legislation on waste electrical and electronic equipment (Directive 2002/96/EC). Consumers should be able to update electronics easily rather than purchasing new systems, and toxic materials should be phased out of production (Iles, 2004). Waste reduction and recycling infrastructure strategies might represent what Gunningham and Grabosky (1998) called "complementary" strategies. If manufacturers are required to pay for recycling, then it might encourage them to advance waste-reduction techniques voluntarily.

Given the ever-growing production of E-waste, failure to develop a corresponding recycling and waste-reduction process is criminogenic in the sense of generating the conditions for transnational crime. However, relying exclusively on industry to make these changes voluntarily absent of any financial incentive may be naïve. Some companies might change practices voluntarily and invest in producing less waste, but in the absence of a credible threat and profit incentive, many will continue with business as usual. The use of alternative interventions and "third-party regulators" might facilitate this type of transformation of business practices (Gunningham and Grabosky, 1998).

Self- and Third-Party Regulation

Consumer and government purchasing power can be used to persuade companies to change current practices. For example, the Clinton Administration indicated that it was in the market for energy-saving products prior to purchasing a significant number of computers. Such signals sent to the market by large prospective customers can achieve significant positive results (Grabosky, 1994). Similarly, knowledge of business practices allows general consumers to factor company record into purchasing decisions. Standards and certification programs for legitimate recyclers could enable the general public to exercise power by choosing higher-performing businesses (Gunningham and Grabosky, 1998). In fact, although the agency itself will not issue certifications (indicating the need for third-party involvement), the EPA supports recycler certification as an alternative to regulation (Tonetti, 2007b). Public awards for zero-waste recyclers are another option for using third parties to improve performance. Directing consumers to legitimate recyclers can create a financial incentive for unethical companies to self-regulate.

In addition to encouraging positive change, large and small consumers alike can provide informal sanctions, which is often a more powerful influence on individual and company behavior than formal sanctions (Paternoster, Saltzman, Waldo and Chiricos, 1983; Simpson, 2002; Vandenbergh, 2007). Government regulators can facilitate this process through information dissemination (Cohen, 2001). In addition to the potential for fines or other sanctions, negative publicity regarding E-waste can be used publicly to shame repeat "offenders" through the association of their brand with export and improper disposal of E-waste. General risk communications to consumers might help the public act as a control on company behavior. Currently, many consumers take strides to dispose of E-waste appropriately with little knowledge of the potential for improper disposal by illegitimate "recyclers" (CBS News, 2008). Communication campaigns might increase public knowledge of the problem.

Oversight

The effective use of "webs of actors" or "third-party regulators" does not preclude the need for significant formal sanction threats; strong legislation is the backstop of smart and responsive regulation (Ayres and Braithwaite, 1992). One option is to amend current RCRA regulations to include E-waste. For example, the EPA definition of "hazardous" could be expanded to be consistent with the international standards of the Basel Convention. Ratifying the Convention also would require U.S. action when nations that restrict or prohibit E-waste imports receive illegal shipments from U.S. recyclers (GAO, 2008b). If these changes occurred, then increased criminal liability might be necessary. The threat of harsh penalties might deter reasoning offenders, particularly owing to the tendency for white-collar offenders to have more to lose than street offenders (Shover and Hochstetler, 2006). Thus, threatened criminal sanctions might suffice in some cases to prevent abuses associated with E-waste.

Without new regulations, innovations in enforcement are the key to disentangling the actors and methods involved in transnational criminal and risky transactions (Hill, 2005). Methods developed in other nations provide models for increasing U.S. efforts. Officials from the Australian Department of Environment, Water and Heritage, for example, visited importing recyclers in developing countries to verify the legitimacy of the operations. Permits to export Australian E-waste are approved only if it is sent to verified recyclers. The United Kingdom uses intelligence-based enforcement to prevent illegal hazardous waste exports. Information gathered using traditional investigative methods is cross-referenced with public and secure databases to establish targets (individuals, companies, and shipments) for more in-depth investigation. Interventions are matched to the actor and nature of the activity to maximize crime prevention and deterrence (Chris Smith, Environment Agency, personal communication, October 2009). Emerging track and trace technologies also might enable authorities to link illegal exports to specific recyclers and thereby increase the likelihood of detection (Wyld, 2005). Such efforts might be advanced through "joined up" enforcement efforts via organizations such as Interpol's Environmental Crime Program (Elliott, 2009).

Risk assessment can be used to define the probability and potential consequence of certain behaviors or actors and target enforcement resources (Kennedy and Van Brunschot, 2009; Renn, 1998). Companies have demonstrated a range of behavior related to E-waste. Some companies willingly violate U.S. regulations, and importing countries have intercepted and returned illegal shipments to the United States (GAO, 2008a, 2008b). Prioritization of E-waste and cooperation among international customs organizations could help identify companies involved in this illegal trade. Other companies, however, engage in extremely prosocial, environmentally responsible behaviors without any legal requirement to do so. Thus, the level of risk might be assessed by examining prior behavior. Additional research might uncover other risk factors that can enhance control of disposal and export practices, perhaps by informing patterns of regulatory review and development of surveillance or early indicator systems. Such methods also might be used to determine whether the EPA's current educational strategies will be effective for specific companies; in some cases, more severe sanctions "higher" in the responsive regulation enforcement pyramid might be necessary (Ayres and Braithwaite, 1992; GAO, 2008a, 2008b). Relying on the enforcement pyramid to use more punitive punishments selectively when necessary might reserve resources for the most egregious and repetitive offenders.

Absent the general and political will to make these large-scale changes, analysis of growth in global business regulation provides a reason for optimism. "Modeling" is a regulation tool that has been used effectively to address other international business transactions, even by actors that have less power in the global arena (Braithwaite and Drahos, 2000). "Rules or principles do not have to be incorporated into state law or international law to have significance. Modelling of self-regulatory principles and the rules of the private justice systems of corporations are crucial to understanding how the globalization of regulation happens" (Braithwaite and Drahos, 2000: 10).

Smart regulation also could be used to police financial transactions. Additional legislation and innovative enforcement will be necessary to prevent the riskiest financial transactions. However, as with E-waste, a complete ban on these transactions might not provide the optimal solution. Financial innovations are important to fuel economic growth (Shiller, 2008). In addition, a complete ban will be met with industry resistance. Rather than promulgating extensive rules that prohibit these transactions, regulatory agencies need to evolve to provide credible oversight of this economic activity. In other words, risk-management institutions must be updated (Shiller, 2008). As with E-waste, a coordinated regulatory and enforcement effort would facilitate oversight of global financial exchanges. In addition, systemic risk regulation has been proposed by the Obama Administration to prevent future financial crises. Specifically, companies will be designated a specific level of monitoring and oversight according to the level of risk posed to the national economic system (Roth, 2009).

Even with innovation, relying exclusively on enforcement efforts will doubtless be insufficient, if only due to the scope and nature of global financial transactions—many occur in cyberspace. Enhanced prevention is needed. Improved information infrastructure is the key to prevent future financial crises (Shiller, 2008). To address the knowledge gap among low-income individuals victimized by subprime mortgages, the U.S. government could subsidize financial assistance. In fact, dissemination of financial advice to the general public could improve their capacity to act as third-party regulators. Coupled with standards and certification programs for approved financial advisors, opportunities for unethical lenders and brokers to swindle consumers could be reduced. Publicizing the performance record of lenders also would allow the public to sanction unethical firms informally. The will of the general public can encourage legitimate practices. Public awards for firms with outstanding financial records, for example, might create a financial incentive for other companies to improve performance voluntarily.

Conclusion

Risky and fraudulent business transactions resulted in a global financial crisis with profound global repercussions. Lure combined with noncredible oversight created significant opportunities for predisposed and tempted individuals and organizations alike to engage in white-collar crime and the externalization of risk. The scale of these transactions and the resulting harm demand innovative responses and present opportunities to learn about the challenges posed by E-waste and other harmful commercial transactions. Smart regulation is a promising approach to intervene in global business transactions. Specifically, drawing on multiple interventions, targeting multiple actors, and advertising the threat of punishment almost certainly will be more effective than primarily relying on state intervention.

Future research should explore the extent to which various mixtures of policies and "regulators" successfully address specific white-collar crimes and risks as well as the extent to which these interventions can be applied to other transnational problems. In addition, explorations of the contexts in which these interventions are effective would inform evidence-based approaches to crime control and prevention. Regardless of the specific set of interventions that ultimately works best to address these issues, the global financial crisis and the harms and risks associated with E-waste demonstrate the need to be more proactive so these threats do not create preventable "international catastrophes."

References

Ayres, Ian and John Braithwaite. 1992. *Responsive Regulation: Transcending the Deregulation Debate.* Oxford, U.K.: Oxford University Press.

Brack, Duncan. 2004. The growth and control of international environmental crime. *Environmental Health Perspectives,* 112: 80–81.

Braithwaite, John and Peter Drahos. 2000. *Global Business Regulation.* Cambridge, U.K.: Cambridge University Press.

Carmassi, Jacopo, Daniel Gros, and Stefano Micossi. 2009. The global financial crisis: Causes and cures. *Journal of Common Market Studies,* 47: 977–996.

Carroll, Chris. 2008. High tech trash. *National Geographic,* January: 64–87.

CBS News. 2008. The electronic wasteland. *CBSnews.com.* Retrieved January 21, 2010 from cbsnews.com/video/watch/?id=4586903n.

Chayes, Abram, Antonia Handler Chayes, and Ronald B. Mitchell. 1998. *Managing* compliance: A comparative perspective. In (Edith Brown Weiss and Harold K. Jacobson, eds.), *Engaging Countries: Strengthening Compliance with International Environmental Accords.* Cambridge, MA: MIT Press.

Cohen, Mark A. 2001. Information as a policy instrument in protecting the environment: What have we learned? *Environmental Law Reporter,* 31: 10425–10431.

Elliott, Lorraine. 2009. Combating transnational environmental crime: "Joined up" thinking about transnational networks. In (Kristiina Kangaspunta and Ineke Haen Marshall, eds.), *Eco-Crime and Justice: Essays on Environmental Crime.* Turin, Italy: Public Information Department of UNICRI.

Faiola, Anthony, Ellen Nakashima, and Jill Drew. 2008. The crash: What went wrong? *Washingtonpost.com.* Retrieved January 21, 2010 from washingtonpost.com/wp-srv/business/risk/.

Felsen, David and Akis Kalaitzidis. 2005. A historical overview of transnational crime. In (Philip Reichel, ed.), *Handbook of Transnational Crime and Justice.* Thousand Oaks, CA: Sage.

Foley, Tony. 2004. *Using a Responsive Regulatory Pyramid in Environmental Regulation.* Presented at the Queensland Environmental Law Association Conference, Cairns, Australia.

Ford, Matt. 2009. Sifting through the mounting problem of Ewaste. *CNN.com.* Retrieved August 21, 2009 from cnn.com/2009/TECH/science/08/02/e-waste.recycling/.

Frean, Alexandra. 2010. *Regulators Were "Blinded" by Wall Street Profits.* Retrieved January 21, 2010 from business.timesonline.co.uk/tol/business/industry_sectors/banking_and_finance/article698416.ece.

Fuller, Thomas. 2006. China trade unbalances shipping. *NYTimes.com*. Retrieved January 21, 2010 from nytimes.com/2006/01/29/business/worldbusiness/29iht-ships.html?_r=1.

Gibbs, Carole, Jennifer L. Melvin, Edmund F. McGarrell, and Mark Axelrod. 2008. *Exploring the Environmental Risks and Environmental Crime Links of Electronic Waste Generated in the United States: An Interim Report to the Interpol Pollution Crimes Committee.* Lyon, France: Interpol Environmental Crime Program Pollution Crimes Committee.

Grabosky, Peter N. 1994. Green markets: Environmental regulation by the private sector. *Law and Policy*, 16: 420–448.

Greenpeace. 2008. Poisoning the poor: Electronic waste in Ghana. *Greenpeace.org*. Retrieved January 21, 2010 from greenpeace.org/international/news/poisoning-the-poor-electroni.

Grossman, Elizabeth. 2006. *High Tech Trash: Digital Devices, Hidden Toxics, and Human Health*. Washington, DC: Island Press/Shearwater Books.

Gunningham, Neil and Peter N. Grabosky. 1998. *Smart Regulation: Designing Environmental Policy*. Oxford, U.K.: Oxford University Press.

Hauck, Maria and Marcel Kroese. 2006. Fisheries compliance in South Africa: A decade of challenges and reform, 1994–2004. *Marine Policy*, 30: 74–83.

Hill, Cindy. 2005. Measuring transnational crime. In (Philip Reichel, ed.), *Handbook of Transnational Crime and Justice*. Thousand Oaks, CA: Sage.

Huo, Xia, Lin Peng, Xijin Xu, Liangkai Zheng, Bo Qui, Zongli Qi, Bao Zhang, Dai Han, and Zhongxian Piao. 2007. Elevated blood lead levels of children in Guiyu, an electronic waste recycling town in China. *Environmental Health Perspective*, 115: 1113–1117.

Iles, Alastair. 2004. Mapping environmental justice in technology flows: Computer waste impacts in Asia. *Global Environmental Politics*, 4: 76–107.

India, the E-Wasteland. 2006. *Physorg.com*. Retrieved on January 21, 2010 from physorg.com/news67098899.html.

Jackson, Anita Sarah, Aaron Shuman, and Gopal Dayaneni. 2006. *Toxic Sweatshops: How UNICOR Prison Recycling Harms Workers, Communities, the Environment, and the Recycling Industry*. Report by the Center for Environmental Health, Prison Activist Resource Center, Silicon Valley Toxics Coalition and the Computer TakeBack Campaign. Retrieved on January 21, 2010 from computertakeback.com/problem/ToxicSweatshops.pdf.

Jickling, Mark. 2009. *Causes of the Financial Crisis*. Retrieved January 21, 2010 from digitalcommons.ilr.cornell.edu/cgi/viewcontent.cgi?article=1605&context=key_workplace.

Kennedy, Leslie W. and Erin Gibbs Van Brunschot. 2009. *The Risk in Crime*. Lanham, MD: Rowman & Littlefield.

Lemieux, Andrew M. and Ronald V. Clarke. 2009. The international ban on ivory sales and its effects on elephant poaching in Africa. *British Journal of Criminology*, 49: 451–471.

Luther, Linda. 2007. *Managing Electronic Waste: An Analysis of State E-Waste Legislation*. CRS Report for Congress. Retrieved January 21, 2010 from ncseonline.org/NLE/CRSreports/08Mar/RL34147.pdf.

Michalowski, Raymond and Kevin Bitten. 2005. Transnational environmental crime. In (Philip Reichel, ed.), *Handbook of Transnational Crime and Justice*. Thousand Oaks, CA: Sage.

National Center for Electronics Recycling (NCER). 2006. A study of the state-by-state E-waste patchwork: An analysis of its economic and other effects on industry, government, and consumers. *Ecyclingresource.org*. Retrieved January 21, 2010 from ecyclingresource.org/UserDocuments/Patchwork%20Study%20final.pdf.

National Center for Electronics Recycling (NCER). 2008. State recycling requirements for CE manufacturers and retailers in 2008. *Ecyclingresource.org*. Retrieved January 21, 2010 from 74.125.95.132/search?q=cache:S8JLyyxA8cMJ:www.ecyclingresource.org/UserDocuments/NERIC%2520Presentation%2520on%2520State%2520Recycling%2520Requirements%2520at%2520CES%25202008%2520FULL%2520final.

O'Hear, Michael M. 2004. Sentencing the green-collar offender: Punishment, culpability, and environmental crime. *Journal of Criminal Law and Criminology*, 95: 133–276.

Palmer, Charles. 2001. *The Extent and Causes of Illegal Logging: An Analysis of a Major Cause of Tropical Deforestation in Indonesia*. Retrieved on January 25, 2010 from eprints.ucl.ac.uk/17588/1/17588.pdf.

Passas, Nikos. 1999. Globalization, criminogenic asymmetries, and economic crime. *European Journal of Legal Reform*, 1: 399–423.

Passas, Nikos. 2001. Globalization and transnational crime: Effects of criminogenic asymmetries. In (Phil Williams and Dimitri Vlassis, eds.), *Combating Transnational Crime: Concepts Activities and Responses*. New York: Frank Cass.

Passas, Nikos. 2002. Cross-border crime and the interface between legal and illegal actors. In (Petrus C. van Duyne, Klaus von Lampe, and Nikos Passas, eds.), *Upperworld and Underworld in Cross-Border Crime*. Nijmegen, The Netherlands: Wolf Legal.

Paternoster, Raymond, Linda E. Saltzman, Gordon P. Waldo, and Ted G. Chiricos. 1983. Perceived risk and social control: Do sanctions really deter? *Law & Society Review*, 17: 457–479.

Pellow, David N. 2007. *Resisting Global Toxics: Transnational Movements for Environmental Justice*. Cambridge, MA: MIT Press.

Puckett, Jim, Leslie Byster, Sarah Westervelt, Richard Gutierrez, Sheila Davis, Asma Hussain, and Madhumitta Dutta. 2002. Exporting harm: The high-tech trashing of Asia. Report by The Basal Action Network and the Silicon Valley Toxics Coalition. *Ban.org*. Retrieved January 21, 2010 from ban.org/E-waste/technotrashfinalcomp.pdf.

Putnam, Tonya L. 2009. Courts without borders: Domestic sources of U.S. extraterritoriality in the regulatory sphere. *International Organization*, 63: 459–490.

Renn, Ortwin. 1998. Three decades of risk research: Accomplishments and new challenges. *Journal of Risk Research*, 1: 49–71.

Roth, Richard. 2009. Systemic risk regulation bill proposed by Administration. *Financialcrisisupdate.com*. Retrieved January 21, 2010 from financialcrisisupdate.com/2009/07/systemic-risk-regulation-bill-proposed-by-administration.html.

Scanlon. 2004. Poison PCs and toxic TVs: A report by Californians Against Waste, The Materials for the Future Foundation and the Silicon Valley Toxics Coalition. *Svtc.org*. Retrieved January 21, 2010 from svtc.org/site/DocServer/ppc-ttv1.pdf?docID=124.

Schmidt, Richard B. 2008. FBI saw threat of loan crisis: A top official warned of widening mortgage fraud in 2004, but the agency refocused its resources elsewhere. *Articles.latimes.com*. Retrieved January 21, 2010 from articles.latimes.com/2008/aug/25/business/fi-mortgagefraud25.

Shiller, Robert J. 2008. *The Subprime Solution: How Today's Global Financial Crisis Happened, and What to Do About It*. Princeton, NJ: Princeton University Press.

Shover, Neal and Andy Hochstetler. 2006. *Choosing White-Collar Crime*. Cambridge, U.K.: Cambridge University Press.

Silicon Valley Toxics Coalition. 2008. Toxics in electronics: 1000s of chemicals are used in electronic production. *Etoxics.org*. Retrieved January 21, 2010 from etoxics.org/site/PageServer?pagename=svtc_toxics_in_electronics.

Simpson, Sally S. 2002. *Corporate Crime, Law, and Social Control*. Cambridge, U.K.: Cambridge University Press.

Theil, Stefan. 2009. The Germans are toxic too: Claims of safer banking now ring false. *Newsweek.com*. Retrieved January 21, 2010 from newsweek.com/id/201749.

Tonetti, Robert. 2007a. EPA's regulatory program for "E-waste." *EPA.gov*. Retrieved February 1, 2008 from epa.gov/epaoswer/hazwaste/recycle/ecycling/rules.htm.

Tonetti, Robert. 2007b. Export of used and scrap electronics: What you need to know. *EPA.gov*. Retrieved February 1, 2008 from epa.gov/epaoswer/hazwaste/recycle/ecycling/rules.htm.

Tonry, Michael H. 1992. Mandatory penalties. In (Michael H. Tonry, ed.), *Crime and Justice: A Review of Research*. Chicago, IL: University of Chicago Press.

Tonry, Michael H. and David P. Farrington. 1995. *Building a Safer Society*. Chicago, IL: University of Chicago Press.

U.S. Environmental Protection Agency (EPA). 2007. Management of electronic waste in the United States. *EPA.gov*. Retrieved January 21, 2010 from epa.gov/waste/conserve/materials/ecycling/docs/fact7-08.pdf.

U.S. Government Accountability Office (GAO). 2008a. Electronic waste: EPA needs to better control harmful U.S. exports through stronger enforcement and more comprehensive regulation (GAO-08-1044T). *GAO.gov*. Retrieved January 21, 2010 from gao.gov/new.items/d081044.pdf.

U.S. Government Accountability Office (GAO). 2008b. Electronic waste: Harmful U.S. exports flow virtually unrestricted because of minimal EPA enforcement and narrow regulation (GAO-08-1166T). *GAO.gov*. Retrieved January 21, 2010 from gao.gov/new.items/d081166t.pdf.

Vandenbergh, Michael. 2007. The new Wal-Mart effect: The role of private contracting in global governance. *UCLA Law Review,* 54: 913–964.

Wood, Jennifer and Clifford Shearing. 2007. *Imagining Security.* Cullompton, U.K.: Willan.

Wyld, David C. 2005. *RFID: The Right Frequency for Government.* Retrieved January 21, 2010 from rfidconsultation.eu/docs/ficheiros/WyldReport4_IBM.pdf.

Yifu Lin, Justin. 2008. The impact of the financial crisis on developing countries. Retrieved April 5, 2010 from crisistalk.worldbank.org/files/Oct_31_JustinLin_KDI_remarks.pdf.

Zonneveld, Norbert. 2007. A treatise on the (illegal) export of WEEE. *Eera-recyclers.com.* Retrieved January 21, 2010 from eera-recyclers.com/member/files/Presentation%20 Treatise%20on%20WEEE%20export.pdf.

Statutes Cited

Commodity Futures Modernization Act, 7 U.S.C. 1 (2000).

Community Reinvestment Act, 12 U.S.C. § 2901 (1977).

Gramm-Leach-Bliley Act, 5 U.S.C. § 6801 (1999).

Resource Conservation and Recovery Act, 42 U.S.C. § 9601 (1976).

Carole Gibbs is an assistant professor at Michigan State University with a joint appointment in the School of Criminal Justice and the Department of Fisheries and Wildlife. Her research interests include corporate environmental performance, environmental justice, and transnational environmental crime. Gibbs is the author of *Corporate Crime* (co-edited with Sally S. Simpson) and recent articles that appear in *Crime, Law, and Social Change* and the *British Journal of Criminology.*

Edmund F. McGarrell is a professor and the Director of the School of Criminal Justice at Michigan State University. His primary research interests are in communities and in crime with a particular focus on gun, gang, and drug market related violence. Additional interests include restorative justice and conservation criminology. Recent publications appear in the *Journal of Experimental Criminology* and *Justice Quarterly.*

Mark Axelrod is an assistant professor at Michigan State University in James Madison College and the Department of Fisheries and Wildlife. His research explores negotiation and implementation of international treaties with a focus on the application of international environmental law at the local level. His chapter regarding how trade law constrains environmental negotiations is forthcoming in *Institutional Interplay and Global Environmental Change: State of the Art and Perspectives* (MIT Press). He also has articles under review regarding global invasive species negotiations and the role of existing international law in subsequent negotiations.

[21]

Gemstone mining in Madagascar: transnational networks, criminalisation and global integration

Rosaleen Duffy*

Centre for International Politics, Manchester University, Oxford Road, Manchester, M13 9PL, UK

rosaleen.duffy@manchester.ac.uk

ABSTRACT

This article examines the ways in which illicit gem mining in Madagascar indicates the highly variable impacts of globalisation in sub-Saharan Africa. It argues that distinct categories such as global/local, legal/illegal and traditional/modern have lost much of their explanatory power. Far from being distinct categories, they are indivisible and constitute a single, complex whole which produces enormous wealth, coupled with high degrees of poverty and marginalisation in precisely the same locations. It is clear that Africa's participation in globalisation has not been just about 'joining' the world economy; instead it has been characterised by highly selective forms of global connection which have been combined with highly visible and very real forms of disconnection.

INTRODUCTION

This article examines the role of transnational criminalised networks in the gem sector in Madagascar, and shows how the very same processes that produce the exclusion and marginalisation evident in the poorest African states also create new forms of integration, especially the development of non-national economic spaces. Africa's participation in globalisation has

* This paper is based on field research conducted in Madagascar in 2004, made possible through funding from the ESRC, grant number RES 000 22 0342. It was previously presented as a conference paper, at 'Redesigning the state? Political corruption in development policy and practice', ESRC/Global Poverty Research Group conference at Manchester University, 25.11.2005. I am grateful for comments made by two anonymous referees.

not been merely about joining the world economy – it has been marked by highly selective and spatially encapsulated forms of global connection which have been combined with highly visible and very real varieties of disconnection and exclusion. As Ferguson (2006: 26) notes, 'when it comes to globalisation, Africa just doesn't fit the story line. It is an inconvenient case.' This article explores one specific way in which Africa has been integrated into the global economy, through an analysis of the inter-related global and local networks involved in informal, or extra-legal, gem trading and extraction in Madagascar. It analyses how the impact of these networks may conform to or contest the notion that exclusion and marginalisation are the *attached twin* (*ibid.*) of more conventional and positive understandings of globalisation.

Since the late 1990s, Madagascar has experienced a boom in gem mining, especially high quality rubies and sapphires. This boom has been largely driven and controlled by illicit mining and transnational gem trafficking. In 1999 a World Bank study found that US$100 million in gems was smuggled out of Madagascar in that year alone (*Focus* 2000; World Bank websites 1, 2). This article examines how such patterns of production and trade are produced by the inter-relationships of a specific locality (Ilakaka, Madagascar) with globalised networks of production and exchange. It then examines the economic, social and environmental impacts of this form of integration into the global economy, especially in mining areas. In sum, it investigates the complex and highly variable dynamics produced by globalisation, and their impacts on Madagascar. In so doing, it provides a more nuanced account of what is meant by global/local, legal/illegal, formal/informal in the context of highly interlinked networks of actors involved in the wide range of exchanges which exist outside the formally recorded economic system.

GLOBAL NETWORKS AND GLOBAL SHADOWS

It is clear that analysing the so-called illicit economy requires us to rethink what is meant by global/local, legal/extra-legal and formal/informal. In general, these terms are used as binary opposites, but an examination of the gem trade from Madagascar indicates that they are far from being distinct categories; rather they are indivisible and constitute a single, complex whole which produces enormous wealth coupled with high degrees of poverty and marginalisation in precisely the same localities. As Callaghy *et al.* (2001) argue, the study of global politics has been infused with a fashionable framework that defines global and local as binary opposites, but this is not enough to explain new *global formations*.

Instead they argue that the really compelling elements lie silently between global and local, namely the structures and relations that emerge *in* the intersection of social phenomena that vary in range as well as in form (see also Nordstrom 2001). In turn, this means that commonly used terms such as local/global, rural/urban, traditional/modern have lost much of their explanatory strength, because sub-Saharan Africa is characterised by numerous places and processes that produce a very diffuse sense of space (materially and mentally) (De Boeck 1998: 799; 2001). In short, it is important to examine how the global and local impact on and shape each other.

In the context of sub-Saharan Africa, it is important to understand the nature of engagement between the continent and external actors. In particular, the contemporary state in Africa is characterised by alliances between elite cliques and global economic interests, including private business, NGOs, donors and illicit trading networks. Bayart (1993) explains this through an analysis of the ways in which the state-imported system by European colonisers was resisted by African societies, which resulted in a complex mix, where African states resemble a rhizome rather than a root system. As a rhizome, the state is organised along patrimonial lines which stretch through society in a horizontal fashion, and has reappropriated the institutions that originated under colonial rule. State–society relations are then characterised by factional struggles, the rhizomatic nature of the state and patronage politics. Bayart calls this the 'politics of the belly', which refers to the way in which political elites use informal and invisible networks to exercise political and economic power. Leading actors in sub-Saharan Africa have compensated for a lack of autonomy by recourse to *strategies of extraversion*, and so the global economy has been turned into a major resource for political elites in Africa (Bayart 1993; 2000: 219). For Bayart, the external environment is important in the structuration of African societies, and the strategies of extraversion are marked by the creation and capture of a rent generated by external dependency (Bayart 2000: 225; Nordstrom 2001, 2004; see also Clapham 1996).

Bayart's analysis demonstrates how sub-Saharan Africa is inextricably interlinked with the global economy. The way in which Africa is integrated with the global system has resulted in the creation of a patchwork of highly globalised areas and networks, which in turn produce real forms of exclusion and marginalisation. As Ferguson notes (2006; see also Hibou 2004), large tracts of territory and rural populations have been abandoned by African central governments, in favour of linking more closely with the economic benefits and rents made available through international integration with donors, international financial institutions, NGOs and private businesses. This is particularly apparent in the ways that resource extraction (of minerals, especially oil) is organised and carried out by interlinked networks of private companies and elite cliques in African states. The impact of such global networks is particularly important for understanding the specific patterns of globalisation and how they are manifested in material ways in sub-Saharan Africa. As De Boeck (1998) notes in his studies of diamond miners from Zaire/Democratic Republic of Congo (DRC) working within Angolan territory, rural areas can be the sites of clear integration with the global economy (through the export of stones and availability of consumer and luxury goods), while also producing new patterns of marginalisation, exclusion, insecurity and violence. For De Boeck (1998: 803; Bayart 2000), the diamond areas on the borders of DRC and Angola reinvent capitalism in their own terms. This is important for understanding dynamics of gem mining and trading in Madagascar, and how this reinvents or engages with globalisation in its own way. The dynamics of diamond production mean that rural areas which are usually thought of as inhabiting the periphery are brought centre-stage in the global economic system through their engagement with global networks of smugglers, gem dealers and traders.

In examining these forms of globalisation, it is no longer useful to concentrate on visible political and economic systems such as the state and the formal economy; instead it is more important to focus on an emergent set of shadow politico-economic systems (Reno 1998). As Ferguson (2006) argues, a shadow is not a poor copy of the original (in this case the 'formal' neoliberal economies of the industrialised world); instead the shadow is an inter-related and *attached twin* of the original. Reno's examination of the growth of informal markets suggests that that these developed partially in response to the decay of central state authority, especially in Africa's weakest states. He argues that high-ranking politicians and businessmen constitute shadow states. Furthermore, they manage to exercise significant political authority through the private control of resources in informal and illicit markets (Reno 1995, 1998; see also Nordstrom 2001, 2004; Roitman 2001). Academic research has rarely focused on the shadow networks that constitute the illicit economy. As Bayart (2000: 230) argues, it is important to understand African societies have both a *pays legal*, a legal or formal structure which is the focus of attention for donors and Western states, and an informal *pays réel* where real power lies. In examining the illicit economy, we can analyse the complex links between the formal and informal economies, criminalised networks and politics in sub-Saharan Africa (Nordstrom 2001, 2004; see also Bayart *et al.* 1999; Roitman 2001). This article now turns to an exploration of the impact of illicit sapphire mining and trading in Ilakaka, to provide an analysis of the contours and dimensions of globalisation as a process which integrates Africa with the rest of the world economy in very specific ways which can be highly destructive, but which also produce highly beneficial outcomes for some individuals and networks (De Boeck 1998).

GEMSTONES IN MADAGASCAR

Since the late 1990s, Madagascar has become identified as a site of rich deposits of gemstones and semi-precious stones. It contains a wide variety of minerals including gold, nickel, bauxite, iron, chromite, titanium oxide, beryl and quartz. The major investors in mining in Madagascar include Qit Minerals Madagascar (a division of Rio Tinto), which is engaged in titanium dioxide mining in southern Madagascar (Rio Tinto website), and a Canadian company, Dynatec, which has invested in a nickel mine in Ambatovy (BBC website 2004; Dynatec website). Until 2003 it was thought that Madagascar had no diamonds, but in that year a mining company with an exploration permit for areas in south-central Madagascar found two diamonds of 23 carats and 9 carats each (Rakotoarimanana int.). Since then, a Canadian mining company, Majescor, has been attracted to Madagascar, after diamonds of up to 23 carats were recovered by sapphire miners engaged in artisanal alluvial diggings; Majescor has joined with De Beers to begin diamond exploration in north-western Madagascar (Majescor website). This has sparked investment in exploration by two other Canadian companies, Pan African Mining and Diamond Fields International (Pan African Mining, Diamond Fields & Resource Investor websites). However, so far, Madagascar's sapphires and rubies have been more important as major sources of revenue: the stones have been judged as the highest quality, and as global demand for coloured gemstones increases they could be a growing source of revenue to the government and private mining companies.

The government of Madagascar, with international actors such as the World Bank and USAID, has argued that if gem mining were properly regulated and carried out by international mining companies, the revenue could be used to invest in economic development for the benefit of Madagascar as a whole (Cushman int.; Razafindretsa int; Rakotoarimanana int.). This is in line with notions of 'developmental states', originally applied to East Asian tiger economies, but more recently used to describe the diamond-driven economic development of Botswana (Taylor 2003). However, Madagascar's sapphires and rubies are found in alluvial deposits, which are so accessible that organised and commercial mining operations are not necessary to extract them. Given this accessibility, gems in Madagascar may constitute 'lootable' resources, the extraction of which is very difficult to control. Nevertheless, the World Bank, in conjunction with the President of Madagascar, Marc Ravalomanana (elected in 2002), have embarked on an ambitious programme to attempt to gain control over gem mining.

THE MINERAL RESOURCES GOVERNANCE PROJECT

Prior to 2002, donors and international financial institutions had little confidence in the then Ratsiraka government in Madagascar. It was regarded as highly corrupt and ineffective, and the post-independence period was marked by the development of what Reno (1998) calls a shadow state Under the Ratsiraka regime, government reluctance to control gem mining and smuggling was considered to be related to the ways that key individuals and their families benefited from the illegal gem trade. This created a perception that decision-making had been moved out of the control of the formal state apparatus and into the domain of an informal and shadow network (see Bayart 2000; Reno 1995, 1998). Madagascar is a former French colony, which gained independence in 1960, but retained close relations with its former colonial power. However, in 2002 President Ravalomanana was elected, and made it clear that he was interested in turning towards the English-speaking world, especially the USA and South Africa, as a source of economic and political support. Furthermore, his election promises included a commitment to greater economic liberalisation, constituting a significant break with past presidents who had a closer relationship with France and state-centric economic policies (IRIN website). Donors and international financial institutions (IFIs) regarded the election of Ravalomanana as a fundamental shift away from the patterns of the past, especially since he indicated a much greater willingness to deal with IFIs. However, despite the claims to increase transparency and reduce corruption, the informal networks that flourished in this period have remained important since the new government took over in 2002. These networks have been sustained by their integration with global networks, which in turn present a challenge to newly established forms of governance, such as the Mineral Resources Governance Project (MRGP).

Since the new government made fighting corruption a major theme of its administration, the World Bank responded by re-engaging with Madagascar, after suspending its support during the 2002 presidential crisis (*FT* 18.8.2001; BBC website 2005). In 2003 it provided a US$32 million loan to help the country manage its minerals more effectively, through the MRGP (administered through the Ministry of Energy and Mines). This is a five-year project which runs from 2003 to 2008 and is funded primarily by the World Bank, with further financial support from USAID, and the South African and French governments. According to the World Bank the main objective of the project is to assist the government of Madagascar in implementing its strategy to accelerate sustainable development and reduce poverty in Madagascar, through the strengthening of governance and transparency in the management of mineral resources, with special emphasis on small-scale and artisanal mining. The project has four components: strengthening transparency and governance in mining; key institutional reforms for the decentralised management of mineral resources; promoting private investment and value-added in the sector; and project co-ordination and management (World Bank website 3). This is a key shift in donor attitudes towards Madagascar; donors had been reluctant to provide much capital in the form of loans and aid to the pre-2002 Ratsiraka regime, but have been more confident about the capacities and transparency of the post-2002 government under Ravalomanana (Cushman int.; BBC website 2005). However, given that the MRGP provides the framework under which a newly installed network of elites can gain control over revenues from a potentially lucrative gem sector, it remains to be seen whether government control over the gem sector leads to genuine investment in national economic development, or if it will merely be used to provide resources to secure support from a specific and narrow set of patronage networks. It is, as yet, difficult to determine whether this constitutes a genuine and long-term shift in the government's position and policy actions.

One aim of the MRGP is to establish a clear legal framework to regulate the application procedures for exploration licences. The Project aims to set up a 'user friendly' legal framework so that Malagasy and foreign investors are encouraged to invest in mineral exploration in Madagascar; as a result the government of Madagascar has established *Socmin* as a 'one stop shop' for potential investors, where they can obtain relevant information on gem deposits and apply for exploration and mining licences. To facilitate this, the Ministry of Mines and Geology has produced a CD-Rom which contains relevant information for foreign and Malagasy businesses interested in mining; the CD-Rom provides advice on how to apply for mining exploration licences in areas outside national parks and forest reserves. The Governance Project is intended to produce transparency and accountability in the gem sector to ensure that new exploration licences are not given on a corrupt basis (Rakotoarimanana int.).

The project has also supported the creation of an Institute of Gemmology linked to the Gemmological Institute of America. The Institute provides training for Malagasy graduates who are interested in working in the mining sector; the aim is to develop a lapidary arts sector in Madagascar to ensure that the country can capture the full value of polished stones for sale to the global gem market (Cushman int.; Razafindretsa int.; Rakotoarimanana int.; IRIN 18.9.2003). The Malagasy state, in conjunction with the World Bank and other donors, has also begun to turn its attention to identifying new gem mining areas, and trying to obtain control over the extraction of mineral resources in those areas from the outset (Cushman int.; Rakotoarimanana int.). Tom Cushman (int.) from the Institute of Gemmology in Madagascar suggested that the new Malagasy government was attempting to 'get ahead of the curve' on future gem rushes, indicating an acceptance that areas where gem rushes have already occurred will remain beyond the boundaries of control.

As part of this, the major portion of the World Bank funding has gone into developing a geological survey of Madagascar, carried out by USAID. In addition, in 2004 USAID produced a map of the country's potentially rich gem areas, which was intended to show which areas would be suitable for the sale of government-controlled prospecting permits to international gem mining companies (Crowley int.; Razafindretsa int.). As a result, some areas have been designated as 'reserved', where companies and individuals can apply for permits to explore under the MRGP (Razafindretsa int.). The aim is to ensure that mining is regulated so that it provides revenue to the government as well as to private mining companies. For a standard exploration permit the company or individual must undertake an environmental impact assessment, and only once this is approved will they be given an exploration licence. For larger-scale mining, the company also has to refer to the Poverty Alleviation Strategy for Madagascar, and provide a plan for how their mining operation will contribute to poverty reduction within the country (Rakotoarimanana int.). The creation of this new legal framework is intended to provide the Malagasy government and private sector with the means to gain control over the gem sector so that they can capture the value of gemstones.

THE DEVELOPMENT OF GEMSTONE MINING IN MADAGASCAR

Despite these recent attempts to gain control, the way in which the gem sector has developed in Madagascar since the late 1990s makes the implementation of formal and transparent governance systems extremely difficult. Even though the new government has backed the MRGP, the major gem deposits are still extracted by miners who work in the extra-legal sector. These miners are interlinked with globalised networks of international dealers and elite cliques who ensure that the stones can be illegally exported for personal financial gain. Such networks engage in *strategies of extraversion* which produce the shadow economy which integrates Ilakaka in Madagascar with the global economy (Bayart 2000; Ferguson 2006; Reno 1998).

The Director of Mines and Geology under the new Ravalomanana government suggested that under the previous regime the allocation of mining licences and exploration permits was done on a corrupt basis which depended on the 'mood' of the minister. He claimed that prior to 2002 approximately 80 % of licences were allocated to the highest bidder, and that licences would be given to one individual or company, and then another licence would be issued to mine the same location because the applicant had paid the minister more money (Rakotoarimanana int.). He also suggested that partly because of the ways that the sector had developed under the previous government, in 2004 about 80 % of gems were still being exported as rough stones, and only 20 % as cut stones; the MRGP set an export target of 80 % cut stones and 20 % rough stones, which should be exported through legal and transparent channels (Rakotoarimanana int.). Though it is understandable that the current minister should criticise the practices of the previous regime, the patterns of corruption associated with the Ratsiraka years still structure the way the gem industry operates. The major benefits from gem extraction still accrue to those who benefited from it under Ratsiraka (especially his political supporters and family members). It has proved difficult for the new government to gain control over existing patterns of gem mining and trading, leading the Ravalomanana government to concentrate on gaining control over new gem areas. The allocation of licences lay with the *pays réel* rather than the *pays legal*, and since Ravalomanana has only been in power for three years, it has not been possible to completely change the personnel operating within the bureaucratic structures of government. Once the new government took over, it still relied on many of the same people who served under Ratsiraka. The networks and dynamics developed in the years preceding 2002 could not be expected to disappear overnight. In fact one ambassador to Madagascar (anonymous int. 6) complained that opposition groups were attempting to undermine the government by placing stories in national newspapers claiming that civil servants still loyal to the Ratisaraka regime were engaged in undermining the new government 'from within'.

It is therefore important to examine the logic of 'gem rushes', and how the gem sector developed into its current form. In this regard the case of Ilakaka is instructive. It echoes the arguments made by Bayart (1993; 2000), Reno (1998), Hibou (2004) and Ferguson (2006), because Ilakaka as a 'locality' is a highly globalised place and thereby disrupts strict definitions of local and global, formal and informal, legal and illegal (De Boeck 1998). Ilakaka town rapidly developed in the late 1990s, after the discovery of high-quality sapphires. It was estimated that its population increased from 30 to 100,000 between 1998 and 2000 (*FT* 18.2.2000; Laurs 2003). By 2004 the gem mining areas covered 4,000 square kilometres (Cushman int.). More recently, as Ilakaka has become a very large mining centre, new areas have been subject to exploration by more recent migrants to the area, especially around Sakahara and the WWF-funded Zombitse-Mahafaly National Park, just south of Ilakaka (Durbin int.).[1] In addition, the staff of Catholic Relief Services working in the area have reported an increase in the use of what they referred to as 'sorcery', where diggers request the services of spiritual leaders to identify sites that are *fady* (taboo), and areas that might contain rich deposits of stones; as a result there are a numerous stories, myths and legends about curses on individuals and suspicions surrounding the reasons why some diggers discover rich gemstone deposits, while others do not (Randrianarison int.).

The sapphires are considered to be amongst the highest quality in the world, and sapphire mining promises opportunities of instant wealth to Malagasy people living in poverty. Serge Rajaobelina (int.), director of a Malagasy NGO, Fanamby, suggested that many of the 3,000 artisanal gold miners from northern Madagascar migrated to the Ilakaka and Sakahara area when news of the gem fields reached them. Since the gemstones can be extracted by individuals and teams of diggers using nothing more complex than a spade, the poorest sections of Malagasy society have been migrating to Ilakaka because of the promise, or hope, of instant riches. However, the money made by diggers is minor compared to the profits made by international gem dealers in Ilakaka town and global gem dealers in Europe and Asia. A World Bank Study in 1999 found that US$100 million in gems was smuggled out of Madagascar in that year alone (*Focus* 2000; World Bank websites 2, 3). One interviewee involved in the gem mining sector estimated that the value of illegal gemstone exports had remained at about the same level since then, but that this was a small amount compared with the profits that might be available to the government from regulating the extraction of industrial minerals such as titanium dioxide by Qit Minerals Madagascar/Rio Tinto (anon. int. 1; Rio Tinto website).

In general, migrant sapphire miners have little ability to judge the quality of the stones they bring into Ilakaka town to sell. This puts the foreign gem dealers into a very powerful position; they are able, for instance, to claim that a stone has imperfections that will make it hard to cut. In general, the diggers get a very low price for the stones they find, but because they are cash-poor even a small amount of money is worth working for (Ramamaonjisoa int.). Since the mining and trade in gems are largely illegal, they have no recourse to appeal if they believe they are getting an unfair price for their stones (Randrianarison int.; *FT* 3.2.2001). The buyers can make large profits from working in Ilakaka because they set the price for stones, and the buyers tend to co-operate to ensure that the prices paid to diggers are low, while the final polished version will sell at the highest price once it has been taken out of Madagascar. The Director of Conservation for WWF-Madagascar, which works in an area adjacent to the Ilakaka gem fields, Isalo National Park, suggested that the buyers co-operate over setting prices to ensure that diggers cannot go from buyer to buyer looking for a good price; instead, he claimed, any buyer who 'broke ranks' and started to offer higher prices to diggers would be in personal danger (Ramamaonjisoa int.). The networks involved in gem extraction in Madagascar have thus gained control over the local economy, and are able to use symbolic or actual violence to enforce that control (Nordstrom 2004; Reno 1998). This process is not disorganised and haphazard. Rather, the mining undertaken by seemingly disorganised and unconnected individuals is structured by the alliances between key members of the Malagasy elite and the international gem dealers who have established gem buying centres and stalls in the Ilakaka area.

GLOBAL NETWORKS AND PARALLEL ECONOMIES

It is useful to use Bayart's (2000) notion of *pays réel* to examine the workings of illicit mining and gem trafficking. Although this may seem anarchic and chaotic, it clearly has a logic and organisational form that operates through networks of miners, gem traders, state officials and international business; these networks move the rough stones from diggers in Ilakaka to jewellers in Europe, Asia and North America, where they reappear as polished stones. During the journey from rough to polished stone the gemstones move in and out of the informal and formal economy, and move from being illicit goods to being 'legitimised' commodities. Furthermore, an analysis of the nature of these networks indicates that it is not useful to think of Ilakaka as a bounded 'locality': it is at once a local site and a global site, characterised by a high degree of integration into the global economy (see De Boeck 1998). It provides an excellent site for studying extra-legal sapphire mining, and its relationship to clandestine networks of international business and local politicians is especially illuminating. The continued ability to mine sapphires around Ilakaka is directly dependent on global networks of foreign gem dealers who traffic the stones out of southern Madagascar (with the assistance of Malagasy individuals) and into the international trade.

The organisation of illicit sapphire mining is complex, and mixes global and local networks. One interviewee who preferred to remain anonymous suggested that under the previous government the Ratsiraka family had organised groups of impoverished diggers as cheap labour to dig big holes searching for rubies in Vatomandry in eastern Madagascar and sapphires in south-central Madagascar, and then sold the gems on the international market for personal profit (anon. int. 2). Another anonymous interviewee claimed that especially under the Ratsiraka government, prominent members of the ruling elite and the president's family were able to exploit ruby deposits with the knowledge and co-operation of foreign companies that were willing to exploit corruption and lack of regulation in the gem sector (anon. int. 3). Economically impoverished Malagasy men travel to the gem areas to seek employment; they either work alone or are organised through clandestine networks headed by individuals within the Malagasy elite. The diggers then sell their unpolished stones to gem dealers (usually Thai, Sri Lankan or Indian, but also African, European and North American), who have established gem buying businesses in the sapphire areas. Finally, the buyers traffic the stones out of Madagascar through airports or by sea, with assistance from key individuals within relevant customs departments, government agencies and local businesses. At this point the gemstones become part of the 'recorded' international economy and obtain legitimacy as a commodity.

Illicit sapphire mining is thus highly dependent on complex clandestine networks that include international actors and Malagasy individuals from all sections of society. However, despite the illegal export of the stones, there were individuals and sections of society within Madagascar which did (and still do) profit from the trade. One anonymous interviewee who worked in the mining sector claimed that 500,000 people were making money in some way from the extra-legal mining industry, which made it the second largest employer in the country behind agriculture. That revenue had an impact on the direction and pace of other developments in Madagascar, particularly in urban areas where new found wealth from the parallel economy in gems was funnelled into purchasing luxury imported goods and property development, including the establishment of new casinos and hotels (anon. int. 1). These networks have proved to be highly resilient, flexible and adaptable, and remain in place despite the change in government in 2002. They have managed to evade attempts at control under the MRGP, partly because they are embedded within globalised networks that cross-cut and challenge the agendas of the formal state apparatus, donors, NGOs and international financial institutions. Sapphire mining in Ilakaka is linked to global networks of gem dealers and smugglers that stretch into sub-Saharan Africa (Rwanda, Mauritania, South Africa and DRC), Asia (Sri Lanka, Laos, Thailand and Burma) (Gem Scoop website; Duffy 2005), and on to Europe. These global networks rely heavily on invisible economic and political networks of elites within Madagascar that intersect with, and are almost indistinguishable from, the formal economy and visible apparatus of the state (Bayart 2000; Bayart *et al.* 1999; Hibou 2004; Reno 1998).

The confused and unregulated situation in and around Ilakaka provides perfect conditions for the development of such globalised networks. The pre-2002 Ratsiraka government failed to determine how many sapphires were in the area, what their value was, or how they were being mined. This allowed for wildcat illegal mining to develop and for Malagasy networks to link up with transnational networks (see *FT* 18.8.2001). Tom Cushman (int.) of the Institute of Gemmology in Madagascar stated that Thai and Sri Lankan buyers have a very clear presence in Ilakaka, but that traders were drawn from all over the world (Gem Scoop website). This is evident from the physical characteristics of Ilakaka town itself: shops in Ilakaka town have names such as Thai-Mada Cooperation, Congo Gems, Colombo Gems and Sri Lanka Saphir. The names of the shops bear witness to Ilakaka's close links with transnational trading routes and broader processes of globalisation. Furthermore, Thailand and Sri Lanka have developed a global reputation for specific expertise in grading, polishing and selling rubies and sapphires in particular (Macfarlane *et al.* 2003: 58–71).

It is impossible to place a precise value on the stones that are traded in Ilakaka each day, but one rough estimate was that US$4 million worth of stones changed hands daily in 2001, when trading in Ilakaka was at its height (Cushman int.; Razafindretsa int.). Despite this massive cash flow in southern Madagascar, the value of the Malagasy franc continued to fall against the US dollar. Rather than feeding into the formal economy, the income generated from the gem sector remains locked in an informal and illegal economy which is populated by gem dealers, criminal organisations, protection racketeers, miners and individuals in the Malagasy elite. While the biggest traders are foreigners, rumours have abounded that top Malagasy officials and members of Ratsiraka's family have been able to siphon off large profits from the illegal gem sector before and after the change in government (anon. int. 4; see also *FT* 18.8.2001). In sum, the illicit economy surrounding Ilakaka is so intimately linked with the global economy as to be indistinguishable from more recognisable forms of globalisation (De Boeck 1998, 2001; Ferguson 2006).

GLOBALISATION, MARGINALISATION AND EXCLUSION

As Ferguson (2006) notes, globalisation in Africa produces benefits for some networks and groups, but its attached twin is characterised by marginalisation, violence and exclusion within specific locations. These forms of globalisation produce locally specific problems in Ilakaka in particular, and in Madagascar more generally. The current structure of the gem mining and trading sectors has created numerous economic and social problems. Ilakaka is not an area that global capital skips over or ignores; nor does it conform to the enclave model that characterises mineral extraction (especially oil) in other parts of sub-Saharan Africa. As such it does not quite fit the models put forward by Ferguson (2006), where there are spatially separated areas of marginalisation (marginal and poverty stricken areas) and integration (extractive enclaves). Instead, the impact of globalisation is highly uneven and variable, so that for certain individuals and networks it means integration in the global economy, plus significant wealth. In contrast, for other individuals and networks, the way that Ilakaka is drawn into the global economy leads to a greater degree of poverty, marginalisation and exclusion. The case of Ilakaka indicates that such zones may not be spatially segregated, but may inhabit precisely the same geographical locations. For example, when miners get a good price for their finds, sale of the stones gives them instant access to cash, which even in small amounts makes a big difference to individuals. Beatrice Olga Randrianarison (int.) of Catholic Relief Services (which has worked in Ilakaka since it experienced its first gem rushes) suggested that the culture surrounding the mining areas means that few people really value money because one day they have nothing and after a good sale they suddenly feel rich and spend the money very quickly. Rumours of sapphires the size of footballs and of fortunes made in a single day have made Ilakaka irresistible. This is also evident in Ilakaka, because the income tends to go on conspicuous consumption: prostitutes, alcohol and gambling (see Walsh 2002, 2003). In Ilakaka this is referred to as *mepoka*, which denotes a desire to get rich quickly (Randrianarison int.).

The growing number of male diggers and dealers with large amounts of disposable income has created a demand for prostitutes. While many of the women working in the Ilakaka brothels and bars have migrated there from elsewhere in Madagascar, because of the promise of easy earnings, local Bara women and girls have begun to be drawn into the town. The discovery of sapphires has thus disrupted and transformed social relations in the area; in line with De Boeck's (1998) findings in diamond areas, rural places have been changed in ways that are detrimental to some and beneficial to others. This has created serious social problems within the Bara communities, as girls leave school in order to become prostitutes. Rates of HIV/AIDS and other sexually transmitted diseases are increasing. Consequently, in 2002 the Ministry of Health designated Ilakaka a 'red zone', a term reserved for 'emergency areas' (Randrianarison int.; Catholic Relief website). Since Ilakaka is located on the main Route Nationale 7, there were fears that truck drivers could become infected with HIV/AIDs and spread it throughout Madagascar.[2] The only visible social welfare organisation in Ilakaka, Catholic Relief Services (CRS), originally became involved in the area to run a project aimed at preventing cholera. However, by 2001 cholera was under control, even if not eradicated. Spurred on by this success, CRS has now turned its attention to curbing sexually transmitted diseases, including HIV/AIDS (Catholic Relief website).

The negative impact of the sapphire boom is clearly illustrated by its impact on public health, and especially water pollution. Prior to the discovery of sapphires the river in the areas was a key resource for the local community as a source of drinking water and irrigation, and for washing (*ibid.*). The impact on the water supply is an example of the social and health problems produced in a context of massive flows of capital through the town; it indicates the ways that the profits made from gem mining and extraction are not used for the benefit of local communities. In Ilakaka, the already poverty stricken miners have to bear the social and environmental costs of mining where profits are extracted for the benefit of elite cliques. Since the area is one of porous sandstone, the local water supply has become polluted with the chemicals that the miners use to wash their stones, in preparation for selling them to the gem dealers. The sandstone had ensured that Ilakaka had very pure water, because it acted as a filter, but since the discovery of sapphires people in Ilakaka have started to buy water from the next village, Ranohira. Water trucks come into the town to sell drinking water to those who can afford it (Randriamampianina int.; *FT* 18.8.2001). Mining has also impacted on the water supply for agricultural areas. The diggers have diverted the river to areas where they wash the stones, significantly reducing the amount of water running downstream to rice-growing areas, so that large volumes of sand are washed downstream onto the rice fields. As a result, people in Ilakaka must buy in rice at inflated prices (Randriamampianina int.; *Focus* 2000). The problems associated with water pollution indicate the ways in which globalised networks produce particular dynamics and impacts in specific localities. These networks can generate massive wealth alongside forms of marginalisation, exclusion, violence and poverty.

As a result of the lack of formal controls over Ilakaka, miners have faced significant hazards and threats to their safety and health. Numerous diggers have been buried as the holes and tunnels they were working in have collapsed; since the digging is unregulated, most deaths among miners go unrecorded and unnoticed (Randriamampianina int.; *FT* 18.8.2001; *Focus* 2000). According to Dominique Rakotomanga (int.) of the International Programme for Elimination of Child Labour, children are often used to mine narrow tunnels where there are regular accidents, and are killed by landslides or collapsing tunnels; the programme has collected some data from ruby mining areas in Antsiranana and Vatomandry in northern and eastern Madagascar, but not as yet on children working in the Ilakaka area.

In line with this, Ferguson (2006) suggests that Africa as characterised by global shadows is also reliant on the symbolic value and actual value of violence (see also Reno 1998). The illegal nature of gem mining and trading has created an industry centred on protection and extortion: it is common for dealers to hire armed protection. The brothels and bars are sites of violence, and are extremely dangerous at night, and the violence can easily erupt into shoot-outs between rival gem dealers and their bodyguards (Jose int.; Randriamampianina int.; Randrianarison int.; *FT* 3.2.2001). One local police officer claimed that during 2000 there were numerous incidences of violence in Ilakaka, and the skirmishes had resulted in more police being deployed to the area and the need to ask the army to intervene. He said 'it is like this every day, shooting, like Texas' (anon. int. 5).[3] This confirms Reno's (1998) argument that players within shadow networks organise their own forms of private protection; a key feature of the shadow state is the development of privatised security as an alternative to the formal security systems, which are generally understood as being the preserve of the state apparatus (see also Ferguson 2006; Nordstrom 2004).

Apart from the political, economic and social impacts of globalised networks in the gem sector, there are also environmental consequences. The Wildlife Conservation Society has become concerned at the potential impact of gemstone mining on biodiverse forested areas. As a result they have been part of a lobbying campaign directed at the Government of Madagascar, to identify and designate 'no-go' areas for mining. The campaign has been articulated in terms of the economic value of forested areas as potential sites of ecotourism development. Helen Crowley of the Wildlife Conservation Society (Madagascar) stated that it was important to demonstrate that the forests could be more economically valuable to the people and government of Madagascar in the long term through their development as protected areas that could become major sources of revenue from tourism. Environmental NGOs in Madagascar have decided that it was best to talk in terms that the mining companies understood, and since they understood the language of the market, the best way to persuade the private sector and the Government of Madagascar to conserve biodiverse forest areas is to argue that the forests will be more profitable in the long term if they are conserved (Razafindretsa int; Conservation International & World Conservation Society websites).

Conservation International and Wildlife Conservation Society both have extremely important 'local chapters' of their organisation based in Madagascar. Both NGOs hold seats on the 'Donor Consortium' that includes the World Bank, the government of Madagascar, World Wide Fund for Nature (WWF), and bilateral donors including Coopération Suisse, Coopération Française, the German development agency GTZ and the Japanese government (see Duffy 2006). This means that they can exercise a great deal of political power within the Donor Consortium, especially when the three international environmental NGOs within the Consortium are able to act in concert. This has induced the Ministries of Water and Forests, Environment and Mining to collaborate to tackle the problem of unregulated gemstone mining (*ibid.*).

The map of potential gemstone areas produced by USAID in 2004 has been a serious cause for concern amongst the conservation community in Madagascar, because it shows that gem areas are contiguous with protected areas and tropical rainforests with high levels of biodiversity. For many conservation NGOs the challenge is to demonstrate to the Malagasy government, donors and private business that ecotourism and the creation of more national parks is financially more sustainable in the long term than exploiting the areas for gems (Crowley int.; Razafindretsa int.; *FT* 15.5.2001; BBC website 2002). Furthermore, since new gemstone areas have been identified in key sites of tropical forest in Madagascar, USAID has lobbied hard for the creation of a Joint Committee on Forests and Mining to guide and determine policy towards potential mining areas (Razafindretsa int.).

However, the plans to designate no-go areas for mining companies still fail to cover areas where illicit mining is carried out in areas of high biodiversity and mining in the vicinity of national parks. Illicit gem mining continues to benefit a narrow section of society in Madagascar, mostly clustered around sections of the political and economic elite. While a few individual gem diggers may derive some economic benefit from the sale of stones within Ilakaka itself, the main beneficiaries are the political and economic elite linked to global networks that trade gems in the international system.

In environmental terms, Ilakaka is significant because it is close to Isalo National Park, a key protected area in Madagascar's conservation sector. The park covers 81,000 hectares and is the country's most important in terms of tourism revenue. It contains numerous different species of lemurs, but a particular attraction is Verreaux's Sifaka, endemic to southern Madagascar. The Parks Department (ANGAP)[4] and other donors involved in the area became concerned about the damage that might be inflicted by illegal, unregulated mining and its rapid expansion into the park. ANGAP park managers are worried that once the gems are exhausted, the landscape will be left with highly visible and unappealing scars from the mining, which could adversely affect the development of tourism in the park and surrounding area (Ravelonandro int.).

The confusion and the rumours surrounding the size and quality of the sapphire deposits also indicate the dynamics produced by globalised networks in Ilakaka. Indeed the rumours – which are almost impossible to control at either global or national level, or through initiatives from international financial institutions – have an important impact. They reveal the ways in which different groups in Ilakaka make sense of and understand the global dynamics that structure and shape their immediate surroundings, especially in terms of understanding what kinds of stones are in high demand. As a result of rumours, the belief spread that the best sapphires had been exhausted in the area immediately around Ilakaka, and that the National Park itself contained bigger stones of even higher quality. Parfait Randriamampianina (int.), former director of Isalo National Park, suggested that the diggers and gem dealers believed that the government knew this, and that was why the area had been gazetted as a National Park in the first place. The illegal miners also believed that he, as the Park Director, knew the location of the biggest and best sapphire deposits. Consequently, his life had been threatened on a number of occasions, and he was transferred to the ANGAP office in the capital as a precaution. Nor were the Malagasy sapphire miners the only problem: as rumours of big deposits spread, foreign tourists were also entering the park with spades and starting to dig for gems. ANGAP responded with a stipulation that all visitors to the park had to be accompanied by a licensed ANGAP guide. This indicates the power of invisible networks, or global shadows, that resist and evade attempts to control their activities: the threats and intimidation directed at ANGAP staff demonstrate the confidence with which these shadow networks regard their own power and influence in the local area and even beyond.

❃ ❃ ❃

This article shows that globalisation has had very specific kinds of impacts in sub-Saharan Africa, and produces integration and wealth in precisely the same locations as it produces exclusion, marginalisation, violence and poverty. This suggests a further refinement of Ferguson's discussion of the impact of globalisation on sub-Saharan Africa: that capital hops and skips across Africa to produce sites of exclusion (poverty and marginalisation) and sites of inclusion (extractive enclaves). Ilakaka clearly blends both of these dynamics in a single and specific locality. An analysis of the gem sector in Madagascar shows that Africa's participation in globalisation has not just been about 'joining' the world economy; instead it has been characterised by highly selective forms of global connection which have been combined with highly visible and very real forms of disconnection.

Despite attempts by the central government, supported by global institutions such as the World Bank and USAID, to gain control of the gem sector in Madagascar, it has so far proved impossible to regulate existing illicit mining areas. The Ravalomanana government claimed a commitment to reducing such forms of corruption, but is itself deeply embedded in and indistinguishable from formal structures of the economy and political networks which intersect with the Malagasy state. This in turn is partly due to the strategies of extraversion exercised by elite cliques within Madagascar who had benefited under Ratsiraka because of his patronage and protection, but which continue to flourish because the new government has been so far unable to wrest control from them. The networks in Madagascar that are engaged in the illicit gem trade are reliant on global networks of traffickers and traders. Criminalisation provides substantial benefits for interest groups and networks that stretch across the formal and informal sectors, and in turn support its continuance. The dependence on strategies of extraversion thus deeply subverts projects of regulation, such as the Mineral Resources Governance Project. Furthermore, such strategies are highly dependent on global trading networks. It is therefore not helpful to think of corruption, criminalisation or the shadow state as bounded by the territories and structures of specific developing states like Madagascar. Rather, it is important to recognise the complex connections between global networks and specific localities. When it comes to globalisation, Africa is indeed an inconvenient case.

NOTES

1. Joanna Durbin previously worked for WWF-Madagascar in the Zombitse-Mahafaly Park.
2. Currently Madagascar has a very low rate of infection, UNAIDs estimates that 0·2–1·2% of the population are living with HIV. See UN AIDS website.
3. On my fieldwork visit to Ilakaka in 2004, I witnessed a violent clash involving hundreds of people on the main road; the single police officer sent to deal with it flagged down our vehicle, and asked us to take him back to his police station because he could not cope and was afraid.
4. Association Nationale pour la Gestion des Aires Protégées (ANGAP).

REFERENCES

Bayart, J.-F. 1993. *The State in Africa: the politics of the belly*. London: Longman.

Bayart, J.-F. 2000. 'Africa in the world: a history of extraversion', *African Affairs* 395, 99: 217–67.

Bayart, J.-F., S. Ellis & B. Hibou. 1999. *The Criminalisation of the State in Africa*. Oxford: James Currey.

Callaghy, T., R. Kassimir & R. Latham, eds. 2001. *Intervention and Transnationalism in Africa: global-local networks of power*. Cambridge University Press.

Clapham, C. 1996. *Africa and the International System: the politics of state survival*. Cambridge University Press.

De Boeck, F. 1998. 'Domesticating diamonds and dollars: identity, expenditure and sharing in southwestern Zaire (1984–1997)', *Development and Change* 29, 4: 777–810.

De Boeck, F. 2001. 'Garimpeiro worlds: digging, dying and "hunting" for diamonds in Angola', *Review of African Political Economy* 28, 9: 549–62.

Duffy, R. 2005. 'Global environmental governance and local resistance: illegal sapphire mining in Madagascar', *Development and Change* 36, 5: 1–19.

Duffy, R. 2006. 'NGOs and governance states: the impact of transnational environmental management networks in Madagascar', *Environmental Politics* 15, 5: 731–49.

Ferguson, J. 2006. *Global Shadows: Africa in the neoliberal world order*. Durham, NC: Duke University Press.

Focus. 2000. 'Sapphires in the Sand', BBC *Focus*, August.

Hibou, B. ed. 2004. *Privatising the State*. London: Hurst & Co.

Integrated Regional Information Network (IRIN). IRIN@irinnews.org

Laurs, B. M. 2003. 'Featured gem news international: update on sapphires, pezzottaite, and other gems from Madagascar', *Gems and Gemmology: the Quarterly Journal of the Gemmological Institute of America* 39, 3, online at: http://www.gia.edu/gemsandgemology/18578/18175/1969/back_issue_article_detail.cfm

Macfarlane, M., A. Tallontire & A. Martin. 2003. *Towards an Ethical Jewellery Business*. Chatham: University of Greenwich, Natural Resources Institute.

Nordstrom, C. 2001. 'Out of the shadows', in Callaghy *et al.*, eds. *Intervention and Transnationalism in Africa*, 216–39.

Nordstrom, C. 2004. *The Shadows of War: violence, power, and international profiteering in the twenty-first century*. Berkeley. CA: University of California Press.

Reno, W. 1995. *Corruption and State Politics in Sierra Leone*. Cambridge University Press.

Reno, W. 1998. *Warlord Politics and African States*. Boulder, CO: Lynne Rienner.

Roitman, J. 2001. 'New sovereigns? Regulatory authority in the Chad Basin', in Callaghy *et al.*, eds. *Intervention and Transnationalism in Africa*, 240–63.

Taylor, I. & G.G. Mokhawa 2003. 'Not forever: Botswana, conflict diamonds and the Bushmen', *African Affairs* 102, 407: 261–83.

Walsh, A. 2002. 'Preserving bodies, saving souls: religious incongruity in a northern Malagasy mining town', *Journal of Religion in Africa* 32, 3: 366–92.

Walsh, A. 2003. 'Hot money and daring consumption in a northern Malagasy sapphire mining town', *American Ethnologist*, 30, 2: 290–314.

Websites

BBC. 2002. 'Madagascar Biodiversity Threatened', 16.01.2002, http://www.bbc.co.uk accessed 08.02.2002

BBC. 2004. 'Madagascar's Conservation Conundrum', 11.04.2004, http://news.bbc.co.uk/1/hi/world/africa/4433817.stm

BBC. 2005. 'Down to Business in Madagascar', BBC News 25.03.2005.: http://news.bbc.co.uk/1/hi/world/africa/4382733.stm

Catholic Relief. http://www.catholicrelief.org/our_work/where_we_work/overseas/africa/madagascar/index.cfm (accessed 15.08.2004)

Conservation International: http://www.conservation.org/xp/gcf/where/ (accessed 22.09.05)

Diamond Fields: http://www.diamondfields.com/s/Madagascar.asp (accessed 10.06.2006).

Dynatec: www.dynatec.com/ca (accesssed 12.06.2006)

Gem Scoop: http://www.thaigem.com/email/gemscoop/gemscoop135.html (accessed 02.06.06)

Impala Platinum: www.implats.co.za (accessed 09.06.2006)

IRIN News: http://www.irinnews.org/report.asp?ReportID=36281&SelectRegion=Southern_Africa (accessed 22.09.2005)

Majescor: http://www.majescor.com/e/properties/madagascar/ (accessed 10.06.2006)

Pan African Mining Corporation: http://www.panafrican.com/home.htm (accessed 10.06.2006)

Resource Investor: http://www.resourceinvestor.com/pebble.asp?relid=9639 (accessed 12.06.2006)

Rio Tinto: http://www.riotinto.com

Wildlife Conservation Society: http://wcs.org/sw-around_the_globe/Africa/Madagascar (accessed 16.11.04)

UN AIDS. http://www.unaids.org/en/ (accessed 25.05.2006)

World Bank 1: http://www.worldbank.org/afr/wps/wp19/1.pdf (accessed 05.09.2002)

World Bank 2: http://www.4.worldbank.org/afr/poverty/pdf/docnav/03298.pdf (accessed 05.09.2002)

World Bank 3: http://web.worldbank.org/WBSITE/EXTERNAL/NEWS/0,,contentMDK:20111634~menuPK:34470~pagePK:34370~piPK:34424~theSitePK:4607,00.html (accessed 02.06.2006)

Newspapers

Financial Times (*FT*) (London).

Interviews

Crowley, Dr Helen, Country Director, Madagascar Programme, Wildlife Conservation Society, Antananarivo, 25.03.2004.

Cushman, Tom, Manager/Adviser, Institute of Gemmology of Madagascar, Antananarivo, 18.03.2004.

Durbin, Joanna, Director of the Madagascar Programme, Durrell Wildlife Conservation Trust, Antananarivo, 31.03.2004.

Jose, Emison, ANGAP guide, Isalo National Park, 25.08.2001.

Rajaobelina, Serge, Director of Fanamby, Antananarivo, 26.03.2004.

Rakotoarimanana, Pomphile, Director of Mines and Geology, Ministry of Mines and Geology, Antananarivo, 16.03.2004.

Rakotomanga, Dominique, International Programme for Elimination of Child Labour, Antananarivo, 16.03.2004.

Ramamaonjisoa, Joseph, Director of Conservation, WWF-Madagascar, Antananarivo, 29.08.2001.

Randriamampianina, Parfait, Director of Parks, ANGAP, Antananarivo, 21.08.2001.

Randrianarison, Beatrice Olga, STD and AIDS Unit Head, Catholic Relief Services – Madagascar, Antananarivo, 30.03.2004.

Ravelonandro, Jose, Head of Ecotourism Development, Isalo National Park, Ranohira, 29.08.2001.

Razafindretsa, Josoa, Environmental Policy Specialist, USAID Madagascar, Antananarivo, 22.03.2004.

Anonymous Interviews

Anonymous interviewee 1, civil servant, Antananarivo, April 2004.
Anonymous interviewee 2, representative of environmental NGO, Antananarivo, March 2004.
Anonymous interviewee 3, representative of environmental NGO, Antananarivo, April 2004.
Anonymous interviewee 4, representative of environmental NGO, Antananarivo, March 2004.
Anonymous interviewee 5, local police officer, Ilakaka, April 2004.
Anonymous interviewee 6, Ambassador, Antananarivo, May 2004.

Part VI
Globalization and Violence: Global Forces and Local Violence

[22]

Dead Certainty: Ethnic Violence in the Era of Globalization

Arjun Appadurai

This article explores the links between globalization and ethnic violence in comparative perspective. By looking at ethnographic material from Central Africa, Europe, India and China, the paper suggests that bodily violence between social intimates may be viewed as a form of vivisection, and as an effort to resolve unacceptable levels of uncertainty through bodily deconstruction. This approach may cast light on the surplus of rage displayed in many recent episodes of inter-group violence. At the same time, the study suggests that the conditions for such extreme and intimate violence may partly lie in the deformation of national and local spaces of everyday life by the physical and moral pressures of globalization.

Under what conditions is group violence between previous social intimates associated with certain forms of uncertainty regarding ethnic identity?[1] In one widely shared perspective, ethnic violence, as a form of collective violence, is partly a product of propaganda, rumour, prejudice, and memory — all forms of knowledge and all usually associated with heightened conviction, conviction capable of producing inhumane degrees of violence. However, there is an alternative approach to ethnic violence, with roots traceable to Durkheim's (1951) work on anomie and Simmel's (1950) ideas about the stranger. This tradition of thinking — which focuses on doubt, uncertainty, and indeterminacy — has surfaced recently in many different ways. It animates the ongoing work of Zygmunt Bauman (1997) on the roles of the stranger, the consumer, the parvenu, and the vagabond as social archetypes of the postmodern world. It appears, too, in the work of Piotr Hoffman (1986, 1989) on doubt, time, and violence. Julia Kristeva's (1991) work on strangers, a philosophical reflection clearly prompted by the renewed fear of xenophobia in France, belongs to this tradition. This line of thought has also been invoked, at least implicitly, in several recent anthropological works on

1. In sketching an approach to this question, I build on an argument against primordialism developed in previous work (Appadurai, 1996) and lay the foundations for a larger study of ethnic violence currently in progress.

ethnic violence. These works have in common the sound intuition that, given the growing multiplicity, contingency, and apparent fungibility of the identities available to persons in the contemporary world, there is a growing sense of radical social uncertainty about people, situations, events, norms, and even cosmologies.

Some of these works discuss the politics of the body in such a world of uncertainty. In others, there is a recognition that what is new about these uncertainties has something to do with the forces of globalization — weakened states, refugees, economic deregulation, and systematic new forms of pauperization and criminalization. This latter connection is especially suggestively made in Bauman (1997). Yet, to my knowledge, no single work has sought to explore the precise ways in which the ethnic body can be a theatre for the engagement of uncertainty under the special circumstances of globalization. This link is an important preoccupation of the essay that follows.

Significant steps to engage these challenges are found in a growing body of work on ethnic violence by anthropologists (Daniel, 1996; Das, 1990, 1995; Desjarlais and Kleinman, 1994; Devisch, 1995; Hayden, 1996; Herzfeld, 1997; Jeganathan, 1997; Malkki, 1995; Nordstrom, 1997; Tambiah, 1996). Part of what emerges from this work is a consensus that the ethnic labels and categories involved in contemporary ethnic violence are frequently products of recent state policies and techniques, such as censuses, partitions, and constitutions. Labels such as 'Yugoslav', 'Sikh', 'Kurd', and 'Muslim', which appear to be the same as long-standing ethnic names and terms, are frequently transformations of existing names and terms to serve substantially new frameworks of identity, entitlement, and spatial sovereignty.

Given the high-level mobilization of such names and terms, three consequences follow. First, given the increasingly porous borders between nation-states in matters of arms, refugees, trade, and mass media,[2] these ethnic names and terms become highly susceptible to transnational perturbation. Second, where local identities and identifications often were far more important than higher-order names and terms, modern state-level forces tend to generate large-scale identities (such as Latino, Scheduled Caste, and Serb), which become significant imagined affiliations for large numbers of persons, many of whom reside across large social, spatial, and political divides. Third, and by extension, the angers, frustrations, and

2. Virtually all borders, however rigidly policed, are porous to some extent. I am not suggesting that all borders are equally porous or that all groups can cross particular borders at will. The image of a borderless world is far from what I wish to evoke. Rather, I wish to suggest that borders are increasingly sites of contestation between states and various kinds of non-state actors and interests and that it is only in respect to some populations, commodities, and ideologies that states succeed in maintaining tight borders. Further, the movement of ethnic populations across national borders, whether in flight or not, is frequently a factor in intranational ethnic conflict.

quarrels of small (face-to-face) communities and larger megaethnic groupings tend to affect each other directly and explosively, so that certain communities, in Robert Hayden's provocative phrase, become unimaginable (1996: 783).

Since the subject of ethnic violence is large and horrifying in its range and variety, this article confines itself to violence involving neighbours, friends, and kinsmen — persons and groups who have some degree of prior social familiarity. Thus the organized violence of police, armed hoodlums, professional torturers and investigators, and paid ethnic militias is not discussed here, except as it directly informs the problem of violence between socially proximate persons.[3] Also, rather than focus on all forms of violent confrontation, the discussion will concentrate on those associated with appalling physical brutality and indignity — involving mutilation, cannibalism, rape, sexual abuse, and violence against civilian spaces and populations. Put simply, the focus here is on bodily brutality perpetrated by ordinary persons against other persons with whom they may have — or could have — previously lived in relative amity.

This focus allows an examination of limiting conditions and extreme cases for testing the idea of uncertainty as a key factor in severe ethnic violence. Focusing on bodily violence between actors with routine — and generally benign — prior knowledge of one another is also a way to illuminate 'threshold' or trigger conditions, where managed or endemic social conflict gives way to runaway violence.

Although transregional contacts and transnational processes have antecedents and anticipations over centuries (Abu-Lughod, 1993; Wallerstein, 1974) in the form of what we refer to as world-systems, there is a widely shared sense that there is something new about these processes and systems in the last few decades. The word globalization (both as a socioeconomic formation and as a term of folk ideology in journalism and in the corporate world) marks a set of transitions in the global political economy since the 1970s, in which multinational forms of capitalist organization began to be replaced by transnational (Rouse, 1995), flexible (Harvey, 1989), and irregular (Lash and Urry, 1987, 1994) forms of organization, as labour, finance, technology, and technological capital began to be assembled in ways that treated national boundaries as mere constraints or fictions. In contrast with the multinational corporations of the middle of the century which sought to transcend national boundaries while working within existing national frameworks of law, commerce, and sovereignty, the transnational corporations of the last three

3. However, I do not wish to imply that these different forms and registers of violence are analytically or empirically insulated from one another. Indeed, Claudio Lomnitz (personal communication) has suggested various ways in which the vivisectionist violence between intimates and the banalized violence of professional torturers (especially in Latin America) may be linked through the politics of identity and the state, and thus of globalization. I hope to pursue these suggestions in future work on this subject.

decades have increasingly begun to produce recombinant arrangements of labour, capital, and technical expertise which produce new forms of law, management, and distribution. In both phases global capital and national states have sought to exploit each other, but in the most recent decades it is possible to see a secular decline in the sovereignty of national states in respect to the workings of global capital. These changes — with accompanying changes in law, accounting, patenting, and other administrative technologies — have created 'new markets for loyalty' (Price, 1994) and called existing models of territorial sovereignty into question (Sassen, 1996).

It is not difficult to see that the speed and intensity with which both material and ideological elements now circulate across national boundaries have created a new order of uncertainty in social life. Whatever may characterize this new kind of uncertainty, it does not easily fit the dominant, Weberian prophecy about modernity in which earlier, intimate social forms would dissolve, to be replaced by highly regimented bureaucratic-legal orders, governed by the growth of procedure and predictability. The links between these forms of uncertainty — one diacritic of the era of globalization — and the world-wide intensification in ethnocidal violence inform this essay and are explicitly addressed in its conclusion.[4]

The forms of such uncertainty are certainly various. One kind of uncertainty is a direct reflection of census concerns: how many persons of this or that sort really exist in a given territory? Or, in the context of rapid migration or refugee movement, how many of 'them' are there now among 'us'?[5] Another kind of uncertainty is about what some of these megaidentities really mean: what are the normative characteristics of what the Constitution defines as a member of an OBC (Other Backward Caste) in India? A further uncertainty is about whether a particular person really is what they claim or appear to be or have historically been. Finally, these various forms of uncertainty create intolerable anxiety about the relationship of many individuals to state-provided goods — ranging from housing and health to

4. It is difficult to make plausible quantitative claims about changes in the incidence of ethnic violence over long periods of time. There is some evidence that intrastate conflict (including ethnic violence) is more frequent today than interstate conflict. It appears that there is a secular increase in extreme forms of bodily violence between ethnic groups, even though many societies are remarkable for their striking degree of ethnic harmony and social order generally. There is no doubt that the amplification of our impressions of ethnic violence through the mass media creates the inherent risk of exaggerating the global occurrence of extreme violence.

5. For a suggestive discussion of the widespread uncertainty concerning the identities of persons, social categories, villages, and even about the link between religion and nationhood during the process of partition in 1947, I am indebted to a draft paper by Gyanendra Pandey, 'Can a Muslim Be an Indian?' delivered at the University of Chicago in April 1997. A similar kind of uncertainty, produced by late colonial and postcolonial politics, is remarked by Quadri Ismail (1995) with respect to Sri Lankan Muslim self-understandings of identity.

safety and sanitation — since these entitlements are frequently directly tied to who 'you' are, and thus to who 'they' are. Each kind of uncertainty gains increasing force whenever there are large-scale movements of persons (for whatever reason), when new rewards or risks attach to large-scale ethnic identities, or when existing networks of social knowledge are eroded by rumour, terror, or social movement. Where one or more of these forms of social uncertainty come into play, violence can create a macabre form of certainty and can become a brutal technique (or folk discovery-procedure) about 'them' and, therefore, about 'us'. This conjecture might make special sense in the era of globalization.

The first step toward such an understanding must be the most obvious and striking feature of such violence, which is its site and target — the body. Even a quick scan of the extensive literature suggests that the human body is the site of the most horrifying acts of ethnic violence. It might seem banal to say that the body is the site of the worst possible infliction of pain, terror, indignity, and suffering, in comparison with property or other resources. Yet it is clear that the violence inflicted on the human body in ethnic contexts is never entirely random or lacking in cultural form. Wherever the testimony is sufficiently graphic (Das, 1990; Feldman, 1991; Malkki, 1995; Sutton, 1995), it becomes clear that even the worst acts of degradation — involving faeces, urine, body parts; beheading, impaling, gutting, sawing; raping, burning, hanging, and suffocating — have macabre forms of cultural design and violent predictability.

The single most forceful anthropological account of such design is Liisa Malkki's 1995 description of the memories of Hutu refugees in Tanzania in the 1980s of the genocidal violence perpetrated against them principally in the early 1970s in Burundi. This study, which brings together themes of exile, morality, memory, space, and nationalism in its effort to interpret genocidal violence, has many points of convergence with the principal arguments made here, but just two issues raised by Malkki directly concern me: the forms of bodily violence and the relationship of purity to identity.

Built around partially standardized accounts (mythico-histories) by Hutu refugees in Tanzania of the ethnocidal violence they experienced in Burundi since the 1960s, but especially in the bloodbath of 1972 directed against the Hutu majority, Malkki shows how questions of identification and knowledge of the ethnic body lay at the heart of the atrocious violence of this moment. Discussing a detailed response to her question of 'how it could be possible to know a person's identity with certainty enough to kill', Malkki shows how earlier colonial efforts to reduce the complex social differences among local ethnic groups to a simple taxonomy of racial-physical signs had come to be elaborated in the 1970s and 1980s. These 'necrographic' maps were the basis for detailed, technical recollections of the ways in which death was administered to victims in specific, humiliating, and drawn-out ways. Malkki (following Feldman, 1991) suggests that these maps of bodily difference are themselves delicately poised between acquired knowledge and techniques of detection. These maps 'help construct and imagine ethnic difference', and 'through violence, bodies of individual persons become metamorphosed into specimens of the ethnic category for which they are supposed to stand' (Malkki, 1995: 88). A slightly different approach to the relationship between 'bodies', 'persons', and 'identities' appears in this essay.

In the account that Malkki presents of the mythico-historical presentation of how Tutsi killers used shared maps of physical differences to identify Hutu, it is clear that the process is racked with instability and uncertainty (even in survivors' views of the uncertainty faced by their killers), so that multiple physical tests have to be applied. Malkki offers a bold interpretation of the specific ways in which Hutu men and women were killed (often with sharp bamboo sticks, using the grid of vagina, anus, and head; often removing fetuses from pregnant women intact and forcing the mother to eat the fetus, and so on). She concludes that these recollected practices, played out on the necrographic maps of the Hutu ethnic body 'seem to have operated through certain routinized symbolic schemes of nightmarish cruelty' (ibid: 92).

It remains to draw out the link between the mapped body of the ethnic other and the peculiar and specific brutalities associated with ethnic murder. While much of Malkki's analysis strikes me as deeply persuasive, what is vital for the present argument is the link between indeterminacy and brutality in the negotiations over the ethnic body.[6] Although it is difficult to be sure (especially for an analyst who is one step away from Malkki's firsthand exposure to these narratives), there is enough evidence to suggest that we are looking here at a complex variation of Mary Douglas's classic arguments about 'purity and danger' (1966) and about the body as a symbolic map of the cosmos (1973). In her classic argument about 'matter out of place' (which Malkki also discusses), Mary Douglas made a symbolic-structural link between categorical mixture, the cognitive anxiety it provokes, and the resultant abhorrence of taxonomic hybridity in all sorts of social and moral worlds. In subsequent work on body symbolism, Douglas showed how and why the body works to compress and perform wider cosmological understandings about social categories and classifications. Several recent analysts

6. This is the appropriate point at which to acknowledge the pathbreaking contribution of Allen Feldman's study of ethnoreligious violence in Ireland (1991). Most subsequent anthropological studies of violence, including several that I cite here, are in his debt. His brilliant examination of the logic of space, torture, fear and narrative in Northern Ireland brings a radical Foucauldian perspective to bear on a series of searing ethnographic observations of militarized ethnic terror. The ways in which Feldman's arguments set the stage for my own are many: they include his observations about interrogation as a ceremony of verification (Feldman, 1991: 115), torture as a technique for the production of power out of the body of the victim (ibid), the medicalization involved in interrogation (ibid: 122–3), and the role of the corpse, or 'stiff', to mark the transfer of larger spatial maps onto the map of the enemy body (ibid: 73). My effort is to shift the focus away from state-sponsored violence to its 'ordinary' forms and agents and to elaborate the links between clarification and purification.

of ethnic violence have made useful recourse to Mary Douglas's ideas about purity and category-mixture (Hayden, 1996; Herzfeld, 1992, 1997) in addressing issues of ethnic cleansing in Europe.

The argument here owes a direct debt to Douglas, but some distinctions are worth making. While Douglas takes a cosmology (a system of categorical distinctions) as culturally given, thus leading to taboos against 'matter out of place', ethnic violence introduces contingency into this logic, for the situations discussed here are explicitly about cosmologies in flux, categories under stress, and ideas striving for the logic of self-evidence. What is more, the sort of evidence presented by Malkki (and supported by similar accounts from Ireland, India, and Eastern Europe) suggests an inversion of the logic of indeterminacy, category-mixture, and danger identified by Douglas. In Malkki's evidence, for example, the body is both a source and a target of violence. The categorical uncertainty about Hutu and Tutsi is played out not in the security of the 'body maps' shared by both sides but by the instability of the signs of bodily difference: not all Tutsis are tall; not all Hutu have red gums; not all noses help identify Tutsi, nor do all modes of walking help identify Hutu.

In a word, real bodies in history betray the very cosmologies they are meant to encode. So the ethnic body, both of victim and of killer, is itself potentially deceptive. Far from providing the map for a secure cosmology, a compass from which mixture, indeterminacy, and danger may be discovered, the ethnic body turns out to be itself unstable and deceptive. It is this reversal of Douglas's cosmologic that might best explain macabre patterns of violence directed against the body of the ethnic other. The peculiar formality — the specific preoccupation with particular body parts — is an effort to stabilize the body of the ethnic other; to eliminate the flux introduced by somatic variation, by mixture and intermarriage; and to evict the possibility of further somatic change or slippage. It is difficult to be sure whether such a shift in the role of the body in ethnic violence is a qualitatively new feature either of modernity or of the most recent decades of globalization or simply an intensification of earlier tendencies. I shall return to this interpretive challenge later.

This sort of brutality belongs to the theatre of divination, sorcery, and witchcraft. It literally turns a body inside out and finds the proof of its betrayal, its deceptions, its definitive otherness, in a sort of premortem autopsy (see also Feldman, 1991: 110–15), which, rather than achieving death because of prior uncertainty, achieves categorical certainty through death and dismemberment. In Peter Geschiere's recent and magisterial analysis of witchcraft in West Africa (1997), with special reference to regional variation in Cameroon, we are presented with a powerful reminder that witchcraft and sorcery, far from being static cultural forms, are elastic and highly flexible moral discourses for bringing to 'account' new forms of wealth, inequality, and power. They both feed and are fed by news of national politics, global flows of commodities, and rumours of illegitimate flows of people and goods. Flourishing in an atmosphere of rumour, deception, and uncertainty, these discourses place large-scale political and economic uncertainties onto maps of kinship and its local discourses of equity and morality. Among the Maka of Cameroon, witchcraft is focused on the frightening figure of the *djambe*, a small creature that occupies the body of the victim and drives him or her to sacrifice their kin, to participate in nocturnal anthropophagic banquets, and thus to 'introduce treason into the most reliable space in Maka society' (Geschiere, 1997: 40), the space of kinship and the household. We shall return to the themes of treason, cannibalism, and morality shortly. For the moment, though this is not Geschiere's principal concern, let us note that the many variations on witchcraft and sorcery studied by anthropologists in sub-Saharan Africa, going back to Evans-Pritchard's classic study (1937) of these matters among the Azande, the sources of witchcraft and sorcery often involve forces and creatures embedded inside the body of the victim/perpetrator, and the establishment of guilt and accountability often involve techniques of bodily investigation, whether of other animals or of humans. Finally, Geschiere is able to show that witchcraft links the world of kinship to the world of ethnicity and politics in Cameroon and is held responsible for the new found wealth and potential power of large ethnic groups. This extension of an idiom of intimacy gone awry to large-scale suspicion of adversarial ethnic groups is a matter that will be re-engaged shortly.

For now, it is sufficient to note that the macabre regularities and predictabilities of ethnocidal violence cannot be taken as simple evidence of 'calculation' or as blind reflexes of 'culture'.[7] Rather, they are brutal forms of bodily discovery — forms of vivisection; emergent techniques for exploring, marking, classifying, and storing the bodies of those who may be the 'ethnic' enemy. Naturally, these brutal actions do not create any real or sustainable sense of secure knowledge. Rather, they exacerbate the frustration of the perpetrators. Worse, they create the conditions for pre-emptive violence among those who fear being victims. This cycle of actual violence and the expectation of violence finds its fuel in certain spatial conditions of information flow, human traffic, and state intervention.

Anthropology has long known about the ways in which the body is a theatre for social performances and productions (Bourdieu, 1977; Comaroff,

7. This may be the place to note the peculiar relationship between spontaneity and calculation in collective ethnic violence. The emphasis in this essay on uncertainty and vivisection may cast new light on this difficult problem. Existing approaches tend to encounter a missing link between the planned (generally politically motivated) forces behind ethnic violence and the undeniable element of spontaneity. The approach taken here suggests that, at least under certain conditions, the vivisectionist response to uncertainty may mimic modern scientific modes of verification just as the planned aspects of ethnic violence may mimic other legitimate modes of politics that stress procedure, technique, and form. There may thus be an inner affinity between spontaneity and calculation in modern ethnic violence which requires further explanation (cf. Tambiah, 1996).

1985; Douglas, 1966; van Gennep, 1965; Martin, 1992; Mauss, 1973). Combining Malkki's material on ethnic violence in Burundi with Geschiere's study of witchcraft in Cameroon, against the backdrop of Douglas's path-breaking work on category confusion, power, and taboo, allows us to see that the killing, torture, and rape associated with ethnocidal violence is not simply a matter of eliminating the ethnic other. It involves the use of the body to establish the parameters of this otherness, taking the body apart, so to speak, to divine the enemy within. In this sense, the fruitful studies of witchcraft logics in Africa might have much wider interpretive salience.

The role of the body as a site of violent closure in situations of categorical uncertainty is closely allied with a theme that has already been touched upon, the theme of deception. The literature on ethnocidal violence is shot through with the related tropes of deception, treachery, betrayal, imposture, and secrecy. Considerable sustenance for this view of the suspicion, uncertainty, and cognitive paranoia about the identity of the ethnic enemy comes from a variety of sources. Benedict Anderson has shown the salience of the Nazi fear about the 'secret agency' of Jews in Germany, and the desperate deployment of all sorts of means to smoke out the 'real' Jews, many of whom seemed 'Aryan' and 'German' in every regard (Anderson, 1991). The murder of Jews under Hitler constitutes a large area of research and of ongoing debate that exceeds the scope of this essay, but the importance of Nazi ideas of racial purity (Aryan-Germanness) for the extraordinary genocidal violence directed against Jews seems beyond debate.

The idea of Jews as 'pretenders' — as ethnic quislings, as a cancer within the German social body — draws our attention to a crucial way in which the Nazi handling of the Jewish body far exceeds the logic of scapegoating, stereotyping, and the like. What it shows is how those needs, under certain conditions, evolve into policies for mass extermination of the ethnic other. This brutally modern fact, which is the peculiarly horrifying feature of the Holocaust (associated with its totality, its bureaucratization, its 'banality', its goal of complete ethnonational purification) is certainly complicated by the special history of European anti-Semitism.[8] However, in its drive for

8. There is a vast literature about the relationship between German nationalism, Jewish identity, and the dynamics of the Holocaust. Some of this literature, including some work produced by the Frankfurt School, recognizes the relationship between modernity, irrationality, and the fear of international cosmopolitanism represented by Nazi anti-Semitism. It is also apparent that the banalization and mechanization of death in Nazi Germany had much to do with the Jewish body as a site of fear about abstract forms of capital and identity. The recent debates surrounding Daniel Goldhagen's study (1996) of the involvement of ordinary Germans in the extermination of Jews in Nazi Germany have reopened many of these questions. The scope of this literature makes it impossible to take it up intensively here. Suffice it to say that Nazi policies toward Jews raise issues about both purity and clarity in ethnonational projects, which are closely connected to the argument of this essay.

purity through ethnocide and its 'medicalization of anti-semitism' (Proctor, 1995: 172) it sets the stage for the ethnic cleansing of, at least, Eastern Europe, Rwanda-Burundi, and Cambodia in the last two decades, the era of globalization. In the case of Nazi racial ideology, the idea of the Jew as secret agent brings together the ambivalence of German Nazis about race, religion, and economy. Jews were the perfect sites for the exploration of Nazi uncertainty about both Christianity and capitalism. Like the Hutu for the Tutsi, the Jews were 'the enemies within', always potential threats to German national-racial purity, secret agents of racial corruption, of international capital (and, paradoxically, of communism).

As Malkki shows, the theme of secrecy and trickery pervaded Hutu ideas about the Tutsi élite that governed Rwanda. Here seen from the vantage point of the victims, their oppressors appear as 'thieves who stole the country from the indigenous Hutu', as innately skilled in the arts of deception (Malkki, 1995: 68). The Hutu were seen as foreigners who hid their origins, as malign tricksters who were 'hiding their true identity' (ibid: 72).

The trope of deception, fake identity, and betrayal finds further support in the context of the violence perpetrated in North India since the 1980s in struggles between Hindus and Sikhs, articulated eventually in powerful demands for an autonomous Sikh state (Khalistan). In the discourse of Sikh militants in India, Veena Das (1995) has shown the importance of concern with 'counterfeit' claims to Sikh identity, even where such claims pertained to identities that were not the most legitimate forms of Sikhness. In a chapter on Sikh militant discourse, Das shows how, in the key years of the early 1980s, a Sikh militant discourse emerged in the Punjab which identified the state with Hinduism and Hindus with a dangerous effeminacy that threatened the community of Sikhs conceived as male. This discourse selectively identified key events in the Sikh past and present so as to play down the crucial tensions between Sikhs and Muslims in favour of the current opposition between Sikhs and Hindus. Das has much to say about history and memory, speech and violence, gender and the state, but her crucial concern is with the ways in which militant discourse both represents and induces the possibility of violence through its graphic mobilization of sexual, personal, and political images and narratives and exhortations. In many ways, Das shows how the public speeches of Sikh militants, such as Sant Bhindranwale, transform the experience of individuals into the shame of the community, and thus all violence committed in the name of the Sikhs is justified as individual action against collective injustice, as a step toward martyrdom. The many rich details of this analysis of Sikh militant discourse cannot be engaged here, but two phenomena concerning identity addressed by Das are highly relevant.

Especially in the speeches of Bhindranwale, as cited by Das, a recurring theme is the question of who the Sikhs really are. One vital issue in mobilizing the uncertainty surrounding what it means to be Sikh concerns a breakaway group among the Sikhs, called the Nirankaris. Here is what Das has to say about Sikh militant violence against the Nirankaris in the 1970s and 1980s:

> There is a huge mistrust of alternative definitions of the Sikh community. This comes to the fore in the relationship between Sikh militants and communities on the peripheries of Sikhism. One such community is the Nirankaris, who may be considered a sectarian development within Sikhism. Since the followers of this sect worship a living guru, this being contrary to orthodox Sikh teaching, they were declared enemies of the panth in 1973 by the priests of the Golden Temple. In April 1978 some of Bhindranwale's followers clashed violently with the Nirankaris on both sides ... Though it acknowledges that they were a sect with close connections with the Sikhs, their present forms of worship are considered unacceptable; they are declared 'counterfeit Nirankaris' ... The Nirankaris are declared to be agents of the Hindu government, whose only mission is to destroy Sikhs. (Das, 1995: 133–4)

So here is a vivid example of having to bring the killing close to home to clarify who real Sikhs are and what the label Sikh really means. Note the ideas of 'counterfeit Nirankaris' and of 'agents' of the hostile group (Hindus), along with the terrible fury against the 'pure' Sikh. We are back here with the theme of purity, first remarked by Douglas (1966), then elaborated by Malkki (1995), Robert Hayden (1996), and Michael Herzfeld (1997) in various directions. In Malkki's account, this ideology of the pure and the counterfeit explains the paradoxical sense among Hutu living in refugee camps in Tanzania that their very exile was the sign of their purity as 'Hutu' (and anticipates Bauman's [1997] reflections on purity, strangers and otherness). While the Nazi case shows the power of the discourse of purity for the powerful majority (often using the idiom of the minority as a 'cancer' within the social body), the Sikh case shows the domino effect of violent efforts to cleanse, as they ripple through the victim group, creating further efforts to cleanse grey areas and achieve complete clarity and purity. Of course, clarity and purity are not identical concerns, nor do they call forth similar forms of motive and commitment. While clarity is a matter of cognition, purity is a matter of moral coherence. These dimensions seem to converge in the collective heat of ethnocide, where the logic of cleansing seems both dialectical and self-perpetuating, as one act of 'purification' calls forth its counterpart both from and within the ethnic 'other'. Likewise, purification and clarification appear to be in a dialectical and productive relationship.

The terror of purification and the vivisectionist tendencies that emerge in situations of mass violence also blur the lines between ethnicity and politics. Indeed, just as ethnocide is the limiting form of political violence, so certain forms of political hysteria lead to a quasi-ethnic preoccupation with somatic strategies. This somatic rendition of political identities offers another angle on the issue of masks, counterfeits and treachery. A powerful example of this dynamic comes from China, where Donald Sutton (1995) interprets the significance of widespread reports of cannibalism in Guangxi Province in China in 1968, toward the tail end of the violent phase of the Cultural Revolution. Again, this complex essay takes up a large range of fascinating issues involving cannibalism in the cultural history of this region, its reactivation under the violent conditions of the Cultural Revolution, the complex relations between regional politics and the politics of Beijing, and so on.

What is striking for our purposes in Sutton's analysis is the issue of violence among persons who live in considerable social proximity to one another. Consider this chilling description of the general forms of events of what Sutton calls 'political cannibalism'. The forces of law and order, not the revolutionary rebels, were the killers and eaters. Moreover, the forms of cannibalistic consumption varied within a narrow range. People agreed on the best body parts and insisted on them being cooked; and the selection, killing, and consuming of victims were relatively systematized (Sutton, 1995: 142).

By closely examining what were referred to in Wuxuan as 'human flesh banquets' and what were known during this period as 'struggles' (ritualized events involving accusation, confession, and physical abuse of suspected class enemies), Sutton is able to show convincingly that, while these episodes involved ostensible political categories of persons, their logic appears fully compatible with the sorts of violence we would usually call ethnic. In analysing a related case from Mengshan, Sutton shows how the designation of a man as a 'landlord' made him such a convincing villain that a neighbour did not warn him of his impending murder by a local group of militia.

Sutton also shows how political labels took on immense somatic force: an urban youth cited in one of his sources says of the former landlords, 'I felt that deep in their hearts they still wanted to overthrow everything and kill all of us. In movies, they had awful faces. And in the village when I saw them I feared them and thought they were repulsive to look at. I guess ugliness is a psychological thing'. This remarkable quotation offers a brief glimpse of how political labels (such as 'landlord', 'class enemy', and 'counterrevolutionary') become powerful bearers of affect, and of how, in at least some cases, verbal propaganda and mass-mediated images can literally turn ordinary faces into abominations that must be destroyed.[9] In a final, crucial piece of data from Sutton's essay, a former party leader, when expelled from the party in the

9. The entire issue of dual identities and split subjectivities has been approached in a highly suggestive manner by Slavoj Zizek (1989) in his creative Lacanian revision of Hegel. As part of this reading, Zizek observes the sense in which anxiety about the resemblance between Jews and German is a key part of anti-Semitism. He also notes the peculiar ways in which Stalinist terror demanded that its victims, in political trials, for example, confess their 'treason' precisely because they are, in some sense, also 'good' communists who recognize the needs of the party for purges and exposures. In both cases, the victims endure the suffering of being both 'us' and 'them' in reference to a totalizing ideology.

Sheila Fitzpatrick first pointed out to me the salience of the Stalinist trials of 'class traitors' to the general logic of my argument. In her own brief essay on autobiographical narratives and political trials in Stalin's Russia, Fitzpatrick shows that the fear of uncertainty about their class histories affected many Soviet citizens at this time, since everyone had some sort of vulnerability: 'Then their Soviet masks would be torn off; they would be exposed as double dealers and hypocrites, enemies who must be cast out of Soviet society. In the blink of an eye, as in a fairy tale, Gaffner the kolkhoz pioneer would become Haffner the Mennonite kulak. A clap of thunder and the face looking back from

early 1980s on the grounds of his earlier cannibalism, says with contempt: 'Cannibalism ...! It was the flesh of a landlord that was eaten, the flesh of a secret agent' (Sutton, 1995: 162).

With this example, we are back again with the problem of identification and uncertainty, the transformation of neighbours and friends into monsters, and the idea that social appearances are literally masks (Fitzpatrick, 1991, 1995), beneath which truer, deeper, more horrible forms of identity may subsist. 'Secret agency' is found in a wide range of sources that deal with ethnic violence, and it is an indicator of the crucial trigger of the sense of betrayal, treachery, and deception that seems to underwrite its most dramatic expressions. This essay about political cannibalism from China casts an eerie light on descriptions from Bosnian concentration camps in which men were made to bite the severed genitals of friends or fellow prisoners and similar hints of forced cannibalism in other contexts.

Ethnocidal violence evidently mobilizes some sort of ambient rage about the body as a theatre of deception, of betrayal, and of false solidarity. Whenever the charge of categorical treachery is made to appear plausible, secret agents are unmasked, impure ethnicities are exposed, and horribly cancerous identities are imputed to what we may call the inner body, numerous collective forms of vivisection seem possible, with the most ordinary of people as their perpetrators.

In many of these forms of violence, we can see a horrible range of intimacies. It is of course true that the most extreme forms of ethnic violence involve major dramas of power, of degradation, of violation, and of emotional and physical pain. It is also true that some of this is explicable as part of a cycle of memory and countermemory, where one remembered atrocity becomes the basis for another. However, something else is present in at least some of these situations: that is, this violence is a horrible effort to expose, penetrate, and occupy the material form — the body — of the ethnic other. This may well be the key to the many ways in which sexuality is implicated in recent global forms of ethnic violence. Eating the liver or heart of the exposed 'class enemy' is surely a horrible form of intimacy, and one does not have to make recourse to deeper structural theories about 'friendly' cannibalism to see that eating the enemy is one way of securing a macabre intimacy with the enemy who was so recently a friend.[10] Making one

---

Ulianova's mirror would be that of Buber the wicked witch, enemy of the Soviet people' (Fitzpatrick, 1995: 232; see also 1991).

10. This sort of brutal intimacy could be viewed as a fatal deformation of the sort of 'cultural intimacy' which Herzfeld (1997) defines as that sense of familiarity, proximity, trust, and inside knowledge that is preserved by local communities in the face of state taxonomies, policies, and stereotypes. Given the delicate line between popular essentialisms and state essentialisms that Herzfeld notes in his larger analysis, it may not be far-fetched to suggest that some sort of intimacy — gone terrifyingly awry, to be sure — is a feature of the vivisectionist quality of much ethnic violence today.

prisoner bite off the genitals of another is an even more grotesque way of simultaneously inflicting deep pain, injury, and insult while imposing a brutal sort of intimacy between enemy bodies.

This may be the place to briefly note that rape in such circumstances is not only tied up with special understandings of honour and shame, and a possible effort to abuse the actual organs of sexual (and thus ethnic) reproduction, but is additionally the most violent form of penetration, investigation, and exploration of the body of the enemy. These factors may account for the renewed salience of rape in ethnic violence. Rape, from this point of view, is the counterpart to the examination of males suspected to be Muslim (in places like Bombay) to check whether they are circumcised. Like the wooden stakes driven through the anus of the ethnic enemy and up into his skull (in the case of Hutu–Tutsi ethnocide reported by Malkki) the penis in ethnocidal rape is simultaneously an instrument of degradation, of purification, and of a grotesque form of intimacy with the ethnic other. This is not of course to suggest that the sexual violence directed against men and women — for example, in recent events in Eastern Europe — is the same either in quantity or quality. It is clear that, in the history of warfare generally and of ethnic violence more recently, women bear the largest burden as victims of sexual violence.[11] Still, it may be worth considering that there is something that links the violence of ethnocidal rape with other forms of bodily violation and disposal.

In the end, when all the horrible descriptions are read and all the large-scale political, social and economic factors are taken into account, the body remains the site of intimacy, and in the many different forms that bodily violence takes in different contexts, there is a common thread of intimacy gone berserk.[12] Looking at the question of uncertainty and vivisection in the context of intimacy returns one to the question of number and abstraction — and thus of globalization — discussed earlier in this essay.

To repeat, one of the key features of the new ethnic categories is their large-scale, officialized quality. In no case of ethnocide of which we have knowledge can it be shown that these categories are innocent of state practices

11. Several colleagues have suggested to me that in the United States and in the advanced industrial societies of Western Europe many of the features that I see in global ethnic violence are strikingly present in domestic abuse directed against women. This comparative insight opens up the wider question of the links between ethnic and sexual violence and of the structural relation between these forms of violence in more and less wealthy societies. In the current context, this link is a reminder that large-scale violence in the context of intimacy is not restricted to the non-European or less-developed countries of the world.

12. This point resonates with the provocative analysis of power and obscenity in the post-colony by Achille Mbembe, where he discusses the dynamics of 'the intimacy of tyranny' (1992: 22). Here the body appears as the site of greed, excess, and phallocentric power among the ruling élites and thus as the object of scatological intimacy in popular discourse. The relation between this sort of political obscenity and the logic of vivisection which I explore here must await another occasion (see also Mbembe and Roitman, 1995).

(usually through the census and often involving crucial forms of welfare or potential punishment). The question is, how can forms of identity and identification of such scope — ethnic labels that are abstract containers for the identities of thousands, often millions, of persons — become transformed into instruments of the most brutally intimate forms of violence? One clue to the way in which these large numerical abstractions inspire grotesque forms of bodily violence is that these forms of violence — forms that I have called vivisectionist — offer temporary ways to render these abstractions graspable, to make these large numbers sensuous, to make labels that are potentially overwhelming, for a moment, personal.[13]

To put it in a sanitized manner, the most horrible forms of ethnocidal violence are mechanisms for producing persons out of what are otherwise diffuse, large-scale labels that have effects but no locations.[14] This is why the worst kinds of ethnic violence appear to call for the word 'ritual' or 'ritualized' from their analysts. What is involved here is not just the properties of symbolic specificity, sequence, convention, and even tradition in particular forms of violence but something even more deep about rituals of the body: they are always about the production, growth, and maintenance of persons. This 'life-cycle' aspect of bodily rituals (remarked upon by Arnold van Gennep and many distinguished successors in anthropology) finds its most monstrous inversion in what we may call the 'death-cycle' rituals of mass ethnocide. These horrible counterperformances retain one deep element in common with their life-enhancing counterparts: they are instruments for making persons out of bodies.[15] It may seem odd to speak of the production of persons out of bodies in an argument that rests on the

---

13. Of course, not all forms of abstraction in social life conduce to violence, nor have such potentially violent forms of abstraction as the map, the census, and models of economic development always led to coercion or conflict. Here, as elsewhere, one needs to examine the multiple vectors of modernity and the particular ways in which they converge and diverge in the era of globalization. In this most recent epoch of globalization, these instruments of abstraction combine with other forces, such as migration, mediation, and secession to create conditions of heightened uncertainty, but that is not an inherent quantitative or structural property of these abstractions.
14. Here and elsewhere in the paper I have preferred the use of person over subject, although the Hegelian idea of subjectivity, as well as its Foucauldian version in respect to violence and agency, is deeply relevant to my analysis. While the idea of the subject is more immediately and explicitly tied to the dialectics of modernity, there is no easy bridge between it and the category of the person that continues to be central to the anthropology of the body and of ritual. I hope to engage more fully with the discursive implications of these key terms in future work on this topic. For now, I can only suggest that my use of the term person is not intended to foreclose the sorts of readings that for some may more comfortably flow from the substitution in such contexts of the idea of the subject.
15. This part of the analysis resonates with many aspects of Feldman's interpretation (1991) of the ceremonial — indeed, sacrificial — overtones of the interrogation and incarceration of political prisoners by state functionaries in Northern Ireland, as well as his account of the transformations of these eschatological procedures by the victims.

presumption of prior social intimacy (or its possibility) between agents and victims. However, it is precisely in situations where endemic doubts and pressures become intolerable that ordinary people begin to see masks instead of faces. In this perspective, extreme bodily violence may be seen as a degenerate technology for the reproduction of intimacy where it is seen to have been violated by secrecy and treachery.

Through this ritualized mode of concretization we can see how the bodily violence of ethnocide is an instrument for the production of persons in the context of large-scale ethnic identities that have, for whatever reason, turned mutually hostile. It may seem frivolous to suggest that such violence produces persons, in the face of the fact that so much of it is not only degrading and deadly but also literally appears to deconstruct bodies (through various forms of mutilation and butchery). This macabre technique for the production of persons is, of course, special. Nevertheless, in the intimacy and intricacy of preoccupation with body parts and wholes, with penetration and with consumption, with exit and with access, these forms of violence are methods of assuring that some bodies are — without doubt — real persons. The horrible negativity of this technology is that the production of 'real' persons out of the bodies of traitors, secret agents, and despised group enemies seems to require their vivisection. Here, too, is the link between intimacy and uncertainty. Where fear about ethnic body snatching and secret agency becomes plausible, then producing 'real' ethnic enemies out of the uncertainty posed by thousands of possible secret agents seems to call forth a special order of rage, brutality, and systematicity, all at once. The problem of fake identities seems to demand the brutal creation of real persons through violence. This is the modification I propose to the suggestion of Allen Feldman (1991), echoed by Malkki (1995), that ethnic violence produces abstract tokens of ethnicity out of the bodies of real persons.

Such examples can be multiplied. They testify to one important fact: as large populations occupy complex social spaces and as primary cultural features (clothing, speech styles, residential patterns) are recognized to be poor indicators of ethnicity, there tends to be a steady growth in the search for 'inner' or 'concealed' signs of a person's 'real' identity. The maiming and mutilation of ethnicized bodies is a desperate effort to restore the validity of somatic markers of 'otherness' in the face of the uncertainties posed by census labels, demographic shifts, and linguistic changes, all of which make ethnic affiliations less somatic and bodily, more social and elective. Mixed marriages, of the sort that have long taken place in many cosmopolitan regions and cities, are the biggest obstacles to simple tests of ethnic 'otherness' (Hayden, 1996). It is such facts that set the stage for the body as a site for resolving uncertainty through brutal forms of violation, investigation, deconstruction, and disposal.

This proposal — linking categorical uncertainty to the bodily brutalities of ethnocide — builds on other components of a general theory of ethnic violence, many of which are already in place: the classificatory policies of many colonial states; the large involuntary migrations created by such powerful states as Stalin's USSR; the confusions created by policies of affirmative action applied by democratic constitutions to quasi-ethnic classifications, such as the 'Scheduled' Castes created by the Indian Constitution; the stimuli of arms, money, and political support involved in diasporic populations, creating what Benedict Anderson (1994) has called 'long-distance' nationalism; the velocity of image circulation created by Cable News Network, the World Wide Web, faxes, phones, and other media in exposing populations in one place to the goriest details of violence in another; the major social upheavals since 1989 in Eastern Europe and elsewhere that have created dramatic fears about winners and losers in the new open market, thus creating new forms of scapegoating, as with Jews and Gypsies in Romania (Verdery, 1990).

These larger forces — global mass mediation, increased migration, both forced and voluntary, sharp transformations in national economies, severed links between territory, citizenship, and ethnic affiliation — return us to the theme of globalization, within which the argument was earlier framed. It is not hard to see the general ways in which transnational forces impinge on local ethnic instabilities. Hayden's (1996) discussion of national populations, censuses, and constitutions in the former Yugoslavia, and the resultant drive to eliminate the 'unimaginable' in new national formations, is one clear demonstration of the steps that lead from global and European politics (and history) to imperial breakup and ethnic meltdown, especially in those zones characterized by the greatest degree of ethnic mixture through intermarriage. However, the road from constitutional mandates to bodily brutality cannot wholly be handled at the level of categorical contradiction. The peculiar and ghastly forms of vivisection that have characterized recent ethnocidal violence (both in Eastern Europe and elsewhere) carry a surplus of rage that calls for an additional interpretive frame, in which uncertainty, purity, treachery, and bodily violence can be linked. This surplus or excess makes sense of the hyperrationalities — noted throughout this essay — that accompany what seems to be the hysteria of these events: the quasi-ritual order, the attention to detail, the specificity of bodily violation, the systematicity of the forms of degradation.

Yet globalization does not produce just one road to uncertainty, terror, or violence. In this essay I have identified a logic for the production of 'real persons' which links uncertainty, purity, treachery, and vivisection. There are surely other 'ethnocidal imaginaries'[16] in which the forces of global capital, the relative power of states, varying histories of race and class and differences in the status of mass mediation, produce different kinds of uncertainty and different scenarios for ethnocide. The examples I have relied on here — the

16. I am grateful to Dipesh Chakrabarty (personal communication) for this striking phrase and for alerting me to the dangers of moving from global questions to globalizing answers.

People's Republic of China in the late 1960s, Central Africa in the 1970s, North India in the early 1980s, and Central Europe in the late 1980s and early 1990s — do not have either the same spatial or temporal relationship to the process of globalization. In each case, the degree of openness to global capital, the legitimacy of the state, the internal and external flow of ethnic populations, and the variety of political struggles over group entitlement were clearly not the same. Though the vivisectionist hypothesis put forward here may not thus apply uniformly in these cases, its critical elements — purity, clarity, treachery, and agency — may well provide key ingredients that might be recombined fruitfully to cast some degree of light on them.

In an earlier effort to analyse the link between large-scale identities, the abstraction of large numbers, and the theatre of the body, I suggested that global forces are best seen as 'imploding' into localities, deforming their normative climate, recasting their politics, and representing their contingent characters and plots as instances of larger narratives of betrayal and loyalty (Appadurai, 1996: 149–57). In the present context, the idea of implosion might account for actions at the most local of globalized sites — the ethnicized body, which, in already confused and contradictory circumstances, can become the most natural, the most intimate, and thus the most horrifying site for tracking the somatic signs of the enemy within. In ethnocidal violence, what is sought is just that somatic stabilization that globalization — in a variety of ways — inherently makes impossible. In a twisted version of Popperian norms for verification in science, paranoid conjectures produce dismembered refutations.[17]

The view advanced here of ethnocidal violence between social intimates is not only about uncertainty about the 'other'. Obviously, these actions indicate a deep and dramatic uncertainty about the ethnic self. They arise in circumstances where the lived experience of large labels becomes unstable, indeterminate, and socially volatile, so that violent action can become one means of satisfying one's sense of one's categorical self. Of course the violent epistemology of bodily violence, the 'theatre of the body' on which this violence is performed, is never truly cathartic, satisfying, or terminal. It only leads to a deepening of social wounds, an epidemic of shame, a collusion of silence, and a violent need for forgetting. All these effects add fresh underground fuel for new episodes of violence. This is also partly a matter of the pre-emptive quality of such violence: let me kill you before you kill me. Uncertainty about identification and violence can lead to actions, reactions, complicities, and anticipations that multiply the pre-existing uncertainty

17. The issues alluded to in these concluding remarks will be pursued more fully in the larger work of which this essay is a preview. Close attention will be paid to the question of what distinguishes situations that share a large number of features with other situations of globalized stress but do not produce ethnocidal violence. Likewise, the complex epidemiology that relates various forms of knowledge (including propaganda, rumour, and memory) to various forms of uncertainty will be explored more fully.

about labels. Together, these forms of uncertainty call for the worst kind of certainty: dead certainty.

ACKNOWLEDGEMENTS

Earlier versions of this essay were presented before audiences in Amsterdam, Cambridge (MA), Chicago, Paris, and Rio de Janeiro. The valuable criticisms and suggestions offered to me on these occasions were too numerous to fully engage in this revision. Many persons who raised valuable questions at these sessions cannot be named here, for the list would be too long. However, I must note the encouragement, queries, and suggestions of the following persons: Anthony Appiah, Fredrik Barth, Jean-François Bayart, Jacqueline Bhabha, Dipesh Chakrabarty, Sheila Fitzpatrick, Susan Gal, Manu Goswami, Michael Herzfeld, Marilyn Ivy, Beatrice Jaguaribe, Pradeep Jeganathan, Rashid Khalidi, David Laitin, Ben Lee, Claudio Lomnitz, Achille Mbembe, Candido Mendes, Birgit Meyer, Federico Neiburg, Peter Pels, Enrique Rodrigues, Janet Roitman, Roger Rouse, Livio Sansone, Doris Sommer, George Steinmetz, Mary Steedly, Ron Suny, Stanley Tambiah, Xiaobing Tang, Katie Trumpener, Peter van der Veer, and Unni Wikan. Special thanks are due to Carol Breckenridge and Peter Geschiere, friendly critics and patient creditors, who urged me to pay equal attention to deadlines and to deliberation.

REFERENCES

Abu-Lughod, Janet L. (1993) *The World System in the Thirteenth Century: Dead-End or Precursor?* Washington, DC: American Historical Association.

Anderson, Benedict R. (1991) *Imagined Communities: Reflections on the Origin and Spread of Nationalism*. London: Verso.

Anderson, Benedict R. (1994) 'Exodus', *Critical Inquiry* 20(2): 314–27.

Appadurai, Arjun (1996) *Modernity at Large: Cultural Dimensions of Globalization*. Minneapolis, MN: University of Minnesota Press.

Bauman, Zygmunt (1997) *Postmodernity and Its Discontents*. Cambridge: Polity Press.

Bourdieu, Pierre (1977) *Outline of a Theory of Practice*. Cambridge: Cambridge University Press.

Comaroff, Jean (1985) *Body of Power, Spirit and Resistance: The Culture and History of a South African People*. Chicago, IL: University of Chicago Press.

Daniel, Valentine E. (1996) *Charred Lullabies: Chapters in an Anthropology of Violence*. Princeton, NJ: Princeton University Press.

Das, Veena (1990) *Mirrors of Violence: Communities, Riots and Survivors in South Asia*. Delhi: Oxford University Press.

Das, Veena (1995) *Critical Events: An Anthropological Perspective on Contemporary India*. Delhi: Oxford University Press.

Desjarlais, Robert and A. Kleinman (1994) 'Violence and Demoralization in the New World Disorder', *Anthropology Today* 10(5): 9–12.

Devisch, Rene (1995) 'Frenzy, Violence and Ethical Renewal in Kinshasa', *Public Culture* 7(3): 593–629.

Douglas, Mary (1966) *Purity and Danger: An Analysis of Concepts of Purity and Taboo*. London: Routledge and Kegan Paul.

Douglas, Mary (1973) *Natural Symbols: Explorations in Cosmology*. London: Routledge.

Durkheim, Emile (1951) *Suicide: A Study in Sociology*. Glencoe, IL: Free Press.

Evans-Pritchard, Edward E. (1937) *Witchcraft, Oracles and Magic among the Azande*. Oxford: Clarendon Press.

Feldman, Allen (1991) *Formations of Violence: The Narrative of the Body and Political Terror in Northern Ireland.* Chicago, IL: University of Chicago Press.

Fitzpatrick, Sheila (1991) 'The Problem of Class Identity in Nep Society', in Sheila Fitzpatrick, Alexander Rabinowitch and Richard Stites (eds) *Russia in the Era of the Nep: Explorations in Soviet Society and Culture*, pp. 12–33. Bloomington, IN: Indiana University Press.

Fitzpatrick, Sheila (1995) 'Lives under Fire: Autobiographical Narratives and Their Challenges in Stalin's Russia', in Martine Godet (ed.) *De Russie et d'ailleurs*, pp. 225–32. Paris: Institut d'Études Slaves.

van Gennep, Arnold (1965) *The Rites of Passage*. London: Kegan Paul.

Geschiere, Peter (1997) *The Modernity of Witchcraft: Politics and the Occult in Postcolonial Africa*. Charlottesville, VA: University Press of Virginia.

Goldhagen, Daniel (1996) *Hitler's Willing Executioners: Ordinary Germans and the Holocaust*. New York: Knopf.

Harvey, David (1989) *The Condition of Postmodernity: An Enquiry into the Origins of Cultural Change*. Oxford: Blackwell.

Hayden, Robert (1996) 'Imagined Communities and Real Victims: Self-Determination and Ethnic Cleansing in Yugoslavia', *American Ethnologist* 23(4): 783–801.

Herzfeld, Michael (1992) *The Social Production of Indifference: Exploring the Symbolic Roots of Western Bureaucracy*. Chicago, IL: University of Chicago Press.

Herzfeld, Michael (1997) *Cultural Intimacy: Social Poetics in the Nation-State*. New York: Routledge.

Hoffman, Piotr (1986) *Doubt, Time, Violence*. Chicago, IL: University of Chicago Press.

Hoffman, Piotr (1989) *Violence in Modern Philosophy*. Chicago, IL: University of Chicago Press.

Ismail, Qadri (1995) 'Unmooring Identity: The Antinomies of Elite Muslim Self-representation in Modern Sri Lanka', in Pradeep Jeganathan and Qadri Ismail (eds) *Unmaking the Nation: The Politics of Identity and History in Modern Sri Lanka*, pp. 55–105. Colombo, Sri Lanka: Social Scientists' Association.

Jeganathan, Pradeep (1997) 'After a Riot: Anthropological Locations of Violence in an Urban Sri Lankan Community'. PhD Thesis. Department of Anthropology, University of Chicago.

Kristeva, Julia (1991) *Strangers to Ourselves*. New York: Columbia University Press.

Lash, Scott and John Urry (1987) *The End of Organized Capitalism*. Madison, WI: University of Wisconsin Press.

Lash, Scott and John Urry (1994) *Economies of Signs and Space*. London: Sage.

Malkki, Liisa H. (1995) *Purity and Exile: Violence, Memory, and National Cosmology among Hutu Refugees in Tanzania*. Chicago, IL: University of Chicago Press.

Martin, Emily (1992) 'The End of the Body?', *American Ethnologist* 19(1): 121–40.

Mauss, Marcel (1973) 'Techniques of the Body', *Economy and Society* 2(1): 70–85.

Mbembe, Achille (1992) 'The Banality of Power and the Aesthetics of Vulgarity in the Postcolony' (Janet Roitman, trans.), *Public Culture* 4(2): 1–30.

Mbembe, Achille and J. Roitman (1995) 'Figures of the Subject in Times of Crisis', *Public Culture* 7(2): 323–52.

Nordstrom, Carolyn (1997) *A Different Kind of War Story*. Philadelphia, PA: University of Pennsylvania Press.

Pandey, Gyanendra (1997) 'Can a Muslim Be an Indian?' Unpublished ms.

Price, Monroe E. (1994) 'The Market for Loyalties: Electronic Media and the Global Competition for Allegiances', *Yale Law Journal* 104(3): 667–705.

Proctor, Robert N. (1995) 'The Destruction of "Lives Not Worth Living" ', in Jennifer Terry and Jacqueline Urla (eds) *Deviant Bodies*, pp. 170–96. Bloomington, IN: Indiana University Press.

Rouse, Roger (1995) 'Thinking through Transnationalism: Notes on the Cultural Politics of Class Relations in the Contemporary United States', *Public Culture* 7(2): 353–402.

Sassen, Saskia (1996) *Losing Control: Sovereignty in an Age of Globalization*. New York: Columbia University Press.

Simmel Georg (1950) 'The Stranger', in Kurt H. Wolff (trans. and ed.) *The Sociology of Georg Simmel*, pp. 402–8. Glencoe, IL: Free Press.
Sutton, Donald S. (1995) 'Consuming Counterrevolution: The Ritual and Culture of Cannibalism in Wuxuan, Guangxi, China, May to July 1968', *Comparative Studies in Society and History* 37(1): 136–72.
Tambiah, Stanley J. (1996) *Leveling Crowds: Ethnonationalist Conflicts and Collective Violence in South Asia*. Berkeley, CA: University of California Press.
Verdery, Katherine (1990) *National Ideology under Socialism: Identity and Cultural Politics in Ceausescu's Romania*. Berkeley, CA: University of California Press.
Wallerstein, Immanuel (1974) *The Modern World-System*. San Diego, CA: Academic Press.
Zizek, Slavoj (1989) *The Sublime Object of Ideology*. London: Verso.

Arjun Appadurai is Samuel N. Harper Professor of Anthropology at the University of Chicago (Pick Hall 116, 5828 South University Ave., Chicago, IL 60637, USA), where he is also Director of the Globalization Project. His most recent book is *Modernity at Large: Cultural Dimensions of Globalization* (University of Minnesota Press, 1996).

[23]

State Terrorism and Globalization

The Cases of Ethiopia and Sudan

Asafa Jalata*

ABSTRACT

This article compares the essence and effects of Ethiopian and Sudanese state terrorism by focusing on the commonalities between the two states. These peripheral African states have used global and regional connections and state terrorism as political tools for creating and maintaining the confluence of identity, religion, and political power. Ethiopia primarily depends on the West, and Sudan on the Middle East, since Christianity and Islam are the dominant religions in these African states respectively. While the Ethiopian state was formed by the alliance of Abyssinian (Amhara-Tigray) colonialism and European imperialism, the Sudanese state was created by British colonialism known as the Anglo-Egyptian condominium. Massive social and cultural destruction and violence have produced and maintained these colonial political structures. These structures, in turn, have racialized identities by facilitating the processes of Abyssinianization and Christianization in Ethiopia, Arabization and Islamization in Sudan, and Africanization and marginalization of indigenous Africans in both states. Furthermore, each state has been involved in ethnonational cleansing, which has been disguised rhetorically as a move toward national self-determination and democracy. Consequently, the racialization and ethnicization of these states, external dependency, and domestic terrorism have prevented the implementation of national self-determination and the construction of legitimate multinational democracies that could solve the political, social, cultural, and economic crises in Sudan and Ethiopia.

Keywords: genocide, globalization, marginalization, massive human rights violations, racism, religion, state terrorism

Introduction

In this article, I examine the essence of state terrorism in Ethiopia and Sudan in regional and global contexts. From the late 19th century to the present, the 'modern' Ethiopian and Sudanese states have been formed, consolidated, and maintained by state terrorism and global connections. The Ethiopian state was created by the alliance of Abyssinian (Amhara-Tigray) dependent colonialism and European imperialism, and the Sudanese state by British colonialism known as the Anglo-Egyptian condominium. In both Sudan and Ethiopia, colonial political structures dominated by persons claiming Semitic descent emerged through a strategy of massive social and cultural destruction and political violence. Although Christianity is the main ideology of the Ethiopian state and Islam is the principal ideology of the Sudanese state, the elites and societies that have dominated the political structures in both countries share a strategy of racializing their own identities and those of indigenous Africans to Africanize and marginalize indigenous population groups and facilitate the process of Abyssinianization and Christianization in Ethiopia and Arabization and Islamization in Sudan. In addition, just as successive Ethiopian state elites have maintained their legitimacy and survival through external connections and domestic political terrorism, the Sudanese state elites that emerged through the process of decolonization in the mid-20th century have depended on external connections and terrorism for their legitimacy and survival.

First, I provide historical background to the processes of state formation in the two countries. Second, I explore the global, regional, and local processes through which the modern Ethiopian and Sudanese states emerged. Specifically, I demonstrate how global connections and state terrorism have been used as political tools for creating and maintaining the confluence of identity, religion, and political power; in other words, I examine the connection between terrorism, globalism, and the process of racialization and ethnicization of state power. Third, I explore state terrorism in Ethiopia and Sudan and conclude that in these two countries there can be no multicultural or multinational democracy, peace, stability, or development without removing the conditions that have facilitated external dependency and domestic terrorism.

Historical Background

Since ancient times, repeated episodes of migration from Arabia have led to a series of conflicts revolving around issues of religion, identity, land, and power between indigenous African population groups and the Africanized Arab descendants in the countries that today are called Ethiopia and Sudan. The modern ideology of the Ethiopian state evolved from what was once the Axumite Kingdom of Abyssinia, which Africanized descendants of Arab settlers formed in the first century AD (Michels, 1991). The Axumite Kingdom accepted Orthodox Christianity in the fourth century through the commercial relationship it developed with the Greco-Romans. However, Muslim Arab immigrants who arrived after the rise of Islam in the seventh century subsequently challenged the Axumites and spread this new religion throughout African coastal towns. As Islamic influence increased, the commerce of the Axumite Kingdom started to decline. In the mid-11th century, the previously colonized Agao people established a kingdom known as the Zagwe Dynasty by overthrowing the Axumite Kingdom. This dynasty lasted until 1270, when it was overthrown by one of the groups that descended from the remnants of the Axumites. These Axumite descendants developed a separate identity known as Amhara.

The Amhara ethnonational group and another group known as Tigray are collectively called Habashas or Abyssinians. The Habashas developed a common religion, tradition, and set of customs, but the Amhara and Tigray have maintained different languages. Although phenotypically and culturally Africanized, the Habashas have suppressed their Africanness by linking themselves to the Middle East and by considering themselves racially and culturally superior to indigenous Africans (Jalata, 2001). Using their state power, the Habashas imposed their Christian religion, their languages – Amharic or Tigragna – and their customs on the peoples they colonized, resulting in Abyssinianization, which I have described as the complete destruction of the identity of the colonized population groups by claiming racial and/or cultural superiority (Jalata, 1993).

Arab immigrants and their Africanized descendants also culturally, politically, and religiously marked the country known as Sudan, the northern part of which was once the famous indigenous kingdom of Nubia. Nubians had trade connections with the Arabs before the emergence of Islam, and with the decline of the Nubian civilization and the division of its kingdom, the number of Muslim Arab immigrants increased in Nubia. A signed treaty with Arabs who colonized Egypt in AD 640 led to the peaceful migration of more Arabs into Nubia, who gradually colonized the kingdom. There were four immigration waves from Arabia to this region: immigration through Egypt in the seventh and eighth centuries (MacMichael, 1967), immigration through Abyssinia in the eighth century, a third immigration wave in the 13th and 14th centuries (MacMichael, 1967), and a fourth immigration wave following the emergence of the Funj Kingdom.

The Funj Kingdom was founded in AD 1504 by the descendants of Arab immigrants who overthrew the Kingdom of Christian Nubia (Adams, 1977). For the Arab immigrants and their descendants, the Funj Kingdom 'became a guarantee of peace and order' (Adams, 1977: 14), but for the original Africans, it became the tool of destruction. Most Nubians remained Christian until the 15th or 16th century, when the newcomers introduced their system of racialized politics and religion. Between 1504 and 1820, the kingdom 'institutionalized Islam and it developed into the official religion' (Ibrahim, 1979: 8). Generally speaking, Arab immigrants and their Africanized descendants developed racialized identities and introduced to the Horn of Africa politicized religions, Orthodox Christianity and Islam, which proved to be problematic for the construction of legitimate and multicultural democratic societies. The original Africans, in particular, were negatively affected by Abyssinianization and Christianization and by Arabization and Islamization, respectively, in the areas that later emerged as Abyssinia/Ethiopia and Sudan.

Indigenous Africans had various social and cultural formations. Different ethnonational communities had varying forms of state formation processes, including kingdoms, democracies, and lineage and kinship political systems. The Oromo were one of the peoples that practiced an indigenous popular democratic system called *Gada*, or Oromo democracy (Legesse, 1973, 2000).[1] American anthropologist Bonnie Holcomb (1991: 1–10) notes that the *Gada* system 'organized the Oromo people in an all-encompassing democratic republic even before the few European pilgrims arrived from England on the shores of North America and only later built a democracy.' Each indigenous society fought but failed to protect its homeland and people from the invaders. Over the last five centuries, conflicts and wars having international dimensions have been frequently recorded in the Horn of Africa (Jalata, 1993). The Arabs and the Ottoman Empire dominated the commercial activities of the Horn until European imperialism expanded to the region.

This capitalist penetration laid the foundations for the modern Ethiopian and Sudanese states. Oromia (the Oromo country) was partitioned between Britain and Ethiopia; Somaliland was divided among Britain, France, Italy, and Abyssinia; Sudan was occupied by Britain; and the Afar country was partitioned between France, Italy, and Abyssinia. While other Africans were denied the opportunity to buy firearms on suspicion that they would be used against Europeans, because of their collaboration with the European imperialists and because of their Christian religion, the Habasha (Ethiopian) rulers were allowed to buy firearms and participate in the Scramble for Africa (Beachey, 1962). The modern Ethiopian state emerged from the alliance of Ethiopian colonialism and European imperialism, while the modern Sudanese state developed after the decolonization of Sudan in 1956.

The Emergence of the Modern Ethiopian and Sudanese States

The practice of creating and supporting a neocolonial state in accordance with the interests of the racialized capitalist world system started with the emergence of the modern Ethiopian state in Africa (Jalata, 1993, 2001). Because of their Christian ideology and the willingness to collaborate with European imperialist powers, successive Habasha rulers received access to European technology, weapons, administrative and military expertise, and other skills needed for the construction of the modern state (Holcomb and Ibssa, 1990; Jalata, 1993). Consequently, Ethiopian warlords participated in the scramble for Africa. The main reason for this colonial expansion was to obtain commodities such as gold, ivory, coffee, musk, hides and skins, slaves, and land. The emerging Ethiopian state committed genocide on peoples such as the Oromo to obtain these materials. Between 1868 and 1900, when Oromia was effectively colonized by Abyssinia, the Menelik forces reduced the Oromo population from 10 to 5 million; war, slavery, famine, and diseases contributed to the destruction of the Oromo people (Bulatovich, 2000;

Jalata, 1993), but we do not know how many Somali, Afar, Sidama, and others were decimated during this colonial occupation. The Haile Selassie, Mengistu and Meles regimes have continued these genocidal practices (Jalata, 1993).

The racialized/ethnicized modern state of Sudan also developed from the expansion of the European-dominated capitalist world economy in the form of British colonization. When, in the mid-1950s, various Sudanese political forces demanded their rights of national self-determination, the British colonial government announced its intention to decolonize Sudan. Since the British relinquished power, successive racialized/ethnicized Sudanese regimes – civil or military – have imposed their political authority through repression and terrorism to possess absolute control over the means of compulsion (the state) and the means of consumption (productive resources). As Besteman (1999: 129) explains:

> global racial categories elaborated during the colonial period reinforced preexisting local ethnic construction, ensuring a national hierarchization of ethnicities and their accompanying privileges, statuses, rights, and meaning within the political community condensed into being by postcolonial state power.

European colonialism and the imperial interstate system have created and consolidated racialized/ethnicized states or 'authoritarian-terrorist' regimes in both countries. Each has been viewed as an authoritarian regime by the respective ethnonation from which it emerged and as terrorist by the racialized political minorities it suppresses and exploits. These authoritarian-terrorist regimes are characterized by extreme militarization and repression; tight control of information and resources in the form of foreign aid, domestic financial resources, and political appointments; and direct ownership and control of all aspects of state power, including security and military institutions, judiciary and other public bodies, and financial institutions (Besteman, 1999; Jalata, 2000). As the Ethiopian state has been Abyssinianized and Christianized to exclude non-Habashas from decision-making power, the Sudanese state has been Islamized and Arabized to exclude indigenous Africans from state power. These authoritarian-terrorist regimes have been supported by powerful global or regional powers and the imperial interstate system.

The Discourse of Racism, Ethiopian State Terrorism, and Global Tyranny

State terrorism is a systematic governmental policy in which massive violence is practiced against a given population group with the goal of eliminating any behavior that promotes political struggle or resistance by members of that group. Any state that engages in terrorism is not a protector of citizens; rather, it violates civil and human rights through assassinations, mass killings, and imprisonments, often along with a display of corpses in the streets so that the remaining population will accept the violent state out of terror and intimidation. The main assumption of such a state is that it can control the population by destroying its leaders and the culture of resistance. States that fail to establish hegemony by accountable democratic political order are unstable and insecure; hence, they engage in state terrorism (Oliverio, 1997).

Successive Ethiopian authoritarian-terrorist regimes have used the discourses of race, culture, and Christianity to link themselves to the Middle East, Europe, and North America and to consolidate their power against fellow Ethiopians and the colonized populations, such as the Oromo, Sidama, Ogaden-Somali, and Walayita. Habashas have effectively used racism, which combines the discourses of biological and cultural differences to justify unequal treatment of different population groups, to destroy or suppress colonized peoples (Jalata, 2001). Globally, the Habashas have used Semitic and Christian discourses to mobilize assistance from Jews, Arabs, Europeans, and Americans who see Habashas closer to themselves than the peoples whom they consider 'real black' (Jalata, 2001) and consider them closer to 'the European race' or members of 'the great Caucasian family' (quoted in Marcus, 1996: 5).[2]

Ancient Ethiopia was the name of the black world as a whole. Because most people do not know the difference between ancient Ethiopia and contemporary Ethiopia, the Habashas have been able to use their blackness to mobilize other Africans, the African diaspora (Scott, 1993), and black US policy elites against the Oromo and other colonized peoples (Jalata, 2001). Recognizing the political significance of the name Ethiopia, the Abyssinians officially adopted the name in the 1930s, although they developed a racialized identity that differentiated them from the original Africans whom they saw as real blacks. Because the Habashas maintained formal political power, Africans who were colonized and enslaved by Europeans wrongly considered contemporary Ethiopia as an island of black freedom. Most blacks 'knew very little about the social and political conditions of Ethiopia. What they wrote or said about Ethiopia was at best a manifestation of their emotional state' (Scott, 1993: 26). Other Africans were unaware that Ethiopia's political power came from allying with the colonizing European powers.

In reality, the Ethiopia that participated in the slave trade and the Scramble for Africa was not an island of black freedom but a 'prison house' in which colonized and enslaved peoples were and still are brutalized. Even though Habashas are black, they present themselves as Semitic to associate themselves with the Middle East and dissociate themselves from Africa, whose peoples they consider both racially and culturally inferior. Sorenson (1993: 29) expresses this racist attitude as 'a multiplicity of Ethiopians, blacks who are whites, the quintessential Africans who reject African identity.' Since the concept of race is a sociopolitical construct, it is essential to critically understand the historical context in which Ethiopian racism is produced and reproduced to denigrate colonized peoples and to deny them access to Ethiopian state power by practicing state terrorism. In Ethiopian discourse, so-called racial distinctions such as Semitic,

Hamitic, Negroid, and Cushitic are manipulated to perpetuate the political objective of Habasha domination of the colonized population groups. Habasha elites have recognized the importance of racial distinctions and used the discourse of racism to mobilize support for their political projects (Sorenson, 1998).

Ethiopian racism and white racism have conveniently intermarried in US policy formulation and implementation in Ethiopia. When policy issues are discussed, ideologies such as Semitic civility, Christianity, and the patriotism of Amharas and Tigrayans are used to valorize and legitimize Habasha dominance and power. Moreover, the façade of barbarism, backwardness, and destructiveness of the Oromo and other indigenous Africans is reinvented to deny them access to state power (Jalata, 2001). The Ethiopian government has historically obtained its political legitimacy and financed its engagement in human rights violations through global connections. Just as Britain supported Ethiopia during the first half of the 20th century, the United States provided financial assistance to the Haile Selassie government from the mid-20th century to the mid-1970s. Subsequently, from the mid-1970s to 1991, the Soviet Union supported the Ethiopian military regime headed by Mengistu Haile Mariam, which brought untold misery, war, famine, and terrorism to various population groups in Ethiopia. The financing provided from these external resources enabled successive Ethiopian states to engage in terrorism.

When the military regime collapsed in 1991, the United States financed the Tigrayan organization, the Tigrayan People's Liberation Front (TPLF), which emerged from the Tigrayan ethnonational group, and diplomatically assisted Meles Zenawi to replace Mengistu Haile Mariam. The successive regimes of Menelik, Haile Selassie, Mengistu, and Meles have been racist and dictatorial and have continuously pursued destructive policies that have intensified war, terrorism, underdevelopment, and poverty and have denied the people subsistence, protection, and development (Shiffman, 1995). Consequently, the people do not have adequate income, food and habitable homes, or access to health and medical services. Moreover, they have no protection from political violence, because the Ethiopian state engages in massive human rights violations and terrorism (Jalata, 2000).

As with the previous states, the current Ethiopian state mainly obtains its political legitimacy from global connections. In addition to financing with Israel the flight of Mengistu in 1991, the United States supported the creation of the Ethiopian People's Revolutionary Democratic Front (EPRDF) by the Tigrayan People's Liberation Front (TPLF) and endorsed the emergence of the Meles regime. Along with other western countries, the United States still provides significant assistance to the regime. *Human Rights Watch/World Report 1999* (1999: 3) states:

> With about $30 million in development aid and $66 million in food aid, bringing the total to about $97 million, Ethiopia remained the second largest recipient

> of US aid in sub-Saharan Africa, after South Africa. The US failed to use its privileged relations with Ethiopia as a leverage for human rights improvements.

US foreign policymakers support regimes like that of Ethiopia in the perceived strategic and economic self-interest of the United States and have no interest in developing a more critical understanding of the political context in which they have become involved.

Currently, the main rationale for the involvement of US policymakers with regard to Ethiopia is to maintain political order and to enlist it in the fight against global terrorism. Ironically, the US government cannot effectively deal with global terrorism because it practices a double standard: It condones the terrorism of friendly states such as that of Ethiopia and Israel while simultaneously complaining about other forms of terrorism. US foreign-policy experts are more concerned with political order, economic reforms, and existence of regimes such as that of Ethiopia at any cost and care less about democracy and human rights. The *Economist* (1997: 36) notes that Meles Zenawi:

> is regarded as one of Africa's 'new leaders': he recently won an award in the United States for good government ... Their [western] governments tend to give priority to the Prime Minister's economic reforms rather than his record on human rights.

The intensification of globalization through various technological and information revolutions has not changed the underlying status of colonized peoples like the Oromo. Rather, it has increased their exploitation and repression by enabling the regime in power to use the Internet and other communication and information networks to keep the Oromo under 'Ethiopian political slavery' and to ally the Ethiopian state with transnational capital. The Oromo and others are denied the freedom of self-expression and self-development and are forced to provide their economic and labor resources to the Ethiopian colonizers and their supporters and to live under deplorable conditions. Using political violence, the Tigrayan authoritarian-terrorist regime has dominated and controlled the Oromo and denied them the freedom of expression, association, and organization, as well as access to the media and related forms of communication and information networks. The Meles regime has used various techniques of violence to terrorize colonized peoples like the Oromo. Former prisoners have testified to incidents of being whipped or tortured, being locked in steel barrels, and being forced into pits where fire was made on top of them; others have reported that large containers or bottles filled with water were fixed to their testicles, or if they were women, bottles or poles were pushed into their vaginas (Fossati et al., 1996). TPLF/EPRDF soldiers have openly shot thousands of people in rural Oromia – leaving their bodies for hyenas, burying them in mass graves, or throwing their corpses off cliffs.

Other methods of killing include burning, bombing, cutting throats or arteries in the neck, strangulation, and burying people up to their necks in the ground. Hassen (2001) estimates that between 1992 and 2001 about 50,000 killings and 16,000 disappearances (euphemism for secret killings) took place in Oromia alone. Further, he estimates that 90 percent of the killings are not reported. To hide these criminal practices from the world community, the Meles government 'does not keep written records of its extrajudicial executions and the prolonged detention of political prisoners' (quoted in Hassen, 2001: 33). The Meles regime has killed Oromo who engaged in peaceful demonstrations. For instance, on 25 March 1992, in the town of Watar, Hararghe, the soldiers of the regime massacred 92 Oromo and wounded more than 300.

Hassan Ali, an Oromo collaborator with the Meles regime who subsequently fled and resettled in the United States, describes the criminal activities of the soldiers as follows:

> The TPLF soldiers and its members are a law unto themselves. Only what they say and what they want is implemented in Oromia to the general exclusion of Oromo interests or wishes . . . Although Oromia is autonomous in name, the government soldiers and secret service agents have total power to do whatever they want in Oromia. They imprison, torture, or kill anyone . . . without any due process of law. They have established several secret detention centers, where thousands of innocent people are kept for years without trial or charge. (quoted in Hassen, 2001: 33)

TPLF/EPRDF soldiers have killed several pregnant women and hundreds of Oromo children between the ages of 12 and 16. According to the Oromia Support Group (1997: 8):

> a 7-month pregnant woman in Robe, Bale, was arrested and beaten . . . She miscarried and later died in custody. When relatives went to claim her body, they were told to replace the remains with a living relative. When asked to explain, the TPLF soldiers said, 'She died with OLF objectives still stuck in her brain and we could not get what we wanted from her.'

The Ethiopian government has used state terrorism to commit genocide on the Oromo and other indigenous peoples.

Article II of the United Nations Convention (1948) defines genocide as 'acts committed with intent to destroy, in whole or in part, a national, ethnical, racial or religious group.' Chalk and Jonassohn identify two major types of genocide (1990): the first type is used to colonize and maintain an empire by actually terrorizing people perceived to be real or potential enemies. In this case, the main purpose of practicing genocide is to acquire land and other valuable resources. The second type of genocide, ideological genocide, involves the maintenance of colonial domination by state elites through the establishment of hegemony practiced through genocidal massacres to prevent the resistance of the dominated groups. Jonassohn (1998: 23) notes that ideological genocide develops 'in nation-states where ethnic groups develop chauvinistic ideas about their superiority and exclusiveness.'

As the Amhara-dominated successive regimes engaged in terrorism and genocide and exploited the resources of the Oromo, Afar, Ogaden-Somali, Sidama and Walayita, the Tigrayan-dominated regime is engaged in similar practices to suppress the national movements of these indigenous peoples in order to continue their domination and exploitation. With the intensification of the national movements of the Oromo, Sidama, Afar, and Annuak, the Tigrayan-dominated regime has been engaged in massive human rights violations, terrorism, and genocide. The Meles regime has been using war, torture, rape, and other mechanisms of violence to fulfill its political objectives. While engaging in political violence in the form of state terrorism, state rape, and hidden genocide to control the Oromo people and others and loot their economic resources, the Tigrayan state elites claim that they are promoting democracy, federalism, and national self-determination. The Meles regime believes that Oromo intellectuals, businessmen and women, and community and religious leaders are the enemy of the 'Ethiopian revolution.' In its propaganda pamphlet known as *Hizbawi Adera* (1996/1997), the regime claims that Oromo leaders have endangered the processes of peace, democracy, and development by promoting what it calls narrow nationalism. *Sagalee Haara* (1998: 6) notes that 'recent murders and disappearances of Oromo and the detention of members of the Macha/Tulama Association and the Human Rights League are part of the implementation of policies put forward in this document.'

When it attempts to eliminate the Oromo elite through hidden genocide to deny the Oromo a leadership, this racist regime prepares the Tigrayan children for the position of leadership by providing better education while denying an appropriate educational opportunity for the Oromo children.[3] Hundreds of Oromo business people have been harassed, killed, or imprisoned and robbed of their properties. Similarly, hundreds of Oromo intellectuals have been harassed or killed or forced into exile. The regime expelled more than 300 Oromo students from the Addis Ababa University and other colleges and imprisoned or killed their leaders for peacefully demonstrating on 21 January 2004. Saman Zia-Zarifi (2004: 1), the academic freedom director at Human Rights Watch, says, 'Shooting at unarmed students is a shameful misuse of government power.'

Despite its adoption in its constitution, the principles of the Universal Declaration of Human Rights and International Covenants on Human Rights, the Meles government engages in terrorism and gross human rights violations. The TPLF/EPRDF government accepts state violence against Oromo, Sidama, Annuak, Somali, and others as a legitimate means of establishing political stability and order. Welsh (2002: 67–8) suggests that since weak states 'lack the capacity to meet the demands and rights of citizens and improve the standard of living for the majority of population,' they engage in political violence and in genocidal massacres to suppress the population groups that struggle for political and economic rights. Because of their economic resources, the size of their population, and their resistance in challenging the racist policy of this regime, the Oromo are targeted for destruction. As Sharlach (2002: 107) attests, genocide occurs when a politically 'dominant group, frightened by what its members perceive as an onslaught of international and internal movements for democracy and socioeconomic change, harnesses the state apparatus to destroy the subordinate group altogether.' The Meles government sees Oromia as part of its empire, controls all Oromian resources, and practices terrorism and genocide against the Oromo people since it perceives them as its potential or real enemies.

The Tigrayan elites are imposing their political ideologies, such as 'revolutionary democracy' and 'federalism,' to legitimate Tigrayan ethnocracy and state power through genocidal massacres to control the Oromo and other population groups and their resources by eliminating their leadership. The regime has been hiding its genocidal practices and terrorist activities. Jonassohn's (1998: 11) description of the conspiracy of 'collective denial' of genocide by perpetrators captures this reality:

> There are many reasons for this: (a) in many societies such materials are not written down, or are destroyed rather than preserved in archives; (b) many perpetrators have recourse to elaborate means of hiding the truth, controlling access to information, and spreading carefully contrived disinformation; and (c) historically, most genocides were not reported because ... there appears to have existed a sort of conspiracy of 'collective denial' whereby the disappearance of a people did not seem to require comment or even mention.

The government of Ethiopia committed genocide on the Annuak people of Gambella in December 2003 and 2004. In the letter it sent to Prime Minster Meles Zenawi on 8 January 2004, the *International Campaign to End Genocide* notes that massacring people:

> because of their ethnic group membership is genocidal. The Genocidal Convention outlaws the intentional destruction of part of an ethnic group, not just the destruction of the whole group ... We ask that you now arrest and try the perpetrators of the December massacre of Annuak in Gambella.

State-sanctioned rape is a form of terrorism in Ethiopia. The use of sexual violence is a tactic of genocide that a dominant ethnonational group practices in destroying the subordinate ethnonational group (Sharlach, 2002). Genocide studies ignore:

> the full extent of the humiliation of the ethnic group through the rape of its women, the symbols of honor and vessels of culture. When a woman's honor is tarnished through illicit intercourse, even if against her will, the ethnic group is also dishonored. The after effects of rape, forced impregnation, psychological

> trauma, degradation, and demoralization go beyond the rape victims themselves. (Sharlach, 2002: 107)

The Tigrayan cadres, soldiers, and officials frequently rape Oromo girls and women to demoralize the Oromo and show that the Tigrayan rulers wield boundless power. Many of the rape survivors have contracted diseases, such as syphilis, gonorrhea, and AIDS. MacKinnon's (1994: 11–12) comment regarding ethnic cleansing in Croatia and Bosnia-Herzegovina applies equally to the rape of Oromo women: 'It is rape to drive a wedge through a community, to shatter a society, to destroy a people. It is rape as genocide.'

The Tigrayan regime has targeted all sectors of Oromo society to destroy the foundation of Oromo nationalism and political struggle. In Ethiopia, where neither freedom of expression nor free media exist, people choose to be quiet to save their lives even if their relatives are killed by the government. The Ethiopian state elites who have been engaged in gross human rights violations and genocide like other criminal leaders in peripheral countries:

> not only go unpunished, they are even rewarded. On the international scene they are accorded all the respect and courtesies due to government officials. They are treated in accordance with diplomatic protocol in negotiations and seated in the General Assembly of the United Nations. When they are finally ousted from their offices, they are offered asylum by countries that lack respect for international law, but have a great deal of respect for the ill-gotten wealth that such perpetrators bring with them. (Jonassohn, 1998: 24)

The Tigrayan-dominated regime banned independent Oromo organizations, including the Oromo Liberation Front, in 1992, and declared war on these organizations and the Oromo people. It even outlawed musical groups and professional associations and closed down Oromo newspapers. Attempting to make the Oromo voiceless, as previous Ethiopian governments have done, the Meles government has left Oromo without any form of organization and institution. Only the organizations and the media that are owned and controlled by the Tigrayan government have remained intact, serving to impose the Tigrayan colonial and racist authority in Oromia and other colonized regions. The regime has engaged in political crimes, genocidal massacres, and state terrorism with little or no opposition from western powers, particularly the United States. How long will international bodies continue to ignore these problems? Are they waiting for a full genocide to emerge? Let us now turn to Sudan and examine the connection between racism, Islamism and state terrorism.

Racism, Islamism, and State Terrorism in Sudan

The modern Sudanese state was created through the broadening of the European-dominated racialized capitalist world system via British colonization.

Since the transfer of state power to the Arabized northern Sudanese elites in 1956, northern Sudanese elites have practiced slavery, colonialism, and continued subjugation on various Sudanese population groups. In these practices, racism and Islamism have been used as twin ideologies. Before the colonization of Sudan by Britain, the Turko-Egyptian conquest laid the foundation for a central state in northern Sudan. A northern Sudanese movement known as the Madhia dismantled the Turko-Egyptian rule and ruled northern Sudan until Britain colonized Sudan. Madism 'was both a religious and a political movement which aimed at a return to the Orthodox Islamic constitution in government, culture, and religion' (El Mahdi, 1965: 19).

Northern Sudanese elites enslaved population groups that they considered unbelievers and racially and culturally inferior; they used the sword and the Koran to commodify human beings. They burned houses and destroyed communities to hunt and enslave the southern and other Sudanese. Arab slave traders from northern Sudan and other countries settled in the south and other places and intensified the slave trade and social destruction with the help of the state. According to Fluehr-Lobban (1991: 73), 'slavery was conducted for both military and commercial purposes. The Turko-Egyptian armies depended on regular slave raiding, and the demand for domestic slaves in Egypt, the Ottoman Empire, and Arabia was continuous.' More than 2 million people were sold during the 19th century (O'Ballance, 1977: 20). Northern Sudanese

> merchants went south demanding huge deliveries of slaves, ivory and feathers and in doing so devastated the area, burning villages and farms, encouraging [inter-ethnonational] wars so that one [ethnonation] made deliveries at the expense of the other. This situation which lasted for . . . [more than] 50 years made stable life and progress impossible in the south. (Garang, 1985: 23)

Slavery created long-lasting historical contradictions in Sudan. Fluehr-Lobban (1991: 72) argues that:

> the complex role that the nineteenth-century slave trade played in laying the foundation for the fear of the foreigner and the trader from the north, together with a belief that the trader was Muslim and condoned by Islam, laid the basis and set the agenda for north-south suspicions and divisions that have continued to define relations from the nineteenth century to present.

Prior to the colonization of Sudan by Britain, the northern Sudanese elites could not effectively occupy the south (Holt and Daly, 1979); however, they sometimes raided it (Woodward, 1994). O'Ballance (1977: 24) notes that 'wherever possible the Mahdi attempted to force the Islamic religion on the southerners, which caused hostility, and also legalized slavery.' During the Turko-Egyptian and Mahdist regimes, 'social progress was arrested in the south, for the same reasons trade flourished in the north, towns appeared along the Nile, and on the Red Sea. This was the beginning of uneven development between the two parts of the country' (Garang, 1985: 22). Further, the Anglo-Egyptian condominium that ruled Sudan from 1899 to 1956 widened the inequality between the north and the south.

Although the British administration abolished slavery, its policies favored the north and expanded colonial capitalist development in that region. In the south and other places, development issues were largely ignored. For instance, there were only five university graduates and one secondary school in the south when Sudan gained its independence in 1956 (Garang, 1985). Thus the southern and other Sudanese were not only economically exploited but denied education by the British. When Britain was forced to leave Sudan by anti-colonial forces, the south and other regions came under the control of the north, and the south's demand for a federation was ignored and a unitary state was imposed. According to Garang (1985: 23–4):

> The British official in the south was replaced by a northern official because Britain had not trained southerners for the job. The southern market fell to northern merchants who bought food and other crops cheaply from the southerners and [in return] sold them expensive European goods.

The system of southern education was changed; Arabic became the official language, and the north practically occupied state power (O'Ballance, 1977). Although decolonization 'itself resulted from an act of the Constituent Assembly, freely and fairly elected in 1953 by any reasonable standard' (Bechtold, 1991: 3), the new Sudanese government 'sought to impose Arabization and Islamization on the south in an attempt to achieve national unity through uniformity' (Deng, 1991: 25).

The southern Sudanese resisted both Turko-Egyptian and northern Sudanese colonialism in the 19th century. They fiercely resisted the Madist army and forced it to withdraw from the south in 1897 (O'Ballance, 1977). Similarly, they opposed British colonialism and its policy of creating a hereditary chief. Numerous revolts occurred during the first half of the 20th century. In the early 1920s, the south began to create protonationalist organizations, such as the Sudanese United Tribes Society and the White Flag League. The south also continued its resistance to northern domination after the modern Sudanese state emerged. Nevertheless, northern politicians ignored the interests of the south and other regions. O'Ballance (1977: 40) states that:

> the increasing pace of Sudanization (which to the southerner means northernization) caused unrest and discontent in the south . . . To the southerners it appeared as if they were being colonized for the second time. Both the army and the police in the south . . . were now heavily officered by northerners.

Grievances such as increasing the number of northern troops in the south and the attempt to transfer southern soldiers to the north led to mutiny. Deng (1991: 24) comments that:

> the conflict erupted in August 1955 when a mutiny by one southern battalion was triggered by a widely shared fear in the south that independence was going to mean a change of masters – from the British to the Arabs – and could entail the return of the slave trade in which blacks were the victims of the Arab north.

The mutineers, who escaped imprisonment and execution by fleeing into the forest, began to initiate guerrilla warfare against the Sudanese state. The continued state repression of the south and indiscriminate killings of civilians for allegedly harboring the guerrilla fighters facilitated the development of southern nationalism. To curb that impulse, the state intensified its Arabization and Islamization policies: it nationalized private schools, prohibited missionary schools in 1957, and, in 1960, replaced the Sunday weekly holiday with Muslim Friday.

With the emergence of a resistance movement and a continuation of the demand for independence or federation, the state increased its political terrorism on the south. Because of brutal repression, many government employees and soldiers deserted the government and joined a movement known as the Anya-Nya. In 1971 the Anya-Nya became the Southern Sudan Liberation Movement (SSLM). This organization reached a negotiated political settlement with the Numayri government in 1972. The south accepted regional autonomy set forth in the Addis Ababa Peace Agreement and abandoned its demand for a separate army. In 1983, President Numaryi changed his mind and introduced the rule of *sharia*, or Islamic law. Numaryi divided the south into three regions thus violating the 1972 Addis Ababa Peace Agreement.

Consequently, the second phase of the struggle of the south started under the leadership of the Sudan People's Liberation Movement (SPLM) and its military unit, the Sudan People's Liberation Army (SPLA). As the resistance increased, the south was exposed to mass poverty, economic and cultural dislocation, unemployment, recurring famine and disaster, war, and state terrorism. This political terrorism manifested itself in the form of summary executions, assassinations, mass imprisonments, rape, forced dislocation into concentration camps, constant destruction of houses, farms, and villages, robbery and theft, and militarization of rural communities (Amnesty International, 1995/96; Prendergast and Bickel, 1994; Walgren, 1994). Today, the Sudanese government continues to use state terrorism and famine to crush the resistance struggles of southern and western Sudan. According to Prendergast (2004a: 1):

> the government's helicopter gunships are blowing bombs and bullets into southern villages, while the opposition Sudan People's Liberation Army conducts ground raids on the oil industry infrastructure that helps pay for the state's helicopters. Relief agencies, banned from many areas by the government, are begging for access to deliver food aid to a million people dependent on them for survival. More bodies are added to the shocking two million victims of violence and famine in Sudan's 19-year civil war.

The conflict between northern and southern Sudanese displaced 4.5 million people, compounded the famine crises, and increased the suffering and misery of the victims (Prendergast, 2004a). The conflict has been:

> between the central government, dominated by a well-armed and well-funded Arab Islamist elite, and southern insurgents opposed to the regime. Sudan's vast oil reserves, currently controlled by the government, are the greatest spoils of the war, but it is also a battle over land, religion, ideology and demands for self-determination. (Prendergast, 2004a: 1)

The conflict in Sudan sometimes goes beyond the south and north and religion and identity. This conflict also has taken place among Muslims, not simply between Christians and Muslims, since 'a small group from the center of the country maintains power by any means necessary' (Prendergast, 2004b: 1). The peoples of west Sudan who are currently facing state terrorism and genocide are Muslims, although they are not Arabized Muslims.

Prendergast (2004b: 1) notes that 'Sudan is Rwanda in slow motion.' The Sudanese state created 'the second largest death toll since World War II (the conflict with the SPLA),' and it 'is responsible for creating the worst humanitarian crisis in . . . Darfur' in 2003 and 2004. When two Darfurian rebel groups in western Sudan, namely, the Sudan Liberation Movement/Army (SLM/A) and the Justice and Equality Movement (JEM), attacked military garrisons in western Sudan in February 2003, the government mobilized, armed, and unleashed a terrorist militia group known as 'Janjaweed' (Arab militia) to collectively punish the peoples of the Fur, Zaghawa, and Massalit. As of 19 November 2004, public television reports from the United States estimate that about 70,000 people have been killed by Janjaweed militia and state soldiers in west Sudan. According to Mozersky (2004: 1), these militia attacks have produced untold human atrocities:

> Part of a scorched-earth government offensive, Janjaweed attacks have led to massive displacement, indiscriminate killings, looting and mass rape. These have been characterized as ethnic cleansing by many observers and compared to the Rwandan genocide by the former head of the United Nations in Sudan.
>
> To date, more than one million residents of Darfur have been displaced, many now living in squalid camps, where they are dying from disease and malnutrition. Another 110,000 have crossed into neighbouring Chad, though even there they are not safe from Janjaweed attacks.

The Arabized Sudanese state has been using state terrorism to resolve the political, social, and economic crises in Sudan. This state receives political and financial support from Arab countries (Oxford Analytica, 2004).

Comparing the Two Cases

State terrorism is associated with the issues of control of territory and resources and the construction of political and ideological domination. Oliverio (1997: 52) explains two essential features of state terrorism:

> First, the state reinforces the use of violence as a viable, effective, mitigating factor for managing conflict; second, such a view is reinforced by culturally constructed and socially organized processes, expressed through symbolic forms, and related in complex ways to present social interests. Within increasing economic and environmental globalization, gender politics, and the resurgence of nationalities within territorial boundaries, the discourse of terrorism, as a practice of statecraft, is crucial to the construction of political boundaries. As such, terrorism is invoked in the art of statecraft when multiple, often conflicting versions of the past are produced and, at particular historical moments, become sites of intense struggles.

Ethiopian and Sudanese state elites have been determined to maintain existing political and economic order by investing meager available resources in building unproductive institutions, such as the army, security infrastructure, and bureaucracy, and using them in imposing state terrorism on their subjects in Ethiopia and Sudan, respectively. The behavior of these elites has been shaped by predatory political cultures that have been tyrannical, racist, and parasitic. Consequently, political elites in the two countries have failed to advance peaceful and meaningful socioeconomic development, to resolve fundamental contradictions between the dominant and the dominated ethnonational groups, and to recognize principles of self-determination and multinational democracy. Rather, they have chosen state terrorism to promote their political objectives.

As Christians, Habashas have been enjoying the sympathy and support of the West, while the northern Sudanese Muslims have been receiving assistance from Muslim states. Consequently, both states have ignored domestic political legitimacy. The identification of the Sudanese government with the Arab world rather than with Africa has strengthened the relationship of this state with the Arab states. For many decades, 'the Arab states have been an important source of economic, military, and political assistance. Such assistance has been especially helpful to Sudan's governments when they have been internationally beleaguered or under pressure in the country's long-running civil war' (Oxford Analytica, 2004: 1). Of all Arab countries, Egypt has the greatest strategic and economic interest in Sudan because of its reliance on the Nile, which originates in Sudan. Following Egypt, Libya and Saudi Arabia have the second greatest interest in Sudan:

> For Libya, Sudan constitutes a potential ally in its on-off rivalry with Egypt. Otherwise its principal interest in Sudan is, as for Saudi Arabia, that the country

> should not be a political threat. Libya and Saudi Arabia therefore share with Egypt a preference for Sudan to be ruled by a stable military regime, rather than a democratic government or, worst of all, a revolutionary Islamist regime such as ruled Sudan in the 1990s and which supported Islamist opposition groups in the region. (Oxford Analytica, 2004: 2)

While Sudan is strategically important for some Arab countries, Ethiopia is strategically significant for western countries in general and for the United States in particular. Therefore, these western countries are more interested in supporting regimes that they can easily maneuver rather than democratic governments that have domestic legitimacy and can resist external dependency (Jalata, 2001). The Meles regime is in power predominantly because it receives financial and military support from the United States and other western countries. For example, *Impact International* (1997: 1) notes that the US government:

> agreed in July 1996 to supply Ethiopia 50 fighter aircrafts and a number of helicopter gun ships. After signing the agreement, a Pentagon spokesman described Prime Minister Meles Zenawi as [a] 'trusted and important friend of America . . . the Ethiopian leader was the only one in the region' whom they could depend upon to counter the menace of fundamentalism.

The United States, other western countries, and Israel use the discourse of Islamic fundamentalism to support the authoritarian-terrorist regime of Meles Zenaw and to suppress the national struggles of Oromo and others for self-determination and multinational democracy (*Africa Confidential*, 1997; Jalata, 2001). The regional and international supporters of these states have directly or indirectly contributed to serious human tragedies that have significant consequences for the Horn of Africa. Although global powers are concerned about the political crisis in Sudan because they oppose the Islamist Sudanese regime, they rarely show any concern about state terrorism in Ethiopia.

As President Numaryi adopted the rhetoric of socialism and regional autonomy and established a temporary peace with the south between 1972 and 1983, the Meles regime established a coalition transitional government with the Oromo Liberation Front (OLF) and other political organizations between 1991 and 1992. Although Numaryi won the confidence of the south during this period and established *consensual domination* (Gramsci, 1971) over the south, he returned to coercive domination by reintroducing the policy of Islamization and terrorism in 1983. According to Fluehr-Lobban (1991: 71), 'Sudan has offered one of the more provocative cases of state-supported Islamization in recent years because of the government's swiftness and readiness to apply the *hudad* punishment after *sharia* was decreed to be national law in September 1983.' Similarly, the Meles regime soon disbanded the coalition transitional government after it consolidated the Tigrayan-based government and started state terrorism as previous Ethiopian regimes. Since this regime emerged from the Tigrayan numerical minority group (estimated at 3.5 million), its terrorism has mainly targeted the Oromo numerical majority (estimated at 35 million), because the Oromo have challenged the Ethiopian racial and ethnic hierarchy and Meles's fake democracy and federalism.

As the Sudanese state currently uses the policies of racism, Islamism, and state terrorism in its attempt to destroy the national movements of the indigenous Africans, the Tigrayan-led Ethiopian regime uses racism and state terrorism to suppress the national movements of the Oromo, Ogaden-Somali, Sidama and others while preaching the rhetoric of 'democracy,' 'federation,' and 'self-determination' to establish the hegemony of the Tigrayan ethnocracy. Ethiopia and Sudan are two of 13 countries in the world that face the threat of genocide; the remaining countries are Iraq, Afghanistan, Myanmar, Burundi, Rwanda, the Democratic Republic of Congo, Somalia, Uganda, Algeria, China and Pakistan (Genocide Alert, 2004).

Conclusion

In Ethiopia and Sudan, state elites have failed in their policies of domination and thus have faced resistance from subjugated ethnonational groups and other sectors. State terrorism and other forms of political repression have intensified crises in these two countries. Global powers that support the authoritarian-terrorist regime of Ethiopia oppose the Islamist-terrorist regime of Sudan. The inclination of the Sudanese state to promote Islamic fundamentalism is turning the West against the country. This creates international conditions favorable for the SPLM of the south, and for the SLA and the JEM of west Sudan. This is clearly not the case for the OLF and other liberation movements in Ethiopia. Further, both radical and moderate Arabs are still more comfortable with their Christian Habasha cousins than with indigenous African groups, even though some Oromo are Muslims. As Arab states ignore non-Arabized Muslim Africans in Sudan and Ethiopia, the Christian West ignores the suffering of Christian Oromo and other Christians by siding with Habashas. Neither Christianity nor Islam necessarily helps indigenous Africans to have global or regional connections because of racism; only some southern Sudanese are benefiting from such connections. In their opposition to the Islamist Sudanese state, Europe and North America support the SPLM; they also sympathize with the organizations of western Sudan for political expediency, although they are Muslims.

As the Soviet Union was committed to help the Mengistu regime, the West, particularly the United States, along with some Arab countries, is committed to keeping the Meles regime in power in Ethiopia. The policies of the West have become major obstacles for the struggle for self-determination and democracy in Ethiopia. Similarly, the policies of Arab states have hindered to some degree the struggles of south and west Sudan. It is paradoxical that the policies of the West that support the struggle for self-determination in southern and western Sudan ignore the consequences of state terrorism and massive human rights violations in Ethiopia.

Without accountable, democratic, and legitimate governments both in Ethiopia and Sudan, various population groups in these countries may soon face dangerous conditions similar to Bosnia, Rwanda, the former Yugoslavia, and Somalia. If the current Ethiopian state terrorism and massive human rights violations are tolerated by countries that support the Ethiopian government and by international organizations that finance the Ethiopian government – such as the World Bank, the International Monetary Fund, and the United Nations – a disaster is imminent in Ethiopia. The current intervention of the West in the crisis of Sudan may avert the emerging disaster there if western leaders are serious about implementing self-determination and a multicultural or multinational democracy in that country. Regional and global powers, nongovernmental organizations, human rights organizations, responsible and progressive faith communities, and democratic individuals and groups have a political and moral responsibility to expose and fight racism, state terrorism, religious persecution, genocide, and other forms of human rights violations both in Ethiopia and Sudan.

Notes

1. The *Gada* system has the principles of checks and balances (such as periodic transference of power every eight years and division of power among executive, legislative, and judiciary branches), balanced opposition (among five parties), and power sharing between higher and lower administrative organs to prevent power from falling into the hands of despots (Legesse, 2000: 2).

2. Historically, Europeans have considered Habashas as a very intelligent people because of their racial affinity with the 'Caucasian race' (Marcus, 1996: 5) and as 'racial and cultural middleman' between black Africa on one side and Europe and the Middle East on the other (Marcus, 1996: 7).

3. According to Hassen (2001: 42):

> Only fractions of the Oromo are educated . . . By 1995, according to government sources, enrollment was only 20 percent for primary and 12 percent for secondary schools respectively . . . Out of an estimated population of thirty million in Oromia 0.1 percent received the third level education in 1994 . . . By 2002, all secondary school students in Oromia will graduate from 10th grade instead of the usual 12th grade. Oromo students start learning English in the seventh grade and they

take [high] school leaving exams in English in tenth grade. Students in Tigray start learning English in second grade and they take [high] school leaving exams in English in 12th grade. They have a better chance of passing [high] school leaving examinations than Oromo students. This means that the Oromo students will not have any more opportunity for college and university level education. Only students in the privileged state of Tigray will have that opportunity in the future. The TPLF dominated regime is deliberately leaving behind Oromo children from the mainstream modern education.

REFERENCES

Africa Confidential (1997) 38(21) October.

Adams, W.Y. (1977) *Nubia: Corridor to Africa.* Princeton, NJ: Princeton University Press.

Amnesty International (1995/96) *Ethiopia: Accountability Past and Present: Human Rights in Transition*. Amnesty International.

Beachey, R W. (1962) 'The Arms Trade in East Africa in the Late Nineteenth Century', *Journal of African History* 3: 451–67.

Bechtold, P.K. (1991) 'More Turbulence in Sudan: A New Politics This Time?', in J.O. Voll (ed.) *Sudan: State and Society in Crisis*, pp. 1–23. Bloomington: Indiana University Press.

Besteman, C. (1999) *Unraveling Somalia: Race, Violence, and the Legacy of Slavery.* Philadelphia: University of Pennsylvania Press.

Bulatovich, A. (2000) *Ethiopia through Russian Eyes: Country in Transition 1896–1898*, trans. R. Seltzer. Lawrenceville, NJ: The Red Sea Press.

Chalk, F. and Jonassohn, K. (1990) *History and Sociology of Genocide*. New Haven, CT: Yale University Press.

Deng, M. (1991) 'War of Visions for the Nation', in J.O. Voll (ed.) *Sudan: State and Society in Crisis*, pp. 24–42. Bloomington: Indiana University Press.

The Economist (1997) 'Ethiopia: Federal Sham', 16–22 August, p. 36.

El Mahdi, M. (1965) *A History of the Sudan.* London: Oxford University Press.

Fossati, B., Namarra, L. and Niggli, P. (1996) *The New Rulers of Ethiopia and the Persecution of the Oromo: Reports from the Oromo Refugees in Djibouti.* Frankfurt: Dokumentation, Evangelischer Pressedienst Frankfurt am Main.

Fluehr-Lobban, C. (1991) 'Islamization in Sudan: A Critical Assessment', in J.O. Voll (ed.) *Sudan: State and Society in Crisis*, pp. 71–89. Bloomington: Indiana University Press.

Garang, J. (1985) 'A Historical Perspective on the Sudan', *Horn of Africa* 8(1): 21–5.

Genocide Alert (2004) 'Iraq, Afghanistan, 11 Other States at Risk of Genocide: Expert', *World-AFP*, 27 January.

Gramsci, A. (1971) *Selections from the Prison Notebooks*, trans. Q. Hoare and G.N. Smith. New York: International Publishers.

Hassen, M. (2001) 'Is Genocide Against the Oromo in Ethiopia Possible?', presented at the Fourth International Biennial Conference of the Association of Genocide Scholars, 10 June, Minneapolis, MN.

Hizbawi Adera (1996/97) An EPRDF Political Pamphlet, 4(7), December 1996–February 1997.

Holcomb, B. (1991) 'Akka Gadaattii: The Unfolding of Oromo Nationalism–Keynote Remarks', in *Proceedings of the 1991 Conference on Oromia*, pp. 1–10. Oromo Studies Association.

Holcomb, B. and Ibssa, S. (1990) *The Invention of Ethiopia*. Trenton, NJ: The Red Sea Press.

Human Rights Watch/World Report (1999) 'Ethiopia: The Role of the International Community' [http://www.hrw.org/hrw/worldreport99/africa/ethiopia3.html].

Holt, M. and Daly, W. (1979) *The History of the Sudan*. Boulder, CO: Westview Press.

Ibrahim, H. (1979) *The Shaiqiya: The Cultural and Social Change of a Northern Sudanese Riverain People*. Wiesbaden: Franz Steiner Verlag GMGH.

Impact International (1997) 'Cleansing "Islamic Fundamentalism" from the Horn', March.

The International Campaign to End Genocide (ICEG), Genocide Watch (2004) 'ICEG Letter to Prime Minister of Ethiopia: Massacres of Annuak in and around Gambela', 8 January.

Jalata, A. (1993) *Oromia and Ethiopia: State Formation and Ethnonational Conflict, 1868–1992*. Boulder, CO: Lynne Rienner.

Jalata, A. (2000) 'U.S.-Sponsored Ethiopian "Democracy" and State Terrorism', in P. Toggia, P. Lauderdale and A Zegeye (eds) *Crisis and Terror in the Horn of Africa*, pp. 64–8. Burlington: Ashgate.

Jalata, A. (2001) *Fighting Against the Injustice of the State and Globalization: Comparing the African American and Oromo Movements*. New York: Palgrave.

Jonassohn, K. (1998) *Genocide and Gross Human Rights Violations*. New Brunswick, NJ: Transaction Publishers.

Legesse, A. (1973) *Gada: Three Approaches to the Study of African Society*. New York: Free Press.

Legesse, A. (2000) *Oromo Democracy: An Indigenous African Political System*. Lawrenceville, NJ: The Red Sea Press.

MacKinnon, C. (1994) 'Rape, Genocide, and Women's Human Rights', *Harvard Women's Law Journal* 17: 11–12.

MacMichael, H.A. (1967) *A History of the Arabs in the Sudan*, vol. I. New York: Barnes and Noble.

Marcus, H. (1996) 'Racist Discourse about Ethiopia Before and After the Battle of Adwa', presented at the Adwa Conference, 5 March, Addis Ababa University.

Michels, J.W. (1991) 'The Axumite Kingdom: A Settlement Archaeological Perspective', *Henok: Journal of Historical and Philosophical Thought* 2 (August): 63–72.

Mozersky, D. (2004) 'Sudan Crisis Crying Out for Solution', *International Crisis Group*, 29 April, pp. 1–2.

O'Ballance, E. (1977) *The Secret War in the Sudan, 1955–1972*. London: Faber and Faber.

Oliverio, A. (1997) 'The State of Injustice: The Politics of Terrorism and the Production of Order', *International Journal of Comparative Sociology* 38(1–2): 48–63.

Oromia Support Group, The 1997 Series.

Oxford Analytica (2004) 'Sudan/Middle East: Arab States Unmoved over Darfur', 13 October.

Prendergast, J. (2004a) 'Sudan's Last Fighting Season?', [http://.crisisweb.org/home/index.cfm?id=2213&1=1], pp. 1–3.

Prendergast, J. (2004b) 'Testimony by John Prendergast to the House Committee on International Relations: Ethnic Cleansing in Darfur; A New Front Opens in Sudan's Bloody War,' *International Crisis Group* [http://.crisisweb.org/home/index.cfm?id=2213&1=1] 6 May, pp. 1–2.

Prendergast, J. and Bickel, S. (1994) 'Sudan: Scorched-Earth War', *Africa Report* (May–June): 38–9.

Scott, W.R. (1993) *The Sons of Sheba's Race: African-Americans and the Italo-Ethiopian War, 1935–1941*. Bloomington: Indiana University Press.

Sagalee Haraara (1998) The Official Newsletter of Oromia Support Group (December), pp. 1–2.

Sharlach, L. (2002) 'State Rape Sexual Violence as Genocide', in K. Worcester, S. Avery Bermanzohn and M. Ungar (eds) *Violence and Politics: Globalization's Paradox*, pp. 107–23. London: Routledge.

Shiffman, R. (1995) 'Urban Poverty: The Global Phenomenon of Poverty and Social Marginalization in Our Cities; Facts and Strategies' [http://www.picced.org/advocacy/poverty.htm] (accessed 2003).

Sorenson, J. (1993) *Imagining Ethiopia: Struggles for History and Identity in the Horn of Africa*. New Brunswick, NJ: Rutgers University Press.

Sorenson, J. (1998) 'Ethiopian Discourse and Oromo Nationalism', in A. Jalata (ed.) *Oromo Nationalism and the Ethiopian Discourse*, pp. 223–52. Lawrenceville, NJ: The Red Sea Press.

United Nations (1948) Convention on the Prevention of the Crime of Genocide, 9 December, Article II.

Walgren, J. (1994) 'The Lost Boys of Southern Sudan', *Africa Report* 40 (May–June): 40–1.

Welsh, B. (2002) 'Globalization, Weak States, and Death Toll in East Asia,' in K. Worcester, S. Avery Bermanzohn and M. Ungar (eds) *Violence and Politics: Globalization's Paradox*, pp. 67–89. New York: Routledge.

Woodward, P. (1994) 'Sudan: State Building and the Seeds of Conflict', in Peter Woodward and Murray Forsyth (eds) *Conflict and Peace in the Horn of Africa: Federalism and its Alternatives*, pp. 78–85. Brookfield, VT: Dartmouth.

Zia-Zarifi, S. (2004) 'Ethiopia: Halt Crackdown on Oromo Students', *Human Rights Watch* [http://www.hrw.org/press/2002/05/ethiopia052202.html].

Asafa Jalata is Professor of Sociology, Global Studies, and Africana Studies at the University of Tennessee, Knoxville. He has published two books and edited two, namely, *State Crises, Globalisation, and National Movements in the North-East Africa* (Routledge, 2004), *Fighting Against the Injustice of the State and Globalization: Comparing the African American and Oromo Movements* (Palgrave, 2001), *Oromo Nationalism and the Ethiopian Discourse: The Search for Freedom and Democracy* (Red Sea Press, 1998), *Oromia & Ethiopia: State Formation and Ethnonational Conflict, 1868–1992* (L. Rienner Publishers, 1993). He has published more than two dozen book chapters and refereed articles. He currently is writing a book entitled *Faces of Terrorism in the Age of Globalization: From Christopher Columbus to Osama bin Laden*. Address: Department of Sociology, University of Tennessee, Knoxville, TN 37996–0490, USA. Email: ajalata@utk.edu

[24]

The Rwandan Genocide: International Finance Policies and Human Rights

Dawn L. Rothe, Christopher W. Mullins, and Kent Sandstrom*

Introduction

THE GENOCIDE OF THE RWANDAN TUTSIS SERVES TO REMIND US OF THE ETHNIC, political, and economic conditions that are typical for postcolonial states. Ethnic identities are often magnified, if not manufactured, by occupying forces or national elites during the colonial period. Once independence has been obtained, ethnic identities are often internally enhanced for the political purposes of the new ruling regime. Like their colonial forebears, the rulers of the new regime often employ the strategy of pitting one ethnic group against the other ("divide and rule"), particularly through their military, human rights, and macroeconomic decisions. Additionally, they often form one-party states that perpetuate conditions of governance similar to those experienced under colonial rule. In turn, these states reproduce or exacerbate the political, economic, and ethnic crises originally resulting from colonial exploitation of regional and national resources (Chossudousky, 1995; Chossudousky and Galand, 1996).

These political conditions contribute to the instability felt throughout postcolonial environments. The new regimes monopolize existing resources, leaving subordinate populations in socioeconomic conditions analogous to (or worse than) those characterizing colonial rule. Widespread inequities of access to social, political, and economic capital are perpetuated by these new social arrangements. The histories of postcolonial states frequently degenerate into civil wars or other internecine conflicts that undermine the fragile forms of social organization built out of the anomic social rubble of colonial decampment. In the most extreme cases, such as Rwanda, genocides arise. Even though the previously oppressed Hutus gained

DAWN L. ROTHE is Assistant Professor at Old Dominion University (e-mail: drothe@odu.edu); she is the author of *Symbolic Gestures and the Generation of Global Social Control* (Lexington, 2006, with Christopher W. Mullins) and co-author of *Power, Bedlam, and Bloodshed: State Crimes in Post-Colonial Africa* (Peter Lang, 2008). CHRISTOPHER W. MULLINS is Assistant Professor of Criminology at Southern Illinois University (e-mail: mullinsc@siu.edu). He is author of *Holding Your Square: Masculinities, Streetlife and Violence* (Willan, 2006) and *Power, Bedlam, and Bloodshed: State Crimes in Post-Colonial Africa* (Peter Lang, 2008, with Dawn L Rothe). KENT L. SANDSTROM is Professor of Sociology at the University of Northern Iowa (e-mail: Kent.Sandstrom@uni.edu). He is the co-author of four books, including *Symbols, Selves, and Social Reality: A Symbolic Interactionist Approach to Sociology and Social Psychology* (Roxbury, 2006).

political positions of power, they were not content to allow the perceived and actual injustices of the past to remain there. As global and local economic situations grew problematic, the Hutus used their new authority to orchestrate widespread efforts to eliminate all Tutsi rivals.

Scholars have written about the Rwandan genocide from a number of disciplinary perspectives. We add to the extant literature by adopting an approach that focuses on human rights and highlights the role played by international finance institutions in setting the stage for genocide. In doing so, we begin with a review of criminological literature that focuses on issues of state criminality and "crimes of globalization" (Friedrichs and Friedrichs, 2007). This review is followed by a brief description of the World Bank, the International Monetary Fund (IMF), and international human rights. We then apply an integrated theory of organizational crime (Rothe and Mullins, 2006) to explain the conditions fostering the Rwandan genocide, including the roles of the World Bank, IMF, and other international finance lenders to show how they bear some culpability for the disaster due to their policies and development demands that altered Rwanda's social, economic, and political structures. We conclude with a discussion of how and why international financial policies for postcolonial states should be dictated by human rights concerns and consideration of the social, cultural, and economic needs of a state and its citizens rather than the exigencies of "free trade," capital mobility, and global capital accumulation.

State Crime and Crimes of Globalization

The subfield of state crime is an outgrowth of Sutherland's (1939, 1949) call to expand the purview of criminology to crimes of the powerful, but its origins are often traced to the "Presidential Address" delivered by William Chambliss at the 1988 Meetings of the American Society of Criminology. Chambliss (1989, 1995) demonstrates that states can play a crucial role in organizing and supporting activities that violate domestic and international laws, such as piracy and smuggling, when doing so fulfills their broader political and economic objectives. His "structural contradictions approach" emphasizes that when presented with "unsolvable" problems, states can be enticed to violate the law to meet broader goals. Criminologists, particularly critical criminologists, have seized upon and extended Chambliss' insights, broadening and enriching understandings of state crime (see Barak, 1991; Kauzlarich and Kramer, 1993; Kramer, 1995; Ross, 1995; Tunnell, 1993). In the process, these criminologists have examined crimes tacitly supported or organized by a sovereign polity, as well as illegal actions committed by states themselves.

With the publication of more case studies and theoretical papers, the subfield broadened its analysis of state criminality to include actions committed by governments that violated domestic, international, or human rights laws (see Kauzlarich and Kramer, 1998; Kauzlarich, Matthews, and Miller, 2001; Mullins and Kauzlarich,

2000; Ross et al., 1999; Ross, 2000a), as well as incidents of states or state agencies that failed to take obligatory actions (Barak, 1991; Kauzlarich and Kramer, 1998; Kauzlarich, Mullins, and Matthews, 2003). Definitional debates continue (see Rothe and Friedrichs, 2006), but the idea of state criminality is firmly entrenched in the field.

The concept of "crimes of globalization" (Friedrichs and Friedrichs, 2007; Friedrichs, 2004) is the newest addition to the list of forms of crime with a cognate relationship to crimes of the state. Informed by Falk's (1993) observation that globalization is driven by the interests of capital over people, "crimes of globalization" refer to mass harms of people, especially within developing countries, that arise as latent consequences of the development and expansion of global capital. According to Friedrichs and Friedrichs (2007: 18), crimes of globalization have characteristics of "state crime, political crime, white-collar crime, state-corporate crime, and finance crime," but do not fit neatly into any of these categories. Specifically, these crimes "involve cooperative endeavors between international financial institutions, transnational corporations, and state or political entities that engage in demonstrably harmful activities in violation of international law or international human rights conventions."[1]

Friedrichs' approach highlights the role of international financial institutions, transnational corporations, and states in the context of criminogenic tendencies within globalization. Friedrichs and Friedrichs (2007) examined the role of policies put forth by the World Bank, the International Monetary Fund, and the World Trade Organization in developing states that result in socially harmful practices and human rights violations. The policies and practices of these international finance institutions can have dramatic societal effects, as reflected in the "structural adjustments" imposed on countries such as Argentina, Senegal, and Rwanda, which destroyed the way of life of large numbers of indigenous peoples (Rothe and Friedrichs, 2006).

International finance institutions may not intend to do harm. Indeed, they claim that their central mission is to alleviate economic and other forms of suffering. But the privileging of transnational corporate interests and the interests of powerful states, coupled with the arrogance with which these institutions implement a "top down" form of globalization, results in immensely harmful consequences that conflict with the ideology and promotion of human rights. Moreover, since international financial institutions work closely and cooperatively with high-level government officials in developed and developing countries, the crimes of globalization they facilitate are inevitably intertwined with crimes of the state (*Ibid.*).

Criminologists face the challenge of examining and explaining how these different cognate forms of crime interact and have reciprocal influences. Following Friedrichs' (2004) call to criminologists to engage with the literature of globalization, Rothe, Muzzatti, and Mullins (2006) conducted research that explored the interrelations between international institutions such as the IMF and World Bank, legacies of colonialism, and foreign policies that set the stage for atrocities, state victimization, and state crime. In turn, they provided an illustration of how and why the sinking of the Senegalese ferry *Le Joola* was a crime of globalization. Most crucially, Rothe, Muzzatti, and Mullins (2006) demonstrated why scholars need to examine the domination of Western capitalism and international finance lenders and institutions and their criminogenic effect on "developing" states.

We hope to extend the focus and insights of criminological analysis by examining the role played by international finance institutions in the Rwandan genocide. In doing so, we incorporate the concepts of crimes of collusion between the state and organizations (Kramer and Michalowski, 1990; Kauzlarich and Kramer, 1998), including organizations such as the IMF and the World Bank. To date, these interconnections have been largely ignored in the literatures on state crime, genocide, and human rights. They have also been ignored in the growing literature on Rwanda and its genocide. An examination of the collusion between the Rwandan government, the IMF, and the World Bank is important for its etiological contributions and because some scholars identify these organizations as key mechanisms for mitigating state and international criminal acts. For example, in the context of state crime among advanced industrialized democracies, Ross (2000a: 4) points out that controls of state crime can be either internal or external to the state. External controls provide "powers of review or sanction" by domestic organizations (e.g., external review boards, extra-agency competition, public opinion, and the media) and/or international organizations (e.g., the media, the World Court of Justice, and the United Nations). Ross suggests that these supra-national structures are central for keeping states in line. Yet, not all commentators concur. Barak (2000: *viii*) suggests that these controls are problematic, since they are subject to "burnout, especially since the benefits of regulating these kinds of crimes seem to be dwarfed by the costs" of control. However, Barak ignores the possibility that the driving ideologies and policies of these organizations might not simply "burn out," but rather may in and of themselves act as catalysts or even lures to criminality.

In the case of international financial organizations, the ability to operate as a control of state crime lies within their capacity to grant or withhold needed capital. Especially in developing states, this capacity could be a strong deterrent to state-sponsored criminality. However, in analyzing the Rwandan genocide, we find that the policies and practices of external controlling bodies, especially the International Monetary Fund and World Bank, served to facilitate rather than constrain criminal activities. Before discussing the nature of these two organizations, as well as their role in crimes of globalization, we discuss the emergence and role of transnational human rights for states and their policies. After elaborating on the diffusion of human rights discourse in recent decades, we consider how human rights have been downplayed and undermined in the broader drive to expand laissez-faire economics based upon deregulated markets and private ownership, particularly by institutions such as the World Bank and the IMF.

International Human Rights

The end of World War II brought new alliances and new attempts to generate and legitimate an international institution designed to foster peaceful cooperation and collective security among nations. The human rights atrocities, genocidal killings, and widespread destruction taking place during World War II provoked both ideological and structural responses. New international institutions, such as the United Nations, World Bank, and the IMF, were founded. These institutions together comprised an effort to strengthen the international arena—at least as it still existed in Western Europe. Initially, the financial entities focused their efforts on rebuilding Europe, expressly avoiding lending to colonial or formerly colonial holdings. Indeed, the World Bank and IMF did not focus their missions toward a broader agenda of economic development until the 1960s.

Beyond the creation of an international political and economic organizational structure, the postwar world also saw a fundamental shift in political discourses. This ideological shift included the articulation of a universal quality of life standard for humanity: international human rights. The transformation of this standard from an ideology to a moral imperative and legal duty has been a slow process. Nonetheless, human rights have been incorporated into several treaties and conventions, including the Universal Declaration of Human Rights (UDHR) of 1948. The UDHR contains 30 articles outlining an array of basic human rights. These include civil and political rights, such as freedom of expression and freedom from unlawful arrest, which are grounded in the notion of the "dignity of the person." Beyond these "first generation" rights, the UDHR includes a broader range of social and economic (or "second generation") rights, as well as community and cultural (or "third generation") rights. Human rights have also been incorporated into the Convention on the Prevention and Punishment of the Crime of Genocide of 1948, the International Covenant on Civil and Political Rights of 1966, the International Covenant on Social and Economic Rights of 1966, the Convention on the Elimination of All Forms of Discrimination against Women of 1981, the Convention against Torture and Other Cruel, Inhuman, or Degrading Treatment or Punishment of 1984, and the Convention on the Rights of the Child of 1989.

Although the merits of the UDHR are widely recognized, critics have pointed out that it is a "soft law," existing largely "as a weak form of customary international law" and having its primary impact as an internationally agreed upon set of standards toward which countries *should* strive (Klug, 2005: 92). However, as with any international laws, soft laws such as the UDHR call upon state governments to mesh their domestic law with international standards and obligations. But governmental failures to observe the standards and obligations of human rights, as well as other forms of public international law, are typically overlooked, unless they reach the level of genocide or crimes against humanity—and even then actions are problematic at best (Adebajo and Sriram, 2001, Rajagopal, 2003). As Klug (2005:

92) asserts, human rights have been most effectively implemented "either through domestic law or more recently through the exercise of humanitarian intervention and the enforcement of international criminal law." Yet intervention and/or enforcement of these violations are rare and often too late in coming. In the late 20th and early 21st centuries, interventions have occurred only well after the perpetration of substantial harms (e.g., Kosovo and Croatia) and frequently under extremely limited rules of engagement (e.g., Somalia, Rwanda, and the Democratic Republic of Congo), if they occur at all (e.g., Darfur).

A main issue within the implementation of human rights emerges in light of the inherent contradiction of the generation of universal principles and standards. Although certain principles of general human rights have been enshrined within international humanitarian law and in the Rome Statute (e.g., genocide, crimes against humanity) or other universally intended agreements (e.g., the convention against genocide), in general human rights have not attained the legal status of *ergo omnes* or *jus cogens*. In other words, these treaties are only binding on those who both sign and ratify treaties and voluntarily submit themselves to the standards. This opt-in approach reduces the power and reach of human rights agreements. But the idea of a universal jurisdiction imposed against the will of a given state directly violates a key principle expressed within the UDHR: sovereignty. Moreover, these treaties and conventions are limited to state acceptance and compliance.

International human rights accords are also challenged by the far-reaching changes taking place in the global economy. As many analysts have highlighted, the process of economic globalization is simultaneously pulling the contemporary world together and apart. Various peoples and regions, regardless of national or geographic boundaries, are being drawn together, largely through the integration of the global market for goods, services, and labor. At the same time, the push for a globalized brand of Western capitalism is promoting fragmentation in many regions by exacerbating problems of inequality, exploitation, poverty, and ethnic strife. This has had profound and contradictory effects on the realization of human rights at the international level. As McCormick (2000) observes, in some ways globalization has aided the promotion of human rights by enabling states, international organizations, and nongovernmental organizations to combine their efforts and do more collectively for human rights than any national government could do on its own. Globalization has also enhanced the "rights explosion" (Epp, 1998) and the emergence of transnational human rights movements and discourses (such as those described in the previous paragraphs). Indeed, the widespread diffusion of the concept of universal human rights has become a key component of the phenomenon of globalization (Boyle and Meyer, 2002). Ironically, even the fragmentation provoked by globalization has, in some respects, contributed to the promotion of human rights (Clohesy and Kuraz, 2000; McCormick, 2000).

On the less favorable side, the forces of fragmentation have torn apart the cultural, political, and economic fabric of many fragile nations and/or states and, in some cases, have removed constraints against longstanding antagonisms, thereby giving rise to brutal violence, civil war, and egregious human rights violations. Examples of the latter include the mass rapes and genocidal crimes that took place in Bosnia and Rwanda during the 1990s and in Darfur at the present time. Regrettably, as McCormick (2000) notes, the forces of fragmentation seem to be more powerful than the forces of unification, and recent attempts to prevent human rights violations around the world have at best met with mixed results.

Fortunately, human rights treaties and laws have attempted to address the fragmentation that has occurred due to the contradictory and destabilizing consequences of globalization. For instance, a series of United Nations resolutions—particularly Resolution 3201: The Declaration of the Establishment of a New International Economic Order—have been designed to generate a more equitable economic experience for "third world" countries. Although some analysts may be inclined to dismiss this declaration as a matter of symbolic politics, it was crafted in response to resistance to the growing hegemony of neoliberal capitalism represented by the World Bank and IMF. Other relevant guidelines have been created, including the Convention on Economic, Social and Cultural Human Rights, the Committee on Economic, Social, and Cultural Human Rights (2003), and the Maastricht Guidelines (1997). The recent Agreement by the Economic and Social Council (2003) addresses the criminal liability of transnational organizations, while specifically mentioning that these organizations (and their representatives) fall under the purview of international law and the International Criminal Court (ICC). The 2003 Norms on the Responsibilities of Transnational Corporations and Other Business Enterprises with Regard to Human Rights Agreement also notes that transnational organizations should fall under the purview of the ICC and be defined as such in the statute (Rothe and Mullins, 2006).

In this article, we frame the conditions of international aid receipt as one set of the many threats to the sovereignty of postcolonial states. We are not alone in this approach. For example, An-Na'im (2003: 13) remarks that the "sovereignty and stability of African states are constantly contested...by the forces of diminished sovereignty over vital national economic and social policy under current structural adjustment polices and unfavorable global trade relations." To be fully agentic in the global political and economic arenas, nations must be able to choose their agendas freely from a number of viable options. Simply, they must be in full control of how they regulate and enact basic economic principles and policies. As we will show in this article, recipients of World Bank and IMF aid must reshape their economic and social polices to the will of institutions of international finance. To gain deeper insight into the struggles surrounding human rights, as well as the significance of enforcing these rights in nations such as Rwanda, it is important to examine the purpose and impact of institutions such as the World Bank and International Monetary Fund, particularly in setting the stage for collective violation of these rights and implementation of far-reaching crimes of genocide.

The World Bank

The World Bank is not a "bank" in the commonly used sense of the term. Rather, it is a specialized financial agency, composed of 184 member countries. Conceived during World War II, it initially helped to rebuild postwar Europe. In 1947, its first loan of $250 million went to France for reconstruction. It once had a homogeneous staff of engineers and financial analysts, based solely in Washington, D.C. More recently, the Bank became a Group, encompassing five closely associated development institutions: the International Bank for Reconstruction and Development (IBRD), the International Development Association (IDA), the International Finance Corporation (IFC), the Multilateral Investment Guarantee Agency (MIGA), and the International Centre for Settlement of Investment Disputes (ICSID) (Rothe et al., 2006).

The World Bank is a closed system based upon investment. Votes allocated to member countries regarding specific programs are linked to the size of its shareholding. Initial membership in the Bank gives equal voting rights, but there are also additional votes. These votes depend on financial contributions to the organization by member states, implying undemocratic decision-making. As of November 1, 2006, the United States held 16.4% of total votes, Japan 7.9%, Germany 4.5%, and the United Kingdom (U.K.) and France both held 4.3%. Rwanda holds .08% of total votes. Within the MIGA, the United States has 15% of total votes, Germany 4.2%, and France and the U.K. had four percent of total votes. By contrast, Rwanda has 398 votes (0.18%). The IFC distribution of votes shows a similarly disproportionate total for Rwanda.

Once its original mission of postwar European reconstruction was finished, the World Bank turned its lending practices to development issues. Its rhetoric was often focused on human rights, human dignity, and infrastructure development, but its operational concerns strongly focused on producing returns for investors. Through the 1970s and 1980s, debtor nations were frequently unable to meet repayment demands. Therefore, during the 1980s the Bank went through an extensive period that focused on issues related to macroeconomic and debt rescheduling. During the latter part of the 1980s, social and environmental issues assumed center stage and an increasingly vocal and active civil society in Europe and the Americas accused the Bank of failing to observe its own policies in some high-profile projects. The World Bank often did not respond directly to the critiques and more human rights-focused concerns of these populations, though it did begin to consider the need for debt restructuring. Yet, as with other actions, the World Bank did not simply accede to the vocal minorities that demanded global policy changes. In return for debt reallocation or admission into forgiveness programs, it demanded that macro-structural political and economic changes occur within the debtor nations. In many cases, the Bank also required recipient countries to adopt certain political measures, such as policies that would foster "democracy," by which they meant opening state holdings to private ownership.

In addition to providing financing, the World Bank Group offers advice and assistance to developing countries on almost every aspect of economic development. Since the mid-to-late 1990s, the Bank Group has used Private Sector Development (PSD) as its strategy to promote privatization in developing countries. Thus, all other strategies must be coordinated with the push toward privatization. Although impoverished governments around the world rely on the World Bank as a contributor of development finance, it has often been criticized for undermining the national and economic sovereignty of recipient countries through its pursuit of economic liberalization. The Bank also operates under the marked political influence of certain countries, notably the United States, that profit from advancing their access to additional markets and to specific resources available in Third World states, such as cheap labor, gold and diamond mining, peanuts, and electric industries. Moreover, G8 member states exercise notable political influence over the World Bank's policies of restructuring, reflected in priorities directed toward private ownership policies. Consequentially, economic enterprises funded by the World Bank are often detrimental to the people they are allegedly designed to help. In many cases, they contradict the needs of specific states and the promotion of human rights (Rothe et al., 2006).

The International Monetary Fund

The International Monetary Fund is also composed of 184 member countries and is headquartered in Washington, D.C. Established in 1945, it sought to promote international monetary cooperation, to foster economic growth, and to provide temporary financial assistance to needy countries. It "is the central institution of the international monetary system—the system of international payments and exchange rates among national currencies." The purposes of the IMF have remained unchanged since it was established, but its operations—such as surveillance (a dialogue among its members on the national and international consequences of their economic and financial policies), financial assistance (loans), and technical assistance (structural adjustment policies)—have changed over time.

The IMF is the international system that encourages countries to adopt what it believes to be "sound economic policies," and what most commentators refer to as neoliberal economics. However, as with the World Bank, the voices represented in such policies are not equally distributed. For example, the United States has 371,743 votes (16.83% of all votes), Japan has 133,378 votes (six percent), Germany has 130,332 votes (5.9%), and France and the U.K. each have 107,635 votes (4.87%). Rwanda holds only 1,051 total votes. Many international observers have been questioning the effectiveness of the remedies embodied in IMF-supported adjustment programs—especially those backed by the ESAF, the facility established in 1987 through which the IMF provides low-interest loans to poor countries that attach specific demands. Borrowing countries must follow requirements concerning currency devaluations and peggings, cut social programs and spending on civil works, and open state-run industries to private, international investment. As noted by the IMF (1999: 1), "some even described these remedies as part of the problem rather than the solution." In part, remedies for countries' economic hardships are constructed in an ideological framework of global capitalism that ignores the primacy of citizens' human rights and the overall social, political, and economic health of a nation. We now turn to these policies within Rwanda.

Rwanda, International Finance Institutions, and Lenders

After its independence in 1962, Rwanda's relations with Belgium, its former colonial power, and with international financial donors became exceedingly complex. The catastrophic impact of structural adjustment policies dictated by the IMF and World Bank, along with the fall in coffee prices on the global market (linked to the adjustment policies and to the International Coffee Organization), played a key role in establishing the socioeconomic context within which the Rwandan crisis emerged. The evolution of the postcolonial economic system played a decisive role in the development of the Rwandan genocide during 1994. From the perspective of Western-inspired capitalism, Rwanda showed "progress" after its independence in diversifying its national economy. However, it still relied heavily on the coffee export economy established under the Belgian administration. Indeed, coffee exports provided the country with approximately 80% of its foreign exchange earnings.

Despite Rwanda's high poverty levels during the 1970s and 1980s, especially in the countryside, general food self-sufficiency persisted. Approximately 70% of rural households cultivated coffee. The food situation started to deteriorate in the early 1980s, however, when a marked decline took place in the per capita availability of food (Chossudovsky, 1995). This decline in food production was linked to broader initiatives to recapture export quantities. For example, subsistence and coffee fields were turned into ranchlands, causing severe soil erosion and the loss of general fertility, much like what happened in Latin America. Additionally, in 1987, the system of quotas established under the International Coffee Agreement started to fall apart. A global glut of coffee had developed and many countries had become dissatisfied with the quotas assigned to them by the ICO.

To meet explosive debt payments to the IMF and World Bank, highly indebted countries attempted to expand production and began selling their product outside the ICO at lower prices. At the same time, the World Bank and IMF were pushing governments to increase the production and export of coffee (e.g., Uganda, Ethiopia, Vietnam, and Kenya), leading to saturation of coffee availability. For example, the World Bank promoted the mass expansion of coffee growing in Vietnam, including the funding of an agricultural rehabilitation project to diversify export income by expanding coffee and rubber exports. In another example, the World Bank (1993) advised the Ugandan government to increase production by claiming that Uganda could double its coffee exports without effecting international prices (Chang, 2002). The massive oversupply of coffee resulted in a price collapse. World prices plummeted and the Fonds d'égalisation (the state coffee stabilization fund) that purchased coffee from Rwandan farmers at a fixed price began to accumulate a sizeable debt.

During 1989, the Rwandan budget was reduced by 40%, which was offset mostly by reducing social services. These cuts were not well received by a peasantry already overburdened with taxes and increased mandatory labor for the government. The situation was worsened by a mini-drought that caused additional famine and sent thousands of others fleeing to Tanzania in search of food. Rwanda's increasing population made land a contentious issue and the peasantry became irritated over stories of governmental land grabbing. Indeed, government appropriation of lands had multiplied and favored the elite and regime. Moreover, the state seized land for the World Bank-funded Gebeka project, which benefited the regime and included the seizure of the last primary growth forests in Rwanda. This reinforced peasant fears of large-scale government land appropriations. Forests were logged to clear the land for grazing European cattle and starting dairy businesses. Although the lands remained public, profits were shared between the "regime and World Bank expatriates that had invested in the scheme" (Prunier, 1995: 88).

During this period, export earnings continued to decline by nearly 50%. When coffee prices plummeted, famine erupted throughout the Rwandan countryside.[2] According to the World Bank, GDP per capita growth declined from 0.4% from 1981 to 1986 to –5.5% from 1987 to 1991 following the fall of the coffee market. In 1988, a World Bank mission went to Rwanda to review its public expenditure program. This review led to a series of recommendations that aimed to put Rwanda back on the track of "sustained economic growth" (Chossudovsky, 1995). Of the two policy options the Bank offered to the Juvénal Habyarimana regime, the first, "No Strategy Change," would have meant remaining with the prevailing system of state planning. The second option was a macroeconomic reform designed to instigate a transition to a "free market." The World Bank concluded that if Rwanda adopted option two, then levels of consumption would increase markedly between 1989 and 1993, alongside a recovery of investment and an improved balance of trade. To accomplish this, other policies would have to be implemented: trade liberalization, currency devaluation, lifting of all subsidies to agriculture, termination of the Fonds d'égalisation, privatization of government-held enterprises, and a general reduction of civil employment.

In June 1989, mere months after the Rwandese government adopted the program, the ICA talks deadlocked due to political pressures from Washington on behalf of the large U.S. coffee traders. At the conclusion of the Florida meetings, coffee prices plunged by more than 50% in a matter of months. For Rwanda, the drop in price wreaked havoc with an already fragile economic situation. Economic foundations remained extremely fragile. With a large share of government revenues dependent upon coffee, the collapse in coffee prices precipitated a crisis in the state's public finances. As the debt crisis unfolded, a larger share of coffee and tea earnings were earmarked for debt servicing, putting further pressure on small-scale farmers to maximize production while receiving less and less profit.

As often occurs in heavily indebted countries undergoing additional economic stressors or near collapse, the Habyarimana regime requested help from the international arena. It accepted the IMF–World Bank's proffered structural adjustment program (SAP). After the adoption of the "With Strategy Change" plan, a 50% devaluation of the Rwandan franc was carried out almost immediately in November 1990. The devaluation was posited as the key to boosting coffee exports by increasing the purchasing power of international trading partners. However, the plunge of the Rwandan franc triggered severe inflation within the Rwandan economy. Outstanding external debt, which had doubled since 1985, increased by another 34% between 1989 and 1992. Import prices soared; yet the price of coffee sold by local producers was frozen by the IMF's SAP requirements. As a result, hundreds of thousands of small coffee farmers were ruined (Maton, 1994).

Like the poorest sectors of the urban population, these destitute farmers became a permanent reservoir of recruits for the Interahamwe militia and the army. Political disintegration of the Habyarimana regime accompanied the fall of the market in the late 1980s. The regime's hardliners channeled the massive social discontent resulting from the devastating economic conditions into implementing their plan for genocide. (For a more detailed account of the Rwanda genocide and Rwanda's history, see also Prunier, 1995.)

By 1990, Rwanda was in a pervasive crisis. With the political system on the verge of collapse, the Franco-African summit was held. Outside forces met with Habyarimana in an attempt to force him to allow a multiparty political system—which he did in July. Conditions were ripe for the Rwandan Patriotic Forces (RPF, a Tutsi militia group) to make their move. After this announcement, a group of intellectuals issued a manifesto demanding democratization and began forming opposition political parties. The manifesto acted as a multidimensional catalyst for political resistance, especially for the RPF in Uganda who were preparing an invasion against the Rwandan ruling elites.

The Rwandan crisis of the early 1990s became a spectacle of donor roundtables in Paris, broken cease-fire agreements, and failed peace talks. Initiatives were closely monitored and coordinated by the economic donors in a tangled web of conditions (Toussaint, 2004). When the fighting started, millions of dollars in balance-of-payments aid from multilateral and bilateral sources came pouring into the coffers of the Central Bank, which was later emptied when the Mouvement Révolutionnaire National pour le Développement (MRND) fled Kigali. Earmarked for commodity imports, a sizeable amount of these loans were diverted toward the acquisition of military hardware. After October 1990, the Rwandan Armed Forces expanded from 5,000 to 40,000 men, requiring a sizeable influx of outside money to pay the new recruits who were drawn from the dramatically increasing number of urban unemployed after the collapse of the coffee market in 1989. Thousands of youth were also drafted into the civilian militia. The stage was set for the upcoming genocide.

International financial institutions became wary of such large military expenditures and demanded that the regime decrease military spending. At the same time, however, they allowed the regime to account for sums loaned by the World Bank and the IMF by presenting old invoices based on a flawed accounting system for all imported goods (Toussaint, 1999). By using invoices instead of receipt-based accounting for imported goods, the dates and amounts were easily altered. This strategy allowed the regime to finance massive arms purchases that would later be used in the 1994 genocide. For example, trucks imported for the army were put on the Transport Ministry's account and fuel used for militia and army vehicles was recorded on the Health Ministry's account (Toussaint, 2004). When the IMF and World Bank suspended lending at the beginning of 1993, they failed to freeze the large sums of money held in accounts in foreign banks, which the Habyarimana regime used to buy more arms. Actions such as these indicate how, through acts of omission, the institutions failed in their duty to monitor loan money. The suspensions should have taken place in early 1992, when they knew that the money was funding exuberant and unprecedented military spending and arms purchases. By continuing to provide financing until early 1993, the IMF and World Bank were complicit in the preparations for genocide.

The economic crisis reached its climax in 1992, when Rwandan farmers uprooted some 300,000 coffee trees. With international coffee markets not providing the needed economic revenues, Rwandans in the hinterlands sought to transform plantations into pasture, hoping that herding cattle would be more viable. Despite soaring domestic prices, the government had frozen the price of coffee at its 1989 level, under the terms of its agreement with the international financial institutions. The government was not allowed to transfer state resources to the Fonds d'égalisation. Further, a significant portion of the existing profit was appropriated to local coffee traders, which put further pressure on the peasantry (Toussaint, 2004). In June 1992, the IMF ordered a second currency devaluation; prices for fuel and consumer essentials rose again. Without coffee revenues, there was nothing for the majority of peasants to fall back on. Traditional subsistence economics had all but disappeared. With trade liberalization and the deregulation of grain markets (as recommended by the SAP), cheap food imports and food aid from the other countries destabilized the few local markets that had managed to sustain themselves. The entire agricultural system was pushed into crisis due to austerity measures and sinking civil service salaries. These policies inevitably exacerbated the overarching climate of insecurity (*Ibid.*).

During this upheaval, a new cabinet was sworn in. For the first time, the MRND had to share power. Policies were put in place that attempted to circumvent many of Habyarimana's practices, such as the abolition of the "policy of equilibrium" that had allowed the government to choose civil service workers based on ethnicity. Habyarimana resigned as the head of armed forces, but the political and social conditions remained tense (Prunier, 1995).

The situation in Rwanda became even more unpredictable in the face of events unfolding in neighboring Burundi. Burundi was similar to Rwanda in economic, ethnic, and colonial experiences. The main difference was an inversion of dominance among ethnic groups. In Rwanda, the majority Hutu had been repressed by the minority Tutsi as a result of the preferences of former colonial powers, but in Burundi the situation was reversed. Minority Hutus were given positions of power and used them to exploit the subordinate Tutsi, who constituted a numerical majority. In June 1993, Melchior Ndadaye, a Hutu, was elected president of Burundi. However, in October he was kidnapped by extremist Tutsis and killed. Several ministers and local civil servants used this event to encourage the Hutu population to take revenge directly on the Tutsi population. Violence erupted in areas, but the Tutsi-controlled army of Burundi moved in and, in heavy-handedly manner, restored order. Within days Burundi experienced over 50,000 deaths, of which roughly 30,000 were Tutsi and 20,000 Hutu (Prunier, 1995: 199). Over 150,000 Tutsis fled to army-controlled areas, while nearly 300,000 Hutu fled across the Rwandan border.

These events had a significant impact on the already tumultuous situation in Rwanda. Hutu extremists viewed it as yet another example of the evil engaged in by Tutsis. The Burundian violence reinforced propaganda initiated in 1992 that called for a final solution to the "ethnic problem." The death of Ndadaye, along with the refugees arriving and spreading tales of horror occurring at the hands of the Tutsi, provided a ripe opportunity for Hutu extremists to rally even the hesitant to their side. The growing hostility and racist notions of a final solution spread quickly even to remote rural areas of Rwanda. This dissemination of hostility, coupled with the heightened increase in arms distributions, should have served as a signal to the U.N. that peace was far from being restored.

Further, the full democratization of Rwanda envisaged by the IMF, World Bank, and the 1993 Arusha Accords was impossible due to the widespread impoverishment of the population. Instead, the objectives of democratization and interethnic solidarity were subsumed to the demands of *Realpolitik*, which meant meeting the conditions of "good governance" imposed by international finance lenders and Habyarimana. The installation of a multiparty coalition government under the trusteeship of Rwanda's external creditors fueled the various political factions within the regime, leading to the assassination of Habyarimana—the oft-cited trigger of the genocide.

Clearly, the international financial institutions did not intend to produce the Rwandan civil war and the 1994 genocide. However, austerity measures and the impact of the IMF-sponsored devaluations contributed to impoverishing the Rwandan people at a time of acute political and social crisis. The deliberate manipulation of market forces destroyed economic activity and people's livelihood, fueled unemployment, and created a situation of generalized famine and social despair (Toussaint, 2004). The anomie developed and intensified by the international financial institutions produced the genocide.

Discussion

In this article we have explored the harmful consequences that developing nations such as Rwanda experience as a result of IMF– and World Bank-imposed financial policies. Though the IMF and World Bank did not intentionally encourage the genocidal event in Rwanda, they did promote the implementation of economic policies that served as a strong catalyst for the emergence of genocidal killings. Both institutions knowingly violated their own standards, as well as international human rights principles, by imposing rigid conditions tied to aid packages. Rather than assisting in the development of an independent and functional Rwandan economy, these policies further exacerbated deteriorating economic conditions and structures in a nation held together by increasingly fragile civil bonds.

The IMF and World Bank did not seek to instigate economic collapse or to catalyze genocide through the policies they promoted in Rwanda, but their systematic inattention to the effects of these policies on Rwandan citizens set the stage for political and economic disaster. Despite presenting a public image of benevolent interest in the reduction of poverty worldwide, the IMF and World Bank have focused mostly on generating investor return and spreading a vision of economic health and development that subordinates developing economies to the markets of long-dominant nations.

The vision and policies of the IMF and World Bank have exacerbated the anomic conditions already encountered by many postcolonial societies. These institutions claim to promote structural adjustments that will ease the social problems associated with harsh impoverishment, yet these policies often destabilize the economic structures of targeted economies. Rwanda illustrates this pattern. For instance, the currency devaluation encouraged by the World Bank precipitated a massive rise in inflation, escalating already growing poverty rates, especially in rural areas. The reduced value of the Rwandan franc benefited trading partners, but was disastrous for local farmers and exporters. Moreover, the mandated opening of publicly owned industries to private (and foreign) investment had similarly harmful consequences in Rwanda and other developing nations.

The push to open and expand exports from these countries can have devastating affects. Such was the case when the IMF and World Bank pushed Uganda, Ethiopia, and Vietnam to increase coffee production for the global coffee trade. This flooded the international market and fostered conditions that precipitated a crash of the coffee market and further devastated a fragile Rwandan economy. The currency devaluation mandated by the international financial institutions, along with a price cap on Rwandan coffee exports, aggravated the problems of an economy near collapse and led to higher poverty rates.

In Rwanda and elsewhere, IMF and World Bank mandates assumed that privately owned industries are more efficient and economically beneficial than their state-run counterparts are, despite the lack of evidence that this is the case. Realizing the benefits of privatization are primarily local elites and foreign investors, who can purchase ownership interest cheaply within established utility grids and the like. Investors can buy into an established infrastructure with a captive clientele at a relatively low investment cost, especially where currency reevaluations decrease the international value of a local monetary system. Such investment adversely affects developing economies since wealth and economic policy choices shift from local hands to Western institutions.

Structural adjustment policies that compel reductions in social program spending have similar ideological roots and social consequences. World Bank and IMF officials presume that lower social spending is economically beneficial, yet the reduction of spending on welfare, health care, education, and other elements of necessary infrastructural development drastically affects the population of developing countries, especially disempowered groups plagued by illness, poverty, and militia-based violence. The perpetuation and escalation of harsh economic inequality not only reduce the quality of life for those living in rural and urban areas, but also create more widespread social disorder. As noted, these conditions are highly criminogenic for individuals, groups (e.g., militias), and states.

Institutions that promote these programs, such as the World Bank and IMF, are aware of the depth of corruption and misuse of the funds they provide to targeted nations in the developing world. For example, in Rwanda the World Bank and IMF knew of the military uses of the grants and loans they provided to the government, but did little to compel a reorientation in spending. Although these institutions allocated no new monies to the Rwandan government, they could have cut off access to finances held in European banks, but did not do so. Their intelligence and NGO reports within Rwanda indicated that ethnic hostility between the Hutus and Tutsis had increased and genocidal rhetoric had become amplified. The World Bank eventually responded by suspending lending in early 1993, but military usages of international funds—specifically the financing of troop increases—had begun in 1989. The Bank's delay in responding to the Rwandan government's misuse of funds allowed a military infrastructure (hardware and personnel) to develop, which facilitated the 1994 genocide.

For scholars of state crime, we call attention to the role of international lending and development finance in establishing the economic relations and macro-level conditions that serve as catalysts for these types of state crimes. The growing literature in the field acknowledges a plurality of effects and influences, yet it has largely ignored the role of the World Bank and IMF in restructuring postcolonial social and economic structures in ways that promote or exacerbate anomic conditions and foster state crime. To better understand and explain how this occurs, students of state crime should focus analytical attention on structures of development finance, especially within postcolonial environments.

In our view, the direct manipulation of a state's economic processes and ownership structures violates core human rights standards, especially as embodied by the 1974 Declaration on the Establishment of a New International Economic Order (UNGA 3201/s-vii), the Convention on Economic, Social and Cultural Human Rights (2003), the Committee on Economic, Social, and Cultural Human Rights, the Maastricht Guidelines (1997), and the Norms on the Responsibilities of Transnational Corporations and Other Business Enterprises with regard to Human Rights Agreement (2003). In this light, the economic manipulations promoted by the World Bank and IMF look far more like neocolonial intervention strategies than philanthropic assistance to global neighbors in need. These manipulations constitute a forceful and direct resubordination of postcolonial economies to former colonial powers and markets. Though it could be argued that global economic reorganization in the postcolonial environment has resulted in the reestablishment of informal colonial relations, structural adjustment programs serve to formalize and crystallize these relationships.

Defenders of the World Bank and IMF suggest that developing nations voluntarily enter into agreements with these institutions and can choose whether to accept their policy recommendations and how to implement them. However, their compliance with IMF and World Bank demands are not purely or genuinely "voluntary," particularly given the nature of the contemporary global economy. The coercive conditions of transnational capitalism and the lingering effects of colonial environments leave many still-developing states with no real choice but to accept proffered development funds and their corollary conditions. States combating poverty and HIV/AIDS, while still attempting to build functional economic, educational, and transportation infrastructures, have significantly limited agency in their financial dealings. Where or how else can they gain access to needed markets? How else can they obtain necessary funds to address their pressing social and economic problems? Indigent states have few options for development aid or other forms of humanitarian assistance. The structures of the global economy, along with the domestic challenges they face, often push them into the arms of international lenders such as the World Bank and IMF.

Unfortunately, the World Bank and IMF are essentially unregulated institutions. The controls placed upon them are all self-imposed. This is a cause for significant concern given the criminogenic effects of the structural adjustment policies they impose on developing economies (see Friedrichs and Friedrichs, 2007, Friedrichs, 2004, Rothe, Muzzatti, and Mullins, 2006). Ironically, the World Bank and IMF are positioned to serve as strong controls or inhibitors of state-orchestrated crimes (see Ross, 2000a, 2000b). Given their extensive resources and ability to provide and direct funds to needy states, they could potentially act as institutions that promote greater justice. However, their prevailing policies and practices have the opposite influence; instead of facilitating justice, they promote conditions that push the leaders of targeted countries toward the commission of state crimes.

To remedy this situation and to serve as more effective agents of international control, the World Bank and IMF could tie their aid packages and lending behaviors directly to a nation's enforcement and honoring of human rights principles. This would require reconfiguring the typical operations of these institutions ideologically, but precedents do exist. For example, during the Carter administration, U.S. foreign policy and aid were structured to reward states that honored human rights issues. The World Bank and IMF could embrace similar measures, thereby bringing their powerful influence to bear in addressing human rights issues. They could also legitimate the idea that human rights should be justiciable conditions. We agree with An-Na'im's (2004: 106) assertion that "there was a time when civil and political rights too were nonjusticiable and nondeterminant, but they were made justiciable and sufficiently determinant through imaginative development of judicial mechanisms and remedies. The same can happen to economic, social, and cultural rights." The process of generating and enforcing human rights has unfolded slowly, but somewhat steadily throughout the 20th and 21st centuries. Hopefully, the general trend of the past 50 years will continue in terms of holding individuals, organizations, and states responsible for their violations of human rights, as well as in terms of expanding the umbrella of available protections into the economic sphere, particularly in regulating the institutions of international finance.

NOTES

1. For a more complete discussion of the typology, see Friedrichs (2004).
2. With falling coffee prices devastating farmers and local economies, the Gebeka project removing farmland formerly used for subsistent living, the mini-drought of 1989, the reduction in social services, and an increasingly impoverished population, the slide from food self-sufficiency to famine was rapid.

REFERENCES

Adebajo, Adekeye and Chandra Lekha Sriram (eds.)
2001 *Managing Armed Conflicts in the 21st Century*. London: Frank Cass.

An-Na'im, Abdullah A.
2004 "The Legal Protection of Human Rights in Africa: How to Do More with Less." A. Sarat and T. Kearns (eds.), *Human Rights: Concepts, Contests, Contingencies*. Ann Arbor: University of Michigan Press. 89–116.
2003 "Introduction: Expanding Legal Protection of Human Rights in African Contexts." A. An-Na'im (ed.), *Human Rights Under African Constitutions: Realizing the Promise for Ourselves*. Pittsburg: University of Pennsylvania Press: 1–28.

Barak, Gregg
2000 "Foreword." Jeffrey Ian Ross (ed.), *Varieties of State Crime and Its Control.* Monsey, NY: Criminal Justice Press: *i–ix.*
1991 *Crimes by the Capitalist State: An Introduction to State Criminality.* Albany: State University of New York Press.

Berry, John A. and Carol P.O. Berry
1999 *Genocide in Rwanda: A Collective Memory.* Washington, D.C.: Howard University Press.

Boyle, Elizabeth Heger and John W. Meyer
2002 "Modern Law as a Secular and Global Model: Implications for the Sociology of Law." Y. Dezalay and B.J. Garth (eds.), *Global Prescriptions: The Production, Exportation, and Importation of a New Legal Orthodoxy.* Ann Arbor, MI: University of Michigan Press: 65–95.

Chambliss, William
1995 "Commentary by William J. Chambliss." *Society of Social Problems Newsletter* 26,1: 9.
1989 "State Organized Crime." *Criminology* 27,2: 183–208.

Chang, Ha-Joon
2002 *Kicking Away the Ladder: Development Strategy in Historical Perspective.* London: Anthem Press.

Chossudousky, Michael
1995 "Rwanda, Somalie, ex Yougoslavie: Conflits armés, génocide économique et responsabilités des institutions de Bretton Woods." Banque, FMI, OMC: ça suffit, CADTM, Bruxelles.

Chossudousky, Michael and Pierre Galand
1996 *Le Génocide de 1994, L'usage de la dette extérieure du Rwanda (1990–1994). La responsabilité des bailleurs de fonds.* Ottawa et Bruxelles. At *globalresearch.ca/articles/CHO403F.html.*

Clohesy, William and Konstanz Kuraz
2000 "Realizing Rights: The Role of NGOs in Universalizing Human Rights." Published in Working Paper Volume, Fourth Biennial Conference, International Society for Third Sector Research, Dublin, Ireland.

Darrow, Mac
2003 *Between Light and Shadow: The World Bank, the International Monetary Fund and International Human Rights.* Oxford: Hart Publishing.

Epp, Charles. R.
1998 *The Rights Revolution: Lawyers, Activists, and Supreme Courts in Comparative Perspective.* Chicago: University of Chicago Press.

Falk, Peter
1993 *Global Visions: Beyond the New World Order.* Boston: South End Press.

Friedrichs, David
2004 "White-Collar Crime in a Globalized World." Presentation at Western Michigan University.

Friedrichs, David and Jessica Friedrichs
2007 "White-Collar Crime in a Postmodern, Globalized World." H.N. Pontell and G. Geis (eds.), *International Handbook of White-Collar and Corporate Crime.* New York: Springer: 163–184.

Hanssen, A.
1989 "Le Desenchantment de la coopération, Enquête au pays des mille coopérants." G. Prunier (ed.), *The Rwandan Crisis: History of a Genocide.* New York: Columbia University Press: 394.

International Monetary Fund (IMF)
1999 *The IMF's Enhanced Structural Adjustment Facility (ESAF): Is It Working?* Online. At *mf.org/external/pubs/ft/esaf/exr/index.htm.*

Kauzlarich, David and Ronald C. Kramer
1998 *Crimes of the American Nuclear State: At Home and Abroad.* Boston: Northeastern University Press.
1993 "State-Corporate Crime in the U.S. Nuclear Weapons Production Complex." *The Journal of Human Justice* 5,1: 1–26.

Kauzlarich, David, Rick A. Matthews, and W.J. Miller
2001 "Toward a Victimology of State Crime." *Critical Criminology: An International Journal* 10,3: 173–194.

Kauzlarich, David, Christopher Mullins, and Rick A. Matthews
2003 "A Complicity Continuum of State Crime." *Contemporary Justice Review* 6,3: 241–254.

Klug, Heinz
2005 "Transnational Human Rights: Exploring the Persistence and Globalization of Human Rights." *Annual Review of Law and Social Science* 1: 85–103.

Kramer, Ronald and Raymond Michalowski
1990 "Toward an Integrated Theory of State-Corporate Crime." Presented at the American Society of Criminology. Baltimore, MD.

Kramer, Ronald
1995 "Exploring State Criminality: The Invasion of Panama." *Journal of Criminal Justice and Popular Culture* 3,2: 43–52.

Maton, J.
1994 *Développement économique et social au Rwanda entre 1980 et 1993. Le dixième décile en face de l'apocalypse.* Université de Gand, Faculté de Sciences économiques: 43.

Michalowski, Raymond
1985 *Order, Law and Crime.* New York: Random House.

McCormick, James
2000 "Human Rights and the Clinton Administration: American Policy at the Dawn of a New Century." Robert Patman (ed.), *Universal Human Rights?* Basingstoke: Macmillan Press and New York: St. Martin's Press: 114–134.

Prunier, Gérard
1995 *The Rwandan Crisis: History of a Genocide.* New York: Columbia University Press.

Rajagopal, Balakrishnan
2003 *International Law from Below: Development, Social Movements, and Third World Resistance.* Cambridge: Cambridge University Press.

Ross, Jeffrey Ian
2000a "Introduction: Protecting Democracy by Controlling State Crime in Advanced Industrialized Countries." J. Ross (ed.), *Varieties of State Crime and Its Control.* Monsey, NY: Criminal Justice Press: 1–10.
2000b "What Have We Learned and What Is the Next Step?" J. Ross (ed.), *Varieties of State Crime and Its Control.* Monsey, NY: Criminal Justice Press: 199–206.
1995 *Controlling State Crime: An Introduction.* New York: Garland.

Ross, Jeffrey Ian, Gregg Barak, Jeff Ferrell, David Kauzlarich, Mark Hamm, David Friedrichs, Rick Matthews, Sharon Pickering, Mike Presdee, Peter Kraska, and V. Kappeler
1999 "The State of State Crime Research: A Commentary." *Humanity and Society* 23,3: 273–281.

Rothe, Dawn L. and David Friedrichs
2006 "The State of the Criminology of State Crime." *Social Justice* 33,1.

Rothe, Dawn and Christopher W. Mullins
2006 *The International Criminal Court: Symbolic Gestures and the Generation of Global Social Control.* Lanham, MD: Lexington Books.

Rothe, Dawn, Stephen Muzzatti, and Christopher W. Mullins
2006 "Crime on the High Seas: Crimes of Globalization and the Sinking of the Senegalese Ferry *Le Joola.*" *Critical Criminology* 14,2: 159–180.

Skogly, Sigrun I.
2001 *The Human Rights Obligations of the World Bank and the International Monetary Fund.* London: Cavendish Publishing.

Sutherland, Edwin
1949 *White Collar Crime.* New York: Holt, Rhinehart and Winston.
1939 "White Collar Criminality. Presidential Address to the American Society of Sociology." Reprinted 1940. *American Sociological Review* 5: 1–12.

Toussaint, Eric
2004 *Rwanda 10 Years on: Uncovering the Financiers of the Genocide.* At *www.redpepper.org.uk/May2004/x-May2004-Toussaint.html.*
1999 *Your Money or Your Life! Tyranny of Global Finance.* London. Pluto Press.

Tunnell, Kenneth
1993 *Political Crime in Contemporary America: A Critical Approach.* New York: Garland.

Treaties, Laws, and Resolutions Cited

1. United Nations General Assembly.
2. Universal Declaration of Human Rights 1948.
3. Convention on the Prevention and Punishment of the Crime of Genocide of 1948.
4. International Covenant on Civil and Political Rights of 1966.
5. The International Covenant on Social and Economic Rights of 1966.
6. Declaration of the Establishment of a New International Economic Order, 1974. Resolution 3201.
7. The Convention on the Elimination of All Forms of Discrimination against Women of 1981.
8. The Convention against Torture and Other Cruel, Inhuman, or Degrading Treatment or Punishment of 1984.
9. The Convention on the Rights of the Child of 1989.
10. The Maastricht Agreement 1997.
11. Committee on Economic, Social, and Cultural Human Rights, 2003.
12. Agreement by the Economic and Social Council, 2003.
13. The Norms on the Responsibilities of Transnational Corporations and Other Business Enterprises with Regard to Human Rights, 2003.

[25]

Murder in Juárez

Gender, Sexual Violence, and the Global Assembly Line

JESSICA LIVINGSTON

On July 7, 1995, seventeen-year-old Silvia Morales left for school and disappeared. Her body was found two months later. In February 1999 thirteen-year-old Irma Angelica Rosales was sent home from her factory job for having left her station. Later that day her body was found in a drainage canal. In September 2001 nineteen-year-old Luna Guadalupe, a student in business administration, disappeared on the way to a friend's house on a Saturday afternoon. The next month twenty-year-old Claudia González arrived to work four minutes late, and the doors of the *maquiladora*, or foreign-owned assembly plant, were locked. She never returned home. Both Luna and Claudia were found in November in a shallow grave with six other women—all eight women had been raped and strangled.[1]

Since 1993 murdered bodies of young women and girls have haunted Ciudad Juárez, the border town that lies across the Rio Grande from El Paso, Texas. By mid-2002 an estimated three hundred women had been murdered, and more women are missing. Rosa Linda Fregoso states:

> Mexican women have been brutally and systematically killed in Ciudad Juárez, Chihuahua. . . . Many [of the victims] have been tortured and sexually violated: raped, strangled or gagged. Mutilated, with nipples and breasts cut off, buttocks lacerated like cattle, or penetrated with objects.[2]

After being dumped in desert gullies or vacant lots, their decomposed bodies are often unidentifiable. Almost a third of the cases seem to follow a pattern suggesting they are the work of one or more serial killers. Most of these victims are young, slender women with long dark hair; they are also poor. These murders are the most extreme form of a general violence against women in the border city. In the first nine months of 1998 alone, women in Juárez reported eight hundred cases of rape and over nine thousand cases of violence, including rape, kidnapping, and domestic violence.[3]

Why have there been so many cases of mysogynic violence in the last decade in Juárez? Chandra Talpade Mohanty argues in *Women Workers and Capitalist Scripts: Ideologies of Domination, Common Interests, and the Politics of Solidarity* that because globalization has complicated class relations nationally and internationally, "issues of spatial economy . . . gain fundamental importance for feminist analysis." She defines these issues of spatial economy as "the manner by which capital utilizes particular space for differential production and the accumulation of capital and, in the process, transforms these spaces and peoples."[4] While ethnicity certainly plays a significant factor in selecting Juárez as a production site, once the factories are operating, gender plays a significant role in both obscuring and maintaining class relations in the new international division of labor.

Within the context of globalization, it is necessary to investigate not just the possible male perpetrators but also the export-processing zone and the city of Juárez itself. After recounting the story of the murdered women in Juárez as it is being reported by U.S. and British Commonwealth journalists, I will place these murders in their socioeconomic and ideological context in order to analyze the gendering of production, the gendering of violence, and the relationship between the two. The murders of the young women result from a displacement of economic frustration onto the bodies of the women who work in the *maquiladoras*. The construction of working women as "cheap labor" and disposable within the system makes it possible, and perhaps acceptable, to kill them with impunity.

BIG-CITY DREAMS: MIGRATING FROM THE COUNTRY TO THE CITY

Most of the newspaper articles about the murders of women in Juárez refer to the victims as *maquiladora* workers. Molly Moore reports that factories have "lured hundreds of thousands of women and girls from their confining homes and remote villages across Mexico, giving them greater financial and social independence than perhaps any other single phenomenon in recent Mexican history."[5] Although *maquiladoras* have operated in Mexico since 1965 under the Border Industrialization Program (BIP), the North American Free Trade Agreement (NAFTA) has helped to create 1.2 million jobs in Mexico since being implemented on January 1, 1994. Over one quarter of these jobs are in Ciudad Juárez.[6]

Alma Vucovich, president of the Mexican Congress' Committee on Sexual Equality, complains about the investigation of murders in Juárez, "Authorities haven't cared because the victims are women and they're poor, and many times they have no family in Juárez."[7] The *maquila* (another name for a *maquiladora*) workers usually come from small villages and rural areas, and move to

Juárez in search of work. Many of the women have worked in family economies, including working on a farm, taking in laundry, or making and selling tortillas. Others have worked for wages in agriculture or as domestics, and some have taken up *maquila* piecework before migrating to Juárez. Often a desire to escape the confines of poverty and domesticity motivates their decision to move to Juárez. Their migration creates "a new phenomenon of mobile, independent—and vulnerable—working women" living in the city.[8]

Many of these migrant women move to Juárez, a city on the U.S.-Mexico border known for its *maquiladoras*, drug cartel, and pollution. Many of the residents of Juárez live on the outskirts of the city in *colonias*, or shantytowns, in makeshift houses constructed from discarded wooden pallets, cardboard boxes, or cement, without running water or telephones. Some landlords illegally provide electricity by tapping into city lines, which often causes power surges that burn appliances. Each day factory workers have to walk through the unlit dirt roads to the company buses that transport them to work. Some women pool their resources and live together, and other women move in with relatives or friends of their family.[9]

Despite the seeming harshness of life in Juárez, the young women keep coming at the rate of forty to sixty thousand a year. They seek jobs in the *maquiladoras*, which pay higher wages than elsewhere in Mexico. Women already living in Juárez also work because the income from the men in the household is insufficient to support the family.

The chance to have an independent social life also attracts many young women to the city and to work in the *maquiladoras*. They come because, like Irma Angelica Rosales, they dream of adventures in the city and want to escape "the tedium that enveloped daily life" in rural Mexico.[10] Leslie Salzinger, a sociologist who worked in a *maquiladora* in Juárez, reports that many girls have told her that "they take *maquila* jobs not for survival but for independence: to buy clothes with their own money and to get out of their houses and socialize."[11] Many young women go out with their coworkers to dance clubs and women-only clubs that feature male dancers. Esther Chavez, director of Casa Amiga, the city's only shelter for abused women, says that *maquila* workers go to the dance clubs despite the crime and violence "to forget the mechanical, dehumanizing work they do."[12]

MAQUILADORAS AND LABOR EXPLOITATION: REGULATING THE LIVES OF FEMALE EMPLOYEES

The *maquiladoras* primarily employ young women. The managers claim that women are better suited to factory work because of their manual dexterity and their ability to tolerate tedious and repetitive work. Despite these "natural abilities," the *maquiladoras* use discriminatory job classifications to hire women for "unskilled" positions and men for "skilled" labor.[13]

In addition to paying the female workers cheaply for long hours, Debbie Nathan reports that the *maquiladoras* also monitor their female employees more closely than male employees. Before hiring new female employees, managers require medical exams and often inquire about their employees' sexual activities. Pregnancy tests are routinely administered. Mexican law requires social security coverage of pregnant women during the third trimester, and the *maquiladoras* would have to pay. Therefore, any woman who is pregnant is dismissed or harassed until she quits. Birth control pills are plentiful at the factories while other health services are scarce. In addition to requiring pregnancy tests, some supervisors even inspect employees' sanitary napkins to ensure that they are not pregnant.[14]

In some *maquiladoras* a woman's appearance receives more attention than her work skills. Supervisors often hire based on a potential employee's attractiveness, and they say, "Girls, utilize your sexuality."[15] Often employees wear miniskirts, high heels, and makeup to work, especially on Fridays when the company buses drop off many of the workers after their shifts at the dance clubs. Supervisors often stalk the assembly lines, playing favorites and asking for dates. The *maquiladoras* also encourage workers to participate in annual industry-wide "Señorita *Maquiladora*" beauty contests. Dance clubs host "Most Daring Bra" and "Wet String Bikini" contests with cash prizes that are more than an entire week's wages.[16]

Supporters of industrialization say that the industrial park and the *maquiladoras* within symbolize modernization for Mexico. One *maquiladora* manager compared globalization to the nineteenth-century industrial revolution, saying: "We are again transforming the world by bringing progress to all people, but especially to women."[17] Yet, working conditions in the *maquiladoras* have deteriorated with NAFTA, and existing labor laws are not enforced.[18] An average starting wage is thirty-five dollars a week.[19] *Maquiladoras* discourage union organizing with dismissals and threats of blacklisting or moving the factory.[20] Often workers' only recourse is to quit and look for a new job, but employees are easily replaced, and new jobs are usually not much better. Because factories consider women to be short-term employees, there is no investment in a stable workforce.

"IF SHE WASN'T A BAD GIRL": THE RESPONSE OF MEXICAN AUTHORITIES

When young women have disappeared, police have frequently suggested to family members that the missing woman left with a boyfriend or have suggested that the woman was at fault, saying, "If she wasn't a bad girl, then why did she leave?" State authorities have assumed that some of the victims were prostitutes and moved slowly on investigations. In 1995, the state assistant attorney general blamed the murders on the "double life" that many young women lead—working by day and going out at night, or even taking up prostitution.[21]

Nathan reports that the Juárez mayor issued statements such as "Do you know where your daughter is tonight?" Some Juárez residents also adopted this attitude, believing that only prostitutes and factory women were at risk of being murdered. Mexican feminists accused the first state appointed prosecutor for the women's murders, Suly Ponce, as being more interested in the victims' reputation than in solving the crimes. Ponce herself admits to investigating the victims' backgrounds and stated, "We were studying the entire family [of the victims] and we couldn't reach any conclusions because many of them were good workers, many of them were students—good girls, clean girls."[22]

Fregoso states:

> [In 1998 the National Commission for Human Rights] issued a report charging gross irregularities and general negligence in state investigations, including the misidentification of corpses, failure to obtain expert tests on forensic evidence, failure to conduct autopsies or obtain semen analysis . . . failure to file written reports, [and] incompetence in keeping records of the rising tide of women murders.[23]

Ponce was hired in late 1998 after this report was issued. On her first visit to a crime scene, she witnessed photographers moving the body, police trampling evidence with footprints and tire tracks, and reporters and bystanders littering the scene with cigarette butts and empty soda cans. Ponce began cordoning off crime scenes, but as recently as November 2001 family members of victims have searched the areas and found evidence, often victims' clothing, where bodies were located after the police have supposedly combed the area.[24]

Under governmental pressure to solve the murders, police have hurriedly arrested suspects and wrapped up cases, only to have the killings to continue.[25] Originally, their investigations primarily focused on one man—Egyptian-born chemist Sharif Abdel Latif Sharif. Arrested in 1995 and convicted for one murder, Sharif is now in jail, but the killings continue.[26] In 1996 the police arrested members from a gang, the Rebels, accusing them of committing murders under Sharif's orders. While on trial, the gang members claimed they were tortured while in custody and showed evidence of physical abuse. In 1999 a fourteen-year-old girl survived after being raped and left for dead in the desert. She identified her bus driver as the assailant. Again authorities attempted to link the murders to Sharif, arresting a ring of bus drivers and claiming that Sharif paid them twelve hundred dollars to kill two women a month to make him look innocent.[27]

Mexican authorities have also considered theories about a serial killer, especially since the murders appear to follow a pattern. Former FBI criminal profiling expert Robert K. Ressler said in 1998 that several serial killers might be involved but that many of the murders appeared to be random crimes. In March 1999, an FBI team aiding Mexican authorities also said the murders do not appear to be related.[28]

Bus drivers were arrested in November 2001 for several murders. Mario Escobedo, the lawyer of one of the drivers, put together a solid defense, "claiming that the confessions were induced by torture and were internally contradictory." On the night of February 5, 2002, police officers in unmarked vehicles pursued Escobedo, who crashed his car before the police shot and killed him. The police claim that they thought they were following a "dangerous fugitive," who shot at them first.[29]

Lourdes Portillo made a documentary investigating the murders and found a "web of complicity" between police and government officials.[30] Feminist organizations that demanded better investigations into the murders have recently come under attack in ads published in local newspapers accusing them of "profiting from the pain" of victims and their families. The ads are "signed by shadowy civic groups," which the women's groups believe are a front for the state government.[31] While police investigations have been inept at best and corrupt at worst, feminist organizations in Juárez believe that a "macho backlash" is responsible for the murders. According to Esther Chavez, this "macho backlash" might be a reaction against the *maquiladoras* for employing so many female workers.[32] It is this connection between the *maquiladoras*, sexuality, and violence that I now want to discuss.

NEGOTIATING BORDERS IN JUÁREZ: RURAL, URBAN, AND NATIONAL

In her work on globalization, Saskia Sassen emphasizes the importance of place and production in an analysis of economic globalization: "Many of the resources necessary for global economic activities are not hypermobile and are, indeed, deeply embedded in place, notably places such as global cities and export processing zones." She argues that globalization includes a "dynamic of dispersal and of centralization."[33] Global capitalism requires the centralization of labor in global cities in the third and first worlds. Structural adjustment policies in Mexico have forced migrations of laborers from rural areas to export processing zones.

After a 1982 debt crisis, Mexico implemented structural adjustment programs to stimulate the economy, including agricultural reforms in the late 1980s and 1990s. Previously, the Mexican government had supported agrarian programs that subsidized resources for farmers. However, structural reforms "based on the deregulation of markets, privatization of state enterprises, and trade liberalization" have increased unemployment in rural areas, causing high levels of male migration to the United States.[34]

In her study of the gendered economic history of rural households, María de los Angeles Crummett analyzes how these structural adjustments affected women's economic roles. She states that women left behind to maintain land rights had to take greater economic responsibility for the household and engage in income-earning activities, such as *maquila* piecework. Daughters, who also assist with income-earning activities, did not necessarily remain in the household. Rather, once in their twenties, these daughters form the largest group of female migrants moving from the subsistence sector to urban areas.[35] Because industry policy maintains low wages and causes a high turnover rate, the *maquiladoras* continually have to recruit young female workers from rural areas and have even begun hiring older women with greater familial obligations as well.[36]

Despite the claim that these export-processing zones would stimulate economic growth in Mexico, the economy has been frustrated in the past few decades. Male unemployment has been particularly high, and workingmen are often underemployed. NAFTA promised jobs and prosperity, but in 1995 Mexico lost more than a million jobs, and the peso devaluation cut the standard of living in half for most workers. While real wages decrease, the cost of living continues to rise. Over the past twenty years, income of Mexican workers has fallen to twenty-five percent of its previous purchasing power.[37]

While Mexico has export processing zones along the border and now even in its interior, Juárez remains the largest. Particularly successful at recruiting multinational corporations, Juárez has developed industrially on a larger and more rapid scale than other cities.[38] In particular, it has attracted many U.S. corporations; historian Emma Pérez reports that 80 percent of the *maquiladoras* in Juárez are U.S.-owned.[39] Because Juárez is a border city, American managers can live in El Paso and commute across the bridge to work. Juárez residents can see the El Paso skyline—a poor city by American standards but wealthy in comparison to Juárez. Living on the border next to the United States makes costs higher while wages remain low. The poverty of the *colonias* and the desolation of the desert surround the industrial park in Juárez.

While some call Juárez the gateway to U.S. prosperity, in actuality, it is the U.S. gateway to cheap labor. Juárez and other border cities operate as the first stage of migration for many immigrants, which benefits U.S. businesses and residents who hire them.[40] Multinational corporations who relocate their factories to Juárez also profit tremendously from the cheap labor, and this labor pool is often the most important factor in the decision to relocate labor-intensive industries to these export processing zones.[41] However, Mexicans resent both the multinationals who profit and the women who work for them.

Sociologist Pablo Vila says that margins connote "pollution and endangerment," and that Mexico's northern border is a particularly symbolic margin because it is where Mexico meets "the country that for many years was considered the historical enemy, the country that, according to Mexican narrative, stole half of the national territories." He claims that *maquiladora* workers, like prostitutes who service foreign men, represent "the openness of the border to the needs of the 'other,'" which threatens Mexico's sovereignty. One particular woman interviewed by Vila, Margarita, views *maquila* work as more corrupt than prostitution, "The *maquilas* are purely pinche puteadero [fucking prostitution], purely pinche corruption. I think that a chingada [fucking] cantina is cleaner than *maquilas*."[42] In "Globalizing Social Violence: Race, Gender, and the Spatial Politics of Crisis," Tryon P. Woods claims, "The *maquiladoras*, representing the commodity exchange relationship of capitalism, come to symbolize prostitution."[43] In this association between *maquiladora* workers and corruption, the women bear the resentment for the United States once again infiltrating Mexico's borders.

"MASCULINE AUTHORITY AND OWNERSHIP": IMPUNITY IN CASES OF SEXUAL VIOLENCE

In their study of prostitution in Tijuana, Debra A. Castillo, María Gudelia Rangel Gómez, and Bonnie Delgado interviewed a woman who, prior to engaging in prostitution, had been raped by her employer. The researchers claim this is a "more violent form of the many stories of sexual harassment in the workplace." They state that the women interviewees "describe a societal structure based on male dominance in the workplace and male rights to women who are perceived as stepping out of their traditional roles, whether by remaining unattached to a male protector or by attempting to enter the realm of paid labor."[44] In fact, the Chihuahua legislature had attempted to enact a law that reduced the minimum sentencing for rape from four years to one year if the defendant could prove that the victim had provoked the attack. Only under threat of intervention from Mexico's Congress did the Chihuahua legislature overturn the law in September 2001.[45]

Mexico's judicial system provides little recourse for women who are victims of male violence, particularly if it is domestic. Fregoso states: "Mexico's regulatory and judicial system, strengthened by traditional cultural values, supports 'the idea of masculine authority and ownership' over the lives of women and grants males impunity in the exercise of violence against women."[46] A woman in Mexico cannot file domestic abuse charges unless her injuries take longer than fifteen days to heal. The courts rarely interfere in the private domestic sphere. Maria Luisa Carsoli was killed by her husband Ricardo Medina while she was at Casa Amiga, the only shelter for abused women in Ciudad Juárez. Before he murdered his wife, he had even boasted that he would not be held accountable by the justice system. Even though eyewitnesses have identified him as the killer, he is not in jail.[47] The *maquiladoras* draw on local patriarchal practices, discourse, and tolerance of sexual violence against women, and thus violence against women has intensified.

THE CONSTRUCTION OF CHEAP LABOR: WOMEN WORKING IN THE *MAQUILADORAS*

Nathan reports that "many coalition activists attribute high sexual assault statistics to gender inequality, and some mention the maquila industry's complicity in fostering it."[48] The *maquilas* are more than complicit in maintaining gender inequality; they are invested in it. Susan Tiano states: "For capitalism to benefit maximally from women's participation in both the capitalistic and domestic modes of production, the gender-based division of labor and the patriarchal relations that support it must be maintained."[49] Central to this gender-based division of labor is the construction of women as cheap labor. Freeman argues that third-world women are neither "naturally" docile nor cheap labor to be tapped. Rather, the multinational corporations "actually create ideal workers" for certain types of production.[50] The *maquiladoras* in Juárez engage in complex negotiations with ideologies of gender to construct and maintain this category of cheap labor.

Women working in the *maquila* industry challenge the ideal of Mexican womanhood, "which holds women to an ideal of femininity symbolized by the Virgin of Guadalupe, the virgin mother."[51] According to this ideology, Mexican women have been expected to center their lives on their children and not engage in waged employment. However, motherhood is being reformulated to include economic support of children as a responsibility. While women are not choosing between the identities of mother and worker but combining them, many still hold motherhood (without waged work) as the ideal. Thus, they feel ambivalent about their roles as wageworkers, which helps to support the gender division of labor.[52]

However, the factories do not want workers to also be mothers because they do not want to pay maternity benefits and because "a child implies a lowering of productivity."[53] By refusing to hire pregnant women and often harassing women who become pregnant to quit, they are discouraging women from performing their traditional roles as mothers. Yet, at the same time, the factories do not want their female employees to assume an identity as permanent workers. Central to this construction of a female workforce is the notion that these laborers are temporary, which justifies their low wages. Factories justify not training female employees for skilled tasks because they are imagined to be short-term workers who will eventually quit to have a family. In a *maquiladora* in Juárez, Melissa W. Wright observes that "in order to preserve the representation of Mexican women as the cheap opposition who outlined the limits of masculine value, [the managers] did not train their new female employees sufficiently for their jobs."[54] Thus, factories use the potential role of motherhood to devalue women's worth as workers while maximizing productivity.

However, if motherhood is not used to distinguish female from male workers, women might begin to expect opportunities for training and advancement equal to men. Thus, the factories must differentiate the women in some way. By encouraging female employees to dress fashionably, to participate in beauty contests, and to go dancing in the clubs, managers are able to feminize, sexualize, and trivialize them as workers. Not only do these sexualized practices distinguish female from male workers, but they also encourage women to become consumers and purchase clothing, cosmetics, jewelry, and entertainment. Consumerism is presented as an appropriately feminine role as opposed to production.

In contrast to the sexualized atmosphere of the *maquiladoras*, the traditional ideology of femininity requires chastity, particularly of young, unmarried women. The Virgin of Guadalupe's "monstrous double" is Malintzin, conquistador Hernan Cortez's Indian mistress and interpreter. Malintzin also has additional names, including La Chingada, which "refers to a woman who is both 'fucked over,' that is, taken advantage of, and one who is literally, 'fucked,' or entered sexually."[55] During the 1980s several scholars, including Maria Patricia Fernandez-Kelly, Gay Young, Annette Fuentes, and Barbara Ehrenreich, commented on the stigma attached to women working in the *maquiladoras*.[56] More recently Wright has described the "managerial narrative of the female Mexican employee," which connects women's dress with prostitution. She states that in her interviews, the "message that you cannot tell the difference between a prostitute and a female *maquiladora* worker was common."[57] *Maquila* managers are complicit with the narrative that equates factory work and prostitution; and they benefit from this connotation, which characterizes not just female labor but female workers themselves as worthless and disposable.

FUELING RESENTMENT: MEN WORKING IN THE *MAQUILADORAS*

Being the breadwinner is a central component of patriarchal manhood. However, unemployment and low wages compromise this masculinity. Furthermore, global capitalism undermines men as workers by defining women as the ideal workers. When rapid growth led to labor shortages in the 1980s, *maquiladoras* began employing more men to work in the assembly lines. Estimates of the current number of male workers in the *maquiladoras* range from 35 to 50 percent.[58] Despite or because men are working in the *maquiladoras*, they perceive their masculinity as threatened. The *maquiladoras* are the national and patriarchal extension of the United States into Mexico; in these spaces Mexican masculinity is considered inferior to American masculinity.[59]

While assembly line jobs are no longer exclusively female, the popular narrative still speaks as if they are in order to maintain the category of cheap labor. The factories make no pretense of a family wage, and they pay men the same low wages as women. Thus Salzinger argues that the Mexican and American managers are:

> reluctant to diverge from the public framework that defines women as appropriate maquila workers, even in the face of their overwhelmingly male workforce. . . . Faced with the choice between questioning maquila pay practices or the manliness of maquila workers, managers choose to question their subordinates.[60]

Salzinger describes two very different work environments at plants in Juárez where the experiences for men differ, but in both she notes, the "amount of work dedicated to the creation of appropriately gendered workers."[61] In the type of *maquiladora* more typically known, the assembly line, is predominantly female, and the physically-segregated men are standing rather than sitting. Sometimes different colored smocks also differentiate between male and female workers. Discriminatory classifications of jobs into categories of "light" tasks and heavier work also help to maintain gender difference. Supervisors interact and flirt with the women workers, who are objectified. The women workers and the supervisors ignore the men working on the assembly line. In this atmosphere, class and gender intertwine, stripping the male workers of their masculinity.[62] When disciplined, the male workers have to work among the women, further feminizing them. It is likely that the men in these plants find their work both demeaning and emasculating.

In an auto parts assembly plant, the managers, who claim a preference for female workers, are unable to attract enough women workers, making men the majority. This plant focuses on finding rather than making good workers, and thus the managerial presence on the floor is conspicuously absent. Men and women wear the same color smocks and frequently interact with each other. In this managerial absence, men constitute masculinity through "activity and aggressiveness vis-à-vis women workers—both in the sphere of sexuality and the sphere of work." While the women construct a femininity that allows them to be both sexually receptive and capable workers, the men sexualize the women through catcalling and disparaging their ability to do the work. This aggressiveness seems rooted in a resentment of the presence of the women workers who transform what would otherwise be to them a masculine atmosphere. Through their sexual aggressiveness, the male workers attempt to put women in their (traditional) place.[63]

RESTRUCTURING OF LABOR: THE EFFECTS ON RELATIONSHIPS BETWEEN MEN AND WOMEN

Although limited, the restructuring of the labor market does contain possibilities for improving women's autonomy and empowerment.[64] Only a few decades ago, women could not socialize with men unchaperoned, and their parents often selected their marriage partners. However, the discourse on the "new *maquila* woman" defines unchaperoned socializing between young men and women at work and in the dance halls as appropriate.[65] Through economic contribution to their household, women have more say over budgeting and domestic decisions. Some women also succeed in requesting help from men in domestic chores.[66] A growing number of working women head their own household; 20 to 30 percent of women workers were household heads by 1984.[67] In addition, women also participate more in the public sphere.[68]

However, women's participation in the public sphere makes them more visible, whether going to work, to the store, or to bars. The presence of so many female factory workers has altered the city. As Chavez states, "Women are occupying the space of men in a culture of absolute dominance of men over women. This has to provoke misogyny."[69] This misogyny motivates a macho backlash, often expressed through violence.

Although the economic contributions of wives and daughters to the household are essential, women are commonly perceived as competitors for jobs. Even though global capitalism relies upon and reinforces patriarchy, men feel threatened when their wives and daughters earn more money. Fernandez-Kelly says that it is assumed that as women spend more time working in the factories, men will have to spend more time helping with domestic work, "with deleterious effects upon their sense of manhood."[70] Sassen notes that women "gain greater personal autonomy and independence while men lose ground."[71]

However, women and men in Juárez most likely could adjust to restructuring of the labor market if it did not undermine men as workers by constructing women in the workplace as cheap labor. Fuentes and Ehrenreich cite "male resentment and hostility" as a factor in the stigmatization of *maquiladora* women; they are also factors in the increased violence against women.[72] Currently, Juárez has the highest rate of domestic violence in Mexico, and it has increased dramatically since 1993.[73] If this male resentment and hostility was not tolerated by Mexican authorities, and if it could also be reduced with more egalitarian and better-paying working conditions, perhaps the murdering of women in Juárez would also cease.

RETURNING TO THE SCENE OF THE CRIME

Although the police investigations have been handled poorly, forensic evidence alone will neither solve nor stop these murders. By analyzing the crime scene, one can deduce that the sexualized murder suggests anger at the increasing sexual independence of young women in Mexico. The mutilated breasts suggest anger at women's use of their bodies for more than mothering and nurturing. The victims are primarily working women, suggesting resentment at women's increasing economic independence. Abandonment of their bodies in the desert like garbage reveals that these women are considered cheap and disposable. What is not apparent at the crime scene is the class hierarchy—embedded in global capitalism and expressed through gender—that plays an integral part in these murders.

Economic restructuring in the last two decades has created a new international division of labor that particularly exploits women in third world countries. Necessary to this division has been the construction of female labor as cheap and disposable when, paradoxically, global capitalism depends upon these women to assemble its commodities. While multinational corporations profit from the *maquiladoras* in Juárez, the murdered women and their families bear the cost of global capitalism.

NOTES

1. Paul de la Garza, "Series of Slayings Baffles City on Mexican Border" (Morales murder), *Arizona Republic*, November 27, 1998, in LexisNexis: News: 2 (database on-

line), available from Reed Elsevier Publishers, Dayton, Ohio; Sam Dillon, "Feminist stokes outcry at brutal string of killings" (Rosales murder), *The Gazette* (Montreal), March 1, 1999, B1 in LexisNexis: News: 2; Jo Tuckman, "Women: Deadly Frontier" (Guadalupe murder), *The Guardian*, March 25, 2002, G2, in LexisNexis: News: parag. 4 and 11; and Kris Axtman, "Border Mystery: 274 Murders in Nine Years" (Gonzalez murder), *Christian Science Monitor*, May 2, 2002, in LexisNexis: News: parag. 31.

2. Rosa Linda Fregoso, "Voices Without Echo: The Global Gendered Apartheid," *Emergences*, 10:1 (2000): 137.

3. Tuckman, "Women: Deadly Frontier" (murder total), parag. 1; Molly Moore, "Young Women Follow Journeys of Hope to Factories—and Then to Violence; Bright Lights, Dark City," *The Washington Post*, June 25, 2000, final ed., A01, in LexisNexis: News: 3; Tuckman, "Women: Deadly Frontier" (serial killer theory), parag. 1; Mary Beth Sheridan, "The Death that Haunts Juárez," *Los Angeles Times*, May 12, 1999, home ed., A1, in LexisNexis: News: 2; and Ricardo Sandoval, "Serial Killings Haunting Mexico; 120 Young Women Slain Since 1993" (statistics of violence), *Times-Picayune* (New Orleans), November 21, 1998, A1, in LexisNexis: News: 2.

4. Chandra Talpade Mohanty, "Women Workers and Capitalist Scripts: Ideologies of Domination, Common Interests, and the Politics of Solidarity," *Feminist Genealogies, Colonial Legacies, Democratic Futures*, ed. M. Jacqui Alexander and Chandra Talpade Mohanty (New York: Routledge, 1997), 5.

5. Moore, "Young Women Follow Journeys of Hope," 6.

6. Moore, "Young Women Follow Journeys of Hope," 2.

7. Almoa Vucovich quoted in Sheridan, "The Death that Haunts Juarez," 2.

8. For Mexican women's work histories see Norma Iglesias Prieto, *Beautiful Flowers of the Maquiladora: Life Histories of Women Workers in Tijuana*, trans. Michael Stone with Gabrielle Winkler (Austin: University of Texas Press, 1997): 46–73. Also see María de los Angeles Crummett, "A Gendered Economic History of Rural Households: Calvillo, Aguascalientes, Mexico, 1982–1991," *Frontiers: A Journal of Women's Studies* 22:1 (2001): 105–25; and Moore, "Young Women Follow Journeys of Hope," 3.

9. Moore, "Young Women Follow Journeys of Hope," 6.

10. Moore, "Young Women Follow Journeys of Hope," 4.

11. Leslie Salzinger quoted in Debbie Nathan, "Death Comes to the *Maquilas*: a Border Story," *Nation*, January 13, 1997, in Infotrac Web: Expanded Academic: parag. 7 (database online), available from Thomson Corp., Stamford, Conn.

12. Esther Chavez quoted in Mark Stevenson, "American Prosperity Trickles Over Border; Signs of U.S. Business Influence Abound in Fast-Growing Juárez," *Arizona Republic*, September 26, 1999, A34, in LexisNexis: News: 4.

13. Nathan, "Death Comes to the *Maquilas*," parag. 11.

14. Nathan, "Death Comes to the *Maquilas*," parag. 10.

15. Prieto, *Beautiful Flowers of the Maquiladora*, 76.

16. Nathan, "Death Comes to the *Maquilas*," parag. 12–14.

17. María Patricia Fernández-Kelly, *For We Are Sold, I and My People: Women and Industry in Mexico's Frontier* (Albany: State University of New York Press, 1983), 134.

18. Jim Sessions, "Cross-Border Blues," *Forum for Applied Research and Public Policy*, 14:1 (1999): 58, in InfoTrac Web: Expanded Academic: parag. 2 and 51.

19. Stevenson, "American Prosperity Trickles Over Border," 1.

20. Prieto, *Beautiful Flowers of the Maquiladora*, 96.

21. de la Garza, "Series of Slayings Baffles City on Mexican Border," 2; Sheridan, "The Death that Haunts Juarez," 5; and Howard La Franchi, "Girls Who Find New Roles in Mexico Also Face Danger," *Christian Science Monitor*, June 4, 1997, in Ebscohost: Expanded Academic Premier: 2, (database online), available from EBSCO Publishing, Ipswich, Mass.

22. Debbie Nathan, "Work, Sex, and Danger in Ciudad Juárez," *North American Congress on Latin America Report on the Americas* 33:3 (1999): 24, in Infotrac Web: Expanded Academic: parag. 10; Tuckman, "Women: Deadly Frontier," parag. 11; Tuckman, "Murder Case Solved," 1; and Moore, "Young Women Follow Journeys of Hope to Factories," 4.

23. Fregoso, "Voices Without Echo," 138.

24. Moore, "Young Women Follow Journeys of Hope to Factories," 3; and "Brutal Juárez Slayings Demand Investigation," *Albuquerque Journal*, March 1, 2002: A14, in LexisNexis: News.

25. In Juárez the National Action Party (PAN) came to power in 1992. The previous long-ruling party, the Institutional Revolutionary Party (PRI), was quick to charge PAN's inability to protect the women in the city. Thus the city faced pressure to catch the supposed serial killer after the elections (Nathan, "Work, Sex and Danger," parag. 7).

26. Ellen Nieves reports that although Sharif's murder conviction was overturned in 2000 due to false evidence, he remains in custody pending further appeals (Ellen Nieves, "To Work and Die in Juárez," *Mother Jones*, May/June 2002: 54).

27. Sheridan, "The Death that Haunts Juárez," 5.

28. Sheridan, "The Death that Haunts Juárez," 4; and Nieves, "To Work and Die in Juárez," 54.

29. Tuckman, "Women: Deadly Frontier," parag. 2.

30. Edward Guthmann, "The Disappeared; Lourdes Portillo's Wrenching Documentary on the Killings of Young Mexican Women in Juárez Exposes Government Incompetence," *San Francisco Chronicle*, August 17, 2002: D1, in LexisNexis: News: parag. 5.

31. "Women's Groups Pressing for Investigation of Border Murders Complain of Official Attacks," *Associated Press State & Local Wire*, January 23, 2002, in LexisNexis: News: parag. 3.

32. Sam Dillon, "Rape and Murder Stalk Women in Northern Mexico," *New York*

Times, April 18, 1998, A3, in LexisNexis: News: 1. Sheridan, "The Death that Haunts Juarez," 5.

33. Saskia Sassen, "The Global City: Strategic Site/New Frontier," *American Studies* 41:2/3 (2000): 79–80.

34. Crummet, "A Gendered Economic History of Rural Households," 105–6.

35. Crummet, "A Gendered Economic History of Rural Households," 120.

36. Robert D. Manning and Anita Christina Butera, "Global Restructuring and U.S.-Mexican Economic Integration: Rhetoric and Reality of Mexican Immigration Five Years after NAFTA," *American Studies* 41:2/3 (2000): 18.

37. David Bacon, "We Are Not at the End of History," *Communication for a Sustainable Future: Labor Research and Action Project Discussion Archive*, October 29, 2001, available from the World Wide Web: http://csf.colorad.edu/forums/labor-rap/current-discussion/msg00814.html (sec. 4–5).

38. Susan Tiano, *Patriarchy on the Line: Labor, Gender and Ideology in the Mexican Maquila Industry* (Philadelphia: Temple University Press, 1994), 7.

39. Emma Perez quoted in Nieves, "To Work and Die in Juárez," 55.

40. Women who have worked in the *maquiladoras* in Juárez often cross the border in search of work as domestics or nannies in El Paso. While wages for such jobs are higher than in Juárez, they can be as low as fifty dollars a week plus room and board. Grace Chang argues that structural adjustment programs in connection with the dismantling of social services in the U.S. "force migrant women into low-wage labor in the U.S." (Grace Chang, *Disposable Domestics: Immigrant Women Workers in the Global Economy* [Cambridge: South End Press, 2000], 125). Sassen calls these cross-border migrations "counter-geographies of globalization," which are also part of the dynamic of centralization (Saskia Sassen, "Women's Burden: Counter-Geographies of Globalization and the Feminization of Survival," *Journal of International Affairs* 53:2 [2000]: 503, in Ebscohost: Academic Search Premier: parag. 1 and 2).

41. Carla Freeman, *High Tech and High Heels in the Global Economy: Women, Work, and Pink-Collar Industries in the Caribbean* (Durham: Duke University Press, 2000), 104.

42. Pablo Vila quoted in Nathan, "Work, Sex, and Danger," parag. 24, 26, and 27. Vila spent more than six years interviewing residents in the El Paso-Ciudad Juárez area beginning in the early 1990s.

43. Tryon P. Woods, "Globalizing Social Violence: Race, Gender, and the Spatial Politics of Crisis," *American Studies* 42:1 (2002): 142.

44. Debra A. Castillo, María Gudelia Rangel Gómez, and Bonnie Delagado, "Border Lives: Prostitute Women in Tijuana," *Signs* 24:2 (1999): 404.

45. Julie Watson, "Mexican Lawmakers Revoke Law Reducing Penalties for Rapists 'Provoked' by Women," *The Associated Press State and Local Wire*, September 19, 2001, in LexisNexis: News. parag. 2 and 5.

46. Fregoso, "Voices Without Echo,"143.

47. "Murders of 'Invisible Women' Grow at Mexican Border," *New Zealand Press Association*, March 5, 2002, in LexisNexis: News. parag. 21–22.

48. Nathan, "Death Comes to the *Maquilas*," parag. 23.

49. Tiano, *Patriarchy on the Line*, 44.

50. Freeman, *High Tech and High Heels*, 103.

51. Susan Tiano and Carolina Ladino, "Dating, Mating, and Motherhood: Identity Construction Among Mexican Maquila Workers," *Environment and Planning A* 31:2 (1999): 307.

52. Tiano, *Patriarchy on the Line*, 44.

53. Prieto, *Beautiful Flowers of the Maquiladora*, 39.

54. Melissa W. Wright, "The Politics of Relocation: Gender, Nationality, and Value in a Mexican Maquiladora," *Environment and Planning A* 31:9 (1999): 1608.

55. Nathan, "Work, Sex, and Danger," parag. 28.

56. Fernandez-Kelly, *For We Are Sold*, 135; Gay Young, "Gender Identification and Working-Class Solidarity among Maquila Workers in Ciudad Juárez: Stereotypes and Realities," *Women on the U.S.-Mexico Border: Responses to Change*, ed. Vicki L. Ruiz and Susan Tiano (Boston: Allen and Unwin, 1987): 110; and Annette Fuentes and Barbara Ehrenreich, *Women in the Global Factory* (Boston: South End Press, 1983), 33.

57. Melissa Wright, " 'Maquiladora Mestizas' and a Feminist Border Politics: Revisiting Anzaldúa," *Hypatia*, 13:3 (1998): 114, in Infotrac Web: Expanded Academic: parag. 19-21.

58. Tiano and Ladino provide the lower estimate and Leslie Salzinger the higher estimate. See Tiano and Ladino, "Dating, Mating, and Motherhood," 309 and Leslie Salzinger, "From High Heels to Swathed Bodies: Gendered Meanings Under Production in Mexico's Export Processing Industry," *Feminist Studies* 23:3 (1997): 549, in InfoTrac Web: Expanded Academic: parag. 6.

59. Wright states that "when an American and Mexican employee share the same title, such as the rank of production supervisor, the American supervisor receives, at a minimum, one third more in wages and also supervises the Mexican supervisor (Wright, "The Politics of Relocation," 1606).

60. Salzinger, "From High Heels to Swathed Bodies," parag. 34.

61. Salzinger, "From High Heels to Swathed Bodies," parag. 13. Salzinger also describes a third *maquiladora* where the women and men work side by side. The atmosphere is more egalitarian, and there is no single line on gender.

62. Salzinger, "From High Heels to Swathed Bodies," parag. 23.

63. Salzinger, "From High Heels to Swathed Bodies," parag. 42.

64. Sassen, "The Global City," 87.

65. Tiano and Ladino, "Dating, Mating, and Motherhood," 312.

66. Sassen, "The Global City," 87.

67. Fuentes and Ehrenreich, *Women of the Global Factory*, 32.

68. Sassen, "The Global City," 87.

69. Chavez quoted in Sheridan, "The Death that Haunts Juárez," 6.

70. Fernandez-Kelly, *For We Are Sold*, 134. Sam Dillon reports that local activist Esther Chavez believes that in Juárez most women continue to perform all of the domestic work. She says, "Women are not liberated, they just have a double workload," (Sam Dillon, "Rape and Murder Stalk Women in Northern Mexico," *New York Times*, April 18, 1998, A3, in LexisNexis News: 3).

71. Sassen, "The Global City," 87.

72. Fuentes and Ehrenreich, *Women of the Global Factory*, 33.

73. Nathan, "Work, Sex, and Danger," parag. 34.

Part VII
Global Networks of Knowledge and Practice: Globalizing Criminology and Criminal Justice

[26]

In search of interactive globalisation: Critical criminology in South Africa's transition

BILL DIXON
Keele University, UK (e-mail: w.j.dixon@keele.ac.uk)

Abstract. Maureen Cain (2000) identifies orientalism and occidentalism as features of much criminological writing on "non-western" societies. As alternatives to these opposite but complimentary tendencies, she argues for the possibility of mutual and reciprocal learning under conditions of interactive globalisation. The purpose of this article is to look for evidence of orientalism, occidentalism and interactive globalisation in the exchange of critical criminological ideas between North and South during the period of South Africa's transition to democracy. The discussion focuses on two bodies of critical criminological work – left realism and nocal governance theory – and traces their development-in-use both as examples of criminological theorising and attempts to reshape the practice of policing. Traces of orientalism and occidentalism are detected in the evolution of critical criminology in South Africa over the last 25 years, but it is argued that the exchange of criminological ideas has been far from unidirectional and can indeed be characterised as a continuing process of interactive globalisation.

Introduction

If recent critics of the project are to be believed, the search for a one-size-fits-all "Third World criminology" is over. The competing accounts of crime and crime control offered by modernisation (Clinard and Abbott, 1973) and underdevelopment (Sumner, 1982) theorists alike have been submerged by a rising tide of criticism. Arthur and Marenin (1995) have called for the "correlationitis" of much comparative work to be replaced by a "case study" approach. Banks (2000) has advocated the development of a new "cultural criminology". And Clegg and Whetton (1995) have grappled with the criminological challenges presented by the neo-patrimonial state form prevalent in much of sub-Saharan Africa.

Moreover, in what is perhaps the most penetrating contemporary analysis of criminology's failure to make sense of societies that, in her words, "self-define as non-western", Maureen Cain (2000: 71) has drawn attention to the opposite (but complimentary) problems of orientalism and occidentalism. The first, and more familiar, of these she describes as

> . . . the discursive constitution of an often romanticized but also wayward and unknowing "other" which . . . requires the guidance and advice of the "us" to find and/or accept its proper place in the world.
>
> (Cain, 2000: 71)

Malign though its wider effects may have been in the past, Cain argues that it is the West that has most to lose from its own orientalist predilections today, not least in the rapidly growing field of informal justice. Much more damaging for the rest of the world and the societies of the southern Caribbean with which Cain is directly concerned in her paper, is the strain to occidentalism which Cain takes to mean: seeing everything from the perspective of the West (or North). Evident in everything from the good governance[1] strings attached to much western economic benevolence to the kind of scholarship that explains rising crime in the Third World as a delayed replay (Sumner, 1982) of a similar trend observable during the First's own industrial revolution, "occidentalism presumes the 'sameness' of key cultural categories, practices and institutions" (Cain, 2000: 71). Occidentalism, she argues, results in a "constant misdiagnosis of problems leading, on occasion, to a misallocation of scarce resources"[2]. What both orientalism and its opposite share, Cain goes on to suggest, are distinct hegemonic tendencies and the ability to infect the thinking and practice of those whose "otherness" they seek either to idealise or elide.

In place of these impoverished approaches to understanding crime and crime control in the countries of the South[3] – and the static and polarising methods of conventional comparative criminology that go with them – Cain (2000: 87) sets out to "demonstrate the possibility of mutual and reciprocal learning". Instead of unidirectional notions of northern hegemony and southern resistance, she detects a more complex, dynamic and dialectical process at work in feminist struggles in the islands of the southern Caribbean. Rather than misrepresent the philosophy and practices of the women she got to know as mere resistance to the hegemony of (in her terms) western feminism, Cain (2000: 88) argues that they formed "the grounds of and result from positive choices". Occidentalist thinking denies the southern "other" the capacity to do more than resist or submit to northern hegemony, whereas Cain's notion of *interactive globalisation* acknowledges that indigenous ideas and activity can not only develop lives of their own in the South, but stimulate new theorising and innovative practices in the North as well.

The purpose of this article is to look for evidence of orientalism, occidentalism and interactive globalisation in the exchange of critical criminological ideas between South Africa and the North over the two decades it has taken for the former to transform itself from a crisis-ridden racist autocracy to a functioning multi-ethnic democracy. Two strands of critical theorising are at the centre of the discussion. The first of these is the left realist strand of "new" criminology developed by Jock Young and others from the late 1970s. The second is what I will call nodal governance theory and can be traced back to the early 1980s in the work (again amongst others) of Clifford Shearing[4]. They have been selected for examination here for rather different reasons: left realism because it was rescued from relative obscurity to become a theoretical cornerstone of the only serious attempt to construct a coherent, and distinctively South African, critical criminology in the immediate post-apartheid period; and nodal governance theory because it involves the (potentially far-reaching) development of a long-standing South African tradition of informalism as part of a radical response to global changes in the supply and demand for security under conditions of late modernity. The development-in-use of these ideas in and beyond South Africa will be traced both as examples of criminological theorising in the broad sense of "organized ways of thinking and talking about crime, criminals and crime control" (Garland and Sparks, 2000: 6) and as attempts to reshape the practice of policing. In the space available here this will be done in the context of a somewhat serendipitous chronology of developments in criminological thought and policing practice in South Africa over the last 25 years. Some concluding observations will then be made on the impact of orientalist and occidentalist thinking on South Africa and the extent to which its relationship with the North reflects processes of interactive globalisation rather than the unfolding of, and resistance to, some neo-colonial hegemonic project.

Prologue: the origins of Afrikaner nationalist criminology

Before we turn our attention to the 1980s and the impact of "new" British criminology on South Africa in what were to be the dying days of apartheid it is both necessary and instructive to look back another 50 years to the 1930s and the part played in its conception by an earlier generation of social theorists schooled in the traditions of European critical thought. It is necessary because the nature of the ideological hegemony that the critical criminologists of the 1980s sought to break can only be understood in the broader historical and political context of apartheid. And it is instructive because the influence of the eminent Dutch neo-Marxist, Willem Bonger, seems so clear in the development of what Dirk van Zyl Smit (1989, 1990, 1999) has called the Afrikaner nationalist tradition in South African criminology. A detailed account of van Zyl Smit's (1989) excavation of the foundations of Afrikaner nationalism is not possible here. But the ironies of the use to which Bonger's former student, Geoff Cronjé, and the equally influential W.A. Willemse, put his work in South Africa are too striking to pass entirely unremarked. Returning to their homeland from Europe in the early 1930s, Cronjé and Willemse were confronted by – and sought to address – what they believed to be two distinct crime problems. The first of these was a facet of a wider social malaise, the capitalist exploitation and cultural degradation of the "poor white" Afrikaner (van Zyl Smit, 1989: 236). In the hands of Cronjé and Willemse, Bonger's deterministic anti-capitalism was blended with essentialist theories of race and nation and the criminogenic effects of racial mixing to explain "poor white" criminality and point the way to its prevention[5]. The second, "non-white", problem was less pressing for Afrikaner nationalist academics and, to their minds, had nothing to with the grinding poverty of the black population. Rather it was a product of the distinctly orientalist notion that, because of "organic differences" between the races, black people were congenitally incapable of coping with the strains and temptations of urban life[6]. The solution to these problems advocated by Cronjé, Willemse and their fellow nationalists lay in the economic and social solidarity of the Afrikaner *volk* in the face of British neo-colonial exploitation and the strict separation and segregation of the white and non-white races to contain the crime threat posed by what Clinard and Abbott might (but would not) have called the "modernised native". Together, these policies were to find their expression in the designs of territorial or "grand" apartheid implemented after the electoral victory of the nationalists in 1948 (cited in van Zyl Smit, 1989: 241).

By the time we take up the story of critical criminology in South Africa half a century later in the 1980s, the Afrikaner nationalist tradition had ossified. With the segregationist ideology of apartheid in retreat its analytical force dissipated to leave the leading texts reliant on what van Zyl Smit (1990: 6, emphasis in original) calls "*middle-range* American criminological theory". In its practical application, this still dominant tradition was Janus-faced. On the one hand it professed some potentially progressive concern for the victims of traditional blue-collar crime. Yet, on the other, it demonstrated – in the form of "military criminology" – an entirely reactionary enthusiasm for mobilising what intellectual strength it could muster in aid of the apartheid state's fight against the liberation movements. Thus it was essentially as a counter-current to the hegemony of this theoretically bankrupt and politically compromised Afrikaner nationalist tradition that left realism filtered into South Africa in the 1980s at the height of the anti-apartheid struggle.

Points of departure: Left realism in Britain

The basic tenets of left realism are too well known to require much exposition here. Having said that, three features of British left realism are worth recalling before we consider its impact in South Africa. The first of these is the characteristically adversarial posture adopted by Jock Young in hammering out the principles and practice of realism in the course of an extended polemic against writers variously characterised (or caricatured) as "left idealists, "administrative criminologists" and "right realists" (Young, 1979, 1986, 1994)[7]. The second, less controversial, feature of the realists' work was their willingness to give their ideas not just a distinctive theoretical shape – most famously (and literally) as the "square of crime" – but practical political substance as, for example, a set of proposals for democratically accountable "minimal" policing (Kinsey et al., 1986). Thirdly and finally, we have the adoption of the local victimisation survey as their data collection instrument of choice, a vehicle for "rational democratic input" into policy-making and a means of uncovering "real" experiences of inner city crime lost in the statistical morass of national surveys (Young, 1992: 49–50).

"A voyage of discovery": *Crime and Power in South Africa*[8]

With South Africa in thrall to the Afrikaner nationalist successors of Cronjé and Willemse, left realism would have passed the country by if it had not been for a group of criminologists based at the University of Cape Town (UCT). Founded in 1977, the Institute of Criminology at UCT had been intended to effect change in the apartheid justice and penal systems from within. However, as Dirk van Zyl Smit records, its researchers soon found the room for manoeuvre afforded by such a narrowly reformist agenda impossibly restrictive while the apartheid authorities took a distinctly dim view of the Institute's research output (Slabbert and van Rooyen, 1978; McLachlan, 1984 and 1986, cited in van Zyl Smit, 1990: 8). Interest in critical criminology among the Institute's staff grew apace in these early years (van Zyl Smit, 1977 and 1983; Davis, 1981; Slabbert, 1981, cited in Davis, 1985). But it was not until the publication of a collection of "critical studies in criminology" (the volume's subtitle) that a concerted effort was made to apply the "new theoretical insights" provided by recent British and American work to South Africa (Davis and Slabbert, 1985).

In his introduction to the volume, Dennis Davis (1985) traced the emergence of a critical sociology of deviance in the work of Becker, Gouldner and others, its synthesis in *The New Criminology* (Taylor et al., 1973) and its application by Stuart Hall and his colleagues in *Policing the Crisis* (1978). For Davis (1985: 7, 11) at least, it was the last of these that was the seminal work. As he and his fellow contributors embarked on their "voyage of discovery" in critical criminology, it was *Policing the Crisis* that examined a society moving into a "crisis of control", and thus provided an analysis "particularly appropriate to modern South Africa". Yet, despite this enthusiasm for the notion of hegemonic crisis central to the work of Hall and his colleagues, Davis (1985: 11) was very much aware of the dangers of borrowing too promiscuously from "First World social theory". State control of black South Africans "did not lend itself to interpretation simply in terms of a hegemonic order". Nor was he oblivious to the criticisms levelled at *Policing the Crisis* by the likes of Sumner (1981, cited in Davis, 1985: 5–6) and the "more sophisticated" analyses of crime – and ways of preventing it short of the establishment of a socialist society – developed by Young (1979) since the publication of *The New Criminology*. What emerges from his discussion then is a qualified but hopeful endorsement of the role that "First World" critical theorising in all its disputatious complexity could play in challenging the dominance of consensual, functionalist thinking common to both the Afrikaner nationalist and liberal wings of South African criminology[9]. If there is something faintly occidentalist in this looting of the conceptual toolbox represented by "new" British critical criminology it is no more than incipient and must be seen in the historical context of long decades of Afrikaner nationalist domination.

Towards justice?: Criminology for a democratic South Africa

Insofar as the central purpose of Davis and Slabbert's "voyage of discovery" was to problematise the role of the South African state and the processes of criminalisation and repression central to the maintenance of apartheid, the left realist canon was not the most obvious place to begin the search for inspiration. Although the state, its police and other agencies of social control form one point of the realist "square of crime", the early left realist literature of the 1980s contained remarkably little in the way of sustained critical analysis of the state and its workings (Jefferson et al., 1991). So it is hardly surprising to find that the major work of empirical critical criminology published in the wake of *Crime and Power* owed little to realism. On the contrary, *Detention and Torture in South Africa* (Foster et al., 1987) was a courageously researched indictment of the treatment of detainees under South Africa's draconian security laws that owed more to the Gramscian analysis of Hall et al. (1978) than contemporary work on policing in Britain by Young and his fellow realists (Lea and Young, 1984; Kinsey et al., 1986)[10]. Against this background, it is hard to take issue with van Zyl Smit's (1990: 1, emphasis in original) view that

> ... when discussing criminological thought, in South Africa in particular, one is often dealing with a form of practical reasoning in which theoretical approaches are used in a somewhat *eclectic* and *pragmatic* manner in order to justify or make sense of current practices.

These words appear in the introduction to a second collection of essays published under the auspices of the Institute of Criminology at UCT some 5 years after *Crime and Power* and entitled *Towards Justice?: Crime and State Control in South Africa* (Hansson and van Zyl Smit, 1990). The central argument of this introduction was that three broad traditions had been instrumental in the development of South African criminology. The first of these was the dominant Afrikaner nationalist current referred to earlier. As one might expect, van Zyl Smit (1990: 10) was sharply critical of this tradition – particularly in its most recent manifestation as military criminology. Indeed he argued that critical criminology should have nothing to do with those who saw their function as providing "techniques for bolstering the power of the South African state". Though careful to point out its contradictions, he was much kinder to the second, legal reformist, tradition that had given birth to the Institute.

But it is what he had to say about the third approach that is of direct concern here. Describing it as "a criminology for a democratic South Africa", van Zyl Smit (1990: 8) saw the critical tradition in which he and his colleagues were working as the product of three distinct influences: the broader context of change in contemporary South Africa; "international developments in criminological theory"; and what he described as "empirically-based conclusions" inconsistent with "the notion of consensus ... central to legal reformism"[11]. Thus the foundation of the Institute of Criminology in 1977, and the commencement of its initially reformist programme of research, coincided not just with the beginning of a long period of domestic political upheaval after the Soweto uprisings of 1976 but also with the flowering of international critical criminologies attentive to the definition and social construction of crime as well as its aetiology. With the future democratisation of South Africa still in the balance (the book was published in 1990 but the papers it contains had been presented at a conference the year before)[12], van Zyl Smit argued that the mission of this new South African criminology was threefold: to continue to expose abuses of state power; to maintain criminology as a serious intellectual enterprise; and, finally, to continue a tradition of practical intervention in the lives of ordinary people. It was only in respect of the last of these tasks that he explicitly referred to left realism and its attempts to resolve the "paradox" of "first generation" critical criminology's disregard for "the *real suffering* of the broader mass of the people, both at the hands of the state and as a result of conventional crimes" (van Zyl Smit, 1990: 10 citing Young, 1986)[13]. On this account, the influence of left realism was marginal to the development of a critical South African criminology. It could serve as a necessary corrective to the excesses of idealism and a timely reminder of the need for criminologists to pay heed to the experiences of their fellow citizens, but for van Zyl Smit writing in the dying days of apartheid it clearly did not do much more than that.

Towards nodal governance: Dual policing and community empowerment in transition

The early 1990s were turbulent times in South Africa. As the negotiations paving the way to democratic elections dragged on, a state of undeclared war existed across much of the country (Taylor and Shaw, 1998). The South African Police (SAP), their surrogates in the townships and equivalents in the nominally independent or self-governing black homelands were at the forefront of the struggle. In the midst of all this a bloodless, but no less intense, contest was going on over the future of policing in a new, democratic South Africa. While the old order generals in charge of the SAP sought to manage and contain the process of reform, civilian activists close to the ANC were busy preparing a blueprint for the future of "the formal policing agency" based on Anglo-American experiences of "community policing" (Marais, 1992: 8; Dixon, 2000; Rauch, 2001). While the continuing significance of collective self-policing *below* rather than *by* government (Loader, 2000) was acknowledged, the central concern of these activists was the reform of policing by the state police. Thus it fell to an expatriate and a foreigner to develop an alternative model of dual policing that put territorial and interest-based "communities" at its centre and relegated the state police to the role of specialist bearers of coercive force to be called upon as one of many resources in the wider enterprise of collective problem-solving (Brogden and Shearing, 1993)[14].

The genealogy of Brogden and Shearing's ideas is slightly harder to trace than those of the left realists, but a number of theoretical and empirical inheritances are evident. If Davis and (at least some of) his colleagues were indebted – via Hall and others – to Gramsci, Brogden and Shearing owed more to Foucault, a quotation from whose work serves as preface to their book. Other obvious sources include the work of Shearing and others on the rebirth of private policing, the growth of mass private property and the resulting pluralisation of both orders and mechanisms of ordering within a rapidly changing world system (Johnston, 1992; Shearing and Stenning, 1983; and Santos, 1992; cited in Brogden and Shearing, 1993: 172)[15]. But perhaps the most striking – and certainly the most loudly protested – contribution to their vision of "policing through civil society" seems to have been made by the ordinary people of South Africa and the myriad informal ordering processes developed in the townships during the apartheid era[16]. Even as Brogden and Shearing (1993: 161) were writing, attempts to "network" the informal justice system – people' courts, street committees and the rest – had collapsed and the institutions themselves were reeling from the state repression of the mid 1980s. Yet, in these institutions – and for all their palpable failings – Brogden and Shearing (1993: 165) detected "the seeds of a more equable ordering system". Policing for a new South Africa, they argued, should be "located primarily in the institutions of civil society" (Brogden and Shearing: 1993: 175–176). It should be understood "as a product of a network of interrelated institutions operating at different levels and with different knowledges and resources" while the use of force should be constitutionally restrained, strictly licensed and concentrated in the hands of the state police. Herein lay a very different, and more radical, blueprint for policing than the one being pored over either by the police generals or the civilian advisers of the post-apartheid ANC government-in-waiting. And herein too lay a preliminary sketch of what one of its progenitors was later to call "networked nodal governance" might look like in a society in transition (Shearing and Kempa, 2001: 206).

Hegemony, deconstruction and progressive realism

Before the story of dual policing on the ground in the townships of the early 1990s is pursued any further, it is important to note that Brogden and Shearing had much in common with the exponents of van Zyl Smit's criminology for a democratic South Africa. Mike Brogden had been a visiting professor at UCT in 1991 and contributors to Hansson and van Zyl Smit's (1990) collection head the list of acknowledgements in *Policing for a New South Africa*. Moreover, Wilfried Schärf and other researchers associated with the Institute of Criminology had long been active in the field of informal justice. Much as Brogden and Shearing (1993) saw processes of ordering developed in the townships under apartheid as an alternative to "doing [policing] the Western way", so Schärf (1989: 230, 232) hoped that they might "prefigure" a democratic structure for post-apartheid social control and act as a "counter-hegemonic" bulwark against the incursion of state-centred community policing[17].

Indeed the interest shown by leading exponents of UCT's criminology for a democratic South Africa in informal justice is evidence of a more general eclecticism and owed more to the exigencies of the political situation in which these researchers found themselves than any imported theoretical tradition. Despite the cautious support of one of its most prominent adherents for a careful, and "realistic", assessment of informal adjudication mechanisms (Matthews, 1988: 23), mainstream British left realism had little time for anything that smacked of "abolitionism", particularly when it came to the crucial gatekeeping function of policing. So, for example, Louk Hulsman

(1986) was taken to task by Young (1992) for suggesting that (in the latter's words) "the informal system of control, which deals with the majority of "problematic situations" should be extended to tackling their totality". Two years later the "left idealist", Phil Scraton (1985), was similarly castigated for arguing that crime control could be left to the community in high crime areas where "no such community exists" (Young, 1994: 115). Prominent though "the public" was in realist thinking, the ordinary citizen tended to be cast very much in a supporting role. It was the job of the police and other "multi-agencies" to control crime and they were dependent on public co-operation in doing so. But the idea of turning substantial parts of that all-important enterprise over to popular institutions in civil society was regularly excoriated in realist writing as dangerously idealistic nonsense.

Such discontinuities between the principles of British left realism and the practices of those engaged in developing a criminology for a democratic South Africa are less immediately apparent if we raise our sights from the day-to-day problems of ordering a society in transition to the struggle for ideological hegemony. For it is at this level that scholars such as Desirée Hansson (1993; 1995) believed that the liberating effects of British critical criminology in general, and left realism in particular, had been most keenly felt.

> Although somewhat eclectic and under-theorized, South African critical criminology has been consistently influenced by the work of British critical criminologists Ian Taylor, Paul Walton and Jock Young. From the mid-eighties this criminology has taken on a more definite shape – that of progressive realism which is akin to British left realism. [...] [O]ver the past five years South African progressive realist criminology has made a number of significant contributions, both theoretical and policy-oriented, to the broad field of the construction and management of social conflict in South Africa. *Perhaps the most significant of these contributions has been to displace conservative [Afrikaner nationalist] criminology from dominance* [by] remapping the boundaries of this individualistic, correctionalist criminology.
>
> (Hansson, 1993: 6–7, emphasis added)[18]

Convinced though she was of the impetus given to South African criminology by British scholarship, Hansson was concerned that the critical edge of progressive realism should not be dulled. As a feminist she was dismayed by its continued "androcentrism" (Hansson, 1993: 9)[19]. And, as a self-conscious realist, she was uneasy at its almost exclusive focus on abuses of state power to the exclusion of "ordinary", "non-political" street and white collar crime (Hansson, 1993: 8–9). But, above all, Hansson (1995: 55; cf. 1993: 10) feared that progressive realism as the replacement hegemonic discourse of a democratic South Africa would abandon critique in its haste to make itself useful to a new ANC-led government:

> In the prevailing frenzy of social reconstruction in South Africa, academics in progressive-realist criminology, both feminist and non-feminist alike, run the very real risk of abandoning the pursuit of theoretical deconstruction in favour of political pragmatism.

We shall see whether these words were to prove prophetic in a moment. But first we must return to the townships and the reform of policing in the immediate post-apartheid years.

"Community policing" for a new South Africa

Brogden and Shearing's (1993: 186) call for a "bottom-heavy" system of policing founded on a "network of civil institutions" was not mere rhetoric. By the time their book appeared, work was already well under way in townships across South Africa first to re-establish self-regulating mechanisms of popular justice and then to articulate them with the burgeoning private sector and an increasingly legitimate state (Nina, 1995). Many of these initiatives were undertaken and/or documented by the Community Peace Foundation (CPF), a non-governmental organisation (NGO) directed by none other than Clifford Shearing[20]. While Daniel Nina and others busied themselves with the practical work of training township activists in policing *without* the state police (Mncadi and Nina, 1994), Shearing (1994b, 1995) himself continued to promote participatory forms of local civil policing as an indispensable corollary to reform of the state system. Unfortunately for him, however, the national tide was turning as the focus of the reform process shifted away from establishing a decentralised, self-regulating, system of preventive *policing* to enhancing first the legitimacy, and then the capacity, of the (state) *police* (Dixon, 2000; Rauch, 2001; van der Spuy, 2001).

Reporting in 1992 on the prospects for community policing in a democratic South Africa, an influential working group of activists and academics close to the liberation movements had taken care to acknowledge the continued significance of self-initiated policing *by* communities (Marais, 1992). This theme was taken up two years later in the first official statement of policing policy issued by the freshly elected ANC-led Government of National Unity:

> We must find points of convergence between the formal and informal systems of justice. Local police commanders must interact with, and accommodate, informal policing systems where they add to the general problem-solving capacity of the community.
>
> (Minister of Safety and Security, 1994: 14)

By 1997, however, the position had changed dramatically. Community Police Forums (CPFs) had been established in all police station areas, principally as a means of legitimising the newly unified (and renamed) South African Police Service (SAPS)[21]. CPFs were closely modelled on arrangements for consultation between the police and the community established in England and Wales a decade earlier in the wake of Lord Scarman's (1981) report into disorders in the Brixton area of South London. Their creation had been provided for in the Interim Constitution of 1993, but their role was restricted to providing "the community" with an opportunity to work in partnership with the SAPS in identifying and solving local problems[22]. Legislation on CPFs was followed in 1996 by the publication of a National Crime Prevention Strategy (Department of Safety and Security, 1996) which also sought to encourage popular participation in the formal criminal justice system, this time by means of a programme of public education. The final endorsement of a state-centred Anglo-American vision of community policing came with the publication in 1997 of a manual (Department of Safety and Security, 1997) littered with references to, and extensive quotations from, the work of leading North American scholars such as Herman Goldstein (1990) and Robert Trojanowicz (Trojanowicz and Bucqueroux, 1990). Where Brogden and Shearing had envisaged the state police as specialist providers of coercive force in a dual system of policing rooted in civil society, the new government clearly saw the "community" as a junior partner in an enterprise dominated by a state agency remodelled in accordance with international best practice. Shamelessly occidentalist though the state-centred conception of community policing promulgated in the 1997 manual undoubtedly was, subsequent research (Pelser, 1999) indicates that its success in gaining approval as the official blueprint for police reform has not been reproduced on the ground where evidence of its implementation is confined to the existence of a network of CPFs and very little else. Despite this evidence of widespread implementation failure it is easy to sympathise with the following gloomy assessment of the state of police reform published a mere five years after the appearance of *Policing for a New South Africa*:

> [W]hile community policing was intended as a programme to ensure that police reform in South Africa would not lead to a reinforcement of the Beccarian model and would shift the focus of policing resources to poor areas, it has not done this. Community policing has rather become a mechanism to achieve better bandit catching, than a way of involving the police in wider strategies to enhance community involvement in crime prevention. (Shaw and Shearing, 1998: 8–9)

From progressive realism to the new administrative criminology?

As we saw earlier, Dirk van Zyl Smit (1990: 11) drew on the left realist tradition in international criminology to advance his argument for South Africans to maintain their commitment to devising "practical responses to current conditions". Writing some nine years later he was able to take stock of the contribution that criminologists and criminological ideas had made over a decade of unprecedented change both inside and beyond the criminal justice system (van Zyl Smit, 1999). The picture he painted was a complex one. For him, the most dramatic changes in criminal justice – the effective abolition by the new Constitutional Court of capital and corporal punishment – had been achieved not by critical criminologists but through the efforts of those he described (in 1999 as in 1990) as "legal reformists"[23]. In contrast to this, he suggested that the fortunes of a critical criminology "committed above all to community involvement" had been mixed (van Zyl Smit, 1999: 206). Public participation in state policing had, as we have seen, been institutionalised in the form of a national network of community police forums. But they had proved difficult to establish and harder still to manage effectively. Despite strenuous efforts, a dysfunctional, and often brutal, system of juvenile justice had proved resistant to reform with the result that many young people continued to be detained in unsuitable police and prison accommodation. Lay assessors had been introduced to add legitimacy and local knowledge to courts alienated from large swathes of the population, but again only with considerable difficulty. And finally, attempts to transform the delivery of correctional services had been derailed by a series of intractable political disputes.

Taking van Zyl Smit's admittedly partial survey of post-apartheid developments in criminal justice as a starting point it is hard to see the practical interventions made by South African critical criminologists as the gradual unfolding of some progressive or, by proxy, left realist blueprint. On the contrary, it requires some ingenuity to detect much evidence of distinctively realist thinking in South African criminology in the immediate post-apartheid period. Consider, for example, van Zyl Smit's (1999: 206) view that "community involvement" in criminal justice and the wider business of social ordering was central to the critical project in those years. To recap what was said earlier, and to put it no higher here, an emphasis on informalism is not typically, and certainly not distinctively, left realist. Consider too that Hansson's (1993; 1995) brave attempts to give van Zyl Smit's (1990) eclectic "criminology for a democratic South Africa" greater coherence, and a more immediately recognisable international pedigree, were to remain a high water mark in the theoretical development of South African critical criminology for the rest of the decade. And consider, finally, that it was not until the second year of the new century that any similarly systematic attempt was made to bring international critical criminological theorising in the realist tradition to bear once again on the South African condition (Dixon, 2001)[24].

Even when we turn to matters like police reform and the measurement of victimisation we find South African practice – with criminologists from the critical tradition in the van – differing significantly from British left realist orthodoxies. So, for example, Kinsey, Lea and Young (1986) strongly opposed forms of community policing based on extending the police mandate to accommodate a proactive problem-solving role[25]. In its place, they argued for "minimal" policing. On this view, priorities would be set at "the collective level" *for* (rather than *by*) the police through the democratic process, while interventions at "the individual level" would be limited to reacting to requests for assistance by members of the public (Kinsey et al., 1986: 190). Yet in South Africa in the 1990s we have seen how post-apartheid police reformers soon signed up to the by then dominant, and far from minimalist, Anglo-American model of state-centred community policing popularised in the work of Goldstein and Trojanowicz.

A slightly different picture emerges if we look at the use of victimisation surveys. The British left realists made large claims on behalf of their favoured empirical device arguing that, in its local form, the victimisation survey was not only a "democratic instrument", but also an important means of uncovering the geographical concentration of crime in inner city areas and countering claims made on the basis of national data that much fear of crime was "irrational" (Young, 1992: 50)[26]. Given the prevailing scepticism about the accuracy of South Africa's official statistics dating back to the apartheid era (Shaw, 2002: chaps. 1 and 3; Louw and Schönteich, 2001), it is not surprising that victimisation surveys were widely used as an alternative source of data after liberation. Considerable energy was devoted to studying the plight of the rural and urban poor (Louw and Shaw, 1997; Schärf et al., 1999; Pelser et al., 2000). Yet much effort also went into national (Hirschowitz et al., 1998) and city-wide surveys (Camerer et al., 1998; Louw et al., 1998; Louw,

1998) that stirred the experiences of people living in the townships into an often insubstantial mixture with those of middle class suburban-dwellers, to produce what Young (1992: 50) might once have dismissed as "blancmange figures of little use to anyone".

All this takes us back to Desirée Hansson's (1995: 43) work and her prediction that progressive realism was about to become "the dominant criminological discourse" of post-apartheid South Africa. With the benefit of hindsight we can see that her confidence was misplaced. By the end of the 1990s – and in the absence of any substantial theoretical development beyond the preliminary sketches offered by Hansson (1993; 1995) herself – talk of progressive realism as a coherent, let alone dominant, discourse had little practical meaning. Adherents of a much more eclectic post-apartheid South African criminology were widely dispersed in government and a flourishing NGO sector, as well as in academia[27]. The connections between this new "can-do" criminology and the three traditions identified by van Zyl Smit (1990; 1999) became complicated as ideas, practices and people changed to meet the challenges of non-racial democracy (Dixon, forthcoming). But it is also clear that criminologists working in the broader critical tradition delineated in their different ways by Davis (1985) and van Zyl Smit (1990) had become preoccupied with the urgent task of nation-building and abandoned "theoretical deconstruction" in the rush to undertake policy-relevant research. Thus as critical criminology and progressive realism shaded into a new administrative criminology for a democratic South Africa[28], the influence of imported left realism became, at most, vestigial.

Networking local capacity nodal governance: from Zwelethemba (and Belfast) to the world

Meanwhile, back in the townships, the attempts by Clifford Shearing, Daniel Nina and others associated with the Community Peace Foundation to build on the institutions and practices of popular justice inherited from the struggle years had foundered. But all was by no means lost and, from the ashes of the CPF, arose a new organisation, the Community Peace Program (CPP) and a renewed commitment to the institutionalisation of "networked nodal governance" (Shearing and Kempa, 2001: 206)[29]. Known to Shearing and his various collaborators as the Zwelethemba model, the CPP's approach to building local capacity in civil policing took its name from the settlement outside the town of Worcester some 120 kilometres from Cape Town where it was first developed (see Shearing, 2001a; Shearing and Kempa, 2001; Roche, 2002; and Johnston and Shearing, 2003: 151–160 for detailed accounts)[30]. The significance of the Zwelethemba model for present purposes is its centrality to a much more ambitious theoretical and political project involving the re-imagination of policing not just in post-apartheid South Africa and other newly democratic societies in the South, but in the old democracies of the North and wherever rising demand for security can no longer be met by the state alone. But before we consider the global implications of Zwelethemba-style nodal local capacity governance, we need to pay slightly more attention to its South African foundations than they have tended to receive thus far.

An initial difficulty with assessing the usefulness and sustainability of the peace committees established in Zwelethemba and their role in facilitating the resolution of a wide range of local problems is that there is very little in the way of independent evaluative data to go on. The only published accounts of what actually happened in Zwelethemba have been written either by author teams including Clifford Shearing himself (Shearing and Kempa, 2001; Johnston and Shearing, 2003) or by researchers using data supplied, as far as one can make out, by Community Peace Program staff (Roche, 2002). This is not to suggest that there is any reason to disbelieve these accounts, or to doubt Declan Roche's (2002: 531) judgement that peace committees "may provide an example of how informal justice can play a constructive role in ameliorating both individual and social injustice". The object here is rather to argue that more exhaustive evaluative studies might help to fill in some important gaps in our knowledge about the operation and impact of the Zwelethemba model. For example, we currently know next to nothing about whether and how the peace committees set up in Zwelethemba have sustained themselves[31]. We also know nothing about the achievements of peace committees in the townships across South Africa to which the Zwelethemba model has been "rolled out" (Roche, 2002: 515, n 3). Filling these gaps becomes all the more important when, among the things that we *do* know, is that the social dynamics and micro-politics of South Africa's townships are neither uniform nor simple. From this we may surmise that a model designed to work in a place like Zwelethemba on the outskirts of a relatively small agricultural town will not readily be replicated in other contexts. In fact, as recent research by Boyane Tshehla (2001; 2002) in Khayelitsha outside Cape Town suggests, peace committees may find it much harder to prosper and preserve their autonomy as new entrants to already highly diversified and ruthlessly competitive security markets in much larger, metropolitan areas.

Tshehla's work also prompts two further thoughts on the Zwelethemba model. The first of these is that, even if the peace gatherings held in South Africa since the CPP began promoting them in 1998 now total well over 1,000[32] the number of (criminal and non-criminal) problems these proceedings can possibly have resolved is dwarfed both by the number of crimes brought to the attention of the police and[33], in all probability, by the disputes handled by the wide range of alternative civil and commercial structures also documented by Tshehla. This leads on to a second point which is that the very existence of such structures, dispensing a very different, and much harsher, form of justice than that on offer from peace committees, is testament to a level of popular demand for retribution – even revenge – that simply cannot be ignored by those anxious to displace the punishment mentality and its associated technologies of coercion[34].

Unfortunately, none of these doubts about the significance of the Zwelethemba model in its land of origin, have been addressed by those eager to promote it as the harbinger of a brave new world of nodal governance. Neither the potential difficulties of replicating the Zwelethemba model in more hostile environments, nor the relative insignificance of "peacemaking" in the flourishing mixed economy of do-it-yourself retributive "justice", nor the immanent problems of regulation raised by the existence of many competing providers of security, have prevented Shearing and others from using the activities of peace committees as evidence that local mechanisms of civil policing can function effectively and equitably as self-regulating nodes in an emergent network of security governance in which the state enjoys no conceptual or political pre-eminence (Johnston and Shearing, 2003; Braithwaite, 2000)[35]. Indeed, together with the wider regulatory frameworks for networked policing sketched out in the Report of the Independent (Patten) Commission on Policing for Northern Ireland (1999), the forward-looking, preventative peace-making (and peace-building) experience of Zwelethemba is taken to represent a globally-relevant model for the subversion and eventual replacement not only of outmoded notions of state-centred security governance but also of the entire retributive "Beccarian punishment paradigm" (Johnston and Shearing, 2003)[36]. While Johnston and Shearing (2003: 160) are wary of offering the Zwelethemba or South African[37] model as an "off-the-peg" solution to the problem of reconfiguring governance applicable "in all places and at all times", Shearing and Kempa (2001: 206) are more bullish, declaring that the plan they outline for realising " 'networked nodal governance' as a mode of optimal democratic policing" in South Africa "can be adapted and transferred to practical use in many nations of the world, including the established democracies of the West"[38]. What we are witnessing here then is the elaboration of criticisms of state centred community policing as a response to the unmet security needs of South Africa's poor (Brogden and Shearing, 1993; Shaw and Shearing, 1998) into a globally-relevant design for overhauling the relationship between the retrospective righting of wrongs – "making good" or "doing justice" in Johnston and Shearing's (2003: 140) epigrammatic formulation – and the prospective prevention of harms – "making safe" or "doing security". And the remarkable thing is that the momentum behind this grand conceptual and practical project is coming as much from the periphery as from the centre, from Zwelethemba as well as from Belfast. The flow of ideas, practices and institutional structures is not unidirectional and the South is no longer the passive recipient of recycled northern criminological theorising and crime control policies but a significant player in a bold attempt to rethink the governance of security on a global scale[39].

Conclusions: Occidentalism, orientalism and the interactive globalisation of critical criminology

This somewhat selective and disjointed history of South Africa's engagement with critical criminology began in the 1930s with Bonger and the rise of Afrikaner nationalism. It ended 70 years later with Shearing and nodal governance. It is easy, perhaps too easy, to see where northern-educated, northern-oriented or simply northern criminologists have either exaggerated or denied the differences between Britain, Europe or North America on the one hand and South Africa on the other. The warped orientalism of Cronjé, Rademeyer and Willemse allowed them to alight on, pathologise and then seek to expel, the "modernised native" as a threat to the moral well-being of the Afrikaner body politic. Almost half a century later, a rising generation of South African criminologists fiercely opposed to the orthodoxy imposed on their discipline by Afrikaner nationalism flirted with "occidentalism" by turning once again to Europe for inspiration in framing a counter-hegemonic discourse. In the 1990s, this flirtation with the criminologies of the north deepened into a more serious relationship when imported models of state-centred community policing – "as American as cherry pie" in Mike Brogden's (1999) memorable phrase – overtook more radical notions of a dual system of policing based in civil society. And finally, in the early years of a new century, it is possible to detect a certain tendency to idealise ordering practices developed in (but not necessarily by) poor "communities" and to wish away the problems of "meta-governance" that even the most rudimentary nodal networks present[40].

So, in Maureen Cain's terms, there undoubtedly are traces of both orientalism and occidentalism in the theory and practice of critical criminology in South Africa over the past 70 years. Yet, as the weight of evidence presented in this paper suggests, the impact of any tendency to romanticise or ignore the differences between Europe and Africa has been limited when northern ideas have bumped up against the harsh realities of the South. Thus, Bonger's economic determinism makes an unexpected appearance in the genealogy of apartheid while "new" British criminology in its various guises provides intellectual ammunition to a generation of South Africans struggling to overthrow the hegemony of Afrikaner nationalism at the height of the liberation struggle. Then, when that struggle has been won, South Africa in the throes of democratic transition becomes a test bed for the development of local capacity governance and the inspiration for new theories of networked nodal policing. As Cain (2000) argues in the case of the southern Caribbean, it would be quite wrong either to ignore the creative use and adaptation of imported critical criminological ideas in the South, or to see their development as no more than resistance to some alien ideological force. The importation, translation, interpretation and implementation of critical criminological ideas is a far more dynamic, reflexive and extended process than it appears if we concentrate too closely on particular orientalist or occidentalist moments. To make sense of the place that Zwelethemba – whatever the weaknesses of the eponymous model may be – occupies in contemporary efforts to re-imagine policing and resist the punitive impulse demands that, along with Maureen Cain, we see the exchange of criminological ideas as a continuing process of interactive globalisation rather than a once-and-for-all deal struck between an overbearing North and an impoverished South.

Acknowledgements

I would like to thank Ian Loader, Dirk van Zyl Smit, Elrena van der Spuy and participants in a staff seminar in the Department of Criminology at Keele University for their comments on this paper in draft form. My thanks also go to the editor of this special issue, Ronnie Lippens and my fellow authors for their contributions to a stimulating seminar, also held at Keele, where this paper was first presented.

Notes

1. See Abrahamsen (2000) for an illuminating critique of the discourses of development and good governance in the African context.
2. Cain cites three examples of occidentalism at work in the southern Caribbean: the assumption that the relationship between age and crime is universal rather than culturally specific; the justification of increased policing of low income groups in terms of their greater exposure to the risk of criminal victimisation; and the promotion of state-sponsored civil policing in the form of neighbourhood watch.
3. Although little better than the First/Third World and western/non-western alternatives, I marginally prefer the North/South binary, if only because it has the merit of geographical accuracy when, as here, the two sides of the inevitably arbitrary global divide are represented by the United Kingdom and South Africa.
4. Whether left realism and nodal governance theory can be described as critical criminologies may be a moot point for some. However, if the contents of a recent collection of essays edited by Carrington and Hogg (2002) are anything go by, the boundaries of critical criminology are neither so tightly circumscribed nor so rigorously policed as to permit the exclusion of the theories discussed here.
5. Van Zyl Smit (1989) speculates that Cronjé's nationalism (and racism) were fostered during his undergraduate days at the University of Stellenbosch where he was a contemporary

of H F Verwoerd, one of the leading architects of apartheid and a future Nationalist prime minister of South Africa.

6. As van Zyl Smit (1989: 241) also observes, mixed-race or "coloured" people were singled out for special attention as an incorrigibly deviant group since they lacked the requisite cultural integrity possessed by the "native" and white populations.
7. See Cottee (2002) for a searching re-examination of Young's attacks on "left idealism" and Sim, Scraton and Gordon (1987: 39) for a robust critique of the role of "idealist straw men" as targets for realist scatology.
8. Davis and Slabbert (1985).
9. A rather crude measure of the limited influence exerted by the British critical criminologists cited by Davis can be gained by scanning the notes and index entries in *Crime and Power* for references to Stuart Hall, Jock Young and other northern theorists such as Stan Cohen and Carol Smart. This reveals that imported critical work was explicitly referred to in no more than a third of the nine chapters, two of which were written by expatriate postgraduate students based at British universities (Durbach, 1985; Albertyn, 1985) and the third by the book's co-editor, the late Mana Slabbert (1985).
10. An obvious example of this is a chapter reviewing the history of detention without trial in South Africa which opens with an approving reference to the concept of hegemonic crisis and a substantial quotation from *Policing the Crisis* about the tendency for temporary disturbances in the balance of class forces to presage not "a revolutionary conjuncture" but "the coming of "iron times"" (Hall et al., 1978: 217 quoted by Davis in Foster et al., 1987: 11).
11. The latter exemplified by the work, amongst others, of Foster et al. (1987).
12. The speech by President F W de Klerk announcing the unbanning of the liberation movements and the return to South Africa of its many political exiles often taken as the point of no return for white minority rule was delivered on 2 February 1990.
13. The basis for levelling such a charge against either first generation scholars such as Stan Cohen or their supposedly "idealist" successors is, at best, debatable (Cottee, 2002; Dixon, 1999).
14. This is not to suggest that Brogden and Shearing (1993) were indifferent to the need for reform of the state police. Indeed they went to some lengths to explain that the transformation of policing should proceed at two levels, one of which was the reform of state policing in line with developing international best practice.
15. As Kelling's (2001) riposte to forensic examinations of his collaboration with James Q Wilson (1992) suggest, attempts to "spot" the contributions of individuals to jointly authored work is rarely illuminating. Suffice to say here that Mike Brogden's earlier work betrays a long-standing interest in the history and governance of colonial and metropolitan forms of state policing.
16. Much is also made in *Policing for a New South Africa* and Shearing's subsequent work (1994a) of the participatory model for policing mass demonstrations proposed by a multinational panel of experts under the auspices of the Commission of Inquiry Regarding the Prevention of Public Violence and Intimidation chaired by Judge Richard Goldstone.
17. See also Schärf and Ngcokoto (1990) and, for a more general overview, the papers collected in Schärf and Nina (2001).
18. Hansson herself pointed out that the Afrikaner nationalist tradition was in the process of repackaging itself as a "fundamental criminology" less concerned with the positivist task of isolating the causes of crime than the "right realist" goal of controlling it effectively. The "right realist" sobriquet is borrowed directly from Jock Young's many critical commentaries on the work of James Q Wilson.

19. She did not, however, share the terminal pessimism about criminology expressed by northern feminists such as Carol Smart (1990).
20. Daniel Nina's (1995) *Re-thinking Popular Justice* contains discussion of the theoretical background to these initiatives as well as detailed accounts of experiments in civil self-regulation from as far afield as KwaZulu Natal, the Eastern Cape and what is now Gauteng.
21. Detailed provision for CPFs was made in the South African Police Service Act 68 of 1995, which also created a single "service" out of the 11 police agencies inherited from the apartheid regime.
22. See s.221 Constitution of the Republic of South Africa Act 200 of 1993 and s.18(1) South African Police Service Act 68 of 1995.
23. See *S v Makwanyane* (1995) 3 SA 391 (CC) and *S v Williams* (1995) 3 SA 632 (CC) for decisions on the death penalty and whipping respectively.
24. By 2001 left realism (and the leading left realists) had moved on to the extent that the present author felt able to suggest that Young's (1999) then most recent work represented a break with realism and a return to his more radical, if not "idealist", roots (Dixon, 2001).
25. The leading British proponent of "maximalism" was a former chief constable, John Alderson (1979).
26. The most widely cited of the many realist local victimisation surveys are those conducted in the inner London Borough of Islington (Jones et al., 1986; Crawford et al., 1990).
27. The speed with which the institutional doors revolved is evident in the career of Mark Shaw who, as the back cover of his recent book (2002) announces, worked in the Department of Safety and Security in between stints at three of the country's leading NGOs, one of which is affiliated to the University of the Witwatersrand in Johannesburg.
28. In this respect at least the South African experience mirrored that of British left realism which, if Downes and Rock (1998: 301) are to be believed, had (by the late 1990s) lost much of its critical force and become "little more than the name taken by mainstream criminology when it appears in radical circles".
29. This new organisation is also directed by the indefatigable Shearing and was established in 1997 with funding from foreign donors and the South African government (Roche, 2002: 515).
30. According to Roche (2002), the essence of CPP's work in Zwelethemba and elsewhere has been to establish peace committees of township residents. These committees then undertake peacemaking and peace-building activities designed both to resolve specific conflicts through convening peace gatherings and to address the social problems of poverty and unemployment believed to lie behind them amongst other things by providing funds to support local micro-enterprises.
31. Johnston and Shearing (2003: 151) tell us that the CPP project team was in the township for two years from 1998 while Roche (2002: 515) says that full-time CPP staff based in Cape Town oversee the maintenance of committees but nothing about what this involves in practice.
32. Roche (2002: 521, n. 15) says that "just over 1,000" such gatherings had been held as of January 2002.
33. According to South African Police Service figures, no fewer than 3,396 murders, 6,808 incidents of rape and attempted rape and 10,747 robberies with aggravating circumstances were reported to the police in the Western Cape (the province in which Zwelethemba is located) in the year 2000 (South African Institute of Race Relations: 2001: 368).
34. For further evidence of the persistence of popular retributiveness, see the research evidence on public attitudes to sentencing and vigilante responses to crime presented by

Schönteich (2000) and Wilson's (2001) discussion of reactions to the work of the Truth and Reconciliation Commission (TRC).

35. In terms of Johnston and Shearing's (2003: 147) cartography of nodal governance, Zwelethemba's peace committees straddle the NGO and informal/voluntary sectors (the others are the state and corporate/commercial sectors).
36. For Clifford Shearing's own reflections on the work of the Patten Commission in Northern Ireland of which he was a member, see Shearing (2000, 2001b); and, for further discussion of the relevance of his work on nodal governance to the future of punishment, see Shearing (2001c).
37. The outlines of an overarching system of regulation for local community dispute resolution structures in South Africa not dissimilar to the framework suggested by the Patten Commission for Northern Ireland were sketched out in a discussion paper published by the South African Law Commission in 1999.
38. According to Roche (2002: 515, n 3), a programme based on the Zwelethemba model has already been established in Argentina.
39. See Karstedt (2001, 2002) for reflections on similar developments in the closely related field of restorative justice.
40. Some of the broader questions to do with the "meta-governance" of nodal security networks and the place of public political institutions in that process, are discussed in a review of Johnston and Shearing's book by Ian Loader and Neil Walker (forthcoming).

References

Abrahamsen, R., *Disciplining Democracy: Development Discourse and Good Governance in Africa* (London: Zed Books, 2000).

Albertyn, C., "Drugs and Moral Panic," in D. Davis and M. Slabbert (eds.), *Crime and Power in South Africa: Critical Studies in Criminology* (Cape Town: David Philip, 1985).

Alderson, J., *Policing Freedom* (Plymouth: MacDonald and Evans, 1979).

Arthur, J. and O. Marenin, "Explaining Crime in Developing Countries: the Need for a Case study Approach," *Crime, Law and Social Change* 1995 (23), 191–214.

Banks, C., "Developing Cultural Specificity for a Cultural Criminology," in Cyndi Banks (ed.), *Developing Cultural Criminology: Theory and Practice in Papua New Guinea*, Sydney Institute of Criminology Monograph Series No. 13. (Sydney: Sydney Institute of Criminology, 2000).

Braithwaite, J., "The New Regulatory State and the Transformation of Criminology," in D. Garland and R. Sparks (eds.), *Criminology and Social Theory* (Oxford: Oxford University Press, 2000).

Brogden, M., "Community Policing as Cherry Pie," in R.I. Mawby (ed.), *Policing Across the World* (London: UCL Press, 1999).

Brogden, M. and C. Shearing, *Policing for a New South Africa* (London: Routledge, 1993).

Cain, M., "Orientalism, Occidentalism and the Sociology of Crime," in D. Garland and R. Sparks (eds.), *Criminology and Social Theory* (Oxford: Oxford University Press, 2000).

Camerer, L., A. Louw, M. Shaw, L. Artz and W. Schärf *Crime in Cape Town: Results of a City Victim Survey*. ISS Monograph 23 (Halfway House: Institute for Security Studies, 1998).

Carrington, K. and R. Hogg (eds.), *Critical Criminology: Issues, Debates, Challenges* (Cullompton, Devon: Willan, 2002).

Clegg, I. and J. Whetton, "In search of a Third World Criminology," in L. Noaks, M. Maguire and M. Levi (eds.), *Contemporary Issues in Criminology* (Cardiff: University of Wales Press, 1995).

Clinard, M. and D. Abbott, *Crime in Developing Countries* (New York: Wiley, 1973).

Cottee, S., "Folk Devils and Moral Panics: 'Left Idealism,' Reconsidered," *Theoretical Criminology* 2002 (6:4), 387–410.

Crawford, A., T. Jones, T. Woodhouse and J. Young, *The Second Islington Crime Survey* (London: Middlesex Polytechnic, 1990).

Davis, D., "Introduction: Criminology and South Africa," in D. Davis and M. Slabbert (eds.), *Crime and Power in South Africa: Critical Studies in Criminology* (Cape Town: David Philip, 1985).

Davis, D. and M. Slabbert (eds.), *Crime and Power in South Africa: Critical Studies in Criminology* (Cape Town: David Philip, 1985).

Department for Safety and Security, *National Crime Prevention Strategy* (Pretoria: Department for Safety and Security, 1996) (Available online at http://www.gov.za/reports/1996/crime1.htm).

Department of Safety and Security, *Community Policing Policy Framework and Guidelines: A Manual for the South African Police Service* (Pretoria: Department for Safety and Security, 1997).

Dixon, B., *Popular Policing? Sector Policing and the Reinvention of Police Accountability.* PhD thesis 1999, Department of Law, Brunel University, Uxbridge.

Dixon, B., *The Globalisation of Democratic Policing: Sector Policing and Zero Tolerance in the new South Africa*, Occasional Paper Series (Cape Town: Institute of Criminology, University of Cape Town, 2000).

Dixon, B., "Exclusive Societies: Towards a Critical Criminology of Post-Apartheid South Africa," *Society in Transition* 2001 (32:2), 205–227.

Dixon, B. (forthcoming), "Crime, Crime Control and Criminology in Transition," in B. Dixon and E. van der Spuy (eds.), *Justice Gained? Crime and Crime Control in South Africa's Transition.*

Downes, D. and P. Rock, *Understanding Deviance*, 3rd edn. (Oxford: Oxford University Press, 1998).

Durbach, A., "Reforming Women: a Case Study of Disintegration," in D. Davis and M. Slabbert (eds.), *Crime and Power in South Africa: Critical Studies in Criminology* (Cape Town: David Philip, 1985).

Foster, D. (with D. Davis and D. Sadler), *Detention and Torture in South Africa* (Cape Town: David Philip, 1987).

Garland, D. and R. Sparks, "Criminology, Social Theory and the Challenge of our Times," in D. Garland and R. Sparks (eds.), *Criminology and Social Theory* (Oxford: Oxford University Press, 2000).

Goldstein, H., *Problem Oriented Policing* (New York: McGraw-Hill, 1990).

Hall, S., C. Critcher, T. Jefferson, J. Clarke and B. Roberts, *Policing the Crisis: Mugging, the State and Law and Order* (Basingstoke: Macmillan, 1978).

Hansson, D., "Feminist Scholarship and Progressive Realist Criminology in Contemporary South Africa – Preferred Relations and Future Directions," Paper delivered at the British Criminology Conference, University of Wales, Cardiff, 28–31 July 1993.

Hansson, D., "Agenda-ing Gender: Feminism and the Engendering of Academic Criminology in South Africa," in Nicole Hahn Rafter and Frances Heidensohn (eds.), *International Feminist Perspectives in Criminology* (Buckingham: Open University Press, 1995).

Hansson, D. and D. van Zyl Smit (eds.), *Towards Justice: Crime and State Control in South Africa* (Cape Town: Oxford University Press, 1990).

Hirschowitz, R., P. Buwembo, J. Serwadda-Luwaga and H. Nasholm *Victims of Crime Survey* (Pretoria: Statistics South Africa, 1998).

Hulsman, L., "Critical Criminology and the Concept of Crime," *Contemporary Crises* 1986 (10), 63–80.

Independent Commission on Policing for Northern Ireland, *A New Beginning: Policing in Northern Ireland* (Belfast: HMSO, 1999).

Jefferson, T., J. Sim and S. Walklate, "Europe, the Left and Criminology in the 1990s: Accountability, Control and the Social Construction of the Consumer," in D. Farrington and S. Walklate (eds.), *Offenders and Victims: Theory and Policy*, British Society of Criminology Conference, Selected Papers Vol. 1 (London: British Society of Criminology/Institute for the Study and Treatment of Delinquency, 1991).

Johnston, L. and C. Shearing, *Governing Security* (London: Routledge, 2003).

Jones, T., B. MacLean and J. Young, *The Islington Crime Survey* (Aldershot: Gower, 1986).

Karstedt, S., "Comparing Cultures, Comparing Crime: Challenges, Prospects and Problems for a Global Criminology," *Crime, Law and Social Change* 2001 (36), 285–308.

Karstedt, S., "Durkheim, Tarde and Beyond: The Global Travel of Crime Policies," *Criminal Justice* 2002 (2), 111–123.

Kelling, G., "Broken Windows, and the Culture Wars: a Response to Selected Critiques," in R. Matthews and J. Pitts (eds.), *Crime, Disorder and Community Safety* (London: Routledge, 2001).

Kinsey, R., J. Lea and J. Young, *Losing the Fight Against Crime* (Oxford: Blackwell, 1986).

Lea, J. and J. Young, *What Is To Be Done about Law and Order?* (Harmondsworth: Penguin, 1984).

Loader, I., "Plural Policing and Democratic Governance," *Social & Legal Studies* 2000 (9:3), 323–345.

Loader, I. and N. Walker (forthcoming), "A State of Denial? Rethinking the Governance of Security," *Punishment and Society*.

Louw, A. and M. Schönteich, "Playing the Numbers Game: Promises, Policing and Crime Statistics," in Jonny Steinberg (ed.) *Crime Wave* (Johannesburg: Witwatersrand University Press, 2001).

Louw, A. and M. Shaw, *Stolen Opportunities: The Impact of Crime on South Africa's Poor*, ISS Monograph Series No. 14 (Halfway House: Institute for Security Studies, 1997).

Louw, A., M. Shaw, L. Camerer and R. Robertshaw, *Crime in Johannesburg: Results of a City Victim Survey*, ISS Monograph Series No. 18 (Halfway House: Institute for Security Studies, 1998).

Louw, A., *Crime in Pretoria: Results of a City Victim Survey* (Pretoria/Halfway House: Idasa/Institute for Security Studies, 1998).

Marais, E., *Community Policing in South Africa: Prospects and Challenges*, Report of the Community Policing Working Group presented to the 2nd Centre for Criminal Justice Conference on "Policing in the New South Africa," 18–21 September 1992.

Matthews, R., "Reassessing Informal Justice," in R. Matthews (ed.), *Informal Justice?* (London: Sage, 1988).

Minister of Safety and Security, *Draft Policy Document* (Pretoria: Ministry of Safety and Security, 1994).

Mncadi, M. and D. Nina, "A Year: a Training Programme in Guguletu on Community Policing," *Imbizo* 1994 (2), 18–24.

Muncie, J., "Reassessing Competing Paradigms in Criminological Theory," in P. Walton and J. Young (eds.), *The New Criminology Revisited* (Basingstoke: Macmillan, 1998).

Nina, D., *Rethinking Popular Justice* (Cape Town: Community Peace Foundation, 1995).

Pelser, E., *The Challenges of Community Policing in South Africa*, ISS Occasional Paper No. 42 (Pretoria: Institute for Security Studies, 1999).

Pelser, E., A. Louw and S. Ntuli, *Poor Safety: Crime and Policing in South Africa's Rural Areas*, ISS Monograph Series No. 47 (Pretoria: Institute for Security Studies, 2000).

Rauch, J., "Police Reform and South Africa's Transition," in Mark Shaw (ed.), *Crime and Policing in Transitional Societies*, Seminar Report (Johannesburg: Konrad-Adenauer-Stiftung, 2001).

Roche, D., "Restorative Justice and the Regulatory State in South African Townships," *British Journal of Criminology* 2002 (42), 514–533.

Scarman, Lord, *The Brixton Disorders 10–12 April 1981*, Report of an Inquiry, Cmnd. 8427 (London: HMSO, 1981).

Schärf, W., "Community Policing in South Africa," *Acta Juridica* 1989, 206–233.

Schärf, W. and B. Ngcokoto "Images of Punishment in the People's Courts of Cape Town 1985–7: from Prefigurative Justice to Populist Justice," in N. Manganyi and A. Du Toit (eds.), *Political Violence and the Struggle in South Africa* (London: Macmillan, 1990).

Schärf, W. and D. Nina, *The Other Law* (Cape Town: Juta, 2001).

Schärf, W., G. Saban, J. Geerlings, R. Röntsch and J. Connolly, *Wetton-Lansdowne-Phillipi Corridor Programme: Crime Study* (Cape Town: Institute of Criminology, University of Cape Town, 1999).

Schönteich, M., *Justice Versus Retribution: Attitudes to Punishment in the Eastern Cape*, ISS Monograph Series No. 45. (Pretoria: Institute for Security Studies, 2000).

Scraton, P., *The State of the Police* (London: Pluto, 1985).

Sim, J., P. Scraton and P. Gordon, "Introduction: Crime, the State and Critical Analysis," in P. Scraton (ed.), *Law, Order and the Authoritarian State* (Milton Keynes: Open University Press, 1987).

Shaw, M., *Crime and Policing in Post-Apartheid South Africa: Transforming under Fire* (London: Hurst, 2002).

Shaw, M. and C. Shearing, "Re-shaping Security: an Examination of the Governance of Security in South Africa," *African Security Review* 1998 (7:3), 3–12.

Shearing, C., "Participatory Policing: Modalities for Lay Participation," *Imbizo* 1994a (2), 5–10.

Shearing, C., "Reinventing Policing: Policing as Governance," *Imbizo* 1994b (1), 1–12.

Shearing, C., "Reinventing Policing: Policing as Governance," in F. Sack, M. Voss, D. Frehsee, A. Funk and H. Reinke (eds.), *Privatisierung Staatlicher Kontrolle: Befunde, Konzepte, Tendenzen* (Baden-Baden: Nomos Verlagsgellschaft, 1995).

Shearing, C., "'A New Beginning', for Policing," *Journal of Law and Society* 2000 (27:3), 386–393.

Shearing, C., "Transforming Security: A South African Experiment," in H. Strang and J. Braithwaite (eds.), *Restorative Justice and Civil Society* (Cambridge: Cambridge University Press, 2001a).

Shearing, C., "A Nodal Conception of Governance: Thoughts on a Policing Commission," *Policing and Society* 2001b (11), 259–272.

Shearing, C., "Punishment and the Changing Face of Governance," *Punishment and Society* 2001c (3:2), 203–220.

Shearing, C. and M. Kempa, "The Role of 'Private Security,' in Transitional Democracies," in M. Shaw (ed.), *Crime and Policing in Transitional Societies*, Seminar Report (Johannesburg: Konrad-Adenauer-Stiftung, 2001).

Slabbert, M., "Violence on Cinema and Television and in the Streets," in D. Davis and M. Slabbert (eds.), *Crime and Power in South Africa: Critical Studies in Criminology* (Cape Town: David Philip, 1985).

Smart, C., "Feminist Approaches to Criminology or Postmodern Woman meets Atavistic Man," in L. Gelsthorpe and A. Morris (eds.), *Feminist Perspectives in Criminology* (Milton Keynes: Open University Press, 1990).

South African Institute of Race Relations, *South Africa Survey* (Johannesburg: South African Institute of Race Relations, 2001).

South African Law Commission, *Community Dispute Resolution Structures*, Discussion Paper 87 (Project 94) (Pretoria: South African Law Commission, 2001).

Sumner, Colin, "Crime, Justice and Underdevelopment: Beyond Modernisation Theory," in Colin Sumner (ed.,) *Crime, Justice and Underdevelopment* (London: Heinemann, 1982).

Taylor, I., P. Walton and J. Young, *The New Criminology* (London: Routledge, 1973).

Taylor, R. and M. Shaw, "The Dying Days of Apartheid," in D. Howarth and A. Norval (eds.), *South Africa in Transition: New Theoretical Perspectives* (Basingstoke: Macmillan, 1998).

Trojanowicz, R. and B. Bucqueroux, *Community Policing: A Contemporary Perspective* (Cincinnati: Anderson Publishing, 1990).

Tshehla, B., *Non-State Ordering in the Post Apartheid South Africa – A Study of Some Structures of Non-State Ordering in the Western Cape Province*, Masters dissertation (Cape Town: Institute of Criminology, University of Cape Town, 2001).

Tshehla, B., "Non-state Justice in the Post Apartheid South Africa," *African Sociological Review* 2002 (6:2), 47–70.

Van der Spuy, E., "Crime and its Discontents: Recent South African Responses and Policies," in M. Shaw (ed.), *Crime and Policing in Transitional Societies*, Seminar Report (Johannesburg: Konrad-Adenauer-Stiftung, 2001).

Van Zyl Smit, D., "Adopting and Adapting Criminological Ideas: Criminology and Afrikaner Nationalism in South Africa," *Contemporary Crises* 1989 (13), 227–251.

Van Zyl Smit, D., "Introduction: Contextualizing Criminology in Contemporary South Africa," in D. Hansson and D. van Zyl Smit (eds.), *Towards Justice?: Crime and State Control in South Africa* (Cape Town: Oxford University Press, 1990).

Van Zyl Smit, D., "Criminological Ideas and the South African Transition," *British Journal of Criminology* 1999 (39:2), 198–215.

Wilson, James Q. and G. Kelling, "Broken Windows: the Police and Neighbourhood Safety," *Atlantic Monthly* 1992 (127: March), 29–38.

Wilson, R., *The Politics of Truth and Reconciliation in South Africa: Legitimising the Post-Apartheid State* (Cambridge: Cambridge University Press, 2001).

Young, J., "Left Idealism, Reformism and Beyond: from New Criminology to Marxism," in B. Fine, R. Kinsey, J. Lea, S. Picciotto and J. Young (eds.), *Capitalism and the Rule of Law* (London: Hutchinson, 1979).

Young, J., "The Failure of Criminology: the Need for a Radical Realism," in R. Matthews and J. Young (eds.), *Confronting Crime* (London: Sage, 1986).

Young, J., "Ten Points of Realism," in J. Young and R. Matthews (eds.), *Rethinking Criminology: The Realist Debate* (London: Sage, 1992).

Young J., "Incessant Chatter: Recent Paradigms in Criminology," in M. Maguire, R. Morgan and R. Reiner (eds.), *The Oxford Handbook of Criminology* (Oxford: Oxford University Press, 1994).

Young J., *The Exclusive Society* (London: Sage, 1999).

[27]

Creating Institutions: Linking the 'Local' and the 'Global' in the Travel of Crime Policies

Susanne Karstedt

Institutions represent the 'technologies of the social.' They are increasingly modelled and transported to other cultures and societies, and criminal justice institutions—traditional, parochial, and local as they are—are no exception to this. Problems of crime and insecurity have engendered the travelling of institutions from the centre to the periphery and vice versa. This paper will explore the problems which arise from travelling and modelling, and from the transport and creation of institutions in the area of criminal justice. An important feature in the travel of criminal justice institutions is the use of 'local knowledge' and its role in this process.

Keywords: Linking Social Capital; Criminal Justice Institutions; Modes of Knowledge Production; Applied and Basic Science; Local Knowledge; Universalism and Particularism in Criminal Justice

Introduction

Recently, people from indigenous communities at the shores of the Amazon River got in touch with the Metropolitan Police of London via the Internet. They wanted advice on the most successful crime prevention policies and policing strategies for deployment in their remote communities. What advice they got, and if they could put it to

---

Susanne Karstedt is Professor of Criminology in the School for Criminology, Education, Sociology and Social Work at Keele University. Her research and publications include cross-cultural and cross-national comparisons of violence and corruption, on white collar and middle-class crime, on democracy, crime and justice, and on transitional justice. Her most recent publications include Special Issues of the *British Journal of Criminology* and of the *Annals of the American Academy of Political and Social Science*. Parts of this paper have been published in Hope and Karstedt (2003), and were written during a Visiting Fellowship at RegNet at the Australian National University, 2004. Correspondence to: Susanne Karstedt, Criminology, CESSW, Keele University, Keele, Staffordshire ST5 5BG, UK. Email: s.karstedt@keele.ac.uk

good use, are not known. What vexed the small audience of criminologists, most of whom were stunned by this story, were two questions: why did they think that strategies of metropolitan policing in the UK had something on offer for their crime problems, and secondly, was there any chance that the most recent inventions of community policing could be useful advice for their small and presumably closely knit communities?

At the beginning of the 1980s, Cohen (1982) had fervently warned against the (then) uncritical transport of Western and First World crime policies to Third World countries. He pointed out the 'iatrogenic' effects of such transport from the centre to the periphery, for instance, that what should heal and solve the problems actually exacerbated them or, in the worst case, produced new and unintended ones. Moreover, while countries in the Third World were in the course of abandoning traditional forms of social control and criminal justice that had been firmly embedded in their communities for centuries, under the pressure of introducing modernized forms of criminal justice, the very countries from which they were going to import these models, were reverting to 'community crime prevention,' and rediscovering the potential of neighbourhoods and communities for more parochial forms of crime control.

Presently, the global travel of crime policies and policing strategies takes many roads and has many faces. First, the routes of travel are neither one-way routes from the centre to the periphery, or back, but can be best described as 'criss-crossing' the globe. The Zwelethemba model of 'Community Peace Committees' in South Africa (Johnston & Shearing, 2003) has been transported to Argentina on a 'South-to-South' route, and exchanges are taking place within Asia and Africa. Second, the types of criminal justice policies that travel are increasingly varied. Restorative Justice in many forms has become one of the most successful travelling models; the agenda of 'What Works' in crime prevention and criminal justice has provided models for community policing, offender treatment, and crime prevention that promise universal applicability independent of the circumstances and environment where they are implanted (see critically Worrall, 2004). Finally, the argument has been made that, in the wake of (neo-liberal) economic policies, the USA is presently the source of the greatest number of exported ideas and practices, having spread its ideas to Western Europe (Jones & Newburn, 2003); to the transitional countries of East and Central Europe, to South Africa (Dixon, 2004); and to Latin America (Wacquant, 2003).

Two other aspects of this global travel need to be mentioned here: the import and export of the most advanced information technologies, and the exchange of knowledge as a most important resource in this process. The pool of knowledge on crime prevention is becoming international and transnational. As a result, the problems, underlying theoretical assumptions, and shortfalls of crime prevention measures and criminal justice programmes in one system are being transported with equal speed into other systems and tend to multiply, often in the form of unintended consequences and failures (see Cohen, 1982; Karstedt, 2001).

This crime policy transfer raises a number of questions (Newburn & Sparks, 2003, p. 4). Specifically, which particular policies, practices, or ideas are transferred? Who is involved in such transfers? What is transferred—are these programmes, instruments, information technologies and their innovative use, institutions, or just ideas? From where do the policies originate? And finally, what are the results of the global spread of policies? Do they work everywhere or is it the case that 'successful interventions do not travel well' (Pitts, 1992, p. 144), and if so, what are the causes of their failure?

The analysis of the development of crime prevention and criminal justice policies in South Africa by van Zyl Smit and van der Spuy (2003) demonstrates how these questions are intricately interrelated. South Africa can be regarded as a showcase of a transitional country, and may harbour lessons for the crime policy transfers of a number of other countries. These authors found that while juvenile justice and prisons made some considerable inroads into change and improvement, these went largely unnoticed. The thrust of policy transfers—extensively driven by international donors and powerful national interest groups—concerned security and policing. This process started with an agenda that focused on community models of crime prevention that had emerged during apartheid, but under internal pressures and external offers of policy models, it soon transformed into the rhetoric and strategies of a 'war on crime.' Realizing that the latter was not very successful, policy makers and police have taken up the former community model again (see Dixon, 2004). South Africa is a perfect demonstration that presently, models and policies of policing and provision of security are the foremost and most visible global travellers.

It has been argued that policy transfers are mainly shaped and influenced by the complexity and feasibility of the policy (or instruments, practices, and programmes) in question. I will argue in contrast (as I have done elsewhere: Karstedt, 2001, 2003) that the cultural, socio-political, and in particular institutional context at the receiving end is decisive for the success and impact of such transfers. If successful interventions neither travel nor settle down well, their failure in cultures and environments different from those where they have been invented and proven a success, seems to be much less the result of specific features, traits, and deficiencies of the intervention, than of cultural, structural, and institutional 'misfits.' Consequently the focus of this paper is on the 'local' and 'particular,' in contrast to the global and universal. While a certain level of convergence between crime policies and a certain measure of universality in the causes cannot be denied, I will focus on local institutions and the key role they play in the travelling of crime policies.

Institutions, in particular criminal justice institutions, are thoroughly local and parochial. The imaginative faculties of collectives such as groups, communities, and nations are most visible in the creation of their institutions. Institutions can be termed as 'technologies of the social,' and the invention of institutions is the field where the 'social creativity' of humankind most visibly thrives. Criminal justice institutions—from penal codes, policing, or security provision to prisons, offender treatment, or restorative justice—are most apt to demonstrate this 'institutional inventiveness' by their sheer diversity across history as well as the globe. Criminal justice institutions (besides family law) may be the most traditional, parochial, and local set of institutions to be found in our age of global exchange. Consequently, the change of institutions is overwhelmingly incremental and path dependent. That is, yesterday's practices and choices are the initial starting point for today's practices and choices, and thus shape future ones to a considerable degree. Or, in other words, the process of learning by which we arrived at today's institutions constrains future choices. This is exactly the reason why the institutional framework of criminal justice is of utmost importance in the transfer of crime policies, and why this framework is decisively local.

Consequently, criminal justice institutions and policies differ widely even between countries that are generally seen as very similar, like Western democracies, and crime policies do not travel easily even between these. Thus, the UK did not adopt 'Megan's Law' from the USA, a law which requires convicted sex offenders to reveal themselves to the community before settling down (Jones & Newburn, 2003). Australia implemented a 'harm reduction' strategy for drug users instead of waging a 'war on drugs' (O'Malley, 2003, 2004), and most Western European countries do not follow the model of the UK by clearly restricting or outrightly rejecting the use of CCTV cameras.

Further, the institutional framework is the place of relevant local and particularistic knowledge for solving crime problems and designing preventive policies. In contrast, when crime policies travel they do so on the assumption that they are founded on 'universal knowledge and theories' that apply mostly independent of specific contexts, or can be adapted to a small number of contextual factors (see Karstedt, 2001). Cognitive behavioural treatment programmes for offenders are based on this assumption (Worrall, 2004), as are programmes targeting early intervention for children at risk. In a similar vein, situational crime prevention programmes like target hardening or other strategies that change the physical environment are assumed to 'work everywhere.' Notably, both early risk intervention and situational (designing out crime) prevention figured prominently in the planning of crime prevention policies in post-apartheid South Africa (Dixon, 2004, p. 170).

This assumption of 'universal foundations' and a small number of universal criminogenic factors was criticized by Cohen (1982) on the grounds that formal criminal justice procedures as well as crime prevention programmes could—like health policies—engender unintended consequences when implanted in different cultural, sociopolitical, and institutional environments. Cohen, at that time, observed that crime prevention programmes were often suggested on purely theoretical reasoning, and nearly all of those transported from the USA or Western European countries had not, even there, been properly evaluated, and any effect remained highly contested. This situation has basically not changed. The 'Broken Windows' theory on which Zero Tolerance policing was based theoretically (besides its managerial and information technology foundation) has been severely challenged in recent research (Eck & Maguire, 2000; Harcourt, 2001; Taylor, 2001). Cognitive Behavioural Programmes for offenders have meanwhile been found to have little or even counterproductive impact in the UK, presumably for very similar reasons why they failed to help Aboriginal offenders in Australia. According to Worrall (2004), in an environment of 300 different Aboriginal languages many Aboriginal offenders can barely speak English. Similarly, one of the reasons for the failure of the programme as per the evaluation report was the lack of literacy skills amongst UK offenders (ibid.). Many 'importing' countries cannot afford expensive evaluation programmes in order to find out how these programmes work in their environment (for South Africa see Dixon, 2004, p. 171). This does not imply that 'universal' knowledge does not exist in the field of crime prevention and criminal justice; the problem seems to be that like all new technologies, the technologies of the social have to be adapted to different environments.

Not incidentally, most critics of travelling crime prevention programmes identify the lack of a functioning framework of criminal justice institutions (for Brazil, see Wacquant, 2003) and of vertical links between the state and its overarching institutions and crime prevention programmes 'on the ground' in communities (for South Africa, see Dixon, 2004) as decisive reasons not only for failure, but for far-reaching and detrimental consequences. Wacquant predicts for Brazil that the dramatic increase in police repression in the wake of the introduction of Zero Tolerance policing has dire 'consequences on the social fabric as well as on state-society-relationships' (Wacquant, 2003, p. 198). He identifies three causes, two of which are directly related to criminal justice policies. First, criminal justice interventions are themselves extremely violent, and firmly embedded in a violent police culture. Second, colour discrimination is endemic to the Brazilian police and judicial bureaucracies, both systematically disadvantaging the poor. Consequently, Zero Tolerance policies—far from offering managerial security solutions—exacerbate the built-in failings of criminal justice institutions. For South Africa, Dixon (2004, p. 170) identifies the lack of established links that vertically connect local communities to resources (of power and participation) as well as authority in civil society as reasons behind the failure of these polices (see also van Zyl Smit & van der Spuy, 2003). However, crime prevention policies might generate similar problems in the exporting countries, and in fact, more convergence in failure and problems than originally assumed seems to exist. As Hope and Karstedt (2003) point out for the UK, the reliance on formal social control or CCTV depletes the 'natural social controls' in communities, and community crime prevention schemes actually are taken up by, and provide security to the better off (and those who live in higher security environments) instead of to those who are most affected by crime in their neighbourhoods. The following sections will address two questions that arise from these various problems and failures: first, what is the role of institutions in the travel of crime policies? Second, how can we tap into and make proper use of 'local knowledge' in crime prevention and criminal justice?

Forging the Links: The Role of Institutions

We find all types of practices, strategies, and technologies of crime prevention travelling around the globe. CCTV is a technology that is spreading rapidly. Private policing has risen to or even overtaken the number of public police nearly everywhere (Braithwaite, 2000; Johnston & Shearing, 2003). A combined package of managerial approaches, new technologies, and theories like Zero Tolerance travels swiftly with doubtful impact. Private prisons or electronic monitoring obviously travel at a much slower pace, even to countries that can provide the necessary infrastructure and cover their costs. Neighbourhood Watch schemes have travelled from Britain to South Africa, linking up there with community and popular justice, while they never became popular in most of the other West European countries. Even if practices, technologies, or packaged programmes seem to travel more or less on their own they need an institutional link to be 'plugged in.' South Africa offered established institutions of community justice which could be dated back to pre-apartheid and were not abolished during this period, for community crime prevention schemes to be 'plugged in.' Germans, for reasons also dating back to their history of authoritarian regimes, are extremely reluctant to subscribe to Neighbourhood Watch schemes.

I will try to explore the role of the institutional/organizational structure in the travelling of crime prevention and justice programmes by analysing 'cases' of success and failure. They will inform us about mechanisms that institutions contribute in the framework of criminal justice: links between people of difference, links between people and institutions, and trust in institutions. I will start by briefly sketching the specific institutional/organizational structure within the field of criminal justice.

Institutions—at the most general level—provide the formal structure that humans impose on human interactions in order to reduce insecurity. As such, institutions are the rules of the game, both formal rules and informal constraints; these are laws, conventions, norms of behaviour, self-imposed codes of conduct as well as the ways in which these are enforced. As such, institutions include our moral codes as well as our formal laws (North, 1996). Institutions create special situations (like trials in court, arrests by police officers, searches, or training of offenders in prison) with a special system of authority, accountability, and responsibility (Stinchcombe, 2003). Organizations are the 'players' in this game by combining the efforts of a group of people under a common objective and regulating their day-to-day operations (North, 1996). Institutions and organizations thus interact in their respective field.

The system of criminal justice and the provision of security can be singled out as a special institutional field or 'matrix' (North, 1996), where organizations are tasked to enforce the rules. 'Legal pluralism' characterizes this field, indicating that enforcement of rules is taking very different shapes, and takes place within highly diverse settings—from courts to informal or 'popular' justice. The institutional matrix of criminal justice and the provision of security further occupy a unique position in the societal framework of institutions. It is intricately linked to the political institutions, and simultaneously embedded in the general belief systems of society, and embodied in communities. Thus, criminal justice can be easily 'captured' by political institutions, but it also mirrors and supports social institutions and deeply rooted belief systems of a wide range. Unlike the market and market institutions, the institutional framework of criminal justice is much less a driving force of social change than reactive toward changes. Markets easily globalize, however, political institutions and belief systems build a set of strong constraints against change into criminal justice, and thus make it a unique institutional environment for the import of practices, programmes, and technologies of crime prevention, security, and justice delivery. Conceptualizing the institutional/organizational framework of the criminal justice field in this narrower way—as attempted here—however, draws attention to imports from other institutional fields within society. Most important in this respect are regulatory institutions that have evolved in the economy (see Braithwaite, 2003; Braithwaite & Drahos, 2002).

Success and the Role of Principles

According to van Zyl Smit and van der Spuy (2003), both prison reforms and reforms of the juvenile justice system in South Africa were partially and moderately successful in introducing profound legal changes, which were the result of modelling legislation from other countries (see Braithwaite & Drahos, 2000; Karstedt, 2003), and of changes driven by the new constitution and the constitutional court. In other words, these were simultaneously exogenous and endogenous changes, which interacted in the process. In particular the endogenous changes encouraged by the new constitution and constitutional court transformed the wider institutional environment. These changes were principled, and less driven by outcome considerations in the form of crime reduction, though constantly in danger of being subjected to tough law and order policies. It is interesting that these were institutional changes that were linked to human rights, international charters and legislation, and sought to establish an institutional framework that was compatible with democratic institutions. However, these in turn led to substantial reforms of prisons and children's justice, which can at least be regarded as a moderate and partial success.

The significance of imports that are driven by principle and not by outcome is pertinently illustrated by a particular 'negative policy transfer,' that is, by the non-adoption of a particular policy (Newburn & Sparks, 2003, p. 5). Western European countries would not import practices of corporal punishment from Singapore, despite the low crime rate in this city. Such an import would not be compatible with their institutional framework in the field of criminal justice, and further, would be in stark contrast to the belief systems on which criminal justice institutions are rested in these countries.

It is the change of the formal rules of the institutional 'game' which made the difference in South Africa. While not ensuring substantial justice, they provide a type of inclusionary links that can ensure formal justice. The rule of law, human rights, and constitutional principles give individuals the opportunity to solve conflicts on an equal basis, provide the prospect that their complaints are heard (even as prisoners), and ensure that their rights are respected. Institutions provide these types of formal links between individuals and groups; they transform the actions and interactions between parties and individuals. Highly developed institutions therefore significantly mitigate the negative effects of social inequality and ethnic diversity (Easterlin, 2001). Imports from countries where these institutional rules are not only well developed and enforced, but also act as safeguards in a number of ways, can easily fail in an environment with less developed institutions in the field of criminal justice. They might not build formal links between social groups, but instead widen the gaps and exacerbate conflicts between them, thus impeding the proper functioning of criminal justice institutions.

As Comaroff and Comaroff show for South Africa, these formal institutions provide a neutral medium for people to deal with conflicts and to make claims on each other and the polity where otherwise irreducible differences exist (Comaroff & Comaroff, 2000, 2003). It is a paradox—and exactly reversed from what Cohen (1982) observed two decades earlier on the travel of crime policies to post-colonial environments—that much of the export from the First World is now in crime prevention projects that are based on the assumption of closely knit communities and that promote traditional and parochial forms of social control, thus neglecting the formal and more universal institutions in criminal justice that provide vital linking functions between different people and different communities. These institutional links will be explored in the next section which focuses on failure.

Failure: Missing Links

In his detailed narrative of the recent history of crime prevention in South Africa, Dixon (2004) identifies the neglect and absence of the 'vertical dimension' in community crime prevention programmes as a major failure. Linking communities vertically to resources, power, and authority in the institutional field is vital for their ability to reduce crime (Hope, 2001). The institutional dimension in parochial social control in neighbourhoods is an essential part of what Sampson, Raudenbusch, and Earls (1997) have termed the 'collective efficacy' of communities to establish social order and prevent crime. Collective efficacy comprises on the one hand the social control of children and young people, and on the other hand the links that individuals (and collectively in the neighbourhood) have established with the local institutions of order and control: police, social services, the authorities, and the polity. These are links of confidence, through which rights are voiced, and requests forwarded, and which provide a minimum of commonweal, recognition, and belonging, where irreducible differences prevail. The capacities of institutions in dealing with differences and providing (formal) routes for individuals and groups to relate to each other beyond differences are vital in producing and nourishing links of confidence. In this capacity, institutions are decisively non-parochial, and non-local, but transcend the conflicts of the local (Karstedt, 2004).

Wacquant's (2003, p. 199) description of the potential impact of Zero Tolerance policing on Brazilian society and its poor provides the lens 'of failure' which allows for focusing on institutional mechanisms of linking. The point is not so much that Zero Tolerance policing might increase an already incredibly high level of lethal violence inflicted by the police, but that police and the courts are discriminating along racial lines, and that their incapacity and 'disinterest' to enforce the law has led to general distrust amongst the population. Zero Tolerance policing, it can be concluded, will further decrease confidence in criminal justice institutions, and increase 'legal cynicism' equally amongst the poor and the rich. Both societal groups will be further alienated from the system of criminal justice, their support for it will dwindle. Private solutions to crime and security problems will prevail, which mostly disadvantage the poor (Hope, 2000). Ultimately, Zero Tolerance will exacerbate the crime problems it was designed to solve.

It is doubtful if community crime prevention practices which focus on highly parochial forms of social control will provide a solution to the soaring crime problems in Latin American cities (Loader & Walker, 2004, p. 227). If anything, they will hardly build institutional links and instil confidence in criminal justice institutions. However, it is exactly the institutional aspect of the Zero Tolerance package that has been left behind in travelling to Brazil. Zero Tolerance was to a not insignificant extent a thorough reform of internal police management, including a crackdown on police corruption (Braithwaite, 2003, p. 21). This managerial package with closer monitoring of police might have made inroads into the use of force by the police, and through this route actually instilled more confidence in the institutions of criminal justice.

The Role of the Local and the Production of Criminological Knowledge

Crime prevention and criminal justice institutions represent an increasingly important arena where criminological knowledge is produced. Projects and programmes are the sites where the expertise of different practitioners in the field, government experts, criminologists, NGOs and, ultimately, citizens, is brought together to provide solutions to crime problems in neighbourhoods, communities, and on the national level. National and international networks for exchange have emerged and, presently, the pool of knowledge on crime prevention is becoming inter- and transnational. Local knowledge is linked and can contribute to the production of 'universal criminological knowledge.' However, it needs to be 'tapped,' stored, and integrated into the common knowledge base (see Karstedt, 2001). Local knowledge is neither superior to, nor does it differ in principle from 'universal knowledge,' but it adds particular types of knowledge: particular historical trajectories, institutional traditions, and cultural practices that help to contextualize 'universal criminological knowledge,' and to identify conditional and qualifying factors, and ultimately make full use of its potential.

The goal of crime prevention measures and criminal justice policies can be defined as responsible decision-making for the public good (whatever is defined as such). Such decision-making has to take inherent scientific uncertainties into account (see Hope, 2001). The decisions about which of the programmes and projects that circulate the globe should be implemented in a specific criminal justice environment, institutional framework, or community, and thus be made local, can neither fully rely on evidence from abroad or on local evaluations. The introduction of mandatory sentencing including a 'third strike' policy in Australian states demonstrates the role of the public good (Worrall, 2004). The decision in the Northern Territory (Australia) to withdraw mandatory sentencing was informed by considerations of its impact on Aboriginal communities, and not by a 'what works' agenda, which at this time was neither available on the exporting side, nor of course the importing one. Responsible decision-making for the public good in each local site needs to properly assess and tap into the local knowledge in order to implement the 'universal programme,' and finally to blend the local with the imported knowledge. The withdrawal of mandatory sentencing programmes in Australia was clearly informed by 'local knowledge' on and from Aboriginal communities, which suffered most from these sentencing principles.

It is also highly doubtful to what extent crime prevention programmes and criminal justice policies are based on genuinely 'universal' knowledge, even if they are travelling as certificated programmes. Community crime prevention programmes might be shaped by their particular institutional, cultural, and political environments, and are thus profoundly 'local' in many respects. On the other hand, Community Peace

Committees, other types of community, or 'popular justice' in South Africa, or Women's Night Patrols in Aboriginal communities in the Australian North seem to be genuinely 'local,' but might have a not-so-visible core of universal knowledge. The boundaries between the 'local' and the 'universal' are blurred in the field of crime prevention and criminal justice. To identify local knowledge and institutions with the 'traditional' or with 'culture' is as wrong as identifying universal knowledge as independent of traditions and cultural environment. Neither particularistic or 'local' knowledge, nor universalistic knowledge as such travels well, and it is doubtful if one has a competitive edge over the other in the global exchange of crime policies. It might be more useful to think of criminological knowledge in crime prevention, sentencing, and offender treatment programmes as multi-site local in principle. The international trade in penal ideas and practices needs a strong foundation in both local and universal knowledge unless they degenerate into mere politics, and little more than symbols are traded.

Responsible public decision-making 'on the ground,' with its inherent uncertainties in the field of crime prevention, is not inimical as such to the production of criminological knowledge. 'Responsible' here implies that the scientific enterprise related to decision-making is organized as a programme of a rationally planned and executed collection of experience and data, thus allowing for reliable, well-founded, justified, and/or proven statements and propositions (Bauman & May, 2001, p. 8). Evidence and theories that are derived in such a 'responsible way' can be agreed upon in scientific discourse including experts, practitioners, politicians, and the public. However, these are theories and propositions that are informed by knowledge of the local. How can, in the process of the export and import of criminal justice and crime prevention programmes, the local knowledge that is thus produced be preserved and contribute to the local as well as to the global stock of criminological knowledge?

Notwithstanding the current effort and amount of evaluation of crime prevention, the production of local knowledge seems to contribute much less to the stock of criminological knowledge than it could. A number of reasons explain this. Politicians and government officials need short-term evaluation and positive outcomes in order to legitimate their policies and efforts, and the process of collecting evidence is much less driven and controlled by the responsible methodologies of science than it is by the demands of governmental decision-making or other vested interests. Consequently, evaluation research focuses on the administration of projects and less on the processes that actually produce their results. That being said, evaluation contributing to our understanding of administration and organizational behaviour in local settings can prove extremely useful in the transport and travel of crime policies. Local evaluations provide the systematic knowledge of institutions, practices, and value patterns that shape the implementation of crime policies, and thus help to accumulate 'multi-site local knowledge.' Consequently, the global exchange of crime and criminal justice policies transforms the 'what works' agenda into the agenda of 'what works under which conditions,' and why it works locally.

Applied research is increasingly identified as a major or even dominant site of knowledge production, and as profoundly changing the general mode of knowledge production. Applied research is embedded locally, and thus makes knowledge production more local. This transformation of inquiry and application has been conceptualized as a transition from (traditional) Mode I production of knowledge to Mode II (Gibbons et al., 1994). Gibbons et al. conceptualize the emerging Mode II and the transition in terms of a coherent set of attributes. The relevant contrast between Mode I and Mode II is 'between problem solving which is carried out following the codes of practice relevant to a particular discipline, and problem solving which is organized around a particular application' (Gibbons et al., 1994, p. 3). Mode I describes the generally traditional context of knowledge production governed by the largely academic interests of a specific scientific community, with a separation of basic from applied research and 'linear' relationships between them. It is organized in a disciplinary way, characterized by homogeneity of approaches, institutions, and controls of evidence and findings. Consequently, it is organized in a hierarchical way, which in particular affects the type and quality of control brought to bear on data and subject matter. In contrast, Mode II is 'trans-disciplinary,' characterized by more heterogeneity; it is less hierarchical and more transient. Mode II is more accountable and reflexive, and it includes a wider, more temporary and heterogeneous set of practitioners and experts involved, who are collaborating on a problem defined in a specific and localized context.

As such, we recognize in Mode II production typical characteristics of local knowledge production, which is situated in crime prevention projects in communities, and in programmes implemented in criminal justice institutions. It is driven by particular local problems and strategies of problem solving, it draws on the 'expertise' of both practitioners and citizens (as in community crime prevention programmes), and it is based on the collaboration and knowledge-sharing mechanisms that evolve in this process. The production (and use) of local knowledge is shaped by a more diverse set of intellectual and social demands than was the case in the more traditional setting of 'applied science.' The global travel of crime policies thus requires and encourages Mode II production of knowledge.

Mode II knowledge production is particularly important for 'multi-site' local knowledge. It increases the number of potential sites where knowledge can be created; it enhances awareness about the variety of ways in which advances in criminological theory and crime prevention can affect the public interest; it encourages problem solutions that do not arise mainly from the application of knowledge that already exists, but to the contrary from the integration of existing and new types of knowledge; it produces solutions comprising both empirical and theoretical knowledge—though these may be embedded in different institutional settings, and need to be linked and fed back into each setting differently. The efficiency of knowledge production in Mode II depends in particular on the interaction, feedback, and relationships between the institutional settings, and on the quality controls that can be established in such transient situations.

Mode I and Mode II are 'types' of knowledge production, but not types of knowledge. Only roughly, they can be equated with 'universal' or 'basic' and 'local' or 'applied' knowledge. Basic science and problem solving were intertwined in many of the great discoveries of science, as for example in the work of Louis Pasteur, who started from basic research but became more and more involved in problem solving in his later years, a context in which he made his most important basic science discoveries. This clearly points to the importance of problem solving for 'basic' criminological inquiry, and to the importance of local multi-site knowledge for those crime policies which are travelling the globe with a claim to universality.

The context of Mode II knowledge production—local communities, criminal justice institutions, police unions, and national governments, just to name a few—is less stable than traditional settings of (mostly academic) knowledge production. It needs to be based on a diligent design of institutional links, networks of research, and problem solving. This particularly includes a set of quality controls that are adaptable to the 'non-hierarchical,' multi-site and transient context, and which help to deal with the vested interests and needs of politicians, experts, practitioners, and ultimately the public, in the field of crime prevention and criminal justice. Strategies of evaluation need to go beyond the 'audit model' that is preferred by governments; this might involve fewer but better evaluations on the one hand, and a diversity of less stringent evaluative strategies on the other hand. Citizens may set up their own audits. Expert and practitioner reports might equally contribute to the overall framework within which the success of the adoption of a specific crime prevention measure is assessed in order to avoid fads in crime prevention policies being adopted and, just as quickly, discarded again.

Local knowledge however, is at once too complex and too important for the public interest to be left solely to a dialogue between (government-sponsored) experts and practitioners. Alternative interpretations of data and outcomes need to be fed back not only within but also outside the specific, localized context of problem solving. New institutional designs, mechanisms, and features of collaboration between criminologists, practitioners, and the public need to be developed that can fulfil this task. Local and multi-site knowledge needs to be linked and networked, both vertically and horizontally. Flows of knowledge have to be balanced in order to feed local results back to the 'export site.' The London Metropolitan Police would have hugely profited for their own crime prevention programme from knowledge fed back to them from a remote community on the shores of the Amazon.

A Plea for Institutional Travel

Any import of crime prevention programmes or technologies into the institutional/organizational framework of criminal justice initiates changes in the 'rules of the game,' and impacts on the underlying belief system. Simultaneously, the programmes undergo a process of adaptation in the new environment. Understanding institutions—the local importing as well as exporting ones—is seminal in this process in order to avoid failure or counterproductive consequences. Tensions emerge between parochial mechanisms of crime and social control and the formal rule of law, between cultural identities and universal practices, and between local and universal knowledge. It is important to realize that the rule of law (and the institutions that are based on it) is a mechanism of governance by distance, not by proximity. This however allows institutions to function as linking mechanisms. The moderate success stories of institutional travelling, adaptation, and imagination reflect conditions where the new and old institutions fulfil their vital functions of linking people with each other and to institutions, and create trust and confidence in criminal justice institutions. The improvements gained might not directly be outcome related, but they might produce changes within the institutional field and of the rules of the game that make other strategies ultimately successful.

Institutional travel, it seems, is more promising than just the exchange of technologies and packages of crime prevention, and institutions should definitely not be left behind It has competitive advantages over the travel of highly parochial and community-based forms of crime prevention and social control, and the principled institutional change seems to have some advantages over a purely outcome-oriented import. Presently, much of institutional change and travelling is initiated and linked to international pressures, coercion, and bargaining in the transnational sphere. This type of travelling might not be the worst kind in criminal justice and crime prevention. The quest for fair, reliable, and impartial criminal justice institutions seems to be a universal one for humankind.

References

Bauman, Z., & May, T. (2001). *Thinking sociologically* (2nd ed.). Oxford: Blackwell.

Braithwaite, J. (2000). The new regulatory state and the transformation of criminology. In D. Garland & R. Sparks (Eds.), *Criminology and social theory* (pp. 47–70). Oxford: Oxford University Press.

Braithwaite, J. (2003). What's wrong with the sociology of punishment? *Theoretical Criminology, 7,* 5–28.

Braithwaite, J., & Drahos, P. (2000). *Global business regulation.* Cambridge: Cambridge University Press.

Braithwaite, J., & Drahos, P. (2002). Zero Tolerance, naming and shaming: Is there a case for it with crimes of the powerful? *The Australian and New Zealand Journal of Criminology, 35,* 269–307.

Cohen, S. (1982). Western crime control models in the Third World: Benign or malignant? *Research in Law, Deviance and Social Control, 4,* 85–119.

Comaroff, J., & Comaroff, J. (2000). Millennial capitalism: First thoughts on second coming. *Public Culture, 12,* 291–343.

Comaroff, J., & Comaroff, J. (2003). Reflections on liberalism, policulturalism and ID-ology: Citizenship and difference in South Africa. *Social Identities, 9,* 445–474.

Dixon, B. (2004). Cosmetic crime prevention. In B. Dixon & E. van der Spuy (Eds.), *Justice gained? Crime and crime control in South Africa's transition* (pp. 163–192). Cullompton: Willan.

Easterlin, W. (2001). Can institutions resolve conflict? *Economic Development and Cultural Change, 49,* 687–706.

Eck, J., & Maguire, E. R. (2000). Have changes in policing reduced violent crime? An assessment of the evidence. In A. Blumstein & J. Wallmann (Eds.), *The crime drop in America* (pp. 207–265). New York: Cambridge University Press.

Gibbons, M., Limoges, C., Nowotny, H., Schwartzmann, S., Scott, P., & Trow, M. (1994). *The new production of knowledge.* London: Sage.

Harcourt, B. E. (2001). *Illusion of order. The false promises of broken windows policing.* Cambridge, MA: Harvard University Press.

Hope, T. (2000). Inequality and the clubbing of private security. In T. Hope & R. Sparks (Eds.), *Crime, risk and insecurity* (pp. 83–106). London: Routledge.

Hope, T. (2001). Community crime prevention in Britain: A strategic overview. *Criminal Justice, 1,* 421–439.

Hope, T., & Karstedt, S. (2003). Towards a new social crime prevention. In H. Kury & J. Obergfell-Fuchs (Eds.), *Crime prevention. New approaches* (pp. 461–489). Mainz: Weisser Ring.

Johnston, L., & Shearing, C. (2003). *Governing security. Explorations in policing and justice.* London: Routledge.

Jones, T., & Newburn, T. (2003). The convergence of US and UK crime control policy: Exploring substance and process. In T. Newburn & R. Sparks (Eds.), *Criminal justice and political culture* (pp. 123–151). Cullompton: Willan.

Karstedt, S. (2001). Comparing cultures, comparing crime: Challenges, prospects and problems for a global criminology. *Crime, Law and Social Change, 36,* 285–308.

Karstedt, S. (2003). Durkheim, Tarde and beyond: The global travel of crime policies. In T. Newburn & R. Sparks (Eds.), *Criminal justice and political culture* (pp. 16–29). Cullompton: Willan.

Karstedt, S. (2004). Linking capital: 'Institutionelle Dimensionen sozialen Kapitals.' In F. Kessel & H.-U. Otto (Eds.), *Soziale Arbeit und soziales Kapital. Zur Kritik lokaler Gemeinschaftlichkeit* (pp. 45–62). Wiesbaden: VS Verlag fuer Sozialwissenschaften.

Loader, I., & Walker, N. (2004). State of denial? Rethinking the governance of security. *Punishment and Society, 6,* 221–228.

Newburn, T., & Sparks, R. (2003). Criminal justice and political cultures. In T. Newburn & R. Sparks (Eds.), *Criminal justice and political culture* (pp. 1–15). Cullompton: Willan.

North, D. C. (1996). *Where have we been and where are we going?* Economic History, Economics Working Paper Archive at WUSTL. St Louis, MO: Washington University.

O'Malley, P. (2003). Globalising risk? Distinguishing styles of 'neoliberal' criminal justice in Australia and the USA. In T. Newburn & R. Sparks (Eds.), *Criminal justice and political culture* (pp. 30–48). Cullompton: Willan.

O'Malley, P. (2004). *Risk, uncertainty and government.* London: Glasshouse.

Pitts, J. (1992). The end of an era. *The Howard Journal of Criminal Justice, 31,* 133–149.

Sampson, R. J., Raudenbusch, S., & Earls, F. (1997). Neighborhoods and violent crime: A multilevel study of collective efficacy. *Science, 277,* 918–924.

Stinchcombe, A. L. (2003). Cultures of discipline: Law teaches Hawaii to become a colony. *Law and Social Inquiry, 28,* 591–608.

Taylor, R. B. (2001). *Breaking away from broken windows.* Boulder, CO: Westview.

van Zyl Smit, D., & van der Spuy, E. (2003). Importing criminological ideas in a new democracy: Recent South African experiences. In T. Newburn & R. Sparks (Eds.), *Criminal justice and political culture* (pp. 184–208). Cullompton: Willan.

Wacquant, L. (2003). Toward a dictatorship over the poor? *Punishment and Society, 6,* 197–205.

Worrall, A. (2004). What works and the globalisation of punishment talk. In G. Mair (Ed.), *What matters in probation* (pp. 327–345). Cullompton: Willan.

[28]

Globalizing risk?

Distinguishing styles of 'neo-liberal' criminal justice in Australia and the USA

PAT O'MALLEY

Carleton University, Ottawa, Canada

Abstract

In the criminal justice arena, the convergence of analyses of 'actuarial justice' and the 'risk society' thesis, has led many to assume that we will experience a global shift towards risk-based models of justice that are statistical, repressive and incapacitating. It is argued in this article that even where we focus on national jurisdictions sharing risk frameworks of justice and the adoption of neo-liberal politics, there is little evidence that actuarial justice has been successfully exported from the USA. By examining recent developments in Australia, it is shown that local political formations and social conditions have meant that models of justice that are both neo-liberal and risk-based in character diverge so much from US models—in form and function—that we cannot make useful global generalizations about the political character or correctional value of such regimes, or about their simple 'transportability' across jurisdictional boundaries.

Key Words

• actuarialism • justice • incapacitation • neo-liberalism
• punishment • risk

The development of risk and 'risk society' themes in current social theory has been associated in criminology with a widespread effort to identify more and more examples of risk-based justice, in more and more countries. In addition to the USA and the UK, risk has been identified as a technique in the criminal justice systems of many countries including Canada, Australia, New Zealand, France, Germany and Italy (e.g. Castel, 1991; Feeley and Simon, 1992; O'Malley, 1992; Hebenton and Thomas, 1996; Beck, 1997; Ericson and Haggerty, 1998; Pratt, 1998; Melossi, forthcoming). Perhaps reflecting Beck's (1992) view that risk is becoming a form of governmental consciousness that is global in its reach and implications, criminologists generally have been content—if often dismayed—to identify more and more examples of risk technique in the governance of crime, affecting more and more people. Consequently there has been much less emphasis on the significance of political and technical differences among risk technologies than on their unity as instances of risk. Yet there is surely a major gulf of form and function separating, say, the 'new vigilantism' of Megan's laws from either the therapeutic interventions of developmental crime prevention or the economically rational criminology that characterizes situational crime prevention.

The partial exception to this overemphasis on risk per se has been the attention paid to the question of how technologies of risk are shaped by the political rationalities with which they are articulated. The contrast between social-liberal (welfare) and neo-liberal approaches to risk, for example, has been one site for such work in criminal justice (e.g. O'Malley, 1992; Rose, 2000). Even this work, perhaps, is affected by a form of globalized thinking, as it is assumed that the meaning or application of 'neo-liberal' is pretty well identical in nature and impact across jurisdictional and national boundaries. Yet the virulently anti-welfare stance of the United States neo-liberalism has little in parallel in 'neo-liberal' countries such as Australia, Canada and New Zealand, where welfare apparatuses are substantially intact, if partially 'translated' into forms more compatible with economically rational sensibilities (e.g. Dean, 1995).

If we attend to such differences in risk techniques and in political rationalities, then we should not expect that risk-based strategies and policies will take on substantially similar forms in all 'neo-liberal' countries. Nor should we assume that variations will be of such minor nature that their 'joint' character as risk-based and neo-liberal will be enough to render them readily transferable among jurisdictions. In this light, I want to examine two closely linked questions. The first is why it is that 'Actuarial Justice', for many criminologists almost the definitive form of risk-based criminal justice, has been almost without impact in Australia. The second concerns why Australia rejected an American-style War on Drugs—a 'war' that has done much to fuel Actuarial Justice in the USA, and that deploys actuarial techniques coercively. Instead of adopting these socially exclusionary technologies of risk, in Australia the most highly developed and visible development of risk-based governance has been a national policy of drug harm minimization that makes a *socially integrative* strategy out of risk.

Actuarial Justice in the United States

Actuarial Justice has been identified as the ascendant strategy of 'risk-based' criminal justice (Feeley and Simon, 1992, 1994). In this form, risk-based justice is predictive and statistical, and is systematically and managerially arranged in terms of internal or system-focused criteria of efficiency (such as speed of throughput rather than reduction in recidivism rates). It also incorporates forms of knowledge and practice that reduce the interventions of justice to merely incapacitating techniques that displace punitive, reintegrative, correctional or deterrent strategies. Examples include the reappearance of curfews managing 'at risk' groups, times and places; the emergence of 'three strikes' laws that abandon proportional sentencing and individual justice in favour of formula-based sentencing according to risk; the massive expansion of prison warehousing and of home detention as purely incapacitating measures. All these, and more, have been examined as part of the formation of knowledge and power that is Actuarial Justice. Accordingly, most academic research and theory—as opposed to much administrative criminology—has regarded the emergence of Actuarial Justice, and of risk more generally, as a blight on criminal justice (Baumann, 2000; Hudson, 2000; Kempf-Leonard and Peterson, 2000; Miller, 2001). Risk appears, explicitly or implicitly, as a negative turn that undermines the modest advances made towards a reconstructive, inclusive and reintegrative criminal justice during the middle ('welfare state') part of the 20th century. By centring insecurity and threat, the governmental grid of risk is seen to work though negation: certain persons are defined primarily in terms of their purely negative and dangerous status as threats to others (victims), and accordingly are merely neutralized and segregated in new gulags of incapacitation.

As is often the fate of major breakthroughs, Feeley and Simon's work on risk in criminal law and penology has been followed by a rush to identify confirming instances, and in the process the specificity of Actuarial Justice has become something of a casualty. Actuarial Justice does not exhaust the play of risk in the field of criminal law and criminal justice, and significant distinctions among strategies of risk-based justice have tended to be overlooked. In this respect, Feeley and Simon themselves provide many insights and observations about the nature and genealogy of Actuarial Justice that should have merited greater caution and finer analytic investigation than they subsequently have been accorded. In the first section of this article I wish to return to their classic analysis and consider more closely some of their arguments. I will suggest that Actuarial Justice appears as a categorically exclusionary strategy of risk, distinct from inclusive and restorative risk technologies and strategies such as insurance and drug harm minimization. As such, Actuarial Justice is profoundly shaped by, and allied with, a tradition of political conservatism—particularly *per medium* of the political invention of the Underclass as the primary problem to be governed through criminal justice.

Actuarial Justice and the politics of exclusion

In their discussion of the context and shaping of Actuarial Justice, Feeley and Simon go to some lengths to emphasize that 'actuarial thinking represents a deeper "pre-political" thought that cannot easily be associated with conventional political labels' (1994: 190). At best, they argue, politics has some impact in shaping Actuarial Justice, and that Actuarial Justice will be employed 'somewhat differently' by different political perspectives. Thus they point out that while conservatism is often associated with Actuarial Justice, traditionally it is associated with a deep-rooted juridical individualism that does not sit well with the statistical and categorical techniques of risk-based justice. The examples of political influence that Feeley and Simon do detect, perhaps in keeping with this sceptical stance, thus are rather indirect—the major instance being the possibility that conservative 'lock-em-up' policies created penal population pressures that facilitated the institutionalization of actuarial techniques.

In their analysis, there is thus little or no constitutive role for politics. This seems surprising at first glance, because the rise of Actuarial Justice historically coincides with the rise of a profoundly anti-correctional politics hostile to what Garland (1985) refers to as the 'welfare sanction'. It sought to empty prisons of social workers, reduce costs and introduce 'truth in sentencing'—but not because of promotion of a pre-political agenda of risk. Rather, it reflected a variety of reasons including a greater acceptance of deterrence as a valid penal philosophy, a hostility to the social sciences and the helping professions and a concern with fiscal accountability and cost-effectiveness (O'Malley, 1992; Rose, 1996). On face value it would seem to many that such political pressures very likely contributed to the formation of tariff-based sentencing and the evacuation of correctional content from prisons, leaving them as the 'cost-effective' warehouses for incapacitation. In other words, these critical elements of Actuarial Justice might have been an explicitly political creation.

However, the weakness of this argument, in turn, is that conservative politics has headed in other more punitive directions as well as mere warehousing, notably the current array of 'emotive and ostentatious' punishments (Pratt, 2000). Likewise, we could add that neo-liberalism would appear to have fostered progressive forms of rehabilitation—including the delivery of 'risk-needs'-based services in prisons and the development of 'enterprising prisoner' schemes—and as this latter example suggests, in some ways mere incapacitation sits ill with the neo-liberal visions of the active subject and switched-on capitalism (O'Malley, 1999b). Hence, Feeley and Simon could be supported in their claim that politics is no more than a facilitating condition, rather than a major constitutive influence, in the formation of Actuarial Justice.

Such an argument certainly reveals weakness in the 'political' case, if by that term we mean—as do Feeley and Simon—the 'pendulum swings' to Right and Left of the political field. Yet it reveals an equally difficult, indeed identical, problem for their own case. That is: if the process is merely technical or pre-political why does risk take the specific shape of Actuarial Justice when there are many other risk-based alternatives to warehousing, such as the identification and treatment of offenders' criminogenic 'risk-needs' in prison? To answer this question, we need to examine elements of the genealogy of Actuarial Justice proposed by Feeley and Simon.

In discussing the possible impact of the law and economics movement in this genealogy, they differentiate 'economic' thinking from 'actuarial' thinking (1994: 189). Both, they stress, emphasize the utilitarian purposes of punishment over the moral purpose. But an 'economic' approach treats the offender as a rational choice actor, whereas Actuarial Justice 'treats the offender as *inert*, from the point of view of influencing decision making' (1994: 189, emphasis added). Economic reasoning thus is associated with deterrence rather than incapacitation, and incapacitation is identified as the 'pure' actuarial response. But what is pure actuarialism? For example, if effective risk reduction is its characteristic, then risk-needs and preventative interventions have been argued to be superior to incapacitation (see O'Malley, 2000). If it is cost-effective risk management, isn't this an economic actuarial argument? And in any case, long-term 'empowerment' has been claimed by some as more cost-effective than incapacitation (Rand Corporation, 1995). In short, it is not clear on what criterion incapacitation can appear as pure or undiluted actuarialism. The point, rather, would appear to be that, as Ewald observes, the technology of risk is highly abstract, so that *any* applications in an institutional setting 'are not *the* application of a technology of risk; they are always just *one* of its possible applications' (1991: 198, emphases added).

We might also consider that it would be difficult to argue that other technologies—such as situational crime prevention—are somehow not 'actuarial' or not fundamentally risk-based simply because they deploy a rational choice actor as their subject (see, for example, Clarke et al., 2000). This point is by no means trivial or marginal to our understanding of the character of Actuarial Justice. As David Garland has argued (1996, 2001), the rational choice actor is the subject of what he terms a 'criminology of the self'. This is a criminology that defines crime as 'normal' in the sense that anyone could be a criminal under the right conditions—the criminal is not a distinctive type of person. Thus Felson and Clarke stress, for situational crime prevention 'nobody is exempt from the temptation to commit crime since human weaknesses are widespread and not confined to any one segment of the population' (1997: 205). Consequently, situational crime prevention and other rational choice-based approaches do not seek to exclude types or categories of persons, or sectors of the population. Rather, they seek to deter abstract and universal potential offenders by rendering the effort and risk of offending greater than the likely benefits. In this way, they converge with judicial deterrence. But they do so as Garland suggests by seeking to govern 'criminogenic situations', that is (more generally) to focus on the risks associated with environmental conditions, rather than with categories or types of person (Garland, 1996).

What does this tell us about the *specific* form of risk approach taken by Actuarial Justice? The critical point again is made by Feeley and Simon when they note that 'the rise of incapacitation and the other instruments of Actuarial Justice [are] a reflection of social forces . . . [pushed] a large portion of the population out of the range of normal economic signals' (1994: 189). In short, deterrence will not work for this social category, and thus Actuarial Justice is to be distinguished from situational crime prevention and related technologies of risk that focus on universal and abstract subjects. In this way Feeley and Simon see the distinction between deterrent models and Actuarial Justice as critical to their case. This social category is the largely Black and Hispanic 'Underclass', seen as permanently excluded from upward social mobility and economic integration by the effects of a global restructuring of the economy (see also Baumann, 2000). Not only is deterrence imagined as unworkable for this category but reintegration and rehabilitation are also rendered irrelevant, for there is nothing to integrate them into. The heavy industrial and related economic sector that once provided for this category's employment has—as a consequence of globalization—disappeared from the local economy. What therefore is installed is a government strategy designed quite specifically to contain this irredeemable, irremediable and dangerous 'other' population.

Looked at in this way, in line with the general tenor of Feeley and Simon's own analysis, Actuarial Justice emerges not as a pure form of pre-political risk management. Rather it is a specific actuarial strategy designed and assembled for a specific governmental—and in this sense, political—purpose. In contrast to the risk technologies that deploy the universal rational actor as their subject, the subjects of this strategy are neither abstract-universal nor 'normal', nor are they subject to normalization. To these others—that are not like us and cannot become like us—the specific strategies of categorically exclusionary risk are applied.

Despite the realist dimensions of their Underclass argument, equally strong is the stress Feeley and Simon place on the inventedness of this category. That is, the Underclass is a governmental category originally created within a 'critical' sociology but appropriated subsequently by (largely conservative) politicians and commentators. Indeed, I would add to this argument the claim that the Underclass appears as the product of a neo-liberal political rationality. The same strategies of global governance that are implicated in relocating the Underclass members' means of employment to the Third World—in the name of competition and efficiency—are also responsible for inventing the spectre of welfare dependency, and of welfare as generating a fiscal crisis of the state. The Underclass was invented and deployed in the USA at the same time that welfare was being withdrawn as 'counterproductive and costly'—and in relation to a population that now could be defined as having become 'dependent', as having lost the will to work and the ability to make an enterprise of their lives. A governmental invention that, on the contrary, defined this population as *a victim* of global restructuring, as Baumann (2000) for example sees them, could well have rendered these people candidates for welfare inclusion and social justice rather than exclusion and incapacitation.

I find two things persuasive about this argument. First, the strategy and techniques of categorically exclusionary risk, to which Actuarial Justice belongs, have subsequently been applied to other categories that fall specifically under the umbrella of irremediable and dangerous otherness. Persistent violent and sexual offenders are the prime candidates. These have become subject to the array of 'Megan's laws', which in various ways notify the community of the identity of former offenders. As Simon himself subsequently has noted, the veneer of technical 'neutrality' of Actuarial Justice is transformed in the risk-based Megan's laws into a politics of vengeance:

> the development of modern institutions, particularly the prison, was aimed at displacing popular emotions from the centre of punishment by extending the control of state based professionals. From a spectacle of solidarity between state and the people against their common enemies, punishment became a vehicle for inculcating habits of order suitable to a democratic society. Megan's law is a shift away from this process of modernization. Starting with its name, and with the central role given to local prosecutors in applying the risk classification, Megan's law advertises itself as a new hybrid of public and private vengeance.
>
> (Simon, 1998: 464)

Thus, while Megan's laws are similar in some respects to such other risk strategies as situational crime prevention, and while certainly mobilized in the name of potential victims taking 'rational' and 'reasonable' steps to protect themselves (Levi, 2000), these risk strategies are distinct. They are aimed at a category of subjects who are politically and governmentally demonized and excluded. These people are not 'inert'—as I think Feeley and Simon mistakenly identify the subjects of Actuarial Justice—but 'other', and in this case, evil. Significantly, as Simon's reference to Megan's laws' movement away from modernist penology indicates, these responses are like those directed at the Underclass in a key respect—they both abandon the modernist project of inclusionary reform and adopt a technology of categorical exclusion.

Actuarial Justice in Australia

The second persuasive issue is that while even in Britain the term 'Underclass' gained some political currency in relation to chronically unemployed youth (Reiner, 1992; Hudson, 2000), this did not happen in countries such as Australia and New Zealand (Pratt, 2000). This was despite the existence of both youth and racial minorities eligible for the label by virtue of their chronic unemployment and high crime rates. In Australia, the early political identification of young people as being systematically exposed to chronic unemployment, and as *victims* of structural changes over which they had no control (notably under the Hawke Labour government in the 1980s), rendered the problem the responsibility of government. Inclusive solutions had to be attempted for 'our' children. The youthful unemployed were imagined as 'like us', but their *situation* was pathogenic and to be remedied. Perhaps more critically, this applies also to the Aboriginal population. Like the US 'Underclass', Aboriginal people do not have substantial access to employment and retain a political profile as culturally and racially distinct from the mainstream. But in this respect they have been understood as falling victim to a pathogenic situation in the legacy of racism and colonialism, and thus they became subject to a bipartisan politics of reconciliation. Neither in word nor form has this population been subject to the exclusionary designation of Underclass. Even the much trumpeted 'racism' of Pauline Hanson's *One Nation Party* centres policies that call for assimilation of Aboriginal people rather than their exclusion.

As a result, I would suggest, Actuarial Justice has gained only a tenuous hold in criminal law in Australia, and much the same is true in New Zealand where similar political conditions have existed (Pratt, 2000). While both Western Australia and the Northern Territory have mandatory sentencing of the 'three strikes' form, this has either been disowned or become the subject of hostile attack by all other state and federal governments, and judicatures (Roche, 1999). Even the Liberal-National (conservative) federal government has attempted to buy the Northern Territory government out of its commitment to three strikes law, as it had become generally regarded as working a racist effect upon the Aboriginal population. And while risk-based sentencing applies to the categories of repeat sexual and violent offenders in a number of other states (e.g. Victoria and NSW, and also in New Zealand), judicial opposition has been effective in marginalizing their impact (Freiberg, 2000).[1] In none of these cases has statistical evidence on recidivism been prominent in justifying the strategies, although risk to the community has certainly been central, so it is not clear that these sentences are examples of Actuarial Justice. More important in this latter respect, where mandatory sentencing does exist, warehousing has not been the principal penological response. Thus, with respect to the Northern Territory, where mandatory sentencing has been associated with the imprisonment of many Aboriginal people, the stress is on 'culturally appropriate' interventions that provide educational and vocational courses, with specific goals of 'reducing recidivism by increasing employment prospects', reduction of alcohol and drug-related harm, developing 'restorative justice' and the development of 'partnership' programmes designed to reintegrate offenders into their communities (see http://www.ourmessage.org.au). Likewise, in the case of sex and violent offenders, whatever the emphasis on risk, treatment and therapy programmes remain critical elements of the correctional programmes set up under this umbrella (Pratt, 1998).

This is not to suggest that these countries are immune to Actuarial Justice in the general sense of a strategy of risk-based categorical exclusion. Moral panics against particular, hated categories such as paedophiles, may yet see the emergence of Megan's laws and other forms of categorically exclusive actuarialism. The imprisonment of illegal migrants (refugees) in a concentration camp in the South Australian desert, although this has little to do with risk per se, certainly suggests that where existing candidates for exclusion are available, categorically excluding responses will be mobilized. But it does suggest that resort to Actuarial Justice and other strategies of exclusion has been substantially limited by the specific political genealogies of these countries, as distinct to that of the United States. In such settings, resort to other kinds of risk strategy (as opposed to Actuarial Justice itself) may still be a major characteristic of crime control and criminal justice. Crime prevention, for example, has maintained a high profile in Australia for several decades (O'Malley, 2000). But the characteristic forms of risk-based intervention are those based on rational choice models of offenders, and more recently—as will shortly be discussed—programmes that deploy revised inclusive techniques and knowledges translated from the welfare-social era. In general it is argued that, in the absence of a politics of the Underclass, inclusive criminologies of the self, rather than categorically exclusionary criminologies of the Other, have informed risk-based justice. This becomes clearer when we consider responses to the government of illicit drug consumption.

The War on Drugs, and harm minimization

The US 'War on Drugs' certainly is not a risk-based *strategy* of justice, in the sense that its central rationale is risk-based governance, but it employs many risk-based or actuarial techniques (such as random drug testing). Most critically, it centres Actuarial Justice in its repertory of weapons, for a large proportion of those imprisoned under three strikes and related legislation are convicted on drug-related charges (Austin et al., 1999). This affinity between Actuarial Justice and a military analogy of government in no small measure lies in their shared categorically exclusionary cores. As with Megan's laws, the militarization of drug policy shifts emphasis dramatically away from any sense of a technically neutral statistical deployment of risk. A threat is created and identified simultaneously as the source of risk and as 'other': whether this is the foreign drug producers; international traffickers from alien countries in the Third World; the drugs themselves and their addictive 'enslaving' properties; or the monstrous (and not coincidentally, frequently Black and Hispanic) dealers, 'addicts' and 'abusers'. Such a moral and military agenda identifies risks with evil. The response is armed exclusion and the destruction or neutralization of those identified with creating such risks. At the borders, the military and quasi-military forces seek to exclude the enemy, while Actuarial Justice excludes the enemy within. Alongside Actuarial Justice, risk-based techniques such as random drug testing extend the strategy of exclusion, even into the recesses of working, sporting and domestic life (O'Malley and Mugford, 1992). In this sense, risk-based techniques appear to be subordinated to the broader politics of exclusion in which those testing positive either are excluded by the criminal justice system or—as Simon has suggested—appear voluntarily to have rendered themselves unfit to labour (Simon, 1987).

But against the American moral War on Drugs, is set the quite contrary risk-based strategy of harm minimization (itself often a target of drug warriors (Broadhead, 1991). In its Australian and New Zealand realizations, this is explicitly associated not only with specific risk *techniques*, such as drug testing and risk identification, but with risk as a *strategy*: that is, its long-range goals and overall mode of operation are defined in terms of risks, of locating and minimizing risks (e.g. HCS, 1993). As with the War on Drugs, much of its character is intelligible once we recognize how and where it identifies risk. For harm minimization the risks are multiple; health risks, risks of corruption, risks to property, risks to productivity and so on. But these risks are not understood as embedded in the nature of particular substances, or of particular categories or types of person. Rather, harm minimization's risks are situationally pathogenic: that is, risks are created by the contexts and ways in which drugs are manufactured, supplied, used and otherwise deployed. For example, intravenous administration of drugs is linked to specific health risks; high intensity policing in turn is identified as a risk factor because it encourages high-risk means and contexts of administration; even effective drug interdiction at the border is seen to generate risks associated with drug adulteration and price increases. Likewise, methadone maintenance programmes take a central role in harm minimization not only because they lower health risks by stabilizing opiate intake, and by reducing risks associated with intravenous administration, but also because the low price of methadone reduces the pressure to commit property crime in order to buy drugs, and because its lengthy half-life allows users to take up paid work more easily—thus having roll-on effects on crime and health risks. (O'Malley, 1999a). As Marsha Rosenbaum indicates, this is quite distinct from the situation in the USA, where 'by the mid 1980s methadone usage has moved essentially from medical treatment to the *containment* of addicts—just as the criminal justice system had moved from rehabilitation to containment of "the rabble"' (1997: 100, emphasis added). Thus even where seemingly identical techniques are deployed, the model of risk is distinct—the one embracing the modernist project of normalization, the other consigning subjects to the excluded status of 'other'.

While linking such risk techniques to a framework of rational choice subjectivities is not a necessary feature of harm minimization, in the

Australian and New Zealand contexts this has become a central characteristic. Actual and potential drug users are addressed as if their drug-taking choices are, for the most part, morally neutral, but they are provided with information on the adverse risks created by drug consumption. It is then assumed they will perform the felicity calculus and many will minimize harms to themselves and others. As well as through deployment of this rational choice 'criminology of the self', illicit drug users are also 'normalized' in other, more explicit ways. Their drug taking is rendered directly comparable with licit drug taking—alcohol, tobacco and pharmaceuticals—each of which is compared unfavourably with illicit drugs in terms of aggregate health risks. They are expressly addressed as 'users' rather than as (irrational) 'addicts' or (morally corrupt) 'abusers'. And any processes that are associated with demonization, pathologizing and exclusion of users themselves are deliberately neutralized (see generally O'Malley, 1999a). In this process, coercion likewise is minimized or displaced, as voluntary participation is strongly preferred. In consequence criminal justice is to be deployed minimally, rather than maximally as in Actuarial Justice, and even then primarily as a conduit to treatment or therapeutic practices rather than as a means to punishment or incapacitation.

Of course, this is not in some sense a 'perfect' arrangement. For example, harm minimization is associated with the progressive encroachment of government of drug consumption as more and more risks are identified and measured more and more minutely. It can also be a form of government by stealth as normalization is deployed only because it 'works', in the sense of most effectively aligning the behaviours of the users with the aims of the strategy. Particular programmes and techniques are deployed not just because in some vague sense they are 'humane', 'enlightened' or 'democratic', but because of their evaluated effectiveness in preventing initial drug use and in drawing into treatment the maximum number of illicit drug users. Thus coercion, punishment and blame are displaced explicitly because current knowledge suggests them to be counterproductive.

Risk and the politics of inclusion and exclusion

It might be convenient and even wise to end the argument here. Having demonstrated the quite contrasting realization of risk in these two countries, the limits of the 'globalization of risk' theses are fairly starkly illuminated. That is, one may seriously ask whether the fact that all of these strategies in some ways have mobilized risk in the context of criminal justice, matters very much. Their respective social impacts, technical forms and political implications are so divergent as to make this shared characteristic of risk almost trivial. As well, the rejection of these major American risk strategies in Australia, and their substitution by interventions of almost polarized form, suggest rather that local political formations and tolerances so colour risk as to dispose also of any idea that the USA has successfully exported a 'new penology' of exclusion and abandonment.

However, while this may be the wise course of action, it is also somewhat trite, for surely a major and unanswered question is left in its wake. How can we reconcile the US 'neo-liberal' politics of exclusionary justice with the equally 'neo-liberal' inclusionary justice that characterizes Australian government?[2] How can both be 'neo-liberal' and yet seemingly be contradictory and even incompatible? In a recent article (O'Malley, 1999b) I argue that attempts to attribute the appearance of an array of volatile and contradictory policies in contemporary criminal justice in terms of the impact of neo-liberalism have been somewhat mistaken. If disciplinary boot camps, chain gangs, the death penalty, prison warehousing, enterprising prisoner schemes, restorative and reintegrative justice and myriad other sanctions are all neo-liberal, as is claimed across the literature, then neo-liberalism must be so all-encompassing as to have little political integrity and/or almost no explanatory power. Yet, despite some variation, neo-liberalism is associated with fairly integrated visions of the rational choice subject, the superiority of markets to deliver efficiencies and goods, freedom of choice, a 'revised autonomy' of the enterprising self, the centrality of innovation and of enterprising individualism, the small and enabling state and so on. And it appears difficult to align such political principles of optimistic 'switched-on capitalism' with strict discipline boot camps, chain gangs, prison warehousing and the death penalty. Rather, these appear much more consistent with the doctrines of a socially authoritarian conservatism, with which neo-liberalism has been allied in some contexts.

In a conservative political rationality a strong and even intrusive state is required to enforce the moral unity that is vital to social harmony, national strength and character. Duty, obedience and self-denial figure prominently. Freedom of choice, market commodification and generalized innovative individualism appear as sometimes valuable but always suspect forces, with the capacity to erode the authority of the moral order and to threaten the discipline essential to the conservative sense of social unity and purpose.

The 'New Right', influential in Britain in the Thatcher years, and largely still so in the USA, is an alliance or hybrid between neo-liberalism and neo-conservatism. While tensions always exist between its conservative and neo-liberal elements, it is held together by agreement on broad principles, notably a preference for markets and a particular take on 'freedom of the individual'. But perhaps most especially, they are linked together by a shared opposition to the welfare state, imagined as generative of dependency, sapping of initiative and enterprise and economically draining.

This interpretation allows both for a volatile and contradictory politics of criminal justice in any state where such a hybrid predominates (for example as mapped out by Garland (1996)), as well as for considerable divergences between such jurisdictions and states. Thus, for example, it can be argued that the United States has a much stronger, and more extreme, tradition of political conservatism than is the case in Australia, and this creates two quite distinctive hybrids and thus distinct polities.

This vision of the US 'conservative neo-liberalism' makes sense of the greater acceptance of categorical exclusion in the USA, and its manifestations in the moral authoritarianism of War on Drugs and social defensiveness of Actuarial Justice. In addition, it can make sense of the fact that the majority of the more 'emotive and ostentatious' (non-risk-based) legal sanctions discussed in the literature, such as chain gangs, the death penalty, military boot camps and mass warehousing *remain* largely or completely characteristic of American criminal justice—and in some of these examples, particularly of the southern states (Pratt, 2000).

Yet it is clear that there are other elements in such hybrid neo-liberalisms. In the Australian environment, the conservative elements are greatly moderated by the impact of a social-democratic tradition (linked to chronic labour shortages, a historically strong labour movement and so on). Indeed, perhaps the current Australian polity (rather like that in New Zealand and Canada) is better thought of in terms of an alliance between neo-liberalism and a social-democratic politics. Thus it was Labour governments that began the push towards neo-liberalism in Australia (the same was true for New Zealand). The direction taken by this neo-liberal hybrid has been not so much hostility to welfare collectivism aimed at dismantling it. Rather there has been a push to render it more economically 'responsible' and accountable, more 'enterprise'-based and more compatible with discourses of the 'active subject' and enterprise (e.g. Dean, 1995). Thus national health care has not been dismantled, but progressive taxation has been implemented both to make the middle classes take more of its economic burden and to push them into private sector medicine. Unemployment relief was not challenged, but linked to programmes of 'job seeking', 'lifelong learning' and the like (O'Malley, 1996). As a result, I suggest, in the criminal justice arena, only in a few instances were there assaults on the provision of *correctional* services—although punishment and deterrence moved up the hierarchy of sentencing principles. Rather, corrections were made increasingly subject to evaluation. Outsourcing of services was implemented, together with some privatization of prisons—linked to performance specifications that retain reform and retraining as central requirements. While such economic 'rationalizing' has led to reductions in service provision, prison warehousing is not generally a description that could be applied to this environment.

In the case of harm minimization, the impact of a hybrid of neo-liberal and social welfare technologies is, perhaps, still more clear. Here, as seen, therapeutic interventions are retained as central elements of the strategy of governing illicit drug consumption, and in many cases these are provided by state institutions and much the same network of agencies that characterized welfare interventions in the mid-1980s when harm minimization was formulated. Yet added to this is a crisply neo-liberal framework in which users and potential users appear as informed choice-makers (thus neutralizing visions of the welfare-dependent subject). As such, they are to be provided with information by the 'empowering' state, with the expectation that more rational activity will follow. In turn, programme evaluation and effectiveness are constant concerns, imposing some degree of 'economic responsibility', while contractual outsourcing to private and charitable agencies has replaced or supplemented state-based provision.[3]

Conclusions

Of course, a comparative analysis of this sort can never be conclusive. Other factors may well have played some role in the Australian and New Zealand rejections of the War on Drugs and the refusal of Actuarial Justice. The scale of the drug problem in the USA is undoubtedly larger (although not on a per capita basis) and this may have provided some impetus towards low-cost warehousing strategies, while in Australasia the smaller scale of the problem made therapeutic responses more feasible. Against this, however, we could equally see the sheer scale of the problem in the USA as one reason for *not* pursuing such a massive policy of social exclusion in the first place. That is, adopting a solution that consigns several million of the population to imprisonment and non-custodial incapacitation would only be regarded as 'cost-effective', or as an acceptable solution, in the light of precisely the style and tradition of conservative (and arguably racist) politics to which I have alluded.

Thus I would suggest that the distinction between the hybrid forms of neo-liberalism in these two countries has played a key role in shaping the nature of the risk-based forms of justice that have emerged. The conservative neo-liberalism of the United States provides an environment in which strategies of categorical exclusion can be directed at very large sectors of the population. The social-democratic tradition in Australia has generated distinctive responses which neo-liberalism has shaped in important ways—but the hybrid form of Australian politics is far more consistent with mentalities of categorical inclusion that render Actuarial Justice and the War on Drugs unlikely to develop as full-blown strategies of criminal justice.

No doubt theoretical priorities and allegiances dictate whether we regard the differences between these various strategies and policies as more important than their commonality in risk. Likewise, it is—for obvious reasons—a matter of political preference that decides which of these inclusive and social-democratic, or exclusive and conservative, neo-liberal modes of institutionalizing risk is regarded as preferable. However, that they are distinct in major ways, and that these distinctions reflect the filtering and translating effects of national politics seems undeniable.

Notes

1. For a 'three strikes' analogue, see also the Crimes (Serious and Repeat Offenders) Act 1992 (WA). In Victoria, the Sentencing Act 1991 (Vic) s. 6A prescribes extended imprisonment for repeat sex and violent offenders, as is also the case in Queensland (the Penalties and Sentences Act 1992 (Qld) s. 163)), Western Australia (Sentencing Act 1995 (WA) Part 14) and Tasmania (Sentencing Act 1997 (Tas) s. 19).
2. Note that this is not exactly the same question as asking the causal question of why the two politics of justice have come to differ. Such a question might be answered in terms of major differences related to the scale of the drug problem, or the existence of large-scale and ghettoized minority populations associated with the drug industry, the influence of religious fundamentalism or the weakness of organized labour (see Mugford, 1993). All of these factors, I suspect, are highly relevant. But in the last analysis, they must all have their effects in the realm of the political in order to shape criminal justice politics, and so it is to the broader political contrast that I attend here.
3. With respect to the first point, fairly typical is this statement by the Victorian government:

   > [a] harm minimisation approach acknowledges that many young people will use drugs at some stage in their life, making it critical that students acquire knowledge and skills that will assist them in making informed decisions about their drug use and so minimise any harmful effects associated with that use.
   >
   > (DSEV, 1995)

References

Austin, J., J. Clark, P. Hardyman and D. Henry (1999) 'The Impact of "Three Strikes and You're Out"', *Punishment and Society* 1(2): 131–62.

Baumann, Z. (2000) 'Social Issues of Law and Order', *British Journal of Criminology* 40(2): 205–21.

Beck, U. (1992) *Risk Society*. New York: Sage.

Beck, U. (1997) *World Risk Society*. London: Polity Press.

Broadhead, R. (1991) 'Social Constructions of Bleach in Combatting AIDS among Injection Drug Users', *The Journal of Drug Issues* 21(4): 713–37.

Castel, R. (1991) 'From Dangerousness to Risk', in G. Burchell, C. Gordon and P. Miller (eds) *The Foucault Effect. Studies in Governmentality*, pp. 281–98. London: Harvester/Wheatsheaf.

Clarke, J., S. Gewirtz and E. McLaughlen (2000) 'Reinventing the Welfare State', in J. Clarke, S. Gewirtz and E. McLaughlen (eds) *New Managerialism, New Welfare?*, pp. 1–26. Milton Keynes: Open University Press.

Dean, M. (1995) 'Governing the Unemployed Self in an Active Society', *Economy and Society* 24(4): 559–83.

DPEC (Drug Policy Expert Committee) (2000) *Drugs: Responding to the Issues, Engaging the Community*. Melbourne: Government Printer.

DSEV (Directorate of School Education, Victoria) (1995) *Get Real. A Harm Minimisation Approach to Drug Education*. Melbourne: Directorate of School Education.

Ericson, R. and K. Haggerty (1998) *Policing the Risk Society*. Toronto: University of Toronto Press.

Ewald, F. (1991) 'Insurance and Risks', in G. Burchell, C. Gordon and P. Miller (eds) *The Foucault Effect: Studies in Governmentality*, pp. 197–210. London: Harvester/Wheatsheaf.

Feeley, M. and J. Simon (1992) 'The New Penology. Notes on the Emerging Strategy of Corrections and its Implications', *Criminology* 30(4): 449–70.

Feeley, M. and J. Simon (1994) 'Actuarial Justice. The Emerging New Criminal Law', in D. Nelken (ed.) *The Futures of Criminology*, pp. 173–201. London: Sage.

Felson, M. and R. Clarke (1997) 'The Ethics of Situational Crime Prevention', in G. Newman et al. (eds) *Rational Choice and Situational Crime Prevention, Theoretical Foundations*, pp. 197–217. Aldershot: Ashgate.

Freiberg, A. (2000) 'Guerillas in Our Midst? Judicial Responses to Governing the Dangerous', in M. Brown and J. Pratt (eds) *Dangerous Offenders. Punishment and Social Order*, pp. 51–70. London: Routledge.

Garland, D. (1985) *Punishment and Welfare*. Aldershot: Gower.

Garland, D. (1996) 'The Limits of the Sovereign State', *British Journal of Criminology* 36(4): 445–71.

Garland, D. (2001) *The Culture of Control*. Oxford: Oxford University Press.

HCS (Victorian Government Department of Health and Community Services) (1993) *Victorian Drug Strategy: 1993–1998*. Melbourne: Health and Community Service, Promotions and Media Unit.

Hebenton, B. and T. Thomas (1996) 'Sexual Offenders in the Community: Reflections of Problems of Law, Community and Risk Management in the USA, England and Wales', *International Journal of the Sociology of Law* 24(4): 427–43.

Hudson, B. (2000) 'Punishment, Rights and Difference', in K. Stenson and R. Sullivan (eds) *Crime, Risk and Justice*, pp. 144–72. Exeter: Willan.

Kempf-Leonard, K. and E. Peterson (2000) 'Expanding Realms of the New Penology. The Advent of Actuarial Justice for Juveniles', *Punishment and Society* 2(1): 66–97.

Kemshall, H. (1998) *Risk in Probation Practice*. Aldershot: Ashgate.

Levi, R. (2000) 'The Mutual Constitution of Risk and Community', *Economy and Society* 29(4): 578–601.

Melossi, D. (forthcoming) 'The Cultural Embeddedness of Social Control. Reflections on the Comparison of Italian and North American Cultures Concerning Punishment', *Theoretical Criminology*.

Miller, L. (2001) 'Looking for Postmodernism in all the Wrong Places. Implementing a New Penology', *British Journal of Criminology* 41(1): 168–84.

Mugford, S. (1993) 'Social Change and the Control of Psychotropic Drugs—Risk Management, Harm Reduction and "Postmodernity"', *Drug and Alcohol Review* 12(4): 369–75.

National Crime Prevention (1999a) *Pathways to Prevention*. Canberra: National Anti-Crime Strategy.
National Crime Prevention (1999b) *Hanging Out. Negotiating Young People's Use of Public Space*. Canberra: National Anti-Crime Strategy.
Nolan, J. (1998) *The Therapeutic State. Justifying Government at Century's End*. New York: New York University Press.
O'Malley, P. (1992) 'Risk, Power and Crime Prevention', *Economy and Society* 21(3): 252–75.
O'Malley, P. (1996) 'Risk and Responsibility', in A. Osborne, T. Barry and N. Rose (eds) *Foucault and Political Reason*, pp. 189–208. London: UCL Press/ Chicago, IL: University of Chicago Press.
O'Malley, P. (1999a) 'Consuming Risks. Harm Minimisation and the Government of "Drug Users"', in R. Smandych (ed.) *Governable Places. Readings in Governmentality and Crime Control*, pp. 191–214. Advances in Criminology Series. Aldershot: Dartmouth.
O'Malley, P. (1999b) 'Volatile and Contradictory Punishment', *Theoretical Criminology* 3(2): 175–96.
O'Malley, P. (2000) 'Risk, Crime and Prudentialism Revisited', in K. Stenson and R. Sullivan (eds) *Risk, Crime and Justice*, pp. 89–103. London: Willan.
O'Malley, P. and S. Mugford (1992) 'Moral Technology. The Political Agenda of Random Drug Testing', *Social Justice* 18(4): 122–46.
Pratt, J. (1998) *Governing the Dangerous*. Sydney: Federation Press.
Pratt, J. (2000) 'Emotive and Ostentatious Punishment. Its Decline and Resurgence in Modern Society', *Punishment and Society* 2(4): 417–39.
Rand Corporation (1998) *Diverting Children from a Life of Crime*. Washington, DC: Rand Corporation.
Reiner, R. (1992) 'Policing a Postmodern Society', *The Modern Law Review* 55(6): 762–81.
Roche, D. (1999) 'Mandatory Sentencing', *Trends and Issues in Crime and Criminal Justice No. 138*. Canberra: Australian Institute of Criminology.
Rose, N. (1996) 'Governing Advanced Liberal Democracies', in A. Barry, T. Osborne and N. Rose (eds) *Foucault and Political Reason*, pp. 37–64. London: UCL Press.
Rose, N. (2000) 'Government and Control', *British Journal of Criminology* 40(2): 321–39.
Rosenbaum, M. (1997) 'The De-medicalization of Methadone Maintenance', in P.G. Erickson (ed.) *Harm Reduction: A New Direction for Drug Policies and Programs*, pp. 97–112. Toronto: University of Toronto Press.
Shearing, C. (1995) 'Reinventing Policing. Policing as Governance', in *Privatisierungstaatliche Kontrolle: Befunde, Konzepte, Tendenzen*. Baden Baden: Nomos Verlagsgesellschaft.
Simon, J. (1987) 'The Emergence of a Risk Society: Insurance, Law, and the State', *Socialist Review* 95: 61–89.
Simon, J. (1998) 'Managing the Monstrous. Sex Offenders and the New Penology', *Psychology, Public Policy and Law* 4: 453–67.
Stanko, E. (1996) 'Warnings to Women. Police Advice and Women's Safety in Britain', *Violence Against Women* 2(1): 5–24.

PAT O'MALLEY is a Canada Research Chair at Carleton University, Ottawa, and formerly was Professor of Law and Legal Studies at La Trobe University, Melbourne. Recent publications include a special issue of the journal *Economy and Society* on 'Configurations of Risk' (2000), and *Crime and the Risk Society* (1998). Current research focuses on the politics of risk and uncertainty in liberal governance.

[29]

East Meets West in Anti-Money Laundering and Anti-Terrorist Finance: Policy Dialogue and Differentiation on Security, the Timber Trade and 'Alternative' Banking

Nicholas Dorn · Michael Levi

Received: 24 August 2007 / Accepted: 7 November 2007 /
Published online: 29 December 2007

Abstract This paper compares and contrasts South East Asian and European Union countries' perceptions of the priorities for anti money laundering (AML) and anti terrorist finance (ATF) in relation to three industries: security goods and services; the timber trade; and 'informal' value transfer and banking services. It might be expected that all countries would equally support each of these aspects of AML/ATF policies, without differentiating between the industries generating the proceeds. As this paper will show, however, historical experiences, contemporary political relations and patterns of trade shape countries' approaches, resulting in distinctive enthusiasms and reservations. In a nutshell, the EU points most strongly to products and services originating in Asia as posing AML/CTF risks, and locates primary responsibility for monitoring and control as falling within Asia - a projection of risk and responsibility that is reciprocated by Asian countries. Asian countries perceive a need for tighter control of dangerous products exported by the west, for example, small arms and light weapons, and of related money laundering circuits. Asian and European policy makers increasingly articulate concerns over illegal logging and related laundering, however European importers and their governments see responsibilities for this as falling primarily within Asia. Finally, the EU (like the US) perceives high levels of laundering risk in 'informal' value transfer/banking services, in which Asian-run businesses have a global competitive advantage. For the future, as the international balance of trade shifts, and as Asia increases its influence in international fora including those concerned with AML/CTF, so the region's policy preferences may be expected to carry more weight.

N. Dorn (✉) · M. Levi
School of Social Science, Cardiff University, Glamorgan Building, King Edward VII Avenue, Cardiff CF10 3WT Wales, UK
e-mail: dornn@cardiff.ac.uk

M. Levi
e-mail: levi@cardiff.ac.uk

N. Dorn
School of Law, Erasmus University Rotterdam, P.O. Box 1738, 3000 DR Rotterdam, The Netherlands

Keywords Alternative money remittance systems · European Union · Illegal logging and timber trade · Money laundering · Policies and regulation · Security at sea · South East Asia · Terrorist finance · Trade in small arms

Introduction

In principle, all countries support all aspects of anti money laundering (AML) and anti terrorist finance (ATF) policies. AML/ATF issues can potentially arise right across the spectrum of economies and cultures. However there are questions to be asked about how that abstract commitment translates into priorities. A possibility explored in this paper is that one country or trade area may place its policy emphasis in relation to one aspect of the economy, whilst another country or trade area may favour stronger action in another sector. Do such policy preferences exist and, if so, what might shape them? In this paper, the authors explore the ways in which political, cultural and economic differences and relations between the South East Asian and European regions shape problematisation of and priority-setting on AML and ATF.

The comparative aim of understanding policy preferences (comparing between regions) is addressed though an exploration of the salience for eastern and western countries of diverse areas of trade in which money laundering or terrorist finance risk may arise. (1) Logging, this being a trade issue in which AML risks are acknowledged by both west and east, however views differ about the primary focus for controls. (2) Value transfer services, including so-called alternative remittance systems, have been a particular focus for regulatory attention, the intention being to exclude funds from crime and/or for terrorism, whilst facilitating transfer/repatriation of small amounts at reasonable cost. Here the east seems to have a competitive advantage that western banks are keen to offset. Lastly (3) in relation to security, whilst all international partners have concerns around seaways, WMD proliferation, terrorism and trade in small arms, the latter has been and remains of particular concern for Asian countries, the main suppliers being outwith the region. These issues - and the contrasts that arise between them - have been chosen for their potential to illuminate differences in perception and priorities between east and west. The authors maintain that, whilst looking 'across' several trades means that no single issue can be dealt with in great depth, it does illuminate the varying regulatory priorities of east and west.

The sources drawn upon by the authors include reports from international and regional bodies, the private sector, NGOs, academic sources, and technical reports from international and regional bodies - which themselves draw upon data from the private sector, Financial Intelligence Units, law enforcement bodies and anti-terrorist services. The presentation proceeds from a sketch of political and economic relations between Asian countries and the European Union, as visible through the prism of the Asia-Europe Meeting (ASEM). Different nuances in policy priorities are then traced through the three economic fields mentioned above. The analysis illustrates how the varying emphases placed by countries and regions in relation to AML and ATF reflect the political and economic salience for them of the substantive fields of activities in which financial flows originate.

Asia-EU Policy Context

Clearly, there are differences between South East Asian and European countries - even if some of those differences are narrowing and additionally the differences between countries within the South East Asian region should not be under-estimated. Our starting point is the context for AML/ATF policy in political and trade relations between Asian and European Union countries, as reflected in an inter-regional forum, the Asia-Europe Meeting (ASEM).[1] Anti-laundering policies are discussed within ASEM in the contexts of its 'economic pillar' and of its 'political pillar' (which includes security issues). An understanding of the interplay between these two broad fields illuminates AML/ATF policies and the various reservations of EU and Asian countries. In terms of specialist anti-money laundering capacity, the primary regional body is the Asia Pacific Group on Money Laundering (APG).[2] In 2005 the ASEAN Secretariat and the APG Secretariat concluded an agreement to enhance the coordination, technical assistance and training in relation to Anti-Money Laundering and Combating Terrorist Financing (APG 2005). Within this context, we were asked to conduct research (see Acknowledgments), some of the less technical and sensitive aspects of which are reported here.

Political, Security, Economic and Development Policy Context

The Asia-Europe Meeting is a dynamic political process, which it is not easy to capture as a snapshot. The following quotation, although somewhat lengthy, usefully encapsulates features of the dialogue. There has been

> [...] a shift towards greater economic, cultural and political ties between Asia and Europe. In the 1980s the world witnessed with surprise the emergence of strong Japanese and Taiwanese economies, followed by other tigers including South Korea, Hong Kong, and Singapore. In the 1990s Malaysia, Indonesia and Thailand have also experienced strong economic growth, though with some slowing due to currency crises through 1997–1998. This economic potential was one of the forces promoting European interest in renewing links with Asian nations through 1998–2004. Trade between Europe and Asia had continued to grow till 1997 [...], while recently a range of Asian nations have demonstrated a concern to diversify their trading partners and sources of technology. [...] The ASEM impetus seems to have slowed somewhat through 2003, but onward cooperation linkages has continued through bilateral contacts. The October 2004 ASEM was able to continue economic cooperation between the two regions, but was unable to reach strong consensus on formally criticizing the human rights situation in Myanmar (Burma), something which has been pressed for by European members. (Ferguson 2005, pp. 8–9)

In terms of security, South East Asia experienced colonialism and its aftermath, various anti-communist interventions, and insurgencies and coups in some countries of the region. Prior to 2005, these countries generally did not see the EU as a credible regional security partner. In an unexpected development, in the aftermath of the 2005 tsunamis and the spirit of reconciliation evoked, EU peace monitors joined with five regional countries in

[1] ASEM is made up of 13 Asian countries - China, Japan, South Korea and all ASEAN countries (Association of South East Asian Nations) members, who are Brunei, Indonesia, Malaysia, Singapore, Philippines, Thailand, Vietnam, Myanmar, Laos and Cambodia - plus all EU Member States and the European Commission.

[2] The members of Asian Pacific Group on Money Laundering (APG) are Australia, Bangladesh, Brunei, Cambodia, Chinese Taipei, Cook Islands, Fiji Islands, Hong Kong, India, Indonesia, Japan, Republic of Korea, Macau China, Malaysia, Marshall Islands, Mongolia, Nepal, New Zealand, Niue, Pakistan, Palau, Philippines, Samoa, Singapore, Sri Lanka, Thailand, United States and Vanuatu. APG is one of several 'FATF-style regional bodies' (FSRBs).

monitoring the ceasefire between the Indonesian government and GAM in Aceh (Ministry for Foreign Affairs and Ministry of Defence 2005). Even so, ASEM's dialogue remains somewhat constrained.

> The Asia-Europe dialogue on security is constrained by [several] asymmetries: The first asymmetry is between the economic rationale of ASEM and the logic of international security. ASEM began [in order] to balance the dominant role of the United States, but in terms of security, the US is the only power with a global reach. Large parts of both Europe and East Asia still depend on US security guarantees. The second asymmetry pertains to different motivations. Asians emphasize economic and financial issues; Europeans favour political dialogue on issues of security and values. (Fort 2004)

Insofar as the EU and ASEAN members of ASEM agree that economic issues are of importance, the issues on which the Europeans and Asians prefer to focus can often differ. For example, at one ASEM forum:

> [The] EU wanted to canvass support for negotiations on trade in information technology and telecommunications, financial services and seek endorsement on the OECD document on promoting multilateral investments. However, several Asian countries were keener to take on issues of protectionism, particularly with regards to "anti-dumping" measures, and to give airing to the notion of "open regionalism". (Yeo 2002, pp 2–3, see also Tay and Yeo 2003)

The reasons for these slightly differing emphases can be understood in terms of the two regions' linked but differing histories of economic and political development. Table 1, below/opposite, touches on these contextual issues, bringing out some Asian specifics in comparison with the EU (as ASEM dialogue partners) and with the US (as an influential player in the region generally as well as in CTF and AML).

Regional Money Laundering Policies

How AML/CTF Translates into Policy Concerns

The security experiences, development paths and economic situations of the Asian and the European partners in ASEM have implications for the enthusiasm with which each 'side' articulates specific AML-related issues. Some AML-related issues - for example intellectual property rights, safeguarding multilateral investments, and opening up markets to full competition within a regulatory framework familiar to western firms (e.g. in money transfer services) - are more energetically put on the AML agenda by the Europeans.

Other issues, for example illegal logging and the international trade in small arms (related to regional insecurity), are brought to the table by Asian partners in the ASEM process and by NGO pressure, with the European side giving an assent in principle but hardly entering into precipitate action. One point to bear in mind is that taking all these issues together, the volumes of turnover and - perhaps - profits from crimes are considerable. (The often unknown but almost certainly unequal distribution of those profits is an important factor in assessing the impact of AML and proceeds of crime confiscation policies.).

Thus, the choice of which area or areas of international and regional economies to focus upon is an invitation to 'take sides' with one or other set of interests. In response to this consideration, the stance taken here is that a study of the landscape of AML should be (a) reasonably politically even-handed in its choice of material and (b) transparent in the

Table 1 Comparative overview of South East Asian, EU & US economic developments and AML stances

	Asia	*Europe*	*US comparison points*
Historical, political and cultural context	Post-colonial or post-communist. . → dash for growth, whilst retaining national characteristics.	Post-war convergence, unification of markets, retaining 'social model'. Now a mature economy.	Biggest economy, committed to free trade, retaining intellectual property.
Industrial strategy and institutional resources – strengths and weaknesses include:	Separate economies, but skilled in bringing together diverse intellectual and physical elements in the manufacturing process; diligent and inexpensive labour force. Vulnerability to energy costs.	Bringing together hitherto segregated national markets; global recognition for luxury brands; skilled, educated but aging and expensive workforce; quite low industrial R&D.	Already an integrated economy; 'new' and 'old' industries; high cost-base; but large home market gives economies of scale.
Financial policies, structures and resources	State support (political and/or financially) for R&D/reverse engineering. Formal banking systems overshadowed by 'informal' sector.	Focus on challenges of enlargement. Historically, some integration of banking and industry (now decreasing).	Seeking entry to new market opportunities. Strong global banking. Strong regulatory framework, with extra-territorial tendencies.
Primary foci for concern about criminal money	ML connected with impediments to economic growth, country development and tax collection, including corruption in specific markets and in regulation.	ML associated with barriers to full market exploitation of intellectual property; expanding pool of non-productive and economically dependent social groups may present vulnerabilities; governmental and industrial icons become potential targets for terrorism.	
Possible successes, difficulties, shaping and displacement effects	Institutional capacities still developing, so AML measures are still developing. Corresponding, displacements may be at early stage.	Some successes due to well developed institutional capacities. Controls expand (e.g., insurance); due to terrorism, privacy and cost issues are overridden. However, displacement of problems to wider channels and jurisdictions is a continuous problem. Reporting may be out-running capacity to analyse, assess and act.	

reasons for the choice. In the view of the authors, it would be inappropriate to select as foci only areas in which the Europeans are urging stronger Asian action - and equally inappropriate to select only areas in which the Asians are urging stronger European action. Of course, it would be possible to detach AML from the contexts in which it occurs, and to discuss technical reporting and estimation issues: whilst such studies are valuable in relation to those specific objectives, they do not aim to understand the wider policy preferences of the actors concerned, this being the aim of this study.

Accordingly, the study makes the choice to compare and contrast various trades in relation to which AML/CTF concerns arise; chooses trades that illustrate differing enthusiasms and reticence of the European and Asian partners in ASEM; and makes the basis for the authors' judgement explicit. The three areas examined are as follows.

- AML/CTF concerns arising around insecurity at sea, the trade in small arms, WMD proliferation and terrorism. Here, action is supported by all countries, albeit with different nuances, interpretations and priorities in practice.
- AML/CTF concerns arising from within illegal logging and closely related corruption and financing. This part of the paper illustrates a situation in which what were domestic issues within producer Asian countries have been accepted in principle as being international issues, however practical action is slow and seems to let western countries 'off the hook' when it come to implementing measures.
- Lastly - and perhaps most famously - AML/CTF concerns arise in relation to so-called 'informal' value transfer channels, including ARS ('alternative' remittance systems), where until recently at least it has been primarily the western countries urging action on Asian partners.

This paper now discusses these issues in the same order.

Some Substantive ML/TF Concerns

ML/TF Related to Security at Sea, the Trade in Small Arms, WMD and Terrorism

As noted above, (in)security concerns have a particular historical resonance in the context of southeast and central Asia.

Security at sea

As a light-hearted 'thought experiment', consider a scenario in 2015 or thereabouts, concerning the English Channel (La Manche as preferred in French), the international waterway through which most shipping goes in order to reach ports including Europe's largest, Rotterdam.

> In August 2015 this waterway becomes declared as risky as an active war zone by leading shipping risk and insurers. Naturally, insurance and management costs increase, trade decreases as worried traders re-route, the competitive advantage of the region declines and its sense of insecurity is heightened. Oh dear! Complaints are made that the risk assessment is unmerited. Mr Sterling-Honeypot, an investor, writes from his home in Bankside, London to The Times: 'Who the devil are these people to mess up my business?'. It turns out that the both shipping insurance and risk ratings are in the hands of 'world class' insurance brokers and security companies based in

the financial centres of Malaysia and Singapore - to where much of London Lloyd's international market migrated in recent years. In media commentaries, Malaysian and other Asian maritime security companies - not unconnected with entities involved in awarding the English Channel such a high risk and financially crippling rating - weep crocodile tears and offer their services for safeguarding regional security and trade in the dangerous European waters. China, the global power, offers to step up cooperation of its naval forces with the Europeans, through deployments and joint exercises in La Manche.

The 'thought experiment' can now end: in fact it was a British security consultancy and Lloyds of London who awarded such a status to Asia's main waterway, the Malacca Straight, in August 2005. The Joint War Committee of Lloyds made the determination (Burton 2005) in the light of a report by Aegis Defence Services, a British-based company whose clients include the US government, international financial institutions and international corporations (Hand and James Brewer 2005). Shipping rates were pushed up, which was bad for local purchasers of oil and other goods (Aegis Defence Systems 2004) - although possibly good for security companies, with one news service reporting that 'Five security companies from Britain and the U.S. have entered the private navy business in the region in the last year, hoping to tap a market that prices security at a minimum of $50,000 per ship' (WorldDailyCom 2005). On the diplomatic level, the United States advanced its proposals for a 'Regional Maritime Security Initiative', evoking mixed reactions from the region (Institute for the Analysis of Global Security 2004). Understandably, there were expressions of 'regret' from leaders in the region and calls for a reversal of Lloyds new insurance ratings from the governments of Singapore, Malaysia and Indonesia (Jana Today 2005).

The Joint War Committee of Lloyds lifted the 'war' rating in mid 2006. This may have been in response to improvements in naval security and/or may have reflected a realisation that the evidence base for the measures was always somewhat open to interpretation. On the one hand, piracy in the Malacca Straight had been described as having become more organised (Countryman & McDaniel 2005) - leading some to speculate that a terrorist seizure of a large vessel such as tanker full of oil could not be ruled out and that a major incident could at least block the quite narrow waterway and at worst cause extensive environmental and other damage. On the other hand, globally, a decline in sea piracy attempts for the first six months of 2005 was reported by the International Maritime Bureau (International Maritime Bureau 2005). From a methodological point of view, IMB data may not be ideal as a way of 'capturing' commonly understood problems of piracy at sea, since they include reported incidents of minor thefts from ships whilst berthed in port or at sea, plus reported attempts to board, where the would-be or actual intruders may or may not be armed with knives or other weapons (Orton 2000). However, such focussed and retrospective reports seem no less worthy of consideration as non-transparent and speculative future scenarios.

The weakness of the evidence base underlines the general point that conceptions of security and risk are construed and contested according to the interests effected. This perspective can be traced through many other elements of Asia-EU security cooperation.

Trade in Small Arms and Light Weapons

There is concern in Asian and other countries about the consequences of availability of 'small arms and light weapons' (SALW, see UN conference 2005), the term referring to weapons that can be carried by a person or an animal such as a donkey; it therefore includes everything from pistols to light missiles. The issues on the international agenda include marking of products so they can be traced back to suppliers, and intermediaries or brokers (Naylor 1995). Given historical and continuing security sensitivities, whilst many ASEAN countries are keen on tightening up on the illegal arms traffic, they may be less keen on outsiders policing their territories.

Speaking on behalf of the Association of South-East Asian Nations (ASEAN), Viet Nam said that the illicit trade in small arms could best be approached through regional mechanisms. ASEAN noted that the illicit trade in South-East Asia was related to transnational crimes such as the production and trafficking of drugs, money laundering and cross-border terrorism, conflict and post-conflict situations, and particularly the problem of armed separatism. (UN non-governmental liaison service 2001).

National sensitivities are not found only in Asia, of course, but also in countries where production of arms has been economically advantageous and/or sometimes the covert international supply of SALW to specific groups has been found politically useful. A 'Small Arms Trade Transparency Barometer' covering many European countries has been published (Small Arms Survey 2005). There is a European Union common position on arms brokering (European Council 2003). However this had led to little practical action, with few EU member states developing legislation on arms brokering (Anders 2005). On the wider international stage, the Small Arms Survey reports 'only limited support for the EU position from other states, with fierce opposition coming from the Arab group, ASEAN countries, China and especially the USA' (Amnistia Internacional et al 2002, p 10). In short, the arena of SALW is beset not only by technical difficulties but also by widespread political ambivalence, for both the ASEAN and EU sides of ASEM (setting side internal differences within those 'blocs').

The amounts of money involved can be considerable, but the implications for AML/CTF are less than straightforward. For example, in those cases in which a government arranges (overtly or covertly) for supply from its own stock, free of charge, then no laundering arises, unless for reasons of non-transparency a third party 'cut out' is used and engages in illegal activity. In other cases, in which governments do not supply the SALW free of charge, some counter-trade may be arranged between intermediaries and suppliers. Sometimes this links the trade with commodities such as drugs, 'conflict' diamonds or agreements on concessions for minerals, oil or other extractive trades. In cases of grant of concessions, the bargain involves conditional transfer of value into the future. Tracking future flows is not easy. Even where direct payments are made, controls of the trade are weak (Naylor 2000).

WMD and Proliferation

Recent events in the US and Europe have eroded some of the differences between WMD and SALW, indeed between armaments of all types and products intended for commercial use, such as aircraft. Nevertheless, the money laundering implications of weapons of mass destruction differ from those of SALW in several respects. Thinking of WMD in the conventional sense, one product alone can have decisive effects, whilst this is rarely true of SALW (outside political assassination). Much attention is focussed upon risks of future use, because of the potential effects, especially on civilian and infrastructure. The term 'catastrophic risk' is sometimes used, to indicate not just the severity of risk in terms of lives but its bunching in time. There is an element of the concern within developed countries that reflects the perceived possibility that WMD would be more likely to be used in such contexts, whereas (India and Pakistan perhaps excepted) SALW are seen as the more pressing problem for developing countries and particularly in less developed countries with weak state and security apparatuses.

Because the power of atomic weapons was first demonstrated against two Asian cities, anti-nuclear proliferation efforts are widely supported in most Asian countries, as well as by the EU side of ASEM. At the same time, however, there is some ambivalence in a few countries of the region, springing from a felt need to provide for self-defence in an uncertain world. Also, as is well known, the potential 'dual use' of some technologies used in civilian atomic power stations, chemical and pharmaceutical industries and biological technologies provide much scope for uncertainty and, where the politics favour conflict, suspicion and accusations.

Money laundering has been more commonly discussed in relation to WMD in terms of sale and purchase, rather than in relation to any financial proceeds stemming from their use. Whilst there has been limited discussion of the possibilities of betting in the financial markets, through futures, options of other instruments - by financial backers of terrorist, or by terrorists themselves, or by those who know of, suspect or simply hear rumours of upcoming WMD strikes - to date the scenario of WMD being used to generate financial proceeds remains fiction. Nevertheless, in 2007, FATF issued Guidance on implementation of financial provisions of UN Security Council resolutions to counter the proliferation of WMD, and Guidance Regarding the Implementation of Activity-Based Financial Prohibitions of United Nations Security Council Resolution 1737.

Terrorism

Counter terrorist finance measures are supported internationally and regionally as a means of reducing terrorism (ASEAN Secretariat 2002). However, there are two caveats. Although some international sources explicitly describe CTF as a successful anti-terrorist strategy (Wayne 2005), not all states or bodies would be as confident as they might like to be about that. The efficacy of CTF has yet to be established, not just because performance criteria are underdeveloped, but also because intelligence and other bodies may be reluctant to share information about what intelligence leads have been useful and at what stage of the process. CTF strategies might have been more useful in the early stage of development of terrorist organisations than they are now, when relatively small and autonomous networks appear to be the common organisational form. Although it might be argued that the current limitation of CTF stem from shortfalls in implementation, there are good reasons to expect effectiveness of such measures to be somewhat context-dependent and also to be low. Context-dependency might result from (1) variations in the level and forms of terrorism and in its financing; and (2) differences in the ways in which states approach anti-terrorism and CTF, reflecting international relations and domestic circumstances.

(1) Briefly, recent events suggest that - by contrast with insurrections involving large quantities of SALW - some terrorist operations can be 'done on the cheap'. Also, the financial dimensions are hard to pick out before the terrorist event. For 11 September 2001, the quite modest funds required were transferred by a variety of commercial means and, prior to the terrorist incident or to prior identification of its perpetrators, would have been indistinguishable from small-scale personal or business transactions (Roth et al 2004). And, whilst some claims have subsequently been made about links between terrorism and informal transfer of funds, in relation to 11 September that appears to have been speculation rather than fact.

> It is worth bearing in mind that despite some claims made in the press about informal methods used by the 9–11 hijackers to transfer their funds, all available evidence points to the use of banks, wire services, credit card accounts and regulated remitters. In many other instances of terrorism (e.g. in the Middle East, South Asia and Africa), militants have indeed used IVTS [informal value transfer systems] for at least some of their fund transfers. It is also true that the small amounts needed for suicide missions can be transferred through both regulated and IVST channels without raising eyebrows. So, while some funding of terrorism does occur through IVST, there is little reason to believe that: a) these would be necessarily or invariably the militants' preferred method, or b) IVST are more vulnerable to abuse than the regulated sector. (Passas 2005a, b, p. 17)

In some other circumstances, for example some attacks principally on foreigners (e.g. Bali) and insurgencies in the Asian regions, pockets of local population may provide funding and practical support. In other instances, particularly high profile conflicts, volunteers may flock from aboard or elsewhere within the jurisdiction to join the fight. Such circumstances give CTF little to bite on and so it seems understandable and, one might go on to say, quite defensible, for enthusiasm about CTF to wax and wane. (See, further, contributors to Biersteker & Eckert 2007.)

(2) States may differ in the way they conceptualise terrorism - and hence CTF - whilst standing shoulder-to-shoulder in the fight against it. One source (Fukuda 2004) explores some of these differences, finding that anti-terrorist policy in a number of Asian countries is driven by domestic circumstances - such as the existence of internal opposition to central government, the strength of support for insurgent groups within a country, the balance of power between government and opposition. For example, in the case of the People's Republic of China (PRC), following 11 September:

> counter-terrorism cooperation with the United States was seen as an opportunity to crack down on their own separatist movements within the country and thus to tighten domestic control. China confronts independence tendencies in Tibet and the western region of Xingjian [...] - two vast regions that occupy about 30 percent of China's land mass and are rich in mineral resources, oil and gas... [Hence] the PRC has initiated counter-terrorism cooperation with the United States, mainly on intelligence sharing, terrorist financing and anti-money laundering. (Fukuda 2004, pp 15–16 and 27)

The PRC has referred on more than one occasion to links between the Uighurs of Xingjian region and Osama bin Laden (Government of PRC 2002, p. 1). From this context, it may be expected that PRC cooperation on CTF/AML would be politically facilitated in cases involving Muslim groups. By contrast in Indonesia, for example, where the balance of power in internal politics was somewhat uncertain, the movement of the then President Megawati was forced to distance itself from certain aspects of international action against terrorism (Fakuda op cit, pp. 20–21). In Malaysia, by contrast, where the then Mahathir government had a relatively strong hand internally, cooperation against Al Qaeda acquired wider public support (ibid).

Summing up the implications from the literature for CTF, it seems that there are two difficulties. The first is the familiar dispute over what behaviour may properly be called 'terrorism'. Is any internal grouping that any state names as terrorist to be accepted as such, or only those activities which specific or all states agree to call terrorist? The second difficulty is the rather weak links between many *operational* terrorist activities and laundering. (The funding of pro-violence education, international travel and of full-time fighters is another matter this may require serious funding from legal or illegal earnings.) As many others have mentioned, although it may be politically understandable for a high priority to be accorded to fighting potential sources of finance for terrorism, that does not necessarily mean that such methods are intellectually compelling, pragmatically appropriate or very effective in practice. Yes, there are some successes stories in relation to terrorism and these may on occasion be linked to efforts on counter terrorist finance. But does that mean that equivalent or even lesser resources, otherwise targeted, would have been any less successful? It is possible that there is an element of the anti-ML community moving quickly, and for understandable institutional and other reasons, to link ML and TF together - whilst in reality they are generally different phenomena (c.f. Biersteker & Eckert 2007; Findlay 2007).

Second Substantive Focus: Illegal Logging, Corruption, Financing Issues

Illegal Logging and Related Corruption - Emergence as a Significant ML/TF Issue

Over the past decade illegal logging, the international trade in tainted timber, the corruption that allows it and the money laundering that results from it have come onto the international policy agenda, particularly in the Asian region (Ant-Lkbn Antara news service 2005). Estimates by a variety of concerned bodies put the proportion of logging that is illegal at about one-fifth of the total for some Asian countries and up to ninety percent for others (Tacconi et al 2003a, b see table on p. 8). The EU and US are sizable customers. European timber users are in process of introducing and/or reinforcing responsible purchasing policies and are exploring methods of reducing use of tainted supplies (see for example Timber Trade Federation 2004), The G8 does not wish to rush into any enforcement action that might take the timber industry and financial institutions by surprise. Nevertheless illegal logging and its related ills have been propelled onto the policy agenda as result of alliances on the topic between governments and anti-corruption agencies in the region (Defensor & Fathoni 2005), some European bodies (Commission of the European Communities 2003), AML and CTF agencies in both regions and NGOs, backed up by media interest.

Taking Indonesia as an example for a rapid overview, illegal logging came onto the domestic agenda after the 1997 Asian financial crisis, a subsequent change of government that put greater distance between the logging industry and government/regulators, and imposition of loan conditions by the International Monetary Fund (IMF), the World Bank, and the Consultative Group on Indonesia (CGI) in the period 1997–2000 (Setiono no date). In practical terms, however, measures taken have been described as being quite limited in their impacts. There are several reasons for this, including the continuing economic incentive to take more timber than is permitted by regulations ('supply push'), an international trade and international demand for timber that are quite vibrant ('demand pull') and some bank-related aspects.

> One important link in the chain of illegal timber trading is Indonesia's banking and financial system. Banks often play the part of financial intermediaries not only for legal forestry transactions, but also in illegal forestry transactions. The assumption is often made that illegal logging in Indonesia is carried out by small-scale actors working on a cash basis with little need for financing. But banks and other financial institutions play an important role in funding both legal and illegal forestry activities. Banks routinely provide working capital and long-term loans for logging activities, plantation investments and timber processing facilities. Often, they guarantee the issue of bonds and commercial financial securities by forest-related companies, buy off

forest-related debts from companies and, of course, accept deposits from forest concessionaires. (Setiono 2003, p. 1)

In terms of Indonesian bank regulation, a 1998 amendment applies.

> "In the extension of credit or financing based on Sharia Principles, banks shall take into account the findings of environmental impact assessments for large-scale and high-risk companies, so that projects being financed continue to protect the sustainability of the environment." The fact that the banks continue to finance an industry that requires six times the amount of legally harvested timber is a very clear indication of how they are contravening the credit extension regulations. [...] Estimates suggest between 60 percent to 80 percent of the timber industry's supplies are obtained illegally. (ibid, p. 2)

In these circumstances it should be clear that, when a bank finances an Indonesian timber concession company, it should obtain information on the company, including ultimate beneficiaries, and monitor transactions as it would with any other account. If there are suspicions of money laundering from illegal timber trading, it should file a suspicious transaction report. If bank fails to do so then, depending on the details of law in the jurisdiction(s) concerned, it may be liable criminally and perhaps civilly (provided that the underlying predicate offence can be proven to the satisfaction of the court). These issues have been debated in meetings in the region. For example, a joint presentation between an NGO and the head of Indonesia's AML agency looked at transfer pricing mechanisms used for concealing proceeds of illegal logging (also an issue that concerns GAFISUD due to illegal deforestation of the Amazon). It also described existing AML powers and made recommendation to the banking industry, calling for cooperation:

> Banks should categorize forestry businesses as high-risk businesses; banks should create a list of high risk customers in the forestry sector; banks should report STR on customers reported by NGOs and the media as being implicated in forestry crimes; the police should begin to investigate the financial backers of illegal logging, by using the AML law; using international AML regimes for curtailing forestry and environment crimes. (Setiono & Husein 2004, p. 12)

The issues also have been debated in several European-wide meetings involving Financial Investigation Units from member states, leading to better understanding of the prospects for suspicious activity reports to FIUs and for AML action in the European context. However, steps being taken towards AML action in Europe are very modest (Federal Ministry on Consumer Protection, Food and Agriculture 2004). In relation to the UK specifically:

> Based on legal advice, it appears that there is a basis for UK anti-money laundering legislation to be used as a tool against both trade in illegally harvested timber and also financing investments that lead to illegal logging. However, in practice there are several constraints to effective implementation. (Speechly 2004, p. 8)

These constraints include the a low level of awareness within UK enforcement agencies of illegal logging issues, the need to establish clearly a parallel offence in UK domestic law (since "illegal logging" not specified as a criminal offence in the UK), limited experience within the enforcement agencies of investigation of similar cases, and the political reality that 'the Crown Prosecution Service has [other] priorities, for example, drug trafficking, people trafficking, arms trafficking and terrorism' (ibid). Similar observations have been made of the UK (and some other developed countries) by the OECD in relation to the inadequate legislation and low resources available to act against transnational bribery.

The EU Action Plan for a Forest Law Enforcement, Governance and Trade agreement (FLEGT) explored several possibilities for action, including the development of assurances of origins of timber (Commission of the European Communities 2003). Somewhat ironically, one predictable and no-doubt unintended consequence of the EU refusal to accept incoming timber unless the shipment has been legally certified would be to make EU importers virtually immune to legal action under money laundering laws. Illegally harvested product would require certification in the exporting countries. That could increase the pressure for corruption amongst the certifying agencies - whilst providing to EU importers, their banks and others connected with the trade the defence they need against allegations of money laundering.

Other areas of concern are whether, given the entrenched nature of the trade, certification is practical; and whether companies should be allowed to enter the certification process without first having gained a 'clean bill of health' about their past activities. Some Asian NGOs want vetting of firms and also possibly land reform to be implemented before certification is introduced (Tacconi et al 2003a, b pp. 24–25). Be that as it may, certification within countries of origin, with a chain of custody through to the end user, seems to be the road that has been found politically feasible. Thus it appears that, whilst AML action has a future in relation to forestry markets, that future may be more imminent within the Asian and other 'countries of origin' than within the EU. Meanwhile, it is clear from official investigations and charges laid in several countries in the region that there are entrenched interests at all level of commercial life and government agencies (Haseman & Lachica 2005; Environmental Investigation Agency 2003).

If historical analogies are felt to be useful, then the early days of action against high level drug trafficking may come to mind. However the fact that illegal logging is seemingly closely integrated into international, regional and local legal trades in timber makes that drugs trafficking analogy less useful. Even the broader term 'corruption' seems to lose much of its force in this context, since connivance in the illegal timber trade is so routinely bound into economic and regulatory routines. Without readier source identification, it is difficult to show that the timber is the product of illegal export, although it should nevertheless be possible to consider whether assets in the possession of businesspeople or public officials are plausibly the product of legitimate activity in Asia or elsewhere.

Third Substantive Focus: Informal Value Transfer, ARS, Banking and Development

This is one of the most challenging aspects for analysis, for reasons that are partly to do with multi-stage transactions and settlement through loosely linked structures, and partly to do with wider economic policy interests.

Balancing ML/TF Risks against other Factors

Informal value transfer systems are widely seen as presenting ML/TF risks, insofar are they continue to be unregulated or are regulated ineffectually compared with other AML risks. As is well known, Financial Action Task Force (FATF) recommendations now refer to the regulation of all hitherto informal value transfer systems/ARS, although implementation varies. However it remains unclear to what extent to which such services present greater or lesser ML/TF risks than do other parts of the economy. Part of the ML/TF concern may relate to the exasperation felt by some financial investigators in trying to trace highly complex transactions, within cultural and business contexts that may not be very familiar. That can lead to an as yet untested suspicion that even when regulated, some of the features of informal value transfer systems may present ML risks that are intrinsically higher than those in 'western' banking. Thus, complexity of settlement between parties in informal value transfer systems may fuel concern about laundering, although normal prudential risks appear to be low, given the rarity with which Hawalladars abscond or otherwise fail to pay their debts. Hitherto, when they do, the losses appear to have been absorbed by counter-parties and the 'offenders' stigmatised and incapacitated from future business in their communities. Of course, 'western' banking also faces settlement issues, which it also manages in quite complex ways, ways that might perhaps perplex a Hawalladar at first sight - so the issues are as much cultural as technical.

Another aspect of concern relates to the recognition that AML/CTF regulation needs to be done with a light touch - otherwise hitherto covert operators would not declare themselves, and hitherto overt operators might be driven underground, which would rather defeat the object. A further risk is that of displacement. As the Passas report for the Dutch government observes, 'over-emphasis and crack-downs on one IVTS [informal value transfer system] or ethnic group may not only be perceived as discriminatory, but also open up opportunities for criminals to take advantage of relative inattention to certain routes or networks for easier and undetected value transfers' (Passas 2005a, b).

Light-touch regulation, on the other hand, might not be enough to squeeze out the ML/CTF risks, not least because the lower customer identification and recording obligations enable them to carry on much as before, while registration allows them to state formal compliance. Because of this, scepticism remains in law enforcement, 'western' banking and policy-making circles. There may continue to be a demand for studies of newly regulated, hitherto informal value transfer systems in many regional settings. It should be noted, however, that there are so many other avenues for value transfer - commodity pricing, for example - that simple transfers of cash or wire transfers outside of commercial import/export transactions are unlikely to account for all the money laundering from illegal-source activities (e.g. timber) or semi-legal source activities (e.g. arms, tax evasion, intellectual property theft).

Commercial Competition and 'Regional Champions' in Financial Services

Informal value transfer systems, due to their reliability, low costs and popularity, are formidable market competitors to western/global banks and money remittance services. (Understandably in these circumstances, some of the studies of risks of ARS and of other informal/unregulated value transfer systems have been sponsored by western/global banks and money remitters.) An unresolved commercial question is to what extent these hitherto informal/unregulated systems might retain their competitive advantages once they become regulated and as they at least partially converge with 'formal' systems. It is only relatively recently that western/global financial entities have begun to develop services that, in relation to relatively developed areas, are competitive in terms of costs and reliability - involving such means as the provision of credit cards posted to countries in which the remitter wishes his family or other associates to be able to withdraw the funds that are created to that account (example, Ikabo, see Mellyn 2003). A related question is how formal and hitherto informal systems are becoming linked, for example through regulated financial institutions ('hubs') in the Middle East whose growth has been rapid. For the foreseeable future, all such banking and quasi-banking systems remain reliant on informal systems for last mile remittances into less developed areas and particularly into 'failed states' and conflict zones:

> In some areas devastated by war or famine there simply is no choice between formal and informal methods: if the often desperately needed money is to reach these areas at all, informal systems are the only option. Even international NGOs in countries like Somalia and Afghanistan use the services of informal remittance companies. (Pieke et al 2005, p. 4)

On those grounds, informal systems should not only be safeguarded, they should be extended and improved, by a variety of means:

> The potential for greater involvement by credit unions, other micro-finance institutions and migrant associations in leveraging remittances for development should be explored and built upon. [...] The study revealed the importance of in-kind transfers in many areas, not only in providing for migrant dependants in times of economic or political crisis, but also as an important modality of trade. [...] Where "formalization" of the remittance sector is pursued, it should seek to complement rather than suppress informal operators, and aim to incorporate their better practices - low cost, speed, accessibility and reliability. (ibid, pp 36–37)

Anonymity may sometimes be an attempt to avoid corrupt 'rake offs' by 'rent-seekers'. Initially, it was thought by AML specialists that anonymity in financial transactions was invariably suspicious, as a marker of ML/TF. More recently however it has become recognised that, in settings in which government officials, political parties or criminal groups may seek informally to 'tax' observable wealth, anonymity can be motivated by the wish to avoid that extortion. As FATF has put this:

> It is worth noting [...] that a desire for anonymity does not necessarily mean that a particular remittance transaction is related to criminal activity. There is evidence that anonymity, in certain instances, may also be a means of circumventing the pressure from government officials that ask the recipient for bribes or try to impose taxes on cross border flows... (FATF 2005, p. 6)

Along the same lines, an APG report refers to 'concerns over corruption in the local banking system' as a reason for avoiding use of the formal banking systems in some countries/areas (APG Typologies Working Group 2005, p. 28). This is a salutary observation and a useful corrective against any assumption that regulated systems are always cleaner than non-regulated systems.

Remittances and Alleviation of Poverty

To what extent does the greater ease of migrant workers' access to informal or lightly regulated value transfer systems, and the relatively low costs thereof, contribute, to poverty reduction in the countries to which funds are remitted? The consensus of research and policy-makers' opinion on this question is generally positive (Pieke et al 2005). However, it is less clear whether these systems have a beneficial or adverse effect on country development: views may be found that are negative (Addy et al 2003), positive (Mellyn 2003) or broadly positive but conditional (Stanton 2003).

Taken together, these policy issues of policy-alleviation, country development, commercial competition, the 'last mile', and attempts to evade corruption/extortion, are clearly non-trivial. AML/CTF considerations need to be reconciled with other issues of interest for the international and regional communities. What this underlines is that, in order to have sufficient leverage to provide impetus to wider policies, AML/CTF needs to be quite politically and commercially sensitive, as well as being technically informed. (See further Levi et al. 2007, for a discussion of the relationship between corruption and money laundering.)

Discussion

International cooperation is the *leitmotiv* of anti money laundering and counter terrorist finance work. However there are differences of understanding on focus and priorities. Whilst these sometimes may be approached as if they are matters of misunderstandings or miscommunications, more is at stake: priorities differ between the parties acting on the international stage. Inevitably, international and regional fora and networks provide laboratories for the containment and management of difficulties and 'stuck' issues. What arise may more fairly be called differences in emphases rather than conflicts; such differences delineate what is possible in international cooperation. This paper has highlighted the ways on which three issues - small arms and light weapons in the context of regional (in)security, illegal logging in the context of local corruption and international trade, and alternative remittance systems in the context of country investment and competition in international financial services - draw from the partners differing emphases in relation to AML/CTF action.

In a nutshell, whereas feeling in many South East Asian countries would be that small arms threaten security and so might usefully be moved further up the ML/TF cooperation agenda (whilst retaining respect for sovereignty), their western counterparts have yet to take radical action to limit the trade and to address the crucial role of brokers who themselves operate transnationally. Also, where western countries strong in international banking tend to see unregulated systems such as ARS as not only a big ML/TF risk but also as unfair price competition, Asian partners and those prioritising development goals stress the benefits of secure and cheap remittance systems and the resulting incoming investment at grassroots level. Finally, where all parties display concern over the accelerating diminution of natural habitats resulting from illegal logging, the EU has not seen fit to give teeth to controls that might adversely affect financers, importers or end-customers of timber products - preferring to rely on voluntary and potentially-manipulable certification schemes that impact most within the region of origin.

The implications are fairly clear. As long as a strong 'demand pull' exists in international markets for certain products, it will be difficult for the region to eliminate or even reduce ML related to corruption and to the markets which stimulate it. To take a historical analogy, such a difficulty eventually became well understood in relation to ML/TF and drug trafficking, leading to a 'balanced approach' in relation to AML measures as well as in relation to the physical trade. Such balance is also accepted in relation to human trafficking and related AML. However the present situation seems not so balanced in relation to ML and some other markets, notably forestry products profiled in this study, where the self-regulatory regimes coming into being at international and country levels would place primarily responsibility on checks in Asian countries. Whether this is realistic would be as much political judgement as a technical one, however clearly there are risks related to the impending policy (im)balance. To combat that risk, work on corruption and on illegal timber deserve fullest practical support - and so does more detailed analysis of how the policy (im)balance arose and how it might be changed. Normative choices need to be made explicit.

Equally sensitive in ASEM context is the export 'supply push' behind the flow of SALW from EU and other developed countries, both officially and more informally/deniably via brokers. The regulatory regimes in place and their slow development in relation to arms brokerage offer little support to AML and CTF efforts. The possibility that some arms are purchased through counter-trades for both illicit goods (e.g. drugs) and licit goods (e.g. gold) adds complexity to this situation. Clearly here are continuing risks to the security of the region and these risks are underlined by internal insurgencies and international terrorism. Ironically, insecurity and terrorism may provide reasons for EU countries to make legitimate shipments of weapons to Asian country security forces - a proportion of such arms later being recycled onto regional/international second hand markets, thus coming into the hands of dissident groups and networks throughout the region. To combat that bundle of risks, consideration might be given by the international community to more vigorous less equivocal action against the trade in SALW and related security and ML/TF problems. That powerful inhibitions are raised against such practical actions, even at a time of generalised concern about security, is hardly reassuring.

In closing, whist there may be technical difficulties in international cooperation against money laundering and terrorist finance, there are also notable structural impediments, grounded in economic interests and political sensibilities. Bargaining over the primary foci of and means of implementing AML/ATF policies reflects wider priorities. Reflecting economic interests and perhaps cultural dispositions, the EU has a tendency to emphasise products and services originating in Asia as posing risks, and to locate responsibilities for monitoring and control as falling primarily within Asia - a tendency reciprocated by Asian partners. As for the future, as the international balance of trade shifts, with Asia increasingly supplying finished goods and higher-value services to the west and increasing its influence in international fora, including the OECD and Financial Action Task Force, so the policy debate can be expected to evolve and pressures for a 'level playing field' to intensify.

Acknowledgments Thanks are due to the ASEM Anti-Money Laundering Project, to UNODC Regional Centre, Bangkok for the opportunity to do the work of which this paper forms a part; to UNODOC for administration of the contract; and to international and national bodies and individuals who facilitated the work. The authors are particularly grateful to the APG, whose experienced Secretariat served as Technical Advisory to the study, and to FATF, whose typologies staff provided documentation and advice at the onset. We also acknowledge the many technical and academic sources drawn upon in the study. A version of this paper was presented at the Organized Crime in Asia Conference, June 28–29 2007 at the National University of Singapore. The authors thank anonymous referees of this journal for comments that were helpful in several respects and that led to a presentational tightening of the reasons for analysing policy preferences. Needless to say, the authors remain responsible for all matters of selection, interpretation and balance.

References

Addy, D., Wijkstrom, B., & Thouez, C. (2003). *Migrant remittances - country of origin experiences; strategies, policies, challenges and concerns, paper tabled at the International conference on migrant remittances: developmental impact and future prospects, organised by DFID, World Bank and IMG, London 9–10 October* (p. 28). Geneva: International Migration Policy Programme. Retrieved on 27 July 2007 from http://www.livelihoods.org/hot_topics/docs/REMITPAPER.doc.

Aegis Defence Systems. (2004). *Aegis 2005 terrorism report, overview* (p. 5). London: Aegis. Retrieved on 17 March 2005 from http://www.aegisdef.com/pdfs/2005Overview.pdf.

Anders, H. (2005). *Implementing the EU common position on the control of arms brokering: progress after two years, Note d'Analyse, 7 July.* Bruxelles: Groupe de recherche et d'information sur la paix et la sécurité. Retrieved on 27 July 2007 from http://www.grip.org/bdg/g4579.html.

Amnistía Internacional and other NGOs. (2002). *The European Union and arms export control: One year on from the UN conference, conference held at NH Hotel Alberto Aguilera, Madrid, 10–11 May, conference report* (p. 30). Geneva: Small Arms Survey. Retrieved on 27 July 2007 from http://www.smallarmssurvey.org/files/portal/issueareas/measures/Measur_pdf/r_%20measur_pdf/European%20Union/EUMadrid%2011052002.pdf.

Ant-Lkbn Antara. (2005). *Integrated [anti-]illegal logging operation in Papua should be just and fair, Minister says, Indonesian government press release, 14 March.* Indonesia: Ant-Lkbn Antara. Retrieved on 27 July 2007 (requires registration) from http://www.accessmylibrary.com/coms2/summary_0286-3914712_ITM.

APG. (2005). *Media release: working to outlaw money laundering and terrorism financing in Asia Pacific* (p. 2). Sydney: Australian Transaction Reports and Analysis Centre. Retrieved on 27 July 2007 from http://www.austrac.gov.au/mr14july.html.

APG Typologies Working Group. (2005). *APG yearly typologies report 2004–05, endorsed by the APG Plenary 14 July 2005* (p. 38). Sydney: Asia/Pacific Group on Money Laundering.

ASEAN Secretariat. (2002). *ARF statement on measures against terrorist financing, by Bandar Seri Begawan, 30 July.* Jakarta: ASEAN. Retrieved on 27 July 2007 from http://www.aseansec.org/12001.htm.

Biersteker, T., & Eckert, S. (Eds.) (2007). *Countering the financing of terrorism.* London: Routledge.

Burton, J. (2005). *'Risky' Malacca strait label fuels criticism, 5 August, p. 4 in hard copy of newspaper.* London: Financial Times. Retrieved on 27 July 2007 from http://news.ft.com/cms/s/5b51fad4-0543-11da-97da-00000e2511c8.html.

Chairman's statement. (2005). *Seventh ASEM foreign ministers' meeting, Kyoto, 6–7 May 2005, notes on EU website. Brussels: European Commission* (p. 8). Retrieved on 27 July 2007 from http://europa.eu.int/comm/external_relations/asem/intro/07_05_05.pdf.

Commission of the European Communities. (2003). *Communication from the Commission to the Council and the European parliament, Forest law enforcement, governance and trade (FLEGT), proposal for an EU Action Plan, 21.5.2003 com (2003) 251 final.* Brussels: European Commission. Retrieved on 27 July 2007 from http://eur-lex.europa.eu/LexUriServ/site/en/com/2003/com2003_0251en01.pdf.

Countryman, & McDaniel. (2005). *Vessel loss dispatches For December 2002.* Los Angeles: Law offices of countryman & McDaniel. Retrieved on 27 July 2007 from http://www.cargolaw.com/presentation_casualties.02.html.

Defensor, M. (2005). *(Secretary, Department of Environment and Natural Resources, Republic of the Philippines) and Fathoni, T. (Secretary of Directorate General of Forest Protection and Nature Conservation, Ministry of Forestry, Republic of Indonesia). Joint statement by Philippines and Indonesia regarding strengthening of the Forest Law Enforcement and Governance process* (p. 1). Jakata: Ministry of Forestry. Retrieved on 27 July 2007 from http://www.dephut.go.id/INFORMASI/FLEGT/Philippines.htm.

Environmental Investigation Agency. (2003). *Environmental investigators expose laundering of illegal Indonesian timber by Malaysia and Singapore, 15 May.* London and Washington: Environmental Investigation Agency. Retrieved on 27 July 2007 from http://www.eia-international.org/cgi/news/news.cgi?t=template&a=133&source=.

European Council. (2003). *Council common position 2003/468/CFSP of 23 June 2003 on the control of arms brokering, 25 June. Official Journal of the European Union L 156* (pp. 79–80). Brussels: European Union. Retrieved on 27 July 2007 from http://www.iansa.org/issues/documents/eu_common_position_on_brokering.pdf.

FATF. (2005). *Money laundering & terrorist financing typologies 2004–2005* (p. 95). Paris: Financial Action Task Force.

Federal Ministry on Consumer Protection, Food and Agriculture. (2004). *EU expert workshop on illegal logging and measures to combat money laundering, Berlin, summary report, September 30/October 1* (p. 7). Bonn: Bundesministerium für Verbraucherschutz, Ernährung und Landwirtschaft. Retrieved on 27 July 2007 from http://www.illegal-logging.info/uploads/Summary_report_of_the_Berlin-workshop.pdf.

Ferguson, R. (2005). *Eurasia: Super-region or zone of conflict? pp 23. Queensland: Bond University* (p. 20). Retrieved on 27 July 2007 from http://www.international-relations.com/wbeurasia/WBEA-2006-Lec1.doc.

Findlay, M. (2007). Terrorism and relative justice. *Crime, Law and Social Change, 47*(1), 57–68, February.

Fort, B. (2004). ASEM's role for co-operation on security in Asia and Europe. *Asia Europe Journal, 2*(3), 355–363.

Fukuda, T. (2004). *Regional cooperation against terrorism in East Asia, technical report number 4, March* (p. 33). Canberra: Strategic and Defence Studies Centre, Research School of Pacific and Asian Studies. Retrieved on 27 July 2007 from http://dspace-dev.anu.edu.au:8080/bitstream/1030.58/13085/1/Regional_Cooperation_against_Terrorism_in_East_Asia.pdf.

Government of PRC, Information Office of the State Council. (2002). *'East Kurdistan' terrorist forces cannot get away with impunity, 21 January.* Geneva: Permanent Mission of the People's Republic of

China to the United Nations Office at Geneva and other international organizations in Switzerland. Retrieved on 27 July 2007 from http://www.china-un.ch/eng/rqrd/jzzdh/t85075.htm.

Hand, M., & James Brewer, J. (2005). *Malacca strait declared a high risk zone by joint war committee, decision could increase premiums in affected area.* Kuala Lumpur: Maritime Institute of Malaysia (MIMA). Retrieved on 27 July 2007 from http://www.mima.gov.my/mima/htmls/mimarc/news/news flash_files/news-cut/jul05.htm.

Haseman, J., & Lachica, E. (2005). *Toward a stronger U.S.-Indonesia security relationship, August* (p. 114). Washington & Jakarta: United States-Indonesia Society. Retrieved on 27 July 2007 from http://www.usindo.org/publications/reports/pdf/Security%20Relations.pdf.

ICC Commercial Crime Services (2005). *IMB report finds piracy declining, 20 July.* Barking (UK): International Maritime Bureau, International Chamber of Commerce. Retrieved on 27 July 2007 from http://www.icc-ccs.org/main/news.php?newsid=51.

Institute for the Analysis of Global Security. (2004). *Chilly response to U.S. plan to deploy forces in the strait of Malacca, 24 May.* Washington: Institute for the Analysis of Global Security. Retrieved on 27 July 2007 from http://www.iags.org/n0524042.htm.

International Maritime Bureau. (2005). *Piracy and armed robbery against ships (book).* Kuala Lumpur and London: IMB, July. No electronic copy: hard copy obtained from http://www.icc-ccs.org.uk/prc/piracy_rep_app.php.

Jana Today. (2005). *Ministers regret categorization of Malacca strait as high-risk zone, Jakarta news item* (p 1). Retrieved 14 August 2005 from http://japantoday.com/e/?content=news&cat=7&id=345290, full item 'expired' but residual remaining and retrieved on 27 July 2007 from http://www.japantoday.com/jp/news/345290.

Levi, M., Dakolias, M., & Greenberg, T. (2007). Money laundering and corruption. In J. Edgardo Campos, & S. Pradhan (Eds.), *The many faces of corruption: Tracking vulnerabilities at the sector level* (pp. 389-426). Washington, DC: The World Bank.

Mellyn, K. (2003) *Worker remittances as a development tool opportunity for the Philippines, report by consultant to the Asian Development Bank, 13 June* (p. 25). Manila: Asian Development Bank. Retrieved on 27 July 2007 from http://www.adb.org/Documents/Reports/Consultant/Worker_Remittances_PHI.pdf.

Ministry for Foreign Affairs and Ministry of Defence. (2005). Sweden to contribute to EU mission in Aceh, Press release, 8 August. Stockholm: Swedish Government Offices, Information Department. Retrieved on 27 July 2007 from http://www.reliefweb.int/rw/rwb.nsf/db900SID/HMYT-6F3LSG?OpenDocument

Naylor, R. (1995) The structure and operation of the modern arms black market. In J. Boutwell, M. Klare, & L. Reed (Eds.), *Lethal commerce: The global trade in small arms and light weapons.* Cambridge: American Academy of Arts and Sciences.

Naylor, R. (2000). The rise of the modern arms black market and the fall of supply-side control. In V. Gamba, S. Meek, & J. Potgieter (Eds.), *Society under siege: Crime, violence and illegal weapons* (pp. 43–72). Cape Town: Institute for Security Studies, PDF retrieved on 27 July 2007 from http://www.iss.co.za/Pubs/Books/SocietyUnderSiege%201.html.

Orton, C. (2000). It's December 15 - do you really know where your cargo is? 12 January. Washington: World Trade Magazine. Retrieved on 27 July 2007 (requires registration) from http://www.worldtrademag.com/CDA/Archives/4aae91c4d5af7010VgnVCM100000f932a8c0____.

Passas, N. (2005a). *Informal value transfer systems, terrorism and money laundering, research report submitted to the US Department of Justice* (p. 137). Rockville: National Criminal Justice Reference Service (NCJRS). Retrieved on 27 July 2007 from http://www.ncjrs.org/pdffiles1/nij/grants/208301.pdf.

Passas, N. (2005b). *Informal value transfer systems and criminal activities* (p. 45). The Hague: Ministry of Justice. Retrieved on 27 July 2007 from http://www.wodc.nl/onderzoeken/onderzoek_179.asp?loc=/.

Patlis, J. (2003). *A new battle front in fighting corruption in the timber sector: Money laundering and the changing role of financial institutions, prepared for and funded by The Center for International Forestry Research, presented at 11th International Anti-Corruption Conference (IACC) Seoul, 25–28 May* (p. 26). Washington and Jakarta: Environmental Law and Law Development Associates. http://www.11iacc.org/download/add/WS6.4/WS%206.4_P2_PatlisPPP.ppt.

Pieke, F., Van Hear, N., & Lindley, A. (2005). *Synthesis study: A part of the report on Informal Remittance Systems in Africa, Caribbean and Pacific (ACP) countries (Ref: RO2CS008), commissioned by DFID, EC-PREP and Deloitte & Touche, 15 January* (p. 43). Oxford: University of Oxford ESRC Centre on Migration, Policy and Society (COMPAS). Retrieved on 27 July 2007 from http://www.compas.ox.ac.uk/publications/papers/Synthesis%20050115.pdf.

Roth, J., Greenburg, D., & Wille, S. (2004) *Monograph on terrorist financing, staff report to the commission* (p. 155). Washington: National Commission on Terrorist Attacks Upon the United States. Retrieved on 27 July 2007 from http://www.9–11commission.gov/staff_statements/911_TerrFin_Monograph.pdf.

Setiono, B. (2003). *Financial institutions and forestry crimes, Jakarta and Brussels: International NGO Forum on Indonesian Development* (p. 6). Retrieved on 27 July 2007 from http://www.infid.be/Forestry.pdf.

Setiono, B., & Husein, Y. (2004). *Creating prudent banks creating prudent banks and sustainable forest-based industries: The anti-money laundering approach, presentation for [conference on] the future of forests in East Asia and China: new markets for ecosystem services & trends in regional forest trade and finance Kuala Lumpur, Malaysia, October 7–8, p 12 of* (p. 12). Retrieved on 27 July 2007 from http://www.cifor.cgiar.org/publications/pdf_files/research/governance/MoneylaunderingKL-7October04.pdf.

Small Arms Survey. (2005). *Small arms survey 2005: weapons at war: reaching for the big picture, chapter 4 summary 'An update on small arms transfers'* (p. 3). Geneva: Small Arms Survey. Retrieved on 27 July 2007 from http://www.smallarmssurvey.org/files/sas/publications/year_b_pdf/2005/2005SASCh4_summary_en.pdf.

Speechly, H. (2004). *Money laundering and illegal logging - application of UK legislation, summary of points made a two seminars held at the Royal Institute for International Affairs, 1 October* (p. 9). London: Royal Institute of International Affairs. Retrieved on 27 July 2007 from http://www.illegal-logging.info/uploads/Money_Laundering_and_Illegal_Logging.doc.

Stanton, D. (2003). *Report & conclusions, International conference on migrant remittances: development impact, opportunities for the financial sector and future prospects, organised by DFID, World Bank and IMG, 9–10 October* (p. 48). London: DFID and World Bank. Retrieved on 27 July 2007 from http://www.livelihoods.org/hot_topics/docs/RemitConfFinal.doc.

Tacconi, L., Boscolo, M., & Brack, D. (2003a). *National and international policies to control illegal forest activities, report by the ministry of foreign affairs, government of Japan* (p. 69). Jakarta, Center for International Forestry Research. Retrieved on 27 July 2007 from http://www.illegal-logging.info/papers/2003_National_and_Int_policies_Illegal-logging.pdf.

Tacconi, L., Obidzinski, K., & Agung, F. (2003b). *Learning lessons to promote forest certification and control illegal logging in Indonesia, report for The Nature Conservancy (TNC) and World Wide Fund for Nature (WWF), sponsored by United States Agency for International Development (USAID)* (p. 88). Jakarta and Bogor (Indonesia): Center for International Forestry Research (CIFOR). Retrieved on 27 July 2007 from http://www.cifor.cgiar.org/publications/pdf_files/Books/BTacconi0401.pdf..

Tay, S., & Yeo, L. H. (2003). Claims and silences: An Asian perspective on the European Union's security strategy. *Challenge* Europe, Issue 10, November. Brussels: The European Policy Centre. Retrieved on 27 July 2007 from http://www.epc.eu/en/ce.asp?TYP=CE&LV=177&see=y&t=42&PG=CE/EN/detail&l=6&AI=316.

Timber Trade Federation. (2004). Responsible purchasing policy, document 10 version 1, risk assessment using choice tables and associated objective evidence (p. 8). London: TTF. Retrieved on 27 July 2007 from http://www.forestsforever.org.uk/sustainability/responsible/Microsoft_Word_-_Document10v1ChoiceTables041101.pdf.

UN Conference. (2005). Greater international cooperation critical to fighting small arms trade, say speakers, as meeting to review 2001 action programme continues, document DC/2977, 13 July. Vienna: United Nations Information Office. Retrieved on 27 July 2007 from http://www.unis.unvienna.org/unis/pressrels/2005/dc2977.html.

UN Non-Governmental Liaison Service. (2001). *NGLS roundup 80, August, The United Nations conference on the illicit trade in small arms and light weapons in all its aspects* (pp. 9–20). New York: UN, July 2001. New York: United Nations. Retrieved on 27 July 2007 from http://www.un-ngls.org/documents/text/roundup/80arms.htm.

Wayne, E. (2005). Money laundering and terrorist financing in the Middle East and South Asia, testimony before the US Senate Committee on banking, housing, and urban affairs, by the assistant secretary for economic and business affairs, July 13. Washington: US Department of State. Retrieved on 27 July 2007 from http://www.state.gov/e/eeb/rls/rm/2005/49564.htm.

World Bank / WWF Alliance for Forest Conservation & Sustainable Use. (2005). *Alliance satisfied with trial of certification assessment tool in Europe, press statement for release on 21 July* (p. 2). Retrieved on 27 July 2007 from http://lnweb18.worldbank.org/ESSD/envext.nsf/80ByDocName/AllianceSatisfiedwithTrialofQACCCertificationAssessmentTool/$FILE/AllianceQACCFindingsPRFINAL.pdf.

WorldDailyCom (Online News Service). (2005). *Private navies combat Malacca strait pirates.* Medford (US): WorldNetDaily.com, Inc. Retrieved on 27 July 2007 from http://worldnetdaily.com/news/article.asp?ARTICLE_ID=45535.

Yeo, L. H. (2002). *The Asia-Europe Meeting (ASEM): from selective engagement to comprehensive partnership. Südostasien Aktuell, special Issue.* Hamburg: Institute for Asian Studies.

Name Index

For Product Safety Concerns and Information please contact our EU
representative GPSR@taylorandfrancis.com
Taylor & Francis Verlag GmbH, Kaufingerstraße 24, 80331 München, Germany

www.ingramcontent.com/pod-product-compliance
Lightning Source LLC
LaVergne TN
LVHW080759011026
849160LV00015B/1490
* 9 7 8 1 1 3 8 3 8 3 5 7 9 *